RELAPSE PREVENTION

THE GUILFORD CLINICAL PSYCHOLOGY AND
PSYCHOTHERAPY SERIES
Michael J. Mahoney, *Editor*

Drawing by Ed Arno; © 1980 The New Yorker Magazine, Inc.

RELAPSE PREVENTION

Maintenance Strategies in the Treatment of Addictive Behaviors

Edited by
G. ALAN MARLATT / JUDITH R. GORDON
University of Washington

Foreword by G. Terence Wilson

THE GUILFORD PRESS
New York   London

For Kit and Colin

© 1985 The Guilford Press
A Division of Guilford Publications, Inc.

Printed in the United States of America

Last digit is print number 9 8 7 6

LIBRARY OF CONGRESS CATALOGING IN PUBLICATION DATA

Main entry under title:

Relapse prevention.

  (The Guilford clinical psychology and
psychotherapy series)
  Includes bibliographies and indexes.
    1. Substance abuse—Treatment. 2. Substance
abuse—Prevention.   3. Behavior therapy.
I. Marlatt, G. Alan. II. Gordon, Judith R.
III. Series. [DNLN: 1. Alcoholism—therapy.
2. Behavior Therapy. 3. Substance Abuse—
therapy. 4. Smoking—prevention & control.
5. Risk-Taking. 6. Obesity—therapy.
WM 274 R382]
RC564.R45 1985   616.86′06   84-19319
ISBN 0-89862-009-0

To give your sheep or cow a large, spacious meadow is the way to control him.

SHUNRYU SUZUKI (1905–1971)

CONTRIBUTORS

EDMUND F. CHANEY, PhD, Veterans Administration Medical Center, Seattle, and Department of Psychiatry and Behavioral Sciences, University of Washington School of Medicine, Seattle, Washington

LARRY DEAN, BA, Butler Hospital, Providence, Rhode Island

DENNIS M. DONOVAN, PhD, Veterans Administration Medical Center, Seattle, and Department of Psychiatry and Behavioral Sciences, University of Washington School of Medicine, Seattle, Washington

EDMUND DUBREUIL, MSW, Butler Hospital, Providence, Rhode Island

JUDITH R. GORDON, PhD, Department of Psychology, University of Washington, Seattle, Washington

JOAN MALTESE, PhD, Department of Psychology, University of California, Los Angeles, California

G. ALAN MARLATT, PhD, Department of Psychology, University of Washington, Seattle, Washington

BARBARA S. MCCRADY, PhD, Rutgers Center of Alcohol Studies, Rutgers —The State University of New Jersey, Piscataway, New Jersey

DAVID RAPKIN, PhD, Department of Psychology, University of California, Los Angeles, California

LAURA READ, BA, Department of Psychology, University of California, Los Angeles, California

BARBARA STERNBERG, PhD, Psychological Services, Weight Watchers International, Inc., Manhasset, New York

SAUL SHIFFMAN, PhD, Department of Psychology, University of Pittsburgh, Pittsburgh, Pennsylvania

SUZANNE SWANSON, RN, Butler Hospital, Providence, Rhode Island

MURRAY E. JARVIK, MD, PhD, Department of Psychiatry, University of California, Los Angeles, California

FOREWORD

It is virtually a truism to note that the addictive disorders are characterized by disturbingly high rates of relapse following initial treatment success. Yet it has been only in the past decade that investigators have directly addressed the problems of facilitating maintenance of treatment-produced change. Primarily under the impact of social-learning theory, it has increasingly come to be realized that effective therapeutic interventions must distinguish between the initial induction of behavior change and its maintenance over time, and accommodate both components if lasting personal change is to result. No one has done more to draw out a conceptual framework for understanding and studying relapse phenomena and their prevention or been as successful in translating a psychological analysis of this sort into broadly usable clinical strategies than G. Alan Marlatt. For close to a decade he has led the field in productive theorizing and research on the analysis of relapse and its determinants. Through his many convention presentations, journal articles, and book chapters, Marlatt has had a major impact on theory, research, and practice in the treatment of addictive disorders, particulaly alcohol abuse. Careful readers of these previous publications and presentations will have observed the subtle changes and additions in Marlatt's thinking as he and his colleagues have pushed ahead with their impressive program of research. Indeed, much of the value of Marlatt's model has been its dynamic quality; it has been refined and developed in response to continually accruing clinical experience and experimental evidence. The present text, jointly edited by Marlatt and Judith R. Gordon, is important because it provides the first formal presentation of the complete model. But the book is also significant in that it lays out in rich detail the theorizing and thinking behind the evolving model, together with the most up-to-date scientific evidence and clinical applications.

Marlatt's own chapters discussing the relapse prevention model are usefully complemented by contributions from other clinical researchers on each of the addictive disorders. These chapters extend Marlatt's model to new areas and provide some measure of its generality. The overall result is more successful than the customary edited anthology, with strongly recommended sections for both practitioners and researchers. The former will find clinically savvy discussions of assessment and treatment strategies for preventing relapse. The latter will discover a heuristic gold mine. It has been my opinion that the study of the addictive disorders, particularly the field of alcoholism, has suffered from an unfortunate insularity. All too often, theory and research have been oddly divorced from developments in experimental psychology. This book offers a persuasive corrective to this conceptual insularity. It provides a refreshing and welcome blending of basic and applied research findings with real-life clinical issues and practice. This is not surprising when it is remembered that over the past decade, Marlatt, in the course of his own work, has made seminal contributions to the study of alcohol use and abuse in such diverse areas as basic methodology (e.g., his influential rediscovery of what is now known as the balanced placebo design), theory (e.g., the role of cognitive factors, such as expectations, in the causes and consequences of alcohol consumption), and clinical assessment and treatment methods (e.g., relapse prevention training).

The scholarship displayed in Marlatt's contributions is of the highest order. The most recent advances in such demanding sub-speciality areas as social psychology, personality psychology, classical conditioning research, social learning theory, and behavior therapy are all smoothly woven together with well-informed and incisive analyses of the nature of the addictive disorders themselves, into an integrative whole. And in addition to this conceptual and substantive accomplishment, several key methodological issues receive expert handling along the way. This outstanding scholarship is all the more commendable when it is remembered that Marlatt has tackled some particularly complex and challenging issues in a field that all too often has been burdened with emotionally charged and extremist claims about the sole source of truth and salvation for the addict.

Marlatt's mastery of mainstream theory and research in psychology, as well as the nature and treatment of disorders such as alcoholism, has made possible the integrative basis of the relapse prevention model as presented in this book. Perhaps the most influential (and controversial) aspect of Marlatt's work has been his steady criticism of traditional notions about alcohol use and abuse, coupled with a highly productive research program that has consistently offered an alternative vision. I believe that Marlatt has achieved more than anyone else in developing a systematic and theoretically sound alternative psychological framework to the disease theory of alcohol use and abuse. We are too close to the unfolding story to know what impact the type of approach Marlatt and his colleagues have fostered will have on the field of alcoholism and other addictive disorders, but I assume that it will be profound. Much research of a critical nature remains to be carried out, and Marlatt's particular relapse prevention model will not escape modification and revision. But the generic value of the sort of rigorous psychological framework espoused in this book, I hazard to predict, will weather the test of time.

A critical feature of Marlatt's model is its overriding emphasis on the psychological commonalities in relapse among the different addictive disorders. The ambitious scope of the model seeks to explain not only relapse in different forms of substance abuse, but also in other forms of addictive behavior, such as gambling, that do not involve the ingestion of potentially self-destructive substances. Identifying both commonalities and differences among these various forms of problem behavior provides a challenging research agenda for years to come.

In my foregoing comments I have understandably stressed the importance of this book for researchers and practitioners in the fields of the different addictive disorders that are covered. But the book goes beyond this audience. Its message transcends the consideration of relapse prevention in the additive disorders. What we have here is a splendid example of the workings of a master exponent of the scientist–practitioner model of clinical psychology. Faithful to Marlatt's past contributions, this book ranges over intellectual terrain encompassing basic research findings, clinical research trials, and actual clinical practice. As such it provides a model of thinking and research for all who are committed to expanding the interaction between science and clinical practice in a balanced and useful manner.

In the book Marlatt draws heavily on the metaphor of the individual client setting out on a highway journey with or without an adequate road map. Readers will be able to experience a trip of another kind as they move through this book. They will travel the route of a creative researcher and his colleagues as they describe how they planned and pursued a program of research that has led to important findings and helped to force a reexamination of traditional views of the addictive process. The path to scientific respectability, as Skinner once said, is steep and thorny. Marlatt and his colleagues have encountered several formidable obstacles as they have progressed in analyzing relapse and its determinants. Obviously, they still have a long way to go. Yet it seems undeniable that they have already arrived at some significant conclusions. And at least as important as the particular facts they discover is the mode of thinking that has guided them in their research. The contributions in this book give the reader a cognitive map with which to follow the intricacies of theory and research on addictive behavior and to better address the problem of facilitating maintenance of behavior change. It will be interesting to look back 10 years from now to see where the map will have taken us.

G. Terence Wilson, PhD
Rutgers University

PREFACE

This book was launched on a ferry ride across Puget Sound from Seattle to Bremerton in January 1980. It was then that the senior author/editor (G. A. M.) began work on the first chapter; a round-trip ferry ride across the Sound seemed at the time to be a good way to begin work on a book, free from the usual hassles of phone calls and other interruptions in the office. As it turned out, the ferry made three 2-hour round-trips before work on the chapter outline and a draft of the first page were completed. It was a clear sunny day and the vista of the snow-capped Olympic Mountain range proved to be somewhat more of a distraction than the constant stream of students knocking on the office door. Many months have gone by since that first day of writing, along with many drafts of the chapters in Part I. Much has happened in the study of relapse since 1980 and several revisions of the text have been necessary in order to bring the material up to date. Chapter 1 was extensively revised in the fall of 1983, and the original first page written on the ferry trip several years ago has long since been replaced. Although it is tempting to continuously update and revise this material as new research and relevant publications become available, one has to stop somewhere—to get off the ferry before it makes yet another round trip across the Sound, so to speak.

Relapse Prevention (RP) is a generic term that refers to a wide range of strategies designed to prevent relapse in the area of addictive behavior change. The primary focus of RP is on the crucial issue of maintenance in the habit-change process. The purpose is twofold: to prevent the occurrence of initial lapses after one has embarked on a program of habit change, and/or to prevent any lapse from escalating into a total relapse. Although the RP model has general implications for habit change with a variety of target behaviors, the main emphasis in this book is on addictive behaviors including problem drinking, smoking, substance abuse, eating disorders, and compulsive gambling. The overarching theoretical orientation throughout the book is that addictive behaviors are conceptualized as overlearned habit patterns rather than addictive "diseases." A key assumption underlying the RP approach is that addictive habit patterns can be changed through the application of self-management or self-control procedures. The role of the therapist is to teach the client to be his or her own "maintenance man" in the habit-change process. Self-control, as represented by the RP approach, encompasses strategies or techniques in three main areas: acquiring adaptive coping skills as alternatives to addictive behaviors; fostering new cognitions (attitudes, attributions, and expectancies) concerning both the nature of habit change and one's capacity to control one's life; and developing a daily lifestyle that includes positive self-care activities and nondestructive ways of achieving personal satisfaction and gratification. The intended audience for this book includes both clinicians (therapists and counselors) and researchers who are working in the addictive behavior field.

Part I is intended to provide an overview of the RP model and its application to addictive behavior problems in general; Part II is devoted to specific applications of this approach in the areas of problem drinking, smoking, and weight control. The material in Chapter 1 is intended to be comprehensive and provides a theoretical rationale for the RP model and its role in the maintenance of habit change, along with an overview of the major assessment and intervention procedures that are described in detail in the remaining four chapters of Part I. Chapter 2 describes methods of assessing high-risk situations for relapse and outlines methods for teaching clients how to cope effectively in these situations. Cognitive factors associated with the relapse process (self-efficacy, outcome expectancies, attributions, and decision making) are discussed in Chapter 3, with an emphasis on background research and theory. Readers who are interested only in the clinical application of cognitive therapy procedures may wish to skip or skim the material in Chapter 3 and go on directly to Chapter 4, which covers cognitive assessment and intervention procedures deriving from the material discussed in Chapter 3. Finally, Chapter 5 is devoted to lifestyle modification procedures and a theoretical discussion of moderation and balance as underlying principles of the RP approach. The material in Part I was written by the senior editor (G. A. M.), although many of the concepts described were developed in collaboration with the co-editor (J. R. G.). Primary responsibility for editing all the chapters in the book was assumed by J. R. G. In our work together we tend to assume the complementary roles of researcher/writer (G. A. M.) and clinician (J. R. G.) with some overlap.

Part II contains four chapters devoted to specific applications of the RP model with selected addictive behavior problems. Chapter 6, by Donovan and Chaney, provides an integrated review of theoretical models of relapse and related intervention procedures in the alcoholism field based on a cognitive social-learning approach. McCrady and her colleagues provide a detailed description of a social-learning-based treatment program for problem drinkers in Chapter 7. Chapter 8, by Shiffman and his associates, describes a comprehensive RP program for smoking cessation. In Chapter 9 Sternberg describes the application of RP in a weight-control program.

Many individuals have contributed to the material presented in this book. First and foremost, we would like to thank the authors and their colleagues who provided the chapters in Part II. Gratitude is also expressed to our own present and former students who contributed to the body of research that has provided the empirical foundation of the RP model; many of their names are included in research citations throughout Part I. We also wish to extend our appreciation and thanks to our clients, whose experiences have provided invaluable insights that we have attempted to incorporate into our work (as evident in the case studies described in Part I). Finally, we wish to express our heartfelt appreciation to Connie Jordan, Barbara Rhudy, and Donald Wood for the extensive work that went into the preparation of the manuscript. Research conducted by G. A. M. and his colleagues described in Part I was supported, in part, by grants from the National Institute of Mental Health (MH 17982), the National Institute on Drug Abuse (DA 02572), and the National Institute on Alcohol Abuse and Alcoholism (AA 03489 and AA 05591). Additional grant support was obtained from the Alcoholism and Drug Abuse Institute of the University of Washington.

G. Alan Marlatt
Judith R. Gordon
Warm Beach, Washington

CONTENTS

PART I

RELAPSE PREVENTION: GENERAL OVERVIEW

1

RELAPSE PREVENTION: THEORETICAL RATIONALE AND OVERVIEW OF THE MODEL

G. ALAN MARLATT

INTRODUCTION

WHAT IS RELAPSE PREVENTION?

Relapse Prevention (RP) is a self-management program designed to enhance the maintenance stage of the habit-change process. The goal of RP is to teach individuals who are trying to change their behavior how to anticipate and cope with the problem of relapse. In a very general sense, relapse refers to a breakdown or setback in a person's attempt to change or modify any target behavior. Based on the principles of social-learning theory, RP is a self-control program that combines behavioral skill training, cognitive interventions, and lifestyle change procedures. Because the RP model includes both behavioral and cognitive components, it is similar to other cognitive–behavioral approaches that have been developed in recent years as an outgrowth and extension of more traditional behavior therapy programs. Descriptions of related cognitive–behavioral research and treatment approaches with a variety of clinical problems are available in a number of recent publications (Beck, Rush, Shaw, & Emery, 1979; Foreyt & Rathjen, 1978; Kendall & Hollon, 1979; Mahoney, 1974; Meichenbaum, 1977).

The RP model described in Part I of this book was initially developed as a behavioral maintenance program for use in the treatment of addiction problems such as alcohol and other drug dependencies (Marlatt & Gordon, 1980). The typical goals of treatment for drug dependency are either to refrain totally from drug use (e.g., to abstain from alcohol), or, in some cases, to impose regulatory controls over the target behavior (e.g., to control or moderate alcohol use). Although much of the material presented in this book is directed toward the treatment of drug dependency problems, the RP model may have applications that extend beyond the traditional categories of "drug addiction." Habit patterns such as excessive drinking, smoking, overeating, or substance abuse may be considered as a subclass of a larger set of what we refer to as *addictive behaviors*. The category of addictive behaviors may be expanded to include any compulsive habit pattern in which the individual seeks a state of *immediate gratification*. With many addictive behaviors (especially drug dependency), the immediate experience of gratification (the pleasure, "high," tension reduction, or relief from distress associated with the act itself) is followed by delayed negative consequences such as physical discomfort or disease, social disapproval, financial loss, or decreased self-esteem. In addition to drug dependency, other examples of addictive behaviors include certain eating disorders (e.g., overeating and binge eating), compulsive gambling, and other "impulse control" problems, including some sexual disorders (e.g., exhibitionism, pedophilia, fetishisms, etc.) and impulsive aggressive acts (e.g., child abuse and rape). Since many treatment programs for these kinds of problems require clients to totally refrain from engaging in the problematic behavior, application of an RP program may turn out to be an appropriate and effective approach. Other possible applications of the RP model are described in the final section of this chapter.

RP procedures can be applied either in the form of a specific maintenance program to prevent relapse or as a more global program of lifestyle change. In the former case, the goals of the program are (1) to anticipate and prevent the occurrence of a relapse after the initiation of a habit change attempt (e.g., to prevent a recent ex-smoker from returning to habitual smoking); and (2) to help the individual recover from a "slip" or lapse before it escalates into a full-blown relapse. Such RP procedures can be used regardless of the theoretical orientation or intervention methods applied during the initial treatment phase. Once an alcoholic has stopped drinking, for example, RP methods can be applied toward the effective *maintenance* of abstinence, regardless of the methods used to *initiate* abstinence (e.g., attending AA meetings, aversion therapy, voluntary cessation, or some other means). In the second more general application of the RP model, the purpose is to facilitate global changes in personal habits and daily lifestyle so as to reduce the risk of physical disease and/or psychological stress. Here, the overall aim is to teach the individual how to achieve a *balanced lifestyle* and to prevent the development of unhealthy habit patterns. The underlying theme of this facet of the RP program is the "middle way." A balanced lifestyle is one that is centered on the fulcrum of moderation (in contrast with the opposing extremes of either excess or restraint). Viewed from this more global perspective, RP can be considered as a component of developing movements such as "health psychology" or holistic medicine (cf. Pelletier, 1979; Stone, Cohen, & Adler, 1979).

PLAN FOR THIS CHAPTER

The material in this chapter is designed to present an overview of the RP model for both the specific and global applications described above. The chapter begins with a general discussion of issues related to the maintenance of habit change, including a discussion of various theoretical models of addiction. Stages of change in the modification of addictive behaviors are then discussed, along with the rationale for a self-control approach to maintenance. The rationale for focusing upon relapse, traditionally considered an indication of failure in the maintenance process, is described in the following section. A theoretical model of the relapse process as it applies specifically to addictive behaviors is presented. The immediate precipitating events that precede a relapse as well as the cognitive and affective reactions associated with its occurrence are outlined. The predispositional factors (covert antecedents and lifestyle pattern) that may set the stage for relapse or increase the probability that a relapse will occur are described. The final major section provides an overview of intervention strategies derived from the RP model. The concluding section provides a brief discussion of the current status and future directions of the RP model.

THEORETICAL MODELS OF ADDICTION

THE DISEASE MODEL AND THE PARADOX OF CONTROL

We are currently approaching a crossroads in our approach to the understanding and treatment of addictive behavior problems. Until recently, the primary approach has emphasized the importance of biological parameters of addiction with a focus on the drug or substance and its pharmacological effects. Implicit in this approach is the assumption that the "addict" cannot voluntarily control his or her drug-taking behavior due to the overpowering influence of internal physiological forces such as compulsions, cravings, or irresistible urges. The fact that contemporary society embraces this view is reflected in dictionary definitions of addiction. *Webster's New Collegiate Dictionary* (1983), for example, defines addiction as the "compulsive physiological need for a habit-forming drug"; compulsion itself is defined as "the state of being compelled" or "an irresistible impulse to perform an irrational act." Thus, an addict is by definition someone who cannot control his or her addictive behavior.

Is it really the case that the addict is incapable of exercising control over the problem behavior? At first glance, behaviors traditionally defined as addictive appear to be under voluntary control. After all, aren't behaviors such as drinking, eating, smoking, or the use of other drugs all activities that we either choose to do or not to do? Excessive use of any substance (or excessive performance of any activity leading to immediate gratification) could be viewed as a problem in "impulse control" in which the individual is apparently lacking in willpower and is thereby unable to exercise appropriate control over the behavior. This line of thinking culminated in the "moral model" of addiction, a view based on Christian morality that dominated thinking in the field until recent years. According to this perspective, an addict is someone who lacks the "moral fiber" to resist temptation. In the case of alcoholism, for example, society came to label the "drunk" as a person lacking in moral character or strength of will, unable to resist the temptation to give in to the evil spirits of alcohol. The moral condemnation of alcoholism reached its height in this country over half a century ago with the unsuccessful experiment of national Prohibition.

Despite recent criticisms of the moral model of addiction that have been advanced by supporters of the *disease model* (described below), there are still many individuals in our society who believe that disorders such as alcoholism are the result of moral failings. Many Christian moralists continue to define drinking as a sinful act. In a recent visit to the wine department at a local supermarket in Seattle, I found the following printed note inserted between two bottles:

CORRECTION: NOT DISEASE BUT STUPIDITY!! Hundreds of columns of newspaper space and millions of dollars have been used in exposing and combating "drug abuse" and "alcoholism." "Drug abuse is what people inflict upon themselves," according to an article in the *Journal of Nervous and Mental Disease*. In other words, considering the consequences, it simply is a case of people using drugs—including alcohol—and abusing themselves. Obviously, then, we should concede that what are so commonly referred to as "drug abuse" and "alcoholism" are not *disease* but the result of the wilful exercise of stupidity. *God's official record adds these facts:* "Do you know that the unrighteous shall not inherit the Kingdom of God? Be not deceived; neither fornicators, not idolaters, nor adulterers, nor effeminate, nor abusers of themselves with mankind, nor thieves, nor liars, nor covetous, nor *drunkards*, nor revilers, nor extortioners, shall inherit the Kingdom of God." It is time to repent!

Subsequent to the general failure of the moral approach, a less judgmental approach to addiction began to surface in the form of the disease model. According to this approach, addictive behaviors are based on an underlying physical dependency and attention is focused on physiological predisposing factors, presumed to be genetically transmitted, as the underlying cause of addiction. The definition of alcoholism as a disease exemplifies this approach. Although the origins of the disease model of alcoholism can be traced back to the early nineteenth century writings of the American physician, Benjamin Rush, the contemporary version of this model was first introduced in the late 1940s by E. M. Jellinek and his associates at the Yale Center for Alcohol Studies (Jellinek, 1960). Jellinek's position was given sanction in 1956 when the American Medical Association officially declared alcoholism a disease. Since then the disease model has been accepted by many prestigious groups from the National Council on Alcoholism to the World Health Organization. Certainly the disease concept of alcoholism offers a number of advantages over the moral model. By attempting to remove the moral stigma associated with drinking problems, the diagnosis of alcoholism as a disease encourages many individuals to seek medical treatment for their disorder. Perhaps one of the main reasons why the disease model has led to increased numbers of individuals seeking help or assistance with their drinking problems is that this approach absolves the alcoholic from accepting personal responsibility or moral guilt for his or her condition. Alcoholics are told, in essence, that they are suffering from a disease similar to other biological disorders, such as diabetes. Are diabetics to blame for their condition? No? Then neither is the alcoholic. The disease process is assumed to be latent even before the alcoholic takes the first drink (due to genetic predisposition) and to remain active (although temporarily "in remission") even if the reformed alcoholic has not taken a drink in years. Alcoholism is often referred to as a "chronically relapsing" condition within this context.

Despite its strengths, there is a major paradox in the disease model of addictive behavior involving the central concept of *control* and how it is defined within the model. On the one hand, the disease model assumes that the alcoholic is unable to exert control over drinking behavior because of the compelling influence of internal physiological factors which underlie the addiction. On the other hand, the alcoholic is told (Catch-22) that the only way to curb the problem is to refrain from drinking, to maintain total abstinence for an indefinite period. Surely the intention or commitment to abstain is itself a form of control. On this basis, an individual can only exercise control while maintaining total abstinence from drinking; to relapse is to *lose* control. The disease model thereby produces a dichotomous restriction on the possible range of treatment outcomes: one is either abstinent (exerting control) or relapsed (losing control). Thus, even though the etiology of alcoholism is described as a disease process which is beyond the control or responsibility of the victim, the major *treatment* mode often takes the form of a moral commandment: Thou shalt not drink! Although they may seem at first glance to be "strange bedfellows," the moral model and the disease model have formed an alliance in recent years. Advocates of Alcoholics Anonymous (AA), for example, endorse the disease model of alcoholism while at the same time advocating the surrender of personal control to a "higher power" as the first step in the process of recovery.

It is ironic that the major strength of the disease model, absolving the addict of personal responsibility for the problem behavior, may also be one of its major shortcomings. If alcoholics come to view their drinking as the result of a disease or physiological addiction, they may be more likely to assume the passive role of victim whenever they engage in drinking behavior if they see it as a symptom of their disease. Some research, for example, shows that individuals who are given a genetic or constitutional explanation for the etiology of a disorder feel they can do less personally to cope with their problem, and are more likely to use alcohol and/or other drugs to relieve emotional distress, than individuals who are given a social learning etiological explanation (Fisher & Farina, 1979). It is possible, on the other hand, that knowing that one is genetically predisposed to alcoholism may motivate one to compensate for this risk by increased vigilance and restraint over drinking. The extent to which the person feels capable of exercising voluntary control within fixed genetic limits (i.e., how much "room to move" the person believes there is) is a significant factor to explore in working with someone who is genetically at risk.

The disease model may be successful insofar as it convinces the alcoholic that he or she is sick, suffering from a medically recognized illness, and no longer capable of drinking without losing control. If the alcoholic accepts this diagnosis and agrees to never take another drink *and does not,* all is well. Unfortunately, the ability to maintain total abstinence from alcohol is a rare outcome in the alcoholism treatment field. A recent comprehensive study conducted by the Rand Corporation evaluated the outcome of over 700 alcoholic patients following their participation in a variety of typical treatment programs. It was found that *less than 10%* of the patients were able to maintain abstinence over a period of 2 years following discharge from the treatment program (Armor, Polich, & Stambul, 1978). These data demonstrate that *relapse* is the most common outcome of alcoholism treatment.

Relapse is the turning point where the disease model is likely to backfire. If an alcoholic has accepted the belief that it is impossible to control his or her drinking (as embodied in the AA slogan that one is always "one drink away from a drunk"), then even a single slip may precipitate a total, uncontrolled relapse. Since drinking under these circumstances is equated with the occurrence of a symptom signifying the reemergence of the disease, one is likely to feel as powerless to control this behavior as one would with any other disease symptom (e.g., a fever or convulsion). The belief in the inevitability of loss of control drinking as a pathognomonic symptom of alcoholism is a dogma strongly held by adherents of the disease model and underlies much of the furor that currently surrounds the mention of controlled drinking as an alternative treatment goal to abstinence in the treatment of alcoholism (Heather & Robertson, 1981; Pendery, Maltzman, & West, 1982; Sobell & Sobell, 1978). In a recent commentary on the controlled drinking controversy (Marlatt, 1983) I discussed the overlap between the disease model and the moral model as an underlying factor in the dispute:

To some observers, the diagnosis of alcoholism carries the moral stigma of a new scarlet letter. Such critics argue that the contemporary disease model of alcoholism is little more than the old "moral model" (drinking as a sinful behavior) dressed up in sheep's clothing (or at least in a white coat). Despite the fact that the basic tenets of the disease model have yet to be verified scientifically (e.g., the physiological basis of the disease and its primary symptom, loss of control), and even though there is a lack of empirical support for the effectiveness of any particular form of alcoholism treatment (including inpatient programs geared toward abstinence), advocates of the disease model continue to insist that alcoholism is a unitary disorder, a progressive disease that can only be temporarily arrested by total abstention. From this viewpoint, alcohol for the abstinent alcoholic symbolizes the forbidden fruit (a fermented apple?) and a lapse from abstinence is tantamount to a fall from grace in the eyes of God. Clearly one bite of the forbidden fruit is sufficient to be expelled from paradise. Anyone who suggests controlled drinking is branded as an agent of the devil, tempting the naive alcoholic back into the sin of drinking. If drinking is a sin, the only solution is salvation, a surrendering of personal control to a higher power. (Marlatt, 1983, p. 1107)

ADDICTIVE BEHAVIORS AS ACQUIRED HABIT PATTERNS

In recent years, a third approach has emerged as an alternative to the moral and disease modes of addiction. Derived from the principles of social-learning theory, cognitive psychology, and experimental social psychology, the addictive behavior model makes a number of assumptions that differ markedly from both the disease and moral models. From a social-learning perspective, addictive behaviors represent a category of "bad habits" including such behaviors as problem drinking, smoking, substance abuse, overeating, compulsive gambling, and so forth. In terms of frequency of occurrence, addictive behaviors are presumed to lie along a continuum of use rather than being defined in terms of discrete or fixed categories such as excessive use (loss of control) or total abstinence. In contrast, *all* points along this continuum of frequency of occurrence, from very infrequent to "normal" to excessive use, are assumed to be governed by similar processes of learning.

Addictive behaviors are viewed as overlearned *habits* that can be analyzed and modified in the same manner as other habits. This position does not imply that continued excessive involvement in an addictive habit is free from any negative physical consequences, however. On the contrary, it is fully recognized by adherents of the addictive behavior model that excessive habits can and often do lead to the development of disease end-states (e.g., cirrhosis of the liver in alcoholics, lung cancer in smokers, etc.). The fact that a disease state is the *product* of a long-term addictive behavior cycle does not necessarily imply, however, that the behavior itself is a disease or that it is caused by an underlying physiological disorder. Does continual, excessive use of tobacco (along with high relapse rates among those who try to quit) necessarily imply that the smoking habit itself qualifies as a disease? It is informative to direct this same question to the habitual use of alcohol.

Those who subscribe to the addictive behavior model are particularly interested in studying the *determinants* of addictive habits, including situational and environmental antecedents, beliefs and expectations, and the individual's family history and prior learning experiences with the substance or activity. In addition, there is an equal interest in discovering the *consequences* of these behaviors, so as to better understand both the reinforcing effects that may contribute to increased use and the negative consequences that may serve to inhibit the behavior. Besides the effects of the drug or activity itself, attention is paid to the social and interpersonal reactions experienced by the individual before, during, and after engaging in an addictive behavior. Social factors are involved both in the initial learning of an addictive habit and in the subsequent performance of the activity once the habit has become firmly established.

One of the central underlying assumptions of this approach is that addictive behaviors consist of overlearned, maladaptive habit patterns. As mentioned earlier, these habit patterns are usually followed by some form of immediate gratification (the "high" state of pleasure or reduction in tension or arousal). In many instances, addictive behaviors are performed in situations perceived as *stressful* (e.g., drinking in an attempt to reduce social anxiety, smoking as a means of "calming the nerves," overeating when feeling lonely or bored, etc.). To the extent that these activities are performed during or prior to stressful or unpleasant situations, they represent *maladaptive coping mechanisms*. Addictive behaviors are maladaptive to the extent that they lead to delayed negative consequences in terms of health, social status, and self-esteem. The performance of these behaviors *per se* is not necessarily maladaptive, providing they are engaged in on an occasional basis, in moderation, and by individuals who choose to do so with a full awareness of the long-term consequences. Responsible moderate use of certain drugs, for example, may be acceptable as long as the behavior does not become a habit or addictive behavior cycle (i.e., frequent, repetitive use with minimal awareness of the activity and its long-term consequences). The topic of moderation as an alternative to addiction is discussed at greater length in Chapter 5.

Habitual behaviors characterized by immediate gratification and delayed negative consequences have been classified by other investigators as "social traps" (Platt, 1973) and "impulsive" behaviors (Ainslie, 1975). These behaviors are not limited to the use of drugs and other substances since they include nondrug activities such as compulsive gambling, compulsive work patterns ("workaholism"), certain sexual problems (e.g., exhibitionism), and some forms of interpersonal relationships like "addictive" love (Peele & Brodsky, 1975). It is important to note that the source of the compulsion is often thought to be rooted in internal body chemistry, especially experiences such as the "physical" craving for a particular drug. An overemphasis on internal physiological factors neglects the possibility that these behaviors are strongly influenced by the individual's *expectations* or anticipation of the desired effects of the activity. Recent research suggests that cognitive and environmental factors such as set and setting often exert greater influence in the determination of drug effects than the pharmacological or physical effects of the drug itself (cf. Marlatt & Rohsenow, 1980). The major implication of this research is that cognitive processes such as expectation and attribution are learned and thereby more open to modification and change than are relatively fixed physiological processes.

One final point needs to be discussed concerning the self-control of addictive behaviors. Some individuals have argued that to accept the fact that addictive behaviors are learned is equivalent to "blaming the victim" in that an addicted individual thereby is held personally *responsible* for his or her condition (cf. Sontag, 1978). Viewed from this perspective, the social-learning account represents a regression to the earlier moral model of addiction. This argument is based on the false assumption that individuals are responsible for their past learning experiences—that they "choose" to engage in these activities perhaps because of some lack of willpower or moral weakness. On the contrary, behavioral theorists define addiction as a powerful habit pattern, an acquired vicious cycle of self-destructive behavior that is locked in by the collective effects of classical conditioning (acquired tolerance mediated in part by classically conditioned compensatory responses to the deleterious effects of the addictive substance), and operant reinforcement (both the positive reinforcement of the high of the drug rush and the negative reinforcement associated with drug use as a means of escaping or avoiding dysphoric physical and/or mental states—including those associated with the negative aftereffects of prior drug use). In terms of conditioning factors alone, an individual who acquires an addictive habit is no more to be held "responsible" for this behavior than one of Pavlov's dogs would be held responsible for salivating at the sound of a ringing bell. In addition to classical and operant conditioning factors, human drug use is also determined to a large extent by acquired expectancies and beliefs about drugs as an antidote to stress and anxiety. Social learning and modeling factors (observational learning) also exert a strong influence (e.g., drug use in the family and peer environment, along with the pervasive portrayal of drug use in advertising and the media). Just because a behavioral problem can be described as a learned habit pattern does not imply that the person is to be held responsible for the acquisition of the habit, nor that the individual is capable of exercising voluntary control over the behavior.

It is important to note, however, that even though an individual's particular habit has been shaped and determined by past learning experiences (for which he or she is not to be held responsible), the process of *changing* habits does involve the active participation and responsibility of the person involved. Through involvement in a self-management program in which the individual acquires new skills and cognitive strategies, habits can be transformed into behaviors that are under the regulation of higher mental processes involving awareness and responsible decision making. As the individual undergoes a process of deconditioning, cognitive restructuring, and skills acquisition, he or she can begin to accept greater responsibility for changing the behavior. This is the essence of the self-control or self-management approach: one can learn how to escape from the clutches of a vicious cycle of addiction, regardless of how the habit pattern was originally acquired. (Additional discussion of addiction as a learned vicious cycle is presented in Chapter 5.)

DIFFERENTIAL ATTRIBUTIONS IN THE PROCESS OF HABIT CHANGE

It is important to reemphasize the distinction between the initial *development* (etiology) of an addictive behavior and factors associated with *changing* these behaviors. In contrast with the disease model and its emphasis on uncontrollable endogenous factors in the etiology of addiction, self-control theorists have emphasized that the individual is capable of exercising control and assuming responsibility for the process of *changing* an addictive habit. One can assume responsibility for becoming actively involved in the change process, much as one does in the acquisition or mastery of any new skill or task. This approach endorses a proactive stance in the habit-change process, in contrast with the more passive, reactive position of personal powerlessness inherent in the disease model. One important premise of the addictive behavior model is that people can learn effective methods of habit change, whether the goal is abstention or moderation, *regardless of how the problem initially developed.* Thus the task faced by the abstaining alcoholic is much the same as the task faced by the ex-smoker or the compulsive gambler. Here the emphasis switches from "why" to "how"—from "Why am I an alcoholic and why should I abstain?" to "How do I get myself out of this trap; how can I stop the old habit and control its occurrence in the future?"

The distinction between attribution of responsibility for the development of a problem (who is to blame for a past event) and attribution of responsibility for a solution (who is to control future events) has been highlighted in an excellent paper by Brickman and his colleagues (Brickman, Rabinowitz, Karuza, Coates, Cohn, & Kidder, 1982).[1] These authors derive four general models that specify the forms of behavior when people try either to help others or help themselves. The essence of their fourfold model is as follows:

In the first (called the moral model because of past usage of this term), actors are held responsible for both problems and solutions and are believed to need only proper motivation. In the compensatory model, people are seen as not responsible for problems but responsible for solutions, and are believed to need power. In the medical model, individuals are seen as responsible for neither problems nor solutions and are believed to need treatment. In the enlightenment model, actors are seen as responsible for problems but as unable or unwilling to provide solutions, and are believed to need discipline. (Brickman *et al.*, 1982, p. 368)

1. Quoted material is from "Models of Helping and Coping" by P. Brickman, V. C. Rabinowitz, J. Karuza, D. Coates, E. Cohn, and L. Kidder, *American Psychologist*, 1982, *37*, 368–384. Copyright 1982 by the American Psychological Association. Reprinted by permission of the publisher and authors.

Let us examine the implications of this analysis for addictive behavior change. In the moral model, people are held responsible for both the development of their problem and its solution. The authors use drinking as an example, "Under the moral model, for example, drinking is seen as a sign of weak character, requiring drinkers to exercise willpower and get control of themselves in order to return to sobriety and respectability" (Brickman et al., 1982, p. 370). The chief limitation of the moral model, as discussed in the previous section, is that people are made to feel guilty and to blame for the development of the problem and that they are somehow lacking in willpower or moral fiber if they do not successfully change their behavior.

The opposite of the moral model, according to Brickman and his colleagues, is the medical model (identical to the disease model in the foregoing discussion) in which neither the illness nor the treatment is the person's responsibility. "The medical model in our sense refers not only to cases in which people are thought to be victims of disease but to all cases in which people are considered subject to forces that were and will continue to be beyond their control" (Brickman et al., 1982, p. 372). The advantage of the medical model is that it allows people to claim and accept help without being blamed for their weakness; the same symptoms that would be punished under another model are entitled to treatment in this approach. The deficiency of this model is that it fosters dependency on outside or external forces in the habit-change process. In terms of addiction treatment, adherents of this model may come to rely upon externally applied treatment (e.g., hypnosis or aversion therapy) as essential to their recovery. Once treatment has ended or the individual perceives the benefits of treatment to be "wearing off," relapse may be imminent and cannot be "controlled" by the exercise of the individual's own resources.

In the enlightenment model, so-called since the central emphasis is placed on "enlightening" participants as to the true nature of their problem, people are considered responsible for the origin of the problem (which they otherwise might deny), but not responsible in the self-control sense for solving the problem. Brickman et al. (1982) cite AA as an example of the enlightenment model:

Alcoholics Anonymous (AA) . . . explicitly requires new recruits both to take responsibility for their past history of drinking (rather than blaming it on a spouse, a job, or other stressful circumstances) and to admit that it is beyond their power to control their drinking—without the help of God and the community of ex-alcoholics in Alcoholics Anonymous. . . . Consistent with the assumptions of the enlightenment model, alcoholics who join Alcoholics Anonymous have been found to have a stronger sense of guilt and responsibility for their past troubles (Trice & Roman, 1970) and a higher need for affiliation and community (Trice, 1959). (Brickman et al., 1982, p. 374)

Thus, although the AA ideology gives lip service to the disease model in terms of etiology, the underlying emphasis according to Brickman is still one of accepting responsibility for the development of the problem. The emphasis on past mistakes evident in the recounting of "drunkalogues" in AA probably reflects this tendency to blame oneself, as do certain "steps" in the AA twelve-step program (e.g., Step Five, "We admitted to God, to ourselves, and to another human being the exact nature of our wrongs," and Step Eight, "We made a list of all persons we had harmed, and became willing to make amends to them all"). Why should someone with an uncontrollable disease feel guilty and responsible for their past misdeeds? Why is there such insistence on admitting that one *is an alcoholic* (instead of accepting the fact that one has experienced problems as a result of excessive drinking) and, at the same time, accepting the veil of anonymity offered by AA or one of the myriad other "Anonymous" groups (e.g., Narcotics Anonymous, Gamblers Anonymous, Overeaters Anonymous, Adulterers Anonymous, Parents Anonymous, etc.)? As Brickman points out:

Representatives of all our models are, to some extent, concerned with instructing people to make the appropriate attributions of responsibility for the causes and solutions to their problems. In the enlightenment model, however, these attributions require people to accept a strikingly negative image of themselves and, in order to improve, to accept a strong degree of submission to agents of social control. Because people tend to resist this position, the emphasis on enlightening them or socializing them to accept it is especially apparent. . . . The deficiency of the enlightenment model lies in the fact that it can lead to a fanatical or obsessive concern with certain problems and a reconstruction of people's entire lives around the behaviors or the relationships designed to help them deal with these problems. This is the criticism that has most frequently been leveled against AA (e.g., Cummings, 1979) . . . and against what dieting means for so many dieters. Alcoholics Anonymous reorganizes people's lives so that they stay away from their old drinking places and drinking partners, but they retain their concern for drinking as an issue in their lives and spend much of their time at AA meetings with new AA friends. . . . Converts are asked to repudiate their old, evil ways and to repeatedly perform acts that bear witness to this repudiation. . . . All bad things are blamed on the residue of the old life and good things credited to the experience of the new: Under these circumstances enormous power lies in the threat to withdraw access to the new life and send people back to the old. In most of the foregoing examples, such as Alcoholics Anonymous, this power is diffused in the hands of a variety of friends and fellow sufferers. In some instances, however, it is concentrated in a single charismatic authority—a Charles Manson, a Jim Jones, a Charles Dederich [the founder of Synanon, one of the first therapeutic communities for the rehabilitation of narcotic addicts]—who seeks increasingly extreme forms of commitment from followers. . . . (Brickman *et al.*, 1982, pp. 373-374)

The final model, one that embodies the principles endorsed in the relapse prevention model, is the compensatory model in which people are not considered responsible for the development of problems (e.g., becoming enmeshed in an addictive habit pattern), but are able to compensate for their difficulties by assuming responsibility for changing their behavior—even in the face of setbacks or apparent "relapses." The underlying theme of this model has been forcefully articulated in recent years by the Reverend Jesse Jackson in his phrase, "You are not responsible for being down, but you are responsible for getting up."

The strength of the compensatory model for coping is that it allows people to direct their energies outward, working on trying to solve problems or transform their environment without berating themselves for their role in creating these problems, or permitting others to create them, in the first place. The compensatory model also allows help recipients to command the maximum possible respect from their social environment. They are not blamed for their problems, but are given credit for coming up with solutions. (Brickman *et al.*, 1982, p. 372)

One is reminded in this respect of the image of the "do-it-yourself" individuals who take active responsibility for understanding and changing things—including their own behavior. Indeed, this metaphor is a good one for relapse prevention: one can learn to become one's own "maintenance man" in the addictive behavior change process, instead of relying upon external treatment programs or the influence of a "higher power" as an agent of change. The person becomes an agent of change while at the same time avoiding either the guilt associated with the moral model or the helplessness and loss of control associated with the disease model.

Self-control programs, even though they are often identified as a kind of behavioral "treatment" approach, differ from most externally-based treatment programs in that they teach the client to eventually become the agent of change. This distinction is crucial to the understanding of the RP model. Here one is reminded of the old adage attributed to Maimonides: "Give a man a fish and he eats for a day; teach a man to fish and he eats for a lifetime." Giving him a fish may provide a temporary solution to the problem, but teaching him how to fish is clearly the best long-term solution. In self-control programs such as RP, the aim is to teach clients how to "do it" on their own. As Brickman and his co-authors conclude:

Finally, we are inclined to see cognitive behavior therapy as embodying the assumptions of the compensatory model. The role of the therapist is the limited but critical one of teaching clients how to alter maladaptive cognitive processes and environmental contingencies. . . . Once taught how to recognize and control these contingencies, clients are expected to set their own standards, monitor their own performance, and reward or reinforce themselves appropriately. . . . (Brickman *et al.*, 1982, pp. 379–380).

COMPARISONS BETWEEN THE SELF-CONTROL AND DISEASE MODELS OF ADDICTION

As a means of summarizing the material presented thus far, let us review the major differences between compensatory self-control and the more traditional disease approach to the treatment of addictive behaviors. The differences are outlined in Figure 1-1.

Topic	Self-control Model	Disease Model
Locus of Control	• Person is capable of self-control	• Person is a victim of forces beyond one's control
Treatment Goal	• Choice of goals: abstinence or moderation	• Abstinence is the only goal
Treatment Philosophy	• Fosters detachment of self from behavior • Educational approach	• Equates self with behavior • Medical/disease approach
Treatment Procedures	• Teaching behavioral coping skills • Cognitive restructuring	• Confrontation & conversion • Group support • Cognitive dogma
General Approach to Addictions	• Search for commonalities across addictive behaviors • Addiction is based on maladaptive habits	• Each addiction is unique • Addiction is based on physiological processes
Examples	• Cognitive-behavioral therapy (outpatient) • Self-control programs • Controlled drinking programs	• Hospital treatment programs (inpatient) • Aversion treatment • AA + Synanon

Figure 1-1. The self-control and disease models: Alternative approaches to the treatment of addictive behaviors.

Locus of Control

The essence of the self-control model is that the individual moves from a position of being the "client" under the direction of a therapist to a position in which the person becomes more able to assume responsibility for the process of change. It may be the case that a preference for a more active role in treatment is associated with an internal locus of control personality orientation (Lefcourt, 1976; Phares, 1976). The disease model, on the other hand, views the individual as a victim of forces beyond personal control. Addiction is viewed as a physical illness or disease brought about by some biochemical, genetic, or metabolic disorder, forces that are not usually considered to be subject to the voluntary control of the individual. A preference for a more passive role in the treatment process may reflect an external locus of control orientation in which the individual perceives behavior as being under the regulation of uncontrollable inner impulses, external forces, or outside circumstances.

Treatment Goal

The disease model strongly advocates abstinence as the only acceptable treatment goal. Commitment to abstinence is not considered a cure, however, since any return to drug use is assumed to trigger the latent disease. In contrast with this view, the self-control model favors a more individualized selection of treatment goals ranging from abstinence to controlled or moderate use. One key implication of the self-control approach is that addictive behaviors are not always successfully treated by insistence upon excessive restraints over these behaviors. The emphasis in the disease model on the dichotomy of abstinence and excess (absolute control vs. loss of control) tends to reinforce the oscillation of addictive behaviors from one extreme to the other by forcing the individual to adopt one or the other of these extreme roles. From the self-control perspective, there is an alternative "middle way" or position of balance between total restraint and total indulgence.

Treatment Philosophy

The traditional disease model often tends to equate the person with his or her disorder: your excessive drinking indicates that you are an *alcoholic*, or your use of heroin indicates that you are a dope *addict*. Adherents of the self-control approach take issue with the notion that a person's behavior (e.g., excessive drinking) should be taken as an indication of the individual's entire identity. We do not label a person who has cancer as a "canceric," so why should we then label a person who drinks to excess as an "alcoholic"? In the self-control model, every attempt is made to foster a sense of detachment between the problem behavior and the person's identity or self-concept. This detachment facilitates an objective, nonevaluative approach to treatment in which the client is trained to become his or her own personal scientist–therapist using objective observation of the target behavior as the essential "data" to work with in treatment (Mahoney, 1977). The emphasis on social learning principles as the basis for the modification of problem behavior illustrates the *educational approach* of the self-control model.

Treatment Procedures

The hallmark of the self-control approach to treatment is a combination of behavioral coping skills and cognitive restructuring techniques (including cognitive coping skills). In addition, lifestyle change procedures are frequently included in this approach. It is assumed that the client eventually will be able to perform newly acquired skills and attitudes without the assistance of external aids such as the continued availability of the therapist or some other support group (e.g., AA). In contrast, the disease model approach often attempts to change the basic personal orientation or belief system of the "addict" through a combination of confrontation procedures and/or conversion techniques (surrender of self-control to a "higher power"). In groups such as AA, the "higher power" is religious or spiritual in nature; in other groups, such as Synanon and some other therapeutic communities for addicts, the power is vested in the organizational hierarchy of the group itself. Once the required behavior change has occurred, it is then reinforced by conformity pressures from a peer group. Since members of such groups provide support and encouragement for continued adherence to the behavioral mandates and philosophy of the organization, any transgression of the rules is often met with punishment and peer rejection. An attempt is often made in such groups to regulate members' behavior by the use of simple slogans, prophecies, and other "cognitive dogma" (e.g., "You are always only one drink away from a drunk," "drink, drank, *drunk*," etc.).

General Approach to Addictions

In the self-control approach, an attempt is made to search for *commonalities* across various addictive behaviors (Levison, Gerstein, & Maloff, 1983). Since addictive behavior problems are assumed to be acquired on the basis of learning maladaptive behavior patterns, there is general agreement among proponents of this model that common factors are involved in the acquisition and maintenance of these behaviors. The present attempt to develop a common model of addictive behaviors is consistent with the search for commonalities. In contrast, the disease model tends to endorse the view that each addiction should be treated as a unique and separate disorder. The tendency to treat each addictive behavior problem as a unique entity is reflected in current American administrative and political policy which encourages the separation and independence of research and treatment programs with different addiction problems. The establishment of separate national institutes for alcoholism (National Institute on Alcohol Abuse and Alcoholism) and for drug addiction (National Institute on Drug Abuse) is an example of this policy, as is the generally accepted tradition of assigning clients with alcohol, drug abuse, smoking, and weight control problems to different types of treatment programs for each "addiction."

From the above discussion, it is clear that the self-control and disease models differ in a number of fundamental ways. The two models hold contrasting basic assumptions about the etiology and treatment of addiction problems on a number of levels. Does this mean that one theory is more "correct" than the other, or that the self-control model is beginning to replace the traditional medical approach; that we are experiencing the beginning of a paradigm shift (cf. Kuhn, 1970) in our basic understanding of addiction? Perhaps. What seems clear, at least, is that we are approaching a new synthesis of behavioral, psychological, and physiological factors that will give us a broader and more harmonious perspective on the basic nature of addictive behaviors and how to treat them. This synthesis may signal a new era in the addictions field, one characterized by a fresh empirical approach that dares to challenge the influence of untested myths and the rhetoric of dogma that have held a tight grip on the addictions field for the past several decades.

ISSUES RELATED TO THE MAINTENANCE OF HABIT CHANGE

STAGES OF CHANGE IN THE MODIFICATION OF ADDICTIVE BEHAVIORS

In the previous section, a distinction was made between attributions of responsibility for the development of a problem and for its solution. The same distinction can be made between the assumed determinants of a disorder (etiology) and factors associated with the treatment of that problem, whether treatment is applied externally or self-initiated. Let us take alcoholism as a case in point. Debates about the etiology of alcoholism (i.e., whether it is a genetically determined biomedical disease or an acquired addictive behavior) have led to a plethora of competing approaches to treatment. Given the assumptions of the disease model, adherents of this approach would probably agree that a consensus of opinion concerning the cause of this disorder would provide a foundation for the development of unified and effective treatment programs. Once the cause of a disease is known, the search for an effective treatment is greatly facilitated. This view is rooted in the assumption that there is a one-to-one correspondence between the discovery of valid etiological factors and the subsequent development of effective treatment procedures. Many supporters of the disease model hold the opinion that a biochemical "magic bullet" derived logically from the discovery of the biomedical etiology of alcoholism will provide an effective cure—much in the same manner as tuberculosis was treated successfully with antibiotics once it was discovered that the disease was caused by a specific microorganism (the tubercle bacillus).

At the present time, however, there is little agreement among adherents of the disease model concerning the underlying physiological basis of alcoholism or any other addiction. Despite this lack of agreement or empirical evidence in support of the disease model, this approach continues to have a profound impact on the process and goals of treatment. As indicated earlier, supporters of this view are uniform in their insistence that alcoholics or other addicts can never exercise voluntary control over their drug-taking behavior and that abstinence is the only acceptable treatment goal.

The absence of an agreed-upon etiology of alcoholism is reflected in the wide variety of treatment methods that are currently promoted by professionals and lay persons working in the field. One can find advocates of almost any treatment approach, ranging from chemical aversion to religious conversion. Treatment programs across the country are characterized by a wide variety of intervention techniques, including individual, marital, and group psychotherapy, dietary regimens, chemical and electrical aversion, confrontation and social pressure, behavioral self-control training, relaxation training and stress management, rational–emotive therapy, religious indoctrination, and so forth. Some programs operate on an inpatient basis, with patients paying thousands of dollars for several weeks of intensive hospital treatment, while others operate on a partial hospitalization basis (e.g., day treatment programs) or are primarily outpatient programs. Some programs treat alcohol-dependent patients along with other addiction problems (e.g., addiction to opiates or cocaine), while most prefer to work exclusively with alcoholics. Many advocates of the AA approach argue that no form of treatment administered by professionals (e.g., psychiatrists or mental health professionals) is as successful as a self-help support group consisting of individuals who have themselves experienced problems with alcohol. One recent study (Orford & Edwards, 1977) provided evidence that at least for some alcoholics, participation in a comprehensive treatment program for alcoholism may be no more effective than a few brief sessions of counseling and advice on how to stop drinking!

In a recent Congressional report sponsored by the Office of Technology Assessment (Saxe, Dougherty, Esty, & Fine, 1983), the costs and effectiveness of alcoholism treatment were assessed in an evaluation of medical technology utilized by the Federal Medicare program. Based on a thorough review of available evidence, the authors conclude:

Despite methodological limitations, the available research evidence indicates that any treatment of alcoholism is better than no treatment. . . . However, there is little definitive evidence that any one treatment or treatment setting is better than any other. Furthermore, controlled studies have typically found few differences in outcome according to intensity or duration of treatment. . . . With respect to treatment setting, there is little evidence for the superiority of either inpatient or outpatient care alone, although some evidence exists for the importance of continuing aftercare as an adjunct to short-term intensive rehabilitation (usually in an inpatient setting). Further research is needed both to specify how to match patient to treatment and setting and to test competing claims of effectiveness. (Saxe et al., 1983, pp. 4–5)

In a related discussion of the wide variety of alcoholism treatment programs currently available the Saxe report notes: "The treatments for alcoholism are diverse, in part because experts have different views about the causes of alcoholism" (1983, p. 4).

Unlike the disease model, the self-control approach provides a model of etiology that does have direct implications for treatment and the process of recovery. Addictive behaviors are defined as acquired habit patterns that can be modified through the application of new learning procedures. Individuals can learn to change and can accept personal responsibility for their own recovery. By viewing recovery as a learning task, it is possible to reframe the process of behavior change associated with treatment and the maintenance of change over time. This reframing involves adopting new assumptions about treatment and behavior change: (1) that the initial development of an addictive habit (etiology) and the process of behavior change (i.e., to abstain or moderate use) may be governed by different factors or principles of learning; (2) that the process of changing a habit involves at least three separate stages—commitment and motivation (preparation for change), implementation of the specific behavioral change (e.g., cessation of drug use), and the long-term maintenance of behavior change; (3) that the third stage, maintenance of change, accounts for the greatest proportion of variance associated with long-term treatment outcomes. Let us examine each of these assumptions in turn.

The first assumption states that factors associated with the initial development of an addictive behavior may be independent of factors associated with changing the behavior. In contrast, if one believes that alcoholism, for example, is caused by a physical defect, deranged metabolism, or genetic aberration, one may come to expect that a change in drinking behavior can only be brought about by biomedical intervention procedures. To illustrate this way of thinking about the presumed relationship between etiology and treatment, consider the following example. During a recent visit to an alcoholism inpatient treatment program in Seattle, I was surprised to find that approximately one-third of the patients were diagnosed as cocaine addicts. Despite the mixture of clientele, all patients were treated by the same regimen, with an emphasis on AA meetings and a change to a low sugar, high protein diet (alcoholism is assumed to be caused by deranged metabolism in this particular program). When I asked the director to explain the rationale for treating cocaine addicts and alcoholics in an identical manner, he said that since it was well known that most cocaine abusers have a family history of alcoholism (common genetic etiology), it made sense to expose them to the same treatment regimen.

The motivation to change may be deleteriously influenced by this kind of focus on uncontrollable causative factors. As an alternative to this pessimistic outlook, clients can be reminded that addiction in general remains a problem of unknown specific etiology, that all existing evidence points to it being a collection of psychosomatic disorders with multiple determinants (psychosocial, biological, developmental, behavioral, and environmental factors all have been found to play a role). Many of these etiological factors are, in fact, controllable, while others are less so.

As an additional incentive to change, it may be helpful to discuss other disorders of unknown etiology in which successful behavior change is possible. One example is stuttering: individuals can learn to control or eradicate a stuttering problem, even though the exact etiology of this disorder remains a mystery. Another example is smoking: many individuals have successfully stopped smoking even though the etiology of tobacco dependence remains an unresolved question (e.g., physiological addiction to nicotine vs. an overlearned habit pattern). The point of these examples is to demonstrate that people can in fact successfully change their behavior and that an addictive habit is a controllable behavior even though the etiology is determined by multiple factors, some of which are not possible to change (e.g., genetic predisposition).

The second assumption states that the process of changing a habit pattern involves at least three separate stages. Other investigators have proposed similar stages in the habit-change process; in a recent paper on the self-change of smoking, Prochaska and DiClemente (1983) describe five stages: precontemplation and contemplation (prior to quitting), action (the act of quitting), maintenance, and relapse (see also Prochaska & DiClemente, 1982). In our own analysis of stages of change, the first stage involves the motivation and commitment to change. A multitude of factors may be involved in an individual's desire to abstain or control consumption, including awareness of long-term negative consequences (negative effects on health, personal well-being, social and family life, employment status, etc.), the failure of drug use to provide beneficial effects despite increased dose levels (increased tolerance), confrontation with significant others, contact with successful ex-addicts, spiritual crisis, significant lifestyle change, and so forth. Once the motivation to stop has developed, the individual may or may not make a specific commitment to change by deciding to begin to abstain or to moderate intake at a specific time and place. Too often people make an impulsive decision to stop without first carefully considering all of the motivational factors involved; as a result, commitment may be weak and short-lived. Those of us in the treatment field need to pay greater attention to the motivation and commitment stage of change in order to improve the "readiness" of clients to embark upon a specific program of change. Unless the ground is firmly prepared and one's commitment to change is solid and based on sound decision making, premature commitment may lead to self-defeating experiences of failure and a reluctance to recommit oneself to the change process.

The second stage of the habit-change process is the implementation of the change itself—the act of quitting or the initial application of control strategies. For those who decide to seek help in the quitting process, this stage corresponds to the basic *treatment* phase. Far too often, clients focus on this aspect of change to the relative exclusion of the motivation/commitment and maintenance stages. For these individuals, the act of quitting becomes the central concern, as though the decision itself to change was equivalent to a successful treatment outcome. Actually, the act of quitting is similar to embarking on a trip when one first leaves home on an extended journey. Here, the act of departure (quitting) is but the *first step* of the journey, the threshold of departure. (The journey metaphor of change is discussed at length in Chapter 4.) Although there are a variety of methods that can be employed to facilitate the initiation of abstinence or control (e.g., aversion, contingency contracting, methods of tapering off, taking a solemn pledge or oath to quit, stimulus control, etc.), it is a mistake to place too much emphasis on this stage of the change process. If the individual believes that change is successfully completed once drug use has ceased, little attention will be paid to the perils and demands of the journey ahead during the maintenance stage. As Mark Twain once said about his ability to stop smoking, quitting itself is an easy task—he was able to do it hundreds of times. Staying off tobacco, however, is a much more difficult undertaking.

The final and most important stage of the change process is the maintenance stage. It is during the maintenance stage (which begins the moment after the initiation of abstinence or control) that the individual must work the hardest to maintain the commitment to change over time. It is during this stage that the person will be faced with a plethora of temptations, stressors, and the pull of powerful old habit patterns. As has been reported in the work of Rudolph Moos and his colleagues (e.g., Cronkite & Moos, 1980; Moos & Finney, 1983), most of the variance associated with long-term outcome in the treatment of alcoholism can be accounted for by events that transpire *after* treatment has been completed and the patient has been discharged from the hospital. Many alcoholics treated in an inpatient setting report that they have few if any urges to drink while they are in the hospital. Such an absence of urges may lead to the illusory impression that treatment has been successful and the urge to drink has been permanently quelled. Return to the pretreatment environment often shakes this illusory confidence as the urge to drink returns in response to old stressors and drinking cues. Failure to anticipate and cope with the return of these urges following treatment may set the person up for an early relapse.

A typical response to the high relapse rate in the field of addiction treatment has been to increase the number of initial treatment techniques and to build a more comprehensive broad-spectrum or multimodal treatment package designed to facilitate cessation of the target behavior. The underlying assumption here seems to be that if we add enough components into the initial treatment program, the effects on treatment outcome will somehow last longer. This trend has become increasingly clear in recent years. With regard to the treatment of problem drinking, for example, behavioral intervention programs have moved from a concentrated focus on one or two primary treatment modalities (e.g., aversion therapy) to a shotgun approach in which every technique that might possibly prove effective is thrown into the hopper. A behavioral multimodal treatment package for alcoholism might include the following components: aversive counterconditioning, relaxation training, systematic desensitization, skill training, stimulus control techniques, videotaped self-confrontation, blood-alcohol level discrimination training, electromyogram (EMG) biofeedback, contingency management and contracting, assertiveness training, and everything else except the kitchen sink. All of this is heavy artillery—yet all it may do is project the cannonball a little bit further before it finally hits the ground.

There are two major drawbacks to the multimodal approach to treatment. First, recent evidence suggests that the more techniques and procedures we apply in any treatment case, the more difficult it becomes for the client to maintain compliance with the program requirements (Hall, 1980). Second, many if not all of the intervention techniques are directed primarily toward initial behavior change only, and not toward the long-term maintenance of this change. Many current smoking treatment programs, to take another example, administer the bulk of procedures *prior* to the target quit date.

What is the best way to conceptualize the maintenance stage of habit change? There are two ways of thinking about this stage. One approach is to consider the maintenance stage as a period following initial treatment during which the effects of the treatment program gradually wear off over time. From this perspective, treatment is maximally effective in the beginning stages, especially right after treatment has been completed. Like a new coat of paint, treatment effects look good at first and only gradually begin to fade as time passes. Viewed in this manner, relapse rates are low to begin with (when residual treatment effects are assumed to be strongest) and increase probabilistically as the time from the end of treatment increases. A good example of this approach is the assumed effectiveness of aversion therapy for alcoholism (Cannon, Baker, & Wehl, 1981). Presumably, the effects of aversion are strongest immediately after treatment; as time passes, however, the conditioned aversion begins to wear out and lose its effectiveness (Marlatt, 1983). One would expect relapse rates to *increase* over time as a result of this erosion of the aversion response unless booster sessions are administered to bolster the effects of the initial treatment. Relapse rates, according to this approach, should resemble the "burn-out" curve (technically known as a Weibul distribution) for mechanical objects such as light bulbs. If one were to plot the time at which light bulbs burn out after continuous use, the resulting curve would show that the bulk of the burn-outs (cf. relapses) occur toward the end of the time period, long after the original manufacture of the bulb (cf. initial treatment period). A similar curve might be predicted for relapse rates following treatment for alcoholism especially if the bulk of the treatment program is geared toward the cessation stage (e.g., aversion therapy).

An alternative conceptualization of the maintenance stage is to view it as an opportunity for new learning to occur. If we view abstinence or moderation as learned forms of control, then the maintenance stage becomes one in which old habits are "unlearned" and new adaptive behaviors are acquired to replace the previously dominant problematic response. Maintenance, from this perspective, must involve a gradual process of new learning. The individual engages in a series of "learning trials" in which new ways of responding to old temptation situations are gradually acquired. As with any new learning (especially when one is attempting to replace an old, well-entrenched behavior with new adaptive patterns), learning during the early stages of maintenance often involves a trial-and-error process as the newly acquired behavior gradually becomes established over time. The task during maintenance is not unlike learning to drive a standard shift car in England when one has learned only to drive an automatic shift car in the United States—imagine an American driver in England faced with learning new responses (demonstrating competence with the gear shift, learning to drive in the left lane instead of the right, etc.) while at the same time inhibiting old, previously dominant response patterns, overlearned through years of prior experience. As with any new and difficult learning task, one would expect the individual to make a number of errors until the new response patterns become firmly established. Lapses in attention can result in risk situations (e.g., forgetting to stay in the left lane) and errors may indeed occur. With each such error, however, the driver learns something new—how to maneuver successfully through the confusing English traffic "roundabouts" or how to make a right turn into oncoming traffic flow. Each mistake carries within it the opportunity for new learning to occur.

Extending this metaphor to the maintenance stage of habit change leads to a new conceptualization of what is to be expected during this period. Unlike the treatment wear-off effect described above with reference to the effects of aversion treatment, the present model suggests that more mistakes (lapses) are likely to occur in the *early stages* of posttreatment recovery, as the individual attempts to consolidate new responses to old stimuli. The rate of errors or lapses during the maintenance stage resembles a classical learning curve in which early errors are gradually reduced as the individual masters the new response pattern. The course of progress is therefore gradually upward as the error rate begins to stabilize, in contrast with the burn-out phenomenon with its basic downward course over time. In the burn-out or treatment wear-off curve, the probability of relapse *increases* over time, whereas in the learning curve, the probability *decreases* as time passes. Analyses of the relapse process over time with various addictive behaviors (e.g., Hunt, Barnett, & Branch, 1971) show that stabilization of the relapse rate following treatment begins approximately 90 days after the initiation of abstinence. Prior to this time, relapse rates are high, particularly within the 1st month. Beginning in the 4th month, however, the probability of remaining abstinent throughout the course of the year stabilizes.

Of central importance in this analysis is what patients or clients expect regarding the course of events during the maintenance stage: Do they expect gradual improvement over time or a deterioration of treatment effectiveness? *Beliefs about the course of treatment outcome* may play a significant role in determining the actual outcome. If, on the one hand, people believe that a lapse indicates the breakdown or failure of abstinence-oriented treatment (presumably determined by uncontrollable endogenous disease factors), they may be more likely to relinquish efforts to change and resign themselves to the inevitable downward course of relapse as predicted by the disease model. On the other hand, if people view a lapse as a mistake, an opportunity for new learning and personal growth, they will be less likely to relinquish control and "give in" to the relapse.

What seems crucial to the recovery process is the individual's underlying theoretical model or "big picture" of how treatment is assumed to work and how it relates to the maintenance stage. It makes more sense in this regard to give our clients an optimistic view of recovery, a view that makes provision for errors and slips as an expected part of new learning during the maintenance stage, than to present a pessimistic view in which high relapse rates are assumed to be caused by internal disease mechanisms or a biochemical "switch" that cannot be controlled by the individual. Another source of negative expectations is that according to normative outcome statistics, one might expect that one has only about one chance in five (20% success rate) to achieve success (e.g., to abstain successfully for 1 year). Faced with an expected relapse rate of 80%, most people would understandably feel pessimistic about their own chances for success. Such relapse rate data are often misleading, however, since they are based on data taken from formal treatment programs and thus do not include rates for self-quitters, but rather, often involve clients who have the least prognostic chance of success (e.g., chronic cases). Finally, even if the chances of success are relatively low in any one treatment attempt, these figures tell us nothing about the *cumulative* effect of multiple attempts to change over time.

If we view each attempt to change an addictive habit as a single "trial," each attempt to change the cumulative effects of learning over trials may bring the individual successively closer to the threshold of a lasting habit change. One may learn for example that certain high-risk situations for relapse must be avoided, or that new ways of coping with social pressure to drink are necessary, or that one must exercise additional vigilance while on vacation trips, and so forth, each time a slip occurs. As this new knowledge accumulates over time and new responses are practiced *in vivo*, the individual may find that eventual success is likely—that the probability of ultimate success *increases* over attempts. This new way of conceptualizing the habit-change process has received support in a study reported by Schachter (1982). Schachter interviewed people in New York concerning their long-term history of success in changing the habits of smoking or overeating. In sharp contrast to the high relapse rates reported for single-treatment trials in the literature, Schachter found that his subjects reported an ultimate success rate, looking back over their lives, that was much higher—in the 60%–70% range. Ultimately, people reported being successful in stopping smoking (usually without formal treatment) or losing weight. Although there are no comparable data available for people who have successfully stopped drinking, some evidence suggests that the same pattern of results may obtain, at least for self-quitters (Tuchfeld, 1981).

How do theoretically different approaches to treatment and maintenance compare in terms of treatment outcome? To illustrate the different outcomes, let us examine the results of two alcoholism treatment outcome studies conducted in our laboratory (details of both studies are given in Chapter 2). The first study (Marlatt, 1973) was an investigation of the effectiveness of electrical aversion therapy conducted with chronic male alcoholics. Patients received daily sessions of aversion therapy (electric shock was paired with the sight and smell of alcoholic beverages on repeated trials) in addition to their usual abstinence-oriented inpatient program. In the second study, also conducted with chronic male alcoholics (Chaney, O'Leary, & Marlatt, 1978), patients received training in relapse prevention in addition to the usual inpatient program (also geared toward abstinence). In the relapse prevention program, patients engaged in group role-playing and discussion in which they rehearsed adaptive responses to high-risk situations for relapse (e.g., coping with frustration and anger, drink-refusal training in social pressure situations, how to cope with urges and craving). In both studies, all patients were followed up for at least a year following treatment. Although in both studies the experimental treatment program (aversion or relapse prevention training) did not produce significant differences in abstinence rates during follow-up compared to control groups, significant differences were obtained when we examined the drinking rates of patients who drank at least one drink during the follow-up period. As can be seen in Figure 1-2, the drinking rates associated with the outcome of the two programs show markedly different patterns.

Patients in the aversion group (left side of Figure 1-2) show a pattern of significant improvement at the initial follow-up period (3 months) relative to the control group, but this difference washes out by the next follow-up conducted a year later (15 months). Drinking rates for patients who received the aversion program actually *increased* relative to controls by the 15-month follow-up, a finding that supports the treatment "wear-off" effect described earlier. Since these patients did not receive any booster treatment sessions after the initial program, initial positive effects appear to deteriorate as time passes. In contrast, patients who received training in relapse prevention

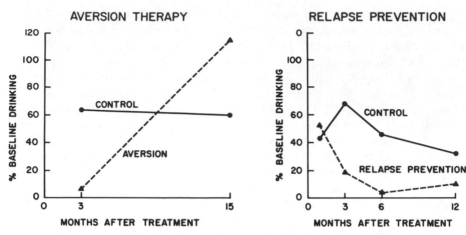

Figure 1-2. Posttreatment drinking rates for nonabstinent patients and controls. Patients received either electrical aversion therapy (left side) or skill training for relapse prevention (right side). Rates represent percentage of pretreatment baseline drinking. From "The Controlled-Drinking Controversy: A Commentary" by G. A. Marlatt, *American Psychologist,* 1983, *38,* 1103. Copyright 1983 by the American Psychological Association, Reprinted by permission.

(right side of the figure) showed a significant improvement during the course of the year following treatment, even though their initial drinking rates (at one month posttreatment) actually exceeded that of the control group who received regular inpatient treatment only. In other words, the drinking rates of the subjects who received skill training for relapse show a *gradual improvement* over time—they appear to get better throughout the course of the year, presumably as their new coping skills become established over time. In both cases, the degree of treatment "success" depends on which part of the posttreatment recovery phase one is looking at: aversion treatment appears to be most effective in the early stages, whereas relapse prevention training does not show up as effective until later in the recovery process. If these results are replicated, it may be the case that a combination of both treatment methods may be even more effective than either given alone. Aversion may be an effective treatment strategy to apply during the cessation stage (to help people quit initially), whereas RP training may facilitate long-term recovery during the maintenance stage.

SELF-CONTROL AS AN APPROACH TO MAINTENANCE

There has been an upsurge of interest in the past decade concerning the application of self-control or self-management programs with a wide variety of behavioral disorders (e.g., Goldfried & Merbaum, 1973; Karoly & Kanfer, 1982; Mahoney & Thoresen, 1974; Stuart, 1977; Thoresen & Mahoney, 1974).

Although early work in this area focused on the use of operant procedures such as stimulus control and self-reinforcement technique (Skinner, 1953), more contemporary approaches have emphasized cognitive components (e.g., cognitive restructuring, training in problem solving and decision making, etc.). The cognitive–behavioral basis of the RP model promotes the combination of selected components from both the behavioral and cognitive domains in the development of an effective maintenance program.

What elements comprise an ideal self-control program for the maintenance of behavior change? Although research on the effectiveness of various combinations of procedures is still in the early stages of development, the following list of ideal characteristics can be taken as a general guideline:

1. The ideal program should prove itself effective in maintaining behavior change for clinically significant periods of time following initial treatment (as demonstrated in long-term follow-up) compared to the best available alternative programs.

2. The ideal program should enhance and maintain an individual's compliance and adherence to program requirements (e.g., continuation of required techniques such as record-keeping, relaxation training, rehearsal of new skills, etc.).

3. The ideal program should consist of a mixture of specific behavioral techniques (e.g., skill training, contingency management, etc.), cognitive intervention procedures (e.g., cognitive restructuring, increased attention to covert ideation such as rationalization and denial, use of coping imagery, etc.), and global lifestyle modification to enhance overall coping capacity (e.g., exercise and stress management procedures).

4. In addition to teaching cognitive strategies, behavioral coping, and lifestyle change, the ideal program should also facilitate the development of motivation and decision-making skills as applied to ongoing changes that occur during the maintenance phase.

5. To increase overall compliance and effectiveness, the ideal program should include a balance of both "right-brain" and "left-brain" intervention components. Theoretical analyses of cerebral hemisphere specialization (cf. Ornstein, 1977) suggests that the left and right hemispheres are associated with different mental operations: the left hemisphere (dominant in most right-handed people) is thought to be the center for linear thought processes (verbalization, mathematical and logical thinking, etc.), whereas the right or nondominant hemisphere is more associated with nonverbal functions (imagery, artistic skills, spatial patterning, and intuition). One of the central precepts of the RP model is that a combination of both verbal and nonverbal (imagery) procedures provides the best protection against relapse.

6. The ideal program should replace maladaptive habit patterns with alternative behaviors and skills, with an emphasis on substitute activities which provide the individual with at least some of the reinforcing consequences (gratification) associated with the old habit pattern. For example, a negative addiction may be replaced by a positive one, especially if engaging in the latter behavior also produces a subjective high or altered state of consciousness (as appears to be the case with meditation and some forms of exercise).

7. The ideal program should enable the individual to cope effectively with new problem situations as they arise, to reduce the probability of relapse. To do this, an effective self-control program should have built-in generalization components designed to teach the client to identify and cope with problems that may not have been specifically dealt with in the initial treatment program. Training in general problem solving, effective decision making, communication skills, and assertiveness skills are some of the more global approaches that can be used to increase treatment generalization effects. In addition to these general coping procedures, effective use of lifestyle engineering and stress-management skills (e.g., time management programs, relaxation training, etc.) may increase the individual's capacity and energy to cope with new problem situations.

8. In addition to increasing generalization effects in new problem situations, the ideal self-control program should teach the client new and adaptive ways of dealing with failure experiences. An attempt should be made to teach the individual that setbacks can be viewed not as failures but as mistakes that can provide valuable information that can then be used to develop more effective coping strategies for the future.

9. The ideal program should make use of client support systems to enhance treatment generalization effects. Every attempt should be made to enlist the cooperative support of other people who are likely to have contact with the client. Members of the client's family or individuals in the client's workplace should be recruited to provide support and encouragement. Recent research on the use of spouses and other family members as providers of support for clients with addictive behavior problems shows considerable promise (cf. Brownell, Heckerman, Westlake, Hayes, & Monti, 1978; McCrady, Paolino, Longabaugh, & Rossi, 1979). In addition, clients with similar problems who share a common theoretical or philosophical orientation can be encouraged to get together in self-help groups where members join to provide support and encouragement in a collective attempt to maintain change.

DETERMINANTS OF RELAPSE AND AN OVERVIEW OF THE RELAPSE PROCESS

In this section, an overview of the theoretical model of the relapse process is provided. Two basic approaches to the understanding of relapse are presented: the disease model and the author's own approach. Relapse curves for various addictive behaviors are discussed and the notion of relapse as a common denominator in the addictive behaviors is put forth. The influence of high-risk situations as immediate precipitants or determinants of relapse along with the hypothetical model of the relapse process are then described. The presentation of the basic relapse model is followed by a description of general lifestyle factors that may increase the individual's vulnerability to the impact of high-risk situations and may be involved in the covert planning or "setting-up" of a relapse episode.

RELAPSE: TWO OPPOSING DEFINITIONS

At a recent workshop for alcoholism and drug counselors, the author asked members of the audience to share their subjective associations to the term *relapse*. Here are some of their replies: "treatment failure," "return to illness," "falling back into addiction," "failure and guilt," and "breakdown." These associations are reflected in one of two definitions of "relapse" given in *Webster's New Collegiate Dictionary* (1983): "a recurrence of symptoms of a disease after a period of improvement." This definition corresponds with the dichotomous view of treatment outcome fostered by the disease model: one is either "cured" (or the symptoms are in remission) or one has relapsed (recidivism). It has been standard practice in the addictions field to view *any* use of drugs following an abstinence-oriented treatment program as indicative of relapse. This all-or-none outlook is reflected in most of the traditional treatment outcome literature, where cases are reported as either successes (e.g., maintaining abstinence) or failures (any violation of abstinence). Relapse is thus seen as an *end state*: the end of the road; a dead end.

There are a number of problems with this rather pessimistic approach to relapse. If the black–white dichotomy of abstinence–relapse is assimilated by the individual while in treatment, it seems likely that this will set up an expectation leading to a self-fulfilling prophecy in which any violation of abstinence will send the pendulum to the extreme of relapse. On one side of this oscillation is the extreme of absolute control or total restraint; the other extreme is that of loss of control or total indulgence. Another problem with the traditional definition of relapse is its association with the return of the disease state. The cause of the relapse is usually attributed to *internal* factors associated with the disease condition. Behaviors associated with relapse come to be equated with the emergence of symptoms signaling the reactivation of the underlying disease, much as the experience of fever and chills serves as a signal of relapse in malaria. This emphasis on internal causation carries the implicit message that there is *nothing much one can do* about the outbreak of symptoms; how does one prevent a fever from breaking out? This outlook tends to ignore the influence of situational and psychological factors as potential determinants in the relapse process. It also reinforces the notion that the individual who experiences a relapse is a helpless victim of circumstances beyond his or her control.

According to some traditional theorists, relapse is the result of "negative forces" that overpower the individual who has lost touch with the protective influence of a "higher power." Consider, for example, the following quotation from a recent publication on relapse:

Sobriety for the alcoholic is, then, an equilibrium, a balance between the forces driving one to drink uncontrollably and the new-found strength to counter them, to keep them in check. The struggle is at first conscious but then submerges into the unconscious with the potential of reemerging into frightening reality. It may be triggered by a variety of stimuli which energize the negative forces leading to an actual relapse. The essential state preceding relapse seems to be one of isolation, of anomie. The existential bonds tying the individual to fellow humans, to one's so-called "higher power," to the mysterious joy of living seem lost or dissolved. The individual is adrift and rudderless and cannot mobilize the positive forces which had so recently been embraced in achieving one's abstinence. As a result, the negative forces become ascendant and powerful enough to effect a relapse. (Weisman, 1983, p. 26)

Here relapse seems to be the result of a battle between one's "higher power" and unconscious negative forces emanating from some kind of "lower power" (the Devil himself?).

There is an alternative approach to the issue of relapse, and it is reflected in the second definition listed in *Webster's*: "Relapse is the *act* or *instance* of backsliding, worsening, or subsiding (1983)." The italics are added here to emphasize that a relapse can be viewed as a *single act* of falling back: a single mistake, an error, a slip. A better word to refer to the singular occurrence of the behavior in question (e.g., the first drink or cigarette following a period of abstinence) would be the term *lapse* (as in a lapse of attention). The same dictionary defines "lapse" as "a slight error or slip . . . a temporary fall esp. from a higher to a lower state." One thinks here of a skater in competition who trips and falls on the ice. Whether or not the skater gets up again and continues to perform depends to a large extent on whether the fall is seen as a *lapse* or a *relapse*—as a single slip (mistake) or as an indication of total failure. By allowing room for mistakes to occur (as opposed to viewing any slip as a symptom of deterioration), one may be able to avoid the oscillation between extremes in which the individual is either perceived as in control (standing up) or out of control (falling down). A primary assumption of the RP model is that the cognitive and affective reactions to the first slip or lapse after a period of abstinence (especially the attribution for the cause of the lapse) exert a significant influence that may determine whether or not the lapse is followed by a full return to the former behavior or habit (relapse).

In the RP approach, relapse is viewed as a transitional process, a series of events that may or may not be followed by a return to baseline levels of the target behavior. Rather than adopting a pessimistic view in which relapse is viewed as a dead end, treatment failure, or a return of the disease state, the

RP model views the occurrence of a lapse as a fork in the road, with one path returning to the former problem level (relapse or total collapse) and the other continuing in the direction of positive change. It is of interest in this regard that the origin of the term relapse comes from the Latin word *relabi*, which means "to slide or fall back." Not every lapse eventuates in a relapse, however. In some cases, we actually *benefit* from a lapse. Just as a child who is learning to ride a bicycle sometimes benefits from a slip or fall (e.g., he or she learns to apply the brakes before going into a turn on the next attempt), so an individual who is attempting to change a habit pattern may sometimes find that a lapse provides useful information about both the cause of the event (e.g., a formerly unknown stressful situation) and how to correct for its occurrence in the future (e.g., to plan remedial action). In such instances, it may be more accurate to define the outcome as a *prolapse* (from the Latin word, *prolabi*, meaning a "slide or fall forward," a term that usually refers to the slipping of a body part from its usual position), since the overall beneficial outcome places the individual in a "forward position" (in terms of new learning). Whether or not a lapse is followed by a relapse or, in some cases, a prolapse, depends to a large extent upon the individual's personal expectations and underlying model of the habit change process.

Many new questions arise when one adopts this alternative perspective of relapse. Many of these questions are rarely even asked by those who adhere to the disease model, with its exclusive emphasis on internal or biological determinants of relapse. Are there any specific situational events that serve as precipitating triggers for relapse? Are the determinants of the first lapse the same as those assumed to govern a total relapse? Is it possible for an individual to covertly plan a relapse by setting up a situation in which it is virtually impossible to resist temptation? At which points in the relapse process is it possible to intervene and alter the course of events so as to prevent a return to the former habit pattern? How does the individual react to and conceptualize the events preceding and following a relapse, and how do these reactions affect the person's subsequent behavior? Is it possible to prepare persons in treatment to anticipate the likelihood of a relapse, so that they may engage in preventive alternative behaviors? To borrow a term from Meichenbaum (1977), can we develop prevention procedures that would "inoculate" the individual against the inevitability of relapse?

In order to answer these and other questions, it is necessary to engage in a detailed microanalysis of the relapse process itself. This fine-grained approach focuses upon the various determinants of relapse, both in terms of the immediate precipitating circumstances and the longer chain of events that may or may not precede the relapse episode. In addition, the role of such cognitive factors as expectation and attribution are examined in detail, particularly in terms of the individual's reactions to the relapse. A microanalysis of the relapse process is justified by the old maxim that *we can learn much from our mistakes.* Rather than being seen as an indication of failure, a relapse can more optimistically be viewed as a challenge, an opportunity for new learning to occur.

THE RELAPSE PROCESS: A COMMON DENOMINATOR IN ADDICTIVE BEHAVIORS?

Recidivism rates are notoriously high across the spectrum of addictive behaviors. In addition to high relapse rates, the temporal patterning of the relapse process also shows considerable consistency for a variety of addiction problems. This consistency is strikingly apparent from an examination of the relapse curves depicted in Figure 1-3. This graph, first published in the early 1970s (Hunt, Barnett, & Branch, 1971), shows the temporal pattern of

Figure 1-3. Relapse curves for individuals treated for heroin, smoking, and alcohol addiction. From "Relapse Rates in Addiction Programs" by W. A. Hunt, L. W. Barnett, and L. G. Branch, *Journal of Clinical Psychology*, 1971, 27, 355. Copyright 1971 by the Clinical Psychology Publishing Co., Inc. Reprinted by permission.

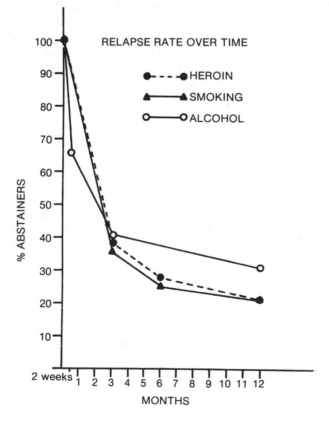

relapse (defined by these authors as *any* drug use) following completion of treatment programs for smokers, alcoholics, and heroin addicts. These curves are based on multiple treatment outcome studies; the curve for smokers, for example, is based on an averaging of data drawn from 84 separate smoking treatment studies. The commonality of relapse rates depicted in Figure 1-3 is quite clear: About two-thirds of all relapses occurred within the first 90 days following treatment.

One traditional interpretation of the data shown in Figure 1-3 is that the similarity in the shape of the curves is due to the fact that these substances are equivalent in some way in terms of their addictive potential. The conclusion is drawn that tobacco, alcohol, and heroin are equally addicting in terms of their effects. Acceptance of this perspective has led investigators on a search for the underlying addictive mechanisms involved.

Others have suggested that the shape of the relapse curves suggests an underlying "extinction" or "forgetting" process described in the learning literature (Hunt *et al.*, 1971; Hunt & Matarazzo, 1970). From this perspective, treatment itself involves the extinction of learned addictive behaviors which then reemerge during the decay of the extinction period. Several cautions must be made concerning models of relapse based on the shape of the relapse curves depicted in Figure 1-3. One possible problem is that since these curves represent relapses among individuals who participated in formal treatment programs, the curves may be misleading because they are based on outcomes from the most difficult cases (most smokers, for example, quit on their own without the benefit of external treatment programs). Similarly, the curves do not show the results of long-term success or failure over repeated treatment trials or self-quit attempts, since they are based only on outcomes for a single cessation attempt (cf. Schachter, 1982).

In addition, as pointed out by researchers at the Addiction Research Unit at the Maudsley Hospital in London (Litman, Eiser, & Taylor, 1979; Sutton, 1979), drawing conclusions about the theoretical nature of the relapse process on the basis of these curves may lead to mistaken conclusions for the following reasons: (1) The curves are based on group averages, and do not necessarily represent the relapse process over time for any given individual. (2) The curves are *cumulative* curves calculated on the basis of the percentage of abstainers remaining at intervals over a given period of time—leading to the often mistaken assumption that once a person has engaged in any drug use after a period of abstinence, regardless of what quantity of how briefly, drug use will continue after that point (the curves in Figure 1-3 represent the time period between treatment completion and the "initial use" or first lapse). (3) Cumulative curves such as those in Figure 1-3 represent the proportion of the total population (all of whom were abstinent at treatment completion) who are still abstinent at given points in time; by their very nature, cumulative data will always take the form of a downward sloping, negatively accelerated curve. (4) Similarly, given individual differences in the probability of remaining abstinent for a given period of time, the probability of survival for the group as a whole will increase over time as a result of a selection process (in each successive interval of time those individuals with a relatively low probability of survival will tend to drop out in favor of those with a relatively high probability of survival).

Many of these problems can be overcome, however, by the use of survival analysis statistical procedures, also known as "life table" or "failure time" analyses (Elandt-Johnson & Johnson, 1980; Kalbfleisch & Prentice, 1980). By the use of such statistical methods, the shortcomings associated with cumulative curves are overcome by the use of the "relapse rate" statistic. Relapse rate is assessed over a given period of time (e.g., a 3-month period) as the proportion of people who have relapsed during this interval to the number of people who were "eligible" for relapse at the beginning of the same time period. Anyone who relapsed prior to this period is not included in the calculation. Use of relapse rate data may have important implications for the timing of treatment interventions during the maintenance stage of the habit change process, since it indicates the relative risk of relapse over different time periods. For a further description of the use of survival analysis in the assessment of relapse, readers are referred to a forthcoming chapter by Goldstein, Marlatt, Peterson, and Lutton (in press).

Relapse rate data confirm the essential findings depicted in Figure 1-3, however; in general, about two-thirds of all initial lapses occur within the first 90 days following initiation of the cessation attempt across various addictive behaviors. The author's conceptualization of these findings yields an alternative theoretical possibility in the interpretation of the relapse process. I hypothesize that there may be common cognitive, affective, and behavioral components associated with the initial lapse itself, regardless of the particular "addictive" substance or activity involved. Although the significance of the individual properties of various substances or activities cannot be ignored, particularly as they influence the development of abuse patterns within user groups, the RP model seeks to uncover the common determinants and reactions to the first lapse and to understand how these factors affect the probability of subsequent relapse or recovery.

In the model to be presented in the following sections, a lapse is defined as any discrete violation of a self-imposed rule or set of regulations governing the rate or pattern of a selected target behavior. The criterion of abstinence, the most stringent and absolute rule one can adopt in this regard, is by definition violated by a single occurrence of the target behavior. From this absolute perspective the occurrence of a single lapse is tantamount to relapse (one cannot be a "little bit" nonabstinent, just as one cannot be a "little bit" pregnant). Although violation of the abstinence rule is the primary form of relapse studied in this author's research, other forms of relapse would also be included within the above definition. The first violation of rules governing caloric intake for someone on a strict diet would also constitute a lapse, as would the initial exceeding of consumption limits imposed in a controlled drinking program. Within this general framework, a distinction thus is being made between the first violation of the rules (the initial *lapse*) and the subsequent *secondary* effects in which the behavior may or may not increase in the direction of the original pretreatment baseline levels (a full-blown *relapse*).

THE RELAPSE PROCESS:
AN OVERVIEW OF IMMEDIATE DETERMINANTS
AND REACTIONS

The material to follow presents an overview of the relapse process focusing on the immediate determinants (precipitating circumstances) and subsequent reactions to the first lapse following a period of abstinence or strictly controlled use. An important constraint in the model is that it applies only to those cases in which the person has made a *voluntary* choice or decision to change; the implications of the theory for enforced or involuntary abstinence have yet to be determined.

In the following overview, only the highlights of the model are presented, since further details are presented elsewhere in this volume (see Chapters 2 and 3). Background research and theory leading to the development of this model can be found elsewhere (Cummings, Gordon, & Marlatt, 1980; Marlatt, 1978, 1979, 1982; Marlatt & Gordon, 1980; Marlatt & Parks, 1982). A schematic representation of the relapse model is presented in Figure 1-4.

To begin, it is assumed that the individual experiences a sense of *perceived control* (self-efficacy) while maintaining abstinence (or complying with other rules governing the target behavior). The behavior is "under control" so long as it does not occur during this period; the longer the period of successful abstinence, the greater the individual's perception of self-efficacy. This perceived control will continue until the person encounters a *high-risk situation*. A high-risk situation is defined broadly as any situation that poses a threat to the individual's sense of control and increases the risk of potential relapse. In a recent analysis of 311 initial relapse episodes obtained from clients with a variety of problem behaviors (problem drinking, smoking, heroin addiction, compulsive gambling, and overeating), researchers identified three primary high-risk situations that were associated with almost three-quarters of all the relapses reported (Cummings, Gordon, & Marlatt, 1980). A table of high-risk situations adapted from the latter source is presented in Table 1-1. A description of the three categories associated with the highest relapse rates follows. A complete description of all categories, along with scoring rules, is presented in Chapter 2.

—> *Negative Emotional States* (35% of all relapses in the sample): situations in which the individual is experiencing a negative (or unpleasant) emotional

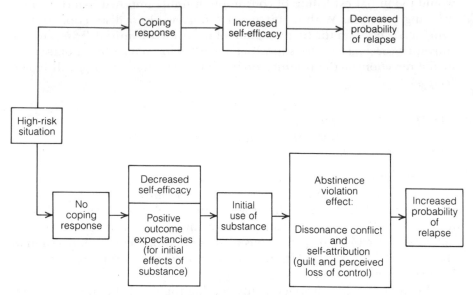

Figure 1-4. A cognitive–behavioral model of the relapse process.

state, mood, or feeling such as frustration, anger, anxiety, depression, or boredom, prior to or at the time the first lapse occurs. For example, one of our smokers gave the following description of a relapse episode: "Everything was going well until I failed my statistics exam. I was feeling low and decided a cigarette would cheer me up." In our scoring system, this category is classified under a major subdivision called *intrapersonal determinants*, which includes all situations that are primarily associated with intrapersonal factors (within the individual), and/or reactions to nonpersonal environmental events. Situations involving another person or group of individuals that is significantly involved in the relapse episode are grouped under the second major subdivision, *interpersonal determinants*; the two following categories both fall within this latter subdivision.

→ *Interpersonal Conflict* (16% of the relapses): situations involving an ongoing or relatively recent conflict associated with any interpersonal relationship, such as marriage, friendship, family members, or employer–employee relations. Arguments and interpersonal confrontations occur frequently in this category.

→ *Social Pressure* (20% of the relapses): situations in which the individual is responding to the influence of another person or group of people exerting pressure on the individual to engage in the taboo behavior. Social pressure may either be direct (direct interpersonal contact with verbal persuasion) or indirect (e.g., being in the presence of others who are engaging in the same target behavior, even though no direct pressure is involved).

Table 1-1. Analysis of Relapse Situations with Alcoholics, Smokers, Heroin Addicts, Compulsive Gamblers, and Dieters

Relapse situation	Alcoholics (n = 70)	Smokers (n = 64)	Heroin addicts (n = 129)	Gamblers (n = 19)	Overeaters (n = 29)	Total (n = 311)
Intrapersonal determinants						
Negative emotional states	38%	37%	19%	47%	33%	35%
Negative physical states	3%	2%	9%	—	—	3%
Positive emotional states	—	6%	10%	—	3%	4%
Testing personal control	9%	—	2%	16%	—	5%
Urges and temptations	11%	5%	5%	16%	10%	9%
TOTAL	61%	50%	45%	79%	46%	56%
Interpersonal determinants						
Interpersonal conflict	18%	15%	14%	16%	14%	16%
Social pressure	18%	32%	36%	5%	10%	20%
Positive emotional states	3%	3%	5%	—	28%	8%
TOTAL	39%	50%	55%	21%	52%	44%

In our analyses of relapse episodes to date (Cummings, Gordon, & Marlatt, 1980; Marlatt & Gordon, 1980), we have found that there are more similarities than differences in relapse categories across the various addictive behaviors we studied. These same three high-risk situations are frequently found to be associated with relapse, regardless of the particular problem involved (problem drinking, smoking, gambling, heroin use, or overeating). This pattern of findings lends support to our hypothesis that there is a common mechanism underlying the relapse process across different addictive behaviors.

If the individual is able to execute an effective cognitive or behavioral *coping response* in the high-risk situation (e.g., is assertive in counteracting social pressures), the probability of relapse decreases significantly. The individual who copes successfully with the situation is likely to experience a sense of mastery or perception of control. Successful mastery of one problematic situation is often associated with an expectation of being able to cope successfully with the next challenging event. The expectancy of being able to cope with successive high-risk situations as they develop is closely associated with the notion of self-efficacy (Bandura, 1977), defined earlier as the individual's expectation concerning the capacity to cope with an impending situation or task. A feeling of confidence in one's abilities to cope effectively with a high-risk situation is associated with an increased perception of self-efficacy, a kind of "I know I can handle it" feeling. As the duration of the abstinence (or period of controlled use) increases, and the individual is able to cope effectively with more and more high-risk situations, perception of control increases in a cumulative fashion. The probability of relapse decreases accordingly. Self-efficacy as a factor in the relapse process is discussed at length in Chapter 3.

What happens if an individual is not able to cope successfully with a high-risk situation? It may be that the person has never acquired the coping skills involved, or that the appropriate response has been inhibited by fear or anxiety. Or, perhaps the individual fails to recognize and respond to the risk involved before it is too late. Whatever the reason, if a coping response is not performed, the person is likely to experience a decrease in self-efficacy, frequently coupled with a sense of helplessness and a tendency to passively give in to the situation. "It's no use, I can't handle this," is a common reaction. As self-efficacy decreases in the precipitating high-risk situation, one's expectations for coping successfully with subsequent problem situations also begins to drop. If the situation also involves the temptation to engage in the prohibited behavior as a means of attempting to cope with the stress involved, the stage is set for a probable relapse.

The probability of relapse is enhanced if the individual holds *positive outcome expectancies* about the effects of the activity or substance involved. Often the person will anticipate the immediate positive effects of the activity, based on past experience, while at the same time ignoring or not attending to the delayed negative consequences involved. The lure of immediate gratification becomes the dominant figure in the perceptual field, as the reality of the full consequences of the act recedes into the background. For many persons, smoking a cigarette or taking a drink has long been associated with coping with stress. "A drink would sure help me get through this," or, "If only I could smoke, I would feel more relaxed," are common beliefs of this type. Positive outcome expectancies are a primary determinant of alcohol use and other forms of substance abuse (cf. Marlatt & Rohsensow, 1980). Outcome expectancies figure prominently as determinants of relapse in our model and are discussed in detail in Chapter 3.

The combination of being unable to cope effectively in a high-risk situation coupled with positive outcome expectancies for the effects of the old habitual coping behavior greatly increases the probability that an initial lapse will occur. On the one hand, the individual is faced with a high-risk situation with no coping response available; self-efficacy decreases as the person feels less able to exert control. On the other hand, there is the lure of the addictive habit, the drink, the drug, or other substance. At this point, unless a last-minute coping response or a sudden change of circumstance occurs, the individual may cross over the border from abstinence (or controlled use) to relapse (uncontrolled use). Whether or not this first excursion over the line, the first lapse, is followed by a total relapse depends to a large extent on the individual's perceptions of the "cause" of the lapse and the reactions associated with its occurrence.

The requirement of abstinence is an absolute dictum. Once someone has crossed over the line, there is no going back. From this all-or-none perspective, a single drink or cigarette is sufficient to violate the rule of abstinence: once committed, the deed cannot be undone. Unfortunately, most people who attempt to stop an old habit such as smoking or drinking perceive quitting in this "once and for all" manner. To account for the reaction to the transgression of an absolute rule, we have postulated a mechanism called the *Abstinence Violation Effect* (AVE) (Marlatt, 1978; Marlatt & Gordon, 1980). The AVE is postulated to occur under the following conditions: Prior to the first lapse, the individual is personally committed to an extended or indefinite period of abstinence. The intensity of the AVE will vary as a function of several factors, including the degree of external justification, the strength of prior commitment or effort expended to maintain abstinence, the duration of the abstinence period, the presence of significant others, the perception of the initial lapse as a voluntary choice of preplanned activity, and the subjective value or importance of the prohibited behavior to the individual. We hypothesize that the intensity of AVE is augmented by the influence of two key cognitive–affective elements: cognitive dissonance (conflict and guilt) and a personal attribution effect (blaming the self as the cause of the relapse).

According to Festinger's original theory (1964), cognitive dissonance is assumed to develop out of a disparity between the individual's cognitions or beliefs about the self (e.g., as an abstainer) and the occurrence of a behavior that is directly incongruent with this self-image (e.g., engaging in the forbidden act). The resulting dissonance is experienced as conflict or guilt ("I shouldn't have, but I did"). This internal conflict acts as a source of motivation to engage in behaviors (or cognitions) designed to reduce the dissonant reaction. To the extent that the problem behavior has been used as a coping response to deal with conflict and guilt in the past, it is likely that the individual will continue to engage in the previously prohibited behavior in an attempt to reduce the unpleasant reactions. An alcoholic, for example, who "falls off the wagon" for the first time may continue to drink after the first lapse in an attempt to relieve the conflict and guilt associated with the transgression itself—particularly if the person used to drink in the past when feeling guilty or conflicted. Continued drinking in an attempt to reduce feelings of guilt may be mediated by negative reinforcement (drinking to escape from unpleasant emotional states).

It is also possible that the individual will attempt to reduce the dissonance associated with the first slip by cognitively altering the self-image so as to bring this in line with the new behavior. Someone who takes the first drink, for example, may reject the former self-image of an abstainer in favor of a new image that is consistent with the emergence of the prohibited behavior: "This just goes to show that I am an alcoholic after all, and that I can't control my drinking once it starts." In either case the result is the same: the probability increases that the lapse will escalate into a full relapse.

The second component of the AVE is a self-attribution effect, wherein the individual attributes the cause of the relapse to personal weakness or failure. Rather than viewing the lapse as a unique response to a particularly difficult situation, the person is likely to blame the cause of the act on such factors as lack of willpower or internal weakness in the face of temptation. People often draw inferences about their own personality traits, attitudes, and motives from the observation of their own behavior (Bem, 1972). To the extent that the person feels personally responsible for "giving in," attribution theory predicts that the person will attribute this failure to internal or personal causes. If the lapse is viewed as a personal failure in this manner, the individual's expectancy for continued failure will increase. If one feels weak-willed or powerless for giving in to the temptation of the first cigarette, for example, the expectation of resisting the second or third cigarette is correspondingly lower. Again the bottom line is the same: an increased probability that the lapse will soon snowball into a full-blown relapse. The hypothesized relationship between the AVE and relapse subsequent to the first slip was confirmed in a recent study of individuals attempting to quit smoking (Goldstein, Gordon, & Marlatt, 1984).

The role of the AVE in the relapse process is further illustrated in Figure 1-5. One way of conceptualizing the relapse process (particularly from the traditional black–white, relapse–abstinence dichotomous perspective) is to view it as a movement or transition between two extremes: absolute control (restraint), on the one side, or loss of control (indulgence) on the

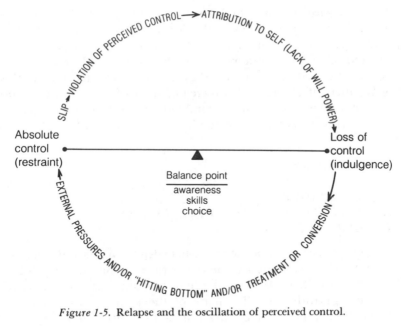

Figure 1-5. Relapse and the oscillation of perceived control.

other. Viewed in this way, the person is at one or the other end of the addictive "seesaw," or is in the process of oscillating between these two extremes (the "revolving door" concept of recidivism). Traditional models of relapse emphasize this oscillation of perceived control in which the addicted individual is either in absolute control (i.e., maintaining faultless abstinence) or has violated this control and, hence, experiences "loss of control." A single slip is taken as evidence that control has been violated; if this violation is attributed to the self (e.g., taken as evidence that one has no willpower), the behavior will go "out of control" (beyond the limits of personal controllability). Recovery from loss of control, from the traditional perspective, can only be achieved through the influence of external pressures (e.g., compulsory treatment, social sanctions and threats, etc.), and/or through the process of "hitting bottom" and relinquishing control to a "higher power" (conversion). The alternative to this dichotomy of oscillating perceived control involves the concept of a "balance point" or a middle-way position between the extremes of restraint and indulgence. Through a combination of increased awareness, coping skills, and the acceptance of personal responsibility and choice, it may be possible to escape from the seesaw of relapse. Material presented in Chapters 3 and 4 provides an elaboration of the AVE in the relapse process.

A final factor to be considered in the relapse process is the subjective effect of the substance or activity experienced by the user following the first lapse. Although these effects differ with the type of drug or other activity, many drugs produce an initial high or state of arousal which is interpreted by the individual as a pleasant or euphoric state. Both alcohol and tobacco, for instance, produce an initial state of physiological arousal (increased heart rate and other autonomic reactions) that may be subjectively experienced by the user as an increase in energy or power (cf. McClelland, Davis, Kalin, & Wanner, 1972). When this increased sense of power is experienced, the use of the substance to counter the individual's prior feelings of personal powerlessness (low self-efficacy) in the high-risk situation is strongly reinforced.

THE RELAPSE PROCESS:
COVERT ANTECEDENTS, LIFESTYLE BALANCE,
AND RELAPSE "SET-UPS"

In the preceding discussion of the immediate determinants and reactions to relapse, the high-risk situation is viewed as the precipitating or triggering situation associated with the initial lapse or first slip following a period of abstinence or controlled use. In many of the relapse episodes we have studied, the first lapse is precipitated in a high-risk situation that the individual encounters unexpectedly. In most of these cases, the person is not expecting the high-risk situation to occur, and/or is generally ill-prepared to cope effectively with the circumstances as they arise. Quite often, people will suddenly find themselves in a rapidly escalating situation. For example, one of my clients (described at length in Chapter 2) who had a serious drinking problem experienced her first lapse after several weeks of abstinence when she treated a new friend to lunch. A last-minute change of plans led them to eat at a restaurant that served alcoholic beverages. Just moments after their arrival, a cocktail waitress approached their table and asked for drink orders. Our client's friend ordered a cocktail first, and then the waitress turned to the client saying, "And you?" She too ordered a drink, the first of a series of events that culminated in a full-blown relapse. As the client said later, "I didn't plan it and I wasn't prepared for it." Suddenly confronted with a high-risk situation (a social-pressure situation, in which she was influenced both by her friend's ordering a drink and by the waitress's asking her for an order), she was unable to cope effectively.

In other relapse episodes, however, the high-risk situation appears to be the last link in a chain of events preceding the first lapse. In another case study, the client was a compulsive gambler who sought therapy for help in controlling his habit that had caused him numerous marital and financial problems. Before therapy, the client had managed to abstain from all gambling for a period of about 6 months, followed by a relapse and an inability to regain abstinence. I asked the client, a resident of Seattle, to describe this last relapse episode. "There's nothing much to talk about," he began. "I was in Reno and I started gambling again." Obviously Reno, Nevada, is a high-risk city for any gambler who is trying to maintain abstinence. I then asked him to describe the events preceding his arrival in Reno. After some prompting, he revealed the following story. Prior to the relapse, he had maintained 6 months of total abstinence from all gambling, a feat that he attributed to his membership in Gamblers Anonymous (GA), a national self-help group patterned closely after the "Twelve Step" format of AA. In his group meetings at GA, he was told that compulsive gambling was an illness or disease, and that the only hope of recovery was to abstain totally from all gambling activities. Even the slightest exception to this rule, such as flipping a coin in a minor coin toss gamble, was considered a violation of the abstinence rule and sufficient to precipitate a total relapse (or, as one of my colleagues commented upon hearing this case, "Even a flip is a slip in GA"). In any case, the client managed to avoid all gambling until the incident occurred in Reno. He and his wife decided to take a car trip down the West Coast, from Seattle to San Francisco. On the return trip, they planned to first drive through the old California gold-mining towns in the Sierras, and then to continue north through Eastern Oregon and on up into Washington State and Seattle.

Everything proceeded smoothly until they were on the road into the mountains east of San Francisco. As they proceeded closer to the California–Nevada border in the gold-rush country, our client began to feel somewhat restless. He and his wife got into an argument about their travel route. He claimed that it would be worth the added time and effort if they would make a slight detour and pass by Lake Tahoe ("To see the amazingly blue waters of the lake," he rationalized) on their route home. They soon found themselves at a junction in the highway. A left turn would take them through Placerville, California ("Safe City"), a destination on their original itinerary; a right turn would take them on the highway leading to the Nevada border and on into Lake Tahoe and Reno. The argument continued for a moment or two at the highway junction before the husband prevailed and made a right turn heading east toward the state line. Although he managed to make it to Lake Tahoe without incident, he did not do as well when they finally arrived in Reno. Along the highway from Tahoe, he observed several billboards advertising gambling casinos and big jackpots in Reno. He parked the car in the downtown section of Reno, directly in front of one of the larger casinos. Needing money for the parking meter, he ventured into the casino to get change for a $5 bill. They gave him four quarters and four silver dollars in change. Since he only needed a quarter for the parking meter, he "decided" to try his luck by dropping one of the silver dollars into a slot machine near the exit, on his way back to the car. The machine gave him a single "cherry" on the payoff line and he won three silver dollars. That was all it took to trigger an episode of "loss of control" gambling—it took his wife almost three days before she could drag him out of town and back on the road home.

By that time, he had wagered away all of their remaining vacation money and they had to make it home on their gas credit card alone. His Reno binge was the start of a prolonged period of gambling which continued for some months until he again sought professional assistance.

The gambler case provides a good illustration of the role of cognitive antecedents in the covert planning of a relapse episode. Looking back over the sequence of events which led him to Reno, a number of significant RP intervention points can be seen. The first major choice-point was the highway junction in California near the Nevada border. Prior to reaching the junction, the client argued with his wife (a high-risk situation in its own right) about their intended route, using a rationalization that the scenery of Lake Tahoe could not be missed; any motive involving gambling was denied. All of these phenomena came together at the highway crossroads, clearly rendering it as an *early-warning junction*. It was at this junction or choice-point that the client engaged in a rationalized decision: he "decided" to turn right, a choice that put him one step closer to a high-risk situation.

A close analysis of this chain of events led us to the conclusion that this client had covertly "set up" or "planned" the relapse. Although he strongly denied his responsibility in this covert planning process, clearly there were a number of choice-points (forks in the road) preceding the relapse where he "chose" an alternative that led him closer to the brink of relapse. The sequence of choice points is illustrated in the "cognitive road map" depicted in Figure 1-6. This road map recreates various choice-points along the way, some of them leading directly to the high-risk situation, others providing various escape routes (U-turn routes and bypasses). The client did not avail himself of these alternative routes, and he ended up in downtown Reno shaking hands with a one-armed bandit, an event that triggered his weekend-long binge of costly gambling. It was as if he had placed himself in a situation that was so risky that it would take a moral Superman to resist the temptation to resume gambling.

Why do some clients seem to plan or set up their own relapse? From a cost–benefit perspective, a relapse can be seen as a rational choice or decision for many individuals (cf. Ainslie, 1975). The benefit is swift in coming: the payoff of immediate gratification (and the chance of hitting the jackpot). For many, the reward of instant gratification far outweighs the cost of potential negative effects that may or may not occur sometime in the distant future (especially if one is a gambler at heart). Why not take the chance—this time it might be different, and perhaps it could be done with impunity. Cognitive distortions such as denial and rationalization make it much easier to set up one's own relapse episode. One may deny both the intent to relapse and the importance of long-range negative consequences. There are also a number of excuses one can use to rationalize the act of indulgence.

One of the most tempting rationalizations is that the desire to indulge is *justified*. This justification is exemplified in the title of a book describing

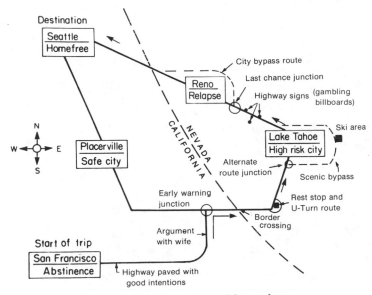

Figure 1-6. A gambler's cognitive road map.

the drinking lifestyles of derelict alcoholics, *You Owe Yourself a Drunk* (Spradley, 1970). My experience in working with a variety of addictive behavior problems suggests that the degree of balance in a person's daily lifestyle has a significant impact on the desire for indulgence or immediate gratification. Here, *balance* is defined as the degree of equilibrium that exists in one's daily life between those activities perceived as external "hassles" or demands (the "shoulds"), and those perceived as pleasures or self-fulfillment (the "wants"). Paying household bills, performing routine chores, or doing menial tasks at work would count highly as shoulds for many people. At the other end of the scale are the wants—activities the person likes to perform, often associated with some form of immediate gratification (e.g., going fishing, taking time off for lunch with a friend, engaging in a creative work task, etc.). Other activities represent a blend or mixture of wants and shoulds. A lifestyle weighted down with a preponderance of perceived shoulds is often associated with an increased perception of self-deprivation and a corresponding desire for indulgence and gratification. It is as if the person who spends his or her entire day engaged in activities which are high in external demand attempts to balance this disequilibrium by engaging in an excessive want or self-indulgence at the end of the day (e.g., drinking to excess in the evening). In order to justify the indulgence, the person may rationalize it by saying, "I owe myself a drink or two—I deserve a break today!" The influence of lifestyle imbalance on the desire for indulgence is illustrated

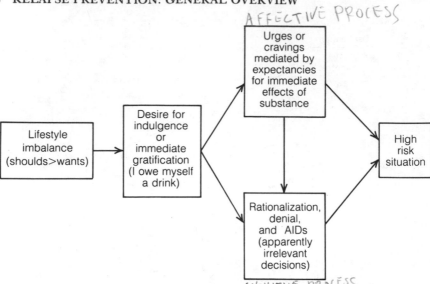

Figure 1-7. Covert antecedents of a relapse situation.

schematically in Figure 1-7. Lifestyle imbalance as a factor in the relapse process is discussed at greater length in Chapter 5.

In addition to a desire for indulgence as a response to the perceived hassles or demands of everyday life, there are other sources of imbalance that can serve as covert determinants of relapse. One such imbalance may involve a reaction against the perceived imposition of external rules or regulations governing the prohibited behavior. Some individuals perceive a commitment to the rule of abstinence as a threat to their personal freedom and choice. This *reactance effect* (Brehm, 1966) may provoke a form of internal "mutiny," in which the person attempts to throw off the oppressive cloak of absolute control by setting up a relapse (see Chapter 3). Such mutinous reactions may be particularly strong in individuals who feel obliged to change in response to the demands of significant others or external social prohibitions.

The desire for indulgence as an attempt to restore balance or equilibrium is often mediated by both affective and cognitive processes as indicated in Figure 1-7. On the affective side the desire for indulgence may be experienced on a somatic level as an urge or craving for the prohibited substance. Both urges and cravings manifest themselves primarily as nonverbal impulses or emotional-affective states. *Urge* is defined here as a relatively sudden impulse to engage in an act (e.g., an impulse to smoke a cigarette). *Craving* is defined in this context as the subjective desire to experience the effects or consequences of a given act. Both urges and craving experiences are assumed to be mediated by the anticipated gratification (immediate pleasure or enjoyment) associated with the indulgent act and its affective consequences, and may be the product of both conditioning (e.g., craving as a conditioned response elicited by stimuli associated with past gratification) and cognitive processes (e.g., expectancy for the immediate effects of a particular act or substance).

In terms of the cognitive antecedents of a relapse episode, three constructs are of central importance: rationalization, denial, and decisions or choices associated with the chain of events preceding the first lapse. A *rationalization* is a cognitive rationale or an ostensibly legitimate excuse to engage in a particular behavior. This conceptualization is similar to traditional psychodynamic theory, which defines rationalization as a defense mechanism allowing the individual to attribute rational or credible motives for a proposed act without a full analysis of the "true" or underlying reasons for this behavior. *Denial* is a similar mechanism. The individual denies or refuses to recognize selected aspects of the situation or set of events. The person may deny the existence of any motive to engage in a relapse, for example, or may deny awareness of the delayed negative consequences of such behavior. Denial and rationalization are both cognitive distortion mechanisms that often go hand in hand in the covert planning of a relapse episode.

Craving and urges do not always result in an immediate impulsive act. In many situations, the consummatory response cannot be carried out immediately due to situational constraints such as unavailability of the substance or the presence of others who may impose negative sanctions. The desire for immediate gratification may be temporarily sublimated, cast in the form of covert planning or fantasies concerning the performance of the taboo activity. Because of the potential for conflict and guilt associated with these covert schemes and plans, the individual is likely to engage in rationalization and/or denial, and these two cognitive distortion mechanisms may then combine to influence certain choices or decisions as part of a chain of events leading ultimately to a relapse. It is hypothesized that a person who is headed for a relapse makes a number of mini-decisions over time, each of which brings the individual closer to the brink of the triggering high-risk situation. An example is the abstinent drinker who buys a bottle of sherry to take home, "just in case guests drop by." Another example is the ex-smoker who decides it would be safe to choose a seat in the smoking section of an airplane. In the gambler case study, a decision was made to expand a vacation driving trip to California to include a visit to the blue waters of Lake Tahoe, just a few miles down the road from Reno, Nevada. One of my colleagues at the University of Washington, Lee Beach (whose area of expertise is decision making), coined the term *Apparently Irrelevant Decisions* (AIDs) to describe these choices.[2] It is as though the person slowly ←

---

2. Because of the unfortunate connotations of the acronym AIDs in connection with the acquired immune deficiency syndrome, a colleague (Robert Marx of the University of Massachusetts) suggested replacing this with a new acronym. SUBTLE (Seemingly Unimportant Behavior That Leads to Errors).

begins to set the stage for a possible relapse by making a series of AIDs, each of which moves the individual one step closer to relapse. A final advantage in setting up a relapse in this manner is that the individual may be able to avoid assuming personal responsibility for the relapse episode itself. By putting ourselves in an extremely tempting high-risk situation, we can claim that we were "overwhelmed" by external circumstances which made it "impossible" to resist a relapse.

RELAPSE PREVENTION:
OVERVIEW OF INTERVENTION PROCEDURES

Most traditional treatment programs for addictive behaviors tend to ignore the relapse issue altogether. There seems to be a general assumption in such programs that even to discuss the topic of relapse is equivalent to giving clients permission to relapse. For example, at a recent lecture given to alcoholics who were about to be discharged from an inpatient treatment program, it was observed that almost all of the 2-hour lecture was devoted to material on the deleterious effects of alcohol on the body's biological systems from the liver to the brain. The captive audience was told in no uncertain terms that alcoholism was a chronic disease that could never be cured, only "arrested" by maintaining total abstinence. As a final comment, the lecturer advised the audience what to do if someone were to offer any of them a drink after they had left the hospital. "Just tell them that your liver is shot, and that you can't drink," was the only suggestion offered. All that input about alcoholism as a disease and the necessity of lifelong abstinence, and only one brief suggestion about how to cope with the temptation to drink! It is reminiscent of those wilderness survival programs in which a volunteer is dropped off somewhere in the mountains miles from the nearest civilization and left alone for several days with only a single matchstick— except in the latter case, the individual involved has already received training in basic survival skills. With most alcoholics, on the other hand, the only "match" they are provided with consists of the single moral imperative: Thou shalt not drink!

I was once told by the director of an alcoholism treatment center in Alberta, Canada, that the best way to handle relapse is to give the patient two marbles upon discharge from the treatment program. "Why the marbles?" I asked. "Two reasons," he replied. "One, the patients carry around the marbles as a reminder of their problems with drinking and the treatment they received with us. Two, if they ever do take a drink, they are supposed to throw away their marbles." When I asked the rationale for this, he replied: "To show them that if they take a drink, they have lost their marbles, of course!"

The rationale that I present to my clients (or to administrators who show some reluctance to focus on relapse issues in their treatment program) is a simple one. I point out that we already have numerous procedures in our society that require us to prepare for the possibility (no matter how remote) that various problematic and dangerous situations may arise. For example, we have fire drills to help us prepare for what to do if a fire breaks out in public buildings or schools. For those who are lucky enough to afford an ocean liner cruise, there are lifeboat drills to teach the passengers what to do in the remote possibility that the ship runs into trouble at sea. Certainly no one believes that by requiring people to participate in firedrills the probability of future fires increases; quite the contrary, in fact, the aim is to minimize the extent of personal loss and damage should a fire break out. The same logic applies in the case of relapse prevention. Why not include a "relapse drill" as a prevention strategy as part of an ongoing treatment program? Learning precise prevention skills and related cognitive strategies would seem to offer more help to the client than relying on vague constructs like willpower or attempting to adhere to the advice embedded in various prophetic slogans such as, "You are only one drink away from a drunk." Other slogans seem much more suited to the RP approach such as, "Forewarned is forearmed," and "An ounce of prevention is worth a pound of cure," or, as any good Boy Scout will tell you, "Be prepared!"

GENERAL APPROACH IN WORKING WITH CLIENTS

Contrary to traditional approaches in the treatment of addictive problems (especially those derived from the disease model), in which therapists often initiate treatment by using confrontation techniques designed to "break through the denial system" and force the client into accepting a particular diagnostic label, the RP approach attempts to foster a sense of objectivity or detachment in our clients' approach to their problem behaviors. By relating to the client as a colleague or cotherapist, we hope to encourage a sense of cooperation and openness in which clients learn to perceive their addictive behavior as something they *do* rather than as an indication of something they *are*. By adopting this objective and detached approach, clients may be able to free themselves from the guilt and defensiveness that would otherwise bias their view of their problem. I also encourage clients to take an active role in treatment planning and decision making throughout the course of treatment. Rather than treating the client as a passive victim of a disease, I facilitate active participation and encourage the client to assume personal responsibility at every stage of the program. The overall goal is to increase the clients' awareness and choice concerning their behavior, to develop coping skills and self-control capacities, and to generally develop a greater sense of confidence, mastery, or self-efficacy in their lives.

Which of the various RP techniques described below should be applied with a particular client? It is possible to combine techniques into a standardized "package," with each subject receiving identical components, if the purpose is to evaluate the effectiveness of a package program. Most readers, however, will be using the RP model with clients in an applied clinical setting. In contrast with the demands of treatment outcome research, those working in the clinical arena typically prefer to develop an *individualized* program of techniques, tailor-made for a particular client. The individualized approach is the one we recommend for implementation with most client problems. Selection of particular techniques should be made on the basis of a carefully conducted assessment. Therapists are encouraged to select intervention techniques on the basis of their initial evaluation and assessment of the client's problem and general lifestyle pattern. In order to evaluate the effectiveness of a particular intervention program in the clinical setting, the use of single-subject designs is recommended (e.g., Jayarante & Levy, 1979; Kazdin, 1976a). By monitoring ongoing progress with the use of single-subject methodology, the therapist should be able to combine procedures into the most effective intervention program for any given client.

To increase the overall impact of the individualized approach, a number of points should be kept in mind. First, in order to enhance the role of the client as colleague or cotherapist, every attempt should be made to assist the client in selecting his or her own combination of techniques. The rationale for selecting one technique over another should follow logically from the assessment phase in which the client plays an active participatory role (e.g., in self-monitoring the target behavior, etc.). Second, the therapist can facilitate the client's general compliance with the self-control program by focusing attention and energy upon a few carefully selected techniques introduced one at a time. Clients are likely to be overwhelmed by being asked to comply with a plethora of procedures which are all introduced at the same time. Along these same lines, adherence to the RP program may be enhanced if the client is able to experience small but progressively incremental successes as the program develops. Self-efficacy is thus enhanced throughout the client's gradual progress, in which each new requirement or assignment is taken "one step at a time." Conversely, the expectation of developing self-control may be demolished in a relatively short period by overloading the client with too many tasks at once. Just as "too many cooks spoil the broth," too many treatment components quell compliance. Finally, the therapist should attempt to develop an intervention program in which there is a balance between prescriptive verbal procedures (e.g., following verbal rules and instructions) and nonverbal techniques (e.g., use of imagery, physical exercise, meditation, etc.).

ASSESSMENT AND INTERVENTION STRATEGIES

This section presents highlights of the RP assessment and intervention strategies that are described at length in the following four chapters. This overview contains a discussion of strategies that are designed to teach the client how to anticipate and cope with the possibility of relapse—to recognize and cope with high-risk situations that may precipitate a lapse, and to modify cognitions and other reactions so as to prevent a single lapse from developing into a full-blown relapse. Because these procedures are explicitly focused on the immediate precipitants of the relapse process, they are referred to collectively as *specific intervention strategies*. The discussion extends beyond the microanalysis of the initial lapse and presents strategies designed to modify the client's lifestyle and to identify and cope with covert determinants of relapse (early warning signals, cognitive distortions, and relapse set-ups). These procedures are referred to as *global self-control strategies*.

Both specific and global RP strategies can be placed in three main categories: skill training, cognitive reframing, and lifestyle intervention. Skill-training strategies include both behavioral and cognitive responses to cope with high-risk situations. Cognitive reframing procedures are designed to provide the client with alternative cognitions concerning the nature of the habit-change process (i.e., to view it as a learning process), to introduce coping imagery to deal with urges and early warning signals, and to reframe reactions to the initial lapse (restructuring of the AVE). Finally, lifestyle intervention strategies (e.g., relaxation and exercise) are designed to strengthen the client's overall coping capacity and to reduce the frequency and intensity of urges and craving that are often the product of an unbalanced lifestyle.

SPECIFIC INTERVENTION STRATEGIES

Figure 1-8 provides a schematic overview of several specific intervention strategies. The boxes along the midline of this figure represent the stages of the relapse process described earlier (see Figure 1-4), from the high-risk situation to the AVE. The circles contain various assessment and treatment procedures that can be used to intervene at successive stages in the relapse sequence.

Let us briefly review the assessment and intervention strategies encircled in Figure 1-8, beginning at the left side of the diagram. The first step to take in the prevention of relapse is to teach the client to recognize the high-risk situations that may precipitate or trigger a relapse. The earlier one becomes aware of being involved in a chain of events that increases the probability of a slip or lapse, the sooner one can either intervene by performing an appropriate coping skill or recognize and respond to the discriminative stimuli that are associated with "entering" a high-risk situation and use these cues both as warning signals and as "reminders" to engage in alternative or remedial action.

To introduce a metaphor that will be used frequently in this presentation, imagine that the client involved in a self-control program is a driver setting out on a highway journey. The trip itinerary (e.g, moving from excessive drug use to abstinence) includes both "easy" and "hard" stretches of road (from the plains to mountain passes). From this metaphorical per-

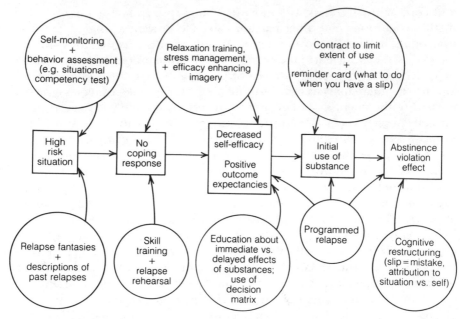

Figure 1-8. Relapse Prevention: Specific intervention strategies.

spective, the high-risk situations are equivalent to those dangerous parts of the trip where the driver must use extra caution and driving skills to keep the car on the road and prevent an accident. The discriminative stimuli which signal a high-risk situation can be thought of as highway signs providing the driver with information about upcoming dangers and risks on the road (e.g., "Icy patches ahead: SLOW to 25"). The responsible alert driver is someone who is trained to keep an eye out for these signs and to take appropriate action to prevent a mishap. So it is with the person who is attempting to refrain from engaging in an addictive behavior: one must be on the lookout for cues that denote the proximity of potentially troublesome situations. These cues can serve as early warning signals that remind the individual to "Stop, Look, and Listen," prior to responding. The sooner these signs are noticed, the easier it is to anticipate what lies around the next bend and take appropriate steps to deal effectively with the situation. ←

There are a number of different methods that can be used to help the clients identify their own high-risk situations. Many of these situations are listed in Table 1-1 and have already been described. Additional details on a wide variety of high-risk situations are provided in Chapter 2. The high-risk situations that my colleagues and I have discovered as part of our research provide a general survey of various categories of relapse episodes, however, and do not necessarily reflect all of the situations that may be high-risk for any particular individual. Although the therapist may make use of the general categories of high-risk situations in Table 1-1 as a starting point, it is important to highlight the need for an individualized assessment procedure to identify unique or idiosyncratic situations that may pose a problem for a particular client. It is also important to emphasize that an evaluation of the client's coping skills is an integral part of the assessment procedure since any given situation can be considered high-risk only to the extent that the person is incapable of responding with an appropriate coping response.

The procedures available to identify high-risk situations differ based on whether or not the client is still engaged in the target behavior at the time of assessment. With many clients, it is possible to obtain an ongoing baseline record of the problem behavior (e.g., smoking or drinking) prior to the cessation date. In the case of most inpatient treatment settings for alcoholism or heroin addiction, however, the therapist has little or no contact with the client until after detoxification has been completed and the client is already abstinent.

In the former condition, the use of *self-monitoring* procedures provides an effective method of identifying potential high-risk situations where access to the ongoing behavior is readily available. Self-monitoring, described at greater length in Chapter 2, is a procedure in which the client keeps an ongoing record of the target behavior as it occurs (e.g., a smoker can be asked to record each cigarette smoked, along with an indication of the time and setting, mood level prior to and after smoking, etc.). Self-monitoring can also be used to monitor urges or intentions to smoke, along with records of coping responses used (if any), and whether or not the urge was followed by an addictive act. Self-monitoring can serve both as an assessment procedure and an intervention strategy, since the client's awareness of the target behavior increases as assessment continues. Awareness of choice-points and alternative responses in the addictive behavior sequence may be one of the most significant allies in the client's coping repertoire. Most habitual behaviors, by definition, are characterized by a low level of awareness. Addictive behaviors such as smoking or drinking often represent "automatic" and overlearned responses. Self-monitoring reintroduces conscious awareness into the process and thereby has a profound dehabitualizing effect.

Other behavioral assessment procedures that can be utilized to identify potential high-risk situations are described in Chapter 2. *Direct observation methods* can sometimes be used, including observation of the target behavior in naturalistic settings and in analogue tasks (e.g., the use of the taste-rating task as a direct behavioral measure of alcohol consumption). One of the most significant self-report assessment measures to identify high-risk situations and self-evaluations of coping capacity for each situation involves the use of *self-efficacy ratings*. Basically this procedure involves presenting clients with a list of specific high-risk situations for relapse and asking them to rate the degree of temptation likely to be experienced and how confident they feel about their capacity to cope effectively (avoid a lapse) in each situation. In a variation on this method, the *Situational Competency Test* (SCT) described in Chapter 2, clients are asked to provide an account (written or oral) of what they would actually do if they were in the high-risk situation described; this procedure also permits an evaluation of their *coping responses*. Self-efficacy ratings and expected coping responses can then be examined to reveal an overall "profile" of strengths and weaknesses across a variety of high-risk situations. Additional assessment procedures in this regard include asking the client to provide an account of *past relapse episodes* and/or descriptions of *relapse fantasies* (e.g., dreams involving drug use or responses to the probe: "I want you to imagine what it would take for you to return to the old habit pattern"). Personal autobiographies that focus upon the client's addictive behavior pattern also can provide clues to potential high-risk situations. Taken collectively, this assessment material can be used to target areas that require special training or attention during the skill-training components of the RP program.

Once the high-risk situations have been identified, the client can then be taught to respond to these situational cues as discriminative stimuli (highway signs) for behavior change. In some cases, it might be best to simply avoid risky situations if possible (take a detour, to follow the highway metaphor). In most cases, however, the situations cannot be easily avoided, and the client must rely on coping skills or alternative strategies to "get through" the situation without a relapse.

The cornerstone of the RP approach is to teach the client coping strategies with *skill-training procedures* (e.g., Chaney, O'Leary, & Marlatt, 1978). For clients whose coping responses are blocked by fear or anxiety, the therapist should attempt to disinhibit the behavior by the use of an appropriate anxiety-reduction procedure such as systematic desensitization. For clients who show deficiencies in their skill repertory, however, the therapist attempts to teach them new skills using a systematic and structured approach. Assessment and training procedures for both behavioral and cognitive coping skills are also described in Chapter 2.

The approach this author favors combines training in general problem-solving ability with specific skill training. Adopting a problem-solving orientation to stressful situations (cf. Goldfried & Davison, 1976) gives people greater flexibility and adaptability in new problem situations, rather than having to rely on the rote learning of a number of discrete skills that may or may not generalize across various settings and situations. Skill-training methods incorporate components of direct instruction, modeling, behavioral rehearsal and coaching, and feedback from the therapist. I also find that the modeling of self-instructional statements (cf. Meichenbaum, 1977) is particularly useful in teaching clients cognitive self-statements to use independently or in conjunction with performance of overt behavioral skills.

In those cases in which it is not practical to practice new coping skills in real-life environmental settings, the therapist can make use of imagery to represent the high-risk situation. This procedure, called a *relapse rehearsal,* is similar to the relapse fantasy technique mentioned earlier. In the relapse rehearsal procedure described in Chapter 2, the therapist goes beyond the imagined scenario related to the high-risk situation and includes scenes in which the client actually imagines himself or herself engaging in appropriate coping responses. This procedure, known as covert modeling (Kazdin, 1976b), can also be used to help clients to cope with their reactions to a slip by rehearsing cognitive restructuring techniques.

In addition to teaching the client to respond effectively when confronted with specific high-risk situations, there are a number of additional *relaxation training and stress management procedures* the therapist can draw upon to increase the client's overall capacity to deal with stress. Relaxation training may provide the client with a global increased perception of control, thereby reducing the stress "load" that any given situation may pose for the individual. Such procedures as progressive muscle relaxation training, meditation, exercise, and various stress management techniques are extremely useful in aiding the client to cope more effectively with the hassles and demands of daily life. These and other lifestyle intervention procedures are described in Chapter 5. (The use of *efficacy-enhancing imagery* procedures, also depicted in Figure 1-8, is described in the section to follow on global self-control strategies.)

Positive outcome expectancies play an influential role in the relapse process and are described at greater length in Chapter 3. After a client has been abstinent for some period of time, a shift in attitudes and beliefs about the effects of the foregone substance or activity often occurs. Positive outcome expectancies for the immediate effects become an especially potent motivating force to resume use when the client is faced with a high-risk situation and is beginning to feel unable to cope effectively (low self-efficacy), or is reacting to an unbalanced lifestyle. In either case, the temptation to "give in" and relinquish control by indulging in the formerly taboo activity is a powerful influence to contend with. As a reminder of its potent effects, I call it the *Problem of Immediate Gratification,* or the PIG phenomenon.

Education about both the immediate and delayed effects of the drug or activity involved may help offset the tendency to see the "grass as greener" on the other side of the abstinence fence. Information about the long-range effects of excessive drug use on physical health and social well-being may help counter the tendency to think only of the initial pleasant short-term effects (i.e., the PIG phenomenon). Recent research and theory about the time-course of effects following the ingestion of many psychoactive substances suggests that the overall response may be *biphasic* in nature: the initial increase of euphoria and arousal (the rush or the high) is frequently followed by a delayed effect in the opposite direction (increased dysphoria and other negative affective states). This biphasic reaction has been observed with alcohol and other psychoactive drugs, and is often cited in association with the *opponent-process* theory of drug-use motivation recently advanced by Solomon and his colleagues (Solomon, 1977; Solomon & Corbit, 1974). The reader is referred to Chapter 3 for a full discussion on the biphasic response and its implications for the development of positive outcome expectancies.

One technique found to be particularly helpful in the assessment of outcome expectancies is the *decision matrix*, illustrated in Figure 1-9 and described in greater detail in Chapter 4. The matrix shown applies to smoking cessation, but it can easily be adapted for other addictive behaviors. The client is presented with the basic format in the form of a three-way table (2 × 2 × 2 matrix) with the following factors: the decision to resume the old behavior or to maintain abstinence, the immediate versus delayed effects of either decision, and, within each of the former categories, the positive and negative consequences involved. The client is then asked (assisted by the therapist) to fill out each of the eight cells of the matrix, listing the effects which are thought to have the greatest impact. The decision matrix should first be administered in the early stages of the habit-change process. It can be a helpful aid in the assessment of motivation to change and can serve as a reminder to the client of the goals or reasons for embarking on the journey of change. It should be noted that the values associated with each specific outcome will probably *change over time* (relative to the point of initial behavior change). The client should thus be reminded to revise the matrix at each significant choice-point in the future, especially if the client is consider-

Figure 1-9. Decision matrix for smoking cessation.

	IMMEDIATE CONSEQUENCES		DELAYED CONSEQUENCES	
	POSITIVE	NEGATIVE	POSITIVE	NEGATIVE
To stop smoking or remain abstinent	increased self-efficacy social approval improved physical state financial gain	denial of gratification withdrawal discomfort frustration + anger weight gain	enhanced self-control improved health (absence of disease) financial gain absence of social disapproval	denial of gratification (becomes less intense)
To continue or resume smoking	immediate gratification removal of withdrawal discomfort consistent with past self-image weight loss	Guilt + attribution of no control social censure negative physical effects financial loss	continued gratification	decreased self-control health risks financial loss continued social disapproval

ing resuming the old behavior. Clients who are on the verge of relapse frequently will attend only to the immediate positive effects at this point (PIG phenomenon), and will overlook or deny the immediate and delayed negative consequences.

What if all else fails, and a lapse occurs? The client can be prepared in advance to cope with this possible outcome, and to apply some behavioral and cognitive "brakes" so that the initial lapse does not "spin out" and become a full-blown relapse. A combination of specific coping skills and a cognitive reframing or restructuring approach offers the greatest advantage in this regard. First, the therapist needs to teach the client behavioral skills to moderate or control the behavior once it occurs. These coping behaviors can be specified ahead of time in a *relapse contract* (see details of relapse contracting in Chapter 4). The purpose of this procedure is to establish a working agreement or therapeutic contract to limit the extent of use should a lapse occur.

→The principal aim of *cognitive restructuring* is to counter the cognitive and affective components of the AVE. Instead of reacting to the first lapse as a sign of personal failure characterized by conflict, guilt, and internal attribution, the client is taught to reconceptualize the episode as a single, independent event and to see it as a mistake rather than a disaster that can never be undone. Various procedures that can be used to reframe lapse and the AVE are described in Chapter 4. As an additional aid to reconceptualization, the client can be given a summary of the cognitive restructuring material in the form of a *reminder card* (see Chapter 4). Reminder cards present a brief list of "emergency procedures" to be followed if a lapse occurs.←

The final intervention procedure indicated in Figure 1-8 is the *programmed relapse*. In this paradoxical intention technique, the client is required to consume the first drink, smoke, or other substance under the direct supervision of the therapist. The goal of the programmed relapse is to help clients (particularly those who report that they are unable to maintain abstinence and plan to resume the old habit pattern) objectively experience the initial return to the target behavior under the guidance of the therapist. By scheduling the "relapse" at a time and place designated by the therapist, it precludes the otherwise dangerous possibility that the client will resume the habit under highly stressful conditions. Details on the use of this procedure are given in Chapter 4.

GLOBAL SELF-CONTROL STRATEGIES

In addition to providing the client with a set of specific skills and cognitive strategies to cope with a variety of high-risk situations, several global strategies can establish a broader framework for the prevention of relapse. Simply teaching the client to respond mechanically to one high-risk situation after another is not enough. It is impossible for the therapist to identify or work with all of the possible high-risk situations that the client may experience. Also, the skill-training sessions described earlier are by necessity quite specific in content, and generalization to other somewhat different situations may not always occur. Teaching general problem-solving skills and advance planning strategies will enhance the generalization process to some degree. To develop a more complete prevention program, however, it is also important to intervene in the client's overall lifestyle so as to increase overall capacity to deal with stress and to cope with high-risk situations with an increased sense of self-efficacy; to train the client to identify and respond to situational and covert early warning signals; and to exercise self-control strategies to reduce the risk level of any situation that might otherwise trigger a slip. Figure 1-10 provides a schematic overview of these global self-control strategies. The midline sequence of boxes represents the covert antecedents leading up to a high-risk situation, as illustrated in Figure 1-7. Various interventions along this sequence of antecedent conditions are presented within the circles.

Recently the author worked with a client who illustrates the impact of *lifestyle imbalance* on an addictive behavior problem. The client in question was a 35-year-old woman who came into therapy seeking help for a drinking problem. When asked to describe the pattern of her daily drinking, she gave the following details. She was employed as a school teacher and was currently living with a man who feared that she might develop an alcoholism problem. Because of his feelings, the client felt a great deal of guilt and usually avoided drinking any alcohol in his presence. As a result, almost all of her drinking was confined to a short period in the afternoon following work. A typical work day for her began at 7:00 A.M. when she got up to make lunch for herself and her partner. Since she slept in until the last possible moment, the morning routine was rushed and frantic. She drove hurriedly to school to meet her first class, a group of rowdy second graders. Instead of taking a lunch break, she chose to monitor the study hall during the noon hour, since doing so meant that she could get off work a bit earlier. The afternoons were much the same as the morning; she taught drama classes and frequently worked under the pressure of deadlines for upcoming plays she directed. By the time she got out of school at 3:00 P.M., she described herself as a "nervous wreck." Her means of coping with this stress was simple and direct. She was in the habit of keeping a fresh half-pint of vodka in the glove compartment of her car and would usually consume all of it on the half-hour commute home. Since she did not want to risk drinking at work, and since her partner viewed her drinking with criticism and disdain, she squeezed all of her alcohol consumption into this one brief period each afternoon. Needless to say, she frequently arrived home in an intoxicated condition.

As indicated earlier in this chapter, an individual whose daily lifestyle is characterized by a preponderance of "shoulds" and a dearth of self-gratifying

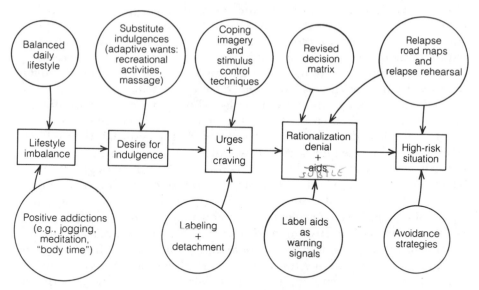

Figure 1-10. Relapse Prevention: Global self-control strategies.

"wants" may come to believe that some form of indulgence is justified as a payoff for responding to external demands and the hassles of everyday life. The client illustrates this principle: she felt that she "owed herself a drunk" since that was almost the only form of self-gratification she allowed herself on a typical work day. She also said that she could hardly wait for the feeling of release that came from the rush provided by the gulped swallows of vodka (for her, the drive home was truly a "rush" hour that she eagerly looked forward to each day).

In working with this client, I began by focusing on two important aspects of her alcohol problem: her partner's attitudes toward her drinking, and her daily lifestyle. Since it was decided on the basis of a careful assessment evaluation that the client would be a good candidate for a moderate drinking program, and since she did not want to give up drinking altogether, the goal of the approach was to bring about a marked change in her pattern of daily drinking. It was agreed that a moderate drinking pattern would involve eliminating the afternoon vodka mini-binges, replacing this behavior with a moderate drinking pattern at home and in other social situations (using wine instead of distilled spirits), and limiting her drinking so as to avoid intoxication. In order to clear the way for her to drink at home, I brought in her boyfriend and discussed with him the possibility that his feelings and attitudes toward the client's drinking may have played an important role in establishing the current aberrant pattern. After some discussion, he began to understand how his fears that she was becoming an alcoholic made her feel guilty to the extent that she had to conceal her drinking from him altogether, confining it to the single rush hour experience. He then agreed to allow her to drink wine at home in his presence without reacting negatively. Almost immediately after her boyfriend came to accept her drinking without responding in a punitive manner, our client reported feeling much less guilt and concern over her consumption of alcohol. Her drinking self-monitoring data showed a drop in consumption of about 25% a week, even in the absence of any additional intervention.

Despite this advance, the client reported that she still felt the need for some form of release after a typical workday. To deal with this desire for immediate gratification, we began to modify her daily activities to restore a balance between her perceived obligatory duties (the "shoulds") and other activities that she found more self-gratifying (the "wants"). As a result, her typical daily routine changed in the following manner. Instead of getting up as late as possible and rushing to prepare lunches for both herself and her boyfriend, she began a new routine of arising an hour and a half earlier in the morning, preparing her lunch (her boyfriend has now learned to make his own lunch), and then stopping off on the way to school at a neighborhood health spa where she enjoyed a leisurely whirlpool bath and massage. She arrived at school relaxed and refreshed to begin the day's work. At mid-morning break, she practiced meditation for twenty minutes, sitting quietly in the school auditorium. At lunch, instead of monitoring the study-hall students, she shared this time with a friend; she and her friend either had a pleasant lunch together or they spent time jogging around a nearby lake.

After the afternoon classes end, the client began devoting an hour to what I call *body time*—time that is set aside exclusively for physical exercise and/or relaxation. Instead of rigidly adhering to an externally imposed exercise regime (e.g., "I must jog every day at 4:00 P.M., no matter what"), she first sat quietly and meditated for a few minutes in order to subjectively intuit what her body "needed" most. Depending on her mood (and often the weather conditions), she then selected an activity from a menu of alternatives consisting of both aerobic activities (jogging, swimming, or bike riding) and meditation–relaxation exercises. In this manner, she chose the activity best suited to her needs on any particular day. If she felt tense and wound-up from the day's work, she might have selected a vigorous exercise such as jogging. On the other hand, if she found herself trapped in compulsive worrying, she may have chosen to meditate instead. (Use of the "body time" concept is described in greater detail in Chapter 5.) Once the client made these lifestyle changes and scheduled them into her routine on a regular basis, her desire for the afternoon vodka rush subsided and was eventually replaced with a need for other more healthy activities. Her drinking decreased dramatically and leveled off at about two to three glasses of wine each evening.

This case illustrates the development of a balanced daily lifestyle. As indicated in Figure 1-10, lifestyle intervention is one of the major global self-control strategies employed in the RP approach. A major goal for lifestyle intervention is to replace drinking or other addictive behaviors with an activity that qualifies as a *positive addiction* (Glasser, 1976). If a "negative" addiction (e.g., excessive drug use) can be described as an activity that feels good at first but causes harm in the long run, a "positive" addiction (e.g., jogging) is an activity which may be experienced negatively at first (especially while one is in the early stages of exercise) but is very beneficial in terms of the long-range effects. Positive addictions often become "wants" as the individual begins to look forward to engaging in the activity, and/or misses the positive effects if the activity or exercise is not engaged in on a regular basis. In addition, since the individual usually must acquire new skills in the development of a positive addiction, self-efficacy often increases as a result. Similarly, since the regular practice of these behaviors is associated with a greater sense of relaxation or improved physical well-being, overall coping capacity is increased; high-risk situations may be more easily dealt with, rather than serving as precipitating triggers for excessive behaviors. Positive addictions, with an emphasis on relaxation and aroebic exercise, are discussed at length in Chapter 5.

Programming periods of free time during the day, when the client can pursue his or her own interests (e.g., going shopping, having lunch with a friend, etc.) may also help provide balance in an otherwise crowded schedule of "shoulds." *Substitute indulgences,* or activities that provide an immediate form of self-gratification (e.g., receiving a massage, sexual activity, eating a gourmet meal, etc.) can also serve as last-minute alternatives or substitute forms of self-indulgence, especially when the temptation to "give in" to the lure of getting stoned on drugs is particularly intense. Lifestyle intervention may also involve therapeutic programs that have a major impact on the client's life—such as marital therapy, employment counseling, or changes in the social or physical environment.

A desire for indulgence stemming from an unbalanced lifestyle may express itself in both affective (usually somatic) and cognitive forms. On the somatic side, the desire may express itself in the form of urges and/or craving responses (anticipation of the effects of immediate gratification). Alternatively, the desire may take the form of cognitive distortions that set the stage or "give permission" for a potential relapse, such as rationalization, denial, or Apparently Irrelevant Decisions (AIDs). Each of these reactions can be countered with RP strategies. To the extent that cravings and urges are elicited by external cues such as the sight or smell of cigarettes, alcoholic beverages, or other substances, the client can exercise a good deal of control by simply removing as many tempting stimuli as possible from his or her everyday living environment. The overall aim of such *stimulus control* procedures can be summarized in the old maxim: "Out of sight, out of mind." Stimulus control techniques are particularly important during the early stages of abstinence (see Chapter 4 for further discussion of stimulus control procedures).

The major point to emphasize here is that craving and urges often take the form of conditioned responses. As with other interoceptive responses (such as a conditioned emotional response), they have a specific course of action, with a given latency of onset, intensity, and duration. The most important thing for clients to remember is that these urges and craving responses will arise and then subside and *pass away* on their own. Individuals who give in or "identify with" these urges may hold the mistaken assumption that the urge will continue to increase in intensity until it becomes impossible to resist. Giving in to the craving or urge at the peak of its intensity, however, increases the probability that the old habit or response will gain in strength. On the other hand, if the individual is able to wait out the waxing and waning of the craving without engaging in the old habit pattern, the internal pressure to respond will eventually fade out through the process of extinction.

The most effective way of coping with craving and urges is to develop a sense of *detachment* with regard to them. Instead of identifying with the urge (e.g., "I really want a cigarette right now"), the client can be trained to monitor the urge or desire from the point of view of a detached observer (e.g., "I am now experiencing an urge to smoke"). By *externalizing and labeling* the craving/urge and "watching" it come and go through the eyes of an observer (much as a meditator learns to passively observe ideas, feelings, and images as they pass through the mind), there will be a decreased tendency to identify with the urge and feel overwhelmed by its power. The situation is analogous to that of an ocean surfer: the urge is similar to the swelling of a wave which the surfer hopes to "ride" without getting "wiped out." In a similar manner, we hope to train clients to "ride" the crest of an urge or craving, maintaining balance until the crest has finally broken and the wave of feeling subsides.

Many clients view repeated experiences of craving as an indication that treatment has been unsuccessful or that relapse is imminent. This defeatist attitude fails to take into account the fact that these responses are to be expected as a natural part of the recovery process. Knowing that these are conditioned responses that will gradually weaken in intensity as the process of extinction continues frees one from the mistaken attribution that one is somehow responsible for their occurrence due to personal weakness or the existence of an "addictive" personality. Clients can be taught that the most effective point to intervene in the chain of events associated with a desire or craving to indulge is the associative linkage between the craving response itself and the subsequent urge or intention to engage in the consummatory response. For a more extensive discussion of cognitive *urge control* strategies (including efficacy-enhancing and coping imagery techniques), the reader is referred to Chapter 4.

Once the client is trained to *recognize and label AIDs as early-warning signals,* what can be done to alter the course of events that might otherwise lead to a relapse? The client can first be instructed to slow down and stop before proceeding any further, to take a "time out" to gain a larger perspective on where all of these actions and thoughts must be leading. To continue the highway metaphor, the client can be encouraged to respond to the danger signals or red flags by pulling over into the nearest rest stop to reconsider the route ahead. Two techniques are particularly helpful as aids to decision making at these important junction points: reviewing the decision matrix and consulting a personalized *relapse "road map"* to locate one's current position with regard to several alternative destinations. Hopefully, this break in the chain of events will enable the client to see the "big picture" of where his or her behavior may be leading, and to take corrective action (e.g., to make a "U-Turn" and go back to an earlier junction, or to plan a "detour" that will avoid nearby or forthcoming high-risk situations, etc.). The relapse road map (see Figure 1-6) is also discussed in the final section of Chapter 4. Just as Tolman's rats were thought to make use of "cognitive maps" to find the goal box at the end of a learning maze (Tolman, 1948), clients can be trained in the use of relapse road maps to assist them in finding their way through the maze of everyday life events to reach their eventual goal. Finally, they can be instructed in the use of "last-ditch" behavioral *avoidance strategies.* Is there a "by-pass" route that can be used to avoid the dangers of encountering a high-risk situation? If so, it should be marked clearly on the client's road map for use in emergencies. In case the high-risk situation cannot be avoided or a last-minute escape is impossible, it is helpful to have clients practice how they would cope in the midst of a stressful or high-temptation situation (*relapse rehearsal;* see Chapter 2).

THE RELAPSE PREVENTION MODEL: CURRENT STATUS AND FUTURE DIRECTIONS

The RP model outlined in this book is still in the formative stages of development. Research and clinical work in support of this approach have emerged largely within the past decade, much of it since 1980. As such, only a few treatment outcome studies have appeared in the literature that have compared the RP model with other approaches to the treatment of addiction or the prevention of relapse. The outcome studies that have already appeared, along with more basic research on the role of expectancies (self-efficacy and outcome expectancies) and coping skills in the habit-change process, have provided generally positive support for the model. Most of these studies are described elsewhere in this book (based on literature reviews through mid-

1983). Despite this emerging empirical support, many of the basic tenets of the model and the effectiveness of the RP approach with various addictive behaviors have yet to be firmly established. The purpose of this book is to provide readers with an account of a theoretical model in the process of growth and development. Refinement of the basic assumptions and clinical applications of the model will undoubtedly occur on the basis of future research.

Many questions remain unanswered at this point. To name but a few:

• What is the role of *motivation* in habit change and how can it be enhanced? If relapse prevention is designed for the maintenance stage or "back end" of the habit-change process, there is a strong need for a corresponding "front end" emphasis on motivation and self-efficacy enhancement.

• What is the *time course* of relapse across various addictive behaviors? Do certain high-risk situations occur earlier than others for most people, and, if so, what is the expected course of such risk situations over time? Examination of relapse rates (based on survivor analysis of time periods preceding initial lapses and/or subsequent relapses) may reveal a distribution of periods of differential risk (e.g., within successive weekly periods after a commitment to abstinence). If so, it may turn out that various RP intervention strategies are effective at different time periods.

• What is the optimum format for the delivery of RP strategies? To what extent is the assistance of trained professional or paraprofessional therapists or counselors necessary or helpful? Can the RP model be effectively applied in the form of self-help manuals, correspondence courses, or other formats? What about individual counseling as opposed to a group treatment format?

• Perhaps the most intriguing question that arises from a comparison of the self-control and disease models of addiction is this: Is one approach more effective than the other for some clients, and vice versa? Do the self-control and disease models reflect the principle of "different strokes for different folks"? It does seem to be the case that the population differs with regard to people's basic orientation toward personal causation and locus of control. Evidence is mounting that people can be placed along a continuum of "perceived personal causation," with those at one extreme believing that they are capable of exercising choice and free will to determine the direction and course of their lives, in contrast with those on the other end who believe that their lives are under the deterministic control of external forces, such as fate, change, and luck (cf. Rotter, 1966). Most people, of course, fall somewhere between these extremes of internal or external control. It remains an open question as to the extent to which these personal differences in perceived control are modifiable for any given individual. Can a therapist change the underlying belief orientation of an individual who is high on the "external" side of this dimension? Can a therapist facilitate a change in such a person by the careful application of procedures designed to enhance self-efficacy? In the meantime, it is tempting to consider the possibility of matching a particular treatment approach with the client's own expectancy system or locus of control orientation. For those clients who strongly believe that their addiction problem is primarily a physical addiction, involving a "compulsive" behavior beyond volitional control, a traditional disease model approach may be more effective. In contrast, clients who reject the notion that they are incapable of exercising control over their behavior and who would prefer instead to learn the skills and attitudes required to modify their lifestyle habits may be more suitable and appropriate for the RP approach.

• A final question concerns the range of application of the RP model. The primary focus in this book is on the application of RP principles to the modification of addictive behaviors in the usual sense of the term: excessive use of alcohol, tobacco, food, or other "substance abuse" problems. The model does, however, seem to have applications in areas other than addictive behavior or substance abuse. One such area is sexual aggression. In the treatment of the sexual aggressor (e.g., rapists), the overall goal is the same as it often is in the treatment of addiction: to abstain from engaging in the taboo behavior. A recent chapter by Pithers, Marques, Gibat, and Marlatt (1983) explores the application of the RP model in the treatment of sexual aggression. A second area of potential application is the "transfer-of-training" problem: how can the effects of new training programs be effectively transferred to and maintained in the target setting? In a recent review paper, Marx (1982) discusses the application of the RP model to managerial training programs. Marx states: "Although organizations invest heavily in training programs to enhance managerial effectiveness, little attention is paid to the transfer of such training from the workshop to the workplace. This paper describes a cognitive–behavioral model that offers a systematic approach to the maintenance of behavior. Relapse prevention strategies are discussed, and implications for management training and research are considered" (Marx, 1982, p. 433). Transfer-of-training problems also arise in the application of other intervention programs, including therapy. In one recent paper, for example, Berlin (1983) examines the effectiveness of RP strategies in a cognitive–behavioral treatment program designed to alter self-criticism. Other potential applications of the RP model await future investigation.

REFERENCES

Ainslie, G. Specious reward: A behavioral theory of impulsiveness and impulse control. *Psychological Bulletin*, 1975, *82*, 463–496.

Armor, D. J., Polich, J. M., & Stambul, H. B. *Alcoholism and treatment*. New York: Wiley, 1978.

Bandura, A. Self-efficacy: Toward a unifying theory of behavior change. *Psychological Review*, 1977, *84*, 191–215.

Beck, A. T., Rush, A. J., Shaw, B. F., & Emery, G. *Cognitive therapy of depression*. New York: Guilford, 1979.

Bem, D. J. Self-perception theory. In L. Berkowitz (Ed.), *Advances in experimental social psychology* (Vol. 6). New York: Academic Press, 1972.

Berlin, S. B. *The effect of relapse prevention on the durability of self-criticism problem change.* Unpublished manuscript, University of Wisconsin, 1983.

Brehm, J. W. *A theory of psychological reactance.* New York: Academic Press, 1966.

Brickman, P., Rabinowitz, V. C., Karuza, J., Coates, D., Cohn, E., & Kidder, L. Models of helping and coping. *American Psychologist,* 1982, *37,* 368–384.

Brownell, K. D., Heckerman, C. L., Westlake, R. J., Hayes, S. C., & Monti, P. M. The effect of couples training and partner cooperativeness in the behavioral treatment of obesity. *Behaviour Research and Therapy,* 1978, *16,* 323–333.

Cannon, D. S., Baker, T. B., & Wehl, C. K. Emetic and electric shock alcohol aversion therapy: Six- and twelve-month follow-up. *Journal of Consulting and Clinical Psychology,* 1981, *49,* 360–368.

Chaney, E. F., O'Leary, M. R., & Marlatt, G. A. Skill training with alcoholics. *Journal of Consulting and Clinical Psychology,* 1978, *46,* 1092–1104.

Cronkite, R., & Moos, R. The determinants of posttreatment functioning of alcoholic patients: A conceptual framework. *Journal of Consulting and Clinical Psychology,* 1980, *48,* 305–316.

Cummings, C., Gordon, J., & Marlatt, G. A. Relapse: Strategies of prevention and prediction. In W. R. Miller (Ed.), *The addictive behaviors.* Oxford, U.K.: Pergamon Press, 1980.

Cummings, N. A. Turning bread into stones: Our modern anti-miracle. *American Psychologist,* 1979, *34,* 1119–1129.

Elandt-Johnson, R. C., & Johnson, N. L. *Survival models and data analysis.* New York: Wiley, 1980.

Festinger, L. *Conflict, decision and dissonance.* Stanford: Stanford University Press, 1964.

Fisher, J. D., & Farina, A. Consequences of beliefs about the nature of mental disorders. *Journal of Abnormal Psychology,* 1979, *88,* 320–327.

Foreyt, J. P., & Rathjen, D. P. *Cognitive behavior therapy.* New York: Plenum, 1978.

Glasser, W. *Positive addiction.* New York: Harper & Row, 1976.

Goldfried, M. R., & Davison, G. C. *Clinical behavior therapy.* New York: Holt, Rinehart & Winston, 1976.

Goldfried, M. R., & Merbaum, M. (Eds.). *Behavioral change through self-control.* New York: Holt, Rinehart & Winston, 1973.

Goldstein, S., Gordon, J. R., & Marlatt, G. A. *Attributional processes and relapse following smoking cessation.* Paper presented at the annual meeting of the American Psychological Association, Toronto, Canada, 1984.

Goldstein, S., Marlatt, G. A., Peterson, A., & Lutton, J. Assessment of relapse in addictive behaviors. In G. A. Marlatt & D. M. Donovan (Eds.), *Assessment of addictive behaviors.* New York: Guilford, in press.

Hall, S. Self-management and therapeutic maintenance: Theory and research. In P. Karoly & J. J. Steffen (Eds.), *Toward a psychology of therapeutic maintenance: Widening perspectives.* New York: Gardner Press, 1980.

Heather, N., & Robertson, I. *Controlled drinking.* London: Methuen, 1981.

Hunt, W. A., Barnett, L. W., & Branch, L. G. Relapse rates in addiction programs. *Journal of Clinical Psychology,* 1971, *27,* 455–456.

Hunt, W. A., & Matarazzo, J. D. Habit mechanisms in smoking. In W. A. Hunt (Ed.), *Learning mechanisms in smoking.* Chicago: Aldine, 1970.

Jayarante, S., & Levy, R. L. *Empirical clinical practice.* New York: Columbia University Press, 1979.

Jellinek, E. M. *The Disease Concept in Alcoholism.* New Brunswick, N.J.: Hill House Press, 1960.

Kalbfleisch, J. D., & Prentice, R. L. *The statistical analysis of failure time data.* New York: Wiley, 1980.

Karoly, P., & Kanfer, F. H. (Eds.). *Self-management and behavior change: From theory to practice.* New York: Pergamon, 1982.

Kazdin, A. E. Statistical analyses for single-case experimental designs. In M. Hersen & D. H. Barlow (Eds.), *Single-case experimental designs*. New York: Pergamon, 1976. (a)

Kazdin, A. E. Effects of covert modeling, multiple models, and model reinforcement on assertive behaviors. *Behavior Therapy*, 1976, 7, 211–222. (b)

Kendall, P. C., & Hollon, S. D. (Eds.). *Cognitive–behavioral interventions: Theory, research, and procedures*. New York: Academic Press, 1979.

Kuhn, T. S. *The structure of scientific revolutions* (2nd ed.). Chicago: University of Chicago Press, 1970.

Lefcourt, H. M. *Locus of control*. Hillsdale, N.J.: Lawrence Erlbaum, 1976.

Levison, P. K., Gerstein, D. R., & Maloff, D. R. (Eds.). *Commonalities in substance abuse and habitual behaviors*. Lexington, Mass.: Lexington, 1983.

Litman, G. K., Eiser, J. R., & Taylor, C. Dependence, relapse, and extinction. A theoretical critique and a behavioral examination. *Journal of Clinical Psychology*, 1979, 35, 192–199.

Mahoney, M. J. *Cognition and behavior modification*. Cambridge, Mass.: Ballinger, 1974.

Mahoney, M. J. Personal science: A cognitive learning therapy. In A. Ellis & R. Grieger (Eds.), *Handbook of rational psychotherapy*. New York: Springer, 1977.

Mahoney, M. J., & Thoresen, C. E. *Self-control: Power to the person*. Monterey, Calif.: Brooks-Cole, 1974.

Marlatt, G. A. *A comparison of aversive conditioning procedures in the treatment of alcoholism*. Paper presented at the annual meeting of the Western Psychological Association, Anaheim, Calif., 1973.

Marlatt, G. A. Craving for alcohol, loss of control, and relapse: A cognitive–behavioral analysis. In P. E. Nathan, G. A. Marlatt, & T. Løberg (Eds.), *Alcoholism: New directions in behavioral research and treatment*. New York: Plenum, 1978.

Marlatt, G. A. Alcohol use and problem drinking: A cognitive–behavioral analysis. In P. C. Kendall & S. D. Hollon (Eds.), *Cognitive–behavioral interventions: Theory, research, and procedures*. New York: Academic Press, 1979.

Marlatt, G. A. Relapse prevention: A self-control program for the treatment of addictive behaviors. In R. B. Stuart (Ed.), *Adherence, compliance, and generalization in behavioral medicine*. New York: Brunner/Mazel, 1982.

Marlatt, G. A. The controlled-drinking controversy: A commentary. *American Psychologist*, 1983, 38, 1097–1110.

Marlatt, G. A., & Gordon, J. R. Determinants of relapse: Implications for the maintenance of behavior change. In P. O. Davidson & S. M. Davidson (Eds.), *Behavioral medicine: Changing health lifestyles*. New York: Brunner/Mazel, 1980.

Marlatt, G. A., & Parks, G. A. Self-management in addictive disorders. In P. Karoly & F. H. Kanfer (Eds.), *Self-management and behavior change*. Elmsford, N.Y.: Pergamon Press, 1982.

Marlatt, G. A., & Rohsenow, D. J. Cognitive processes in alcohol use: Expectancy and the balanced placebo design. In N. K. Mello (Ed.), *Advances in substance abuse* (Vol. 1). Greenwich, Conn.: JAI Press, 1980.

Marx, R. D. Relapse prevention for managerial training: A model for maintenance of behavior change. *Academy of Management Review*, 1982, 7, 433–441.

McClelland, D. C., Davis, W. N., Kalin, R., & Wanner, E. *The drinking man*. New York: Free Press, 1972.

McCrady, B. S., Paolino, T. J., Longabaugh, R., & Rossi, J. Effects of joint hospital admission and couples treatment for hospitalized alcoholics: A pilot study. *Addictive Behaviors*, 1979, 4, 155–165.

Meichenbaum, D. *Cognitive-behavior modification*. New York: Plenum, 1977.

Moos, R. H., & Finney, J. W. The expanding scope of alcoholism treatment evaluation. *American Psychologist*, 1983, 38, 1036–1044.

Orford, J., & Edwards, G. *Alcoholism: A comparison of treatment and advice, with a study of influence of marriage* (Maudsley Monographs No. 26). New York: Oxford University Press, 1977.

Ornstein, R. E. *The psychology of consciousness* (2nd ed.). New York: Harcourt Brace Jovanovich, 1977.

Peele, S., & Brodsky, A. *Love and addiction.* Los Angeles: Taplinger, 1975.

Pelletier, K. R. *Holistic medicine: From stress to optimum health.* New York: Delacorte/Seymour Lawrence, 1979.

Pendery, M. L., Maltzman, I. M., & West, L. J. Controlled drinking by alcoholics? New findings and a reevaluation of a major affirmative study. *Science,* 1982, *217,* 169–174.

Phares, E. J. *Locus of control in personality.* Morristown, N.J.: General Learning Press, 1976.

Pithers, W. D., Marques, J. K., Gibat, C. C., & Marlatt, G. A. Relapse prevention with sexual aggressives: A self-control model of treatment and maintenance of change. In J. G. Greer & I. R. Stuart (Eds.), *The sexual aggressor: Current perspectives on treatment.* New York: Van Nostrand Reinhold, 1983.

Platt, J. Social traps. *American Psychologist,* 1973, *28,* 641–651.

Prochaska, J. O., & DiClemente, C. C. Transtheoretical therapy: Toward a more integrative model of change. *Psychotherapy: Theory, Research and Practice,* 1982, *19,* 276–288.

Prochaska, J. O., & DiClemente, C. C. Stages and processes of self-change of smoking: Toward an integrative model of change. *Journal of Consulting and Clinical Psychology,* 1983, *51,* 390–395.

Rotter, J. B. Generalized expectancies for internal versus external control of reinforcement. *Psychological Monographs,* 1966, *80*(1) (Whole No. 609).

Saxe, L., Dougherty, D., Esty, J., & Fine, M. *The effectiveness and costs of alcoholism treatment* (Congressional Office of Technology Assessment case study, Publication No. 052-003-00902-1). Washington, D.C.: U.S. Government Printing Office, 1983.

Schachter, S. Recidivism and self-cure of smoking and obesity. *American Psychologist,* 1982, *37,* 436–444.

Skinner, B. F. *Science and human behavior.* New York: Macmillan, 1953.

Sobell, M. B., & Sobell, L. C. *Behavioral treatment of alcohol problems.* New York: Plenum, 1978.

Solomon, R. L. An opponent-process theory of acquired motivation: IV. The affective dynamics of addiction. In J. J. Maser & M. E. P. Seligman (Eds.), *Psychopathology: Experimental models.* San Francisco: W. H. Freeman, 1977.

Solomon, R. L., & Corbit, J. D. An opponent-process theory of motivation: I. Temporal dynamics of affect. *Psychological Review,* 1974, *81,* 119–145.

Sontag, S. *Illness as metaphor.* New York: Farrar, Straus, & Giroux, 1978.

Spradley, J. P. *You owe yourself a drunk.* Boston: Little, Brown, 1970.

Stone, G. C., Cohen, F., & Adler, N. E. *Health psychology.* San Francisco: Jossey-Bass, 1979.

Stuart, R. B. (Ed.). *Behavioral self-management: Strategies, techniques, and outcomes.* New York: Brunner/Mazel, 1977.

Sutton, S. R. Interpreting relapse curves. *Journal of Consulting and Clinical Psychology,* 1979, *47,* 96–98.

Thoresen, C. E., & Mahoney, M. J. *Behavioral self-control.* New York: Holt, Rinehart & Winston, 1974.

Tolman, E. C. Cognitive maps in rats and men. *Psychological Review,* 1948, *55,* 189–208.

Trice, H. The affiliation motive and readiness to join A.A. *Quarterly Journal of Studies on Alcohol,* 1959, *20,* 313–320.

Trice, H., & Roman, P. Sociopsychological predictors of successful affiliation with A.A. *Social Psychiatry,* 1970, *5,* 51–59.

Tuchfeld, B. S. Spontaneous remission in alcoholics: Empirical observations and theoretical implications. *Journal of Studies on Alcohol,* 1981, *42,* 626–641.

Webster's new collegiate dictionary. Springfield, Mass.: G. & C. Merriam, 1983.

Weisman, M. N. Relapse. In M. N. Weisman & L. B. Robe, *Relapse/slips: Abstinent alcoholics who return to drinking.* Minneapolis, Minn.: Johnson Institute, 1983.

2

SITUATIONAL DETERMINANTS OF RELAPSE AND SKILL-TRAINING INTERVENTIONS

G. ALAN MARLATT

In this chapter, situational determinants of the relapse process are described in greater detail and a number of skill-training Relapse Prevention (RP) techniques are outlined. Cognitive and affective reactions associated with relapse are discussed in Chapter 3, and cognitive intervention strategies are covered in Chapter 4. Lifestyle factors associated with relapse along with related intervention procedures are described in Chapter 5. Two main topics will be reviewed in this chapter: (1) identification of high-risk situations as immediate determinants of relapse; and (2) training in alternative coping skills to deal effectively with high-risk situations.

IDENTIFYING HIGH-RISK SITUATIONS

This section begins with a brief historical account of high-risk situations as precipitating factors in relapse. Other theoretical models of relapse, with an emphasis on those postulating a conditioned "craving" response as a major determinant of relapse, are briefly reviewed and critically evaluated. A detailed description of a current taxonomy of high-risk situations is then presented, along with a scoring system for assigning specific relapse situations to categories. A case study is introduced as a means of illustrating the influence of high-risk situations in the relapse episode of a problem drinker. Finally, the section concludes with a review of procedures that can be used to identify high-risk situations in the clinical setting.

HIGH-RISK SITUATIONS: DEFINITION AND ROLE IN THEORIES OF RELAPSE

The author's interest in looking at the situational factors associated with relapse dates back to a research study conducted to determine the effectiveness of electrical aversion as a treatment procedure for alcoholism (Marlatt, 1973).

In this study, 65 male alcoholics were exposed to an aversive conditioning program with electric shock as the aversive stimulus. To increase the generalization of the treatment effects, treatment sessions were conducted in a simulated bar since it was hypothesized that the contextual cues of the drinking setting could also acquire aversive properties through the mechanism of higher-order conditioning. Follow-up assessments were conducted at periods of 3 and 15 months following discharge from the hospital. In summary, the overall results showed that the conditioning program produced significant decreases in drinking rates at the 3-month follow-up, compared to control subjects who did not receive aversion training, but that these differences tended to wash out at the 15-month follow-up. It became clear that something extra needed to be added to the conditioning program itself in order to augment and maintain the treatment effects obtained. The clue to that "extra" ingredient became apparent in a close examination of the relapse data for all patients who began drinking again during the follow-up period.

In most treatment studies published at that time, follow-up data usually consisted of no more than simple statements of rates of abstinence or relapse (e.g., 78% of the sample relapsed during the first year, whereas 22% remained abstinent during this period). Little or no information was provided concerning the precipitating circumstances of the relapse or about differences in rate of drinking among relapsed patients. Treatment outcome was thus assessed as a simple binary event: the patient was either abstinent or had relapsed.

There was also a paucity of publications on the topic of relapse. The sparse literature that was available suggested that relapse was a result of an internal compulsive need or craving for alcohol experienced by the abstinent alcoholic (e.g., Isbell, 1955). Mardones (1955) defined craving as "an urgent and overpowering desire to drink alcoholic beverages." Although craving had often been described as a desire for alcohol experienced by an alcoholic undergoing withdrawal following a prolonged drinking bout (craving for the "hair of the dog" to alleviate the distress and agony of hangover and withdrawal), it was also suggested that craving was a factor in precipitating the first drinking experience in an abstinent alcoholic. Most adherents of the medical model assume that alcoholism is a progressive disease, one that grows worse over time even if the individual abstains from alcohol for long periods. This latent disease process may express itself via the symptom of craving, thereby increasing the possibility of relapse. If the individual succumbs to this craving and takes a drink, the craving will increase in intensity to the point where the drinker is unable to exert voluntary control and stop after the first drink or two.

The idea that craving is augmented following the consumption of the initial drink has been used extensively as a theoretical model to explain "loss of control drinking" or the sudden increase in consumption following the first drink. The loss of control phenomenon is considered to be a key symptom in the disease theory of alcoholism since it provides an explanation for why the compulsive alcoholic cannot exercise voluntary control over drinking. According to this view, the ingestion of alcohol in the first drink serves as a trigger for physical craving and subsequent loss of control over consumption. "Loss of control means that as soon as a small quantity of alcohol enters the organism, a demand for more alcohol is set up which is felt as a physical demand by the drinker" (Jellinek, 1952, p. 679).

Apart from the theoretical literature on craving as a determinant of relapse, only a few studies had actually examined the process of relapse itself in alcoholics. In a paper describing characteristics of the relapse situation of alcoholics treated with aversion therapy, Burt (1974) reported that about 80% of his sample (30 men and 4 women) took their first drink in a location that differed from their preferred drinking settings prior to treatment, but no detailed descriptions of these settings are given in the paper. Hore (1971) followed a group of 22 alcoholic patients receiving treatment in an outpatient clinic for periods ranging up to 6 months. He attempted to relate relapses in this group to significant life events reported by the patients in the same general time period. Hore analyzed these life events and assigned them to the following categories: personal interaction, or disturbances in an emotional relationship (33%); work events, involving a change in the patient's working life (33%); events involving a health change in the patient or in members of the family (20%); and events involving a change of residence (13%). Physical craving was not mentioned as a major determinant of relapse in Hore's analysis.

In my study of aversion therapy (Marlatt, 1973), I was interested in the relapse process in alcoholic patients as a source of information concerning the generalization of treatment effects. Specifically, I wanted to know whether relapsed patients took their first drink in a situation that differed from that of the treatment environment (a simulated tavern setting) and whether the first alcoholic beverage consumed was the same or different from those used in the aversion treatment. Aversion therapy would have limited application if the effects were restricted to the specific beverage and setting used in the initial treatment (e.g., if a patient developed an aversion to drinking whiskey in a tavern setting but experienced no difficulties drinking wine in a restaurant). With this rationale in mind, very detailed descriptions of relapse episodes were obtained from patients during the follow-up interviews. During the first 90 days of the follow-up period, 48 of 65 patients consumed at least one alcoholic drink. Each of these patients was interviewed in person within a few days of the relapse episode. An attempt was made to determine the exact circumstances of the situation associated with the first drink episode, including information about the physical location, time of day, presence or absence of others, beverage consumed, a description of any external (environmental) or internal (subjective) events occurring in that general time period, and the patient's feelings and emotions on the day of the relapse. The descriptions of the relapse episodes were then sorted into independent, operationally defined categories. Raters were trained to assign specific episodes to categories until they achieved a high level of interrater agreement.

Surprisingly, it was found that all of the relapse cases could be assigned to relatively few categories. These categories are listed in Table 2-1. Although some evidence was found for treatment generalization effects in terms of the beverage and physical setting, even more impressive was the fact that a common pattern of psychological and situational factors emerged from the analysis, suggesting that some situations were more "high risk" than others in terms of potential for relapse. As indicated in Table 2-1, the first two categories, accounting for over half the cases, usually involved an interpersonal encounter. Most of the situations in the first category (29%) involved an episode in which the patient was frustrated in some goal-directed activity (typically by another person who criticized him), and reported feelings of anger. Rather than expressing this anger in a constructive manner, however, the patient ended up taking a drink. In the second category (23%), the patients reported being unable to resist either direct or indirect attempts by others to engage him in drinking (social pressure). The other two major categories, accounting for about a third of the cases, were basically intrapersonal in nature. Temptation situations were quite common (21%); these relapses may have been triggered by craving experiences, although it is possible that the sudden "urge" to drink was determined by other environ-

Table 2-1.   Analysis of Situations for Relapse in Aversion Treatment Study

Situation category	Example	n	%
Frustration and anger	Patient tried to call his wife (they were separated); she hung up on him; he became angry and took a drink.	14	29%
Social pressure	Patient went with the "boys" to a bar after work. They put pressure on him to "join the crowd" and he was unable to resist.	11	23%
Intrapersonal temptation	Patient walked by a bar, and "just unconsciously walked in, no real reason"; could not resist the temptation to take a drink.	10	21%
Negative emotional state	Patient living alone, no job; complained of feeling bored and useless; could see no reason why he should not take a drink.	5	10%
Miscellaneous other situations	Patient reported that everything was going so well for him that he wanted to celebrate by having a drink.	5	10%
No situation given or unable to remember		3	7%

Note. Based on Marlatt (1978b).

mental or emotional factors that were not identified in the assessment interview.

What are we to make of these findings? At first it appeared that the relapse episodes uncovered were unique to the particular population under study, namely chronic male alcoholics treated in an inpatient setting. Since then, however, essentially similar results have been found in subsequent analyses of relapse episodes with other populations, not only with other alcoholics (Chaney, O'Leary, & Marlatt, 1978), but also with cigarette smokers, heroin addicts, individuals in weight-loss programs, and even compulsive gamblers (Cummings, Gordon, & Marlatt, 1980; Marlatt & Gordon, 1980). Although there are important differences among each of the problem areas mentioned in terms of the relative frequency of occurrence of each high-risk category, there appears to be a common thread running through these situations that make them high risk for relapse. What is this common thread? How can a high-risk situation be defined?

Regardless of the specific underlying mediating variables involved, it is the individual's own subjective definition of "risk" that characterizes a high-risk situation. In this sense, a high-risk situation is defined broadly as any situation that poses a threat to the individual's sense of control (self-efficacy) and increases the risk of potential relapse. Perceived control or self-efficacy refers to the person's subjective expectancy of being able to "make it through" or cope effectively with the situation without giving in to the temptation of the old addictive coping behavior. What constitutes a high-risk situation varies as a function of several variables.

Temporal factors constitute one such variable. In the very early stages of abstinence, some individuals experience various degrees of physical withdrawal, although others report little or no withdrawal distress. Withdrawal from heroin or other opiates is often associated with a fixed syndrome of physical reactions although situational factors or expectancies may attenuate this effect. Abstention from alcohol or tobacco, on the other hand, may or may not be accompanied by pronounced physical reactions, depending on various individual factors. For those persons who are susceptible to physical withdrawal reactions, the first few days of abstinence may constitute a continual high-risk time period. Physical craving for alcohol may be experienced as a result of either withdrawal (and the desire to alleviate this distress by continued drug use) or exposure to the drug or drug-related cues that elicit conditioned anticipatory reactions. Direct exposure to these cues (the "Downtown Reno" situation described in Chapter 1) almost always constitutes a high-risk situation, especially in the early stages of abstinence. Many relapses that occur in the first few days of abstinence may be associated with physical withdrawal symptoms or conditioned anticipatory responses elicited by drug cues (cf. Pomerleau, Fertig, Baker, & Cooney, 1983). A more extensive discussion of the role of classical conditioning in the relapse process is presented in the next chapter.

$\rightarrow$ Following the initial high-risk period for relapse based on either physical withdrawal or conditioned craving responses, the individual is faced with a variety of other high-risk situations that do not involve physical symptoms as the primary determinant of risk. In most cases, these situations (such as the experience of frustration and anger or social pressure described in our first study) are those in which the individual has made extensive use of the drug or problem behavior as a means of attempting to cope with similar situations in the past. To the extent that excessive drinking, smoking, eating, or other indulgent behaviors have been performed habitually in these situations, most individuals will have developed strong positive expectancies about the drug or activity as a coping strategy. This tendency is likely to be most pronounced in those situations perceived as stressful by the individual. Many persons come to believe that they cannot cope with certain stressful events (e.g., handling anger or the threat of negative social evaluation, etc.) unless they are able to lean on some drug or substance as a coping crutch.

Just as Disney's Dumbo the elephant believed he needed to carry a magic feather in his trunk in order to fly, so many people believe they need to have a cigarette or a drink in their hands in order to be able to perform adequately in a stressful situation. One person may feel he needs to have a cigarette whenever he is faced with a tension-producing event in order to calm his nerves. Another individual believes she cannot relax and open up at parties without a couple of drinks to pave the way. A writer faces an empty page in the typewriter and is convinced that a cigarette break will stimulate the creative muse. Most of these individuals rarely experience these situations without their indulgent crutch and so have no way of knowing whether or not they could cope without it. In fact, each time the person gets through a stressful situation or a period of emotional turmoil, the perceived power of the crutch increases: "I never could have gotten through all that without a cigarette to lean on"; or "Whenever I am feeling bummed out, I need a joint in order to detach from my feelings and gain a sense of perspective." Such attributions of "coping power" to the substance or activity strengthen positive expectancies for indulging in that behavior in similar future situations.

When the person decides to eliminate the old habit, the high-risk situations may become even more stressful. In addition to the stress inherent in the situation itself (e.g., facing the prospect of a difficult interpersonal encounter), there is the additional stress caused by the absence of the coping crutch. The combined impact often culminates in a pronounced state of agitation and conflict. Since this high arousal state is experienced in part as unpleasant physical sensations, the individual may label these sensations as craving for the old habit or drug. As research by Schachter and others has indicated (cf. Schachter & Singer, 1962), individuals who are in an elevated state of physiological arousal or emotional distress cognitively label or "explain" the arousal based on existing environmental events and/or their own expectancies and attributions. Logical errors frequently occur in this process. One such error is to attribute the "cause" of one's feelings in a given high-risk situation to internal craving or physical need for a particular substance. To give in to this need by leaning on the addictive crutch at the peak of the craving or stress experience will make it much more difficult for the individual to regain control in similar future situations. By giving in, the person's belief that he or she cannot cope without the crutch will be strengthened even further.

The most important factor that serves to decrease the risk of an otherwise high-risk situation is the availability of an alternative coping response. If the individual has learned new ways of coping with stressful situations and has had the opportunity to practice these new skills without the aid of the former habit crutch, self-efficacy will be strengthened and the probability of relapse will decrease. Although other life experiences may render the person more vulnerable to temptation (e.g., an addictive lifestyle or a covert desire to resume the old habit pattern), the availability of an adaptive coping response will enhance one's perception of control in the high-risk situation. Every time a situation is dealt with effectively by the use of an alternative coping response, the desire for the old crutch decreases. Eventually the person learns that he or she can perform adequately without the aid of crutches and the situation can no longer be considered high-risk.

HIGH-RISK SITUATIONS: IDENTIFICATION AND CLASSIFICATION

Following my initial attempt to categorize high-risk situations in the alcoholism aversion treatment study (Table 2-1), I began to study relapse episodes involving other addictive behavior problems. In one report (Marlatt & Gordon, 1980), we analyzed 137 relapse episodes drawn from three samples: alcoholics, heroin addicts, and cigarette smokers, all of whom were followed up after participation in abstinence-oriented treatment programs. In a second report (Cummings, Gordon, & Marlatt, 1980), we expanded this first sample by adding 174 more relapse episodes ($n = 311$), including some obtained from women in a weight-control program and some from men who were members of Gamblers Anonymous (GA), a national self-help program for compulsive gamblers. The results of this second analysis are reported in Chapter 1 in Table 1-1 (p. 39).

The descriptions of the relapse episode were solicited in the following way. Each person was first asked to give the date and time of the episode (the first drug use for the alcoholics, heroin addicts, or smokers; the first period of uncontrolled eating in the weight-control subjects; the first gambling activity in the compulsive gambler group). Next we asked about the physical setting in which the episode occurred, the location where the event occurred, and the presence or absence of other people. Additional setting factors focused on the presence or availability of the taboo substance or activity, including whether or not the person used alcohol or other drugs (e.g., a smoker who relapses after having a few drinks), or if other individuals in the setting were engaged in the target behavior (e.g., a relapse that occurs in a restaurant, where other people are drinking, smoking, and eating). We asked the following open-ended questions to provide a description of additional possible determinants of the relapse episode:

1. What would you say was the main reason for taking that first drink (or cigarette, etc.)?

2. Describe any inner thoughts or emotional feelings (things within you as a person) that triggered off your need or desire to take the first drink at that time.

3. Describe any particular circumstances or set of events, things that happened to you in the outside world, that triggered off your need or desire to take the first drink.

Once we had obtained descriptions of the relapse episodes, our next step was to develop a revised classification system in order to assign each relapse episode to an independent category. Descriptions of similar episodes were grouped and regrouped, using the basic principles of content analysis (Kiesler, 1973), until a discrete set of categories was developed. The final set of categories, each defined in detail with examples, is presented in Table 2-2. Although refinement of this classification system continues, the system outlined in Table 2-2 has been found to be reliable and reasonably comprehensive for most purposes. Reliability was assessed by training two raters in the classification system until a high degree of agreement between raters was attained. In a reliability check, each rater independently assigned a large group of relapse episodes to the categories listed in Table 2-2; the interrater agreement was found to be 88% for category assignment.

Inspection of Table 2-2 reveals that the relapse episodes are first assigned to one of two major categories. The first major category, *intrapersonal–environmental determinants* (Category I), is used whenever the relapse episode involves a response to primarily intrapersonal forces, either psychological or physical in nature, or to an environmental event that does not primarily involve other people. The emphasis is on precipitating events in which another person or group of individuals is *not* mentioned as a significant factor. The second major category, *interpersonal determinants* (Category II), applies whenever the relapse episode involves the significant influence of other individuals (e.g., an argument with a spouse, social pressure, party celebrations, etc.). It is sometimes difficult to distinguish clearly between the intrapersonal and interpersonal categories. To resolve such difficulties in ambiguous cases, we assigned an episode to the interpersonal category only if the individual describing the incident reported that another person or persons exerted a significant influence either prior to the relapse (e.g., an employee is criticized by the boss an hour or two before the drinking episode began) or at the same time the relapse occurred (e.g., a smoker is influenced by the presence of other smokers in a bar or tavern). Just being in the presence of others at the time of the relapse episode does not necessarily imply that the episode is assigned to the interpersonal category unless it is reported that these individuals exerted a significant influence. Similarly, an event is not assigned to the intrapersonal category simply because the person was alone at the time of the relapse; he or she may still be responding primarily to an interpersonal situation that has occurred in the relatively recent past (e.g., recent loss of a girlfriend or boyfriend).

Table 1-1 shows the percentage of relapse episodes falling into the eight main categories of Table 2-2 (five intrapersonal and three interpersonal categories) for a total of 311 relapse episodes described by alcoholics, smokers, heroin addicts, compulsive gamblers, and overeaters. Although the various subcategories (e.g., Categories 1 and 2 listed under the main categories I-A, I-B, II-A, and II-B) are not included in Table 1-1, use of these narrower categories provides additional information that may be useful in treatment planning. In the following sections each of the major and subcategories in the relapse classification system will be reviewed briefly.

Coping with Negative Emotional States (Category I-A)

Relapses often occur when the individual is emotionally upset. Feelings of anger, sadness, anxiety, boredom, depression, guilt, and apprehension over some forthcoming event, are all included in this category. In some cases, these feelings are elicited by a nonpersonal environmental event or series of events (e.g., one alcoholic took his first drink after being unable to start his car one cold winter morning; he reported feeling upset and angry about not showing up for his first day on the job). More typically, however, the individual is upset about past or present relationships with others. Someone who is living alone and feeling sad and lonely may try to cope with this empty feeling by returning to alcohol or drug use. Alcohol is frequently consumed by problem drinkers or alcoholics when they are experiencing feelings of helplessness or powerlessness in their lives. Some research has suggested that men who drink experience an increase in personal fantasies of feeling stronger and more powerful in the presence of others (McClelland, Davis, Kalin, & Wanner, 1972). Drinking as a response to feelings of helplessness may be true for women as well. In a newspaper account of the divorce of Ted and Joan Kennedy (MacPherson, 1981), Joan Kennedy was interviewed about her reactions to her husband's extramarital affairs and how they affected her problems with alcohol. "'They went to the core of my self-esteem,' she said several years ago. 'When one grows up feeling that maybe one is sort of special and hoping that one's husband thinks so, and then

Table 2-2. Categories for Classification of Relapse Episodes

I. *Intrapersonal–Environmental Determinants.* Includes all determinants that are primarily associated with intrapersonal factors (within the individual), and/or reactions to non-personal environmental events. Includes reactions to interpersonal events in the relatively distant past (i.e., in which the interaction is no longer of significant impact).

  A. *Coping with Negative Emotional States.* Determinant involves coping with a negative (unpleasant) emotional state, mood, or feeling.

    1. *Coping with Frustration and/or Anger.* Determinant involves an experience of frustration (reaction to a blocked goal-directed activity), and/or anger (hostility, aggression) in terms of the self or some nonpersonal environmental event. Includes all references to guilt, and responses to demands ("hassles") from environmental sources or from within the self that are likely to produce feelings of anger.

    2. *Coping with Other Negative Emotional States.* Determinant involves coping with emotional states other than frustration/anger that are unpleasant or aversive including feelings of fear, anxiety, tension, depression, loneliness, sadness, boredom, worry, apprehension, grief, loss, and other similar dysphoric states. Includes reactions to evaluation stress (examinations, promotions, public speaking, etc.), employment and financial difficulties, and personal misfortune or accident.

  B. *Coping with Negative Physical–Physiological States.* Determinant involves coping with unpleasant or painful physical or physiological reactions.

    1. *Coping with Physical States Associated with Prior Substance Use.* Coping with physical states that are specifically associated with prior use of drug or substance, such as "withdrawal agony" or "physical craving" associated with withdrawal. (Note: References to "craving" in the absence of withdrawal are classified under Section E below.)

    2. *Coping with Other Negative Physical States.* Coping with pain, illness, injury, fatigue, and specific disorders (e.g., headache, menstrual cramps, etc.) that are *not* associated with prior substance use.

  C. *Enhancement of Positive Emotional States.* Use of substance to increase feelings of pleasure, joy, freedom, celebration, and so on (e.g., when traveling or on vacation). Includes use of substance for primarily positive effects—to "get high" or to experience the enhancing effects of a drug.

  D. *Testing Personal Control.* Use of substance to "test" one's ability to engage in controlled or moderate use; to "just try it once" to see what happens; or in cases in which the individual is testing the effects of treatment or a commitment to abstinence (including tests of "willpower").

  E. *Giving in to Temptations or Urges.* Substance use in response to "internal" urges, temptations, or other promptings. Includes references to "craving" or intense subjective desire, in the absence of interpersonal factors. (Note: References to "craving" which are associated with prior drug use or withdrawal are classified under Section B-1 above.)

    1. *In the Presence of Substance Cues.* Use occurs in the presence of cues associated with substance use (e.g., running across a hidden bottle or pack of cigarettes, passing by a bar, seeing an ad for cigarettes). (Note: Where other individuals are using the substance, refer to Category II-B below.)

    2. *In the Absence of Substance Cues.* Here, the urge or temptation comes "out of the blue" and is *followed* by the individual's attempt to procure the substance.

II. *Interpersonal Determinants.* Includes determinants that are primarily associated with interpersonal factors: reference is made to the presence or influence of other individuals as part of the precipitating event. Implies the influence of present or recent *interaction* with another person or persons, who exert some influence on the user (reactions to events that occurred in the relatively distant past are classified in Category I). Just being in the presence of others at the time of the relapse does not justify an interpersonal classification, unless some mention is made or implied that these people had some influence or were somehow involved in the event.

A. *Coping with Interpersonal Conflict.* Coping with a current or relatively recent conflict associated with any interpersonal relationship such as marriage, friendship, family patterns, employer–employee relations.

   1. *Coping with Frustration and/or Anger.* Determinant involves frustration (reaction to blocked goal-directed activity), and/or anger (hostility, aggression) stemming from an interpersonal source. Emphasis is on any situation in which the person feels frustrated or angry with someone and includes involvement in arguments, disagreements, fights, jealousy, discord, hassles, guilt, and so on.

   2. *Coping with Other Interpersonal Conflict.* Determinant involves coping with conflicts other than frustration and anger stemming from an interpersonal source. Feelings such as anxiety, fear, tension, worry, concern, apprehension, etc., which are associated with interpersonal conflict, are examples. Evaluation stress in which another person or group is specifically mentioned would be included.

B. *Social Pressure.* Determinant involves responding to the influence of another individual or group of individuals who exert pressure (either direct or indirect) on the individual to use the substance.

   1. *Direct Social Pressure.* There is direct contact (usually with verbal interaction) with another person or group who puts pressure on the user or who supplies the substance to the user (e.g., being offered a drug by someone, or being urged to use a drug by someone else). Distinguish from situations in which the substance is obtained from someone else at the request of the user (who has already decided to use).

   2. *Indirect Social Pressure.* Responding to the observation of another person or group that is using the substance or serves as a model of substance use for the user. If the model puts any direct pressure on the individual to use the substance, then the lapse should be categorized under II-B1, above.

C. *Enhancement of Positive Emotional States.* Use of substance in a primarily interpersonal situation to increase feelings of pleasure, celebration, sexual excitement, freedom, and the like. Distinguish from situations in which the other person(s) is using the substance *prior to* the individual's first use (classify these under Section II-B, above).

Scoring Rules

For each relapse episode, only one category can be used for scoring. When multiple categories seem to apply, choose the most significant precipitating event for scoring (the event *immediately* preceding the relapse). When it is impossible to decide between two equally likely categories, assign the score on a priority basis: Category I takes precedence over Category II; within each major category, the ordering of categories (A before B, etc.) indicates the priorities.

---

suddenly thinking maybe he doesn't . . . I began thinking, well, maybe I'm just not attractive enough, and it was awfully easy to say . . . if that's the way it is, I might as well have a drink.'"

Two subcategories are included in this category: coping with frustration and/or anger (I-A1) and coping with other negative emotional states (I-A2). Frustration and anger are separated out from other negative emotional states because of their relatively high rate of occurrence in this author's original study of relapse in alcoholics (Table 2-1 indicates that 29% of the relapses in that sample fell into this category). In the first classification system described in Table 2-1, I did not separate out intrapersonal versus interpersonal determinants as major categories. In the revised system (Table 2-2), frustration and anger is listed as a subcategory both in the intrapersonal (I-A1) and interpersonal (II-A1) sections. In the latter category, the frustration and anger must arise from a relatively recent or ongoing interpersonal conflict, such as an argument, an episode of jealousy, or other resentment. The data in Table 1-1 indicate that 35% of all relapses occurred in the intrapersonal negative emotional states category (I-A) and 16% occurred in the interpersonal conflict (II-A) category. A further analysis of these findings in terms of subcategories reveals an interesting pattern. In the *interpersonal* category, almost all (82%) of the relapse episodes involved coping with frustration and anger; the results were reversed in the *intrapersonal* category, where emotional states other than frustration and anger accounted for 85% of the relapses. These results seem to indicate that frustration and anger associated with relapse stem primarily from interpersonal sources (arguments with others, etc.), whereas other negative emotional states (fear, depression, etc.) seem to predominate as determinants of relapse when significant other individuals are not involved. A more detailed review of frustration and anger as determinants of relapse will be provided in a later section of this chapter.

Coping with Negative Physical–Physiological States (Category I-B)

This category is included to assess the role of physical withdrawal or craving for a substance to alleviate the unpleasant symptoms associated with withdrawal distress. A subcategory (I-B1) is included specifically for classification of relapse episodes associated primarily with physical withdrawal symptoms (craving in the absence of physical withdrawal is included in Category I-E, however). Determinants involving negative physical states other than those associated with withdrawal are included in Subcategory I-B2 (e.g., relapse in response to physical pain, injury, fatigue, headache, etc.). The data presented in Table 1-1 show that very few relapses (3%) were assigned to the negative physical states category, and most of these were given by subjects in the heroin addiction group (accounting for 9% of all relapses in this group). These results must be interpreted with caution, however, since the time period between initial abstinence and the subsequent relapse may play an important mediating role.

In the analysis of relapse episodes in Table 1-1, no comparison was made between relapse episodes that occurred within a relatively short time period following the initial quit date and those that occurred at a later time interval. Part of the difficulty in making such a comparison among different addictive behavior problems is that treatment programs differ with regard to the date of initial abstinence. An alcoholic who is admitted to an inpatient treatment center, for example, is usually abstinent from the time of admission, even though discharge from the program may be a month later; a smoker, on the other hand, may have a quit date that coincides with the last day of a treatment program. Opportunities for relapse increase at the termination of treatment, regardless of the initial date of quitting or abstinence.

In the author's own sample (Table 1-1), subjects relapsed within a relatively short time after completion of their respective treatment programs. The average number of days between beginning abstinence (for the smokers) or completing a treatment program (for the alcoholics and heroin addicts) and the subsequent date of initial drug use was 17 days for the smokers, 30 days for the alcoholics, and 32 days for the heroin addicts. These figures are difficult to interpret, however, because of differences among the treatment programs involved. For the alcoholics and addicts, for example, abstinence was enforced from the start of the inpatient treatment program—often many weeks prior to release. Some of the heroin addicts were maintained on methadone during treatment, while others took part in an abstinence-oriented therapeutic community. Some of the smokers in the sample took part in a program in which rapid smoking was a key component of treatment (Gordon, 1978) and was used as a self-control intervention procedure during the posttreatment phase by some subjects, thus making it difficult to define a period of "pure" abstinence. More work is needed in this area to clarify the impact of different treatment programs (e.g., inpatient vs. outpatient programs, voluntary vs. involuntary treatment, specific treatment modalities, etc.) on the duration of abstinence or controlled use with each of the major addictive behaviors.

A related problem in analyses of relapse is the question of defining a minimum period of abstinence before one can conclude that a relapse has occurred (vs. continual but intermittent use). In a recent study (Marlatt, Goldstein, & Gordon, 1983) of smokers who attempted to quit smoking on their own without participating in any formal treatment program, we decided arbitrarily that an individual must have stopped smoking for at least 24 hours in order to be included in the abstinent category. Clearly, many persons who intended to quit smoking were only able to do so for a few hours before resuming their habit. Many of these "immediate relapsers" complained of physical withdrawal as a reason for their being unable to maintain abstinence. We are currently comparing these early relapsers with those who have relapsed after a longer period of abstinence. Our hypothesis is that the relapse process across individuals and time may take the form of a bimodal distribution. In this hypothetical model, those who relapse early may do so primarily because of physical discomfort associated with withdrawal, while those who relapse at a later time interval may smoke in response to more psychological or situational factors. This analysis applies only to those addictive behaviors in which there is a high probability of experiencing physical withdrawal following initial abstinence (e.g., most heroin addicts and many alcoholics and smokers).

Enhancement of Positive Emotional States (Categories I-C and II-C)

Some relapses occur when the individual is feeling good instead of bad. The use of a substance or activity to enhance positive emotional states accounted for relatively few relapses overall in the analysis presented in Table 1-1 (12% of the total, combined over the intrapersonal and interpersonal categories). In the intrapersonal category, only 10% of the heroin addicts, 6% of the smokers, 3% of the overeaters, and none of the alcoholics or gamblers reported their initial lapse in this type of situation. Most of the heroin addicts described a desire or need to get high or to enhance their mood state by taking narcotics. The individual's feelings or emotional state prior to taking the drug must be carefully evaluated before assigning a relapse episode to this category. The person must report taking the drug or engaging in the activity to enhance an already existing positive mood state (e.g., "I was feeling so good, I wanted to feel even better," or "I just got some great news, and I was in the mood to celebrate"). Taking a drug to alleviate feelings of boredom or restlessness, on the other hand, would not be included in this category since the primary determinant is to avoid or escape a negative emotional state. Frequently, relapses in the positive emotional states category occur in conjunction with a special event (holiday, birthday, good fortune) or a vacation or trip away from home. Some smokers, for example, report taking their first cigarette when they are out of town to attend a convention or are embarking on a vacation trip. It is very tempting in this type of situation to make a "special exception" and give oneself permission to smoke for the duration of the trip; intentions to quit again upon returning to the normal routine are rarely honored, however.

People involved in a weight-loss program are particularly susceptible to interpersonal influence in the enhancement of positive mood states (Category II-C). Table 1-1 reveals that fully 28% of the overeaters (second only to the negative emotional states category) reported going off their diets in this type of situation. Clearly the prevailing mood at birthday and wedding parties and family gatherings at Thanksgiving and Christmas is one of celebration and joy. It is extremely difficult to resist the pull of the crowd and the upbeat mood of the moment on such festive occasions. For many would-be dieters, the holiday seasons are the most difficult to deal with.

Many individuals feel good about their initial progress in a behavior change program. After the alcoholic has gone a month without alcohol, or the smoker a month without cigarettes, there is a sense of having "made it"—of having escaped from the bondage of the old habit pattern. Members of Alcoholics Anonymous (AA) refer to this initial blissful state as a "pink cloud" stage, in which the ex-drinker begins to feel that he or she has finally won the battle and can begin to let down the guard. Often this positive reaction is accompanied by a feeling of no longer being hooked by the old behavior, coupled with a sense of being able to "take it or leave it"—a false sense of confidence that may precipitate a relapse. The impulse to indulge may also be bolstered by a sense of self-congratulation: "I've done so well and I've been so good for so long—I owe myself at least one reward for all of this good behavior." All too often the reward turns out to be indulging in the very behavior one set out to control in the first place!

Testing Personal Control (Category I-D)

Table 1-1 shows that 5% of all relapses fell into this category, including 9% of the alcoholics, 16% of the compulsive gamblers, and 2% of the heroin addicts. Such cases usually involve an attempt to test out one's ability to "just try it once" without losing control. Often such tests are described as tests of "willpower" or "internal fortitude." This category appears most often with behaviors that are associated with a "loss of control" philosophy—that one cannot engage in the act even once without losing control. Traditionalists in the alcoholism field frequently emphasize this loss of control reaction: "One drink, then drunk," "An alcoholic can never be cured because he or she can never take a drink without losing control," are statements that reinforce this notion. In traditional alcoholism circles, it is presumed that loss of control is triggered by the physical presence of alcohol in the bloodstream. In this regard, it is interesting to note that GA, a self-help group for compulsive gamblers that patterns itself after the philosophy of AA, also stresses loss of control as a central factor, even though there is no underlying "drug" presumed to trigger the reaction. Consider the following quotes taken from the *Gamblers Anonymous Handbook* (1976):

The first small bet to a problem gambler is like the first small drink to an alcoholic. Sooner or later he falls back into the same old destructive pattern. Once a person has crossed the invisible line into irresponsible gambling he *never* seems to regain control. After abstaining a few months some of our members have tried some small-bet experimentation, always with disastrous results. The old obsession invariably returned. . . . (p. 3)

We know that no real compulsive gambler ever regains control. All of us felt at times we were regaining control, but such intervals—usually brief—were inevitably followed by still less control, which led in time to pitiful and incomprehensible demoralization. We are convinced to a man that gamblers of our type are in the grip of a *progressive illness*. Over any considerable period of time we get worse, never better. . . . (p. 13)

The emphasis on the inevitable consequence of losing control after the first episode of gambling or drinking seems to pose a kind of challenge to some individuals, as though their willpower or inner strength is put to the test. To quote from one of our gambler's relapse episodes: "I gambled just to see if I could start and stop when I wished; just to see if I could control it." Often the initial use precipitated by such thoughts ends in a total relapse—

probably more as the result of a self-fulfilling prophecy than any internal "illness" reaction. To equate total abstinence with total control and any deviation from this absolute standard as indicative of loss of control is to load the dice in favor of relapse should a slip occur.

Urges and Temptations (Category I-E)

Sometimes a relapse is precipitated by the experience of a sudden urge or temptation that seems to overpower the person. This category is to be assigned only when other situational or intrapersonal factors have been ruled out. It is possible that some individuals will have forgotten the circumstances that preceded the urge, or that lifestyle factors (such as an over-demanding work schedule) have predisposed the person to greater vulnerability to sudden impulses of this type. As such, "urges and temptations" may represent a kind of "wastebasket" category, to be assigned when all other attempts to pin down the exact antecedent fails.

There are two situations that appear to trigger valid urges, however, each of which is listed as a subcategory in Table 2-2. The first subcategory (I-E1) applies when an urge is experienced in the presence of substance cues—for example, an alcoholic who suddenly runs across a bottle that had been hidden during some earlier state of intoxication. If the person is alone at such a time, the temptation to take a drink may exert a very powerful influence. In one example of this type, an ex-smoker began smoking again while she was driving to work one day; she stopped suddenly at a red light only to discover a previously dropped cigarette that had rolled out from under her seat, providing her with a tempting offer she could not refuse. Table 1-1 shows that less than 10% of all relapses were assigned to the urges and temptations category; most of these fell into the first subcategory.

The second subcategory (I-E2) involves urges that occur in the *absence* of substance cues—those that seem to come "out of the blue." This category was originally included to tap into relapses that seemed to be the result of an intense subjective desire or "craving" for a substance, perhaps triggered by an environmental cue or conditioned stimulus previously associated with earlier experiences of withdrawal or craving. In the sample of relapse episodes, however, this category was used only in rare instances. It seems clear that most "urges" do not suddenly arise out of nowhere or as a response to conditioned stimuli associated with prior withdrawal; rather, an urge is experienced as a response to a specific stressful situation—a state of arousal or tension that comes to be labeled as an urge or state of craving.

Interpersonal Conflict (Category II-A)

Table 1-1 shows that 16% of all relapses occurred in this category, and that these relapses were evenly distributed across the five addictive behaviors. By far the largest number of relapse episodes in this grouping occurred in interpersonal situations involving frustration and anger (Subcategory II-A1) rather than other emotional states such as fear or anxiety (Subcategory II-A2). With regard to the first subcategory, it seems likely that feelings of frustration and anger deriving from an argument or other disagreement are often expressed in the relapse episode itself. A typical scenario: an ex-drinker has an argument with his wife, both of them become very upset, and the husband feels "done in" by the wife. The husband, knowing that his past drinking was a cause of great distress to his wife, takes a drink in her presence, thereby touching off another fight. In the course of the ensuing battle, the husband strikes out at his wife. Later, after things have calmed down, he apologizes for having hit her, but disclaims "authorship" or responsibility for his aggressive behavior because he was "drunk" and "wasn't myself at the time." It is also possible that the husband initiated the first argument in order to provide himself with an excuse to begin drinking. In such a covertly planned relapse, the decision to start the first fight was an Apparently Irrelevant Decision (AID) to set up a high-risk situation in which drinking was a likely outcome. Research supports the notion that there is a strong linkage between anger and drinking. Studies to be reviewed in detail later in this chapter show that heavy drinkers consume more alcohol when they are feeling frustrated and angry (Marlatt, Kosturn, & Lang, 1975), and that the belief that one has consumed alcohol increases the probability of subsequent aggressive behavior (Lang, Goeckner, Adesso, & Marlatt, 1975).

Other research conducted in our laboratory shows that interpersonal evaluation, or the anticipation of possible negative criticism by others, can also be a significant determinant of drinking. In one study (Higgins & Marlatt, 1975), we investigated the influence of social evaluation on the drinking rates of males who were heavy social drinkers. Drinking was assessed in a procedure called the Taste-Rating Task (Marlatt, 1978a), in which subjects are free to consume alcoholic beverages (usually wine) on an ad-lib basis during the course of making comparative taste ratings. Although the "cover story" emphasizes that the purpose of this task is to evaluate individual differences in taste acuity, the real purpose is to provide an unobtrusive measure of alcohol consumption. Subjects in the interpersonal evaluation condition were led to believe that following participation in the Taste-Rating Task, they would be evaluated by a group of college women who would be rating the men on a number of personal dimensions, including personal attractiveness. Subjects in this group consumed significantly more alcohol than subjects in the control condition who did not anticipate being evaluated. It is interesting to note that in a related study, male alcoholics and a matched control group of social drinkers who anticipated a *physically* painful event (receiving an electric shock) did *not* consume more alcohol in the Taste-Rating Task, compared to subjects in a low-threat control condition (Higgins & Marlatt, 1973). The results of these two studies are summarized in Figure 2-1. It appears that stress or threat that is *interpersonal* in nature serves as an impetus for drinking, but that heavy drinkers do not

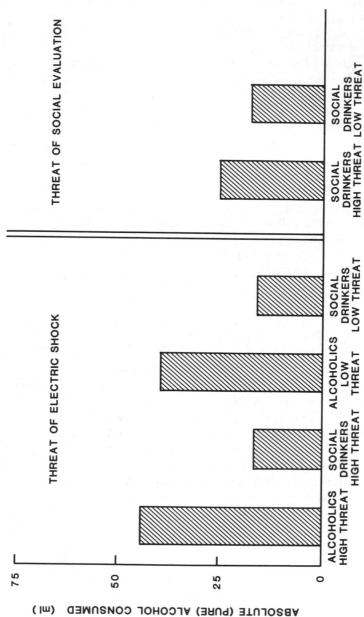

Figure 2-1. Amount of absolute alcohol consumed by subjects threatened by electric shock (left side) and by social evaluation (right side) in a 15-minute Taste-Rating Task. (Note that 1.5 oz of 80 proof spirits = 17.7 ml of absolute alcohol.) Based on data from Higgins and Marlatt (1973, 1975).

increase consumption in other stressful situations (such as anticipation of pain), contrary to predictions from a global tension-reduction model. For further discussion of tension-reduction theory as it applies to alcohol consumption in humans, the reader is referred to papers by Higgins (1976) and Marlatt (1976), and a recent edited volume by Pohorecky and Brick (1983).

Social Pressure (Category II-B)

Approximately 20% of all the relapse episodes categorized in Table 1-1 are classified in the social pressure category. Two subcategories are included here: situations in which some form of direct social pressure (verbal persuasion or providing direct access to a drug or activity with pressure on the person to partake) is involved (Subcategory II-B1), as contrasted with situations in which the mere presence of other people engaged in the behavior acts as a kind of indirect pressure mediated by a social modeling effect (Subcategory II-B2).

Whether the influence of social pressure is direct or indirect interacts in an important way with the substance or activity involved. For alcoholics and heroin addicts, the predominant relapse situation in this category involved *direct* social pressure, with actual contact between users (e.g., meeting an old drinking buddy who put pressure on the person to begin drinking again; or the addict who runs across someone who offers some of his or her stash). For the sample of alcoholics who reported relapsing in a social pressure situation (18% of the 70 episodes reported), most began drinking again under direct social pressure (14%), and only a few under indirect pressure (4%). For the smokers studied, however, the findings were reversed; of the relapses in the social pressure category (32% overall), most occurred in *indirect* pressure situations. In a typical high-risk situation of this type, an ex-smoker relapses in a bar, restaurant, or other social situation in which there are a number of other people who are smoking.

Whether the social pressure is direct or indirect is important in terms of treatment planning, since different coping responses are involved: in the former case, the person must be trained to give an appropriate refusal response, whereas in the latter instance, the person should be instructed in how to identify and resist the subtle influence of observing others who are engaged in the prohibited activity. Another factor that has an impact on the type of social pressure involved is the public acceptability of the behavior itself—smoking is a far more public behavior, for example, than is the illicit use of narcotics.

Laboratory research underscores the impact that social influence exerts on drinking behavior. Several studies have been conducted to investigate the role of modeling in the interpersonal drinking situation. Research on this question began in our laboratory with a rather simple analogue study (Caudill & Marlatt, 1975). In this experiment, male heavy social drinkers took part in a taste-rating task in the presence of a confederate "subject" who played the role of either a heavy drinker (guzzling down the equivalent of a full bottle of wine during the 15-minute period) or a light drinker (who sipped slowly and consumed only one-seventh of a bottle). Control subjects took part in the task without a partner. Results showed a significant modeling effect: as indicated in Figure 2-2, those subjects who were paired with a heavy drinking model drank significantly more wine than subjects who drank alone or who were paired with the light drinking model.

In a subsequent study (Lied & Marlatt, 1979), we found that the modeling effect was most pronounced in male heavy drinkers who were paired with a heavy drinking model of the same sex. Female heavy drinkers and both male and female light social drinkers did not show an increase in drinking when paired with a same-sex model. The results of this study, depicted in Figure 2-3, suggest that males are particularly vulnerable to the modeling influence with alcohol, perhaps because of the cultural stereotype of heavy drinking as

Figure 2-2. Amount of wine consumed in a 15-minute Taste-Rating Task (ml of 12% table wine; a 26-oz bottle of wine contains 770 ml) by male social drinkers exposed to heavy- and light-drinking models or a no-model condition. Heavy-drinking models consumed 700 ml of wine compared to 100 ml consumed by light-drinking models. Based on data from Caudill and Marlatt (1975).

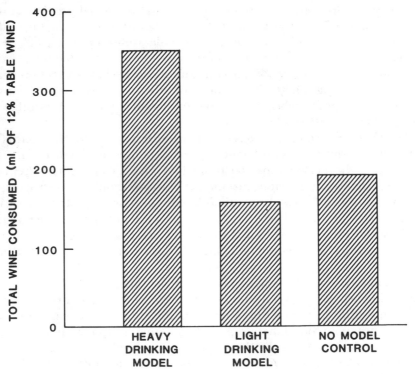

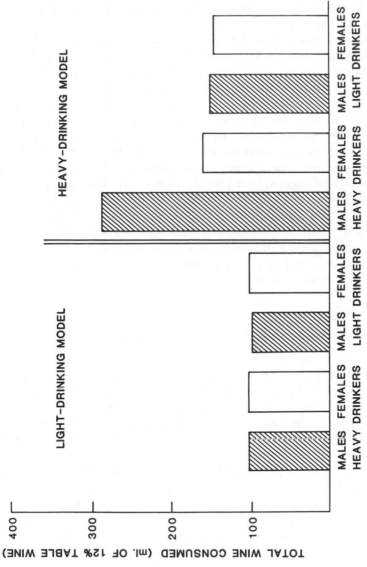

Figure 2-3. Amount of wine consumed by male and female subjects classified as either heavy or light social drinkers, exposed to either a heavy-drinking model (consumption of 700 ml) or light-drinking model (consumption of 100 ml) of the same sex, in a 15-minute Taste-Rating Task. Based on data from Lied and Marlatt (1979).

a sign of masculine prowess (the "macho modeling effect"). Collins and Marlatt (1981) provide a review of studies investigating the modeling phenomenon with drinking behavior. Similar modeling effects have been found to occur with both smoking (Antonuccio & Lichtenstein, 1980; Kniskern, Biglan, Lichtenstein, Fry, & Bavry, 1983) and eating behaviors (Rosenthal & McSweeney, 1979).

Analogue research with social drinkers plays an important role in understanding the relapse process in problem drinkers. Research such as the social modeling studies reinforces the assumption that both social and problem drinking can be placed along the same continuum, and that factors which have been found to increase drinking rates in heavy social drinkers (frustration and anger, social evaluation, peer modeling, etc.) also precipitate relapse in formerly abstinent alcoholics. By the same token, research identifying factors that are associated with *decreased* drinking in social drinkers have important implications for the prevention of relapse. For example, in one study we found that angered social drinkers who were given the opportunity to express their anger prior to drinking drank significantly *less* than angered subjects who did not express their anger (Marlatt et al., 1975). Since frustration and anger is one of the most common high-risk situations associated with relapse in alcoholics, it follows that treatment which includes instruction in anger management (e.g., assertiveness training) should be an effective component in a Relapse Prevention (RP) program.

HIGH-RISK SITUATIONS:
PHYSICAL SETTING AND TEMPORAL FACTORS

In addition to the classification of high-risk situations described above, a number of other points of interest emerged from our study of relapse determinants with alcoholics, smokers, and heroin addicts (Marlatt & Gordon, 1980). Two significant factors emerging from this analysis were the physical setting and the time of day in which the relapse episode occurred. Physical setting varied as a function of the drug used. Alcoholics, as might be expected, took their first drink in a bar or tavern (63% of the relapses in our sample). The next largest groupings began drinking in their own homes (12%) or in the homes of friends or relatives (9%). The remainder of relapses in this group was spread over a wide variety of settings (e.g., hotel rooms, outdoors, while driving, etc.). For the smokers one's own home was the primary setting for relapse (44%), followed by the work environment (19%), restaurants and bars (13%), and parties (6%). Because of the illegal nature of heroin addiction, the settings for relapse with this drug are much more limited; almost all of these relapses occurred in private homes or apartments. In our addict group, heroin was obtained primarily in one of two ways: by purchase from a sought-after connection, or obtained without cost from friends or other users.

Time of day when the relapse occurred was obtained from the alcoholic and smoking group subjects (these data were not available for our addict sample). Subjects were grouped in accordance with whether they took their first drink or cigarette in the morning, afternoon, or evening hours. As might be expected, relatively few subjects relapsed in the morning (12% of the alcoholics and 22% of the smokers). For the alcoholics, relapses were about evenly distributed between afternoons (42%) and evenings (46%). Smokers showed a greater tendency to relapse in the evening (61%) than in the afternoon period (17%).

Physical setting and temporal factors are often important in planning an RP program, especially with clients who have shown a tendency to relapse or who report strong urges in particular settings (e.g., bars or restaurants) or at particular times (e.g., urges to smoke after the evening meal). Treatment effectiveness may be enhanced in many cases by conducting individual or group sessions in actual or simulated high-risk situations. Smokers or drinkers who are exposed to a setting such as a tavern or bar as part of a "dry run" session have the opportunity to practice coping with urges in the real-life environment, thereby increasing generalization of treatment effects.

HIGH-RISK SITUATIONS AND RELAPSE: A CASE STUDY

In order to illustrate the role of high-risk situations in precipitating a relapse, let us examine an actual case study (Marlatt, 1978b). Miss L was a client in our Center for Psychological Services at the University of Washington. A 30-year-old single woman who lived in a self-contained apartment in her parents' home in Seattle, Miss L was a senior undergraduate student majoring in psychology. In the months prior to our first contact, her drinking began to interfere with her studies. Rather than devoting time to her assignments, she would spend most of her evenings alone, sipping vodka and watching television. She did not have a steady boyfriend and spent most of her free time either alone or with her parents, claiming that she could not relate comfortably to most people unless she had been drinking. A 2-week daily diary of her alcohol intake revealed that she was consuming almost a full quart of vodka each day, along with a variety of tranquilizers.

When we confronted her with the seriousness of her condition, she agreed to undergo a period of voluntary hospitalization to provide medical supervision for her detoxification from both alcohol and the other drugs she had been taking. Before she was released from the hospital, she committed herself to complete abstinence from alcohol for at least 1 year. All went well for the first few weeks, and she was able to maintain abstinence during this initial period. On the 58th day following her discharge from the hospital, however, she experienced a "slip" and consumed one drink during a luncheon date with a female friend. On the 78th day, she repeated this

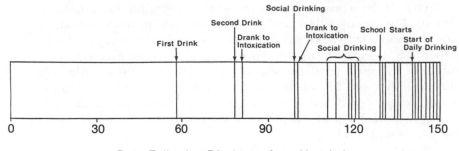

Days Following Discharge from Hospital

Figure 2-4. The course of Miss L's drinking from the beginning of treatment. From "Craving for Alcohol, Loss of Control, and Relapse: A Cognitive–Behavioral Analysis" by G. A. Marlatt, in *Alcoholism: New Directions in Behavioral Research and Treatment* (p. 274), edited by P. E. Nathan, G. A. Marlatt, and T. Løberg, New York: Plenum, 1978. Copyright 1978 by Plenum Press. Reprinted by permission.

experience, and consumed her second drink under identical circumstances. Finally, on the 81st day, she drank to the point of intoxication during a weekend evening alone in her apartment. The course of her drinking during the first 150 days after her hospitalization is presented in Figure 2-4. An examination of this figure shows the pattern of a typical relapse. After becoming intoxicated on the 81st day, Miss L again refrained from any drinking for about 2 weeks, followed by another occasion of "social drinking" (limiting herself to no more than two drinks), and shortly thereafter, another bout of intoxication. With the start of classes in the fall, her drinking began to increase until it almost equalled the rate of intake she reported prior to treatment. Eventually she was able to regain control and maintain abstinence.

We asked the client to keep a running account of her experiences during the period following her discharge from the hospital. As these reports were written within a few days of the events, they would appear to be reasonably accurate accounts of what actually occurred. The following excerpts are taken directly from her written account. The luncheon date reported for July 17 was the first social event of any importance Miss L had participated in since her release from the hospital. Her luncheon companion was a woman who lived in the same neighborhood, although they were not close friends at the time.

July 17, 58th day since leaving the hospital: The first drink. Lunch with neighbor Mrs. S. Mrs. S and her husband are in their middle 60s, retired, with no children. When I asked her to lunch I told her that I thought it would be nice to wander through the shops in Old Mill Town, and then have lunch. I had no intention of having a drink nor did I think about how I'd handle the situation. It never occurred to me that it would be a problem, particularly since it was I who was paying for the lunch. This was, however, the first time I had invited anybody to dine with me as my guest since I had gotten out of the hospital, and more importantly, Mrs. S knew nothing about my problem drinking. I picked her up at 10:30 A.M., and we went to Edmonds. Both of us were dressed up, and I felt very at ease, cheerful, and confident. I had tentatively planned to eat in Edmonds, but Mrs. S suggested or commented that she enjoyed eating at Frederick and Nelson in Aurora Village, so I agreed that we go there. Throughout the entire time we were together, there was pleasant and interesting conversation. When we were seated the waitress came by and asked if we wanted cocktails. Since I was taking her to lunch, I said, "Would you like a cocktail?" She ordered Scotch and soda, and then the waitress looked at me and said, "And you?" "Gin and tonic, please," just came out. I didn't plan it and I wasn't prepared for it. The cocktails came and we ordered lunch. I was extremely cognizant of the effect the alcohol had on me. The first sip was so strong it literally shocked me. It was difficult for me to finish the drink. I am not entirely sure whether or not I imagined some of the physical effects, perhaps because of guilt, or if it was real. I tend to believe that it was the latter. Mrs. S finished her drink before the lunch even came. I was just finishing when we were ready to leave which was approximately 45 minutes to 1 hour from start to finish. I got a headache, my nose got stuffy, my thoughts were tangled, and my voice and actions were abrasive. There were several things that came from this that did help me. One thing was that committing myself to one year of abstinence from alcohol from an inebriated state of some duration was a difficult reality to keep after a month or so because there is no reality in inebriation. Therefore, I was especially vulnerable to the unreality of alcoholic romanticism used in advertising, television, and movies. This sounds trivial but it was a stimulus for envy and anxiety. Alcohol consumption is so intermeshed in the structure of society that it is very difficult not to feel the influence. For me, what was going through my mind was that a social drink at parties, lunches, dinners, etc., is condoned and exploited, making me feel extremely self-conscious for not participating. But, when one gets into the predicament of drug and alcohol abuse, as myself, society doesn't fail to ostracize and condemn.

In terms of the high-risk situations outlined in Table 2-2, the circumstances leading to Miss L's first drink experience would be classified as a *social pressure* situation (Category II-B). The components of this situation include the influence of Miss L's romanticized image of herself as a drinker and the role that alcohol plays in social situations ("For me, what was going on through my mind was that a social drink at parties, lunches, dinners, etc. is condoned and exploited, making me feel extremely self-conscious for not participating"), and the influence of Mrs. S, who acted as a powerful model when she ordered the first drink. The social pressure was indirect since Mrs. S did not pressure Miss L to take a drink. The waitress, however, did exert a form of direct social pressure when she asked for her drink order. One of the most important features to be noted in this account is the sudden and unexpected occurrence of the high-risk situation. In this case, it seems unlikely that Miss L's taking of the first drink was an event that was covertly planned in advance.

Twenty days later, on August 6, Miss L again invited Mrs. S out for lunch, and once again she consumed a single mixed drink. In contrast to the first occasion, however, Miss L considered the possibility of having a drink in advance of the luncheon. The experience of July 17 had brought about a shift in her attitudes toward drinking, as she observes in the following passage:

I can't deny that the first situation was spontaneously reinforcing, greater than I had realized. I would only be kidding myself if I were to say that repeating the same scene, i.e., having one drink at lunch, was not planned; at least I had no real intentions of *not* having that drink. Having this drink was more of a pain than a pleasure. I didn't feel good about having that drink. It lowered my self-esteem and did create some guilty and remorseful feelings.

Three days later, Miss L consumed enough alcohol to become intoxicated.

August 9, 81st day: The first intoxication experience. I got up early, and I felt content and at ease. I went down to the den and played the organ for several hours. I know that I felt mentally and physically well that morning because I have little indicators that give me an indication or realization of what is going on in me that I may not be aware of. Playing the organ is one of them. When I can play the organ to my satisfaction, i.e., not making too many mistakes and enjoying playing, I know that at that particular time I'm happy and not depressed or worried, and that is what I felt like that morning. I then put some records on which I hadn't done since I came home from the hospital. Unfortunately, as I recollect now, the records started some or rather initiated my change in moods. Music has always played a very important part in my life. Although I enjoy all musical forms, classical to hard rock, music has always been an escape and expression of how I am feeling. Well, it never occurred to me that the music conditioned specific moods in me without being aware of it. So, as I played some records and sang along, after, well even during, my mood became melancholy and I began to feel sorry for myself and ill at ease, but I wasn't really cognizant of it happening. The point at which I noticed my "free-floating anxiety" came around 4:00 in the afternoon. I have my little fantasies. This is not easy to write, I don't know how to write without sounding like I belong in a mental institution. My fantasy is to take a real person (male) whom I don't know personally, but through TV, etc., and, well, to imagine that we are together. So, suddenly, about 4:00, his face just popped into my mind. This really affected my mood, because, well, I was alone in the house, it was Saturday, and I knew I was going to be alone for the evening. I had no plans for doing anything that night, and I began to feel sad about being alone. After a while, I began to feel more and more anxious about this.

At first, I thought I would feel better if I could take a tranquilizer so I searched all over the house for the pills my mother had hidden. I couldn't find them, which made me all the more upset. What I did find, though, was two bottles of airline Scotch, miniature bottles like you buy on the plane, hidden in a teapot in the kitchen. I also found three bottles of beer in the fridge upstairs. At first, I tried to ignore them, but I couldn't get the liquor out of my mind.

Finally, I took out the two bottles of Scotch, and put them on the table. I just looked at them for a long time, without even touching them. After about half an hour, and even after resisting the thought of calling my therapist on the phone, I finally opened one of the bottles and poured it into a glass with some ice. I sipped the drink, but didn't feel anything, at first, so I poured in the other one and drank that too. After that, I drank the bottles of beer in the fridge and then I don't remember what happened. I woke up later that night with a hangover, and I felt terrible about what I had done.

In the above episode, the primary determinant of Miss L's drinking appears to be her feelings of loneliness and anxiety that were triggered by the music and by the knowledge that she was going to be alone that evening— events that would be classified in the intrapersonal *negative emotional state* category (specifically, Subcategory I-A2, coping with negative emotional states other than frustration or anger). A secondary component in this episode would seem to be *testing personal control* (Category I-D) in her last-ditch effort to exert willpower and resist the temptation of taking a drink after she had placed the bottles of Scotch on the table.

HIGH-RISK SITUATIONS: ASSESSMENT PROCEDURES

In this section, a number of assessment procedures for identifying potential high-risk situations are discussed. The situations discussed previously are those identified as problematic for clients with a variety of addictive behavior problems. Although the list of high-risk situations presented in Table 2-2 may be useful as a starting point in an assessment program, it is important for the therapist to conduct an in-depth systematic assessment program in order to identify unique or idiosyncratic situations that may increase the risk of relapse for the individual client. The material to follow describes several useful techniques that can be employed in the assessment of high-risk situations. Use of any particular procedure will depend on the circumstances in working with a given client. One important consideration is whether or not the client is still engaging in the target behavior at the time of assessment. With many clients, it is possible to obtain an ongoing baseline record of the behavior prior to the beginning of treatment (e.g., smoking or eating). In the case of most inpatient treatment settings for alcoholism or heroin addiction, however, the therapist has little or no contact with the client until after detoxification has been completed and the client is already abstinent.

It is important to note that the assessment of high-risk situations is actually a two-stage process. In the first stage, an attempt is made to identify specific *situations* that may pose a problem for the client in terms of future risk for relapse. The use of self-monitoring procedures (keeping records of the occurrence of the target behavior), self-efficacy ratings (expectations of one's capacity to cope with specific situations), autobiographical statements, descriptions of past relapses, and related assessment measures are all techniques that can be used in this first stage. The second stage involves an assessment of the client's existing *coping skills* or capacity to respond effectively in a given high-risk situation. Procedures to evaluate coping skills will be presented in the next section of this chapter; the following presentation focuses on assessment of potential high-risk situations. Since the author has defined a specific situation as high-risk only to the extent that the person is incapable of responding with an appropriate coping response, a comprehensive assessment strategy includes both the identification of potential risk situations and the client's capacity to cope in these situations.

Self-Monitoring

Self-monitoring procedures provide the best method of identifying potential high-risk situations for cases in which access to the ongoing behavior is possible. Self-monitoring is a relatively simple technique in which the client is asked to keep a continuous (usually daily) record of the target behavior, along with a brief description of such additional factors as time of occurrence, situational context or other antecedent factors, and the consequences (e.g., mood change) following the behavior itself. Detailed descriptions of self-monitoring as a general behavioral assessment strategy can be found in a number of sources (cf. McFall, 1977). The procedure can be used with any ongoing target behavior such as smoking, drinking, eating, heroin use, or compulsive gambling.

As an example of the use of self-monitoring in a clinical setting, consider a procedure I often use with problem drinkers (Marlatt, 1979). The procedure is applicable for those cases in which it is possible to gain access to the client's drinking prior to abstinence or beginning a controlled drinking program. I usually ask the client to begin keeping self-monitoring records immediately after the first interview or intake session. To enhance interest in this procedure and to motivate the client to keep accurate and comprehensive records, I enlist the client's cooperation by defining his or her role as that of a colleague or cotherapist—someone who is adopting a "scientific" (detached, objective) attitude toward observing his or her behavior. Many clients react very positively to this approach, since it allows them to discuss their problem with a sense of empirical detachment and peer rapport (as if client and therapist were two radiologists going over a patient's x-rays), instead of reacting in a guilty and defensive manner.

The client is asked to keep an ongoing record of drinking in order to provide a valuable source of information not only for the therapist (for treatment planning and evaluation of outcome) but also for the client (as a means of enhancing awareness about the antecedents and consequences of drinking). The *Daily Drinking Diary* (Figure 2-5) requires clients to record the exact amount of alcohol consumed each day, the time period for each drinking occasion, the social and situational setting in which drinking occurs, and the antecedents and consequences of each drinking act. A similar

Time (When did drinking begin?):	Setting (Where? Who was present? Doing what?):	Antecedents (What was happening? How were you feeling prior to drinking?):	Amount consumed (Be specific–give exact ounces of beer, wine, or liquor consumed):	Consequences (What happened? How did you feel after drinking?):	Time (When did the drinking end?):

Daily summary

Total time spent drinking: _____ Minutes _____ Hours
Total ml of absolute alcohol consumed: _____ ml
Average blood–alcohol level for time spent drinking: _____ %
Peak blood–alcohol level obtained during day: _____ %

Figure 2-5. The Daily Drinking Diary. From "Alcohol Use and Problem Drinking: A Cognitive–Behavioral Analysis" by G. A. Marlatt, in Cognitive–Behavioral Interventions: Theory, Research and Procedures (p. 339), edited by P. C. Kendall and S. D. Hollon, New York: Academic Press, 1979. Copyright 1979 by Academic Press. Reprinted by permission.

form, called the *Alcohol Intake Sheet*, has been developed by Sobell and Sobell (1973). The client is urged to record the information required as soon as possible following each drinking episode and to avoid reliance on retrospective accounts that may be distorted by memory problems or emotional factors. To facilitate immediate recording, clients can be asked to keep the information in a small pocket notebook or similar device (smokers can keep the monitoring sheet wrapped around a cigarette pack with an elastic band). When the validity of the client's self-monitoring is in doubt, the cooperation of a significant other person who is asked to keep an independent record of the client's drinking (with the client's permission) may be needed. Similar monitoring forms can be devised for clients with other addictive behaviors.

In most cases, a period of at least 2 weeks of daily record-keeping is required in order to obtain a representative sampling of the target behavior. A variety of findings can be obtained from the self-monitoring data. As noted at the bottom of Figure 2-5, the data from the *Daily Drinking Diary* can be summarized in the form of the total time and amount of drinking each day; these data, along with the individual's weight, can be used to calculate average and peak blood-alcohol levels for each day (see Miller & Muñoz, 1982, for details on calculating blood-alcohol levels). An additional source of information that can be derived from self-monitoring records of this type is a *drinking situations bar graph*. A bar graph of this type is illustrated in Figure 2-6. This chart, taken from one of our recent clients was constructed by having the client keep records of all drinking for a period of 2 weeks. For each week, alcohol consumption rates (in ounces of pure alcohol) were listed for each major situation or setting in which drinking occurred. For this particular client, the major drinking situations were drinking at home alone after work, drinking in work-related settings (business meetings over cocktails), drinking in social situations (e.g., parties), and drinking when visiting his wife and children (he and his wife were recently separated). The height of each bar on the graph was determined by adding the consumption rates in each situation over the 2-week period, then dividing by two to yield an average weekly consumption rate in each situational category. The bar graph tells us that for this client, drinking when visiting his family represents a particularly difficult high-risk situation that may be associated with relapse or uncontrolled drinking in the future. The client reported feeling very tense and irritable when he visited his wife, although he was unaware how much this influenced his drinking until he constructed the bar graph.

Although self-monitoring may produce an initial reactive effect in that the target behavior may be influenced by the act of continual recording, most clients are able to provide reasonably accurate data when the therapist takes the time to explain the rationale and instructions. Many clients find the procedure an interesting and informative one and have no difficulty in carrying out the task of keeping detailed records over relatively long periods of time. For these clients, the increased awareness they develop concerning

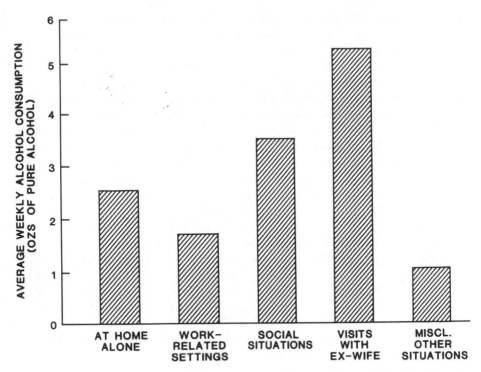

Figure 2-6. Drinking situations bar graph. Data taken from case history. (Note that 1.5 oz of 80 proof spirits = .60 oz of pure alcohol.)

their own behavior serves as an intrinsic reinforcer and a source of motivation. Willingness to keep accurate self-monitoring records is often a good predictor of future compliance and adherence to treatment procedures in our clients. Clients who are unable to comply with requests for record-keeping often do not follow up on other required program commitments. Thus, use of self-monitoring as an initial step in treatment planning often provides a kind of "barometer reading" for future client compliance.

Direct Behavioral Observation Procedures

Direct observation of the target behavior will often provide valuable information concerning situational and interpersonal determinants, although implementation of this approach may not always be feasible or practical. Basically, these methods involve the observation of the behavior *in situ* or in a simulated naturalistic environment. In the author's own research on determinants of drinking, for example, the Taste-Rating Task, an unobtrusive measure of drinking, is frequently used (Marlatt, 1978a). Earlier in this chapter, several experiments that made use of the Taste-Rating Task as a measure of drinking were described (see Figure 2-1). Although this task is particularly appropriate as a dependent measure of ad-lib drinking in laboratory research studies, it can also be used as part of an individualized assessment procedure for client evaluation. One of the chief advantages of this method is that it appears to be sensitive to factors that may increase consumption (e.g., the social context) even when the subject is apparently unaware of this influence. Various situational and interpersonal factors can then be manipulated to determine effects on drinking—such as the presence of others who are drinking, feelings of anger or fear, and so on. One study showed that the amount of alcohol consumed by alcoholics in a similar ad-lib drinking task conducted during an inpatient treatment program was a reliable predictor of treatment outcome (Miller, Hersen, Eisler, & Elkin, 1974). In addition to providing a measure of drinking, the Taste-Rating Task has also been used as a laboratory task to assess eating behavior (Schachter, Goldman, & Gordon, 1968).

Other direct observational approaches include observing the client in the naturalistic setting (e.g., actual restaurants, bars, or in the home environment), or in simulated environments (e.g., research bars) where it is possible to have greater control over the experimental manipulations. More detailed descriptions of direct observational methods that have been used in the assessment of addictive behaviors are available elsewhere (e.g., Donovan & Marlatt, 1980; Sobell & Sobell, 1976).

Self-Efficacy Ratings

Self-efficacy refers to the individual's subjective expectancy concerning his or her capacity to perform a specific response, such as an effective coping response, in a specific situation or task (Bandura, 1977, 1981). Self-efficacy ratings can also be used to identify potential high-risk situations. The procedure is a simple one: the client is presented with a series of descriptions of specific situations and is asked to rate each in terms of how difficult it would be to experience the situation without engaging in the problem behavior. The results can be evaluated by scoring the overall efficacy scores across all situations and by examining ratings for each situation to detect particularly problematic situations. In addition to the items provided by the therapist, the client can be asked to provide additional items to rate, based on prior experience or estimates of unique problematic situations. Since self-efficacy is primarily a cognitive construct, detailed descriptions of this assessment method are described in Chapter 4 (pp. 220–224).

Autobiographies

One of the first "homework assignments" I ask clients to complete following the initial intake interview is to write a brief autobiographical statement (5–10 pages), describing the history and development of their problem. Here, the emphasis is on the client's subjective image of himself or herself as a drinker, smoker, excessive eater, and the like. Often the romantic image of oneself as a smoker, for example, will reveal elements of future high-risk situations (e.g., smoking as a sign of masculinity or as part of a debonair lifestyle). Problem drinkers are asked to emphasize the following points: description of parents' drinking behavior during the client's childhood, the first drinking experience and the first "drunk" episode, the role of drinking in the client's development as an adult (during school years, in the military, and as a part of important personal relationships), factors associated with the development of drinking problems, one's self-image as a drinker, and so forth. We also ask clients to write a brief description of how they would view themselves as an ex-drinker. Comparison of the future self-image compared with the image associated with past problems often will reveal areas of discord that will have to be dealt with in treatment (e.g., an obese person who encounters difficulties with the future image of oneself as "thin"). An autobiography written by one of our clients with a drinking problem, published in a text by Sarason (1976, pp. 540–542), provides a good example of this assessment procedure.

Descriptions of Past Relapses and Relapse Fantasies

Asking the client to describe *past relapses* (if any) will often provide important clues concerning future high-risk situations. If the client has attempted abstinence or controlled substance use prior to the current attempt, information should be obtained concerning the events associated with resuming the problem behavior: What were the situational or intrapersonal determinants, and how did the client react to the relapse? Clients' attitudes toward relapse and their ability to control their own behavior will assist the therapist in structuring the intervention program. Many people, for example, who have tried and failed to change their behavior on repeated occasions in the past have developed very negative attributions about their own capacity to change they may feel devoid of any willpower or self-control abilities, and fear the prospect of yet another failure. These attitudes can be discussed and hopefully modified in discussions with the therapist.

A related procedure is the use of *relapse fantasies*, described briefly in Chapter 1. One of my male clients who recently quit smoking provided the following relapse fantasy:

I see myself at midnight, standing on a railway platform somewhere in the Midwest, waiting for a train. Or, maybe I missed the train and I'm left on the platform alone; it's late and no one is in the station. It starts to rain and I am feeling lonely and lost, and very much sorry for myself. Wait! I think I see a cigarette machine on the platform. I reach into my pocket for change and find, to my relief, that I have enough to buy a pack. I drop the coins in the slot and a package of my old friends, *Lucky Strikes*, slides out ready to do me service. I light one up, inhaling deeply, and I immediately begin to feel better. The rain falls harder, but it is okay now. I am not alone anymore. I put the collar of my coat up around my ears, and exhale a long stream of smoke. I feel like Humphrey Bogart.

Based on this fantasy, a number of ingredients of potential high-risk situations can be ascertained: feelings of loneliness and self-pity, being alone in a strange place, being on a trip, feeling "lost" while waiting—most of them in the intrapersonal negative emotional states category. Also, the lure of a competent, self-assured smoking model (Bogart) may play an important cognitive role in future relapse episodes.

ASSESSMENT AND TRAINING OF COPING SKILLS

This section focuses on methods to train clients in basic coping skills to deal with high-risk situations. The underlying rationale and background research that provide a basis for our emphasis upon skill training as an essential component of RP are presented. The role of frustration and anger as a typical high-risk situation for potential relapse and the use of assertiveness training as a coping skill to deal with this situation are highlighted here as an example of the skill-training approach. Other coping skills are described as additional examples, followed by a discussion of assessment strategies that can be used to evaluate clients' existing skills. The major portion of this section is devoted to a description of various skill-training methods and associated techniques.

COPING SKILLS:
RATIONALE AND BACKGROUND RESEARCH

In an earlier discussion of the relapse determinants that were discovered in a follow-up study of alcoholics who were treated with electrical aversion procedures (see Table 2-1), it was stated that almost one-third of the patients in this initial sample began drinking again following an experience that made them feel frustrated and angry. The majority of relapses in this category occurred in an interpersonal situation, frequently involving a disagreement or argument between the individual and a significant other person. For many of the patients studied, the chain of events was quite similar. The patient would first report feeling frustrated and angry about an event involving another person. Rather than expressing this anger or engaging in a constructive assertive response, the alcoholic turned to a drink instead. In one case, for example, a man reported that he tried to contact his estranged wife after he had been out of the hospital for a week or so to make arrangements to visit his children. Once his wife recognized his voice on the telephone, she hung up on him. When asked about his reaction to this frustrating event, he said that he felt furious and overcome with anger toward "that bitch!" How did he respond to this high-risk situation? After the abrupt termination of the call, he went down to the corner liquor store and bought himself a fifth of vodka. Frequently in such cases, it seems as though drinking takes the form of a symbolic act of aggression—a "slug of booze" coupled with an "I'll show you" defiant attitude.

The model of relapse presented in Chapter 1 predicts that the performance of an assertive response that enables the individual to cope effectively with this type of high-risk situation will decrease the probability of relapse. Successful coping with frustration and anger will increase one's sense of self-efficacy, and will thereby bolster perception of ongoing control. For many alcoholics, however, an adequate coping response may be unavailable (i.e., it was never acquired as part of the behavioral repertoire) or it may be inhibited by anxiety or some other blocking emotion. Some research with this population has shown, in fact, that alcoholics are deficient in general assertive response skills (Miller & Eisler, 1977), although other research has questioned this finding (Monti, Corriveau, & Zwick, 1981). A deficiency in coping skills increases the probability that the alcoholic will take a drink when confronted with frustration and angry feelings. A full-blown relapse may ensue, not only because of the motivating influence of the Abstinence Violation Effect (AVE), but also because of the effects associated with the consumption of alcohol. Some research suggests that men who are heavy drinkers experience an upsurge of personal feelings of power or control when they have consumed alcohol (McClelland *et al.*, 1972). Perhaps this enhancement of psychological control is mediated by the increase in physiological arousal associated with the initial effects of alcohol. In any case, the increase in perceived power or control serves as a strong reinforcement for individuals who drink when they are feeling deprived of control. Feelings of powerlessness or low self-efficacy may provide an incentive for drinking if the drinker expects alcohol to bolster his or her sense of control. The attribution of power-enhancing qualities to alcohol further increases the individual's dependency upon alcohol as a maladaptive coping response. The role of frustration and anger as a determinant of relapse in alcoholics is illustrated in Figure 2-7.

The results of an analogue drinking study provide support for the theoretical model described above. This experiment (Marlatt *et al.*, 1975) is one of a series of studies investigating determinants of alcohol consumption in heavy drinkers. An underlying assumption in these analogue experiments is that the same learning variables (situational determinants, expectation, reinforcement process, etc.) exert an influence on drinking behavior in general, and that drinking rates in the population can be ordered along a continuum ranging from light or infrequent drinking at one end and heavy or problem drinking at the other. In contrast with the traditional disease model of alcoholism, a position that assumes a noncontinuous dichotomy

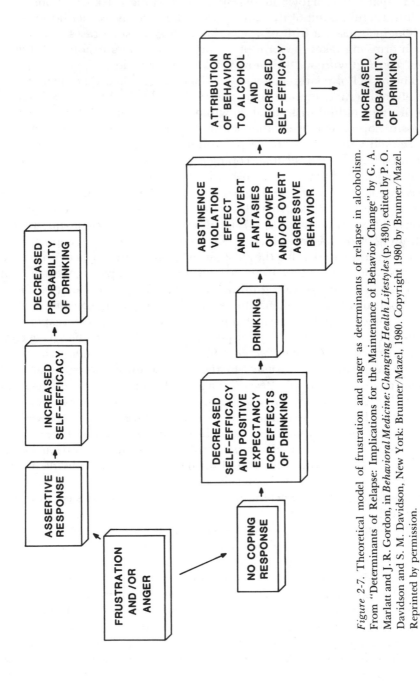

Figure 2-7. Theoretical model of frustration and anger as determinants of relapse in alcoholism. From "Determinants of Relapse: Implications for the Maintenance of Behavior Change" by G. A. Marlatt and J. R. Gordon, in *Behavioral Medicine: Changing Health Lifestyles* (p. 430), edited by P. O. Davidson and S. M. Davidson, New York: Brunner/Mazel, 1980. Copyright 1980 by Brunner/Mazel. Reprinted by permission.

between the drinking behavior of social drinkers and alcoholics, the social-learning approach assumes that the same factors often influence drinking rates in both normal and problem drinkers, and that individual differences exist with regard to the rate or amount of drinking along a continuous (vs. discrete or dichotomous) dimension.

In the Marlatt *et al.* (1975) study, the subjects included both male and female college students who were classified as heavy social drinkers. Subjects were first placed in a situation in which they were deliberately angered and provoked by a confederate subject prior to taking part in a drinking task in which alcoholic beverages were freely available. Some subjects were allowed to respond forcefully to the subject who had provoked them, thus allowing us to assess the effects of this alternative coping response on subsequent drinking.

At the beginning of the experiment, subjects were told that the study was designed to evaluate the role of intelligence on people's abilities to make taste discriminations among various wines. Subjects were randomly assigned to one of three groups. In two groups, each subject was insulted and criticized by the confederate subject while both were ostensibly taking part in a difficult anagrams task, presented as the measure of intellectual ability. Subjects in the third control group experienced a neutral interaction with the confederate during the anagrams task. In one of the angered groups, subjects were given the opportunity of "retaliating" against the confederate subject. In this condition, the angered subject was allowed to deliver a fixed number of electric shocks to the confederate in a standard "teacher–learner" paradigm (the real subject served as the "teacher" for the confederate subject who played the role of "learner" in a memory task; the "teacher" was thereby permitted to deliver "shocks" to the confederate whenever the latter made prearranged errors on the memory task). Although no shocks were actually administered, the procedure was rigged in such a way that the real subject believed he or she was actually aggressing against the other subject. Following this initial procedure, all subjects were presented with the Taste-Rating Task in which they were asked to make a number of discrimination ratings of the taste qualities of three wines.

Our hypothesis was that if the angered subjects were given the opportunity to "get back" at their provoker by retaliating against him (balancing the "score" by making a direct counterresponse), they would drink less than subjects who were deprived of the opportunity to retaliate. The results of the study, depicted graphically in Figure 2-8, supported our predictions. Angered subjects who did not retaliate against the confederate subject (no coping response) consumed the most alcohol in the wine-tasting task. In contrast, subjects who were allowed to express their anger by shocking the confederate, drank significantly less wine compared to the no-retaliation group. The consumption level of the nonangered control subjects fell between the other two groups. These findings supported our hypothesis that heavy drinkers

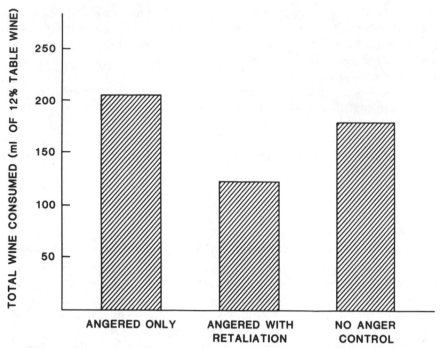

Figure 2-8. Amount of wine consumed (ml of 12% table wine) by male and female heavy social drinkers in the angered only (no opportunity for retaliation), angered with retaliation, and non-angered control conditions, in a 15-minute Taste-Rating Task. Based on data from Marlatt, Kosturn, and Lang (1975).

who are provided with a means of coping with a problematic social situation frequently associated with drinking will show a marked decrease in consumption. Overt retaliation may also have reduced the perceived inequity of the interpersonal situation as viewed by subjects who had been put "one-down" by the confederate (cf. Carver & Scheier, 1983).

In the above study, the coping response consisted of performing a retaliative action against the person who had provoked the subject to anger. In general, we define a *coping response* as any response that enables the individual to "get through" (or around) a high-risk situation without experiencing a relapse. In simple terms, anything the person does that is successful in this sense constitutes a coping response. The use of the term *response* does not imply that only overt behavioral acts are classified as coping responses. Cognitive strategies based on coping self-statements or other thought-regulation techniques are also included.

Coping responses vary in complexity and quality, ranging from simple avoidance responses (e.g., deliberately bypassing a specific high-risk situa-

tion) to complicated cognitive strategies (e.g., the use of meditative detachment to cope with urges). The overall quality or complexity of the coping
response may be less important than the basic question of whether or not *any*
coping response is engaged in (Shiffman, 1982; see also Chapter 8). Research
in our laboratory has shown, for example, that in male alcoholics the
duration of the delay period (latency interval) between being presented with
a problematic high-risk situation and being able to perform a coping response in a role-played task is significantly related to measures of treatment
outcome and relapse (Chaney *et al.*, 1978; see also Chapter 6). The results of
this study strongly suggest that the effectiveness of any coping response is
enhanced if it is performed quickly (short latency) in a high-risk situation.
Failure to respond in a timely manner is likely to produce an outcome in line
with the old maxim that "he who hesitates is lost."

ASSESSMENT OF COPING SKILLS

Basically the purpose here is a simple one: to determine the extent to which
an individual is capable of engaging in a coping response when confronted
with a high-risk situation. The logistics of actually implementing this
assessment strategy are more complicated, however, since coping responses
vary from covert cognitive processes to overt behavioral acts. In addition, the
individual's response may be evaluated in either "real-life" actual situations
or in simulated or contrived situations. Furthermore, it is frequently important to ascertain the person's general capacity to cope with problems as they
arise (problem-solving abilities), regardless of the specific high-risk situation
involved. Space does not permit an exhaustive coverage of all possible
assessment strategies due to the sheer magnitude of different approaches.
Instead, general issues associated with assessment of coping skills will be
focused upon and some examples of procedures used in the author's research
will be described. Further information on the assessment of skills in specific
problem areas (drinking, smoking, and overeating) are provided in later
chapters. For the reader who wishes more detailed information on behavioral
and cognitive assessment procedures, attention is directed to recent works by
Barlow (1981), Hersen and Bellack (1981), Kendall and Hollon (1980), Marlatt
and Donovan (in press), and Merluzzi, Glass, and Genest (1981).

Naturalistic Observation

It may be possible in some cases to assess an individual's coping skills as they
occur in real-life situations. One obvious procedure is for the therapist to
observe a client's behavior when confronted with actual problem situations
—for example, while in a restaurant or bar, at a stressful social gathering,
and so on. This procedure is frequently impractical, however, for reasons of
cost and convenience. Another shortcoming of this method is that it fails to

yield information about the client's covert coping strategies (or lack thereof). One alternative procedure that may be useful in this regard is to have the client keep an ongoing record of his or her responses, both overt and covert, to high-risk situations as they occur on a day-to-day basis. This information could be included along with self-monitoring records of the occurrence of the target behavior problem as described in the previous section. Observations made by significant other individuals (family, friends, work associates, etc.) concerning the client's coping abilities may also prove very useful in the assessment process.

Coping Responses in Simulated High-Risk Situations

In most cases, it is neither practical nor cost-effective for the therapist to observe a client's coping skills in real-life situations. An alternative is to evaluate coping skills in simulated or analogue high-risk situations. The client is presented with a situation and asked to respond as if it had really occurred. The situations can be presented via several different formats including role-playing, staged encounters set up by the therapist, or in written or oral form. Responses to these situations can also be assessed in terms of various response modalities: observation of overt behavior (live or on videotape), self-report (written or oral), or even psychophysiological monitoring.

An example of an assessment procedure in which clients are asked to respond to simulated high-risk situations is the Situational Competency Test (SCT) (Chaney et al., 1978; see also Chapter 6). Although this test was developed initially for use in an inpatient alcoholism program, the format can be adapted for use with other addictive behavior problems. As originally developed by Chaney and other members of our research team, the SCT requires a verbal response to a high-risk situation presented by a narrator on audiotape. We chose an oral response recorded on tape rather than a written response format for several reasons. Many clients are either unwilling or unable to provide a written description of what they would do when faced with a problematic situation due to deficits in motivation or writing skills. In addition, there is no easy way to monitor response latency or reaction time in a written format.

In the initial version of the SCT, the client was presented with 16 different situations drawn from 4 major categories of high-risk situations (developed on the basis of earlier research findings): frustration and anger, interpersonal temptation, negative emotional states, and intrapersonal temptation situations. Two examples of these situations follow. In the frustration and anger category, a situation is described in which the person experiences the blocking of a goal-directed activity and/or hostility toward some person or external event. Four such situations in this category are presented by a narrator on audiotape. An example: "Before you entered the alcoholism treatment program, your employer, who knew about your drinking problem, said that you could have your job back when you got out of the hospital. When you leave the program, you find that the company has hired someone to take your place." A second example, drawn from the intrapersonal temptation category (situations in which the individual experiences a desire or compulsion to drink in the absence of specifically identified external or internal factors): "You have been out of the hospital a couple of months now and haven't taken a single drink. However, you've been wondering how well the treatment really worked, and you get to feeling like taking a drink to test it out."

The tape-recorded vignette was followed with the question, "What would you do or say?" At the start of the test, the subject was instructed to imagine that the situation was actually occurring and to say the words or describe the action that he would use to respond to the situation. Raters score the audiotaped responses for preselected characteristics. In the initial use of the SCT, Chaney and his associates selected four scoring measures: latency, duration, compliance, and specification of new behavior. Latency is defined as the elapsed time from the termination of the recorded situation to the beginning of the subject's verbal response. Response duration is taken as the frequency of words in the response. Compliance is a dichotomous score indicating whether or not the subject gave in to the situation without attempting to engage in an alternative coping response. Specification of new behavior is also a dichotomous score indicating whether the description of the problem-solving behavior or coping response was given in enough detail so that someone else could use the description as a guide to perform the behavior. The SCT can be modified for use with other addictive behavior problems by using the same general format as described above and including high-risk situations that are geared to the specific behavior under study: As an example, the Smoking Situational Competency Test is described in Chapter 8. It is also possible to assess self-efficacy at the same time by asking clients to rate their expectancy of being able to cope with each high-risk situation.

The basic principles of the SCT can be extended to other assessment formats in addition to the audiotape version. A questionnaire can be devised listing a variety of high-risk situations and asking the respondent to provide written descriptions of coping responses. A multiple choice questionnaire can also be prepared that requires the respondent to choose a coping response from among several options listed for a given high-risk situation. Again, ratings of self-efficacy can also be included in a questionnaire of this type. Although such a questionnaire might be useful as a preliminary screening device, the written format has a number of limitations, including its dependence on the respondent's writing skills and the fact that the response latency cannot be ascertained.

In some cases, it may be useful to include standardized questionnaires designed to evaluate specific coping skills. An example is the Rathus Assertiveness Schedule (Rathus, 1973), a questionnaire that has been frequently used as a measure of assertive responding.

Role Playing

A final assessment strategy to be considered is the use of role-playing pro-cedures (Flowers, 1975) in which the client is asked to role-play his or her responses to a high-risk situation enacted by a small group of fellow clients and/or therapists. As an example, a client with a drinking problem can be asked to role-play responses to a social situation in which other members of the group exert pressure on the client to take a drink. Smokers could role-play responding to a difficult interpersonal encounter, to take another example. In order to gain access to the client's covert cognitions, the client can be asked to verbalize or "think out loud" thoughts and reactions as they occur during the role-play enactment (Genest & Turk, 1981). Role-plays can be videotaped for later scoring and analysis. Role playing offers an important advantage over procedures that require clients to say or write what they would do in a given high-risk situation since it requires the performance of actual behavior (vs. the statement of intentions). Frequently there is a dis-crepancy between what people say they are going to do and what they actually do in a given situation.

In some cases, the discrepancy between stated intentions and actual performance in a high-risk situation may be due to anxiety or apprehension that is inhibiting the client's capacity to perform. In such cases, the client may have learned an adequate coping response (and can state this as an intended coping response for a given situation) but is unable to perform this behavior in real-life setting. Anxiety may interfere with access to the coping response, resulting in hesitation, conflict, and the possible emergence of the problem behavior as a maladaptive attempt to cope with the anxiety and stress. In contrast with other individuals who are unable to come up with an adequate coping response on measures such as the SCT (because of a past learning deficit), clients whose responses are inhibited by anxiety will show a marked discrepancy between their stated intentions to cope and their actual performance in a high-risk situation. When this occurs, the therapist must first engage the client in an anxiety-reduction program such as systematic desensitization or other relaxation techniques (Goldfried & Davison, 1976).

SKILL TRAINING

A thorough behavioral assessment of the client's responses to a spectrum of representative high-risk situations will yield a profile of the individual's relative strengths and weaknesses for various coping responses. Once the high-risk situations have been identified, the client can be taught to respond to cues (that either anticipate or coexist with a high-risk situation) as discriminative stimuli for performing a coping response. It should be em-phasized here again that the earlier one intervenes in the chain of events leading up to a high-risk situation, the easier it will be to prevent relapse. In many cases, it is possible to anticipate a high-risk situation far in advance of its actual occurrence. Examples here would include such events as an upcoming party, vacation period, stressful work periods, loss of an important relationship, and the like. Clients should be trained to be on the lookout for impending high-risk situations and to take preventive action at the earliest possible point. In many cases, clients can make a relatively simple decision to either avoid a particular risky situation or to make advance plans about how they will deal with it when it occurs. Along these lines, many clients will find it helpful to sit down once a week (Sunday evenings before the new week begins is a particularly good time for this) and go over the events that are likely to occur during the forthcoming week. What situations are likely to prove difficult in terms of potential for relapse? What plans can be made in advance to deal effectively with each high-risk situation? What decisions can be made now to circumvent or avoid particularly dangerous situations? This method of *advance planning* increases the client's sense of personal responsibility and self-efficacy by underscoring the advantage of early decision making in the process of RP.

Not all high-risk situations can be identified in advance, however. Many situations arise suddenly without warning. Examples here include events such as the sudden death of a loved one, a traffic accident, unforeseen criticism from a friend or employer, and unexpected access to a particularly desirable substance or activity. In this type of situation, the individual must rely on previously acquired coping responses. Here the importance of *skill training* cannot be overemphasized. Skill training implies the actual acquisition of new behavior through overt practice and rehearsal. The individual must learn to give up reliance on the old coping habit and learn a new and different method of dealing with the situation. Simply telling someone what to do by providing a verbal description of a coping response is not enough. One does not acquire a new behavioral skill (e.g., learning to ride a bicycle) by verbal means alone. On the contrary, one must actually perform the new behavior by getting up on the bike and learning to ride while maintaining balance. "Practice makes perfect," as the old saying goes. Actual practice of coping skills is essential in order for the client to acquire and maintain the new behavior.

The approach recommended here in skill training is a combination of practice in both general *problem-solving skills* and specific *coping responses*. I have found the work of Goldfried and his colleagues particularly helpful in problem-solving training (D'Zurilla & Goldfried, 1971; Goldfried & Davison, 1976). These authors have broken the problem-solving process into several stages: (1) orientation to the problem situation, (2) definition of the problem itself, (3) generation of alternative solutions to the problem, and (4) verification of the effectiveness of a chosen alternative. Clients are given training in this general approach to problems before they are introduced to specific skill-training procedures. This sequence allows the client more flexibility in dealing with new problem situations (including responses to unique high-risk situations that may not be covered in the skill-training procedure), rather than relying on rote learning of discrete skills that are tied to specific problem situations. Problem-solving training programs (Spivack, Platt, & Shure, 1976) have been used successfully in their own right in the treatment of addictive problems. Intagliata (1978) has reported, for example, that this approach significantly improved the problem-solving skills of hospitalized alcoholics as well as the specificity of their posthospitalization planning as assessed in a discharge interview.

This author's approach to skill training is based on the research of Goldstein (1973), McFall (1976), and other investigators who have specialized in methods of teaching social skills. The approach to skill training utilizes a combination of behavioral training methods including direct verbal instruction, modeling of appropriate skills, behavioral rehearsal and practice, combined with coaching and feedback provided by the therapist. For a more detailed presentation of skill-training methods, the reader is referred to recent books by Curran and Monti (1982) and Eisler and Frederiksen (1980).

To illustrate the skill-training method, the procedures used by Chaney and his colleagues with chronic alcoholic patients in an inpatient setting will be examined. The training consisted of 8 semiweekly sessions, each 90 minutes in length. Groups of patients (three to five members per group) met with two therapists (male and female team). Skill-training sessions were "added on" to the patient's regular inpatient treatment program. The procedure used in the skill-training groups was as follows:

After giving a general orientation to problem-solving procedures, therapists read a description of a problematic situation. Subjects discussed how they viewed the situation and generated possible ways of responding to it. The therapists pointed out when group members defined the situation differently and what the consequences of different definitions were for problem solving. The probable consequences of different alternatives proposed by members were discussed, and, if necessary, the therapists proposed alternatives. For interpersonal situations, one therapist chose an alternative, explained the basis of this choice in terms of probable consequences, and then modeled a response, with the cotherapist playing the other person in the situation. For intrapersonal situations one of the therapists engaged in a monologue, explicitly defining the problem, generating alternative solutions, deciding which one would maximize long- and short-term gains and could be performed, and outlining steps to implement the solution. After this initial phase, each group member decided on a particular response and rehearsed it, receiving feedback from the group on the probable consequences of his response. If the therapists and group felt that the response was not likely to solve the problem that the situation presented, the subject was required to repeat his performance. After each subject had rehearsed, a member summarized the method for generating and evaluating an adequate response to that situation. Two prepared situations were introduced during each session. . . . Subjects also rehearsed one or two situations of their own devising that they felt might be problematic after discharge from the hospital.

In summary, skill-training groups incorporated instruction, modeling, behavioral rehearsal, and coaching, both of actual response behavior and of the cognitive process for generating the response. Subjects were taught how to define the problem that a situation presented by specifying the elements and to generate alternatives and think about the long- and short-term consequences. Finally, the behavior rehearsal phase of training provided practice in carrying out adaptive responses and served as a role-playing form of verification, assessing the adequacy of the problem-solving process. (Chaney *et al.*, 1978, p. 1096)

In this treatment outcome study, skill training was compared to two control groups: a discussion-only group and a no-treatment group (in which patients received only the regular inpatient treatment program). The purpose of the discussion-only group was to control for the additional time and attention patients received in the skill-training condition. The discussion groups were similar in format to psychodynamically oriented group therapy. High-risk situations were introduced for discussion in these group meetings, but instead of teaching the patients new coping skills as described above, the therapists focused on eliciting *feelings* that patients might experience in problematic situations (e.g., anxiety, anger, depression, etc.) and examining the patient's reactions and motivations relevant to their experiences in similar past situations. Thus, in the discussion groups, after the therapists introduced the same high-risk situations covered in the skill-training group, they encouraged expression and discussion of feelings engendered by these situations but did not engage in any instruction or training in new coping skills.

All patients were followed up on a continuous basis for 1 year after termination of their treatment program. The skill-training group proved to be more effective than either control group, showing a significant improvement on such outcome measures as number of drinks consumed, days of continuous drinking before regaining abstinence, and number of "drunk" days (intoxication). For a summary of these results, see Figure 2-9. It is important to note that the discussion-only control group did not differ significantly from the group that received only the regular hospital program. This finding supports the view that actual overt practice and rehearsal is necessary for new learning to occur, at least in this population of chronic male alcoholics. Simply talking about high-risk situations does not seem to be sufficient for the acquisition of new coping behaviors.

As noted in Chapter 1, it is interesting to compare the treatment outcome results for the subjects in the electrical aversion study (Marlatt, 1973) with those who participated in the skill-training study. As indicated in Figure 1-2, the drinking rates associated with the outcome of the two programs show markedly different patterns. The drinking rates of the subjects who received skill training for relapse show a gradual improvement over time—they appear to get better throughout the course of the year, presumably as their new coping skills become established. Aversion treatment, in contrast, ap-

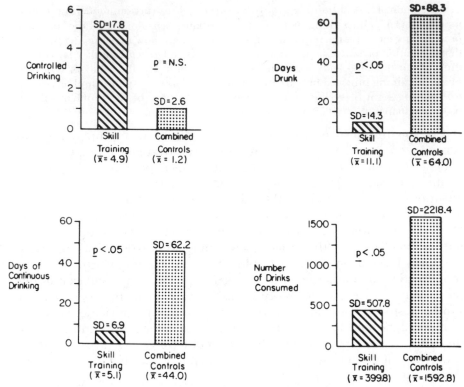

Figure 2-9. Relapse prevention (skill training) with alcoholics: 1-year follow-up results. Based on data from Chaney, O'Leary, and Marlatt (1978).

pears to be most effective in the early stages; RP training does not show up as effective until later in the recovery process. As noted in Chapter 1, this process of gradual improvement found in the RP condition resembles a standard learning curve for the acquisition of other new skills (e.g., learning to play a musical instrument for the first time): more mistakes (lapses) occur in the early stages of the learning process, followed by a stabilization period as the new learning consolidates.

A similar pattern of consistent improvement over time for patients receiving skill training or cognitive restructuring combined with skill training in the treatment of problem drinking has been reported by Oei and Jackson (1982). In this study, patients treated for alcohol dependency received either social skill training, cognitive restructuring (changing beliefs regarding social skill deficits), a combination of both, or a control condition (traditional support group). All patients were followed up for a year after treatment. Results showed that alcohol consumption was significantly lower at the 6- and 12-month follow-ups for subjects in all three experimental groups (compared to the control group), with the combined social skill training and cognitive restructuring group reporting the least consumption of all four groups. The authors conclude that, "The continued, almost linear, improvement in social skills for the [cognitive restructuring and combined skill-training and cognitive restructuring group] patients suggests that the cognitive changes (attitudes, beliefs, and covert self-instructions) manifest themselves as continued improvement in overt social behavior . . ." (p. 545).

A similar point was made in a study by Jones, Kanfer, and Lanyon (1982). In this study, an attempt was made to replicate the skill-training package developed by Chaney et al. (1978) with a group of alcoholics of higher socioeconomic status than those studied by Chaney and his colleagues. Alcoholic patients were randomly assigned to either a skill-training program patterned after Chaney's procedures, a discussion group that discussed the potential relapse-precipitating events without practicing or rehearsing specific responses, or a control group that received only standard inpatient treatment. Results at a 1-year follow-up showed that both the skill-training and discussion group patients reported less drinking and fewer days intoxicated than subjects in the control group. The authors speculate that patients with a higher level of socioeconomic status may respond equally well to a specific skills-oriented approach (with overt practice and rehearsal) or a more cognitively oriented approach that focuses on high-risk situations and the patients' emotional responses to these situations, even though no specific skills are practiced overtly. The possibility that skill training can be transmitted effectively through discussion and verbal analysis alone, particularly with patients or clients who possess advanced verbal skills, remains to be empirically confirmed. In the meantime, the use of overt rehearsal and practice in acquiring new coping skills is recommended with all clients, regardless of socioeconomic or educational differences. Research continues to show that successful outcome in alcoholism treatment is closely associated with demonstrated capacity to cope with situations that are associated with temptations to resume drinking (Jones & Lanyon, 1981; Rosenberg, 1983).

Dry Runs

The general skill-training methods described above may be modified in several ways for use with various client populations. One strategy that has a number of advantages is to take the client or a group of clients to an actual high-risk situation for a *dry run* practice session. This can be done after the client has learned the basic essentials of new coping skills in the treatment setting (inpatient or outpatient). Clients are then taken to a real-life setting where they practice their new skills as a kind of graduation exercise. Clients who are attempting to give up smoking or drinking can be taken to an actual tavern or bar where they exercise their new alternative coping skills surrounded by other people who are actively modeling the target behavior (cf. Blakey & Baker, 1980). Clients sit together over coffee or soft drinks while discussing their reactions to the situation and providing each other with support while they practice their newly acquired skills. Other dry run settings include a party situation, a job interview, a dating experience, and the like. The dry run practice session offers an additional advantage in that it could serve as a cue exposure or "flooding" experience in which previously learned urges and other consummatory responses are extinguished in the stimulus situation (Hodgson & Rankin, 1976, 1982).

Covert Modeling

An additional skill-training method that may be useful with many clients is covert modeling (Kazdin, 1976, 1979). This procedure is recommended for those cases in which it is not practical or possible to practice new coping skills in a group session or in actual real-life environmental settings. In the covert modeling procedure, the client is asked to imagine himself or herself encountering a high-risk situation and engaging in a successful coping response. The client is encouraged to visualize the scene as vividly as possible and to experience the kind of thoughts and feelings that would occur if the person was actually in the situation. The client should be instructed to focus both on the execution of the coping response and on the positive conse- quences that are generated as a result of successful coping (e.g., increased self-esteem, social approval, absence of negative health consequences, etc.). In addition to providing covert self-reinforcement for the coping response, the emphasis on positive consequences provides a positive self-image that contrasts sharply with the sense of loss or deprivation that otherwise might preoccupy the client who has recently given up an addictive behavior. Here, the emphasis is on the self-image of a person who has *gained something beneficial* by changing a behavior, rather than of someone who has given up or lost an old habit. The use of positive coping imagery in which the self is imagined as an active, responsible force that triumphs over adversity may be an effective strategy with clients who otherwise see themselves as victims of an external disease.

Relapse Rehearsal

Covert modeling can also be used to help train clients to cope with an initial slip and prevent it from escalating into a total relapse. In this procedure, which we refer to as relapse rehearsal, the client is asked to imagine that an actual slip has occurred in a particular high-risk situation. The client is instructed to experience reactions to the slip, including the possible feelings of guilt and self-blame that are associated with the AVE. Instead of giving in to these feelings and sliding into the old habit pattern, the client is encouraged to engage in the covert modeling of appropriate coping behavior (e.g., to analyze the situational determinants of the slip, to "wait out" the reaction until it passes, to seek assistance from friends or therapists, etc.).

Skill training can be incorporated at two stages of the treatment process. The first stage involves training clients in relapse prevention skills during their initial treatment program. They are introduced to the general self-control approach and to the components of the relapse model. Specific skill training and cognitive restructuring in selected high-risk situations follows. The second stage is presented after the initial treatment program has been completed and clients are involved in the maintenance or follow-up period. Here clients can meet together in a group format at regular weekly intervals during the follow-up period. These groups can be scheduled during the most "dangerous" periods for potential relapse (the first 3 months following treatment). In addition to providing valuable group support and encouragement, the agenda for the group meetings can include such topics as reenactment of any slips group members might have experienced with an emphasis on rehearsing new coping responses; how to deal with exceptions and unusual events as they occur in each client's ongoing life experiences; planning ahead for upcoming high-risk situations; sharing new information on lifestyle change or relationship issues; and so forth. Such meetings should serve to strengthen and support the new skills and attitudes acquired in the initial treatment stage.

STRESS AND COPING: A TRANSACTIONAL APPROACH

Coping skills have been discussed in this chapter from the specific perspective of coping with high-risk situations for relapse. The author's approach to this topic is consistent with a general model of stress and coping developed by Lazarus and his colleagues (Lazarus, 1966; Lazarus & Folkman, 1984; Lazarus & Launier, 1978; Roskies & Lazarus, 1980). It would seem useful at this point to summarize the main points of this model and to consider potential applications of this approach to RP. In addition to a description of the basic assumptions of the model, the following includes brief discussion of various coping typologies that have derived from this approach, along with associated assessment and treatment procedures.

Transactional Coping

Lazarus has defined coping as "efforts, both action oriented and intrapsychic, to manage (that is, to master, tolerate, reduce, minimize) environmental and internal demands and conflicts among them which tax or exceed a person's resources" (Lazarus & Launier, 1978, p. 311). This definition has several important implications: (1) The reference to "taxing demands" limits this concept of coping to stressful transactions (e.g., high-risk situations), rather than including the general process of adaptation. (2) The definition is *process oriented*, as opposed to other approaches that focus on generalized dispositions or traits or on hierarchies of coping and defense mechanisms. (3) The definition describes coping as a *transactional relationship* between the person and the environment. This last point is emphasized in a recent article by Coyne and Lazarus (1980):

Psychological stress is now viewed as a general rubric for somewhat different though related processes of person–environment transaction, in which demands tax or exceed the resources of the person. Such stress is neither simply an environmental stimulus, a characteristic of the person, nor a response, but a balance between demands and the power to deal with them without unreasonable or destructive costs. Our model of stress is explicitly cognitive–phenomenological, emphasizing how the person appraises what is being experienced and uses this information in coping to shape the course of events. This appraisal of the significance of an ongoing relationship with the environment for one's well-being leads to coping processes consistent with personal agendas. The effects of the coping are in turn appraised and reacted to as part of the continuous flow of psychological, social, and physiological processes and events. Stressful commerce with the environment thus involves extensive psychological mediation and reciprocal feedback loops, which cannot be reduced to stimulus and response terms. The nature of stress phenomena therefore requires that any comprehensive model of it be developed within a transactional, process-oriented perspective. (p. 145)

Coping Processes

Lazarus and his colleagues stress the role of *cognitive appraisal* in the coping process: appraisal in this sense refers to the individual's judgments about demands and constraints in ongoing transactions with the environment and the resources or options available for managing them (Coyne & Lazarus, 1980). *Primary appraisal* refers to the appraisal of a given situation in terms of the person's well-being: "Am I okay or in trouble in this situation?" Situations are appraised in this manner as either irrelevant (no personal significance), benign–positive, or stressful (judgments of harm–loss, threat, or challenge). *Secondary appraisal* refers to the person's ongoing judgments concerning coping resources, options, and constraints in the situation. If primary appraisal asks, "What is at stake in this situation?" then secondary appraisal can be seen as an answer to the question, "What can I do about it?" When that which is at stake is meaningful (primary appraisal) and coping responses are judged less than adequate for managing the situation (secondary appraisal), psychological stress is experienced. From this perspective, secondary appraisal is similar to judgments of self-efficacy or perceived control as discussed earlier in this chapter. Similarly, a high-risk situation for relapse consists of a situation that is primarily appraised as stressful and for which inadequate coping resources or other constraints are perceived in the secondary appraisal stage.

In their discussions of appraisal and coping, Lazarus and his group emphasize the distinction between two major functions of coping: coping that is directed at managing or altering the source of stress itself, called *problem-focused coping*, and coping with the emotional response elicited by the problem situation, called *emotion-focused coping* (cf. Folkman & Lazarus, 1980; Lazarus, 1981). Problem-focused coping refers to one's efforts to deal with the sources of stress, either by changing one's own behavior or by changing environmental conditions. Emotion-focused coping refers to coping efforts aimed at reducing emotional distress and maintaining an effective internal state for processing information and action. Both forms of coping include both cognitive and behavioral strategies. "Problem-focused coping, for example, includes strategies directed at analysing the situation and strategies involving action. Similarly, emotion-focused coping includes cognitive strategies such as looking at the bright side of things as well as behavioral strategies such as seeking emotional support or having a drink" (Folkman, 1982). These two coping functions often occur simultaneously; both forms may facilitate each other (e.g., a person might feel it necessary to control an emotional response such as anger or anxiety before being able to engage in problem-solving activity) or, in some cases, may impede each other (e.g., a person engages in denial of emotional reaction that may inhibit needed problem-focused activity).

The implications of this two-stage model of coping are clearly important. In this chapter, we have primarily been concerned with problem-focused coping in our discussion of skill training for high-risk situations for relapse (problem solving and the acquisition of new cognitive and behavioral coping skills). Drug use or other addictive behaviors that occur in high-risk situations, on the other hand, can be considered as *emotion-focused* coping behaviors or attempts to deal with the affective feelings engendered by the high-risk situation. Later chapters include discussion of cognitive strategies to reduce this emotional reactivity, such as attribution of a slip to situational as opposed to intrapersonal factors (Chapter 4) and lifestyle change procedures (e.g., relaxation and exercise) that serve as general stress-reducing activities (Chapter 5). Since drug use is often the primary maladaptive coping strategy employed by individuals with an addictive behavior problem, it is important to develop skill-training programs that provide both alternative coping responses to deal with the problem directly (e.g., assertiveness training to refuse drinks in social pressure situations) and strategies designed to replace or alter the tendency to use drugs to cope with stressful emotions evoked by the high-risk situation.

Coping Taxonomies and Assessment

In recent years, several attempts have been made to classify various coping responses employed in stressful situations. Some authors have made a distinction between *coping resources* and *coping responses*. Coping resources refer to existing beliefs or environmental factors that increase the individual's overall capacity to cope (e.g., strong prior commitment or belief, social support, etc.), whereas coping responses refer to cognitive or behavioral strategies or acts that are employed in a specific risk situation. In Chapter 8, Shiffman and his associates describe such an instrument, the Coping Response Survey, for use with smokers. Other authors have attempted to classify various appraisal and coping responses (Lazarus & Launier, 1978; Moos, 1976, 1977; Pearlin & Schooler, 1978), although no single classification scheme has been generally accepted in the literature.

One classification scheme that may be useful as a means of conceptualizing coping has been presented by Moos and Billings (1982). In accordance with the overall model outlined by Lazarus and his colleagues, Moos and Billings organize dimensions of appraisal and coping into three domains: appraisal-focused coping (attempts to define the meaning of a situation), problem-focused coping (attempts to modify or eliminate the source of stress, to deal with the tangible consequences of a problem, or to actively change the self and develop a more satisfying situation), and emotion-focused coping (efforts to manage the emotions aroused by stressors). Noting that these categories are not mutually exclusive, Moos and Billings offer a preliminary classification scheme based on these three categories. This classification scheme is presented in Table 2-3.

An additional assessment procedure to assess coping strategies in a specific stress situation has been developed by Folkman and Lazarus (1980; Folkman, 1982). This assessment procedure, called the Ways of Coping Questionnaire, includes a broad range of behavioral and cognitive strategies an individual might use in a specific stressful episode. The Ways of Coping checklist consists of 64 items that can be answered in a yes/no format and are taken from the domains of defensive coping (avoidance, intellectualization, isolation, suppression), information-seeking, problem solving, palliation, inhibition of action, direct action, and magical thinking. Two scales are derived in the scoring procedure: a problem-focused scale (P-scale) and an emotion-focused scale (E-scale). Examples of items from the P-scale are: "Got the person responsible to change his or her mind"; "Made a plan of action and followed it"; and "Stood your ground and fought for what you wanted." Examples from the E-scale are: "Told yourself things that helped you feel better"; "Let your feelings out somehow." Since the items on the scale are geared toward coping with a specific stressful situation, the Ways of Coping test may be particularly useful as a means of asking clients how they have coped (or plan to cope) with specific high-risk situations for relapse.

Treatment Applications

The transactional model of stress and coping developed by Lazarus, Moos, and other investigators is appealing because it provides a conceptual link between stress research in general and contemporary cognitive–behavioral treatment strategies (Cameron & Meichenbaum, 1982; Roskies & Lazarus, 1980). The development of comprehensive coping skills treatment programs have, for the most part, been developed by cognitive and cognitive–behavioral

Table 2-3.   Classification of Coping Processes

Appraisal-Focused Coping

   1. *Logical Analysis.* Strategies in this category include trying to identify the cause of the problem, paying attention to one aspect of the situation at a time, drawing on relevant past experiences, and mentally rehearsing possible actions and their consequences.

   2. *Cognitive Redefinition.* This category includes cognitive strategies by which an individual accepts the basic reality of a situation but restructures it to find something favorable. Such strategies involve reminding oneself that things could be worse, thinking of oneself as well off with respect to other people, concentrating on something good that might develop from a situation, and altering values and priorities in line with changing reality.

   3. *Cognitive Avoidance.* Included here are such strategies as denying fear or anxiety under stress, trying to forget the whole situation, refusing to believe a problem really exists, and engaging in wishful fantasies instead of thinking realistically about a problem.

Problem-Focused Coping

   4. *Seeking Information or Advice.* Responses in this category involve seeking more information about a situation; obtaining direction and guidance from an authority; talking with one's spouse, other relatives, or friends about a problem; and asking someone to provide a specific kind of help, such as lending money.

   5. *Taking Problem-Solving Action.* These strategies include making alternative plans, taking specific action to deal directly with the situation, learning new skills directed at the problem, and negotiating and compromising to try and resolve an issue.

   6. *Developing Alternative Rewards.* This strategy involves attempts to deal with a problematic situation by changing one's activities and creating new sources of satisfaction. Examples are building alternative social relationships, developing greater autonomy and independence, and engaging in "substitute" pursuits such as doing volunteer work or studying philosophy or religion.

Emotion-Focused Coping

   7. *Affective Regulation.* These strategies involve direct efforts to control the emotion aroused by a problem by consciously postponing paying attention to an impulse (suppression), experiencing and working through one's feelings, trying not to be bothered by conflicting feelings, maintaining a sense of pride and keeping a "stiff upper lip," and tolerating ambiguity by withholding immediate action.

   8. *Resigned Acceptance.* This category includes such responses as waiting for time to remedy the problem, expecting the worst, accepting a situation as it is, deciding that nothing can be done to change things, and submitting to "inevitable" fate.

   9. *Emotional Discharge.* Included here are verbal expressions to let off steam, crying, smoking, overeating, and engaging in impulsive acting out. These responses may involve a failure of affective regulation, but we categorize them separately in order to distinguish persons who alternate between emotional control and emotional discharge.

Note. From "Conceptualizing and Measuring Coping Resources and Processes" by R. H. Moos and A. G. Billings, in *Handbook of Stress* (pp. 218–219), edited by L. Goldberger and S. Breznitz, New York: The Free Press, 1982. Copyright 1982 by The Free Press, a Division of Macmillan, Inc. Reprinted by permission.

theorists (e.g., Beck, Rush, Shaw, & Emery, 1979; Goldfried, 1980; Meichenbaum, 1977). The coping skills approach to stress management that is most consistent with an RP approach has been termed *stress inoculation training* (Meichenbaum, 1977; Meichenbaum & Jaremko, 1983). According to a recent overview of this approach (Cameron & Meichenbaum, 1982), stress inoculation involves three phases: (1) conceptualization, in which the client's appraisal of the situation in terms of a coping approach is ascertained and modified; (2) skill acquisition and activation, in which new adaptive coping skills are initially acquired; and (3) rehearsal and application, in which the client practices and applies the newly acquired skills. The stress inoculation approach has been adapted for use with a variety of clinical problems, including speech anxiety (Meichenbaum, Gilmore, & Fedoravicius, 1971), anger reactions (Novaco, 1975), and pain (Holroyd, 1980; Turk, Meichenbaum, & Genest, 1983). The application of the stress inoculation model as part of a general program of relapse prevention is an important objective of this volume.

REFERENCES

Antonuccio, D., & Lichtenstein, E. Peer modeling influences on smoking behavior of heavy and light smokers. *Addictive Behaviors*, 1980, *5*, 299–306.

Bandura, A. Self-efficacy: Toward a unifying theory of behavior change. *Psychological Review*, 1977, *84*, 191–215.

Bandura, A. Self-referent thought: A developmental analysis of self-efficacy. In J. H. Flavell & L. D. Ross (Eds.), *Cognitive social development*. New York: Cambridge University Press, 1981.

Barlow, D. H. (Ed.). *Behavioral assessment of adult disorders*. New York: Guilford, 1981.

Beck, A. T., Rush, A. J., Shaw, B. F., & Emery, G. *Cognitive therapy of depression*. New York: Guilford, 1979.

Blakey, R., & Baker, R. An exposure approach to alcohol abuse. *Behaviour Research and Therapy*, 1980, *18*, 319–325.

Burt, D. W. Characteristics of the relapse situation of alcoholics treated with aversion conditioning. *Behaviour Research and Therapy*, 1974, *12*, 121–123.

Cameron, R., & Meichenbaum, D. The nature of effective coping and the treatment of stress related problems: A cognitive–behavioral perspective. In L. Goldberger & S. Breznitz (Eds.), *Handbook of stress*. New York: Free Press, 1982.

Carver, C. S., & Scheier, M. F. A control-theory approach to human behavior, and implications for problems in self-management. In P. C. Kendall (Ed.), *Advances in cognitive–behavioral research and therapy* (Vol. 2). New York: Academic Press, 1983.

Caudill, B. D., & Marlatt, G. A. Modeling influences in social drinking: An experimental analogue. *Journal of Consulting and Clinical Psychology*, 1975, *43*, 405–415.

Chaney, E. F., O'Leary, M. R., & Marlatt, G. A. Skill training with alcoholics. *Journal of Consulting and Clinical Psychology*, 1978, *46*, 1092–1104.

Collins, R. L., & Marlatt, G. A. Social modeling as a determinant of drinking behavior: Implications for prevention and treatment. *Addictive Behaviors*, 1981, *6*, 233–240.

Coyne, J. C., & Lazarus, R. S. Cognitive style, stress perception, and coping. In I. L. Kutash & L. B. Schlesinger (Eds.), *Handbook on stress and anxiety*. San Francisco: Jossey-Bass, 1980.

Cummings, C., Gordon, J. R., & Marlatt, G. A. Relapse: Strategies of prevention and prediction. In W. R. Miller (Ed.), *The addictive behaviors: Treatment of alcoholism, drug abuse, smoking and obesity*. Oxford, U.K.: Pergamon Press, 1980.

Curran, J., & Monti, P. (Eds.). *Social skills training*. New York: Guilford, 1982.

Donovan, D. M., & Marlatt, G. A. Assessment of expectancies and behaviors associated with alcohol consumption: A cognitive–behavioral approach. *Journal of Studies on Alcohol*, 1980, *41*, 1153–1185.

D'Zurilla, T. J., & Goldfried, M. R. Problem solving and behavior modification. *Journal of Abnormal Psychology*, 1971, *78*, 107-126.

Eisler, R. M., & Frederiksen, L. W. *Perfecting social skills*. New York: Plenum, 1980.

Flowers, J. V. Simulation and role playing methods. In F. H. Kanfer & A. P. Goldstein (Eds.), *Helping people change: A textbook of methods*. New York: Pergamon, 1975.

Folkman, S. An approach to the measurement of coping. *Journal of Occupational Behaviour*, 1982, *3*, 95-107.

Folkman, S., & Lazarus, R. S. An analysis of coping in a middle-aged community sample. *Journal of Health and Social Behavior*, 1980, *21*, 219-239.

Gamblers Anonymous. *Gamblers Anonymous handbook*. Los Angeles, 1976. (Available from Gamblers Anonymous, P.O. Box 17173, Los Angeles, Calif. 90017.)

Genest, M., & Turk, D. C. Think-aloud approaches to cognitive assessment. In T. V. Merluzzi, C. R. Glass, & M. Genest (Eds.), *Cognitive assessment*. New York: Guilford, 1981.

Goldfried, M. R. Psychotherapy as coping skills training. In M. J. Mahoney (Ed.), *Psychotherapy process*. New York: Plenum, 1980.

Goldfried, M. R., & Davison, G. C. *Clinical behavior therapy*. New York: Holt, Rinehart & Winston, 1976.

Goldstein, A. P. *Structured learning therapy*. New York: Academic Press, 1973.

Gordon, J. R. *The use of rapid smoking and group support to induce and maintain abstinence from cigarette smoking*. Unpublished doctoral dissertation, University of Washington, 1978.

Hersen, M., & Bellack, A. S. (Eds.). *Behavioral assessment* (2nd ed.). New York: Pergamon, 1981.

Higgins, R. L. Experimental investigations of tension-reduction models of alcoholism. In G. Goldstein & C. Neuringer (Eds.), *Empirical studies of alcoholism*. Cambridge, Mass.: Ballinger, 1976.

Higgins, R. L., & Marlatt, G. A. The effects of anxiety arousal upon the consumption of alcohol by alcoholics and social drinkers. *Journal of Consulting and Clinical Psychology*, 1973, *41*, 426-433.

Higgins, R. L., & Marlatt, G. A. Fear of interpersonal evaluation as a determinant of alcohol consumption in male social drinkers. *Journal of Abnormal Psychology*, 1975, *84*, 644-651.

Hodgson, R., & Rankin, H. J. Modification of excessive drinking by cue exposure. *Behaviour Research and Therapy*, 1976, *14*, 305-307.

Hodgson, R., & Rankin, H. J. Cue exposure and relapse prevention. In P. Nathan & W. Hay (Eds.), *Case studies in the behavioral treatment of alcoholism*. New York: Plenum, 1982.

Holroyd, K. Stress, coping, and the treatment of stress-related illness. In J. R. McNamara (Ed.), *Behavioral approaches in medicine: Application and analysis*. New York: Plenum, 1980.

Hore, B. D. Life events and alcoholic relapse. *British Journal of Addiction*, 1971, *66*, 83-88.

Intagliata, J. Increasing the interpersonal problem-solving skills of an alcoholic population. *Journal of Consulting and Clinical Psychology*, 1978, *46*, 489-498.

Isbell, H. Craving for alcohol. *Quarterly Journal of Studies on Alcohol*, 1955, *16*, 38-42.

Jellinek, E. M. The phases of alcohol addiction. *Quarterly Journal of Studies on Alcohol*, 1952, *13*, 673-684.

Jellinek, E. M. *The disease concept of alcoholism*. New Brunswick, N.J.: Hillhouse Press, 1960.

Jones, S. L., Kanfer, R., & Lanyon, R. I. Skill training with alcoholics: A clinical extension. *Addictive Behaviors*, 1982, *7*, 285-290.

Jones, S. L., & Lanyon, R. I. Relationship between adaptive skills and outcome of alcoholism treatment. *Journal of Studies on Alcohol*, 1981, *42*, 521-525.

Kazdin, A. E. Effects of covert modeling, multiple models, and model reinforcement on assertive behaviors. *Behavior Therapy*, 1976, *7*, 211-222.

Kazdin, A. E. Imagery elaboration and self-efficacy in the covert modeling of unassertive behavior. *Journal of Consulting and Clinical Psychology*, 1979, *47*, 725-733.

Kendall, P. C., & Hollon, S. D. (Eds.). *Assessment strategies for cognitive-behavioral interventions*. New York: Academic Press, 1980.

Kiesler, D. J. *The process of psychotherapy: Empirical foundations and systems of analysis.* Chicago: Aldine, 1973.

Kniskern, J., Biglan, A., Lichtenstein, E., Fry, D., & Bavry, J. Peer modeling effects in the smoking behavior of teenagers. *Addictive Behaviors*, 1983, *8*, 129–132.

Lang, A. R., Goeckner, D. J., Adesso, V. J., & Marlatt, G. A. The effects of alcohol and aggression in male social drinkers. *Journal of Abnormal Psychology*, 1975, *84*, 508–518.

Lazarus, R. S. *Psychological stress and the coping process.* New York: McGraw-Hill, 1966.

Lazarus, R. S. The stress and coping paradigm. In C. Eisdorfer, D. Cohen, A. Kleinman, & P. Maxim (Eds.), *Theoretical bases for psychopathology.* New York: Spectrum, 1981.

Lazarus, R. S., & Folkman, S. Coping and adaptation. In W. D. Gentry (Ed.), *Handbook of behavioral medicine.* New York: Guilford, 1984.

Lazarus, R. S., & Launier, R. Stress-related transactions between person and environment. In L. A. Pervin & M. Lewis (Eds.), *Perspectives in interactional psychology.* New York: Plenum, 1978.

Lied, E. R., & Marlatt, G. A. Modeling as a determinant of alcohol consumption: Effect of subject sex and prior drinking history. *Addictive Behaviors*, 1979, *4*, 47–54.

MacPherson, M. Ted and Joan part as friends. *The Seattle Times*, February 3, 1981, p. B-1.

Mardones, R. J. "Craving" for alcohol. *Quarterly Journal of Studies on Alcohol*, 1955, *16*, 51–53.

Marlatt, G. A. *A comparison of aversive conditioning procedures in the treatment of alcoholism.* Paper presented at the annual meeting of the Western Psychological Association, Anaheim, Calif., 1973.

Marlatt, G. A. Alcohol, stress, and cognitive control. In I. G. Sarason & C. D. Spielberger (Eds.), *Stress and anxiety* (Vol. 3). Washington, D.C.: Hemisphere Publishing Co., 1976.

Marlatt, G. A. Behavioral assessment of social drinking and alcoholism. In G. A. Marlatt & P. E. Nathan (Eds.), *Behavioral approaches to alcoholism.* New Brunswick, N.J.: Rutgers Center of Alcohol Studies, 1978. (a)

Marlatt, G. A. Craving for alcohol, loss of control, and relapse: A cognitive–behavioral analysis. In P. E. Nathan, G. A. Marlatt, & T. Løberg (Eds.), *Alcoholism: New directions in behavioral research and treatment.* New York: Plenum, 1978. (b)

Marlatt, G. A. Alcohol use and problem drinking: A cognitive–behavioral analysis. In P. C. Kendall & S. D. Hollon (Eds.), *Cognitive–behavioral interventions.* New York: Academic Press, 1979.

Marlatt, G. A., & Donovan, D. M. (Eds.). *Assessment of addictive behaviors.* New York: Guilford, in press.

Marlatt, G. A., Goldstein, S., & Gordon, J. R. *Self-initiated attempts in smoking cessation: Process and outcome.* Unpublished manuscript, University of Washington, 1983.

Marlatt, G. A., & Gordon, J. R. Determinants of relapse: Implications for the maintenance of behavior change. In P. O. Davidson & S. M. Davidson (Eds.), *Behavioral medicine: Changing health lifestyles.* New York: Brunner/Mazel, 1980.

Marlatt, G. A., Kosturn, C. F., & Lang, A. R. Provocation to anger and opportunity for retaliation as determinants of alcohol consumption in social drinkers. *Journal of Abnormal Psychology*, 1975, *84*, 652–659.

McClelland, D. C., Davis, W. N., Kalin, R., & Wanner, E. *The drinking man.* New York: Free Press, 1972.

McFall, R. M. Behavioral training: A skill-acquisition approach to clinical problems. In J. T. Spence, R. C. Carson, & J. W. Thibaut (Eds.), *Behavioral approaches to therapy.* Morristown, N.J.: General Learning Press, 1976.

McFall, R. M. Parameters of self-monitoring. In R. B. Stuart (Ed.), *Behavioral self-management: Strategies, techniques, and outcomes.* New York: Brunner/Mazel, 1977.

Meichenbaum, D. *Cognitive-behavior modification.* New York: Plenum, 1977.

Meichenbaum, D., Gilmore, B., & Fedoravicius, A. Group insight vs. group desensitization in treating speech anxiety. *Journal of Consulting and Clinical Psychology*, 1971, *36*, 410–421.

Meichenbaum, D., & Jaremko, M. E. *Stress reduction and prevention*. New York: Plenum, 1983.

Merluzzi, T. V., Glass, C. R., & Genest, M. (Eds.). *Cognitive assessment*. New York: Guilford, 1981.

Miller, P. M., & Eisler, R. M. Assertive behavior of alcoholics: A descriptive analysis. *Behavior Therapy*, 1977, *8*, 146–149.

Miller, P. M., Hersen, M., Eisler, R. M., & Elkin, T. E. A retrospective analysis of alcohol consumption on laboratory tasks as related to therapeutic outcome. *Behaviour Research and Therapy*, 1974, *12*, 73–76.

Miller, W. R., & Muñoz, R. F. *How to control your drinking* (2nd ed.). Albuquerque, N.M.: University of New Mexico Press, 1982.

Monti, P. M., Corriveau, D. P., & Zwick, W. Assessment of social skills in alcoholics and other psychiatric patients. *Journal of Studies on Alcohol*, 1981, *41*, 526–529.

Moos, R. H. (Ed.). *Coping with life stress*. Lexington, Ky.: Heath, 1976.

Moos, R. H. (Ed.). *Coping with physical illness*. New York: Plenum, 1977.

Moos, R. H., & Billings, A. G. Conceptualizing and measuring coping resources and processes. In L. Goldberger & S. Breznitz (Eds.), *Handbook of stress*. New York: Free Press, 1982.

Novaco, R. *Anger control: The development and evaluation of an experimental treatment*. Lexington, Mass.: D. C. Heath, 1975.

Oei, T. P. S., & Jackson, P. R. Social skills and cognitive behavioral approaches to the treatment of problem drinking. *Journal of Studies on Alcohol*, 1982, *43*, 532–547.

Pearlin, L. I., & Schooler, C. The structure of coping. *Journal of Health and Social Behavior*, 1978, *19*, 2–21.

Pohorecky, L. A., & Brick, J. (Eds.). *Stress and alcohol use*. New York: Elsevier, 1983.

Pomerleau, O. F., Fertig, J., Baker, L., & Cooney, N. Reactivity to alcohol cues in alcoholics and non-alcoholics: Implications for a stimulus control analysis of drinking. *Addictive Behaviors*, 1983, *8*, 1–10.

Rathus, S. A. A thirty-item schedule for assessing assertive behavior. *Behavior Therapy*, 1973, *4*, 398–406.

Rosenberg, H. Relapsed versus non-relapsed alcohol abusers: Coping skills, life events, and social support. *Addictive Behaviors*, 1983, *8*, 183–186.

Rosenthal, B., & McSweeney, F. K. Modeling influences on eating behaviors. *Addictive Behaviors*, 1979, *4*, 205–214.

Roskies, E., & Lazarus, R. S. Coping theory and the teaching of coping skills. In P. O. Davidson & S. M. Davidson (Eds.), *Behavioral medicine: Changing health lifestyles*. New York: Brunner/Mazel, 1980.

Sarason, I. G. *Abnormal psychology* (2nd ed.). Englewood Cliffs, N.J.: Prentice-Hall, 1976.

Schachter, S., Goldman, R., & Gordon, A. Effects of fear, food deprivation, and obesity on eating. *Journal of Personality and Social Psychology*, 1968, *10*, 91–97.

Schachter, S., & Singer, J. Cognitive, social and physiological determinants of emotional state. *Psychological Review*, 1962, *69*, 379–399.

Shiffman, S. Relapse following smoking cessation. *Journal of Consulting and Clinical Psychology*, 1982, *50*, 71–86.

Sobell, L. C., & Sobell, M. B. A self-feedback technique to monitor drinking behavior in alcoholics. *Behaviour Research and Therapy*, 1973, *11*, 237–238.

Sobell, M. B., & Sobell, L. C. Assessment of addictive behavior. In M. Hersen & A. S. Bellack (Eds.), *Behavioral assessment: A practical handbook*. New York: Pergamon, 1976.

Spivack, G., Platt, J. J., & Shure, M. B. *The problem-solving approach to adjustment*. San Francisco: Jossey-Bass, 1976.

Turk, D. C., Meichenbaum, D., & Genest, M. *Pain and behavioral medicine*. New York: Guilford, 1983.

3

COGNITIVE FACTORS IN
THE RELAPSE PROCESS

G. ALAN MARLATT

In this chapter, the role of cognitive factors in the relapse process is described. The discussion focuses on the relative contributions of self-efficacy, outcome expectancies, and attributions of causality as interactive determinants of relapse. Decision-making processes and cognitive defense mechanisms associated with them are also described as important factors in the covert planning or "setting up" of relapse episodes.

As indicated in the overview of the relapse model presented in Chapter 1, three interlocking cognitive mediators play significant roles in the relapse process. The first, *self-efficacy*, refers to the individual's perception of his or her ability to cope with prospective high-risk situations. Successful coping with a variety of high-risk situations increases one's sense of self-efficacy and decreases the probability of relapse, whereas failure experiences have the opposite effect. To the extent that one's inability to cope with a high-risk situation is associated with a perception of decreased efficacy, the attraction to the old "coping crutch" or addictive substance will increase. This increase in attraction or temptation is mediated by positive *outcome expectancies* for the effects of the addictive substance or activity, the second cognitive factor in the relapse sequence. If the individual then engages in the taboo activity, the third cognitive process, *attribution of causality*, becomes important in determining whether the first lapse or slip precipitates a full-blown relapse. The magnitude of the reaction to the first slip, that is, the intensity of the Abstinence Violation Effect (AVE), will be determined in part by whether the individual attributes the "cause" of the slip to internal (self-related) or external (situational) factors. In the following sections, each of these cognitive processes is described in turn. The chapter concludes with a discussion of how *decision-making processes* may be involved in the covert planning or setting up of a relapse episode. Intervention strategies for each of these cognitive determinants are presented in Chapter 4.

SELF-EFFICACY

GENERAL DEFINITION

The concept of self-efficacy as an important cognitive mediator of behavior has been elaborated by the social-learning theorist, Albert Bandura (1977, 1981, 1982). In a recent review article, he states that "Self-efficacy is concerned with judgments about how well one can organize and execute courses of action required to deal with prospective situations that contain many ambiguous, unpredictable, and often stressful, elements" (Bandura, 1981, pp. 200–201). Self-efficacy is defined as a cognitive process since it deals with perceived *judgments* or evaluations people make about their competency to perform adequately in a specific task situation. Bandura differentiates self-efficacy from related concepts such as self-esteem or the self-concept (cf. Rogers, 1959; Wylie, 1974) by noting that the former term deals with perceived performance competency in *specific situations*, whereas the latter terms refer to a *global self-image* across a wide variety of situations. These global and specific expectancies may often be inconsistent with each other. As an example, consider an individual who although harboring a very positive overall self-image may judge himself or herself to be incapable of performing specific acts (e.g., to play the piano, write poetry, or stop smoking). The emphasis on judgments of self-efficacy for specific tasks or situations is consistent with recent theoretical movements in psychology that emphasize the significance of contemporaneous *states* (the here-and-now interaction of the person and the immediate environment) in contrast with the traditional global concept of *traits* (long-term dispositional tendencies) as determinants of behavior.

Bandura also differentiates self-efficacy from *effectance motivation* (White, 1959) and related concepts that define an individual's degree of striving for competency or mastery of the environment as an intrinsic motivational or drive state. Because of their intrinsic source, drive states such as effectance motivation do not vary as a function of the specific task or situation involved—the emphasis is on the internal, dispositional tendency toward mastery or competence across all situations. Self-efficacy judgments, on the other hand, always are geared specifically toward the situation at hand. "Some situations require greater skill and more arduous performances, or carry higher risk of negative consequences than do others. Judgments will vary accordingly. Thus, for example, the level and strength of perceived efficacy in public speaking will differ depending on the subject matter, the format of the presentation, and the types of audiences to be addressed" (Bandura, 1981, p. 227). This distinction is important to keep in mind, since there is a tendency to equate self-efficacy judgments with a general measure of motivational strength, such as commitment to change or willpower.

What are the effects of self-efficacy on performance? Bandura (1981, 1982) states that perceived efficacy can have diverse effects on behavior, thought patterns, and emotional arousal. In terms of behavior, efficacy judgments influence choice of activities in that people are likely to avoid situations that they believe exceed their capacities and to seek out those in which they feel competent. The effort expended in a given situation is also determined by self-efficacy judgments: "In the face of difficulties people who entertain serious doubts about their capacities slacken their efforts or give up altogether, whereas those who have a strong sense of efficacy exert greater effort to master the challenges" (Bandura, 1981, p. 201). Thoughts and feelings are also affected by self-efficacy. An individual with low efficacy in a particular task or situation is more likely to engage in frequent self-appraisals of inadequacy and to perceive the task as more difficult than it really is, thereby creating a disruptive state of increased arousal that impairs performance. People with a strong sense of efficacy, on the other hand, are able to exert their skills to the demands of the task without undue doubts or negative self-appraisals.

According to Bandura, self-efficacy judgments are based on four main sources of information: one's own performance accomplishments, vicarious observation of the performance of others, the influence of external persuasion and social influence, and states of emotional arousal. Information from any of these sources is cognitively appraised by the individual; individual differences in the manner by which people selectively attend to certain information or arrive at inferences concerning their judgments of competency will influence their ratings of self-efficacy.

In terms of the Relapse Prevention (RP) model, the most important source of information for inferring self-efficacy judgments concerns the individual's performance accomplishments—the successes and failures experienced in coping with high-risk situations. We shall elaborate upon this point shortly. Vicarious experiences also influence self-efficacy judgments related to one's ability to modify addictive habits. Observing the successes or failures of others as they try, for example, to stop smoking, may have considerable impact. Modeling is also an important ingredient in skill-training programs; competent models can teach observers effective strategies for coping with high-risk situations. The third source of information, social persuasion, is probably the least effective in enhancing self-efficacy with regard to habit control. Although an individual may be motivated to stop smoking by repeated exposure to social pressure and disapproval, this information will probably have little impact on efficacy judgments related to one's capacity to maintain abstinence. The final source of efficacy information, physiological arousal, exerts an important influence in that people often rely on their state of physical arousal in judging their capacities to respond to stress. "Because high arousal usually debilitates performance, individuals are more likely to expect success when they are not beset by aversive arousal than if they are tense and viscerally agitated" (Bandura, 1981, p. 204). Since most high-risk situations for relapse are emotionally stressful, they pose serious threats to the individual's perception of control.

SELF-EFFICACY, MOTIVATION, COMMITMENT, AND WILLPOWER

It is important to make a clear distinction between the constructs of self-efficacy and motivation as they influence success or failure in changing an addictive behavior. As an illustration of this distinction, consider the following anecdote. I was interviewed recently on a television talk show on the topic of habit control. The host told me that he planned to quit smoking that day (in fact he lit up his "last" cigarette during the program). In order to ascertain his level of motivation or commitment, I asked him the following question: "Can you tell me how strongly motivated you are to quit and stay off cigarettes for at least a week, using a scale of 1–10, with 1 indicating the lowest strength and 10 the highest strength of motivation?" He reflected for a moment and then replied, "Seven." I thought to myself, "That's too low." A week later when I had the occasion to speak to him again, I asked him how he was doing. He was smoking, having only managed to stay off cigarettes for a few hours.

In the terminology of the relapse prevention model presented in this book, the television host gave me a rating of his *motivation* or strength of commitment to stop smoking. From a motivational point of view, the overall goal is to stop smoking and maintain abstinence. For many people, degree of commitment to this global goal is measured in terms of *willpower*. The very word "power" as used in this phrase connotes images of drive strength or intensity of motivation. (*Webster's New Collegiate Dictionary*, 1983, for example, defines willpower as "energetic determination or resoluteness.") But how is this goal met—what are the means to be taken in arriving at this goal? If one responds to this question from a purely motivational perspective (as many people do), the answer is something like the following: "I will resist the temptation to smoke by exercising my willpower," or, "As long as I can maintain control by not giving in to urges, I will succeed." Here the means to the goal takes the form of *inhibiting the target behavior*, "keeping the lid on it" by the exertion of sheer "will" or "control." Should a failure occur under these circumstances and a cigarette is smoked, the person is likely to ascribe the failure to a lack of willpower or a corresponding loss of control.

From the perspective of relapse prevention, motivation is only half the story when it comes to changing addictive habits. Motivation is particularly important as it relates to the *commitment* one makes to achieving a particular goal. The strength of one's motivation to stop drinking, for example, is determined by a wide range of factors including the payoff matrix of the immediate and long-term benefits and costs involved, the events precipitating the decision to quit at a particular time, the individual's history and outcome of prior attempts to change, availability of treatment programs, social support, and so forth. Whereas motivation influences the decision to stop and the degree of commitment to this goal, it sheds little light on the *means* one uses to achieve the goal. Motivation alone is not enough, since it leaves the person relying upon ill-defined resources such as "willpower" to carry out the task. One is reminded here of the old saying, "Where there's a will, there's a way." For people who rely on willpower as the sole means of changing a behavior, the "will" becomes the only "way." Certainly motivation (will) is an important and necessary first step, but one also needs a way to proceed that goes beyond motivational drive. Coping responses and the confidence one has to use them in high-risk situations (self-efficacy) are the best way to go.

High levels of both motivation and self-efficacy are important ingredients in a successful RP program. In many cases, a particular coping response may fail to be executed despite high levels of motivation if the individual has low self-efficacy concerning his or her capacity to engage in the behavior. The converse is equally true, of course; an individual may fail to engage in a specific behavior despite high levels of self-efficacy if the motivation for performance is low or absent ("I knew what to do, but I just didn't feel like doing it").

To summarize, self-efficacy is concerned with the individual's perceived ability to perform a coping response, an active behavior to deal effectively with the specific situation, and not with one's general ability to exercise control or resist the temptation to give in to internal urges. The failure to conceptualize the task of changing an addictive habit as involving *both* motivational factors (commitment to the overall goal) and self-efficacy (for coping with high-risk situations as a means to achieving this goal) often leads to a self-defeating overemphasis on willpower as the sole means of coping with temptation.

SELF-EFFICACY AND COPING WITH HIGH-RISK SITUATIONS

In terms of the relapse model presented in this book, self-efficacy refers to the judgments or expectations about one's capacity to cope with specific high-risk situations. In Chapter 2, a high-risk situation was defined as any situation that poses a risk or threat to the individual's perception of control. *Perception of control* or self-efficacy as used in this context, means the person's subjective sense of mastery or control over temptations or urges to engage in the taboo behavior. Until a high-risk situation is encountered, there is little threat to this perception of control since urges and temptations are minimal or absent. When a high-risk situation occurs, there is a *conflict of motives* between a desire to maintain control and the opposing temptation to give in or yield to the impulse. As defined here, self-efficacy is concerned with the person's perceived ability to perform a coping response to deal with the high-risk situation, and *not* with one's general ability to exercise willpower or sheer resistance to temptation. The exercise of willpower is a nonbehavior and is the antithesis of performing an active coping response. If a pot boiling over on the kitchen stove can be taken as a symbolic representation of a high-risk situation, a willpower approach attempts to keep the lid on by suppressing the steam by sheer force of will or mental opposition. An active coping approach, on the other hand, involves either turning down the heat, moving the pot to another location, or, to paraphrase Harry Truman's adage, getting out of the kitchen altogether when the heat gets too intense.

The probability of relapse in a given high-risk situation decreases considerably when the individual harbors a high level of self-efficacy for performing a coping response. If a coping response is successfully performed, the individual's judgment of efficacy will be strengthened for coping with similar situations as they arise on subsequent occasions. Repeated experiences of success strengthen self-efficacy and reduce the risk that occasional failure or slips will precipitate a relapse. According to Bandura (1981):

Successes raise efficacy appraisals; repeated failures lower them, especially if the failures occur early in the course of events and do not reflect lack of effort or adverse external circumstances. After a strong sense of efficacy is developed through repeated success, occasional failures are unlikely to have much effect on judgments of one's capabilities. Indeed, failures that are overcome by determined effort can instill robust percepts of self-efficacy through experience that one can eventually master even the most difficult obstacles. (p. 203)

The degree of change in self-efficacy is tied in with the specific circumstances of coping (or failing to cope) with a particular high-risk situation. Bandura (1981) notes that the extent of increase in self-efficacy associated with successful performance depends on such factors as the perceived difficulty of the task, the amount of effort expended, the degree of external aid received, and the situational circumstances under which the response is performed. Similarly, performance failures may not lead to significant decreases in self-efficacy if the failures are discounted on the grounds of insufficient effort, adverse situational conditions, despondent mood, or debilitated physical condition. This topic will be discussed in more detail later in this chapter when the role of attributions in the relapse process is described.

If an individual fails to cope with a high-risk situation, the probability of relapse increases. The perceived capacity to cope with the situation, often low to begin with, sinks even further. This drop in confidence may be even more pronounced for those individuals who have come to rely upon willpower as their sole means of dealing with conflict situations, since there is nothing they can "do" to cope. There may be an increased sense of failure or helplessness ("I can't cope with this," etc.) as the situation gets "out of control." It is at this low point in the situation that the person may feel overcome with cravings that give rise to urges to reach out for the old crutch, much as a drowning man will clutch at a straw to keep from going under. These cravings are mediated by positive outcome expectancies for the immediate effects of engaging in the taboo behavior. If the individual has come to believe that the cigarette, drink, or related behavior is an effective way of alleviating the stress and discomfort experienced in the high-risk situation (including feelings of helplessness or lowered self-efficacy), even as a short-term stopgap attempt, the probability of relapse increases greatly.

SELF-EFFICACY AND THE PREDICTION OF RELAPSE

Two recently published studies from the smoking treatment literature provide empirical support for the theoretical model described above. Both studies (DiClemente, 1981; Condiotte & Lichtenstein, 1981) were designed to investigate whether self-efficacy is predictive of relapse for individuals who attempted to stop smoking. Since the results of both studies were essentially similar, only the results of the Condiotte and Lichtenstein paper will be summarized here.

The subjects in the Condiotte and Lichtenstein (1981) study consisted of 78 male and female individuals who took part in either of two smoking cessation programs. All subjects filled out a self-efficacy rating scale twice: at the beginning of treatment (before the quit date) and at the completion of the treatment program. Subjects were assessed for smoking rates and other measures for a period of 3 months. Self-report data on smoking rates were corroborated through contacts with significant others who acted as informants. By the end of the follow-up period, 44 of the 78 subjects had relapsed (defined as smoking one cigarette or more each week). An attempt was then made to relate the self-efficacy ratings taken at posttreatment with treatment outcome.

The self-efficacy questionnaire consisted of a list of 48 smoking situations, originally developed by Best and Hakstian (1978) (sample situations: "When you feel frustrated," "When you see others smoking," "When you have finished a meal or snack," and the like). For each item, subjects were asked to designate on a 100-point scale (expressed in percentage units) the probability that they would be able to resist the urge to smoke in that situation. A cluster analysis was used to obtain seven clusters or categories of situations from the original 48 items (the seven clusters are similar in many ways to the categorization system for high-risk situations described in Chapter 2).

The results included several significant findings. Participation in the smoking treatment programs produced a significant increase in self-efficacy ratings when the pre- and posttreatment measures were compared. This finding is important since it shows that efficacy enhancement may be a useful measure of the extent to which treatment "takes" and produces increased efficacy for posttreatment adjustment.

The results also demonstrated a strong relationship between self-efficacy ratings and treatment outcome during the follow-up period. Subjects' scores on the seven clusters of the self-efficacy scale administered at posttreatment were used as predictor variables in a multiple regression analysis to predict which subjects would relapse and the duration of abstinence prior to relapse. The regression analysis revealed that the higher the level of perceived self-efficacy at the completion of treatment, the greater the probability that subjects would remain abstinent throughout the follow-up or would remain abstinent for longer periods of time prior to relapse. These relationships were highly statistically significant. Of even greater interest was the finding that there was an extremely high correspondence between the cluster of smoking situations in which relapsed subjects experienced a low degree of self-efficacy (at the time of quitting) and the situation in which relapse first occurred. Condiotte and Lichtenstein (1981) state: "Careful measurement of posttreatment efficacy state made possible extremely accurate predictions of the circumstances under which individual subjects would relapse" (p. 656). It is as if the subjects were able to predict almost the exact circumstances under which they would relapse. The implications for intervention are obvious: efficacy ratings taken during treatment should enable the therapist to identify a client's weak areas and to take appropriate steps to increase self-efficacy in these areas. The major results of this study have recently been replicated by McIntyre, Lichtenstein, and Mermelstein (1983); these results, along with similar findings reported by DiClemente (1981), demonstrate the utility of self-efficacy as a significant construct in predicting relapse for ex-smokers. Clearly there is a need for similar studies with other addictive behaviors to extend the generality of these important and provocative findings.

A recent study by Rist and Watzl (1983) extends the predictive findings of self-efficacy reported in the smoking area to treatment outcome findings in the alcoholism field. These authors describe a study in which 145 female alcoholics were asked to provide self-efficacy ratings of how difficult it would be not to drink in various social pressure situations involving alcohol. All subjects also completed a general questionnaire to assess assertiveness in nondrinking situations. Self-efficacy and general assertiveness ratings were obtained prior to and following a social skills training program which was part of a 3-month inpatient treatment program. Patients who relapsed

3 months after discharge from the treatment program rated the risk situations at pretreatment as significantly more difficult to refrain from drinking in (lower self-efficacy) than abstinent patients. The relapsed patients did not differ from abstinent patients in self-rated assertiveness in nonalcohol-related situations, however. Thus, in this study, specific self-efficacy ratings in high-risk social drinking situations were predictive of posttreatment functioning, whereas ratings of general assertiveness were not predictive of outcome.

OUTCOME EXPECTANCIES

When a man lifts a cup, it is not only the kind of drink that is in it, the amount he is likely to take and the circumstances under which he will do the drinking that are specified in advance for him, but also whether the contents of the cup will cheer or stupify . . . induce affection or aggression, guilt or unalloyed pleasure. These and many other cultural definitions attach to the drink, even before it touches the lips. (Mandelbaum, 1965, p. 282)

GENERAL DEFINITION

This section is devoted to a discussion of outcome expectancies: how they are defined, their determinants, and the role they play in the relapse process. As the above quote suggests, there is a wide range of possible effects that can occur when a person takes a drink. Bandura (1977) distinguishes between two types of expectancies that are closely associated with the performance of any given behavior: efficacy expectancies (concerning one's capacity to perform the behavior, as discussed in the previous section) and outcome expectancies (expectancies of what will happen as a result of engaging in the behavior). Both types of expectancy play a key role in understanding the relapse process. Although self-efficacy and outcome expectancies also influence the performance of an effective coping response in a high-risk situation (in which case the expected outcomes are associated with the long-term benefits of resisting the urge to indulge), this section focuses on outcome expectancies as determinants of relapse.

Outcome expectancies are based on the anticipated effects of engaging in a particular behavior. The range of possible effects is determined by a multitude of factors. In the case of drug use, these effects are manifested in different *response systems*: physical effects (changes in sensations and feelings associated with the physiological effects of the drug), psychological effects (altered cognitions and emotional states), and behavioral effects (changes in overt acts and behavior). Any given effect is also experienced along a continuum of *reinforcement value*, ranging from highly rewarding to highly aversive. In addition, the effects differ in terms of *temporal delay*, with some effects occurring immediately and others delayed. Finally, some effects derive from *environmental reactions* (e.g., social disapproval) to the individual's drug-taking behavior.

It is extremely important to remember that the *actual* effects of taking a drug may not correspond with the *expected* effects. The expectations one holds about the effects (perceived outcome) often exert a greater influence than the actual or "real" effects of taking a drug. In terms of the relapse process in particular, *positive outcome expectancies* are more important than the actual effects experienced after the drug is consumed.

As an example, consider the case of an abstinent male alcoholic who is faced with the temptation of drinking in a high-risk situation. He may hold a variety of positive outcome expectancies. In terms of physical effects, he may expect that a drink will alleviate the stress associated with the high-risk situation by making him feel more relaxed through alcohol's tension-reducing effects. On a psychological level, he may believe that alcohol will enhance perceptions of control (via increased feelings of power or energy), thereby reducing or eliminating his sense of helplessness in the high-risk situation. He may also believe that drinking will enable him to cope more effectively with the situation—that he will be able to behave more aggressively or spontaneously due to the disinhibiting effects of alcohol. Individuals are likely to focus on these expected immediate "specious" effects and neglect the potential delayed negative effects (cf. Ainslie, 1975). Research conducted with alcoholics has emphasized this discrepancy between the expected positive effects of alcohol and the actual effects that occur after alcohol has been consumed (cf. Tamerin, Weiner, & Mendelson, 1970). Other research has shown that alcoholics who report positive expectancies of drinking and drunkenness show a higher probability of relapse than those with negative expectancies (Eastman & Norris, 1982).

CRAVING, URGES, AND POSITIVE OUTCOME EXPECTANCIES

It is important to note that an expectancy has both cognitive (informational) and motivational (incentive) components (cf. Bolles, 1972; Reiss, 1980). The cognitive or informational component is associated with what the person "knows" or expects to happen as a result of engaging in a given behavior. The incentive component, on the other hand, concerns the desirability (reinforcement value) of the specific outcome or effect. A drinker, for example, may have acquired the belief that alcohol consumption will increase feelings of relaxation. This is a cognitive belief or expectancy about an anticipated outcome, regardless of whether or not this belief is "true" in terms of the objectively assessed outcome. This expected outcome also has an incentive component in that relaxation is likely to be a desired effect, one that is positively reinforcing for the individual. In terms of the incentive component, positive outcome expectancies are those associated with a positive or desired outcome, in contrast with negative outcome expectancies in which the outcome is considered undesirable or unrewarding. The incentive component provides a motivational impetus: to engage in behaviors with expected positive effects and to avoid or inhibit behaviors that are expected to yield negative outcomes.

Craving is defined here as a subjective state that is mediated by the incentive properties of positive outcome expectancies. In other words, craving is a motivational state associated with a strong desire for an expected positive outcome. The opposite of craving, from this standpoint, would be a motivational state of *aversion* or a desire to avoid or escape a negative outcome. Craving can be considered in this context as a useful mediational construct, similar to other psychological constructs such as anger or anxiety. To the extent that one is able to specify the operations used to measure both antecedent events that serve to increase craving (e.g., deprivation or being in a stressful high-risk situation) and the subsequent consummatory behavior (e.g., drinking), craving can be considered an intervening variable. Craving, in this sense, is not unlike other motivational states that can be defined operationally (e.g., fear or hunger). On the other hand, if the construct is not operationally defined by specifying the relevant independent and dependent variables, craving can easily become a tautological concept that is assumed to be the "cause" of overt behavior—as is the case when craving is referred to as the cause of loss of control drinking in alcoholics (Mello, 1975). Within the medical model of alcoholism, craving is viewed as a symptom assumed to arise through an internal physiological or tissue "need" for alcohol (cf., Isbell, 1955; Mardones, 1955); as such, craving has become reified as the cause of relapse, much as willpower has become reified as the apparent cause of continued abstinence. On a technical level, it may be useful to distinguish between craving and urges. Craving is equated with the subjective desire for the effects of a drug, whereas *urges* represent behavioral intentions to engage in a specific consummatory behavior (e.g., a sudden urge to smoke in response to craving). Most often, however, the terms *craving* and *urges* are used interchangeably.

SOURCES OF POSITIVE OUTCOME EXPECTANCIES

How do positive outcome expectancies arise? There are several possible sources, including exposure to conditioned stimuli associated with prior drug experiences (classical conditioning), physical dependency, the influence of personal and cultural beliefs about drug effects, and situational–environmental factors. Let us examine each of these possible sources in turn.

Classical Conditioning

Classical or Pavlovian conditioning has often been described as a primary source of craving. According to this approach, drug cues (situational or temporal) that have been repeatedly paired with the drug-taking experiences in the individual's past learning history come to serve as conditioned stimuli. During the conditioning process, unconditioned stimuli associated with the "active ingredients" of the drug (presumably pharmacological properties of the drug that elicit unconditioned drug effects) are continuously paired with other cues that acquire conditioned stimulus properties. These other cues include both stimuli that are similar in appearance to the real drug (unconditioned stimulus) as well as stimuli that are associated in time and place with the drug-taking behavior (setting and temporal factors). The former cues become conditioned on the basis of stimulus generalization (cues that are similar to the sight, taste, touch, and smell of the unconditioned stimulus), whereas the latter are subject to the influence of higher-order conditioning (the physical and social setting, time of day, etc.). Unless extinction of responses to these cues has occurred, exposure to the conditioned stimuli will elicit a conditioned anticipatory response much in the same way that Pavlov's dogs showed a conditioned salivary response to the sound of a bell previously associated with a food reward. The conditioned response will in most cases have both somatic and cognitive components and will be experienced subjectively as craving.

Conditioned craving has been postulated as a primary determinant of relapse by some theorists in the addictions field (Grabowski & O'Brien, 1981; O'Brien, 1976; Pomerleau, 1981; Poulos, Hinson, & Siegel, 1981; Wikler, 1965, 1976). One such theoretical model has been put forth as an explanation of relapse in alcoholics. According to this group of investigators (Ludwig & Stark, 1974; Ludwig & Wikler, 1974; Ludwig, Wikler, & Stark, 1974), craving in the abstinent alcoholic is mediated by conditioned responses elicited by stimuli formerly associated with withdrawal distress in the individual's past drinking history. According to this view, craving is considered to be strongest during withdrawal when the drug user desires the substance to alleviate the agony of physical withdrawal. As a result of classical conditioning, environmental or internal cues present during earlier withdrawal come to serve as conditioned stimuli for craving when and if they are encountered at some later date by the abstinent alcoholic. In a direct analogy with craving for narcotics, Ludwig and Wikler (1974) consider "craving for alcohol, comparable to craving for narcotics, as representing the psychological or cognitive correlate of a 'subclinical' conditioned withdrawal syndrome" (p. 114). These authors consider craving to be similar to a "mini-withdrawal" experience: "The more frequent and severe the prior withdrawal experiences, the greater the predisposition to conditioned withdrawal symptoms with consequent desire for relief (i.e., "craving through drink") (p. 115).

From Ludwig and Wikler's perspective, craving is defined as an *aversive* state mediated by the elicitation of unpleasant physical symptoms associated with prior withdrawal. The symptoms (the "subclinical conditioned withdrawal syndrome") are thought to be elicited by cues associated with prior withdrawal, and not the initial drug-taking experience. What is the evidence in support of this theory? Although the investigators report an analogue experiment designed to test the validity of their assumptions (Ludwig *et al.*, 1974), there are a number of serious flaws with the study and the results are not inconsistent with an alternative cognitive interpretation (see Marlatt, 1978, for a detailed critique of this research). If the Ludwig and Wikler model were correct, alcoholics would experience the greatest craving in treatment centers where they have undergone detoxification and withdrawal. Clinical experience shows, however, that most patients in treatment centers report their craving to be low or virtually nonexistent.

One of the few studies to test the conditioned withdrawal theory of relapse in human narcotic addicts was reported recently by McAuliffe (1982). The study consisted of structured interviews with 40 street addicts, all of whom had at least one period of abstinence outside of an institution. Of this sample, only 11 subjects (27.5%) reported having experienced conditioned withdrawal by taking drugs, and one ultimately relapsed as a result. McAuliffe concludes:

Since all of the 40 subjects had relapsed at least once, conditioned withdrawal sickness does not appear to explain a large proportion of the relapses that street addicts experience. . . . In the present study, *desire for euphoria* was the most commonly mentioned reason for relapse, even among addicts who had experienced conditioned withdrawal sickness. (1982, pp. 29–30; italics added)

In a related study of relapse in opiate addicts, Chaney, Roszell, and Cummings (1982) reported that only 16% of 38 relapse episodes studied could be attributed to conditioned withdrawal (negative physiological states not associated with prior substance abuse).

Does this mean that classical conditioning is not an important factor in the relapse process? In our view, classical conditioning does play an important role, but not in the same way posited by the conditioned withdrawal theory described by Ludwig and Wikler. If a former drug user is exposed to drug-related cues (actual exposure to the drug itself or stimuli associated with prior drug use), it seems likely that this will elicit conditioned positive outcome expectancies or craving. This process is illustrated in Figure 3-1, using smoking as an example. However, the conditioned craving response is not *aversive* in quality (as predicted by the conditioned subclinical withdrawal syndrome model); to the contrary, it is *appetitive* or positive in nature. Exposure to drug cues will elicit positive expectancies and an increased desire for the effects of the drug. It is as though the individual can

Figure 3-1. Hypothetical anatomy of an urge to smoke. Craving (positive outcome expectancy) and the urge to smoke (behavioral intention) are shown as covert mediators of the consummatory response (smoking behavior). (CS = conditioned stimulus; CR = conditioned response.)

almost taste and feel the effects of the first drink or injection, much as we assume that dogs anticipate the taste of food when they are salivating in response to a conditioned stimulus. Some narcotic addicts will actually give themselves injections of inert substances (e.g., water or saline solutions) when narcotic drugs are unavailable so as to experience a conditioned "high." Clearly these "needle freaks" would not engage in this behavior if they thought it would elicit the aversive experience of a conditioned withdrawal syndrome.

Although classical conditioning may be an important determinant of relapse for those cases in which the individual is directly exposed to drug cues (as in the case of the alcoholic who passes by an old drinking haunt or the ex-smoker who finds himself surrounded by others who are smoking in a bar or restaurant), in most of the relapse episodes we have studied, craving occurs in the absence of drug-related cues. Positive outcome expectancies (craving) are more frequently reported when the individual is confronted with a high-risk situation for which he or she lacks an appropriate coping response. As reported in Chapter 2, the percentage of lapses in high-risk situations such as negative emotional states and interpersonal conflict are far greater than for negative physical states or urges and temptations. How do positive outcome expectancies arise in these high-risk situations?

The relapse process model assumes that the attraction toward the old coping crutch increases in a high-risk situation to the extent that the individual lacks an alternative coping response and is experiencing decreased self-efficacy. Under conditions of stress, the previously dominant response in the coping hierarchy is likely to rise to the fore, especially if an alternative coping response is not well established. An individual in these circumstances is likely to think, "I could cope better with this situation if only I had a cigarette" (or drink, etc.). Also, because of the stress associated with most high-risk situations, there may be a strong desire for the effects of the drug or other addictive behavior if the person believes that this activity will reduce tension and stress. Along these same lines, the individual who is experiencing increased emotional arousal in a high-risk situation may misinterpret this reaction as craving for the drug rather than attributing it to the stress of the situation itself. Craving will be of greatest intensity, of course, when both the stress of a high-risk situation and the presence of substance cues (the availability of alcohol, cigarettes, etc.) occur together or in close proximity.

Physical Dependency

What role does physical dependency play as a source of craving? Some investigators have suggested that physical dependency may be an important mediator of craving and relapse in alcoholics (Chick, 1980; Hodgson, 1980; Skinner & Allen, 1982). Researchers at the Addiction Research Unit at the Institute of Psychiatry in London, for example, have developed a questionnaire designed to measure degree of physical dependency (Stockwell, Hodgson, Edwards, Taylor, & Rankin, 1979). Items on this questionnaire refer to various physical symptoms associated with periods of heavy drinking (the "shakes," perspiration, etc.) along with drinking patterns assumed to reflect dependency (e.g., morning drinking and amount consumed). Presumably, alcoholics who show high scores on this questionnaire are more physically dependent and will experience greater withdrawal and craving for alcohol after periods of heavy drinking. These investigators have demonstrated that alcoholics who are assessed as severely dependent on the basis of the physical dependency questionnaire evidence greater craving (defined operationally as the speed by which they consume drinks containing alcohol) after having consumed a high-dose "priming" alcoholic beverage (Hodgson, Rankin, & Stockwell, 1979; Stockwell, Hodgson, Rankin, & Taylor, 1982).

Although the previously cited studies show that physical dependency may be an important mediator of craving (as measured by speed of consuming alcoholic beverages), these results do not necessarily imply that physical dependency is a significant determinant of relapse in the formerly abstinent alcoholic (cf. Shaw, 1979). A recent study by Heather, Rollnick, and Winton (1983) demonstrated that a measure of physical dependency (the Stockwell *et al.*, 1979, questionnaire) administered to a sample of alcoholics during a hospital treatment program was *unrelated* to treatment outcome and relapse rates. Since strength of physical dependency is assumed to be highly correlated with the intensity of physical withdrawal, these findings provide little support for the notion that dependency or withdrawal are significantly associated with relapse. In fact, the study reported by Heather *et al.* (1983) shows that a cognitive measure of *beliefs* about the inevitability of loss of control drinking after the first drink was the only measure that was significantly related to relapse following treatment.

Attitudes and Beliefs

Cultural and personal beliefs about the effects of a given drug or substance are important determinants of outcome expectancies. On a cultural level, people are constantly being exposed to depictions of drug effects in newspapers, magazines, books, and the visual media. Many religious groups have vocalized their strong beliefs, usually about the harmful effects of drug use. Children are exposed to the effects of drugs on a vicarious level through exposure to the drug use and beliefs about drug effects expressed by peers and parental figures. Beliefs about drug effects also vary from one society to another (e.g., the striking differences between attitudes toward drinking in contemporary American society compared to Islamic cultures in which drinking is seen as a mortal sin). In addition to general *cultural* beliefs, each individual in a society has formed a set of *personal* beliefs about the effects of various drugs. These beliefs are based on a variety of influences including one's own past experiences with drugs, educational background, personal values, and so forth. There may not necessarily be a high correlation between an individual's knowledge of cultural beliefs and his or her own personal beliefs about the effects of a particular drug. Someone may believe, for example, that although drinking increases aggressive behavior for most people, it decreases anger and aggression for that particular individual. Also, it is important to remember that these beliefs may not always be in accord with the actual effects obtained with drug use.

Investigations of personal beliefs about drug effects have appeared in the literature in recent years. Many of these reports have examined cultural and personal beliefs about the effects of alcohol. In a classic treatise, MacAndrew and Edgerton (1969) have provided a thorough review of cultural beliefs about the effects of drinking and intoxication in various societies around the world and how these beliefs influence drinking behavior and "drunken comportment." Personal beliefs about the effects of alcohol have also been described in recent papers (Brown, Goldman, Inn, & Anderson, 1980; Christiansen & Goldman, 1983; Christiansen, Goldman, & Inn, 1982; Rohsenow, 1983; Russell & Mehrabian, 1975). In the Brown *et al.* study (1980), factor analysis of questionnaires administered to both male and female subjects of widely diversified drinking backgrounds revealed six independent expectancy factors: that alcohol transforms experiences in a positive way, enhances social and physical pleasure, enhances sexual performance and experience, increases power and aggression, increases social assertiveness, and reduces tension. In a related study with adolescent subjects (ranging in age from 12 to 19 years), alcohol expectancies were pitted against demographic background variables in the prediction of adolescent drinking behavior. The results showed that expectancies at least equalled and even added to the predictive power of the background variables (Christiansen & Goldman, 1983).

A recent paper by Southwick, Steele, Marlatt, and Lindell (1981) studied personal beliefs about the effects of alcohol in subjects who were classified as either occasional, moderate, or heavy social drinkers, or who reported that they abstained from all alcohol use. Since dose level or amount of alcohol consumed is assumed to be an important factor influencing expectancies, subjects were asked to describe their personal expected effects from consuming both a moderate amount and "too much" alcohol. Expected effects were reported on a series of bipolar rating scales using adjectives obtained in a pilot study. The results, in brief, showed that subjects expected moderate drinking to result in relatively greater stimulation, perceived dominance, and pleasurable disinhibition; for heavy drinking they expected a greater degree of behavioral impairment. Expectancies also differed in terms of the individual's drinking experience. Heavy drinkers expected greater stimulation and pleasure from moderate drinking than those who were lighter drinkers, for example. The fact that expectancies differed both in terms of the subject's own drinking experience and the expected dose level of alcohol is consistent with the hypothesis that the effects of alcohol are biphasic in nature, with enhanced arousal and pleasure at low dose levels and increased behavioral impairment and dysphoria at higher dose levels. Biphasic drug effects are described in more detail in the following section.

Situational–Environmental Factors

The physical and social setting or environment also influence expectancies about the effects of a drug. In our society, we have come to associate certain settings with particular drug effects. In intimate bars and taverns, for example, we assume that drinking will enhance romantic thoughts and feelings, possibly facilitating sexual arousal and amorous conquests. In contrast, drinking at competitive sports events (football, soccer, rugby, etc.) is often associated with outbreaks of violence. Smoking marijuana in a party setting is thought to enhance enjoyment of music and "trippy" conversation for many people. Whether one is alone or with others when a drug is used also shapes beliefs about the anticipated effects. Research by Pliner and Cappell (1974) has shown, for example, that the effects of drinking will vary depending on whether the drinker is alone or is interacting in a social situation. Solitary drinkers described the effects primarily in terms of physical symptoms (feeling dizzy or numb), in contrast with drinkers in a social setting who described the effects primarily in psychological or interpersonal terms (feeling more extraverted or friendly) even though the same amount of alcohol was consumed by all subjects.

POSITIVE OUTCOME EXPECTANCIES AND BIPHASIC DRUG EFFECTS

In the Southwick *et al.* (1981) study previously described, personal beliefs about the effects of alcohol were investigated. Subjects expected a moderate dose of alcohol to produce greater stimulation and pleasurable euphoria, whereas heavy drinking was expected to produce relatively unpleasant effects (impairment and dysphoria). These results are consistent with research showing that the effects of alcohol and other psychoactive drugs are frequently *biphasic* in nature, depending on dose level and temporal factors. Research on the physiological effects of alcohol (heart rate, skin conductance, central nervous system arousal, etc.) show that low doses of alcohol (approximately 1 or 2 oz of whiskey, for example) produce an initial stimulatory effect of *increased arousal* (cf. Docter, Naitoh, & Smith, 1966; Garfield & McBrearty, 1970; Grenell, 1972; Hamwich & Callson, 1972; Mello, 1968). This initial increase in arousal and stimulation is experienced subjectively by the drinker as a high—a feeling of excitement, increased energy, and perceptions of the self as more powerful (cf. McClelland, Davis, Kalin, & Wanner, 1972). As dose level increases and time passes, however, the physical and emotional effects begin to change and to swing in the opposite direction. Instead of increased stimulation, the drinker begins to experience depressant effects such as fatigue, nausea, physical impairment, and dysphoric emotional states (Bach-y-Rita, Lion, & Ervin, 1970; Cameron, 1974; Madden, Walker, & Kenyon, 1976; Nathan & O'Brien, 1971; Ritchie, 1965). This second stage of the biphasic reaction is also experienced by the drinker as the blood-alcohol level begins to decrease after the cessation of drinking (Jones & Vega, 1972).

A biphasic response may also underlie the development of tolerance to the initially rewarding effects over prolonged periods of drug use. According to a theoretical model developed by Solomon and his associates (Solomon, 1977, 1980; Solomon & Corbit, 1974), the nervous system reacts automatically to the initial (unconditioned) effects of a drug such as heroin with a *compensatory response* that is opposite in direction to the drug effect itself. According to this *opponent-process* theory, the compensatory response increases in strength with repeated drug use, thereby reducing the impact of the initial drug effects. This mechanism is thought to account for the development of tolerance in the chronic drug user; increased dosages are required to overcome the compensatory response in an attempt to reinstate the initial high experienced in the early states of drug use. The compensatory response can become conditioned to previously neutral stimuli with repeated administrations of the drug. As a result, drug-taking cues and associated environmental stimuli may elicit a conditioned compensatory response that is opposite in direction to the unconditioned physical effects of the drug itself. Research with animals supports the conceptualization of tolerance to opiates (morphine) as a classically conditioned learned response; tolerance is therefore modifiable by changes in environmental conditioned stimuli (Poulus *et al.*, 1981; Siegel, 1975, 1977, 1979). Further implications of opponent-process theory for understanding alcohol dependence are presented in Chapter 6.

Much of the research associated with the opponent-process model and the development of compensatory responses is based on animal research, and the majority of these studies have been conducted with opiate drugs such as morphine and heroin. As such, the implications for understanding human drug use and abuse, particularly for other drugs such as alcohol, remain speculative at this point. Human cognitive processes probably interact with or in some cases may even override the effects of compensatory physiological responses in ways that only future research can reveal. If the validity of the biphasic response theory is substantiated by future studies with human subjects, some of the apparent contradictions in our current knowledge about drug use may be resolved.

Some of the implications for human alcohol use may be examined as an example. The principal reinforcing effects of drinking may be associated with increased excitation or euphoria in the initial phase of the biphasic response, rather than decreased tension or anxiety postulated by advocates of the "tension-reduction" hypothesis (the belief that drinking is reinforced through the physically tranquilizing effects of alcohol). Thus, the drinker may be correct in saying that he or she drinks to get high; alcohol's initial effects may be more in the form of an "upper" followed by the "downer" of the second-stage depressant effects. In the analysis of alcohol's reinforcing properties, the immediate pleasurable effects have the greatest impact on learning and on the shaping of the drinker's outcome expectancies (cf. Southwick et al., 1980). The dysphoric effects of the second stage have less of an impact because of their delayed occurrence, a finding that is in accord with the temporal gradient of reinforcement effect. Thus, although the eventual outcome of any excessive drinking episode is primarily negative, the initial reinforcing high of the biphasic response accounts most for the drinker's motivation to indulge. The initial stage of the biphasic response may underlie the immediate gratification effect that many individuals seek in their use of drugs.

Expectation of the positive effects of a drug may persist even though the individual may be experiencing the dysphoric effects of the second stage of the biphasic response. If so, this persistence of positive expectancies may explain why some individuals continue to drink or use other substances despite the fact that the predominant quality of the ongoing drug experience is negative. A heavy drinker, for example, who is experiencing the dysphoric stage of the biphasic response (due to a high dose of alcohol and/or the effects of increased tolerance) may attempt to "drink through" the negative effects in a vain attempt to escape or avoid the inevitable unpleasant consequences. Bouts of prolonged drinking or binges may result from this tendency. Unlike physiological reactions to drug use that change over time in accordance with the biphasic model, outcome expectancies are more likely to persist in their initial robust positive form. In other words, cognitive expectancies for drug effects do not show the same "tolerance" effect as somatic responses.

RESEARCH ON OUTCOME EXPECTANCIES:
THE BALANCED PLACEBO DESIGN

In any study of drug effects with human subjects, three major parameters must be taken into consideration: expectancy (set), situational factors (setting), and drug administration procedures (dose level, frequency of administration, etc.). Any observed drug effects may be influenced by one or more of these parameters, often in an interactive fashion. Expectancy effects are particularly salient in research using psychoactive drugs with human subjects. The individual's beliefs about the effects of a particular drug are at least as significant as the pharmacological–physiological effects and must be carefully evaluated. Beliefs and expectancies play an even stronger role when the drug is one with which the individual has considerable prior experience (e.g., alcohol vs. a relatively unknown experimental drug). The setting in which the drug is taken will have an important influence, including both the physical environment (e.g., a sterile hospital research ward vs. a comfortable room in one's own home) and the social context (e.g., alone vs. with others who may be either friends or strangers).

Expectancy effects have traditionally been assessed in most human drug research by the use of the double-blind placebo design. In the traditional use of this design, the subject is given either the real drug (containing the active ingredients) or a placebo (an inert substance with the same overall appearance as the real drug). If neither the subject nor the individual administering the substance knows whether or not the real drug or the placebo has been given (both are "blind" concerning the actual ingredients), it is called a double-blind procedure. This procedure has two main purposes: to eliminate the possibility that the experimenter will selectively bias the results (via expectations about the effects of the real drug or the noneffects of a placebo) and to provide a control for the subject's own expectancies about the relative effects of receiving either the real drug or a placebo. It is important to note, however, that the extent to which this method controls for the subject's expectancies about the medication or procedure depends on the *instructions* given by the experimenter to the subject. Until recently, it was common practice for the placebo to be presented as if it were the real drug, so that the subject had no knowledge that a placebo might be administered. Contemporary research ethics, on the other hand, require that the subject be informed in advance that he or she may receive a placebo. When this procedure is employed, the double-blind administration becomes a guessing game for the subject, who may focus attention inward to physical or psychological cues in an attempt to discover whether an active or an inert substance has been administered.

The double-blind design, although it is an excellent procedure for the control of experimenter bias, is not an acceptable design for the control of subject expectancies. Even if the subject expects to receive the real drug in all cases, this procedure fails to provide a mechanism to test for the "pure" pharmacological or physiological effects of the drug alone, unconfounded by the subject's expectancies of receiving that drug. What is the effect of the active drug alone, without the added effects of the subject's expectancies? Carpenter (1968) was among the first investigators to note that the traditional placebo control design fails to provide a test of the pharmacological effects of a drug, independent of the subject's expectancy for receiving that drug. He suggested the use of an "antiplacebo" procedure, in which both the placebo and the active drug are administered under conditions in which the subject expects to receive an inert subtance. If the two groups of the "antiplacebo" procedure (expect placebo–receive drug; expect placebo–receive placebo) are combined with the traditional placebo design groups (expect drug–receive drug; expect drug–receive placebo), we have a four-group design that enables the investigator to parcel out the independent influences of both expectancy and pharmacological effects. This design has come to be called the *balanced placebo design* (Marlatt & Rohsenow, 1980, 1981; Rohsenow & Marlatt, 1981).

Although the balanced placebo design was first suggested in the early 1960s (Ross, Krugman, Lyerly, & Clyde, 1962), it was not utilized by investigators until a decade later when two groups of investigators (Engle & Williams, 1972; Marlatt, Demming, & Reid, 1973) independently applied the design in human alcohol research. At the time, both groups were interested in investigating "loss of control" drinking in alcoholics. The disease model of alcoholism proposed initially by Jellinek (1960) describes loss of control drinking as a primary symptom of alcoholism. According to this theory, the ingestion of one or two drinks containing alcohol triggers an underlying physiological addictive mechanism that is experienced subjectively by the alcoholic as an intense craving for more alcohol. Unable to resist this craving, the alcoholic loses the voluntary capacity to resist and a bout of loss of control consumption (i.e., a binge) is likely to occur. In our study (Marlatt *et al.*, 1973), we wanted to test the basic assumptions of the loss of control hypothesis. The question we asked was this: Could the alcoholic's expectancy of receiving alcohol mediate this phenomenon, or do the pharmacological effects of alcohol itself primarily act as a biological trigger for craving? Perhaps the alcoholic engages in excessive initial consumption because of the expected reinforcing effects of alcohol, but these effects are delayed due to absorption latency and increased tolerance. Because of this delayed reinforcement, initial consumption may be rapid and excessive and appear to be "out of control" to the observer. Previously, we have described this effect as Rapid Alcohol Consumption Effect drinking (RACE) (Marlatt & Rose, 1980). The rapid drinking exhibited by some alcoholics, if mediated by expectancy of reinforcement, is not unlike the behavior of the Las Vegas gambler who pulls the handle of a slot machine in rapid succession in anticipation of hitting the jackpot. If expectancy of reinforcement serves as a primary determinant of rapid consumption, then high rates of drinking could be predicted for any beverage the alcoholic *believed* to contain alcohol, regardless of the actual presence or absence of alcohol in the drink.

In order to test this hypothesis using the balanced placebo design, we needed to find a beverage in which the presence or absence of alcohol could not be reliably detected. We ruled out procedures that had been used by other investigators (e.g., disguising the taste of alcohol by mixing it with peppermint flavoring), since we wanted to select a beverage that most drinkers would already be familiar with. After considerable experimentation, we finally settled on a mix of one part vodka to five parts tonic water; pilot testing revealed that the presence or absence of alcohol using this combination could not be correctly identified on a better than chance level. The balanced placebo design is presented in Figure 3-2.

In the experiment itself, the volunteer subjects consisted of 32 male alcoholics (who had relapsed following completion of a hospital treatment program for alcoholism) and a matched control group of male social drinkers. All subjects were asked to participate individually in a Taste-Rating Task in which they would compare the taste properties of either alcoholic or non-alcoholic beverages. Subjects in the "expect alcohol" conditions were led to believe that they would compare three brands of vodka (mixed with tonic), while subjects in the "expect no alcohol" groups were told that they would

Figure 3-2. The balanced placebo design.

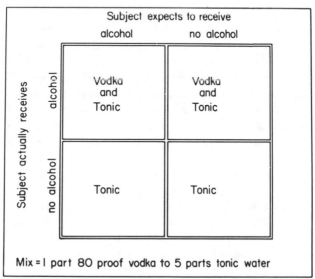

compare three brands of tonic water. Half the subjects in each of these two conditions were actually given alcohol (vodka and tonic), while half received only tonic water, as depicted in Figure 3-2. All subjects were provided with three full decanters of each beverage, and were asked to sample each on an ad-lib basis while making the comparative taste ratings. The results showed that the only significant determinant of the total amount consumed, for both alcoholics and social drinkers, was the expectancy factor. Subjects who were led to believe they were sampling an alcoholic beverage drank significantly more in the tasting task (and estimated that their drinks contained more alcohol in a manipulation check after the taste-rating task) than did subjects who expected only tonic water—regardless of the actual presence or absence of alcohol in the drinks they consumed. These results are depicted in Figure 3-3. The finding that expectancy factors exert more influence than the physiological effects of alcohol in determining alcohol consumption casts a serious shadow of doubt over the validity of the loss of control drinking hypothesis advanced by advocates of the disease model of alcoholism.

Since the publication of the above study in 1973, numerous other experiments have been conducted using the balanced placebo design; the results of some of these studies are reviewed by Marlatt and Rohsenow (1980). In most of these investigations, the beverages are administered first (as the independent variable) and then the effects are assessed for a given target behavior (dependent variable). As an example, let us consider the question of alcohol's effect on aggressive behavior. In our society, there exists a common belief that alcohol "causes" outbreaks of aggression, particularly in male drinkers. Alcohol has been implicated as a causative factor in the commission of aggressive criminal activities such as rape and homicide (e.g., Collins, 1981; Shupe, 1954; Wolfgang & Strohm, 1956). At least two competing hypotheses have been advanced to explain how drinking affects the expression of aggression. The disinhibition hypothesis proposes that an aggressive drive exists in humans but that its expression is normally inhibited by anxiety, guilt, or social restraints. Alcohol is thought to disinhibit or release the aggressive drive, presumably by its effects on higher cortical centers and a corresponding reduction of fear and anxiety concerning the consequences of any aggressive outbreak. A parallel notion is often advanced by psychoanalytic theorists who support the notion that the superego is "dissolvable" in alcohol. The second hypothesis commonly cited is that alcohol has an overall energizing effect on the general activity level of the organism, and that drinking will increase the probability of aggressive fantasies and "power needs" (cf. McClelland et al., 1972); higher doses may stimulate overt aggression. Although a number of studies show that alcohol consumption does indeed increase aggressive responding, there is little direct evidence that would support either hypothesis showing that this effect is mediated primarily by the physiological effects of alcohol. Most of these studies have failed to adequately control for expectancy effects.

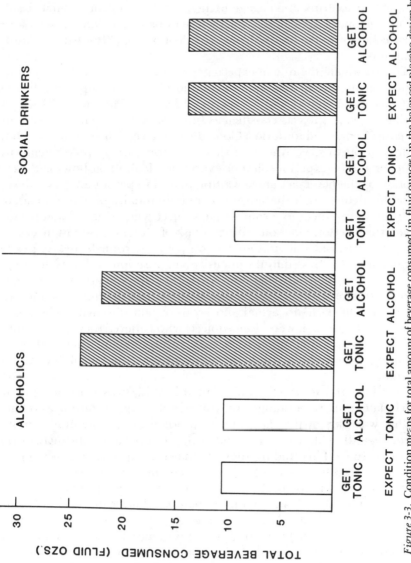

Figure 3-3. Condition means for total amount of beverage consumed (in fluid ounces) in the balanced placebo design by male alcoholics and matched social drinkers. Based on data from Marlatt, Demming, and Reid (1973).

An alternative hypothesis is that the alcohol–aggression link is mediated by expectancies and beliefs about how alcohol affects aggressive behavior. Alcohol may provide a culturally acceptable excuse for engaging in behaviors that are normally socially unacceptable—including aggression (MacAndrew & Edgerton, 1969; Wilson, 1978). From this point of view, individuals who drink and engage in aggressive or violent acts may be able to avoid personal responsibility for their actions by attributing the "cause" of their behavior to the physical effects of alcohol (e.g., "It wasn't my fault—I was drunk").

To investigate the role of expectancy as a possible mediating factor in the alcohol–aggression linkage, we conducted a study employing the balanced placebo design (Lang, Goeckner, Adesso, & Marlatt, 1975). In this experiment, male subjects classified as heavy social drinkers were administered either vodka and tonic (to a blood-alcohol level of 0.10%, the legal limit of intoxication in most American states), or tonic only, under one of two instructional sets (expect alcohol or expect no alcohol). Following the consumption of the beverages and a waiting period to permit adequate absorption of the alcohol, half the subjects were individually provoked to aggression by exposing them to a confederate subject who criticized and insulted them for their performance on a difficult task of motor coordination. Control subjects experienced a neutral interaction with the confederate. Aggression was subsequently assessed by the intensity and duration of shocks the subject administered to the confederate on a modified Buss aggression apparatus (although this procedure was designed to appear as though the confederate subject was shocked, no actual shocks were administered). The results, presented in Figure 3-4, were clear: subjects who believed they had consumed alcohol behaved more aggressively than subjects who believed they had consumed a nonalcoholic drink, regardless of the actual alcohol content of the drink.

An additional measure obtained in this study was reaction time (the subject's latency in responding to the confederate's signals during a decoding task that was part of the experimental procedure). The administration of alcohol, regardless of expectancy condition, produced a significant reduction in reaction time. This finding suggests that the expectancy effect operates more strongly with behaviors for which there are existing beliefs about the effects of alcohol, particularly when these effects are considered desirable (in terms of immediate gratification) in some way for the drinker. The results of several balanced placebo studies reviewed by Marlatt and Rohsenow (1980) and Wilson (1981) tend to support this generalization. A summary of these experiments indicates that expectancy effects predominate over the pharmacological–physiological properties of alcohol for both consummatory behaviors (craving for and actual consumption of alcohol) and certain interpersonal or social behaviors. Males show increases in beverage consumption, aggressive responding, sexual arousal, and decreased levels of

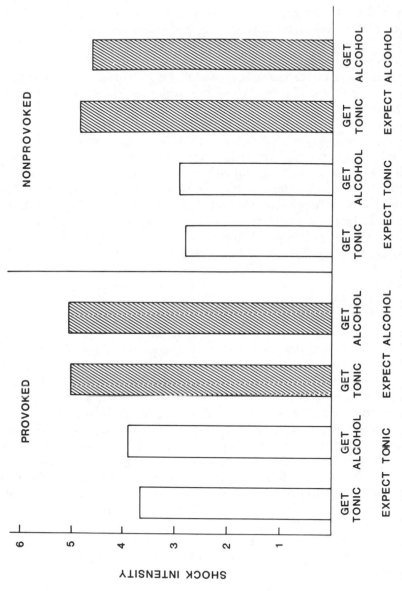

Figure 3-4. Condition means for shock intensity delivered by subjects (male social drinkers) to the confederate (ostensible shock intensity range from 1 to 10, with higher numbers indicating more painful shocks) in both the provoked and non-provoked groups. Based on data from Lang, Goeckner, Adesso, and Marlatt (1975).

anxiety when they are led to believe the drinks they consumed contain alcohol, regardless of the actual presence or absence of alcohol in the drinkers. The pattern for female subjects is more complex and reflects beliefs about the differential effects of alcohol on the behavior of men and women. On the other hand, expectancy effects are minimal or absent altogether with such nonsocial behaviors as reaction time, motor coordination, and memory tasks. With these responses, alcohol itself has a deleterious effect, regardless of the expectancy manipulation.

From this perspective, it would appear that if for a given target behavior, the effects of alcohol are believed to be *positive or desirable* for the drinker, the expectancy effect is more likely to override the influence of alcohol itself. The evidence with male subjects supports this hypothesis for such behaviors as beverage consumption (Marlatt *et al.*, 1973), reduction of tension or anxiety in evaluative social situations (Wilson & Abrams, 1977), increased aggression (Lang *et al.*, 1975), and increased sexual arousal when exposed to erotic stimuli (Briddell, Rimm, Caddy, Krawitz, Sholis, & Wunderlin, 1978; Wilson & Lawson, 1976). In contrast, for those behaviors for which drinking would have a *negative or undesirable outcome*, the expectancy manipulation seems to have minimal impact (Miller, Adesso, Fleming, Gino, & Lauerman, 1978; Rimm, Sininger, Faherty, Whitley, & Perl, 1982; Vuchinich & Sobell, 1978).

It is obvious to most observers that heavy drinking impairs physical and motor coordination—such as the ability to walk a straight line or maintain balance when standing on one foot. Many individuals extrapolate from this observation and conclude that alcohol has an equally deleterious effect on social and "moral" behaviors (MacAndrew & Edgerton, 1969). Because of our exposure to drinking models presented in both real life and the media, we have come to expect that people will sometimes do things under the influence of drugs that they would never do while sober. Alcohol, for example, is frequently consumed in relaxed, convivial settings in which sexual advances are often considered appropriate behavior. In these settings, alcohol often acts as a cue or a discriminative stimulus for sexual behavior (Carpenter & Armenti, 1972; Wilson, 1978). The permission-giving cue effects (the dim lights of a bar, sensual music, clinking of glasses) exert a powerful influence in their own right, regardless of the pharmacological properties of alcohol, as long as the individuals involved believe that alcohol is indeed present and an active ingredient in the interaction.

There are obvious implications here for predicting which classes of behavior would be most strongly affected by expectancy effects. Social behaviors that usually provide immediate gratification (e.g., sexual advances, aggressive outbursts, etc.), often accompanied by delayed social disapproval, seem to be most affected. As such, in most of these cases some form of approach–avoidance conflict is involved. There is considerable secondary gain for the individual who attributes the cause of such behaviors to alcohol itself. Whatever the outcome, the drinker can disclaim "authorship" of the behavior by blaming alcohol as the causative culprit ("Don't blame me—I was under the influence of booze at the time"). Certain antisocial behaviors such as rape, which combine both aggressive and sexual components, are frequently performed under the influence of alcohol (Rada, 1973); perhaps alcohol is consumed partly under the belief that it will act as a disinhibitor (to fortify courage, etc.) and partly because it serves as an explanation or excuse for the act. In contrast, motor skills and complex cognitive activities are less likely to be performed under similar conditions. Whereas a man who drinks may wish to act out his aggressive or sexual drives, he does not want to impair his cognitive and motor abilities to the same extent. Alcohol itself will impair these skills, regardless of the expectancy set.

The role of alcohol as a disinhibitor was discussed at a recent conference sponsored by the National Institute on Alcohol Abuse and Alcoholism (Room & Collins, 1983). An interdisciplinary group of researchers, including physiologists, psychologists, anthropologists, sociologists, physicians, and legal specialists, gathered together to address the question of whether alcohol releases or disinhibits behaviors that are normally under some form of inhibition or control. A team of physiological psychologists (Woods & Mansfield, 1983) reviewed evidence on the effects of alcohol on brain functioning. They concluded that there were no firm data supporting the notion that alcohol disinhibits emotions or behaviors through its selective effect on the cerebral cortex since ethanol has an equally deleterious effect on *all* brain functions (including areas in the midbrain thought to be associated with such "base" emotional behaviors as aggression and sex). An anthropologist (Marshall, 1983) reported his observations of youthful drinking among Turk Islanders; young males were found to be capable of acting in an intoxicated manner years before they had ever actually consumed alcohol. This "pseudo-intoxication" effect, acquired on the basis of observing the drunken behavior of older males in the social group, often occurred when the younger boys simply sniffed an empty liquor bottle. The resulting drunken comportment and "crazy" behaviors were attributed to the effects of drinking by adult observers, even though no alcohol had actually been consumed by any of the "drunk" boys (see also, Marshall, 1979). Other anthropologists discussed alcohol's role as a cue or stimulus for "time out" behavior—as an opportunity for escaping from the demands and responsibilities of daily work routines. Social psychologists described research showing the social payoff for naming alcohol as the "cause" of many behaviors that are normally under social restraint. Reference was made to those members of the United States Congress and Senate who were accused of taking bribes in the ABSCAM investigations and who then blamed alcohol as the cause of their downfall. Research was also presented showing that alcohol or other drug use can be used as an excuse or a "self-handicapping" explanation of performance decrements or disinhibition effects (cf. Berglas & Jones, 1978; Jones & Berglas,

1978). By the conclusion of the conference, very little evidence was found to support the notion that alcohol *per se* exerts a disinhibiting effect through its pharmacological or physiological effects. In terms of disinhibition, alcohol seems to be more a catalyst than a causative agent.

One conclusion that can be derived from the foregoing analysis is that many outcome expectancies concerning the effects of drugs are shaped by *attributions of causality* we make about a drug's capacity to alter or change behaviors. Evidence from the balanced placebo design clearly shows that many of these attributions are misinformed and inaccurate. Alcohol as a drug has been attributed as the "cause" of an amazingly wide range of behavioral effects, including increased aggression, decreased anxiety, increased sexual desire, decreased sexual performance, increased socialization, decreased motor coordination, and so on. As such, alcohol seems to qualify as a magical elixir, capable of transforming *any* emotion or behavior in *any* direction (Fingarette, 1983; Marlatt, 1984). How can alcohol itself have such a plethora of specific effects, many of which seem quite contradictory, on so many different behaviors? This question becomes even more significant when we realize that the physiological effects of alcohol *per se* (e.g., if consumed in a solitary neutral setting by the average drinker) are generally diffuse and nonspecific. This observation, coupled with research findings showing that many of the behavioral changes attributed to alcohol can also be produced by a nonalcoholic placebo drink, provide strong support for the influence of both set and setting as determinants of the drug experience. Attributions of causality may influence one's set or outcome expectancies in a feedback loop operation. Based on observations and personal experiences, one comes to expect or believe that a drug "causes" a certain outcome (X); if X occurs after the drug is consumed, this is taken as evidence that X is "caused" by the drug. In this sense, outcome expectancies often operate in a manner similar to that of self-fulfilling prophecies.

Before leaving the topic of outcome expectancies, one final question must be addressed. Is there a possible physiological basis for the expectancy or placebo effect found in the balanced placebo design alcohol studies? Classical conditioning theory suggests that this may indeed be the case. Since individuals who drink regularly are frequently exposed to both unconditioned stimuli (the pharmacological properties of alcohol) and conditioned stimuli associated with drinking (drinking setting and associated cues), it seems reasonable to assume that a placebo beverage (expect alcohol–receive placebo) will serve as a conditioned stimulus to elicit a conditioned state of arousal or intoxication. Just as Pavlov's dogs learned to salivate at the sound of a bell that had been previously associated with a food reward, so the experienced drinker may achieve a conditioned high when presented with the cue properties (sight, smell, taste, etc.) of a drink, regardless of whether the drink actually contains alcohol. Further research is needed to clarify the impact of classical conditioning in balanced placebo studies. It is possible, for example, that the placebo condition elicits some form of conditioned compensatory response that is opposite in direction to the unconditioned drug response (cf. Siegel, 1977, 1979).

The balanced placebo design is an ideal research vehicle to investigate the role of classical conditioning as a possible determinant of drug effects. The four cells of the design provide adequate control for assessing the effects of both *conditioned stimuli* (CS) and *unconditioned stimuli* (UCS). Using alcohol as an example, the design permits evaluation of both UCS and CS effects combined (expect alcohol–receive alcohol), CS alone (expect alcohol–receive placebo); UCS alone (expect placebo–receive alcohol), and a control group in which neither UCS nor CS are presented (expect placebo–receive placebo). Research using this paradigm may show, for example, that a placebo drink (expect alcohol–receive placebo) acts as a conditioned stimulus to elicit a conditioned response of diffuse physiological arousal. The individual may then label this reaction as one of mild intoxication and attribute alcohol as the "cause" of these feelings. Other behaviors (increased aggression, sexual arousal, etc.) which then occur may also be attributed to alcohol.

From this perspective, the possibility of a classically conditioned arousal state with subjects who are led to believe that they are consuming alcohol is consistent with this attributional analysis. Conditioning theory predicts a conditioned arousal reaction only in the expect alcohol conditions, and not in the expect tonic–receive alcohol condition. In both of the expect alcohol groups in the balanced placebo design, a state of arousal is elicited that can then be attributed to the ingestion of alcohol. Since in the studies reviewed by Marlatt and Rohsenow (1980) there was rarely any significant difference between the expect alcohol–receive alcohol and the expect alcohol–receive placebo conditions, it may be the case that the effects of alcohol *per se* on arousal, in the absence of a congruent expectancy set, are diffuse and relatively minimal in impact. At low dose levels at least, the effects of alcohol in the expect no alcohol–receive alcohol condition may be insufficient to produce an associated cognitive appraisal of having consumed any alcohol at all.

ATTRIBUTIONS

GENERAL DEFINITION

I recently took a friend to a restaurant to sample some Pacific Northwest seafood. To start off the dinner we ordered fresh oysters on the halfshell. As our conversation turned to more personal issues, I noticed tears coming to my friend's eyes. I immediately became sympathetic and attentive, commenting that, "Things have been pretty upsetting in your life lately." "What makes you say that?" my friend queried. "Well, you're obviously upset," I replied, as I began settling into a therapist role. "I don't know about being upset, but have you tried any of this horseradish with your oysters? It's so strong, it brings tears to my eyes." We both laughed and went on to discuss how easy it is to make errors in attribution when trying to understand causes of behavior—both with others as well as with oneself.

Attribution theorists study the process of inferred causality individuals engage in while attempting to "explain" the reasons why an individual (the self or others) behaves in a given way. Originating with the works of Heider (1958), attribution theory has received wide attention in recent years by social psychologists interested in social perception (e.g., Jones & Nisbett, 1972; Kelley, 1967, 1971) and achievement behavior (Weiner, 1974; Weiner, Frieze, Kukla, Reed, Rest, & Rosenbaum, 1971). The literature in this area has expanded at such a rapid rate that three volumes have appeared recently with the title *New Directions in Attribution Research* (Harvey, Ickes, & Kidd, 1976, 1978, 1981). Attribution theory has also been applied by clinical psychologists to the analysis of deviant behavior such as depression (Abramson, Seligman, & Teasdale, 1978; Janis & Rodin, 1979).

The purpose of this section is to discuss the implications of attribution theory for relapse prevention. The section begins with a description of an initial theoretical model of attributional effects associated with the first lapse or violation of an abstinence rule, the AVE, as first presented in the literature (Marlatt, 1978). Then follows a discussion of recent advances in attribution theory that have important implications for the understanding of the relapse process. Using this new information as a guide, the concept of the AVE is reformulated and expanded, potential cognitive components of a first lapse are analyzed in detail, and the possible attributions that the individual can make about the "causes" of the lapse are also investigated. Predictions are made about the types of attributions made and how they may determine whether the lapse either escalates into a full-blown relapse or remains a "single slip."

THE ABSTINENCE VIOLATION EFFECT: INITIAL FORMULATION

When the AVE concept was first introduced (Marlatt, 1978), it was described as a possible common *psychological* reaction among individuals who had violated a self-imposed abstinence rule. In Chapter 2, we presented a description by one of our problem drinker clients (Miss L) of her intense physical and psychological reactions to her first drink after almost 2 months of abstinence. Since her drink was a gin and tonic that contained little more than 1 oz of alcohol, it seems unlikely that the alcohol itself triggered such a wide range of reactions, and Miss L herself vacillated between attributing the experience to physical or psychological factors ("I am not entirely sure whether or not I imagined some of the physical effects, perhaps because of guilt, or if it was real"). Although adherents of the disease model of alcoholism have focused on the physiological effects of alcohol as the major precipitating factor in relapse, the AVE was introduced to highlight the influence of the psychological–emotional reactions triggered by an initial lapse. From this point of view, it may have been Miss L's *guilt* that exacerbated the "potency" of the drink and its effects on her (headache, stuffy nose, tangled thoughts, and abrasive actions).

The idea that the AVE might be a common psychological reaction to violating an absolute rule was supported by our investigations of a wide variety of relapse episodes with addictive behaviors in addition to problem drinking, including cases in which no actual drug was involved—e.g., violations of a strict dietary regimen and relapses among compulsive gamblers who were members of Gamblers Anonymous (GA). Many of these reactions appeared similar in nature to those the author studied in problem drinkers or heroin addicts. In one recent study, a significant proportion (30%–40%) of high-frequency gamblers were even found to demonstrate withdrawal-type symptoms (depressed mood, irritability, restlessness, etc.) upon cessation of gambling when they became members of GA (Wray & Dickerson, 1981). Note, for example, the account given by a member of GA describing his reactions to his first gambling lapse after a period of abstinence:

I knew I was doing something I shouldn't have been doing. Nevertheless, I felt powerless, like there was nothing I could do to stop it. I had been contemplating it for a long time and I don't think I realized the severity of it 'til it was too late. I had tremendous guilt about it. It doesn't matter whether the bet lost or won—the damage was done. (Cummings, Gordon, & Marlatt, 1980, p. 314)

In our initial review two features stood out: most individuals reported feelings of guilt or self-blame, and/or reactions of emotional conflict and agitation. It is important to note that these reactions were described most often by individuals who went on to experience a full-blown relapse after the first slip. As we shall emphasize later in this section, the type of reaction experienced and the attributions made by the individual to account for the lapse may determine, in part, whether or not the initial lapse leads to a relapse regardless of the nature of the substance or activity involved. How the individual copes with the AVE itself is also of crucial importance in this regard.

The AVE concept was first described in a paper presenting a cognitive-behavioral account of the relapse process in alcoholics:

To account for the similarity of the relapse process across different consummatory behaviors, we have postulated a common cognitive denominator: the Abstinence Violation Effect (AVE). (The term itself was first introduced by John L. Rogers, a student in an alcoholism seminar given at the University of Washington.) The AVE is postulated to occur under the following conditions: (a) The individual is personally committed to an extended or indefinite period of abstinence from engaging in a specific behavior; (b) The behavior occurs during this period of voluntary abstinence. The intensity of the AVE will vary as a function of several factors, including the degree of commitment or effort expended to maintain abstinence, the length of the abstinence period (the longer the period, the greater the effect), and the importance or value of the behavior to the individual concerned. We hypothesize that the AVE itself is characterized by two key cognitive elements: (1) A cognitive dissonance effect (Festinger, 1957, 1964), wherein the occurrence of the previously restricted behavior is dissonant with the cognitive definition of oneself as abstinent. Cognitive dissonance is experienced as a conflict state, and under what most people would define as guilt for having "given in to temptation." (2) A personal attribution effect (cf. Jones, Kanouse, Kelley, Nisbett, Valins, & Weiner, 1972), wherein the individual attributes the occurrence of the taboo behavior to internal weakness or personal failure (e.g., to "lack of willpower" or "insufficient personal control" over one's behavior), rather than to external situational or environmental factors. (Marlatt, 1978, pp. 297–298)

Implicit in this initial formulation of the AVE is a two-stage process: (1) To the extent that people attribute the first lapse to internal personal causes such as lack of willpower, they will feel powerless to regain control and keep the lapse from escalating into a relapse. (2) The guilt and conflict associated with this attribution of self-blame have motivational or drive properties (as postulated in Festinger's cognitive dissonance theory) that energize behaviors or changes in cognitions designed to reduce the aversive state of dissonance or conflict. If an individual feels that the lapse has "blown it" and made it technically impossible to regain abstinence (now violated), one way of reducing the dissonance is to redefine oneself as "relapsed" (or addicted, or a victim of disease mechanisms beyond personal control) and allowing one's behavior to go "out of control" (e.g., binge eating or loss of control reactions).

Since the original formulation of the AVE appeared, attribution theory has undergone considerable growth and redefinition and has served as the impetus of numerous research studies in social psychology. The following material provides a review of those areas of contemporary attribution theory relevant to the analysis of the AVE.

RECENT DEVELOPMENTS IN ATTRIBUTION THEORY

Weiner (1972, 1974, 1976) is among the forefront of investigators who have applied the principles of social perception and attributional processes to human motivation, particularly with regard to achievement motivation. Along with Atkinson (1964), Weiner's attributional analysis is integrated within an *expectancy–value theory of motivation.*

Expectancy–value theorists maintain that the intensity of aroused motivation is determined jointly by the expectation that the response will lead to the goal and by the attractiveness of the goal object. The greater the perceived likelihood of goal attainment and the greater the incentive value of the goal, the more intense is the presumed degree of positive motivation. (Weiner & Litman-Adizes, 1980, p. 39)

As is clear from the foregoing statement, Weiner's approach is primarily cognitive; along with other cognitive theorists (e.g., Estes, 1975), Weiner believes that behavior is guided by cognitive processes and that individuals are best described as seekers and processors of information. Unlike Schachter (1964), who has argued that emotional states of arousal become interpreted by subsequent cognitive labeling processes, Weiner aligns himself with investigators such as Lazarus (1966) and Valins (1966) who hold that cognitions are "necessary and sufficient causes of emotion" (Weiner, Russell, & Lerman, 1978, p. 84). The notion that emotional states are primarily determined by cognitive processes ("you feel the way you think") is also shared by contemporary cognitive-behavior therapists such as Ellis (1974) and Beck (1976; Beck, Rush, Shaw, & Emery, 1979).

In addition to the assumption that cognitive processes determine affective reactions, these theorists also assume that certain cognitions interlock with each other. In particular it is felt that attributions of causality have an influence on subsequent expectations of future performance capabilities in similar situations (cf. Abramson, Garber, & Seligman, 1980; Abramson et al., 1978). As will be discussed in greater detail below, the degree to which attributions shape subsequent expectations increases when attributions associated with prior task performance are linked with internal or stable factors (e.g., lack of ability or personal shortcomings) as opposed to external or transient factors (e.g., specific environmental constraints, bad luck, etc.). Expectations shaped by prior attributions will influence the extent to which performance in a similar task is enhanced or debilitated. Attributions of causality for past performance are among the primary determinants of self-efficacy judgments for future performance in similar situations. Low self-efficacy associated with personal helplessness, for example, leads to a variety of performance deficits. "The attribution predicts the recurrence of the expectations whereas the expectation determines the occurrence of the helplessness deficits" (Abramson et al., 1980, p. 18).

Attributional Dimensions of Causality in Achievement Tasks

In his initial analysis of perceived causality in achievement-related contexts, Weiner (1972, 1974) postulated four causes that individuals may use to explain a prior success or failure in a given task: level of *ability*, the amount of *effort* expended, degree of *task difficulty*, and the direction of experienced *luck*. Although other perceived causes of success and failure exist (e.g., fatigue, mood, illness, etc.), Weiner has found that the first four causes listed are those most frequently perceived in achievement settings in this culture.

Weiner (1974) described a three-dimensional taxonomy that subsumes the perceived causes of success and failure. These causal dimensions are "second-order concepts" used by attribution theorists to organize the causal concepts of the layperson and are not intended to represent the "first-order" attributions given by the "naive" individual. The first dimension, *locus of causality*, refers to the internal versus external description of causes described originally by Rotter (1966) in his analysis of locus of control. "Ability, effort, mood, and patience, for example, are properties internal to the person; whereas task difficulty, [and] luck . . . are external or environmental causes" (Weiner *et al.*, 1978, p. 61). The second dimension, *stability*, characterizes perceived causes along a continuum ranging from stable (invariant) to unstable (variant):

Ability, the difficulty of the task, and patience are likely to be perceived as relatively fixed, whereas luck, effort, and mood are more unstable: Luck implies random variability; effort may be augmented or decreased from one episode to the next; and mood typically is conceived as a temporary state. (Weiner & Litman-Adizes, 1980, p. 38)

Locus of causality and stability are thought to be orthogonal or independent dimensions.

The third dimension is termed *controllability* by Weiner, although others have referred to it as intentionality (Maselli & Altrocchi, 1969). This dimension refers to causes that are perceived as being either under volitional control or uncontrollable. The dimension of controllability is not independent from the dimensions of locus of causality or stability:

Intentionality implies volitional control, which implies instability. Unstable causes need not be perceived as controllable (e.g., fatigue and mood), but causes subject to volitional control are likely to be perceived as unstable. Furthermore, effort is the single internal cause that appears to be under volitional control. . . . (Weiner *et al.*, 1978, p. 61)

Other theorists have suggested additional causal dimensions that may be important in attributional analyses. In the reformulation of learned helplessness theory presented by Abramson and her colleagues (Abramson *et al.*, 1978, 1980), attribution theory plays a central role. These authors have suggested the addition of a *global–specific* dimension, described as orthogonal to the locus of causation and stability factors: "Global factors affect a wide variety of outcomes, but specific factors do not. A global attribution implies that helplessness will occur across situations, whereas a specific attribution implies helplessness only in the original situation" (Abramson *et al.*, 1978, p. 57).

In addition, these authors have redefined the criteria for making internal versus external attributions of causality. Unlike Heider (1958) and Rotter (1966), who defined internal factors as those that reside "within the skin" of the individual and external factors as those that reside "outside the skin," Abramson and her colleagues posit the *self versus other dichotomy* as the central criterion for internality–externality.

When individuals believe that outcomes are more likely or less likely to happen to themselves than to relevant others, they attribute these outcomes to something about themselves—internal factors. Conversely, when individuals believe that outcomes are as likely to happen to themselves as to relevant others, they make external attributions. (Abramson *et al.*, 1980, p. 9)

The "relevant other" concept refers to either one's friends or peers (vs. a "random other" individual or group) or to one's ideal self. The self–other distinction is at the basis of the difference between what these authors refer to as *personal versus universal helplessness*:

Universal helplessness is characterized by the belief that an outcome is independent of all of one's own responses as well as the responses of other people [e.g., "No one, including myself, could have passed that difficult exam"]. Personal helplessness, on the other hand, is the case where the individual believes that there exist responses that would contingently produce the desired outcome, although he or she does not possess them [e.g., "Although other people seem to be doing OK on this exam, I seem to be failing"]. (Abramson *et al.*, 1980, p. 11)

It is hypothesized that personal helplessness leads the individual to make *internal* attributions, whereas universal helplessness leads to *external* attributions. As we shall see later, this distinction has important implications for understanding the conditions under which some people "set up" relapse situations in such a way as to avoid making internal attributions (or accepting personal responsibility) for their actions.

Another attributional dimension, that of *importance*, has been suggested by Miller and Norman (1979). Importance refers to the value or meaning the person assigns to an event and is thought to primarily influence the magnitude of the affective and performance deficits associated with the attributional process. A related dimension has been described by Wortman and her colleagues: an individual may assign a "philosophical" reason for an event's occurrence that gives the event a special meaning in contrast to focusing on the "mechanical causality" of the incident itself.

A person who was paralyzed by a drunken driver may make an external, unstable specific attribution (the other driver was drunk). The person may simultaneously conclude, however, that God had a reason for the accident because God wanted him or her to slow down, or that the accident was deserved because he or she had done a lot of bad things in life. Both the *mechanical and philosophical levels of causality* may influence the person's subsequent reactions to the uncontrollable event. (Wortman & Dintzer, 1978, p. 78; italics added)

Wortman also makes a distinction between *immediate versus prior causality*:

When asked to make a causal attribution for his or her performance, a person may identify an immediate cause for the outcome. However, causes can also have causes . . . and the prior causes may be a more important determinant of subsequent deficits than the immediate ones . . . A person who is exhausted because of staying out too late at a party may respond differently from a person who is exhausted because he or she has chronic leukemia. (Wortman & Dintzer, 1978, p. 79)

Before turning to the topic of how attributions for failure or success influence emotions, cognitions, and performance, a few final points concerning attribution theory need to be made. First, there is some evidence that suggests that *attributions for failure may change over time*. An individual who makes an internal attribution for failure that leads initially to feelings of guilt and shame may shift to an external attribution (e.g., blaming others or particular external events) over time, particularly if the shift is "face-saving" in its effects (cf. Lazarus, 1966; Wicklund, 1975). Second, *attributions may differ depending on whether they are made by the individual "actor" or by an observer*. Jones and Nisbett (1972) have shown experimentally that an individual actor leans toward interpretations of causality based on external or environmental contingencies, whereas passive observers are more likely to see the behavior as stemming from the actor's internal dispositions or traits. Finally, evidence exists showing that individuals differ with regard to their *attributional style* or tendency to give similar causal attributions across a variety of life situations; attributional styles may also differ between men and women and across different cultural groups (cf. Ickes & Layden, 1978).

Affective Consequences of Causal Attributions

Weiner has stated in several of his writings that the affective or emotional impact of any event depends on the locus of causality dimension of causal ascription. One experiences increased positive or negative affect when causal attributions are made to internal factors; external attribution diminishes the degree of emotional impact. According to Weiner:

Pride and shame, as well as interpersonal evaluations, are absolutely maximized when achievement outcomes are ascribed internally and are minimized when success and failure are attributed to external causes. Thus, success attributed to high ability or hard work produces more pride and external praise than success that is perceived as due to the ease of the task or good luck. In a similar manner, failure perceived as caused by low ability or lack of effort results in greater shame and external punishment than failure that is attributed to the excessive difficulty of the task or bad luck. In sum, locus of causality influences the affective or emotional consequences of achievement outcomes. (Weiner, 1976, p. 183)

Weiner reviews a series of research studies showing that attributions for failure result in greater emotional impact when the perceived cause is ascribed to *lack of effort* rather than to lack of ability. Although both effort and ability are internal factors, Weiner states that "effort attributions elicit moral feelings—trying to attain a socially valued goal is something that one 'ought' to do" (Weiner et al., 1978, p. 65). Also, since effort is believed to be under greater volitional control than ability, it is associated with more intense affective reactions; ability is perceived as relatively nonvolitional and stable over time. In one study, Weiner and his colleagues asked subjects to describe their affective reactions to descriptions of failure experiences associated with various causal factors (reported in Weiner *et al.*, 1978). The results showed that ascription of failure to lack of effort generated reactions of *guilt and shame*. The most dominant affective reactions to failure given a lack of ability, on the other hand, were feelings of incompetency and inadequacy.

If effort is considered under volitional control, failure ascribed to lack of effort is more likely to elicit reactions of perceived loss of control. The relation between internal attributions for failure and loss of control experiences has also been emphasized by Wortman and Brehm (1975):

Individuals who attribute their failure to exert control to their own shortcomings may be more affected by loss of control than those who make attributions to external factors. If we assume that individuals are motivated to view themselves positively, and avoid self-attributions that reflect negatively on their self-esteem . . . we might expect that individuals who attribute failure to exert control to their own shortcomings will react more intensely than those who make external attributions of causality. (p. 321)

Attributions of self-blame and associated perceptions of loss of control are hardly conducive to the performance of adequate coping skills. Perceived loss of control is equivalent to low self-efficacy; individuals who feel they have "lost control" and blame themselves for this shortcoming are unlikely to harbor expectations of increased coping capacity. In a study of victims of serious accidents (e.g., auto accidents and injurious falls), Bulman and Wortman (1977) found that over half of the sample blamed themselves for the accident—especially if they were alone at the time of the accident and had voluntarily chosen the activity in which they were engaged. The extent to which self-blame interfered with subsequent coping depended on whether the accident victim believed that future events were changeable or controllable. In a related study reported by Abrams and Finesinger (1953), personal attributions for uncontrollable negative outcomes were found to impair coping. Cancer patients who reported attributions of self-blame and feelings of guilt and inferiority were less likely to cope effectively with their condition.

Perceptions of loss of control and/or inability to cope are also considered central concepts in the reformulation of learned helplessness theory (Abramson *et al.*, 1978, 1980). The cornerstone of the learned helplessness hypothesis is that learning that outcomes are uncontrollable (i.e., a perception of noncontingency between an individual's response and the desired outcome) results in three deficits: motivational, cognitive, and emotional. Mere exposure to uncontrollability is not sufficient to produce helplessness; the individual must come to *expect* that future outcomes are uncontrollable for the deficits to occur. Helplessness is described as the basis of at least one kind of depression: "When highly desired outcomes are believed improbable or highly aversive outcomes are believed probable, and the individual expects that no response in his repertoire will change their likelihood (helplessness), depression results" (Abramson *et al.*, 1978, p. 68). In addition to depressed affect, helplessness also is associated with decreased motivation to initiate voluntary responses (a consequence of the expectation that responding is futile) and deficits in cognition (difficulty in learning that responses produce outcomes).

The distinction between personal and universal helplessness has already been noted. Personal helplessness is associated with another deficit, low self-esteem. The distinction between personal and universal helplessness is based on social comparison (comparison of self vs. other). Abramson *et al.* (1980) state that

individuals who believe that desired outcomes are not contingent on responses in their repertoire, but are contingent on responses in the repertoires of relevant others, will show lower self-esteem than will individuals who believe that desired outcomes are neither contingent on acts in their own repertoire nor contingent on acts in the repertoires of relevant others. (p. 16)

In other words, if the person feels that the response is controllable in general (i.e., that relevant other people could exercise control by engaging in the desired response), but that the desired outcome is not contingent upon the individual's own responses, personal helplessness and decreased self-esteem will result.

Of the four attributional causes described by Weiner (effort, ability, task difficulty, and luck), *effort* is the one cause that is considered readily controllable, since it is unstable (changeable), internal, and specific in terms of the attributional dimensions described above. Personal helplessness attributed to lack of effort elicits a particular form of self-esteem deficit, according to Abramson *et al.* (1978): ". . . we note that the phenomena of *self-blame, self-criticism, and guilt* (a subclass of the self-esteem deficits) in helplessness (and depression) follow from attribution of failure to factors that are considered controllable. Lack of effort as the cause of failure probably produces more self-blame . . ." (p. 62; italics added). These authors define *failure* itself as a subset of personal helplessness associated with "unsuccessful trying" (p. 55) or lack of effective effort. The degree to which helplessness deficits, including decreased self-esteem, generalize across situations and over time depends on the attributional dimensions involved for a particular act:

An attribution to global or stable factors predicts that the expectation [of uncontrollability] will recur even when the situation changes or even after a lapse of time, respectively. Alternatively, an attribution to specific or unstable factors predicts that the expectation need not recur when the situation changes or after a lapse of time, respectively. (Abramson *et al.*, 1980, p. 18)

There are numerous empirical findings that provide support for the preceding analysis (see reviews by Garber & Seligman, 1980; Kirschenbaum & Tomarken, 1982; McFarland & Ross, 1982). Depressed individuals, for example, have been shown to make internal, global, and stable attributions for failure on various experimental tasks; success experiences are more likely to be attributed to external, specific, and unstable attributions (Hammen & Krantz, 1976; Klein, Fencil-Morse, & Seligman, 1976; Rizley, 1978). Rizley's (1978) findings also support Beck's (1967) hypothesis that depressed individuals exaggerate their causal responsibility for failure experiences and deny causal responsibility for evaluatively positive events. Recent studies with alcoholic patients show that alcoholics tend to make greater internal attributions for their own drinking than do nonalcoholic control subjects (Vuchinich, Bordini, Tucker, & Sullwold, 1982).

Attribution Processes and Emotional Exacerbation of Dysfunctional Behavior

The foregoing heading is the title of a paper by Storms and McCaul (1976), who describe a theoretical model showing how internal attributions for dysfunctional behavior serve to exacerbate or increase subsequent occurrences of the same behavior. This theory has important implications for understanding how an initial slip or lapse may escalate into a full-blown relapse.

In terms of this model, an individual observes some unwanted or uncomplimentary aspect of his own behavior for which he makes a dispositional self-attribution. This self-attribution often takes the form of inferences about real or imagined inadequacies, psychological disorders, character flaws, lack of self-control, personality deficits, deviant tendencies, and so on. These negative views of the self give rise in turn to a variety of unpleasant emotions—anxiety, guilt, frustration, perhaps even self-hatred. These emotions, then, promote increases in emotional behaviors which began the whole process. For convenience, we can refer to this syndrome as exacerbation and propose two essential steps in the model. First, attribution of dysfunctional behavior to negative dispositions in the self produces an increased emotional state. Second, increased emotionality exacerbates the occurrence of some dysfunctional behaviors. (Storms & McCaul, 1976, pp. 147–148)

The model presented by Storms and McCaul draws upon Duval and Wicklund's (1972) theory of *objective self-awareness*. This theory states that at any one time an individual is in one of two conscious states: attention is either directed inward toward the self (objective self-awareness) or directed outward toward the environment (subjective self-awareness). The distinctiveness of one's behavior determines whether attention is focused inward or outward; to the extent that one's behavior stands out, is noticeably different, or unique, the individual is pushed toward objective self-awareness. Objective self-awareness usually leads to increased negative affect to the extent that the individual compares his or her own behavior at the time to internalized standards of ideal behavior. This theory is similar to the cybernetic model of self-attention processes developed by Carver and his colleagues (Carver, 1979; Carver & Scheier, 1981, 1983). As noted by Wicklund (1975):

We assume that the person in self-reflection will typically find shortcomings in himself. If the dimension of occupational success is the focus of attention, discrepancies will be found between attainment and aspiration. Similarly, when the obese individual focuses on his eating habits he will discover that his gluttony falls short of the ideal abstinence. (p. 234)

Research designed to test the predictions of the theory has shown that objective self-awareness associated with a negative discrepancy (based on a comparison between actual and ideal self-image or behavior) elicits negative affect, often in the form of self-criticism or lowered self-esteem (Duval & Wicklund, 1972; Wicklund, 1975). Researchers in this area stress the need for *immediate* assessment of these self-image changes since self-criticism may be followed by attempts to reduce self-blame:

It should be noted that self-focused attention has two potential outcomes when that attention is inescapable. First comes a self-critical reaction, manifested in an increased sense of responsibility for unwanted outcomes. But there should be an accompanying motivation to reduce this discrepancy and if there is a viable means of accomplishing this, objective self-awareness may ultimately result in decreased self-blame. This, of course, would follow the initial reaction, which is one of heightened self-blame. (Wicklund, 1975, p. 244)

Commenting further on the negative affect elicited by objective self-awareness, Storms and McCaul (1976) point out that perceived *loss of control* is one of the most damaging consequences:

The objective self-awareness state enhances a tendency to make dispositional self-attributions of inadequacies and lack of control. Emotionally, the state is aversive, unpleasant, and affectively negative. If the objectively self-aware individual is psychologically upset by dispositional attributions of inadequacy, he may be even more traumatized by implications that he has lost self-control. In terms of exacerbation cycles, an examination of examples and case studies . . . suggests that one of the most damaging effects of self-attribution is a perceived loss of control. (pp. 149-150)

Anxiety will increase even further with perceived loss of control if the individual anticipates stressful consequences that are likely to occur as a result of this inadequacy.

The anxiety and other negative affect states serve to exacerbate the unwanted dysfunctional behaviors that initially triggered the objective self-awareness experience. Storms and McCaul describe three aspects of anxiety that may produce this exacerbation effect: (1) increased physiological arousal that may impede adequate performance; (2) anxiety acting as a drive state to energize overlearned, dominant, habitual responses—the higher the level of anxiety, the more likely dominant, habitual responses will be emitted over any other responses (cf. Spence & Spence, 1966); (3) increased covert verbalizations of self-depreciation that distract the individual and have a debilitating effect on performance. The drive properties of anxiety and their energizing effects on habitual behaviors have particularly important implications for addictive behaviors, as Storms and McCaul (1976) point out: ". . . behaviors which are habitual, well-learned responses may be increased by anxiety. This category may include various addictions, alcoholism, overeating, and perhaps other typical responses to stressful situations" (p. 154). Commenting on alcoholism as an example, these authors state:

> If the drive properties of anxiety can be generalized to emotional behaviors, as we have suggested, exacerbation cycles should occur whenever an individual has a dominant emotional response to a particular situation. Paradoxically, when the individual becomes concerned about changing that emotional response, if his concern takes the form of increased anxiety, he is even less likely to succeed . . . [when] the alcoholic is made more aware of the unattractiveness of his drunken behavior, he becomes more anxious. Unfortunately, his habitual response to anxiety is to reach for another drink. (Storms & McCaul, 1976, p. 153)

Recent research has supported the assumption noted in the preceding paragraph that self-attention (objective self-awareness) intensifies negative affect, particularly in those individuals with low self-efficacy or negative failure expectancies (Carver, Blaney, & Scheier, 1979; Kirschenbaum & Tomarken, 1982).

THE ABSTINENCE VIOLATION EFFECT: A REFORMULATION

In this section, the concept of the AVE is reformulated based on the theoretical developments in attribution theory described above. In this analysis, relapse is viewed as a two-stage process. The first stage consists of the initial lapse or slip; whether or not the lapse is followed by "loss of control" (leading to a full-blown relapse) in the second stage will depend to a large extent on the individual's perceptions of the cause of the first lapse. The section begins with a discussion of the implications of choosing abstinence as a self-control requirement or rule. Potential determinants of the initial lapse are then reviewed and placed within an attributional framework. The consequences of various perceived causes of the first slip are discussed, drawing upon recent developments in theories of attribution and self-awareness. Finally, a potential prototype for the AVE based on the biblical treatment of temptation is presented.

Abstinence as a Potential Determinant of Relapse: Reactance Effects

Webster's New Collegiate Dictionary (1983) defines "abstinence" as "1: voluntary forbearance esp. from indulgence of an appetite or craving or from eating some foods: abstention 2: habitual abstaining from intoxicating beverages." The verb *abstain* carries this definition: "to refrain deliberately and often with an effort of self-denial from an action or practice." It is important to note that these definitions stress the "voluntary" or "deliberate" component of abstinence often associated with an "effort of self-denial." For most individuals, adherence to abstinence requires a voluntary effort of self-denial—usually conceptualized as *willpower*. The consequences of attributing failure to maintain abstinence to a lack of willpower will be reviewed shortly.

In the realm of addictive behaviors, abstinence may be applied in an *absolute* sense as a restriction against *any* use of a particular substance (e.g., to abstain from all use of alcohol or tobacco), or in a *conditional* manner, as with individuals who are attempting to control their behavior in certain situations or under certain conditions (e.g., a dieter refrains from eating certain foods or from consuming more than a predetermined caloric level; or a client in a controlled drinking program abstains from alcohol in certain situations or after a preset consumption level has been obtained). Even when abstinence is applied only under certain conditions, however, the basic requirement remains an absolute one: to refrain from *any* activity that would violate the abstinence rule. There can be no "exceptions" under this absolute abstinence rule. Abstinence is a dichotomous, all-or-none requirement in the eyes of most individuals—one is either abstinent or nonabstinent; it is impossible to be in both states at once. Furthermore, once the border is crossed, there is no going back. In the strictest sense, even a slight excursion over the border (a single puff on a cigarette or the first sip of an alcoholic beverage) is sufficient to violate the absolute requirement of abstinence. Or to put it in the words of an acquaintance who tried unsuccessfully to abstain from the use of marijuana: "One toke over the line and I was a goner."

The absolute requirement of abstinence as a self-control goal may in itself increase the probability that a lapse will escalate into a complete "loss of control" relapse. There are several good reasons why this may be the case. Unlike other achievement goals, such as learning a new skill or changing one's behavior in therapy, the goal of abstinence allows no room for error: 'one strike and you're out!" Just as there are no "degrees" of abstinence (either one is or one is not), individuals often come to see relapse in the same dichotomous way: if one is not abstinent, one must therefore be relapsed. Treatment program philosophies often set up this all-or-none dictum, presumably to convince the patient of the necessity to remain abstinent and that *any* violation of this requirement will result in total banishment to "Relapse-land." (An example of this banishment occurred recently in Seattle when a director of a local alcoholism treatment program was fired from his job because he was seen in a restaurant drinking a glass of wine.) Traditionalists in the addictions field do not readily accept the fact that there can be "degrees" of relapse, ranging from a single lapse to periods of nonproblem consumption and/or uncontrolled use. The recent uproar about the results of the Rand reports (Armor, Polich, & Stambul, 1978; Polich, Armor, & Braiker, 1981) showing that a significant proportion of previously treated alcoholics engaged in nonproblem drinking over a 4-year period testifies to this dichotomous rigidity; by definition, *any* drinking in a "recovering" alcoholic is tantamount to total relapse (cf. Marlatt, 1983). Repeated exposure to this party line by patients in treatment is likely to set up a powerful outcome expectancy that may act as a self-fulfilling prophecy propelling the individual to "loss of control" once any violation of abstinence occurs. Imagine if the same absolute requirement of error-free performance were applied to the acquisition of any other new skill—this would be akin to expecting a music student to sit down at the piano for the first time and play flawlessly without a single missed note!

A second important reason why an abstinence requirement may increase the probability that a lapse will snowball into a relapse involves the "forbidden fruit" phenomenon and the subjective experience of deprivation of freedom that is associated with this condition. Just as the ex-marijuana smoker referred to above told me that "grass is much greener on the other side of the abstinence fence," so the ex-alcoholic or restricted dieter may experience enhanced attraction to the now-forbidden substance or activity. In recent years, a body of research and theory has been developed that deals with the effects of being deprived of personal freedom to choose among available alternative courses of action. The theory of *psychological reactance* (Brehm, 1966; Brehm & Brehm, 1981) "holds that a threat to or loss of freedom motivates the individual to restore that freedom. Thus the direct manifestation of reactance is behavior directed toward restoring the freedom in question" (Brehm & Brehm, 1981, p. 4). The requirement of abstinence obviously eliminates one's freedom to engage in the taboo behavior; the eliminated freedom may lead to a state of reactance and enhanced attraction of the forbidden activity. According to Brehm and Brehm (1981), "The arousal of reactance . . . is maximal when a freedom is eliminated altogether. That is, even when there is no way to restore the freedom, reactance is aroused and has the consequence of making the lost option more desirable" (p. 4). Mahoney and Mahoney (1976) coined the term "cognitive claustrophobia" to refer to a similar subjective reaction experienced when one's available options or choices are curtailed (e.g., going on a diet).

One of the possible consequences of reactance is a desire to test one's personal control as an attempt to regain the lost freedom imposed by abstinence. *Testing personal control* is one of the high-risk situations for relapse described in Chapter 2. "Control" in this sense implies freedom to choose. Brehm and Brehm (1981) have stated in this regard that

control is the ability to affect the probability of occurrence of a potential outcome. To the extent that one has this ability, one has a freedom. To the extent that this ability is reduced, exercise of the freedom is made more difficult. Hence, reduction in control arouses reactance, and reactance impels the individual to try to restore control. (p. 6)

Attempts to restore perceived control can take several forms. Wortman and Brehm (1975) list three possibilities. (1) The individual attempts to engage in the eliminated behavior (e.g., testing personal control by having the first drink, cigarette, etc. after a period of abstinence). (2) The individual engages in related behaviors that suggest, by implication, that one could engage in the eliminated behavior (e.g., an abstinent drinker may choose to hang around bars and taverns; an ex-smoker may exercise his or her freedom to indulge in other addictive behaviors such as overeating, increased drinking, or the use of other drugs such as marijuana). (3) The individual experiences hostile or aggressive feelings toward the perceived "responsible agent" (if the person feels that the abstinence rule has been imposed on the basis of pressure from family members or treatment staff, he or she may express anger toward these individuals—e.g., by dropping out of treatment). Feelings of hostility and anger have been found, in fact, to be one of the most frequent high-risk situations associated with relapse. According to the above analysis, the source of much of this anger (at least for some individuals) may stem from reactance elicited by the absolute abstinence rule.

What if the individual attempts to restore perceived freedom by engaging in the previously taboo behavior? To the extent that the individual experiences an AVE reaction (described in detail below), accompanied by internal attributions of guilt, self-blame, and perceived loss of control, he or she may give up and stop trying. In other words, the end result of testing personal control (motivated by reactance) may be a learned helplessness reaction in which the person comes to expect that the outcome (e.g., controlled use without loss of control) is basically uncontrollable. Evidence in support of this two-stage process (reactance followed by helplessness) has been reviewed by Wortman and Brehm (1975). In their account, "helplessness training" involves experiences that lead the individual to expect that the desired outcome (e.g., moderation) is basically uncontrollable. Because of the influence of prior beliefs (e.g., that one drink will lead to a drunk) and subsequent attributions (e.g., guilt and perceived loss of control following attempts to test personal control), the individual may give up trying and succumb to the relapse process:

If a person expects to be able to control or influence outcomes that are of some importance to him, finding those outcomes to be uncontrollable should arouse psychological reactance. Thus, among individuals who initially expect control, the first few trials of helplessness training should act as a threat to their freedom. They should experience increased motivation to exert control, and improved performance should occur. The more important the uncontrollable outcome, the more reactance should be experienced. But despite his increased motivation to do so, the individual comes to learn through extended helplessness training that he cannot control the outcome. *When a person becomes convinced that he cannot control his outcomes, he will stop trying.* (Wortman & Brehm, 1975, p. 308)

Potential Determinants of the Initial Lapse

Before discussing the various attributions that individuals might use to explain the "cause" of a lapse, let us briefly review the potential determinants or antecedents as viewed by an objective observer. The perceived cause of a lapse given retrospectively by the individual who has experienced the lapse may or may not correspond with the determinants as viewed by an outside observer (cf. Jones & Nisbett, 1972). An objective observer may come up with very different perceptions of the antecedents of a lapse than those perceived by the individual under observation. It should be emphasized that of all the potential antecedents described below, only a subset may be involved in the determination of any one particular relapse episode. Different antecedents may interact in a unique manner for any given individual. In addition, some of the antecedents are *proximal* (immediate precipitating factors involved at the time of the lapse) and others are *distal* (factors that occur earlier in the time sequence); this distinction is similar to the immediate versus prior analysis of causation described by Wortman and Dintzer (1978).

In describing the potential determinants, we will modify the attributional system introduced by Weiner (1974, 1976). As will be recalled, Weiner described four attributional factors: effort, ability, task difficulty, and luck; the first two factors are considered internal (within the person) and the latter two external (outside the person). These factors can be modified to fit the relapse process in the following manner. In terms of the two internal factors, "effort" refers to *motivational and incentive factors* (including initial commitment and the influence of positive outcome expectancies) and "ability" refers to the individual's repertoire of *coping skills*. For the external factors, "task difficulty" includes elements of the *high-risk situation* (stress, social factors, availability of substance), and "luck" refers to *factors perceived as beyond one's control* (e.g., the influence of physical dependency and withdrawal). Each of these four factors may involve several component elements, as indicated below. The external factors are described first, followed by the two internal factors.

HIGH-RISK SITUATIONS
(parallel to Weiner's external task-difficulty factor)

Descriptions of high-risk situations associated with relapse (e.g., negative emotional states, interpersonal conflict, social pressure, etc.) are presented in Chapter 2. The difficulty of these external tasks varies as a function of the degree of stress or challenge to the individual's continued adherence to abstinence. The most stressful high-risk situations include those situations that previously (prior to abstinence) were associated with the occurrence of the addictive habit as an attempt to cope with stress. Situations such as negative emotional states and interpersonal conflict are more stressful from this perspective than other situations (e.g., enhancing positive states). The presence of social support (individuals who provide support or encouragement) lessens the risk involved; absence of social support increases risk. Similarly, the presence of individuals who are engaging in the taboo behavior and the availability of the substance or activity involved will also enhance risk. Social or situational constraints, on the other hand, may decrease the probability of a lapse. Factors included in the category of high-risk situations are external determinants, since they exert immediate influence in the precipitation of a lapse. Unless preventive actions are taken to avoid high-risk situations, this factor can be considered to be uncontrollable and unstable (situations change over time).

FACTORS PERCEIVED AS BEYOND ONE'S CONTROL
(parallel to Weiner's external luck factor)

Although an individual could conceivably attribute a lapse to an episode of "bad luck" (e.g., "Just before my first drink, a black cat crossed my path"), luck can hardly be considered a viable determinant in the eyes of an objective observer. Personal misfortune or bad luck may be perceived retrospectively as a "cause" of why a particular high-risk situation occurred, however, by the individual involved in the lapse. There are other factors in addition to luck that are usually considered to be beyond one's personal (internal) control and that may serve as actual antecedents or determinants of relapse. These factors include the influence of physical dependency or withdrawal—often perceived as uncontrollable symptoms of an underlying addictive mechanism or disease state. Despite attributional frameworks that focus on the internal causation of physical craving, recent evidence suggests that cravings and urges are often elicited by conditioned stimuli in the external environment. Although the role of physical dependency and/or withdrawal has yet to be thoroughly investigated as a determinant of relapse, most of the research reviewed elsewhere in this book suggests that physical dependency plays a relatively minor role except during the period immediately following cessation of drug use. Factors in this category may be considered uncontrollable external factors by an objective observer since they are usually considered to be beyond the individual's personal (internal) control. They are also proximal and unstable; the immediate effect changes over time.

MOTIVATIONAL AND INCENTIVE FACTORS
(parallel to Weiner's internal effort factor)

There are several motivational factors to be considered in this category, ranging from the influence of relatively distal events to proximal factors that are active at the time the lapse occurs. The strength and degree of overtness of one's prior *commitment* to the goal of behavior change (cf. Levy, 1977) can be considered as an important distal factor (since presumably the commitment to abstain or to moderate one's behavior is made some time prior to the lapse); the prior commitment may serve as a proximal determinant, however, if the individual brings the commitment factors (e.g., the consideration of positive and negative outcomes) to mind in the high-risk situation. The strength of one's commitment often shifts or changes as time passes; the initial commitment may be weakened by subsequent events and experiences.

Psychological reactance to the perceived loss of freedom associated with adherence to an abstinence regimen may motivate the individual to test control (attempt to reassert freedom). The probability of a lapse increases with the degree of reactance, as indicated in the previous section.

Another factor that will influence motivation is the individual's *lifestyle balance*: One who feels deprived of personal rewards (too few "wants" among too many "shoulds") may succumb to the lure of immediate gratification associated with an addictive substance or activity (see Chapter 5). Fatigue and illness are additional lifestyle factors that may have a negative effect on one's motivation to abstain. Similarly, the use of psychoactive drugs such as alcohol or marijuana may increase the probability of relapse with other behaviors (e.g., eating or cigarette smoking). An ex-smoker who has consumed alcohol at a party, for example, may be more vulnerable to relapse because of alcohol's effects on motivation and decision making.

Motivation may also be affected by the individual's beliefs and outcome expectancies about the effects of the initial lapse: strong positive outcome expectancies (e.g., craving for the immediate effects) may outweigh the previous motivational constraints associated with negative expectancies about the long-range effects of indulgence. Similarly, beliefs about the inevitability of loss of control as a consequence of a slip will also influence the probability that a relapse will occur. Some or all of the above motivational factors interactively determine the degree of effort the individual will "put forth" in the temptation situation. Motivational factors can be considered controllable, internal, and unstable determinants (acting in both distal and proximal manner).

COPING SKILLS
(parallel to Weiner's internal ability factor)

The extent to which motivational effort is translated into effective action or ideation will depend on the individual's repertoire of coping skills. Unlike Weiner's ability factor in achievement settings (in which the ability of intelligence is considered an internal, stable, and uncontrollable factor), coping ability is an internal *controllable* (unstable) factor. Individuals are capable of acquiring new skills to cope with high-risk situations. Coping skills are also situation-specific; one may have acquired the skill to refuse drinks in a social situation but may be unable to cope constructively with feelings of frustration and anger. The individual's perceived ability to cope with various high-risk situations is reflected in situation-specific self-efficacy judgments.

Consequences of Attributions of Causality for the Initial Lapse

The probability that an initial lapse will be followed by further use of the substance or involvement in the addictive activity depends to a large degree on the type of attribution made. In contrast with the determinants listed above, which an independent observer might identify, the individual who has the first slip may retrospectively attribute its cause to one or more of the following factors.

HIGH-RISK SITUATIONS

It is hypothesized that attributions of causality for the initial lapse to external situational or environmental factors will decrease the probability of further use, relative to other attributional factors (cf. Kirschenbaum & Tomarken, 1982). Because high-risk situations are considered external factors, there will be less self-blame and guilt associated with the lapse. The individual may be able to perceive the situation as a unique and specific event, an exception to the "general rule" of abstinence. Because of this situation-specificity, the probability decreases that the individual will over-generalize the effects of a single lapse to *all* situations. For example: One ex-smoker commented that "Just because I had a slip while visiting with an old friend who still smokes, doesn't mean that I can now smoke in other situations. This was a special isolated case." Self-efficacy judgments across other high-risk situations need not drop just because a lapse has been experienced in one particular kind of situation. The individual who focuses on situational factors is more likely to conclude, "It's not my fault; I slipped in this one situation, but I can learn from this experience. How can I cope more effectively with this type of situation in the future?" Thus, although a particular high-risk situation may be seen as uncontrollable, situations change (unstable factor), thereby increasing the sense of future controllability.

The degree of stress experienced in the high-risk situation is another factor that may influence the probability of relapse. In situations of high stress (e.g., intense negative emotional states, personal crises, etc.), it is more likely that the individual will attribute greater coping powers to the addictive habit when a lapse occurs (e.g., "I don't think I could have made it through the divorce hearing without a cigarette"). In contrast, a relatively low-stress event (e.g., smoking with an old friend or while on vacation) may decrease the likelihood that the lapse will escalate into further use—providing the individual makes an appropriate situational attribution.

FACTORS PERCEIVED AS BEYOND ONE'S CONTROL

It is hypothesized that attribution of causality to factors such as an underlying physiological addiction or the pharmacological effects of a drug will *increase* the probability of relapse. To believe that a lapse is the result of physical craving stemming from a disease or addictive mechanism is to attribute the lapse to internal, uncontrollable, stable, and global factors. Some individuals who have undergone a treatment program for their addiction problem may attribute the emergence of craving to the fact that the effects of treatment have "worn off" or that treatment has failed. When the individual perceives this to be the case, the lapse and the events that follow are no more subject to volitional control than the symptoms of any other physiological or genetic disorder. Research has shown, related to this point, that individuals who are given a biological explanation of a mental disorder (e.g., that the problem is due to genetic and/or somatic causes) are less likely to cope constructively with subsequent problems than individuals provided with a social learning model of etiology (Farina, Fisher, Getter, & Fischer, 1978; Fisher & Farina, 1979).

From the disease model perspective, the "symptom" of the underlying disorder is defined as "loss of control." How can then one exert control over a loss of control reaction associated with physical craving and/or the effects of a drug? Although the emphasis on the physical basis of uncontrollability may to some extent alleviate the individual from feelings of guilt or self-blame for the lapse, the overall impact of such an attribution is to surrender one's control to overpowering physiological/pharmacological forces. The expectation of regaining control in the future (self-efficacy) will be low in this case, since the powers of the addiction or disease are thought to be independent of situational or temporal changes (especially when the underlying mechanism is perceived to be a "progressive disease").

MOTIVATIONAL AND INCENTIVE FACTORS

It is hypothesized that attributing the cause of a lapse to motivational deficits will also *increase* the probability of relapse. This hypothesis is consistent with theory and data reviewed earlier showing that attributions associated with lack of effort are more likely to elicit feelings of self-blame, guilt, and perceived loss of control. It seems important, however, to modify this hypothesis to some degree. Lapses attributed to deficits in *willpower* (a stable, global deficit) will make it more difficult to resume control than attributions that focus on transitory fluctuations of perceived effort (an unstable, specific deficit). Although all attributions to motivational deficits are usually considered internal and controllable, those associated with deficiencies in willpower may have the greatest negative influence, particularly for those individuals who consider *willpower to be a stable personality trait or disposition*. Many people believe that willpower is a constitutional character trait—that some individuals are by nature "strong-willed" while others are lacking in willpower and are more likely to give in to temptation. If an individual attributes a lapse to a global deficiency in willpower (a personality trait deficiency), the probability of relapse will increase in comparison with someone who attributes the lapse to a temporary lack of effort (e.g., due to the effects of lifestyle imbalance, fatigue, or illness).

Social comparison processes are also important in the analysis of willpower deficits. To the extent that a person believes that relevant other people have the willpower to resist temptations that the individual has difficulty with, a *personal helplessness* reaction will be elicited. For example, a person might conclude: "I must really be lacking in willpower, since I was the only person at the dinner party who lit up a cigarette; everyone else seems to show much greater control." Research shows that the belief that others have greater willpower than oneself may be spurious or inaccurate. People are more likely to explain the behaviors of other individuals in terms of the influence of personality traits or dispositions—even though the observed individuals may attribute their own behavior to entirely different causes (cf. Jones & Nisbett, 1972). Attributions of a willpower deficit may be far fewer or less intense, on the other hand, in situations perceived as very difficult or extremely tempting for relevant others as well as for oneself. In such cases of *universal helplessness*, everyone is equally tempted, and the individual does not "stand out" as an exception. For example, a person attending a festive New Year's Eve party who experiences a drinking lapse when offered an inviting glass of champagne may conclude: "Everyone else is drinking, why shouldn't I?" In this case, it seems unlikely that the individual would attribute the lapse to a willpower deficit to the same extent that one might if no one else were drinking at the party.

Personal helplessness reactions are also more likely to occur with individuals who experience a lapse in a failed attempt to "test personal control." Testing personal control is more likely to be attempted by individuals who show heightened psychological reactance to the requirement of absolute abstinence. Tests of willpower that fail lead to attributions of "lack of willpower" and a perceived inability to cope with reactions to the initial lapse. To the extent that the individual perceives the desired outcome (to exercise control as an expression of restored "freedom") as uncontrollable, personal helplessness and loss of control will follow.

Finally, a lapse may be attributed to the motivational deficit of *commitment*. The effects of giving up on one's initial commitment to abstinence will vary as a function of whether the commitment is given up in its entirety ("I changed my mind and am going to be a smoker again") or only partially in the form of an exception or "time out" from the general rule of abstinence ("This slip is an exception to my overall commitment to abstinence"). Of critical importance here is whether the change in commitment is made *prior to or following the lapse.* Changes in commitment that are made well in advance of the lapse and include plans to make up for the exception are less likely to result in a total relapse than attributions made just after the lapse has occurred. An individual who claims, after the fact, that the lapse was due to a change in commitment ("I changed my mind and decided to drink") is probably motivated by a desire to "save face" and attribute the lapse to a last minute decisional change. Such individuals are more likely to relapse since it will be more difficult for them to reaffirm their initial commitment to abstinence.

COPING SKILLS

According to our hypothesis, attributing the cause of a lapse to a deficit in coping skills *decreases* the probability of a relapse. Unlike the global concept of willpower, coping skills are specific to the high-risk situation involved. Coping skills are also controllable: new skills can be acquired to cope with future high-risk situations. A failure attributed to a coping deficit in a specific high-risk situation is less likely to be generalized to *all* potential high-risk situations, since different skills are required for each category of risk. A failure to cope with interpersonal conflict on one occasion does not imply that one is less likely to cope successfully in social pressure situations, for example. Unlike the "all-or-none" flavor of willpower, there are many diverse coping skills and the temporary ineffectiveness of one does not mean that all the others have failed.

The Reformulated Abstinence Violation Effect: Definition and Summary

The AVE is assumed to occur under the following conditions: The individual is personally committed to an extended or indefinite period of abstinence and a lapse occurs during this time period. The AVE is a cognitive–affective reaction to an initial slip that influences the probability that the lapse will be followed by an increased use of the substance or activity. Rather than an all-or-none reaction, the AVE is a dimensional construct: the greater the AVE, the greater the probability of relapse or an exacerbation effect following the initial lapse. There are two components to the AVE: a cognitive attribution as to the perceived cause of the lapse coupled with an affective reaction to this attribution.

An increased AVE is postulated to occur when the individual attributes the cause of the lapse to internal, stable, and global factors that are perceived to be uncontrollable (e.g., lack of willpower and/or the emergence of the symptoms of an underlying addictive disease). The intensity of the AVE is decreased, however, when the individual attributes the cause of the lapse to external, unstable (changeable), and specific factors that are perceived to be controllable (e.g., a transitory deficit in coping with a specific high-risk situation). Although coping is considered to be an "internal" factor (within the individual) the emphasis here is on the external situation that is rendered "controllable" through the exercise of coping skills.

How does the AVE increase the probability of relapse? When a lapse occurs, the individual's attention is directed inward, shifting to a state of objective self-awareness (Duval & Wicklund, 1972) or increased self-attention (Carver & Scheier, 1981, 1983). The lapse is evaluated in terms of the individual's degree of responsibility for the event; it is as if the individual asks why the lapse occurred (cf. Abramson *et al.*, 1978). If the attribution is directed toward external, unstable, and specific factors (e.g., a momentary lapse in coping with a specific high-risk situation), the AVE will be minimal or decreased and the individual will retain a perception of control (self-efficacy will remain relatively unaltered). If, on the other hand, the individual attributes the lapse to internal, dispositional factors, he or she will experience a negative emotional reaction. Objective self-awareness theory holds that this negative affect is elicited by a comparison of one's immediate behavior (the lapse) to internalized standards of ideal behavior (to maintain abstinence). The larger the perceived discrepancy between the actual behavior and the idealized standards, the greater the reactions of guilt and self-blame. Relevant to this point, drinkers who are rated as high in "self-consciousness" (more susceptible to objective self-awareness) may drink more following a failure experience or be more prone to relapse when confronted with negative self-relevant events than drinkers who are rated low in self-consciousness (cf. Carver & Scheier, 1983; Hull & Young, 1983). If the attribution for the lapse is made to internal, stable, and global factors (e.g., lack of willpower or to physical addictive disease mechanisms), perception of increased loss of control (decreased self-efficacy) will also occur. The experience of guilt, self-blame, and perceived loss of control is an aversive, unpleasant state that has motivational or energizing properties. This aversive reaction is similar to Festinger's description of cognitive dissonance in which the individual experiences a dissonant conflict between one's ideal self-image (abstinence) and one's discrepant behavior (the lapse). The resulting state of dissonance serves to motivate cognitive or behavioral responses designed to reduce this conflict (Festinger, 1964; Steele, Southwick, & Critchlow, 1981).

The aversive affective reaction increases the probability that the dysfunctional behavior that triggered the reaction (the lapse) will increase (a relapse will occur), in line with the emotional exacerbation effect described by Storms and McCaul (1976). One or both of the following mechanisms may occur to produce this exacerbation effect; the first is a behavioral reaction and the second is primarily cognitive. (1) *Behavioral reaction*: The negative reactions (increased guilt, frustration, and anxiety) will energize the overlearned, dominant, habitual response (cf. Spence & Spence, 1966), and the old addictive habit pattern is more likely to occur. To the extent that the individual has learned to rely upon the addictive habit as an attempt to cope with similar negative emotional reactions in the past (e.g., drinking to cope with feelings of guilt or anxiety), the exacerbation effect is even more likely to occur. This reaction may snowball into a vicious circle in which the person attempts to cope with the reactions to the initial slip by repeating this same dysfunctional behavior; a total relapse or binge reaction may then occur. (2) *Cognitive reaction*: The individual may attempt to cope with the negative emotional conflict state and perceived loss of control by cognitively redefining the self-image to bring it in line with the ongoing dysfunctional behavior. Depending on the person's belief system, he or she may redefine the self as an addict or victim of a disease state beyond self-control. The definition of self as a helpless victim is consistent with this experience of loss of control and may lead the individual to "give up" altogether. Perception of uncontrollability (personal helplessness) increases the exacerbation effect.

The exacerbation effect, in summary, is associated with an oscillation of perceived control (as illustrated in Chapter 1 in Figure 1-5). The perception of control that exists prior to the initial lapse oscillates to the other extreme in which the individual's perception is one of loss of control. Perception of loss of control is the central factor in the AVE concept.

Because an intense AVE reaction involves attributions that are internal, stable, and global, the individual is likely to show a generalized decrement in expectations of future coping (Abramson *et al.*, 1978). The effects of a single slip are more likely to generalize across situations and over time. Deficits in willpower and/or being caught in the clutches of an addictive disease are transsituational; differences in specific high-risk situations are of little import from this global perspective. From the global viewpoint, "one swallow *does* make a summer" (the specificity of each situation is "wiped out" through the global generalization effect). The overall effect is similar to a confabulatory whole response (*dW*) on the Rorschach in which the individual generalizes from one small detail on the inkblot to define the whole percept.

An important additional factor to be considered as a potential determinant of relapse is the *subjective effect of the substance or activity* following the initial lapse. While these effects will differ with the type of drug or other activity, many drugs act in such a way as to produce an initial high or state of arousal—the excitatory rush associated with the first phase of the biphasic drug reaction. The initial rush may be even more intense due to the decreased tolerance associated with a prolonged period of abstinence. The increase in physiological arousal may be labeled by the user as a feeling of enhanced power or control. To the extent that this reaction occurs, the use of the substance to counter the individual's prior feelings of low self-efficacy in the high-risk situation is strongly reinforced. Perceptions of the substance or activity as an effective coping strategy may be particularly enhanced in stressful high-risk situations associated with the initial lapse. Once the stress of the situation has subsided, the individual may make a spurious attribution to the drug as the main stress-reducing agent. Even though the stress associated with the high-risk situation will eventually subside whether or not the individual resorts to drug use as a coping strategy, the drug may end up receiving the greatest "credit" for the reduction in stress (e.g., "I could not have made it through that crisis without a cigarette"). The substance used may also contribute to a greater probability of relapse because of the deleterious effects of some drugs on information processing, decision making, or the individual's ability to execute an adequate coping response.

Temptation in the Garden of Eden: A Prototype for the Abstinence Violation Effect?

Why, one may ask, do people often respond with such self-blame and guilt to a single transgression of abstinence? What is the underlying basis of this essentially moralistic and judgmental reaction? Such reactions to these acts of transgression are based on many factors including personal experience, the observation of others (family, peers, media figures), stories, legends, and myths (e.g., fairy tales with a clear "moral to the story"), and religious teachings. Of all these potential determinants, many if not most of our beliefs and expectations concerning morality stem from religious beliefs. The Judeo-Christian moral teachings, the dominant religious influence in our culture, are usually based on interpretations of biblical writings. Although the Bible contains much material that is allegorical and often ambiguous, contemporary religious teachers often have no difficulty in translating it into clear and unambiguous moral commandments. A current example of this process is the "Moral Majority" movement, proponents of which are unambiguously clear about what is "right" and "wrong" in the realm of human behavior.

Prior to the advent of the disease model of alcoholism, excessive drinking was considered to be a moral sin—a sign of moral depravity or spiritual weakness. Descriptions of drinking as a sinful behavior were promulgated in the late nineteenth and early twentieth centuries by members of various religious temperance movements (e.g., the Women's Christian Temperance Movement). Prior to the activities of the Temperance Movement, a force that eventually led to the adoption of Prohibition in the United States, the consumption of alcohol was not necessarily considered to be a sinful act (Levine, 1983).

Excessive use of alcohol came to be viewed as a sin primarily because of the apparently *voluntary* nature of drinking behavior. Since drinking appears to most observers to be under voluntary control, excessive consumption was thought to be a result of the individual's inability to exercise voluntary restraint or control. As a result, the problem drinker was viewed in the same light as others who seemed unable or unwilling to resist temptation, such as criminals and adulterers. Alcoholism (or as it was then called, chronic inebriation or intemperance) became, like adultery, a "Scarlet Letter" that elicited much social disapproval and disgrace.

Is there a religious basis for this moral view? Is there a prototype of the relapse process that might help explain why a *single act* of transgression is associated with feelings of guilt, shame, and loss of control? What comes to mind here, of course, is the great abstinence violation that occurred in the Garden of Eden. Although there are many interpretations of the allegorical tale of Adam and Eve, it is interesting to view this episode within the framework of relapse theory.

As we all know, God created the Garden of Eden as the initial home for Adam and Eve. In the center of the garden, He planted two trees: the tree of life and the tree of knowledge of good and evil. God then gave Adam His first commandment in the form of an absolute abstinence rule:

And the Lord commanded the man, saying, Of every tree of the garden thou mayest freely eat: But of the tree of the knowledge of good and evil, thou shalt not eat of it: for in the day that thou eatest thereof thou shalt surely die. (Gen. 2:16–17)

It did not take very long for the first temptation to arise. After God then created Eve and all the animals and birds, one of the animals paid Eve a visit:

Now the serpent was more subtil than any beast of the field which the Lord God had made. And he said unto the woman, Yea, hath God said, Ye shall not eat of every tree of the garden? (Gen. 3:1)

For the purposes of our present analysis, we can consider the snake as a symbolic representation of an urge or craving to give in to temptation. The urge also has a strong cognitive component in the form of a seductive rationalization or argument for indulgence. The serpent's rationalization was indeed difficult to resist. After Eve told the serpent that she and Adam were forbidden to eat of the tree of knowledge on the penalty of death, the serpent replied:

Ye shall not surely die: For God doth know that in the day ye eat thereof, then your eyes shall be opened, and ye shall be as gods, knowing good and evil. And when the woman saw that the tree *was* good for food, and that it *was* pleasant to the eyes, and a tree to be desired to make one wise, she took of the fruit thereof, and did eat, and gave also unto her husband with her; and he did eat. (Gen. 3:4–6)

In one sense, the serpent offered Eve the promise of wisdom and enlightenment if she were to take the plunge. Since God Himself possessed the wisdom to know good and evil, eating from this forbidden fruit should result in Eve and Adam having this same wisdom. Such positive outcome expectancies proved too much for Eve and she took the first bite, unable to resist the temptation. Adam soon followed her lead. Although we are told nothing about Eve's interaction with Adam before he succumbed, we must assume that neither made any active attempt to cope with the forbidden fruit temptation. (Adam could, presumably, have changed the course of history at that point by a simple coping statement such as, "Not now, Eve—I'd rather have a banana.")

The reaction that followed the abstinence violation was immediate. Although some individuals might argue that there was something chemical or biological about the forbidden fruit itself (traditionally assumed to be an apple, although the specific fruit is not mentioned in the Bible) that caused the ensuing reaction (e.g., perhaps the apple had already fermented into high-proof cider), it seems more likely that the reaction was tied to the first couple's knowledge that they had committed an evil act in direct opposition to God's commandment. The reaction itself, not unlike the AVE, was characterized by self-blame and guilt. Suddenly aware that they were naked, Adam and Eve quickly dressed themselves in aprons of fig leaves. Hearing the voice of God walking in the garden, they both became ashamed and hid themselves among the trees:

And the Lord God called unto Adam, and said unto him, Where *art* thou? And he said, I heard thy voice in the garden, and I was afraid, because I *was* naked; and I hid myself. And he said, Who told thee that thou *wast* naked? Hast thou eaten of the tree, whereof I commanded thee that thou shouldest not eat? (Gen. 3:9–11)

Neither Adam nor Eve seemed willing to accept personal responsibility for the lapse:

And the man said, The woman whom thou gavest *to be* with me, she gave me of the tree, and I did eat. And the Lord God said unto the woman, What *is* this *that* thou hast done? And the woman said, The serpent beguiled me, and I did eat. (Gen. 3:12–13)

The rest is history: Adam and Eve were expelled from Paradise, man's innocence was lost forever in the fall from grace. There are, of course, many interpretations of this rich and fascinating allegory. On a fundamentalist level, the meaning is straightforward: man committed a sin by giving in to temptation and was severely punished for it. Violation of the Great Abstinence Rule resulted in guilt, shame, and eviction from the Garden of Eden. On another level, however, the end result was a kind of knowledge or discriminative awareness concerning good and evil: the birth of self-consciousness or self-awareness (cf. Wilber, 1981). Prior to the final eviction, a transaction occurred that raises the possibility that the overall outcome was a positive one: a possible "prolapse" instead of a sinful relapse:

Unto Adam also and to his wife did the Lord God make coats of skins, and clothed them. And the Lord God said, Behold, the man is become as one of us, to know good and evil: and now, lest he put forth his hand, and take also of the tree of life, and eat, and live for ever: Therefore the Lord God sent him forth from the Garden of Eden, to till the ground from whence he was taken. (Gen. 3:21–22)

Although any parallel between Adam and Eve's experiences in the Garden of Eden and the relapse process may seem farfetched to some readers, this preliminary analysis may help explain, in part, why religion plays such an important role in certain treatment programs or self-help groups for addictive problems. Religious concepts certainly play a major role in Alcoholics Anonymous (AA) and other "Twelve Step" programs (e.g., GA, Overeaters Anonymous, etc.). These groups may be particularly attractive to individuals who experience a considerable amount of guilt or self-blame concerning their problem. Christian doctrine teaches us that man can alleviate his sense of guilt through confession of his sins and gaining forgiveness in the eyes of God or Christ. To do this, however, he must give up his sense of personal control to a "higher power." The alcoholic, for example, gives up the notion that he or she can control one's drinking and relinquishes control to a higher power. By means of this conversion of control and alleviation of personal guilt, many alcoholics have been able to stop drinking altogether.

DECISION MAKING

RELAPSE AS A DECISION-MAKING PROCESS

From a traditional disease model perspective, it makes little sense to discuss the role of decision making in relapse. Few people would suggest that the recurrence of symptoms associated with an underlying pathology such as malaria or genital herpes is brought on by a conscious choice or decision on the part of the afflicted individual. Extending this analysis to the addictive disorders, adherents of the disease model often tend to ignore or downplay the influence of higher-order cognitive processes in the precipitation of a relapse, instead emphasizing the causative influence of internal states such as physical withdrawal. With this orientation, the individual involved is likely to conceptualize a lapse as something that "just happened"—often with an emphasis on the influence of overwhelming internal or external circumstances. There is an obvious payoff associated with this explanation of relapse, since it minimizes the costs of social disapproval and self-blame associated with the taboo act and may provide a "legitimate" excuse for continuing to indulge in the activity.

From a social-learning viewpoint, however, it makes considerable sense to emphasize the influence of decision making as an important component in the chain of events that both precedes and follows the occurrence of an initial lapse. According to this approach, decision making is a key concept in both the initiation of a habit-change program (i.e., arriving at a decision to abstain from tobacco) and the "volitional breakdown" associated with relapse (Sjoberg & Johnson, 1978; Sjoberg, Samsonowitz, & Olsson, 1978). In the latter case, prior to the initial lapse, the individual is faced with a choice: to smoke or not to smoke. Although the person may not conceptualize it as a decision-making process, there are a number of choice points or forks in the road that occur in the sequence of events in any habit-change endeavor. Some of these forks or branches lead further away from situations associated with an increased risk of relapse, while others are more likely to lead closer to the brink. In this section, we will discuss the role of decision making as an important cognitive process associated with relapse. We begin with a brief overview of a conflict theory of decision making developed by Janis and Mann (1968, 1977) that has direct implications for relapse prevention. The influence of stress on decision making in high-risk situations is then discussed. The main emphasis in this section, however, focuses on the role of decision making in the covert planning or setting up of a relapse. The concept of Apparently Irrelevant Decisions, or AIDs, is described in some detail, followed by an analysis of the "downtown Reno" effect as an example of covert planning that attempts to minimize the apparent influence of personal responsibility or choice in the relapse process.

THE CONFLICT MODEL OF DECISION MAKING

In recent years, a conflict model of decision making has been developed by Janis and Mann (1968, 1977; Mann & Janis, 1982). Unlike other theoretical approaches, which attempt to predict choices people make in rational decision-making situations, the conflict model focuses on how the psychological *stress of decisional conflict* influences ways in which people go about making choices; as such, it is a theory of decision making, and not a theory of choice behavior. A central assumption in the conflict model is that the prospect of making choices that have important consequences produces stress or conflict for the individual involved.

The act of decision is viewed as a form of conflict resolution. Psychological stress arising from decisional conflict stems from two principal sources. First, the decision maker is concerned about the material and social losses he might suffer from whichever course of action he chooses—including the costs of failing to live up to prior commitments. Second, he recognizes that his reputation and self-esteem as a competent decision maker are at stake. (Mann & Janis, 1982, p. 343)

Here, the first source of conflict relates to the expected gains and losses intrinsic to the alternatives themselves—for example, the expected pleasure of immediate gratification versus the long-range health costs of resuming an addictive habit. The second source of stress concerns the expected consequences of the decision as a whole (both in terms of how one goes about making the decision and its outcome)—for example, approval or disapproval from both self and relevant others. In a recent paper, Janis (1983) has outlined the effects of social support (e.g., working with a supportive counselor) on adherence to stressful decisions such as reducing smoking or overeating.

The conflict theory proposed by these authors describes the following five different *decisional coping patterns* that people engage in when making significant decisions:

1. *Unconflicted adherence.* The decision maker complacently decides to continue whatever he or she has been doing, which may involve discounting information about risk of losses.

2. *Unconflicted change* to a new course of action. The decision maker uncritically adopts whichever new course of action is most salient or most strongly recommended.

3. *Defensive avoidance.* The decision maker escapes the conflict by procrastinating, shifting responsibility to someone else, or constructing wishful rationalizations to bolster the least objectionable alternative, remaining selectively inattentive to corrective information.

4. *Hypervigilance.* The decision maker searches frantically for a way out of the dilemma and impulsively seizes upon a hastily contrived solution that seems to promise immediate relief. The full range of consequences of the choice are overlooked as a result of emotional excitement, perseveration, and cognitive constriction (manifested by reduction in immediate memory span and simplistic thinking). In its most extreme form, hypervigilance is known as "panic."

5. *Vigilance.* The decision maker searches painstakingly for relevant information, assimilates information in an unbiased manner, and appraises alternatives carefully before making a choice. (Mann & Janis, 1982, pp. 344-345)

One of the most salient factors influencing the selection of one of these coping patterns is the degree of *stress* associated with a particular decisional conflict. Defective coping patterns are associated with both extremely low and extremely intense levels of stress, whereas intermediate levels of stress are more likely to be associated with vigilant coping and information processing. Extremely high levels of stress have a markedly disruptive effect on cognitive processes—immediate memory span is reduced, thinking becomes overly simplified, and fewer judgment categories are considered in the decision-making process. Unlike the relatively "cool" decisions related to matters of little personal importance (e.g., as in hypothetical situations or intellectual exercises), decisional conflicts with meaningful personal consequences elicit what Janis and Mann call *hot cognitions*—emotionally arousing thoughts and judgments that have considerable impact on the coping pattern employed.

MALADAPTIVE DECISIONAL COPING PATTERNS ASSOCIATED WITH RELAPSE

Of the five coping patterns outlined by Mann and Janis (1982), two seem particularly relevant to the relapse process: defensive avoidance and hypervigilance. The latter pattern may be elicited by the stress engendered by particular high-risk situations. An individual who experiences the hot cognitions associated with the stress of an ongoing high-risk situation (e.g., a heated argument with one's spouse) may show the panic reaction associated with a hypervigilant coping pattern. Instead of a careful weighing of alternatives and searching for relevant information associated with the vigilant coping pattern of decision making, the person may hastily choose to engage in an addictive behavior as a last-ditch coping effort. Both the emotional arousal and cognitive restriction associated with the stressful high-risk situation may prompt the individual to impulsively seek out a hastily contrived solution that seems to promise immediate relief.

The second maladaptive coping pattern, *defensive avoidance*, is also directly relevant to understanding the relapse process. According to Janis and Mann, there are three major forms of defensive avoidance: procrastinating, shifting responsibility onto others, and bolstering the least objectionable alternative in the decision-making process. The tactic of *bolstering* is particularly germane to relapse since it involves various defenses that enable the decision maker to construct *rationalizations* and/or to engage in *denial* regarding the alternative selected. Bolstering tactics involve distortion of the utility or value of a decisional outcome or distortion of the probability of an outcome. Examples include (1) *exaggeration*, or playing up the reward value of the favorable consequences of the chosen alternative (e.g., "This cigarette will enhance my ability to cope with this situation by greatly reducing my level of tension or anxiety"); (2) *minimization*, or playing down the magnitude of loss from unfavorable consequences of the chosen alternative (e.g., "Just having one cigarette cannot possibly cause me much harm"); and (3) *denial* of aversive feelings, for example, when an individual denies the importance of long-range negative outcomes and focuses instead on the anticipated positive immediate effects of engaging in the addictive habit. An illustration of the second example given above which has particular relevance for relapse is *minimization of social surveillance*. The person assumes "it is very likely that others will take little or no notice of his choice, and even then will place no demands on him. This tactic refers to the expectancy of being permitted to get away with something that ordinarily entails social obligations" (Mann & Janis, 1982, p. 353). The bolstering tactics associated with the maladaptive coping pattern of defensive avoidance have important implications for understanding how an individual engages in covert plans designed to "set up" a relapse.

Defensive Avoidance and the Covert Planning or "Setting Up"
of Relapses

For someone who has previously made a commitment to abstain or set strict limits on an addictive habit, the decisional process associated with the possibility of resuming the taboo behavior involves two critical conflicts. The first relates to the expected immediate and long-term gains and losses intrinsic to the alternative of either remaining abstinent or resuming the old behavior. Typically there is a conflict between the expected immediate gratification and the long-range negative health risks involved. Because of the greater incentive or motivational pull of expected immediate gratification ("relief is just seconds away"), the person may attempt to reduce the anticipated long-range costs (possible death from lung cancer, etc.) by engaging in defensively motivated rationalizations. Denial or minimization of loss is one such rationalization. The individual who is tempted to resume smoking, for example, may minimize either the *chances* of long-range negative effects (e.g., "Only those who are genetically predisposed to develop cancer will get it, and there is no history of lung cancer in my family") or the extent or "seriousness" of the resumptive act (e.g., "Just this one time can't possibly hurt me").

The second conflict involves disapproval or blame from both the self and significant others that the individual expects as a result of the transgression. Fear of external social disapproval is likely to be most intense for those who have made a public commitment to change or where there is a high probability of being observed by significant others while performing the taboo act. Here the tactic of minimization of social surveillance is likely to be employed, for example engaging secretly in the addictive behavior, either alone (e.g., sneaking drinks on the sly) or in a location far removed from significant others. The temptation to resume an addictive habit while on a vacation or trip, especially if one is travelling solo, often stems from this factor.

For most people, however, it is almost impossible to resume an addictive habit on a more-or-less regular basis without being observed sooner or later by relevant others in the form of friends, family, or acquaintances. How can one minimize the risk of negative social disapproval and/or self-blame under these circumstances? The anticipated blame and guilt will increase to the extent that the individual perceives the initial lapse to be the result of a "free choice" situation, that is, when there are few or no significant mitigating circumstances that one can point to as being the "cause" of the relapse. On the other hand, to the extent that the individual can come up with a cause that is perceived to be beyond one's personal control, the risk of self-blame or social disapproval is minimized. The desire to reduce self-blame and negative social sanctions may motivate the individual to engage in covert planning to set up a relapse episode that appears justified or even acceptable in the eyes of the self and significant others.

Such planning is considered to be "covert" in the sense that it is a game plan necessarily kept hidden from self and others (otherwise the "game would be up" and the person would be exposed as a manipulator). The individual involved avoids being aware of the game plan through the distorting effect of denial and other defensive avoidance strategies. As Mann and Janis state:

Occasionally, an important consideration may be temporarily preconscious, but readily accessible to consciousness if someone calls it to the decision maker's attention. . . . In exceptional instances, the individual remains unaware of an important consideration that is shaping his decision, because of the operation of repression and other psychological defense mechanisms. (1982, p. 355)

In the covert planning or setting up of a relapse episode, individuals select a high-risk situation or other "causative" element for a relapse that shifts the locus of responsibility from their own volition or free choice to an *ostensibly justifiable cause.* Justifiable causes include both internal events (e.g., addictive craving stemming from an underlying disease pathology) and external situations (e.g., an apparently catastrophic environmental event). One such strategy is to set up an *impossibly tempting high-risk situation,* the type of situation that only a "moral Superman" could resist. Earlier, in Chapter 1, we discussed such a situation in reference to the compulsive gambler who experienced a relapse in downtown Reno. How can you blame someone for gambling in Reno? "Everyone else is doing it—why shouldn't I?" In this case, our gambler has transformed the nature of the relapse episode from one in which he would have to accept maximum personal responsibility (e.g., if he began gambling in his home town of Seattle) to one in which his degree of personal responsibility is minimized. Gambling is the *norm* in Reno; it would be "abnormal" not to engage in it while there. By this gambit, the gambler lets himself off the hook, compared to the social and self-disapproval he would otherwise experience. This strategy of setting up an impossibly tempting situation brings to mind the distinction made earlier in this chapter between personal and universal helplessness (cf. Abramson *et al.,* 1978) in attribution theory. Our gambler shifted the responsibility from a personal to a universal cause by placing himself in a situation where gambling is the "universal" expectation, thereby facilitating an external attribution in place of the otherwise internal attribution associated with a "personal" causative factor.

Other impossibly tempting situations include the following examples: (1) The abstaining alcoholic who happens to find himself on a tour of a Napa Valley winery where free samples of varietal wines are offered in the tasting room. (2) The ex-smoker who ends up drinking with an old friend who pulls out a pack of Winstons, the brand they both used to smoke together in the "good old days." (3) The dieter who ends up on a Caribbean cruise ship where hopelessly tempting gourmet foods are served around the clock. (4) The pedophile who obtains a job working across the street from a school playground. (5) The "reformed" adulterer who ends up in the hotel room of an attractive member of the opposite sex while out of town on a convention trip (someone once asked: "Why do they put the Gideon Bible in the hotel *room*—it should be placed conspicuously in the lobby where it still might do some good!"). Downtown Reno situations usually do not suddenly turn up "out of the blue." Rather, the person must take a series of steps in advance in order to set up the situation. Our gambler, in order to play the slot machines, had to first travel over a thousand miles to get to Reno. In the covert planning of relapses of this kind, the person frequently will engage in a series of "mini-decisions" or Apparently Irrelevant Decisions (AIDs) to set the stage for the final act.

Apparently Irrelevant Decisions (AIDs)

Let us begin with a personal example. During my own drawn-out process of learning to stop smoking over the past several years (a skill I have finally mastered), I have had numerous opportunities to observe my own relapses. The following episode illustrates the role an AID can play in setting up a relapse. Prior to this particular occasion, I had successfully abstained from cigarettes for a period of several months. After a long series of stressful work experiences lasting for several weeks, I was scheduled to make a business trip. Arriving at the airport in Seattle about 30 minutes before the flight was to depart, I went to the airline counter to obtain a seat reservation. It was a clear day and I wanted to get a window seat so I could get a good view of Mt. Rainier and what was left of Mt. St. Helens on the flight east. "Smoker or nonsmoker?" asked the clerk. Although I had not consciously thought about smoking in several weeks, I replied: "It really doesn't matter so long as I get a window seat on the right side of the plane." The clerk checked the computer and said, "I have only one window seat left on that side—but it's in the smoking section." "That'll be fine," I said.

The airlines have a fixed ritual about when one can and cannot smoke on the plane. When you first board the aircraft, there is a strict abstinence rule in effect. Signs clearly state NO SMOKING, a rule reiterated by the flight attendant over the intercom while the plane is taxiing down the runway. Once the plane finally becomes airborne, however, it is usually only a few moments before the flight attendant announces: "The Captain has turned off the no smoking sign; you are now free to light up. The smoking section on this aircraft is in rows 21–35. . . ." In my case, while the "you are now free to smoke" announcement was being made (presumably endorsed by an authority no less than the Captain himself, since it was he who turned off the no smoking sign), the man sitting next to me immediately pulled out a pack of Camels. Along with almost everyone else in the smoking section, he lit a cigarette and took a deep, satisfying drag. All around me, folks were flicking their Bics and I was soon surrounded by the familiar pale blue cloud. Since I was still vulnerable to the old familiar aroma of tobacco smoke, the cloud filled my head with positive outcome expectancies. My neighbor, observing that I was the only person in rows 21–35 who was *not* smoking, turned to me and said, "Would you care for one?" He offered his pack, a cigarette jutting out enticingly waiting to be plucked. A quick rationalization passed through my mind: "Why not? Just one won't hurt. Besides, I deserve it—I have been working hard for days reviewing grant applications and this is my first chance to relax." "Well, thanks, I don't mind if I do," I said to my friendly companion. As with many smokers in these days of considerable antismoking sentiment, he seemed pleased with my response, as if I had communicated a sense of common brotherhood in our mutual addiction, and offered me a light. While smoking the cigarette, my mind came up with additional rationalizations in an attempt to cope with the guilt (AVE) I experienced: "Well, it's okay to do this under these special circumstances. Let's make a specific exception to the no smoking rule—while it is still not permitted to smoke while I'm on the ground, it's okay to have a cigarette now and then while I'm flying; as soon as touchdown occurs, that's it, no more." Later that day, I found myself making the following pitch: "Actually, I think it is permissible to smoke for a day or two during this trip, but only while I'm out of state. Washington, D.C. is okay since no one here really knows me, but smoking in Washington State is definitely out." And so on, until I had made enough "special exceptions" that almost any event, place, or time was covered. In all, it was several weeks before I was again off the weed.

Looking back on this episode, I can trace the origins of the relapse to the "decision" I made concerning my seat reservation at the Seattle airport. By choosing to sit in the smoking section, I took the first step in setting up a high-risk situation. The term Apparently Irrelevant Decision describes the mini-decisions that lead the individual closer to the brink of relapse. In my case, a single AID was sufficient to set up the high-risk situation (direct social pressure) for my smoking lapse. In other cases, a series of AIDs may be involved, each one moving the person a little closer, much as checker players make one move at a time as they move the checkers slowly across the board.

As is the case with the defensive avoidance coping pattern in decision making, the individual may not be fully aware of the motivation behind making an AID. It is as though the person makes a move in the direction of relapse that is "small enough" or distal enough to be apparently irrelevant both in one's own eyes and in the eyes of significant others. I chose the window seat in the smoking section because, I rationalized, I wanted to see Mt. Rainier and maybe even an eruption of Mt. St. Helens. Our gambler managed to get himself into Nevada by telling his wife that Lake Tahoe was considered to be one of the most beautiful lakes in the world, and that they should not pass up the opportunity to see it since they were in the general area anyway. If the rationalizations succeed in convincing everyone that the AID is "justified" (without triggering any alarms of guilt or embarrassment), the individual may "suddenly" be confronted with an impossibly tempting situation. "It's not my fault that this is happening," one says as the champagne is poured and the cigarettes are lit.

REFERENCES

Abrams, R. D., & Finesinger, J. Guilt reactions in patients with cancer. *Cancer*, 1953, *6*, 474–482.

Abramson, L. Y., Garber, J., & Seligman, M. E. P. Learned helplessness in humans: An attributional analysis. In J. Garber & M. E. P. Seligman (Eds.), *Human helplessness: Theory and application*. New York: Academic Press, 1980.

Abramson, L. Y., Seligman, M. E. P., & Teasdale, J. Learned helplessness in humans: Critique and reformulation. *Journal of Abnormal Psychology*, 1978, *87*, 49–74.

Ainslie, G. Specious reward: A behavioral theory of impulsiveness and impulse control. *Psychological Bulletin*, 1975, *82*, 463–496.

Armor, D. J., Polich, J. M., & Stambul, H. B. *Alcoholism and treatment*. New York: Wiley, 1978.

Atkinson, J. W. *An introduction to motivation*. Princeton, N.J.: Van Nostrand, 1964.

Bach-y-Rita, G., Lion, J., & Ervin, F. Pathological intoxication: Clinical and electroencephalographic studies. *American Journal of Psychiatry*, 1970, *127*, 698–703.

Bandura, A. Self-efficacy: Toward a unifying theory of behavioral change. *Psychological Review*, 1977, *84*, 191–215.

Bandura, A. Self-referent thought: A developmental analysis of self-efficacy. In J. H. Flavell & L. Ross (Eds.), *Social cognitive development: Frontiers and possible futures*. Cambridge: Cambridge University Press, 1981.

Bandura, A. Self-efficacy mechanism in human agency. *American Psychologist*, 1982, *37*, 122–147.

Beck, A. T. *Depression: Clinical, experimental and theoretical aspects*. New York: Hoeber, 1967.

Beck, A. T. *Cognitive therapy and the emotional disorders*. New York: International Universities Press, 1976.

Beck, A. T., Rush, A. J., Shaw, B. F., & Emery, G. *Cognitive therapy of depression*. New York: Guilford, 1979.

Berglas, S., & Jones, E. E. Drug choice as a self-handicapping strategy in response to noncontingent success. *Journal of Personality and Social Psychology*, 1978, *36*, 405–417.

Best, J. A., & Hakstian, A. R. A situation-specific model for smoking behavior. *Addictive Behaviors*, 1978, *3*, 79–92.

Bolles, R. C. Reinforcement, expectancy, and learning. *Psychological Review*, 1972, *79*, 394–409.

Brehm, J. W. *A theory of psychological reactance*. New York: Academic Press, 1966.

Brehm, S. S., & Brehm, J. W. *Psychological reactance: A theory of freedom and control*. New York: Academic Press, 1981.

Briddell, D. W., Rimm, D. C., Caddy, G. R., Krawitz, G., Sholis, D., & Wunderlin, R. J. The effects of alcohol and cognitive set on sexual arousal to deviant stimuli. *Journal of Abnormal Psychology*, 1978, *87*, 418–430.

Brown, S. A., Goldman, M. S., Inn, A., & Anderson, L. R. Expectations of reinforcement from alcohol: Their domain and relation to drinking patterns. *Journal of Consulting and Clinical Psychology*, 1980, *48*, 419–426.

Bulman, R. J., & Wortman, C. B. Attribution of blame and coping in the "real world": Severe accident victims react to their lot. *Journal of Personality and Social Psychology*, 1977, *35*, 351–363.

Cameron, D. The psychopharmacology of social drinking. *Journal of Alcoholism*, 1974, *9*, 50–55.

Carpenter, J. A. Contributions from psychology to the study of drinking and driving. *Quarterly Journal of Studies on Alcohol*, 1968, Supplement 4, 234–251.

Carpenter, J. A., & Armenti, N. P. Some effects of ethanol on human sexual and aggressive behavior. In B. Kissin & H. Begleiter (Eds.), *The biology of alcoholism* (Vol. 2). New York: Plenum, 1972.

Carver, C. S. A cybernetic model of self-attention processes. *Journal of Personality and Social Psychology*, 1979, *37*, 1251–1281.

Carver, C. S., Blaney, P. H., & Scheier, M. F. Reassertion and giving up: The interactive role of self-directed attention and outcome expectancy. *Journal of Personality and Social Psychology*, 1979, *37*, 1859–1870.

Carver, C. S., & Scheier, M. F. *Attention and self-regulation: A control-theory approach to human behavior.* New York: Springer-Verlag, 1981.

Carver, C. S., & Scheier, M. F. A control-theory approach to human behavior, and implications for problems in self-management. In P. C. Kendall (Ed.), *Advances in cognitive–behavioral research and therapy* (Vol. 2). New York: Academic Press, 1983.

Chaney, E. F., Roszell, D. K., & Cummings, C. Relapse in opiate addicts: A behavioral analysis. *Addictive Behaviors*, 1982, *7*, 291–297.

Chick, J. Is there a unidimensional alcohol dependence syndrome? *British Journal of Addiction*, 1980, *75*, 265–280.

Christiansen, B. A., & Goldman, M. S. Alcohol-related expectancies versus demographic/background variables in the prediction of adolescent drinking. *Journal of Consulting and Clinical Psychology*, 1983, *51*, 249–257.

Christiansen, B. A., Goldman, M. S., & Inn, A. Development of alcohol-related expectancies in adolescents: Separating pharmacological from social-learning influences. *Journal of Consulting and Clinical Psychology*, 1982, *50*, 336–344.

Collins, J. J. (Ed.). *Drinking and crime.* New York: Guilford, 1981.

Condiotte, M. M., & Lichtenstein, E. Self-efficacy and relapse in smoking cessation programs. *Journal of Consulting and Clinical Psychology*, 1981, *49*, 648–658.

Cummings, C., Gordon, J. R., & Marlatt, G. A. Relapse: Prevention and prediction. In W. R. Miller (Ed.), *The addictive behaviors.* New York: Pergamon, 1980.

DiClemente, C. C. Self-efficacy and smoking cessation maintenance. *Cognitive Therapy and Research*, 1981, *5*, 175–187.

Docter, R., Naitoh, P., & Smith, J. C. Electroencephalographic changes and vigilance behavior during experimentally induced intoxication with alcoholic subjects. *Psychosomatic Medicine*, 1966, *28*, 605–615.

Duval, S., & Wicklund, R. A. *A theory of objective self-awareness.* New York: Academic Press, 1972.

Eastman, C., & Norris, H. Alcohol dependence, relapse and self-identity. *Journal of Studies on Alcohol*, 1982, *43*, 1214–1231.

Ellis, A. Rational emotive therapy. In A. Burton (Ed.), *Operational theories of personality.* New York: Brunner/Mazel, 1974.

Engle, K. B., & Williams, T. K. Effect of an ounce of vodka on alcoholics' desire for alcohol. *Quarterly Journal of Studies on Alcohol*, 1972, *33*, 1099–1105.

Estes, W. K. *Handbook of learning and cognitive processes* (Vol. 1). Hillsdale, N.J.: Erlbaum, 1975.

Farina, A., Fisher, J. D., Getter, H., & Fischer, E. H. Some consequences of changing people's views regarding the nature of mental illness. *Journal of Abnormal Psychology*, 1978, *87*, 272–279.

Festinger, L. *A theory of cognitive dissonance.* Stanford: Stanford University Press, 1957.

Festinger, L. *Conflict, decision and dissonance.* Stanford: Stanford University Press, 1964.

Fingarette, H. Implications for research and action: Discussion. In R. Room & G. Collins (Eds.), *Alcohol and disinhibition.* Rockville, Md.: National Institute on Alcohol Abuse and Alcoholism, Monograph No. 12, 1983.

Fisher, J. D., & Farina, A. Consequences of beliefs about the nature of mental disorders. *Journal of Abnormal Psychology*, 1979, *88*, 320–327.

Garber, J., & Seligman, M. E. P. (Eds.). *Human helplessness: Theory and applications*. New York: Academic Press, 1980.

Garfield, Z., & McBrearty, J. Arousal level and stimulus response in alcoholics after drinking. *Quarterly Journal of Studies on Alcohol*, 1970, *31*, 832–838.

Grabowski, J., & O'Brien, C. P. Conditioning factors in opiate use. In N. K. Mello (Ed.), *Advances in substance abuse*. Greenwich, Conn.: JAI Press, 1981.

Grenell, R. G. Effects of alcohol on the neuron. In B. Kissin & H. Begleiter (Eds.), *The biology of alcoholism* (Vol. 2). New York: Plenum, 1972.

Hammen, C. L., & Krantz, S. Effect of success and failure on depressive cognitions. *Journal of Abnormal Psychology*, 1976, *85*, 577–586.

Hamwich, H. E., & Callson, D. A. The effects of alcohol on evoked potentials of various parts of the CNS of the rat. In B. Kissin & H. Begleiter (Eds.), *The biology of alcoholism* (Vol. 2). New York: Plenum, 1972.

Harvey, J. H., Ickes, W., & Kidd, R. F. *New directions in attribution research* (Vols. 1, 2, & 3). Hillsdale, N.J.: Erlbaum, 1976, 1978, 1981.

Heather, N., Rollnick, S., & Winton, M. A comparison of objective and subjective measures of alcohol dependence as predictors of relapse following treatment. *British Journal of Clinical Psychology*, 1983, *22*, 11–17.

Heider, F. *The psychology of interpersonal relations*. New York: Wiley, 1958.

Hodgson, R. J. The alcohol dependence syndrome: A step in the wrong direction? *British Journal of Addiction*, 1980, *75*, 255–263.

Hodgson, R. J., Rankin, H. J., & Stockwell, T. R. Alcohol dependence and the priming effect. *Behaviour Research and Therapy*, 1979, *17*, 379–387.

Hull, J. G., & Young, R. D. The self-awareness reducing effects of alcohol consumption: Evidence and implications. In J. Suls & A. G. Greenwald (Eds.), *Psychological perspectives on the self* (Vol. 2). Hillsdale, N.J.: Erlbaum, 1983.

Ickes, W., & Layden, M. A. Attributional styles. In J. H. Harvey, W. Ickes, & R. F. Kidd (Eds.), *New directions in attribution research* (Vol. 2). Hillsdale, N.J.: Erlbaum, 1978.

Isbell, H. Craving for alcohol. *Quarterly Journal of Studies on Alcohol*, 1955, *16*, 38–42.

Janis, I. L. The role of social support in adherence to stressful decisions. *American Psychologist*, 1983, *38*, 143–160.

Janis, I. L., & Mann, L. A conflict-theory approach to attitude change and decision making. In A. Greenwald, T. Brock, & T. Ostrom (Eds.), *Psychological foundations of attitudes*. New York: Academic Press, 1968.

Janis, I. L., & Mann, L. *Decision making*. New York: The Free Press, 1977.

Janis, I. L., & Rodin, J. Attribution, control, and decision making: Social psychology and health care. In G. C. Stone, F. Cohen, & N. E. Adler (Eds.), *Health psychology: A handbook*. San Francisco: Jossey-Bass, 1979.

Jellinek, E. M. *The disease concept of alcoholism*. New Brunswick, N.J.: Hillhouse Press, 1960.

Jones, B. M., & Vega, A. Cognitive performance measured on the ascending and descending limb of the blood alcohol curve. *Psychopharmacologia*, 1972, *23*, 99–114.

Jones, E. E., & Berglas, S. Control of attributions about the self through self-handicapping strategies: The appeal of alcohol and the role of underachievement. *Personality and Social Psychology Bulletin*, 1978, *4*, 200–206.

Jones, E. E., Kanouse, D. E., Kelley, H. H., Nisbett, R. E., Valins, S., & Weiner, B. (Eds.). *Attribution: Perceiving the causes of behavior*. Morristown, N.J.: General Learning Press, 1972.

Jones, E. E., & Nisbett, R. E. The actor and the observer: Divergent perceptions of the causes of behavior. In E. E. Jones, D. Kanouse, H. H. Kelley, R. E. Nisbett, S. Valins, & B. Weiner (Eds.), *Attribution: Perceiving the causes of behavior*. Morristown, N.J.: General Learning Press, 1972.

Kelley, H. H. Attribution theory in social psychology. In D. Levine (Ed.), *Nebraska symposium on motivation*. Lincoln: University of Nebraska Press, 1967.

Kelley, H. H. *Attribution in social interaction*. Morristown, N.J.: General Learning Press, 1971.

Kirschenbaum, D. S., & Tomarken, A. J. On facing the generalization problem: The study of self-regulatory failure. In P. C. Kendall (Ed.), *Advances in cognitive-behavioral research and therapy* (Vol. 1). New York: Academic Press, 1982.

Klein, D. C., Fencil-Morse, E., & Seligman, M. E. P. Learned helplessness, depression, and the attribution of failure. *Journal of Personality and Social Psychology*, 1976, *33*, 508–516.

Lang, A. R., Goeckner, D. J., Adesso, V. J., & Marlatt, G. A. The effects of alcohol on aggression in male social drinkers. *Journal of Abnormal Psychology*, 1975, *84*, 508–518.

Lazarus, R. S. *Psychological stress and the coping process*. New York: McGraw-Hill, 1966.

Levine, H. G. The good creature of God and the demon rum. In R. Room & G. Collins (Eds.), *Alcohol and disinhibition*. Rockville, Md.: National Institute on Alcohol Abuse and Alcoholism, Monograph No. 12, 1983.

Levy, R. L. Relationship of an overt commitment to task compliance in behavior therapy. *Journal of Behavior Therapy and Experimental Psychiatry*, 1977, *8*, 25–29.

Ludwig, A. M., & Stark, L. H. Alcohol craving: Subjective and situational aspects. *Quarterly Journal of Studies on Alcohol*, 1974, *35*, 899–905.

Ludwig, A. M., & Wikler, A. "Craving" and relapse to drink. *Quarterly Journal of Studies on Alcohol*, 1974, *35*, 108–130.

Ludwig, A. M., Wikler, A., & Stark, L. H. The first drink: Psychobiological aspects of craving. *Archives of General Psychiatry*, 1974, *30*, 539–547.

MacAndrew, C., & Edgerton, R. B. *Drunken comportment*. Chicago: Aldine, 1969.

Madden, J. S., Walker, R., & Kenyon, W. H. *Alcohol and drug dependence*. New York: Plenum, 1976.

Mahoney, K., & Mahoney, M. J. Cognitive factors in weight reduction. In J. D. Krumboltz & C. E. Thoresen (Eds.), *Counseling methods*. New York: Holt, Rinehart, & Winston, 1976.

Mandelbaum, D. G. Alcohol and culture. *Current Anthropology*, 1965, *6*, 281–294.

Mann, L., & Janis, I. Conflict theory of decision making and the expectancy–value approach. In N. T. Feather (Ed.), *Expectations and actions: Expectancy–value models in psychology*. Hillsdale, N.J.: Erlbaum, 1982.

Mardones, R. J. "Craving" for alcohol. *Quarterly Journal of Studies on Alcohol*, 1955, *16*, 51–53.

Marlatt, G. A. Craving for alcohol, loss of control, and relapse: A cognitive–behavioral analysis. In P. E. Nathan, G. A. Marlatt, & T. Løberg (Eds.), *Alcoholism: New directions in behavioral research and treatment*. New York: Plenum, 1978.

Marlatt, G. A. The controlled drinking controversy: A commentary. *American Psychologist*, 1983, *38*, 1097–1110.

Marlatt, G. A. *Alcohol, the magic elixir: Stress, expectancy, and the transformation of emotional states*. Paper presented at the Seventh Annual Coatesville Jefferson Conference, VA Medical Center, Coatesville, Pa., March 1984.

Marlatt, G. A., Demming, B., & Reid, J. B. Loss of control drinking in alcoholics: An experimental analogue. *Journal of Abnormal Psychology*, 1973, *81*, 223–241.

Marlatt, G. A., & Rohsenow, D. J. Cognitive processes in alcohol use: Expectancy and the balanced placebo design. In N. K. Mello (Ed.), *Advances in substance abuse* (Vol. 1). Greenwich, Conn.: JAI Press, 1980.

Marlatt, G. A., & Rohsenow, D. R. The think–drink effect. *Psychology Today*, 1981, *15*, 60–93.

Marlatt, G. A., & Rose, F. Addictive disorders. In A. E. Kazdin, A. S. Bellack, & M. Hersen (Eds.), *New perspectives in abnormal psychology*. New York: Oxford University Press, 1980.

Marshall, M. *Weekend warriors: Alcohol in a micronesian culture*. Palo Alto: Mayfield, 1979.

Marshall, M. "Four hundred rabbits": An anthropological view of ethanol as a disinhibitor. In R. Room & G. Collins (Eds.), *Alcohol and disinhibition*. Rockville, Md.: National Institute on Alcohol Abuse and Alcoholism, Monograph No. 12, 1983.

Maselli, M. D., & Altrocchi, J. Attribution of intent. *Psychological Bulletin*, 1969, *71*, 445–454.

McAuliffe, W. E. A test of Wikler's theory of relapse: The frequency of relapse due to conditioned withdrawal sickness. *International Journal of the Addictions*, 1982, *17*, 19–33.

McClelland, D. C., Davis, W. N., Kalin, R., & Wanner, E. *The drinking man*. New York: The Free Press, 1972.

McFarland, C., & Ross, M. Impact of causal attributions on affective reactions to success and failure. *Journal of Personality and Social Psychology*, 1982, *43*, 937–946.

McIntyre, K. O., Lichtenstein, E., & Mermelstein, R. J. Self-efficacy and relapse in smoking cessation: A replication and extension. *Journal of Consulting and Clinical Psychology*, 1983, *51*, 632–633.

Mello, N. K. Some aspects of the behavioral pharmacology of alcohol. In D. H. Efron (Ed.), *Psychopharmacology: A review of progress, 1957–1967*. Washington, D.C.: U.S. Government Printing Office, 1968.

Mello, N. K. A semantic aspect of alcoholism. In H. D. Cappell & A. E. LeBlanc (Eds.), *Biological and behavioural approaches to drug dependence*. Toronto: Addiction Research Foundation, 1975.

Miller, I. W., & Norman, W. H. Learned helplessness in humans. *Psychological Bulletin*, 1979, *86*, 93–118.

Miller, M. E., Adesso, V. J., Fleming, J. P., Gino, A., & Lauerman, R. The effects of alcohol on the storage and retrieval processes of heavy social drinkers. *Journal of Experimental Psychology: Human Learning and Memory*, 1978, *4*, 246–255.

Nathan, P. E., & O'Brien, J. S. An experimental analysis of the behavior of alcoholics during prolonged experimental drinking: A necessary precursor of behavior therapy? *Behavior Therapy*, 1971, *2*, 455–476.

O'Brien, C. P. Experimental analysis of conditioning factors in human opiate addiction. *Pharmacological Reviews*, 1976, *27*, 533–543.

Pliner, P., & Cappell, H. Modification of affective consequences of alcohol: A comparison of social and solitary drinking. *Journal of Abnormal Psychology*, 1974, *83*, 418–425.

Polich, J. M., Armor, D. J., & Braiker, H. B. *The course of alcoholism: Four years after treatment*. New York: Wiley, 1981.

Pomerleau, O. F. Underlying mechanisms in substance abuse: Examples from research on smoking. *Addictive Behaviors*, 1981, *6*, 187–196.

Poulos, C. X., Hinson, R. E., & Siegel, S. The role of Pavlovian processes in drug tolerance and dependence: Implications for treatment. *Addictive Behaviors*, 1981, *6*, 205–211.

Rada, R. T. Alcoholism and forcible rape. *American Journal of Psychiatry*, 1975, *132*, 444–446.

Reiss, S. Pavlovian conditioning and human fear: An expectancy model. *Behavior Therapy*, 1980, *11*, 380–396.

Rimm, D. C., Sininger, R. A., Faherty, J. D., Whitley, W. H., & Perl, M. B. A balanced placebo investigation of the effects of alcohol and alcohol expectancy on simulated driving behavior. *Addictive Behaviors*, 1982, *7*, 27–32.

Rist, F., & Watzl, H. Self assessment of relapse risk and assertiveness in relation to treatment outcome of female alcoholics. *Addictive Behaviors*, 1983, *8*, 121–127.

Ritchie, J. M. The aliphatic alcohols. In L. S. Goodman & A. Gilman (Eds.), *The pharmacological bases of therapeutics*. New York: MacMillan, 1965.

Rizley, R. Depression and distortion in the attribution of causality. *Journal of Abnormal Psychology*, 1978, *87*, 32–48.

Rogers, C. R. A theory of therapy, personality, and interpersonal relationships, as developed in the client-centered framework. In S. Koch (Ed.), *Psychology: A study of a science* (Vol. 3). New York: McGraw-Hill, 1959.

Rohsenow, D. J. Drinking habits and expectancies about alcohol's effects for self versus others. *Journal of Consulting and Clinical Psychology*, 1983, *51*, 752–756.

Rohsenow, D. J., & Marlatt, G. A. The balanced placebo design: Methodological considerations. *Addictive Behaviors*, 1981, *6*, 107–122.

Room, R., & Collins, G. (Eds.). *Alcohol and disinhibition.* Rockville, Md.: National Institute on Alcohol Abuse and Alcoholism, Monograph No. 12, 1983.

Ross, S., Krugman, A. D., Lyerly, S. B., & Clyde, D. J. Drugs and placebos: A model design. *Psychological Reports,* 1962, *10,* 383–392.

Rotter, J. Generalized expectancies of internal versus external control of reinforcement. *Psychological Monographs,* 1966, *80* (Whole No. 609).

Russell, J. A., & Mehrabian, A. The mediating role of emotions in alcohol use. *Journal of Studies on Alcohol,* 1975, *36,* 1508–1536.

Schachter, S. The interaction of cognitive and physiological determinants of emotional state. In L. Berkowitz (Ed.), *Advances in experimental social psychology* (Vol. 1). New York: Academic Press, 1964.

Shaw, S. A critique of the concept of the alcohol dependence syndrome. *British Journal of Addiction,* 1979, *74,* 339–348.

Shupe, L. M. Alcohol and crime. *Journal of Criminal Law, Criminology, and Police,* 1954, *44,* 661–664.

Siegel, S. Evidence from rats that morphine tolerance is a learned response. *Journal of Comparative and Physiological Psychology,* 1975, *89,* 189–199.

Siegel, S. Morphine tolerance acquisition as an associative process. *Journal of Experimental Psychology: Animal Behavior Processes,* 1977, *3,* 1–13.

Siegel, S. The role of conditioning in drug tolerance and addiction. In J. D. Keehen (Ed.), *Psychopathology in animals: Research and treatment implications.* New York: Academic Press, 1979.

Sjoberg, L., & Johnson, T. Trying to give up smoking: A study of volitional breakdowns. *Addictive Behaviors,* 1978, *3,* 149–164.

Sjoberg, L., Samsonowitz, V., & Olsson, G. Volitional problems in alcohol abuse. *Gotteberg Psychological Reports,* 1978, *8,* No. 5.

Skinner, H. A., & Allen, B. A. Alcohol dependence syndrome: Measurement and validation. *Journal of Abnormal Psychology,* 1982, *91,* 199–209.

Solomon, R. L. An opponent-process theory of acquired motivation: IV. The affective dynamics of addiction. In J. Maser & M. E. P. Seligman (Eds.), *Psychopathology: Experimental models.* San Francisco: W. H. Freeman, 1977.

Solomon, R. L. The opponent-process theory of acquired motivation: The costs of pleasure and the benefits of pain. *American Psychologist,* 1980, *35,* 691–712.

Solomon, R. L., & Corbit, J. D. An opponent-process theory of motivation: I. Temporal dynamics of affect. *Psychological Review,* 1974, *81,* 119–145.

Southwick, L., Steele, C., Marlatt, G. A., & Lindell, M. Alcohol-related expectancies: Defined by phase of intoxication and drinking experience. *Journal of Consulting and Clinical Psychology,* 1981, *49,* 713–721.

Spence, J. T., & Spence, K. W. The motivational components of manifest anxiety: Drive and drive stimuli. In C. D. Spielberger (Ed.), *Anxiety and behavior.* New York: Academic Press, 1966.

Steele, C. M., Southwick, L. L., & Critchlow, B. Dissonance and alcohol: Drinking your troubles away. *Journal of Personality and Social Psychology,* 1981, *41,* 831–846.

Stockwell, T. R., Hodgson, R. J., Edwards, G., Taylor, C., & Rankin, H. The development of a questionnaire to measure alcohol dependence. *British Journal of Addiction,* 1979, *74,* 79–87.

Stockwell, T. R., Hodgson, R. J., Rankin, H. J., & Taylor, C. Alcohol dependence, beliefs and the priming effect. *Behaviour Research and Therapy,* 1982, *20,* 513–522.

Storms, M. D., & McCaul, K. D. Attribution processes and emotional exacerbation of dysfunctional behavior. In J. H. Harvey, W. Ickes, & R. F. Kidd (Eds.), *New directions in attribution research* (Vol. 1). Hillsdale, N.J.: Erlbaum, 1976.

Tamerin, J. S., Weiner, S., & Mendelson, J. H. Alcoholics' expectancies and recall of experiences during intoxication. *American Journal of Psychiatry,* 1970, *126,* 1697–1704.

Valins, S. Cognitive effects of false heart-rate feedback. *Journal of Personality and Social Psychology*, 1966, *4*, 400–408.

Vuchinich, R. E., Bordini, E., Tucker, J. A., & Sullwold, A. F. A comparison of alcoholics' causal attributions for drinking behavior. *American Journal of Drug and Alcohol Abuse*, 1982, *9*, 95–104.

Vuchinich, R. E., & Sobell, M. B. Empirical separation of physiological and expected effects of alcohol on complex perceptual motor performance. *Psychopharmacology*, 1978, *60*, 81–85.

Webster's new collegiate dictionary. Springfield, Mass.: G. & C. Merriam, 1983.

Weiner, B. *Theories of motivation: From mechanism to cognition*. Chicago: Rand McNally, 1972.

Weiner, B. (Ed.). *Achievement motivation and attribution theory*. Morristown, N.J.: General Learning Press, 1974.

Weiner, B. An attributional model for educational psychology. In L. Shulman (Ed.), *Review of research in education* (Vol. 4). Itasca, Ill.: Peacock, 1976.

Weiner, B., Frieze, I., Kukla, A., Reed, L., Rest, S., & Rosenbaum, R. M. *Perceiving the causes of success and failure*. Morristown, N.J.: General Learning Press, 1971.

Weiner, B., & Litman-Adizes, T. An attributional, expectancy–value analysis of learned helplessness and depression. In J. Garber & M. E. P. Seligman (Eds.), *Human helplessness: Theory and applications*. New York: Academic Press, 1980.

Weiner, B., Russell, D., & Lerman, D. Affective consequences of causal ascriptions. In J. H. Harvey, W. Ickes, & R. F. Kidd (Eds.), *New directions in attribution research* (Vol. 2). Hillsdale, N.J.: Erlbaum, 1978.

White, R. W. Motivation reconsidered: The concept of competence. *Psychological Review*, 1959, *66*, 297–333.

Wicklund, R. A. Objective self-awareness. In L. Berkowitz (Ed.), *Advances in experimental social psychology* (Vol. 8). New York: Academic Press, 1975.

Wikler, A. Conditioning factors in opiate addictions and relapse. In D. Wilner & G. Kassebaum (Eds.), *Narcotics*. New York: McGraw-Hill, 1965.

Wikler, A. Symposium on conditioning and addiction. *The Pavlovian Journal of Biological Sciences*, 1976, *11*, 191–194.

Wilbur, K. *Up from Eden: A transpersonal view of human evolution*. Garden City, N.Y.: Anchor/Doubleday, 1981.

Wilson, G. T. Booze, beliefs, and behavior: Cognitive processes in alcohol use and abuse. In P. E. Nathan, G. A. Marlatt, & T. Løberg (Eds.), *Alcoholism: New directions in behavioral research and treatment*. New York: Plenum, 1978.

Wilson, G. T. The effects of alcohol on human sexual behavior. In N. K. Mello (Ed.), *Advances in substance abuse* (Vol. 2). Greenwich, Conn.: JAI Press, 1981.

Wilson, G. T., & Abrams, D. Effects of alcohol on social anxiety and physiological arousal: Cognitive versus pharmacological processes. *Cognitive Research and Therapy*, 1977, *1*, 195–210.

Wilson, G. T., & Lawson, D. M. Expectancies, alcohol, and sexual arousal in male social drinkers. *Journal of Abnormal Psychology*, 1976, *85*, 587–594.

Wolfgang, M. E., & Strohm, R. B. The relationship between alcohol and criminal homicide. *Quarterly Journal of Studies on Alcohol*, 1956, *17*, 411–425.

Woods, S. C., & Mansfield, J. C. Ethanol and disinhibition: Physiological and behavioral links. In R. Room & G. Collins (Eds.), *Alcohol and disinhibition*. Rockville, Md.: National Institute on Alcohol Abuse and Alcoholism, Monograph No. 12, 1983.

Wortman, C. B., & Brehm, J. W. Responses to uncontrollable outcomes: An integration of reactance theory and the learned helplessness model. In L. Berkowitz (Ed.), *Advances in experimental social psychology*, 1975, *8*, 278–336.

Wortman, C. B., & Dintzer, L. Is an attributional analysis of the learned helplessness phenomenon viable? A critique of the Abramson–Seligman–Teasdale reformulation. *Journal of Abnormal Psychology*, 1978, *87*, 75–90.

Wray, I., & Dickerson, M. G. Cessation of high-frequency gambling and "withdrawal" symptoms. *British Journal of Addiction*, 1981, *76*, 401–405.

Wylie, R. C. *The self-concept: A review of methodological considerations and measuring instruments*. Lincoln: University of Nebraska Press, 1974.

4

COGNITIVE ASSESSMENT AND INTERVENTION PROCEDURES FOR RELAPSE PREVENTION

G. ALAN MARLATT

This chapter is devoted to a discussion of various cognitive assessment and intervention procedures that can be applied in a Relapse Prevention (RP) program. First, the underlying rationale for adopting cognitive methods in the treatment of addictive behavior problems is presented. This is followed by an elaboration of a basic therapeutic principle: the maintenance of behavior change is enhanced to the extent that the client is provided with an understanding of the theoretical model and assumptions underlying the RP approach. By seeing the "big picture" of how the model integrates determinants of relapse with self-control procedures designed to prevent the occurrence of relapse, the client is enabled to assume personal responsibility for his or her behavior and to learn the "tools of the trade" that will facilitate successful long-term maintenance. The bulk of this chapter is devoted to descriptions of cognitive assessment and intervention procedures designed to (1) enhance *self-efficacy* concerning one's capacity to cope with high-risk situations; (2) develop techniques to deal with urges and craving experiences mediated by *outcome expectancies* of immediate gratification; (3) facilitate cognitive restructuring or reframing of causal *attributions* associated with relapse; and (4) improve *decision-making* strategies in the relapse process. The foregoing material will be presented in a metaphorical context that describes the process of habit change as an ongoing "journey"—a *process* of change over time.

RATIONALE FOR COGNITIVE INTERVENTION: TEACHING THE CLIENT THE "BIG PICTURE"

In adopting a cognitive–behavioral approach to the treatment of addictive behaviors, sooner or later one is forced to respond to the challenge of critics who argue along the following lines: "How can you justify the use of cognitive treatment methods with a problem that is primarily based on physiological responses to biochemical agents? Shouldn't we place our main focus on somatic treatment methods such as aversion therapy or the development of new therapeutic medications?" In addition to this criticism (frequently proffered by advocates of the disease model of addiction), a radical behaviorist might offer quite a different objection: "Since behaviorists in the operant tradition have argued convincingly that higher mental processes are merely epiphenomenal in nature and cannot be considered 'causes' of behavior, shouldn't we place our treatment focus on the manipulation of environmental contingencies, such as the selective application of reward and punishment, to modify the addictive behavior?"

In response to such criticisms, I am not saying that physiological processes or biochemical effects associated with drug use or other addictive behaviors are of minimal significance, nor that environmental contingencies do not exert significant influence. It is obvious to all workers in the addictions field that drugs have pharmacological properties that create significant physiological effects. Also clear to most of us is that environmental reinforcement contingencies and related stimulus cues exert considerable impact on the acquisition and maintenance of addictive behaviors. Factors both "within the skin" and "outside the skin" clearly play significant deterministic roles. In terms of human addiction problems, however, there may be an effective meta-level cognitive approach that subsumes physiological and environmental factors. A central assumption derived from this meta-level analysis is that addictive habits are governed by cognitive *perceptions* of internal and external events. In other words, how the individual cognitively perceives and reacts to both physical sensations and environmental contingencies is of central importance in understanding the development and modification of addictive habits. Viewed from this perspective, the individual's beliefs, expectations, attributions, and decision-making capacity constitute the major cognitive arena in which change occurs.

The addictions field is characterized by a mind–body dichotomy. From this either/or perspective, addictions are considered to be either primarily somatic in origin (e.g., the result of constitutional factors associated with a particular genetic pattern, underlying biological disease pathology, etc.) or due to psychological processes (e.g., learning, psychological dependence, etc.). A basic assumption associated with the RP model is that addiction is a *both/and* phenomenon—both body *and* mind are involved in an interactive reciprocal relationship. Drug use and other addictive behaviors clearly involve important somatic experiences—the physical arousal associated with the initial rush, the mediating influence of tolerance, and the pain of withdrawal. Much can be learned from the study of underlying physiological processes, such as the way in which drugs influence neurochemical transmission or impede the functioning of various physical organs (brain, liver, fetal development, etc.).

One thing is clear, however: many of the physical concomitants of addictive behaviors are experienced *subjectively* by the individual on a cognitive–affective level. The experience of getting high, for example, is a subjective affective state associated with the occurrence of pleasurable physical sensations, presumably elicited by the drug or other addictive stimuli. These subjective effects have important cognitive correlates; the individual develops preferences for the high state and will engage in instrumental behaviors in order to recreate the experience. Expectancies and attributions about the drug or other agent as the "cause" of these pleasurable experiences exert an important cognitive influence. It is not long before the individual's thoughts, feelings, choices, and overall lifestyle become increasingly dependent on the addictive experience. Eventually the person becomes "hooked" by the addiction, developing a strong psychological dependency on or attachment to the addictive substance or activity. The mind becomes victimized by the desire (craving) for immediate gratification. Pleasurable physical sensations associated with the addictive behavior become the focus of much cognitive activity. Plans and decisions become increasingly tied to expectancies of addictive experiences. Attributions about drugs or other addictive agents as the cause of desired subjective experiences become firmly entrenched. From this perspective, addiction is a physically based phenomenon that manifests itself primarily in subjective conscious experience. Along with Weil (1972) and other authors who have stressed the importance of subjective experiences in the study of drug use, we believe that the key to the addictive lock can be found in the mind.

If cognitive processes play such a key role, why cannot the addicted individual simply "decide" to abstain or moderate drug use? Most people are aware of the long-range negative consequences associated with excessive drug use, and yet these attitudes and beliefs often seem to have little or no effect on ongoing addictive habits. Two factors are important with regard to this issue: the conflict stemming from the addictive behavior itself, and the debilitating effects of drugs and other addictive activities on cognitive functioning.

Most addictive behaviors involve a *conflict of motives.* The desire for immediate gratification is often in direct conflict with a desire to avoid delayed negative effects (self- and social disapproval, long-range health risks, etc.). In psychoanalytic theory, the addictive conflict is defined as a competition between unconscious demands for immediate gratification (pleasure principle) and the awareness of the real dangers involved (reality principle). Learning theory defines the struggle involved as an approach–avoidance conflict (cf. Ainslie, 1975). Regardless of one's theoretical orientation, it seems clear that conflict often generates a variety of *defensive reactions,* many of which are cognitive in nature. Some of these defense mechanisms were described in Chapter 3 when we discussed the role of decision making in the relapse process. Janis and Mann (1977) described the negative influence of defensive avoidance in decision making. Rationalization and denial are two of the defenses often elicited in a conflictual choice situation. Individuals with an addictive habit will often attempt to minimize the conflict involved by attempting to justify the behavior (rationalization) or by becoming increasingly secretive in attempts to "hide" the significance of the behavior from both self and significant others (denial). Other defense mechanisms such as projection (seeing the problem as stemming from other people or external events) and repression (denial and complete distortion of negative events and feelings associated with the addiction) also may occur. Because of the collective impact of these cognitive defensive reactions, the individual involved is unable to gain an objective, clear view of the entire addictive process. Instead of "seeing the big picture," the person is "blinded" by the cognitive distortions and defense mechanisms associated with the conflict. One of the principal goals of cognitive therapy is to draw back the defensive "curtains" that are blocking the client's view of the truth.

The effect of drugs on cognitive functioning also interferes with clear perception. A large body of literature attests to the general conclusion that both the acute and chronic effects of many psychoactive drugs impair cognitive processes. Acute use of drugs such as alcohol and marijuana has often been found to impair memory, either through deficits in short-term memory storage (Birnbaum & Parker, 1977; Loftus, 1980) or, as in the case with alcohol, through the influence of memory blackouts (cf. Goodwin, 1977).

In addition to the acute effects, chronic drug use may have relatively long-lasting effects on brain functioning. Repeated, excessive, long-term use of alcohol, for example, has been shown to correlate with several indices of cognitive dysfunction, including impaired ability to engage in abstract reasoning, solve problems, and acquire new behavior (cf. Kleinknecht & Goldstein, 1972; Parsons, 1975; Tarter, 1975; Wilkinson & Sanchez-Craig, 1981). As the chronicity of the addictive behavior increases, so does the risk of cognitive dysfunction. In short, both acute and chronic drug effects may seriously interfere with the user's ability to cognitively appraise the addictive process.

As reliance on the addictive substance increases, and the individual comes to depend more and more on the drug or activity as a means of coping with both life's vicissitudes and the ups and downs of drug use itself, there is a narrowing of the perceptual field: the user focuses attention more on the acquisition and use of the addictive substance and less on other aspects of life. The individual can no longer see the overall pattern of what is happening, the global "forest" of addiction, as he or she becomes increasingly lost in the individual "trees" of each addictive experience.

How does an individual become lost in the forest of addiction? One relies on a variety of sources of information in order to find one's way through the journey of life. In addition to the usual social and cultural norms (both prescriptive and proscriptive), the individual comes to rely on his or her own internal feelings and emotional states as a guide to one's behavior. Affective reactions such as pride, guilt, shame, anger, fear, and love influence motivation and direction along the way. Often these internal feeling states are equated with a sense of intuition, a subjective compass that helps as a guide along the path. It is important to note that many of these emotional states are perceived in the form of various physical or somatic sensations. If attention is turned inward when one is feeling angry or frustrated, for example, one may perceive sensations of tightness, constriction, and perhaps a sense of increased heat (e.g., "burning up with anger"). When anxious or fearful, the individual may notice "falling" or "sinking" sensations in the gut, perhaps accompanied by changes in heart rate or body temperature (e.g., "cold fear"). Emotions such as love and joy, on the other hand, are often associated with sensations of lightness, increased tactile responsiveness, and perhaps a "warm glow" feeling. All of these sensations, including those experienced as aversive or unpleasant, serve an extremely useful function in guiding the direction and course of life. Negative sensations often serve as warning signals or early indicators that a change in course is necessary for both basic survival and/or psychological well-being. Positive sensations associated with emotional states such as pride or joy act as feedback cues, indicating to the individual that he or she is on the right track. Mindful attention to both positive and negative emotional states gives a sense of direction, a feeling of being "found" as opposed to "lost."

Drugs and other potentially addictive activities also elicit a spectrum of physical sensations, ranging from the highly euphoric (the initial rush or high) to the intensely dysphoric (as in the withdrawal or "abstinence agony" often associated with prolonged opiate use). As already noted in the discussion of the role of outcome expectancies (Chapter 3), addictive behavior is frequently mediated by positive outcome expectancies experienced as craving, a desire or longing for the pleasurable sensations. The intensity of this desire increases in direct proportion to the magnitude of the negative emotional state experienced by the individual prior to engaging in the addictive behavior. Although the emotional state prior to addictive use may sometimes be affectively neutral or even positive (e.g., enhancement of positive emotional states), in most cases the antecedent state is affectively negative. Research reviewed in Chapter 2, for example, testified to the salience of negative emotional states as determinants of drug use and relapse. People involved in an addictive behavior pattern becomes "lost" to the extent that they *increasingly come to rely upon the addictive activity as a means of attempting to cope with "natural" emotional reactions, especially those judged as unpleasant or aversive.* When this happens, the "signal value" of these otherwise normal emotional reactions becomes covered up or replaced by the sensations elicited by the addictive activity.

To use an analogy of the mind as a radio receiver, signals are picked up that come in from various "stations" located both inside and outside the body. The internal station that normally provides the individual with sensitive information concerning his or her affective reactions (i.e., the intuitive station) becomes overlaid with static (or is drowned out by the loud "rush" of rock music) when the "listener" takes a drug or engages in any affectively intense behavior. Sensations that normally provide directional cues become masked by the artificial sensations engendered by the addictive activity. As a result, the addicted individual loses touch with a key feedback and guidance system based on the normal experiences of everyday life. Instead of reacting to anger or fear as an important informational signal, the individual learns to "turn on" a new station that drowns out the old one. A new form of "control" over emotions is apparently acquired, since it becomes possible to alter sensations at will simply by "dropping" a drug and "turning on." Yet this control is illusory, since the person has actually lost touch with the internal guidance provided by unadulterated emotional reactions. Although seeming to have gained control, the person actually loses control and becomes lost in the process.

What can be done when one is lost in the forest? First, it is necessary to admit that one is indeed lost, and that all resources must be focused on finding a way out. For the addicted individual, this admission often is the result of a self-confrontation or "breakthrough" experience, in which the usual defensive strategies of denial and rationalization are no longer effective or utilized. Once one is committed to finding a way out of the forest, two important initial steps are necessary. The person must first try to establish a "sense of direction" to get oriented to the lay of the land. One might look for a hill or climbable tree in order to gain some overall perspective and to look for familiar landmarks or signs of civilization. Once an overall perspective is gained, it is then necessary to find a means or way of getting free—an escape route, perhaps in the form of finding a trail or following a riverbed, or devising a way of calling for help. In summary, both a commitment to getting free and a means of escape are necessary when one is lost.

The ideal solution when lost, of course, is to find the location on a *map*. A detailed map is ideal because it provides information concerning the surrounding territory. By consulting a map, it may be possible to discover just how one became lost in the first place; by carefully retracing one's steps, it may be possible to get out of the forest. Sometimes the map will indicate a short-cut to freedom—showing the locations of a nearby ranger station where assistance may be obtained. Equally important, a good map will indicate potential pitfalls, areas to avoid such as dead-end trails, dangerous cliffs, quicksand swamps, and other danger spots. One can then plan a safe route to freedom.

The primary purpose of this metaphorical excursion through the woods is to highlight a basic assumption underlying the use of cognitive strategies in relapse prevention. Basically we are assuming that the effectiveness of the various cognitive procedures described in this book (cognitive reframing, modification of outcome expectancies, imagery techniques to cope with urges, etc.) is enhanced by providing the individual with a global "map" or conceptual model of the entire addictive process. The purpose of this map or model is to give the person an overall perspective or clear view of both how one can get lost or "stuck" in an addictive trap and how one can escape. The RP approach differs from most traditional treatment programs for addictive problems in this regard. Whereas traditional programs often involve the utilization of externally applied treatment techniques designed to arrest or modify the underlying addiction (e.g., aversion therapy, dietary regimens, etc.), the RP model favors a self-management approach in which the individual is given both a theoretical overview of the addictive process and the means of escape. The advantage of this approach is that it not only assists people to escape from the immediate addictive trap, but it also enables them to keep from falling back into the trap or getting hooked on other addictive activities.

Maps and models of the big picture are essential to many of life's journeys. As is the case with lost hikers who require a map to get their bearings, there are many potentially dangerous or relatively unknown situations that we confront in life for which guidance is necessary. In Clavell's novel *Shogun*, John Blackthorn, the chief protagonist, is depicted as one of the first men to sail from Europe to Japan (Clavell, 1975). As the pilot of the ship, Blackthorn's feat of navigation was made possible by his possession of the invaluable *rutter*—a collection of maps and navigational aids obtained from others who had made the trip (or portions of it) before. Navigation across unknown and potentially dangerous waters requires both the *rutter* for global navigation and planning the overall course and the skillful use of the ship's own *rudder* for moment-to-moment adjustments in direction. The helmsman must make a pull on the wheel to avoid hitting a log or other obstacle not marked on the navigational charts. In the RP method, the rutter is the theoretical model or map that outlines the territory that must be crossed in order to attain the goal (to escape from the addictive trap); the rudder consists of the individual skills and cognitive strategies the person uses as navigational aids (e.g., making a detour so as to avoid a particularly dangerous high-risk situation).

The importance of teaching clients the big picture was first impressed on me by an experience I had during my internship in clinical psychology (1967–1968) at Napa State Hospital in California. Our internship director arranged a field trip to visit an alcoholism treatment program at another state hospital in Mendocino. According to various rumors, the program was reputed to be among the first to apply behavioral principles to the treatment of alcoholism. Since behavioral approaches in the treatment of alcoholism were relatively innovative at the time, I found myself eagerly looking forward to the field trip. I imagined scenes involving the application of aversive conditioning (the main behavioral intervention of the day), perhaps in a simulated bar setting.

When we finally arrived at the Mendocino State Hospital, one of the first sights to meet our eyes was that of a small group of patients sitting on the lawn outside the alcoholism treatment building, each with their own Skinner box and white rat. It was immediately clear from my graduate school experiences that these patients were attempting to shape operant bar-pressing responses using food pellets as the positive reinforcement. At first, this was a very puzzling sight; instead of receiving electric shocks at a simulated bar, these alcoholics were training their rats to press a bar in the Skinner box! Instead of being the "subjects" in a treatment study, these patients were playing the role of experimenter. The patients also each had their own personal copy of an operant conditioning workbook in which they recorded their observations while shaping the rats' behavior.

Confused and amused by this scene, I approached the director of the program (a bearded psychologist from San Francisco whose name I can no longer remember) and asked him to describe the rationale behind his approach. He replied that his goal was to teach his patients the principles of operant conditioning and the power of reinforcement to shape behavior. He believed that reinforcement contingencies were of central importance for the alcoholic, in terms not only of how drinking behavior is learned and maintained, but also how the application of reinforcement was an essential feature of interpersonal and social behavior. He said that the Skinner box experience teaches the alcoholic the effectiveness of positive reinforcement—that a smile or a warm handshake has the same impact on behavior that a food pellet has on a hungry rat—and also that drinking may be negatively reinforced to the extent that one drinks to try and escape or avoid unpleasant life experiences. He intended to teach his patients that these principles could be applied to their everyday life upon leaving the hospital.

Some years later, I had another experience that reminded me of the Mendocino visit. In the fall of 1980, I was asked to give a presentation at Sea Pines Behavioral Institute, located on Hilton Head Island, South Carolina. The director of the Institute is Dr. Peter Miller, an eminent behavior therapist and current Editor-in-Chief of the journal *Addictive Behaviors*. Among the programs offered by the Sea Pines Behavioral Institute is a weight-loss program based on behavioral principles. Individuals who sign up for the program spend a month or so living in the Sea Pines Plantation (luxurious condominiums located in a choice oceanside setting) while learning a variety of new self-management skills designed to teach them how to lose weight and adopt new eating patterns and other lifestyle changes (exercise, etc.) to maintain the weight loss. The program is an excellent one and is based on the latest behavioral and self-control techniques (cf. Hodgson & Miller, 1982; Miller, 1978).

I was asked to give a kind of "graduation talk" as part of a scheduled follow-up program offered to clients some months following completion of the initial treatment program. During the follow-up session, clients return to the center after spending the intervening months in their regular life routines for a refresher course consisting of a variety of maintenance-enhancing procedures. My role was to give a lecture on relapse prevention and to discuss various strategies with the graduates. When I first got up to begin my talk and looked over the people in the room, it became abundantly obvious which graduates were relatively successful in their attempts to maintain the initial weight loss and which were less successful. Unlike graduates of other addictive behavior treatment programs (e.g., for smoking or problem drinking), the success or failure of those who have completed a long-range weight-loss program stands out clearly to the observer. After giving my talk, I decided to spend some time talking to representatives from both the winning and losing sides of the battle of the bulge. I find that it is often extremely informative to talk to both the survivors and relapsers of any treatment program for addictive problems. They can provide a unique inside view of the habit-change process—how strategies are employed by some and not by others, how they perceive the process of change and the problems of "breakdown," how they attribute successes and failures to various internal and external factors. Such was the case with my conversations with the Sea Pines graduates.

Some of those who were unsuccessful said that although they were able to make great strides in their weight management during the in-house treatment program they were basically unable to maintain the same healthy behaviors when they returned to their regular life routine. One of them made the following comments:

Hilton Head Island is a wonderful place to lose weight. There are beautiful jogging trails by the sea, we all ate balanced meals together each day, and there was plenty of group support and encouragement. I lost over 30 pounds during the month, and it was a very pleasant experience overall. When I got back to my home in Chicago, however, I just couldn't seem to keep on top of my old eating patterns—it was just too stressful, going back to the kids and the job and the Chicago weather . . . all that seemed a far cry from the peaceful gardens of Sea Pines. I put on weight as soon as the program here wore off.

In sharp contrast was the account given to me by one of the "star students" of the program, a woman who had not only maintained her initial weight loss but had also lost an additional 25 pounds during the months prior to the follow-up meeting. When I asked her to explain how she had been so successful she launched into an enthusiastic description of her experiences:

I have become a true behavior modifier. All this stuff about reinforcement, self-control, and stress management was new to me when I first got here this past summer. When I first came, I knew nothing about any of this—my history had been one of going from one crash diet to the next, always feeling guilty and excessively constrained about my eating behavior. When Dr. Miller gave his first lectures on behavioral control, it was like a light bulb flashing on inside my head—suddenly I realized that there was an entirely different way to approach this problem, that there was more to it than willpower and starving myself on one fad diet after another. I learned to control my behavior! I remember the day when I finally understood the principles behind the various strategies and techniques we were taught. I realized that these principles could be used to modify all kinds of different behaviors, not just eating. Why, at home these past few months, I taught these principles to my husband and the kids, and we now use them in all sorts of ways—to help the kids manage their homework, to work on my personal problems when they're still small enough to be managed instead of waiting for them to get big enough to serve as an excuse for another eating binge. I also learned the importance of planning ahead for change. I knew that it was going to be different when I left Hilton Head to go back to my home and job in Baltimore, that all kinds of stress and problems would arise that might get in the way of my continuing to lose weight. So I began the regular routine of sitting down each Sunday night and looking at my schedule for the upcoming week. Where were the dangerous spots—the luncheons with friends, the trips out of town where eating is limited to restaurant meals, the weather problems that might limit my exercise program? And then I would make specific plans about how I would deal with each of these potential problems to keep them from throwing me off track. I even allowed myself certain freedoms—to eat a gourmet meal at a French restaurant on special occasions—so long as I made up for it by limiting my intake on other days. Life is full of change. The secret is to plan ahead and not be thrown off—to alter the principles I learned to fit the situation at hand.

The moral of her success story is clear. She did not see herself as the *recipient* of treatment; she saw herself as the active *agent* of change. She had mastered the principles of self-control and was able to apply them with a variety of different behaviors, altering the application of these methods to changes in her life routine. Once she had learned the big picture, she was able to use this model as a guide or rutter to chart her course through the ever-changing situations of daily life. In contrast, those who were less successful in maintaining their weight loss tended to speak in terms of the program's effects "wearing off" after the initial program ended. They were less able to *generalize* what they had learned in treatment to their ordinary life experiences. For them, treatment was something that was externally applied by professionals, much as a new coat of paint is applied to the exterior of a house. Perhaps if they had learned the basic principles of self-control, their efforts during the maintenance phase would have been greatly enhanced. Without the aid of the big picture to serve as a navigational guide, one may lose grip on the rudder and end up drifting in circles.

What is the best way to teach someone the big picture or overall theoretical model? Although the approach will differ from one individual to the next, and from one addictive behavior to another, the following guidelines seem appropriate. One might begin by giving clients a summary or overview of the RP model. Since the process of addiction is often poorly understood by many people, asking them to share their existing beliefs and preconceptions prior to the presentation of the model may provide an opportunity to compare and contrast different theoretical views as well as to challenge concepts that appear to be inaccurate or self-defeating. Since the RP big picture stresses the importance of cognitive factors and self-control (vs. an emphasis on physiological processes with a corresponding inability to exercise self-control), a therapist might suggest the analogy of the mind as a "black box." Explication of the psychological processes inside the box (self-efficacy, expectancies, and causal attributions) can be described as providing information about the "wiring" of the box and how different processes influence each other and one's behavior. The implication here is that once one knows the "wiring diagram" one is better able to control the operations of the black box.

Emphasis should be placed on how physiological processes impact psychological factors—for example, on how the biphasic drug response influences outcome expectancies. In addition, one can point out the obverse, how internal attributions for failure enhance feelings of guilt, shame, and self-esteem. The main point to emphasize concerning the interaction between mental and physical states is that it is easier to grab the psychological reins (vs. the physiological ones); that is, that people are capable of being the agents of control rather than perceiving themselves as the victims of forces beyond their control. Clients can be taught how cognitive defense mechanisms operate to distort their perceptions, such as the defensive avoidance strategies of denial and rationalization. If they understand *how* these defensive mechanisms operate, they will be better equipped to be on the lookout for them when they occur, and to take remedial action. Defensive maneuvers can be "red-flagged" by the client when they first occur, rather than allowing them to take over and "push" the client toward a possible relapse. Cognitive maps can be provided that enable the client to plot his or her own route out of the addictive trap.

METAPHORS FOR HABIT CHANGE

A few words are in order concerning the use of *metaphor* as a vehicle for communicating important elements of the big picture to clients. Metaphor is a powerful communicative tool, and the use of metaphorical strategies in therapy has been stressed in the recent literature (e.g., Gordon, 1978; Rosen, 1982). An ideal self-control program should include a balance of both "right-brain" and "left-brain" components. Clients are easily overwhelmed (if not bored completely) by presentation of material that relies exclusively on linear, verbal, left-brain channels of communication. Attention and retention are both facilitated by the use of a blend of both left- and right-brain inputs. The use of metaphor and other imagery techniques appears to enhance right-hemisphere processing and storage (cf. Ornstein, 1977). Metaphorical descriptions are used intentionally throughout this book as illustrations of this approach. As such, metaphorical imagery both "brightens up" the material and provides a short-hand method of retaining important principles in the RP model. By the same token, adages, proverbs, homilies, and slogans can be used to consolidate important principles and assumptions associated with the big picture (e.g., "Where there's a will, there's a way").

The single metaphor that encompasses most of the examples we have cited (e.g., escaping from the forest of addiction or the navigational use of the rutter and rudder in a sea voyage) is the *journey* metaphor. The journey metaphor is a particularly useful one for relapse prevention because it illustrates habit change as a *process over time* instead of focusing on the single act of quitting. On a journey, the "quitting" stage occurs at the *beginning*, as one finally embarks on the trip. The most important part of the journey is still to come—the process of travel to one's ultimate destination. Whether or not the individual arrives safely at the final destination (*maintenance* of the behavior change) depends to a large extent on what happens after the initial embarkation, as well as the degree of preparation and planning one has made prior to leaving.

To illustrate the journey metaphor, an example I have developed recently for use in an RP smoking program can be examined. In this program, the following story, entitled "A Journey from Tobacco Road to Freedom Mountain," is told to the clients (group format) at the beginning of the first group meeting, in order to provide an overview and framework for the overall RP program.

The Journey from Tobacco Road to Freedom Mountain

By making a decision to stop smoking, you have taken the first important step in a journey that leads to increased freedom, greater self-esteem, and a longer, healthier life. The most important part of any journey is setting the goal, making the commitment to embark on the trip. By making the commitment to leave smoking behind, you have indicated the strength of your *will* to change. But by itself, the commitment to change cannot transport you instantly to your journey's ultimate destination. You must actually take the journey of change yourself. Our program of Relapse Prevention (RP) is designed to help you make the journey; the RP program is like a guide whom you have hired to assist you by providing maps and navigational assistance, and by pointing out dangers and pitfalls along the route.

The purpose of our program is to provide you with a *means* of attaining your goal; you have the *will* (by making the commitment to quit), RP offers the *way* to reach your goal. Many people who set out on this journey of quitting make the mistake of thinking that their will is all they need to reach their goal—that they will overcome all obstacles on the path through the sheer strength of their willpower. This makes about as much sense as the naive explorer who sets out across unknown territory without the aid of a compass, map, or other essential gear. In most cases, these inexperienced travelers become lost along the way or find themselves unable to get more than a few steps from basecamp before turning back. Usually, the first time they encounter signs of trouble on the trail, they find that their will is not enough to get them through successfully (e.g., meeting a grizzly bear and trying to "stare it down" in a battle of wills). The first troublespot often escalates into a total failure, as the naive explorer gives up and heads back to familiar territory.

Quitting smoking is a journey in its own right—in fact, it's quite a trip! It's a bit like getting divorced and moving to another city. In this case, however, you have decided to divorce an old dependency: tobacco. After living with cigarettes (or pipes, cigars, etc., depending on your preferences) for many years on Tobacco Road, you finally make the decision to leave, to set out on your own for the fresh air and vistas of Freedom Mountain. Although you have many mixed feelings about leaving your friends in Tobacco Road (after all, you went through a lot of hard times together), you feel an increasing need for independence and freedom, to strike out on your own instead of just striking another match. What are you leaving behind, after all? The cigarettes with whom you have lived for so long on Tobacco Road are becoming an increasingly heavy burden. Although they appear to promise friendship and relaxation, you become increasingly aware that the cigarettes are stealing from you behind your back—they steal your strength, your time, your money, often your friends, and eventually they may demand your life. Although it sometimes seems as though you have the cigarette denizens of Tobacco Road under your control (after all, aren't you in charge?), you realize more and more that you have fallen under their control —you feel like a prisoner, you have become "hooked," unable to move about freely on your own without the constant presence and "protection" of your cigarette buddies. It is time to escape.

As you make your escape plans, you discover that the only vehicle you can obtain for your journey is a bicycle; to make matters worse, it has been a long time since you last rode a bike. The territory ahead seems unknown and fraught with dangers. Doubts loom in your mind: "Will I make it? What if I get lost or fail? I don't think I can make it on my own," and so on. These doubts are the natural precursors of any important journey, but they can be reduced to the extent that you are *prepared* in advance for the journey—that you have the right *tools* (e.g., maps, bicycle maintenance tools, proper clothing, and supplies); that you have mastered the appropriate *skills* (learning to ride the bike, use the tools, etc.), and that you have the right *attitude* about the trip (knowing that it really is a journey with ups and downs and adventures along the way—and that it will take some time to reach your destination). The RP program is designed to equip you for the journey (by providing the necessary tools and skills) and to help guide you through the early stages of the trip. Unlike other smoking treatment programs, RP does not just drop you at the city limits of Tobacco Road and leave you to your own resources; we will accompany you through the first difficult stages after you have left the cigarettes behind. Our experience as guides comes from working with many people (including ourselves) who have attempted to make the trip before. We have learned much from both the successful survivors and from those who have experienced difficulties. It's a journey we all have to take sooner or later if we want to reach the cool forests and clear skies of Freedom Mountain.

Specifically, the RP program consists of the following components designed to help you on your journey:

1. RP teaches you coping strategies (constructive ways of thinking and behaving) to deal with the immediate problems that arise in the early stages of the trip, namely, coping with the urges and craving for tobacco.

2. RP provides you with *maps* showing the location of various temptation situations, pitfalls, and danger spots along the way that can throw you off course with the lure of temptation. (In this connection, one is reminded of Homer's *Odyssey*, in which Odysseus had to cope with the lure of the Sirens to keep his ship from becoming wrecked on the rocks.) RP will give you information on detours to avoid temptation situations where possible and to help you to acquire the skills to cope with them successfully without giving in or giving up.

3. RP helps guide you through the tricks our minds sometimes play on us when we have doubts along the way. We will teach you to recognize the *early warning signals* that alert us of the danger of relapse including the psychological tricks of making *Apparently Irrelevant Decisions* (AIDs) that are secretly designed to set us up for trouble and often bring us closer to situations that are extremely tempting and difficult to resist (e.g., deciding to arrange a meeting with an old friend who smokes). We will show how our minds often play tricks such as denial and rationalization that increase the danger of relapse and how we can learn to cope with these inner temptations.

4. RP will help you make important changes in your day-to-day *lifestyle*, so that the gratification you have obtained from smoking is replaced with other non-destructive and ultimately more satisfying activities. Smoking becomes an addiction or dependency for most of us because we use tobacco as a means of *coping* with life's continual ups and downs: we smoke to relax when we're feeling tense, but we also smoke to increase our enjoyment when we're feeling good or celebrating. It becomes increasingly difficult to just *let things be*, without increasing or decreasing the intensity of our experiences by smoking. When we stop smoking we begin to learn that we can trust our inner feelings and experiences, without trying to hide them behind a smoke screen. RP teaches you new methods of coping with stress, such as relaxation or meditation, exercise, and increasing the number of "wants" or desirable, self-fulfilling activities in your daily lifestyle. The development of these so-called *positive addictions* will serve as a growth-enhancing replacement or substitute for the negative addiction of smoking. The RP lifestyle motto is: COPING WITHOUT SMOKING.

5. Finally, RP will help you anticipate and be prepared in advance for possible breakdowns or relapses along the route. Many people begin their journey with very high expectations and demands for themselves. They frequently expect themselves to act perfectly without a single error, so that if they have *any* difficulty they think this proves they do not "have what it takes." Remember when you first learned a new skill such as riding a bicycle? Were you able to get your balance perfectly the first time? Most of us had to take a painful spill or two before getting the hang of it—but these were mistakes that we learned from (e.g., we learned to apply the brakes the next time to keep from going into a spin). The same applies to the journey from Tobacco Road to Freedom Mountain. Although most of us hope we will make it through the first time without any problems, an unrealistic expectation of perfection may set us up for failure; we may be tempted to give up altogether the first time we have a problem or slip along the way. If we find that our bike gets a flat tire on the road, should we give up and start hitch-hiking back to Tobacco Road? Or, to take a more realistic approach, shall we learn to anticipate and cope with the road conditions that might otherwise cause a blowout (e.g., by taking an alternative route)? And, if all precautions fail, shall we find out how to patch up a flat, learn from the experience, and continue on the path ahead? RP favors this approach. Just as fire drills and lifeboat drills are used as a means of teaching people what to do to save themselves in case of

emergency, so RP offers relapse drills designed to teach you what to do in case a fire breaks out (and lights the end of your cigarette).

Not everyone is able to make the trip successfully the first time. Instead of reacting to problems with a sense of self-blame and failure, RP treats these so-called setbacks or relapses as *prolapses*—mistakes that we can learn from to improve our eventual chances of success. For some, the change process is slow and laborious and it takes many attempts before the goal is attained. Others will find that the way is easier, perhaps based on the experiences they have gained in previous quit attempts. Whether you feel you have succeeded or failed in your attempts on this particular journey, the goal of RP remains the same: to help you from lighting up the next cigarette—even if you have just smoked one in your first "slip" since setting out on the trip.

How long does it take to complete the journey to Freedom Mountain? People differ tremendously in terms of how long it takes to get there, but for most of us, the trip will take approximately 3 months. The toughest part of the trip is the beginning—especially the first few days, when the temptations to return to the familiar comforts of Tobacco Road are the strongest. Each step you take on the journey will increase your confidence or self-efficacy, the feeling that you can cope without smoke as you head for the clear mountain air. Setbacks along the way need not leat to impossible dead-ends or impassable cliffs; alternative route-planning is always possible. And if you don't make it on this particular attempt, you can always try again. Each time you try, you learn a little more about how to do it. Happy trails to you!

STAGES OF THE JOURNEY OF HABIT CHANGE

The foregoing metaphorical journey provides a convenient framework for ordering the components of the RP program along a time-line sequence. As a further illustration of this approach, the various cognitive procedures outlined in this chapter are presented as components of a trip or journey and are described in order of occurrence. In addition to emphasizing the importance of the process of change over time, presentation of the material in this form provides an answer to the question of when to do what. The journey metaphor permits a focus on different assessment and intervention procedures as appropriate for various stages of the trip. Another advantage, as stated earlier, is that the journey metaphor presents the otherwise technical material in a form that is relatively easy for clients to understand and remember.

The remainder of the chapter is divided into sections corresponding to each segment of the journey of habit change. The first phase, preparation for departure, is concerned with issues related to motivation (reasons for taking the trip), commitment (making and implementing the decision to leave), and preparation for making the journey itself (including self-efficacy assessment and acquisition of coping skills). The second phase focuses on departure itself (the actual quitting). The third phase involves the actual process of traveling on the journey: coping with urges and temptations as they occur on the road (e.g., dealing with positive outcome expectancies), coping with breakdowns and failures *en route* (e.g., cognitive restructuring regarding slips and the Abstinence Violation Effect [AVE]), and learning to recognize and deal with seductive psychological forces that may pose problems for the traveler (e.g., coping with Apparently Irrelevant Decisions [AIDs], rationalizations, and other cognitive defense mechanisms). Changes in personal lifestyle and adoption of new attitudes and values that are designed to enhance maintenance of change once the initial journey has been completed are topics that will be covered in Chapter 5.

PREPARATION FOR DEPARTURE

Motivation and Commitment to Making the Journey

The issue of motivation to change was introduced in Chapter 3 in the section on self-efficacy. We made a distinction between motivation (degree of commitment to the goal of change) and self-efficacy (expectancy of capacity to cope with particular high-risk situations), which is important since many people tend to equate motivation to achieve a given goal with the *means* of goal attainment. In terms of the present discussion, the issue of motivation involves two components: the reasons *why* one wishes to make the journey (incentives to change) and, in addition, the overall *strength* of the motivation to change. These two components may or may not be highly correlated. One may claim, for example, that one is motivated to quit smoking because of health reasons, but unless the strength of this motive is high enough, the motivation will be insufficient to "spill over" into an actual change in behavior. Almost everyone who smokes is aware of the health risks involved, but unless this is a particularly potent factor for any given individual (e.g., the person begins to experience symptoms of emphysema), the motivation to change often remains below threshold.

Let us assume that for any individual involved in an addictive habit pattern there exists a hypothetical *threshold of motivation* such that a commitment to behavior change only occurs when that threshold is exceeded. Because of vast individual differences and the lack of empirical findings that bear on this issue, social scientists are only beginning to be aware of the factors that contribute to this threshold shift. Many potential incentives come to mind, such as increased risk or damage to one's physical or psychological well-being; feelings of guilt or dissatisfaction at being hooked or dependent on a substance or activity; social disapproval by one's friends, family, or peers; economic costs, etc. In any case, when the motivational threshold is reached, the probability increases that the individual will make a decision to change. Here again, however, unless there is a firm *commitment* to implement this decision in the form of an actual quit date or behavior-change plan, the decision may have little or no impact on behavior. One may get caught up in the old rationalization: "I'll quit tomorrow, or on my next birthday, or as soon as my life settles down, or after I graduate," and so on. *Webster's New Collegiate Dictionary* (1983) gives this definition of commitment: "an agreement or pledge to do something in the future." Thus, in order for a well-motivated decision to have any effect, one must make a firm commitment to *implement* the decision, to agree or pledge to change at a particular point in time. In terms of our metaphor, the client must make a commitment to leave, to embark upon the journey to freedom. It is important to set a departure date sufficiently ahead of time so that one can make adequate preparations for the journey, however. The sudden impulsive commitment to depart immediately (e.g., stop smoking) or shortly after making the commitment may work for a few individuals ("I just threw my last cigarette away, and that was it!"), but for most of us acting on sudden impulse is a sure way to set ourselves up for a failure experience ("I tried, but I only made it for a few hours; I guess I'm just lacking in willpower"). The more prepared one is to make the journey, the greater the chances of eventual success. For most people, the delay between a commitment to make the journey and the actual departure date should be at least 2 weeks, so as to allow time for adequate preparation.

The *decision matrix* (Figure 1-9) is a useful way for clients to organize and prioritize their motivational reasons for embarking on the journey. The decision matrix provides a format by which the client can list, with the therapist's assistance, the anticipated positive and negative consequences (both immediate and long-term effects) associated with the decision either to change (e.g., initiate abstinence) or to maintain or resume the old habit. In addition to the usual anticipated changes (e.g., improved health), the therapist should make sure to probe for any unique or idiosyncratic reasons that the client believes might be important. Such probing may often reveal rationalizations or inaccurate beliefs that can be challenged by the therapist. Recently, a client in one of our smoking groups stated that she felt that she would be at *increased* risk for developing colds and flu after she quit smoking. Upon further questioning, she explained that she had read somewhere that low doses of nicotine dissolved in water made an excellent insecticide if sprayed on plants. "If nicotine kills bugs on plants," she went on, "it probably has the same effect in my body, killing off bugs that would otherwise get me sick." She seriously believed that the "bugs" in her body would flourish once she stopped smoking! It did not take long for other members of the group to challenge her logic on this point. (Group discussion of the reasons each member has for changing their habits is often a very effective strategy, since motivational factors brought up by one member are often adopted—or rejected, as in the above example—in the course of discussion.)

Once the decision matrix is completed, a copy should be given to the client as a reminder of the reasons why he or she has decided to embark on the journey of habit change. The therapist should emphasize that the various reasons given prior to departure will, in all likelihood, shift and change over time as the journey progresses. Certain negative consequences that apply *prior* to quitting smoking, (extensive coughing, feeling of constriction in the chest, etc.) will lose their impact once the person has quit and begins to experience a decrease in the unpleasant physical symptoms previously exacerbated by smoking. The individual may mistakenly conclude that because these symptoms no longer occur, he or she may now resume smoking with impunity—forgetting that resumption of smoking will retrigger the problem. When motivational doubts such as these occur "on the road," clients should be encouraged to consult the original decision matrix as a reminder of all the relevant reasons why they chose to set out on the journey of quitting in the first place. It should be noted that the decision matrix is similar in format to the "decisional balance sheet" developed by Janis and Mann (1977).

In addition to the motivational reasons for habit change, the individual's *self-image* vis-à-vis the addictive behavior is an important topic to explore during the preparation period. Some clients have considerable difficulty imagining themselves as nonsmokers, ex-drinkers, and so on. Their self-image frequently is intimately tied up with the old habit pattern, often with unrealistically romantic imagery. Smokers often talk about their identification with Humphrey Bogart or Lauren Bacall; drinkers sometimes like to see themselves as similar to Winston Churchill or Dean Martin. Younger clients may be attracted to the devil-may-care attitude exemplified by the punk movement and discount the long-range positive consequences of quitting smoking ("What's the difference—we're all going to be blown up anyway").

The best way to get at these self-image issues (often deeply rooted) is to ask the client to write or describe an *autobiography* of their personal history as a smoker, drinker, or whatever. Details of the autobiography method are given in Chapter 2. In addition to providing an historical account of how they view themselves as a smoker or drinker, clients should also be asked to describe how they see themselves as a nonsmoker or nondrinker. The therapist should help those clients who have difficulty in coming up with a clear future self-image, or who focus on aspects of deprivation or loss associated with the habit change ("All I can see is a big hole or space in my image where smoking used to be"), develop a new self-image. Through the use of imagery and covert self-modeling techniques, the therapist and client may be able to construct a new self-image of an active, coping, independent individual who has finally thrown away the crutch of dependency. Residents of "Tobacco Road" can imagine themselves to be free spirits exploring the delights of "Freedom Mountain." Work on modifying the self-image should continue throughout the program until the new behavior patterns are well established.

Clients who harbor negative expectancies concerning their own chances of successful habit change often base their subjective estimates of failure on their own "track record" of previous change attempts (e.g., assuming that unsuccessful prior attempts predict negative outcomes on future attempts), and/or descriptions of high relapse rates in addiction treatment programs. To counter these negative attitudes, the therapist should point out the following facts: (1) One of the best predictors of eventual success is the number of prior quit attempts: the more times one has tried to quit in the past, the better the odds that the next attempt will succeed (cf. Rose & Hamilton, 1978), presumably because one learns valuable information from each prior attempt (attitudes, skills, etc.). (2) Despite the pessimistic outcome associated with any single attempt or treatment program, recent evidence suggests that people are often successful in changing their own behavior *over the long run.*

In a recent provocative report, Schachter (1982) interviewed 161 people in New York State concerning their past attempts to either stop smoking or lose weight. Overall, life-long success rates were surprisingly high: 64% of those who attempted to quit smoking were ultimately successful, and 63% of subjects who attempted to lose weight (and who were previously obese) had succeeded in the long-run. The pattern of results reported by Schachter (1982) provides a much more optimistic outlook on one's chances of successfully changing an addictive behavior problem—even in the absence of a formal treatment program. As Schachter notes in the interpretation of his results:

If it is assumed that the proportion of successful quitters cumulatively increases with successive attempts, it becomes clear why the generalizations that have been made from the results of single therapeutic attempts to cure are probably unwarranted. For example, assume that for any single attempt to quit, 10% of those who try succeed permanently—a figure in line with cure rates reported in most therapeutic studies. Assume further that at a later time, all of those who failed try again. Again, 10% succeed. Cumulatively, then, 19% of those who have tried twice will have succeeded. A third attempt to quit, again assuming a 10% success rate, would yield a cumulative total of 27% success. And so on. Obviously, depending on the exact parameters assumed for rate of success per attempt, rate of recidivism, and the proportion of people who try repeatedly, one could derive virtually any cumulative success rate. However, the general line of reasoning makes it seem likely that retrospective interviews with people who have at some time sought help will yield higher cure rates than those reported in studies on one-shot therapeutic intervention. (Schachter, 1982, p. 443)

Finally, motivation and commitment will also be enhanced by providing an overall *orientation* (the big picture) to the habit-change process. As described earlier in this chapter, clients are taught the overall rationale and theoretical model associated with the RP approach. The gradual process of change over time and the definition of habit change as a skill acquisition process can be emphasized by sharing with clients the journey metaphor and the stages of change (preparation, departure, stages of the journey). Clients often embellish the journey metaphor with their own contributions, thereby further personalizing the imagery. With this general framework in place, the therapist and client can move on to the actual preparations for departure.

Assessment of Self-Efficacy

In essence, the goal in the assessment of self-efficacy is to provide the client with a list of "trouble spots" that are likely to be encountered along the journey by evaluating the client's ability to cope with high-risk situations. Once areas of weakness or vulnerability have been identified, the therapist can begin the process of teaching the client new coping skills (both cognitive and behavioral) to handle anticipated difficulties. The process of skill training for coping with high-risk situations, already described in detail in Chapter 2, continues throughout the program, both prior to and following the departure date. In the preparation stage, all that may be necessary is to forewarn clients concerning potential problem areas and to provide them with some basic coping strategies such as avoidance of high-risk situations, simple distraction techniques, and substitute activities. As treatment progresses and the client begins coping with a wide variety of high-risk situations, additional skill-training methods such as role playing, dry runs, and relapse rehearsals (all described in Chapter 2) can be introduced.

The assessment of self-efficacy is a relatively new endeavor, and the development of specific measurement procedures is still ongoing. Readers who wish to review a variety of approaches to the general area of cognitive assessment should consult the recent volumes by Kendall and Hollon (1981) and by Merluzzi, Glass, and Genest (1981). In the addictive behaviors field, several investigators have recently attempted to develop self-efficacy questionnaires associated with the assessment and treatment of smoking and alcoholism. This work, described below, should provide investigators and clinicians with a general framework for the construction of additional measures suited to their own client populations. To date, however, there is much work still to be done in the construction of self-efficacy measures along with appropriate reliability and validity checks. Before describing measures that have already been developed, a few general points need to be emphasized. Readers may wish to review the theoretical material on self-efficacy presented in Chapter 3 before proceeding.

Self-efficacy is not a global, cross-situational construct like self-esteem or locus of control, but rather refers to expectations or judgments people make about their capacity to cope with *situation-specific* events. As such, self-efficacy is a *state* measure (specific to particular person–situation inter-actions) and not a *trait* measure (i.e., self-esteem is often described as a general trait that generalizes over many situations). As Mischel has noted recently:

Self-efficacy is assessed by asking the person to indicate the degree of confidence that he or she can do a particular task, which is described in detail. . . . Although expectancies seem to be clearly central person variables, it would be a mistake to transform them into generalized traitlike dispositions by endowing them with broad cross-situational consistency or by forgetting that they depend on specific stimulus conditions and on particular contexts. . . . If we convert expectancies into global traitlike dispositions and remove them from their close interaction with situational conditions, they may well prove to be no more useful than their many theoretical predecessors. Construed as relatively specific (and modifiable) subjective hypotheses about behavior-outcome contingencies and personal competencies, however, expectancies may be readily assessed and may serve as useful predictors of performance. (Mischel, 1981, pp. 489–490)

According to Bandura (1977) self-efficacy can be assessed along three dimensions: level, strength, and generality. Level involves a dichotomous yes/no judgment made by the client as to whether or not he or she has the ability to perform the target behavior (such as a coping response in a specific high-risk situation); strength refers to a self-rating of the degree of confidence the client has in that judgment; and generality refers to the similarity in strength ratings across similar situations. For our present purposes, self-efficacy questionnaires for use with addictive behavior problems usually involve a rating scale format in which clients are presented with a series of potential high-risk situations and asked to rate how confident they are that they would be able to resist the urge to engage in the addictive activity. Note that they are not asked what they would actually do to cope with the situation, since this involves an assessment of coping skills and not self-efficacy. Of course, self-efficacy and coping skills are closely related, and there is no reason why they could not be assessed in the same measurement package. Assessment of coping skills (e.g., the use of the Situational Competency Test) is described in Chapter 2.

One example of a recent self-efficacy questionnaire developed for use with an alcoholic clientele is the *Situational Confidence Questionnaire* (SCQ) developed by Helen Annis of the Addiction Research Foundation in Toronto (Annis, 1982a). The SCQ consists of 100 items covering major areas of difficulty experienced by alcoholics in terms of excessive drinking or relapse. A pool of items was initially developed drawing upon a large variety of sources including existing questionnaires and discussions with other clinicians, former alcoholics, and alcoholic clients at the Addiction Research Foundation. The resulting items were classified using the system for high-risk situations described in Chapter 2 (Table 2-2). Clients who are administered the SCQ are given a booklet containing the 100 items. For each item the client is asked to "imagine yourself as you are right now in each of these situations. Indicate on the scale provided how confident you are that you will be able to resist the urge to drink heavily in that situation." The confidence ratings range from 100% confidence (very confident) to 0% (not at all confident). Sample items within each classification category follow:

Intrapersonal–Environmental Determinants
1. Negative Emotional States (20 items)
   • If I were depressed about things in general
   • If I were angry at the way things had turned out
2. Negative Physical States (20 items)
   • If I felt shaky and sick
   • If I were in physical pain
3. Positive Emotional States (10 items)
   • If I felt things were going to work out well for me at last
   • If I would want to celebrate special occasions like Christmas or birthdays
4. Testing Personal Control (10 items)
   • If I would decide to test my willpower by showing that I really could stop after one or two drinks
   • If I would start thinking that I was finally cured and could handle alcohol
5. Urges and Temptations
   • If I would see an advertisement for my favorite booze
   • If I would unexpectedly find a bottle of my favorite booze

Interpersonal Determinants
6. Interpersonal Conflict (20 items)
   • If I had an argument with a friend
   • If pressure would build up at work because of the demands of my supervisor
7. Social Pressure to Drink (10 items)
   • If I would be invited to someone's home and they would offer me a drink
   • If someone would pressure me to "be a good sport" and have a drink
8. Positive Emotional States (10 items)
   • If I would be out with friends "on the town" and wanted to increase my enjoyment
   • If I wanted to heighten my sexual enjoyment

Annis also developed a parallel form of the questionnaire called the *Inventory of Drinking Situations* (Annis, 1982b). This inventory consists of the identical 100 items included in the SCQ, but clients are asked to indicate for each item whether they drank heavily in that situation during the past year using a 4-point scale (never/rarely/frequently/almost always). The assumption is that situations associated with heavy drinking in the past will probably represent high-risk situations for future abstinent periods. A similar but alternative measure of self-efficacy for treatment planning with alcoholics has been reported recently by DiClemente, Gordon, and Gibertini (1983).

In the area of smoking treatment, a similar self-efficacy measure has been developed by Condiotte and Lichtenstein (1981). In a study designed to assess the predictive validity of self-efficacy as a predictor of relapse among smokers participating in a cessation treatment program (results of this study are described in Chapters 3 and 8), Condiotte and Lichtenstein developed a pool of items drawn from a list of smoking situations originally developed by Best and Hakstian (1978). Subjects were provided with this 48-item list and asked to designate on a 100-point probability scale (expressed as a percentage in 10-interval units), the probability that they would be able to resist the urge to smoke in that situation. In order to obtain reliable groupings of the self-efficacy situations presented, the investigators applied a cluster analytic procedure (similar to factor analysis) to the questionnaire data. The analysis yielded seven moderately intercorrelated clusters: restlessness, intrapersonal negative mood states, smoking as a crutch activity, time structuring, social situations, interpersonal negative mood states, and self-image. The classification system yielded by the cluster analysis yields categories that are somewhat similar to those described in Chapter 2, although different terminology and labels are used. As reported in Chapter 3, the self-efficacy scores for smokers in this study turned out to be valid and accurate predictors of subsequent relapse.

One potential problem that arises with the use of self-efficacy measures administered to clients in treatment is that some clients show what might be called a "blanket overconfidence bias" when filling out the questionnaire. Clients showing this bias are likely to rate *every item* on the self-efficacy list with a 100% confidence rating—indicating that they anticipate no situation to be more difficult than any other in terms of resisting the urge to indulge in the addictive behavior. Such a "ceiling effect" on self-efficacy ratings is probably given by clients who may misinterpret the questionnaire as an overall test of motivation. Alcoholics in treatment, for example, often show this overconfidence bias: they fully expect that they will never drink again, *under any circumstances,* and thus they do not provide relative ratings of their self-efficacy in different risk situations; all items are scored identically with maximum confidence.

In order to eliminate or reduce this potential source of bias, several possible strategies might be employed. Clients could be instructed, for example, that although their overall confidence is very high, they are to provide estimates of relative levels of difficulty with coping in various situations just in case a problem were to occur in the future. Alternatively, such clients could be asked to rate each item in terms of how much the situation influenced their drinking in the past (e.g., use of the Inventory of Drinking Situations developed by Annis, 1982b). Another strategy would be to ask clients to rank order the items in terms of difficulty in anticipated coping, from most to least difficult. Development of a forced-choice format may be an effective means of reducing overconfidence bias, since the client would then be presented with pairs of items and asked to rate which of the two would be the most difficult to cope with. Clients who demonstrate the blanket overconfidence bias may require special attention in treatment, especially if this bias represents a naive estimate of the future risks involved in maintaining abstinence. Overconfidence in this respect may represent an underlying reliance on willpower as the sole means of coping with temptations. Since many clients believe that willpower is an all-or-none trait or ability, it follows that they would apply this concept in a blanket way across all temptation situations. Such clients may be at greater risk for relapse as a result, since the first time they encounter a risk situation that they cannot control, they may give up altogether.

Efficacy-Enhancement Procedures

The purpose of the self-efficacy assessment procedures described above is to provide a kind of inventory of the client's relative strengths and weaknesses in coping with high-risk situations. The next step in preparing for the journey of habit change is to fortify the client's coping repertoire with a variety of behavioral and cognitive intervention strategies. Behavioral skill-training methods have already been described in Chapter 2. To summarize briefly, once deficits in self-efficacy have been determined, the therapist's next task is to further assess the client's existing coping skills (if any) relevant to the low self-efficacy situations. Coping skills can be assessed by the use of one or more of the following procedures (see Chapter 2 for details): behavioral observation in naturalistic high-risk situations, assessment of coping responses in simulated situations (e.g., the Situational Competency Test), and role-playing methods. Here, the therapist's goal is to determine if the client possesses the requisite coping skills (along with the quality of such skills) or whether the performance of these skills is blocked by fear or anxiety. The therapist then begins the skill-training program in order to bolster the client's coping defenses. The material in Chapter 2 describes these behavioral training methods, including general problem-solving instructions and specific skill training (overt practice and role playing in coping with high-risk situations, relapse rehearsal, and dry runs). In addition to these behavioral techniques, a number of cognitive methods can be employed to enhance self-efficacy (see Goldfried & Robins, 1982).

As with the behavioral skill-training component, cognitive procedures can be employed both prior to and following the client's "departure" on the journey of self-change. The exact ordering of intervention techniques will depend on the particular client and treatment setting. For outpatient clients who are seeking help in order to quit smoking, for example, many of these procedures can be applied prior to the quit date, as part of the preparation stage. Inpatient alcoholic clients, on the other hand, usually have already stopped drinking by the time the therapist comes into contact with them. For the latter population, many of the RP training components can be applied while clients remain in the inpatient setting, readying them for "departure" to the outside world. The important thing to emphasize here, however, is that the training in skill acquisition should continue *after* the client has stopped smoking or has been discharged from the inpatient setting, since this is the time when the client must learn to apply these skills in actual high-risk situations.

Perhaps the most significant goal of efficacy enhancement is to facilitate a change in the client's self-image from "victim" to "victor." Many clients with addictive behavior problems come into treatment with a pronounced attitude of helplessness and victimization, seeing themselves as victims of forces or events beyond their control (e.g., genetic predisposition or biological addictive mechanisms). With such an attitude, it is not unusual to find that such clients react to a failure experience with increased feelings of helplessness, much as victims of other diseases do when confronted with a relapse (e.g., a second heart attack, return of a malignancy, etc.). The "good news" about relapse with addiction problems, the central theme of the RP approach, is that the client can, in fact, exercise control so as to minimize the "damage" and perhaps even turn the relapse into a positive growth experience (prolapse). How can the therapist help the client to shift the emphasis from victim to victor (from low self-efficacy to high self-efficacy)?

Some of the efficacy enhancement techniques have already been described in earlier sections of this volume. To review briefly, these methods include the following:

1. The therapist relates to the client as a *colleague* instead of the usual doctor–patient relationship. By doing so, the client begins to adopt the role of objective observer, working along with the therapist as a co-investigator. Instead of feeling "one down" and guilty in the eyes of the therapist, the client begins to get some distance from the problem and is more likely to see it objectively and to realize that some control over the behavior is possible. Self-monitoring and other forms of behavioral assessment often will facilitate this sense of disidentification and detachment as clients begin to see the addiction as a habitual behavior instead of equating it directly with their self-image ("I can monitor and see changes in my drinking behavior," vs. "My drinking proves that I *am* an alcoholic"). The decrease in guilt and self-blame that derives from this more objective approach is less likely to trigger defensive mechanisms such as denial and resistance to treatment. Increasingly, as a result, the client begins to accept greater responsibility for the behavior and the habit-change endeavor. This increased sense of personal responsibility can be enhanced further if the client and therapist work together in the choice of treatment goals (abstinence vs. moderation, etc.) and individualized treatment methods.

2. The therapist instructs the client that the process of changing one's habits involves a *skill acquisition* procedure instead of a "battle of the will" with willpower as the only weapon. By emphasizing the learning of new skills, the image of the addictive habit as an "immoral" activity is neutralized as an attitude of anticipated mastery begins to emerge in its place. The client begins to see the process of change as not unlike other skill acquisition experiences he or she has experienced, such as learning to ride a bicycle, ice skate, or play a musical instrument. Again, the end result is one of enhanced self-efficacy and the acceptance of personal responsibility in the habit-change process.

3. Changing a bad habit is described to the client as a gradual process over time, a voyage or journey that has several stages. The overall task that may at first appear formidable to the client ("How can I change after I've been a chain smoker for 35 years?") appears more approachable if the task is broken down into smaller subtasks. Just as a novice pianist must first learn the scales and to read music before learning to play his or her first piece, so the client must acquire some basic skills before success in changing habits can be attained. As Bandura has stated (1977), self-efficacy can be strengthened if the individual breaks the task down into subcomponents and then tackles one subgoal at a time. Instead of focusing on the distal end goal (e.g., maintaining lifelong abstinence), the client is encouraged to make the trip one step at a time by the use of *proximal goal-setting*. Proximal goals can be set up for each week of the treatment program: the goals for one week, for example, may include only the learning of a relaxation technique and acquiring skills to deal with social pressure situations. Setbacks can thus be dealt with as a subgoal problem and are not taken as indicative of total breakdown. In addition to breaking down the distal goal into proximal subgoals, the temporal dimension of the task can also be broken down into more manageable units. Instead of focusing on "forever" ("I'll never be able to smoke again," or "My goal is to stop drinking forever, once and for all"), the client can be encouraged to adopt the oft-quoted slogan of members of Alcoholics Anonymous (AA): "One day at a time." Since self-efficacy is closely tied to performance enactments, successful mastery of subgoals taken one at a time is the best strategy to enhance feelings of self-mastery.

4. Self-efficacy can also be enhanced by providing clients with *feedback* concerning their performance on any new task, including tasks that at first appear to be unrelated to the addictive behavior problem. For some clients, low self-efficacy engendered by their failure to cope with the addiction problem has generalized to the extent that they feel incapable of dealing

effectively with *any* problem area in their lives. Such clients are likely to see themselves as victims of fate, circumstance, or heredity, and are convinced they are doomed to failure when it comes to mastering any new behaviors— particularly coping with stress without an addictive crutch. With such cases, the therapist may wish to consider the possibility of involving the client in learning a new activity or task that enables the person to gain a sense of mastery, thereby enhancing self-efficacy. Activities that involve the acquisition of new skills and that can be mastered with a high probability of success are recommended, including the development of a new hobby or artistic ability, an exercise program, working on a craft, becoming a volunteer helping others in a social agency, and the like. If the client is encouraged to take on this new activity slowly, one subtask at a time, under careful supervision and encouragement, the chances of premature giving up or failure will be minimized. Successful accomplishment, even for a relatively simple task, may greatly enhance the client's self-efficacy. Enhanced efficacy may then generalize to the task of changing the addictive habit as the client gains increased confidence that he or she is actually capable of mastering new skills.

As an example of how mastery of a new task can generalize to coping with an addictive problem, consider the following article that appeared originally in the *Seattle Times* (February 23, 1982). Written by a staff reporter, Marjorie Jones, the headline for the article read "Alcoholics Go Over the Edge for a New High":

Scared and shaking, with hearts pounding and excitement pumping everyone into a natural high, the small group clustered at the top of the 100-foot, rocky precipice. The 13 would descend that cliff supported only by what appeared to be an inadequately thin rope and a trust in their Maker and in those at the top, not necessarily in that order. None ever before had even contemplated belaying 100 feet down a jagged face of a cliff. The highest most ever had gotten before was on a bar stool. All but two of the 13 were alcoholics, residents of the Northwest Treatment Center. . . . They walked down the face of the cliff backward, then walked down backward carrying each other in a rescue technique. This kind of activity is reserved normally for macho mountain climbers in top physical shape, not recovering alcoholics. It all was part of a new pilot program for alcoholics conducted here by the Northwest Outward Bound of Portland. The idea is to give experiences that the alcoholics can work through and feel good about. They are placed in stressful, anxiety-filled situations. When they succeed, as in belaying down a cliff, the experience reinforces the idea that they don't have to turn to alcohol every time they face stress. They get an immediate payoff. Richard Ernst, Outward Bound projects director, said the three-day course was modeled after St. Luke's Hospital Alcoholism Outward Bound program in Denver. . . . To establish trust, they were led on a blindfold hike up a trail edged with steep slopes and over slippery rocks. They also fell backward from a five-foot stump into the arms of the others. Their first real problem was climbing over a simulated electric wire without touching it. The challenge brought out personality conflicts, anger, temper and frustration. The problem took an hour and a half to solve but ended with everyone feeling a boost in confidence. (Jones, 1982, p. B1)

Not everyone, of course, would be willing or able to participate in an Outward Bound program as a means of building confidence—although the above account clearly indicates that some individuals may greatly benefit from this approach. Others may wish to pursue less rigorous means of enhancing self-efficacy. In addition to participation in new activities, there are a number of additional strategies that can be employed to build a sense of mastery. One such strategy, the use of coping imagery, will be discussed shortly when we come to the topic of urge control. Another group of strategies will be discussed in Chapter 5 in the general context of changing lifestyle (use of "positive addictions" to enhance overall levels of confidence). Efficacy-enhancement procedures are appropriate at all stages of the "journey of change" process. For some clients, however, the preparatory stage is the most crucial one for working on self-efficacy, particularly for those who otherwise feel they are incapable or unable to even embark on the initial stages of the journey. These clients are likely to demonstrate an attitude of hopeless helplessness—"It's no use, I just can't quit smoking," or "Nothing I have ever tried has worked in the past and I doubt anything will work for me this time." For clients who express these kind of feelings, the therapist must work on the self-efficacy deficiency before any steps are taken on the habit-change journey. One needs to develop a shift from low self-efficacy to a sense of confidence symbolized by the children's tale about "the little train that could." As some readers will recall, the little train was eventually able to conquer an otherwise impossible hill by repeatedly saying to itself, "I think I can, I think I can," until the crest of the hill was successfully reached ("Now I *know* I can").

DEPARTURE: THE STAGE OF QUITTING

To paraphrase Mark Twain's oft-cited remark about his own attempts to stop smoking, quitting is the easiest part of the habit-change process; after all, he quit on thousands of occasions. The RP approach downplays the emphasis on quitting itself, emphasizing that the main difficulty is not cessation itself but the prevention of relapse. Every time someone puts out a cigarette or finishes a drink, that person has in fact "quit" for a period of time. Sooner or later, however, the act is repeated and the person becomes a user again. So the issue becomes one of *not starting* rather than quitting *per se*. Quitting with the intention of not starting again is viewed as the act of *departure*, the first day of the journey of change. As with any journey, the moment of departure is an important one, often deserving of ceremony and celebration. For the client who is adequately prepared for the journey, the departure day should be a joyful occasion despite the normal apprehension and anxiety that people feel whenever they are about to embark upon a trip of uncertain outcome. Although the details concerning departure will differ depending on the nature of the addictive problem and the client's general circumstances, several topics are important to keep in mind: methods of quitting, enlistment of social support, stimulus control, and the departure ceremony. Each will be considered briefly in this section.

Methods of Quitting

Much has been written in the literature concerning the relative merits of different cessation procedures with various addictive behaviors. Many treatment procedures focus on cessation techniques as the primary emphasis (e.g., aversion, contingency contracting, sensory deprivation, etc.), as shown throughout this book. Since the RP model favors acceptance of personal responsibility and self-agency as the focus of change, the use of such cessation techniques that involve a therapist's application of external procedures to a passive client is not encouraged. Rather, the client who is well prepared is asked to voluntarily set a date for departure and to mark the act of cessation as an important first step in the trip. There are no special procedures designed to "make" the client quit or reinforce cessation with the application of external agents such as drugs or threats of punishment (e.g., monetary fines or public humiliation). One simply accepts the responsibility of departure and gets on with it.

Clients often ask whether they should quit by cutting down on a gradual basis (fading), or just doing it "cold turkey" with an abrupt cessation. Although evidence on the relative merits of these two approaches is mixed, this author recommends that the client use a quitting method that he or she *believes* will work. If a client is convinced that cutting down gradually on smoking will help alleviate physical withdrawal symptoms, then any attempt made to convince the individual of the merits of "cold turkey" quitting is bound to set up a meaningless controversy. With clients who are ambivalent about choosing a particular cessation method, the therapist should discuss the pros and cons of each approach before a final decision is made. Although gradual fading may offer some advantages for the degree of subsequent withdrawal, it suffers from the disadvantage that the reduced level of consumption may in fact enhance the enjoyment value of the addictive activity thereby making it more difficult to make the final cut. A smoker who is restricted to only two or three cigarettes a day during the final stages of the fading process may find those cigarettes to be immensely reinforcing and more difficult to leave behind than a smoker who continues to smoke at normal levels until the day of quitting. Often smokers in the latter category will begin to complain about the negative aspects of heavy consumption and will look forward to quitting as a means of redemption.

Asking smokers to double their rate of normal smoking during the week prior to quitting will often enhance this satiation effect. If one method of quitting meets with initial failure or client disapproval, another method can be tried. The important thing is to emphasize that quitting is a transition stage between preparation and the making of the journey, and not the end point or final destination itself.

Enlistment of Social Support

Although the client essentially must take the journey alone, the trip can be made much easier by enlisting social support and assistance along the way. Family members, friends, colleagues, employers, and others can all help to make the journey easier and more enjoyable. Social support can be helpful in many ways. Clients can be given encouragement, support, and other forms of social reinforcement; people can be helpful by not tempting the client with the taboo activity (e.g., fellow smokers or drinkers can be asked not to offer the client a cigarette or drink); clients can inform others that they may be difficult to deal with during the early stages of the journey and may need additional understanding or support during this period. It often helps if the client is able to ask others for particular kinds of support or inform them how they can be helpful. For example, the client can ask for help in coping with additional stress and can ask others not to nag about initial failures, and so on. Spouses or significant others can be particularly helpful in this regard, and their assistance is to be encouraged. Social contacts can also be harmful, of course, particularly when the client's spouse or other close contacts are still engaging in the taboo activity (thereby providing a constant source of access and temptation) or when the significant other is in some way dependent on or invested in the client's continuing to be involved in the addictive activity (i.e., a spouse whose own perception of power or control depends on the client maintaining a "sick" role or helpless dependency). Care should be taken in these cases to ensure that the client is not sabotaged by others in the habit-change process.

Participation in a group composed of clients who are all working on the same problem can provide considerable social support. Many self-help groups in the addictions field (AA, Narcotics Anonymous, Overeaters Anonymous) or professional treatment programs that employ a group format (Weightwatchers, SmokEnders, etc.) have capitalized on the benefits of group support among individuals who are working to change an identical addiction. Clients can be paired together as "buddies" who agree to exchange phone numbers and provide each other support and consultation at all hours of the day or night. In a group format, clients can share experiences and provide each other with suggestions for coping with stress and temptation.

Some clients state that they do not wish to enlist social support because they would rather work on their problem "in secret" and not tell anyone that they are involved in an attempt to change their behavior. These clients often speak of a need to "lick this problem on my own" and that they don't need anyone's help to do it. Although in some cases this "lone wolf" approach to change may be successful, for most clients a desire for secrecy masks an underlying fear of failure and social disapproval ("The more people who know I am attempting to quit, the more will know about it if I don't make it"). By adopting this stance, the client may in fact make it easier not to succeed, since the impact of failure is minimized if no one but the client is aware of the meaning of the act. Making a public commitment to change and enlisting social support, on the other hand, enhances the chances of success (Levy, 1977). As an example of a rationale for seeking social support along with specific instructions concerning how to enlist help from others, Table 4-1 contains a handout on this topic that we have used recently with clients in an RP smoking group.

Stimulus Control

As the day of departure approaches, clients should be advised to prepare their environment to reduce temptation and possible backsliding by removing all traces of the addictive substance and associated paraphernalia. Such stimulus control procedures represent both wise precaution and a marker of one's commitment to embark upon the journey unencumbered by reminders of the past. Tobacco smokers should get rid of all cigarettes, butts, ashtrays, and lighters; marijuana smokers should throw out or give away their stashes, roaches, and roach clips; drinkers should remove all alcoholic beverages; those who wish to lose weight should clean their cupboards of all tempting foods, and so on. Many clients welcome the opportunity to get rid of all tempting stimuli. One client recently described the procedure of throwing out his cigarettes, ashtrays, and his ever-present Bic lighter (he had flicked his last Bic) as similar to the freedom he felt after an accident earlier in his life when he was finally able to walk freely without the aid of crutches. Others says they enjoy the freedom of not having to haul around the "excess baggage" to support their habit.

On the other hand, some clients are ambivalent about taking such precautions, perhaps because they see it as a sign of weakness or lack of willpower. One client who planned to quit smoking told me she wanted to keep an unopened pack of her favorite cigarettes in her purse after she quit so as to "prove to myself that I can resist the temptation to smoke even when a cigarette is always readily available." Another client, a problem drinker who wished to abstain, told me that he planned to continue visiting his old tavern haunt, to sit at the bar and order a ginger ale, just so he could prove to

Table 4-1.   Strategies Recommended for Client: Enlisting Support for Quitting Smoking

Why You Should Enlist Social Support for Quitting Smoking
One of the things that researchers have discovered is that people who have more social support from spouses, friends, co-workers, relatives, and others have more success at losing weight, quitting smoking, and other behavior change efforts. In our own research we have found that people's social circles have a strong effect on their efforts to quit smoking. For instance, people who are surrounded by other smokers often have a harder time quitting than those who are not.

Enlisting people who can help you in your efforts to quit smoking can have a powerful effect on helping you to stay quit. In this handout we will talk about whose support you should enlist, how to enlist it, and how it can help you to quit and stay quit.

Whom You Should Ask to Help
There are two categories of people who can be most helpful in your efforts to stay quit. One of these is people you are closest to such as your spouse or partner, your family, your close friends. Because they are so close to you these people can have a great impact on your smoking. The other category is people you have a lot of contact with. Examples would be co-workers, housemates, and so on. Although you may not be that close to these people, they can exert a strong impact on you because they are around you a great deal.

The first thing you should do in deciding whose help to enlist is to assess who in your life either already has a great impact on your smoking, or could have a great impact. (This impact may be negative such as a person at work who always offers you a cigarette.) Who in your life could offer you a lot of support? Who in your life could help you by stopping some of the negative things they do?

How to Ask People for Social Support
Now that you have decided whom to ask, how do you ask them? The most important thing is to ask them to help you in specific ways. This lets people know how to help you. The best way to ask is directly. Say something like, "Hello. I'm going to be quitting smoking on [date], and I'd like your help and support in staying quit. Let me tell you a little bit about how I'd like you to help me, and then you can decide if you would be willing to help. Okay?" Then you can describe what kind of help you would like and they can decide.

What People Can Do to Help You
Assuming they are willing, what do you ask them to do? This depends on whether they currently do things that make it hard for you not to smoke, such as smoking themselves. If they already affect you in a negative way, then you should ask them to stop. For instance, you might ask them to stop offering you cigarettes. Or you might ask them if they are willing to not smoke when you are around. Of course, this will be the most effective if you ask nicely and still allow them to be able to smoke. Or you might ask someone at work who often gives you a lot of work at the last minute to give you advance notice of work for a couple of weeks after you first quit so that you won't have as much stress. A good way of phrasing this kind of request is: "Hello. I'm going to quit smoking on [date] and I would like it very much if you could help me by not leaving cigarettes on my desk and, as much as possible, by not smoking when I'm around. Would you be willing to do this for a couple of weeks after I quit?"

You will probably want to enlist some positive support, too, especially from those you are closest to. Some possible requests are for emotional support, tolerance of irritable behavior, rewarding you for not smoking, talking with you about difficulties you are having, and so on. It is a good idea to enlist a little bit of time. You might say something like, "I'm going to be quitting smoking on [date] and I expect that I might be pretty hard to get along with for a bit after I quit. Would you be willing to help me by giving me a little extra support and tolerance during that period?"

You might also want to set up a "buddy system." This involves finding someone who is willing to be your confidante whom you can talk to daily or almost daily, who will listen to you as you discuss problems you are having and give you support. It is a good idea when you ask people to tell them what you would like them to do. For instance, you might say, "I'm quitting smoking on [date] and I would really like your help. What I'd like is to be able to talk to you for a few minutes every day for the first week I quit. I'd like to talk about how I'm doing and have you give me some emotional support. Would you be willing to do that?"

What to Do if You Live with a Smoker
We strongly recommend that if you live with smokers you work out some kind of agreement you can both feel good about. For example they could agree not to leave cigarettes lying around the house, and/or to not smoke in your presence, and/or to not offer you cigarettes, and/or to not tease you or undermine your efforts, all in return for your not pressuring them or being critical of their smoking.

What to Do if Someone Doesn't Want to Help
If you ask someone to help who doesn't want to, that's okay, just find someone else who is willing. However, if the person is actively hindering your efforts to quit, then you must do something about it. Be assertive! Don't get angry but simply repeat your request. When people don't want to change what they are doing it may be because they feel you have no right to ask them not to smoke around you. In this case you may want to try for a compromise. For instance, perhaps some of the time you could work at another location, and the rest of the time they would not smoke when you were near them. Most people will usually agree to some sort of reasonable compromise.

Good luck. Remember, the more help you can enlist, the more support you will have for not smoking!

---

himself that he was "strong enough to meet the challenge." Clients who insist upon proving their willpower by continuing to deliberately tempt themselves are setting the stage for relapse. Underlying this need to "meet the challenge" may be a fear of letting go totally of the old crutch—just in case it is needed. This makes about as much sense as keeping a pair of crutches in the trunk of one's car just in case one ends up with a broken leg. Therapists should emphasize the need to make a full and complete departure when embarking on the journey of habit change—to make a clean break, to wipe the slate clean of all traces of the old habit pattern.

Another important stimulus control procedure is to encourage clients to stock up on a variety of *substitute activities* that will facilitate the transition of departure. Substitute activities include any event, substance, or activity that would provide a readily available substitute for the addictive habit, particularly during the first few days of the journey. Smokers may wish to stock up on a supply of oral substitutes such as toothpicks, mints, or chewing gum. Those who express a fear of not knowing what they will do with their hands (especially during social interactions) should obtain some small articles that they can "fiddle with," such as a rubbing stone, marble, or puzzle. Drinkers should be encouraged to purchase a variety of their favorite nonalcoholic beverages such as soda water, fruit juices, or tonic. Care must be taken, however, to avoid substituting one potentially addictive behavior for another. Smokers should be cautioned against excessive use of alcohol as a substitute for cigarettes; many smoking relapses occur when individuals have been drinking and their resolve becomes dissolved in alcohol. Drinkers should stay away from the use of tranquilizers as an alternative means of coping with tension, since this greatly increases the probability of a new dependency. Planning pleasant activities also may serve as a positive substitute activity to compensate in part for the sense of deprivation and loss that are often experienced in the early days of the journey. Such activities as attending a movie or concert, having a massage, purchasing a new outfit or gift for oneself, reading an engrossing book or magazine, engaging in pleasurable sexual activity, or taking a brief vacation are particularly effective in this regard, since they involve a sense of pleasure that may help compensate for the loss of immediate gratification associated with the addictive habit. Funds for some of these activities may be obtained through the savings made possible by cessation of the addictive behavior.

Departure Ceremony

Choice of the final date of departure should be made with care. If at all possible, one should avoid selecting a departure date that coincides with periods of stress or unusually high temptation. To quit smoking on a Monday morning at the start of a stressful work week is to invite trouble. Similarly, departure should not coincide with stressful life events such as a divorce, a difficult examination, or personal misfortune. On the other hand, avoidance of stress can also be used as an excuse for continual postponement of the departure date (the "I'll quit when my life settles down completely" excuse). Obviously it is impossible to rid oneself of all sources of stress before quitting, and there is no perfect time for departure. Some times are, however, better than others. Good times for departure include weekend or vacation days, special holidays or events (particularly those with a symbolic value such as New Year's Day, Independence Day, or one's birthday), or times of relatively low stress. Planning a date that coincides with departure on an actual trip or vacation (e.g., a trip to Europe) may also be a good idea, providing the destination does not increase the probability of relapse (gamblers should stay away from Monte Carlo as well as downtown Reno).

The actual date of departure should be an occasion for celebration. After all, one is embarking on a journey that will lead to greater freedom, improved health, and an increased sense of accomplishment and self-mastery. The event should be marked with some form of *ceremony* to highlight the significance of the occasion. Choice of an appropriate ceremony is best made by the client, possibly with the assistance and advice of the therapist. The purpose of an individualized ceremony is to draw one's attention to the importance of the moment of actual departure, much as the ceremony that signifies the moment when an ocean liner finally is untied from the pier and begins its voyage (complete with a band playing joyfully while passengers on the upper decks throw streamers down to the well-wishers on the dock below). Smokers may wish to bring in all their remaining cigarettes and paraphernalia and set fire to them as a final parting gesture. Drinkers may wish to toast themselves off to a pleasant journey with a final glass of champagne. For others, a "going away party" may be the best way to mark the occasion. At the very least, the individual should be encouraged to sign a statement of commitment, formally stating the reasons for making the journey and describing the final goal. The moment the statement is signed, the journey begins. The border is crossed at last.

Some therapists recommend the use of a signed contract to formalize the commitment process. Others recommend that such a contract include contingencies describing penalties for violation of the contract (e.g., paying a monetary fine or forfeiting a deposit in the event of relapse). Contingency contracting may be an effective strategy, particularly as a method of increasing the "response cost" of relapse during the initial stages of the journey. Some clients agree in advance to pay their relapse fines to an undesirable individual or political group (e.g., the Ku Klux Klan or the American Nazi Party) as an additional incentive. However, the ultimate outcome of such external restraints may be a backfire effect in which relapse is more likely to occur when the contract expires or the effects of the contingencies lose their incentive appeal. Until future research clarifies the conditions under which contingency contracting is effective, therapists should use caution when considering the use of this procedure.

ON THE JOURNEY: COPING WITH CRAVING AND URGES

The remainder of this chapter is devoted to a discussion of various cognitive intervention strategies that can be employed during the journey of habit change. The three main problem areas to be discussed are coping with positive outcome expectancies, coping with slips, breakdowns, and potential setbacks along the way, and coping with faulty cognitions associated with relapse "set-ups" (covert planning, Apparently Irrelevant Decisions [AIDs], rationalizations, and other cognitive defense mechanisms). Attention will also be paid to the use of behavioral coping strategies where appropriate.

Once the individual has embarked, the initial problem one must cope with is dealing with craving and urges to return to the prior addictive behavior pattern. In some cases, these internal urges become so intense that the client gives up very early on the trip. In a recent study conducted in our laboratory of smokers who attempted to quit on their own, fully 17% were unable to stay off cigarettes for more than 24 hours after quitting (Marlatt, Goldstein, & Gordon, 1984). Clearly the first few days following departure mark the greatest risk period in terms of succumbing to urges. Before going on to describe relevant assessment and intervention methods for coping with these urges and temptations, let us briefly review the theoretical model and definition of positive outcome expectancies described in Chapter 3.

In addition to self-efficacy expectancies, an important expectancy system associated with the relapse process involves the operation of *positive outcome expectancies*—the individual's beliefs or expectations concerning the perceived outcome associated with a particular activity. Of particular interest are expectancies regarding the physical (biological), psychological (cognitive and emotional states), and behavioral effects of engaging in the addictive habit. Even though the actual or real effects may differ from one's expectations, the perceived or *expected outcomes* are the ones that carry the greatest incentive value and are therefore the target of intervention in the RP approach.

An outcome expectancy consists of both cognitive and incentive components. The cognitive component is associated with information concerning the nature of the expected outcome (whether positive or negative), whereas the incentive component involves the degree of motivational attraction (desire or aversion) for the expected outcome. *Craving* is defined within this theoretical framework as the degree of desire (incentive value) for the immediate positive outcomes one expects as a function of engaging in the addictive behavior. In this sense, craving refers to the subjective desire for immediate gratification (the Problem of Immediate Gratification [PIG] phenomenon). An *urge* is defined as an intention to engage in instrumental activity designed to gratify or satisfy craving (thus a distinction is made between craving as a subjective motivational state and the urge as a behavioral intention that "translates" the craving state into a potential overt act of indulgence). In the material to follow, we use the term *urge* as a general catch-all phrase to represent positive outcome expectancies and craving experiences.

According to the theoretical framework presented in Chapter 3, craving and urges derive from several potential sources: (1) classical conditioning, in which direct exposure to drug cues or other stimuli previously associated with the addictive behavior serve as conditioned stimuli that elicit a conditioned craving response (the emphasis in the RP model is on *appetitive conditioning* associated with expected positive outcomes in contrast with other theories that emphasize the influence of aversive conditioning, e.g., conditioned withdrawal symptoms as the basis for craving); (2) exposure to high-risk situations coupled with low self-efficacy for coping (considered to be the primary source of craving associated with most relapses); (3) physical dependency or withdrawal (although the influence of this factor differs with various addictive substances, physical withdrawal seems to play a relatively minor role as a determinant of relapse); (4) cultural and personal beliefs about the expected effects of the addictive behavior; and (5) environmental setting (e.g., social setting, tavern environments, etc.).

Assessment of Outcome Expectancies

In planning intervention strategies for urge control, the therapist must assess both the content of the client's outcome expectancies (the nature of the belief structure) and the rate of occurrence of the expectancies under various circumstances (determinants of frequency and intensity of urges). Although the development of behavioral and cognitive strategies to assess outcome expectancies is still in its infancy, several procedures that may be useful are described in the following paragraphs. Included in the discussion are self-monitoring of urges, assessment of expected outcomes for specific risk situations, evaluation of personal beliefs about the effects of various addictive acts, and direct exposure to stimuli associated with the addictive behavior.

Perhaps the simplest and easiest method of asssessing outcome expectancies is to ask the client to keep an ongoing record of urges or experiences of craving for a period of time. Self-monitoring data should include a brief description of the situation in which the urge occurs, along with a rating of the client's mood or emotional state at the time. In addition, the client can be asked to rate the intensity and duration of the urge (intensity can be rated on a 7-point scale for "strength of urge" and duration can be indicated by the length of time the urge lasted). Analysis of the situations in which urges occur should provide information concerning the nature of specific high-risk situations for potential relapse. Instead of focusing on self-efficacy or perceived ability to cope with the high-risk situation, the emphasis here is on the client's expected outcomes for engaging in the addictive behavior in that particular situation.

Once the urge situations have been defined through the process of self-monitoring, the therapist should query the client concerning his or her expectations of how the addictive activity would influence the client's behavior (overt actions), physical state, feelings, and thought processes. By doing this, the therapist will be able to assess situation-specific expectancies (cf. Mischel, 1981) or what the client believes to be the effects of the addictive behavior in various risk situations. For example, if a problem drinking client reported strong urges when feeling angry, the therapist might ask: "If you were to take a drink when you're angry, how do you think the alcohol would affect you? Would you feel different emotionally? How would it influence your actions—would you be more or less likely to act out your aggressive feelings? Would it influence the way you think when you're angry? How would the drink make you feel physically? What would be your first reaction to the alcohol and how would the effects change over time?" Similar questions could be asked about other urge situations such as social pressure, negative interpersonal conflict, negative physical states, and environmental temptations. By examining the client's perceived functional utility of the addictive act in specific situations, alternative (nonaddictive) methods of attaining the desired outcome may become apparent.

Assessment of personal beliefs about the effects of the addictive substance or activity may also be accomplished by the use of various questionnaires and rating scales. The problem with most existing questionnaires that are designed to assess the expected effects of various drugs is that they fail to take into account the situational factors (setting, set, mood, etc.) involved at the time of use. Obviously, people have different expectancies about how alcohol will influence their mood or feelings in situations that differ markedly from each other. Compare, for instance, beliefs about how drinking would make one feel at a wedding party to drinking as an attempt to cope with feelings of sadness or depression. Or compare using a drug while feeling angry to using a drug while feeling sexually excited. A second problem is that some questionnaires fail to discriminate between the respondent's knowledge of expectations shared by the members of a common culture (shared societal beliefs) and *personal expectancies* (how the individual expects the drug will make him or her feel, not what he or she believes the effects will be for people in general) (Rohsenow, 1983). Recently, several questionnaires have been developed that show promise for the assessment of expectancies associated with the use of alcohol. These include the Alcohol Expectancy Questionnaire for use with adults (Brown, Goldman, Inn, & Anderson, 1980) or adolescents (Christiansen, Goldman, & Inn, 1982; Christiansen & Goldman, 1983) developed by Mark Goldman and his colleagues at Wayne State University. In our own laboratory, we have developed a rating scale questionnaire that can be used to assess the effects of both moderate and heavy amounts of alcohol (Southwick, Steele, Marlatt, & Lindell, 1981). Similar questionnaires have yet to be developed for use with other addictive behaviors.

A final assessment procedure, one that is just beginning to receive experimental attention in recent years, involves exposing the client directly to the addictive substance or related cues and assessing various response systems including psychophysiological arousal (e.g., heart rate, salivation, skin conductance, and perhaps pupillary diameter), self-reported craving, and instrumental activity related to the acquisition of the desired substance (e.g., number of operant level presses the client is willing to perform in order to obtain the desired substance). The main purpose of direct exposure techniques is to assess the classically conditioned components of craving (Cooney, Baker, & Pomerleau, 1983; Pomerleau, Fertig, Baker, & Cooney, 1983). The main problem with this method, as noted previously in connection with general expectancy questionnaires, is that they often fail to manipulate or control for situational factors such as set and setting. Simply having an alcoholic respond to the smell and sight of an alcoholic beverage presented in a neutral laboratory environment may not provide an accurate predictor of the client's response to alcohol when confronted with a high-risk situation in the natural environment. Future research is needed to provide clarification of these issues.

Urge Control: Cognitive–Behavioral Intervention Methods

The first step in teaching cognitive methods for coping with craving and urges is to give the client a theoretical framework that provides a context for the intervention techniques described in this section. Many individuals assume that all cravings and urges are manifestations of physical withdrawal symptoms and thus arise from "internal" sources that cannot be controlled. To counter this belief, the therapist should point out that although physical withdrawal may elicit some urges in the initial stages following cessation for some individuals, most urges are triggered by *external* factors such as exposure to drug cues or related stimuli (via classical conditioning) and involvement in high-risk stress situations. Often the stress reactions engendered by high-risk situations such as negative emotional states or interpersonal conflict are misinterpreted or mislabeled as symptoms of physical withdrawal. When this appears to be the case, the client should be encouraged to reframe the craving as a desire for the addictive crutch as a means of attempting to cope with stress. Rather than interpreting an urge or craving experience as a physiologically based need for the addictive substance or activity, clients can be taught that these experiences reflect their desire for immediate gratification associated with the first phase of the biphasic response (e.g., enhanced feelings of power or control associated with increased arousal).

Another misbelief that often needs to be corrected is that the occurrence of urges is an indication that treatment has failed or that the effects of the initial treatment program have "worn off." The tendency to perceive urges as a sign of imminent relapse is likely to be particularly strong with clients who have undergone treatment programs that claim to remove or recondition underlying urges. Many programs for alcoholism, smoking, or obesity often advertise that they will free the individual of all urges to engage in the addictive behavior through the application of treatment methods such as aversion, hypnosis, or chemical medication. Inpatient treatment programs for alcoholism may inadvertently create the impression among their clientele that their urges to drink have subsided or gone away altogether. This seeming disappearance of urges is an illusion created by the protective stress-free environment of the typical inpatient setting, many of which resemble luxury resorts or peaceful sanatoriums far removed from the day-to-day stress of everyday life. Patients discharged from such programs are often dismayed to find that their craving for alcohol and urge to drink return in full force as soon as they become reinvolved in their "real life" environment.

To counter such defeatist beliefs, clients should be given an alternative explanation of the role of urges in the recovery process. The experience of urges following cessation of the addictive habit should be considered a normal reaction, and not a signal of treatment failure or an indication of imminent relapse. Craving and urges are likely to recur whenever the individual is exposed to stimuli previously associated with the addictive behavior, such as the sight and smell of cigarettes, alcohol, and so on. These urges often represent conditioned responses and are a natural product of the conditioning process. If these conditioned craving responses are not reinforced by resumption of the addictive behavior, they will eventually fade away through the mechanism of extinction. Other urges are elicited by high-risk situations and can be considered a source of valuable information since they provide an intuitive signal or discriminative stimulus that the individual is experiencing stress and needs to come up with an effective coping response. In other words, urges can provide important feedback cues that something is "wrong" and needs attending to. Instead of attempting to block out these stress signals by a cigarette smoke screen or an alcoholic haze, the client can use the urge as a cue for positive coping; in the long run this will lead to a decrease in stress as the client learns to understand and cope with the stressful situation. The urge thereby becomes a signal for active coping instead of passive yielding and relinquishing control.

The most effective cognitive coping strategy with craving and urges is to develop a sense of *detachment* with regard to these experiences. Most clients tend to "identify" with the urge; they equate the urge with a volitional desire to indulge in the addictive behavior. Identification with the urge makes it more difficult to resist the temptation to indulge, whereas to "remove oneself" from the experience is to gain some control over it. The client is likely to think, "I'm dying for a cigarette," instead of "I am experiencing an urge to smoke—this is a useful signal to me that I need to cope with the situation." The best way to facilitate "disidentification" with the urge is to *externalize* it—to perceive it as a response to some external cue or situation instead of stemming from an internal physical source. By externalizing the urge, the client is more likely to assume an objective position of detached awareness instead of a subjective identification with the experience.

People need experience and training to cope with urges in this manner. Several strategies are useful. The client first needs to recognize craving and urges when they occur, and to label them accurately. The diagram presented in Figure 3-1 (p. 141) illustrates a hypothetical model of the process involved. In this example, the craving response is a conditioned response to the sight of a pack of cigarettes (perhaps one left invitingly open on a coffee table at a party). The client should be taught, as discussed above, that it is quite natural to experience conditioned craving responses for some time after abstinence has begun, and that it is pointless to attempt to suppress the craving and the corresponding urge to indulge. Instead of either trying to suppress the urge through the exercise of willpower or passively giving in to the urge by indulging in the addictive act, the client should simply allow the urge to occur without giving in to it. Just because the urge is an automatic conditioned response that cannot be controlled or suppressed does not imply that the consummatory response (addictive indulgence) is also automatic and therefore must occur. One can learn to experience urges without necessarily yielding to their influence. The best strategy is for the client to simply observe the urge when it occurs, to assume an objective stance of detached awareness, and to "let it be" without reacting to it.

The key ingredient in this intervention process is to teach the client to accurately label the urge when it occurs; one practical method is to suggest that the client make a brief mental notation whenever the response occurs (i.e., to note to oneself, "craving response" or "urge response"). The most important error of interpretation that can be made is to conclude that the craving or urge will continue to increase in intensity and pressure until it is relieved by resuming the old habit. One client who was attempting to stop smoking described his urge as a balloon lodged inside his stomach that continued to increase in size; he felt that unless he gave in and smoked a cigarette, the craving would increase the size of the balloon until it eventually broke and he would "go crazy" as a result. This belief is shared by many: that urges continue to increase in intensity in a monotonic fashion and unless they are indulged in, some disastrous outcome will occur ("losing my mind," "going crazy"). Clients need to be reminded forcefully that any attempt to relieve the urge by giving in to it (e.g., by taking a few puffs from a cigarette or having a sip or two of alcohol) will actually serve to strengthen the intensity of the urge and increase the probability of its recurrence. On the other hand, if one does not "feed" the urge in this way, it will eventually weaken and lose its urgency.

To counter the belief that an urge will increase in intensity unless it is indulged in, the therapist can describe the urge as a response that grows in intensity, peaks, and then subsides—as long as the individual does not respond by giving in. In this sense, the craving or urge response is similar to an ocean wave: it starts small, builds to a crest, and then breaks or subsides in intensity. The wave analogy is a useful externalization technique and facilitates detachment from the experience. An imagery technique based on this analogy is *urge surfing*. The client is instructed to imagine that an urge is like a wave and that he or she is learning to be a surfer—to "ride" the wave with balance instead of being "wiped out" by its force. As with any new skill, urge surfing may take some time and practice before the client learns to attain a position of balance.

Another related imagery technique is the *Samurai* image. The client is instructed to visualize the urge as an externalized "enemy" or threat to one's life. As soon as the Samurai warrior (the client) recognizes the presence of the urge, it is disposed of immediately with an active response (e.g., "beheaded with the sword of awareness"). The client as Samurai is warned that urges may assume a variety of "disguises" to avoid being detected. Although some urges may be easy to detect and deal with since they are externally visible (e.g., an open pack of cigarettes on a table), others may be more subtle and disguise themselves as an internal voice or prompter that seems to come from within (e.g., having a thought such as "I could really use a drink at a time like this"). These "internalized" urges are more difficult to deal with, since the Samurai must first externalize them in order to reveal their true identity. The more "macho" clients may wish to visualize cutting a notch in their belt for each vanquished urge.

Because of the strong link between craving and urges and the initial phase of the biphasic response, it may be possible to neutralize the urge to some extent by countering it with thoughts or images related to the downside or delayed negative component of the two-stage reaction. Some clients report that as soon as they have an urge, they imagine the negative consequences of the addictive behavior, such as impaired health, hangovers, or social disapproval. To help remind clients of the delayed negative reactions, a "referenting" procedure can be employed. Each time they think of the immediate positive outcomes, clients are instructed to immediately use that as a referent for the long-range negative consequences. As an example, a smoker who begins to think how nice it would feel to inhale a drag to quell an urge can use this thought as a referent or reminder of the negative effects of tobacco dependency—sore throat, coughing, and increased susceptibility to disease. In order for referenting to be effective, the association between the immediate and delayed effects must be continuously repeated, like paired associates in a verbal learning task. Educating clients about the nature of the biphasic response or opponent-process theory will help facilitate the referenting effect.

In addition to these cognitive intervention methods, there are several behavioral coping strategies that can be used to cope with craving and urges. Most of these techniques have been described in Chapter 2 and will only be briefly reviewed here. The most obvious and relevant behavioral strategy is, of course, the execution of overt coping responses in high-risk situations. If clients report feeling intense urges when experiencing frustration or anger, an assertive coping response clearly is called for. Similarly, an overt refusal response may be the most effective way to reduce urges in social pressure situations. Often the simple exercise of an avoidance or escape response in a high-risk situation will be sufficient to reduce or eliminate the urge to indulge. Distraction, such as engaging in a substitute activity (e.g., taking a walk, having a massage, seeing a movie, thinking about something different, etc.) are also recommended. Although the use of stimulus control procedures is often very effective, particularly in the early stages of a behavior change program, it would be naive to assume that a client will be able to avoid all the stimuli that might trigger an urge to resume the old behavior. For any overlearned habit such as smoking or drinking that is comprised of responses performed on countless occasions, there are just too many situations and stimuli to avoid altogether. In our society, people are constantly bombarded with stimuli and cues arising from the observation of other people's behavior, from advertising and the media, from associations and memories of past behaviors, all of which form a strident chorus of voices urging the individual to "DRINK ME! SMOKE ME! EAT ME!" How can we assist the client to cope with all of these tempting lures? Although it is tempting to follow the lead of Odysseus, who had the ears of his rowers plugged with wax to block out the Sirens' song of temptation, this solution hardly seems practical in contemporary society. Instead, a balanced presentation of cognitive and behavioral coping strategies may be the best weapon against temptation.

One behavioral intervention program that may be effective in modifying craving and urges is called *cue exposure* (Hodgson & Rankin, 1976; Cooney et al., 1983). Based on classical conditioning theory (e.g., Pomerleau, 1981), cue exposure is based on the assumption that direct exposure to substance cues (e.g., liquor, cigarettes, etc.) will elicit conditioned craving responses in the addicted individual; if these craving responses are not reinforced by subsequent consumption or increased use of the substance, they should eventually subside through the mechanism of extinction. Alternatively, cue exposure may be effective because it enhances self-efficacy; clients may feel more confident that they can be exposed to drug cues without losing control. Treatment programs that utilize cue exposure procedures may be able to experimentally induce and modify craving responses prior to discharging the client back into an environment in which substance cues are commonly encountered.

Most current work with cue exposure has been conducted with alcoholic clients. Some investigators have used a procedure in which the client is first administered a priming dose of alcohol (to heighten craving) and then prevented from engaging in subsequent drinking (response prevention) in order to facilitate extinction of craving (e.g., Hodgson & Rankin, 1976, 1982; Rankin, 1982). Other investigators have simply presented the client with alcohol-related cues (sight and smell of various beverages) to elicit craving without having the client actually consume alcohol (Cooney et al., 1983; Pomerleau et al., 1983). In one study, alcoholic patients were gradually exposed to a variety of individualized cues, including trips to their favorite pubs where they observed others drinking while they consumed soft drinks. At the end of the treatment sessions (up to 40 exposure trials were given), clients reported little or no desire to drink (reduced craving) in cue-exposure situations (Blakey & Baker, 1980). Future treatment programs may find that a combination of behavioral cue exposure and the cognitive urge control techniques described above may be a particularly effective combination, as suggested by Cooney et al. (1983).

ON THE JOURNEY: COPING WITH SLIPS AND
POTENTIAL SETBACKS

The aim of the intervention methods described in this section is to prevent the lapse or initial setback from escalating into a total relapse. Almost all journeys involve minor setbacks, frustrations, and disappointments. To return to the road analogy, sooner or later most people develop engine trouble, a flat tire, or other form of breakdown on the road. When this occurs, all movement forward grinds to a halt and one finds oneself stuck. As Robert Pirsig commented in his book, *Zen and the Art of Motorcycle Maintenance*, this can be a very unpleasant and unsettling experience, "This is the zero moment of consciousness. Stuck. No answer. Honked. Kaput. It's a miserable experience emotionally. You're losing time. You're incompetent. You don't know what you're doing. You should be ashamed of yourself" (1974, p. 279).

Many individuals are tempted to give up at this point of the journey. They tend to blame themselves for the breakdown (e.g., see it as a failure of willpower or personal shortcoming) and assume that all is lost, the road has led to a dead end, and there is nothing to do but to turn back and head for home. Because of their unrealistic expectations of perfection—that the journey would proceed smoothly, without a hitch—they are often unprepared to cope with such setbacks; they don't expect problems and are unprepared when they arise. They often lack both the knowledge of what to do and the skills that are needed to correct the problem.

But being stuck or experiencing a lapse does not necessarily mean that one has reached a dead end or that relapse is the only possible outcome. It can be an occasion for growth, understanding, and learning—a prolapse rather than a relapse. The Chinese character for the word "crisis" consists of a combination of two ideograms, one representing "danger" and the other "opportunity." Certainly a lapse is an indication of danger (potential relapse), but it is also an opportunity for growth and the development of new coping skills (potential prolapse). A breakdown on the road offers an opportunity to understand what went wrong and how to remedy the problem. Instead of saying, "I blew it—it's all over," one can ask, "What went wrong? Did I take a wrong turn? What can I do to fix the problem? Is there a place to go for help, or is there someone who can assist me? Is there a manual and tool-kit handy—a map to help me get my bearings?" and so on. The individual can adopt an objective approach to the problem and engage in active attempts to find a solution instead of reacting subjectively to the lapse with a sense of failure and doom. This section includes a review of a variety of methods that can be used to help the waylaid traveler back on the road to freedom. The primary focus will be on cognitive reframing or the restructuring of attributions associated with potential setbacks. Attention is also paid to the use of the programmed relapse as a paradoxical intervention procedure that may serve as a useful clinical strategy when a relapse seems imminent or unavoidable. First, however, the use of these procedures will be justified in response to critics who may argue that to focus on the potential for relapse is equivalent to "permission-giving" and may therefore actually increase the probability of treatment failure.

Rationale for Anticipating and Coping with Lapses

As stated in Chapter 1, many traditional treatment programs for problems like alcoholism do not include any training or preparation for coping with potential slips. The entire focus is on fostering a firm and absolute commitment to abstinence as the one and only treatment goal. From this perspective, teaching clients how to deal with lapses somehow implies that slips are to be expected, even permitted by the treatment staff. Instead, many programs take the opposite tack and assume a hard line against any drinking that may occur: Anyone found drinking in the treatment center or admitting to sneaking a drink on a weekend pass is punished by being expelled from the program.

To counter objections that preparing clients to anticipate and cope with potential slips is coddling and permissive, the following rationale is suggested. It is generally known that in the treatment of addictive behavior problems there are high relapse rates, often running in the 70% 80% range within the first 6 months following treatment. It is therefore somewhat unrealistic and potentially self-defeating to somehow assume that most patients will be totally successful in their attempts to maintain total abstinence. To the extent that clients adopt this absolute criterion for success, the first time a slip occurs they are likely to feel like a total failure, abnormal, aberrant, or unique, even though from a statistical standpoint the experience of an initial lapse is highly probable and not at all abnormal. But what if the client were taught "emergency procedures" to deal with a slip should one occur? Most people understand that the purpose of having fire drills or other preparations for emergencies is to teach survival skills in case an emergency occurs, not to give people permission to light fires. In this sense, to be prepared is to be ready to cope with emergencies: forewarned is forearmed. If preparation for relapse is built into the treatment program, it may facilitate self-regulatory behavior that prevents a lapse from escalating into relapse–collapse. In this regard, an ounce of prevention is definitely worth a pound of cure!

The clinical and research literature supports the notion that preparation and forewarning are frequently effective treatment strategies. In a recent review, Wortman and Dintzer (1978) state:

Uncontrollable outcomes that are expected may produce less serious deficits than uncontrollable events that occur suddenly and without warning. If individuals realize that a certain outcome may occur, they have the opportunity to gradually

absorb the news, explore various possibilities, and begin reevaluating the outcome
. . . most studies suggest that having some advance warning facilitates long-term
coping with uncontrollable life events. (p. 83)

Informing clients about the process of relapse, the triggering events, and
subsequent reactions may lessen the impact of the event should it occur.
Knowing that something can be done to intervene in case a lapse occurs may
reduce stressful reactions to the event. Studies by Glass and Singer (1972a,
1972b) support the notion that if individuals know beforehand that there is
something they can do to alleviate the distress of an unpleasant event (e.g.,
push a button to terminate a noxious tone), there is a significant decrement
in the stress-producing effects of the event—even if subjects do not actually
engage in the escape activity.

Giving the client advance warnings about the possibility of a lapse and
the emotional reactions usually associated with such an event may increase a
perception of control—a sense of knowing that something can be done even
in the face of apparent failure. Perception of control has been found in
several studies to have stress-reducing effects (see review by Janis & Rodin,
1979). In addition, preparing clients for their emotional reactions to a lapse,
the AVE, has the effect of informing them that these reactions are *normal
and to be expected* (cf. Rodin, 1976). Such advance knowledge also has the
effect of reducing the impact and stress of the emotional reaction. In a review
of this literature, Janis and Rodin conclude:

Field experiments repeatedly indicate that preparatory communications containing
forewarnings combined with realistic reassurances can function as stress inoculation
to increase patients' adherence to difficult decisions (see Girodo, 1977; Janis, 1958;
Janis & Mann, 1977; Meichenbaum, 1977). Preparatory information functions as a
form of stress inoculation if it enables a person to increase his or her tolerance for
postdecisional stress by developing effective reassurances and coping mechanisms.
. . . A number of laboratory studies indicate that people are less likely to display
strong emotional reactions or extreme changes in attitude when confronted with a
disagreeable experience if they have already been made aware of the unpleasant event
beforehand (for example, Epstein & Clarke, 1970; Lazarus & Alfert, 1964; Staub &
Kellett, 1972). We expect, therefore, that giving realistic preparatory information
about the potential threats that are likely to materialize will likewise have positive
effects, enabling the inoculated person to cope more effectively with whatever predicted setbacks occur. (Janis & Rodin, 1979, pp. 515–516)

Nonetheless, one must be careful to warn clients about the possibility
that they may be tempted to use preparatory information about slips and
lapses as a rationalization to indulge—for example, "If almost everyone else
experiences a slip, why shouldn't I?" or, "If it is possible to recover from a
slip and that it's not the end of the world if I have a lapse, then why
shouldn't it be okay for me to go ahead and have a drink?" Rationalizations

such as these illustrate the old adage that a little knowledge is a dangerous thing. Clients may in fact find themselves tempted by a "little knowledge" about relapse. Preparatory knowledge and forewarnings are effective to the extent that the individual has made a firm prior commitment to change, but can backfire or have detrimental effects in the absence of a strong prior commitment (cf. Kiesler, 1971).

The essential aspect of the RP program is to emphasize to clients that along with the preparatory information goes the notion of assuming *personal responsibility* for the best use of this material. To use normative information about the relapse process as an excuse or rationalization to indulge is to abdicate personal responsibility for this behavior and to act as if relapse is determined by factors beyond one's personal control. If, on the other hand, clients are forewarned about the temptation to use the preparatory information as a "cop-out" or excuse for relapse, they cannot back out of assuming personal responsibility for this behavior—they are fooling no one but themselves. On the other hand, for therapists to avoid the topic of relapse altogether for fear that it will be used as a rationalization is to leave the client unprepared to cope when and if a lapse occurs.

Initial Lapses and the Abstinence Violation Effect

As discussed in Chapter 3, an initial lapse may or may not escalate into a total relapse, depending in part on the magnitude of the individual's cognitive–affective reaction to the slip, that is, the magnitude of the AVE. An increased AVE is postulated to occur when the individual attributes the cause of the lapse to internal, stable, and global factors that are perceived to be uncontrollable (e.g., lack of willpower and/or the emergence of the symptoms of an underlying addictive disease). The intensity of the AVE is decreased, however, when the individual attributes the cause of the lapse to external, unstable (changeable), and specific factors that are perceived to be controllable (e.g., a transitory deficit in coping with a specific high-risk situation).

To review briefly, the AVE influences the probability of relapse in the following manner. The experience of an initial lapse causes the individual's attention to be drawn toward the self (objective self-awareness state). An attribution is then made as to the perceived "cause" of the lapse. If the lapse is attributed to external factors (e.g., a coping skill deficit in a specific high-risk situation), the resulting AVE will be minimal and the person is more likely to regain control and thereby stave off a full-blown relapse. If, on the other hand, the person attributes the lapse to an internal cause, such as lack of willpower, a reaction of guilt and self-blame will occur. The intensity of the guilt and self-blame will vary as a function of the evaluated discrepancy between one's actual behavior (the lapse) and one's ideal state (e.g., to be an abstainer). This emotional reaction serves to increase the probability of relapse by exacerbating the dysfunctional behavior (energized by the strength of the high arousal reaction) and/or by triggering a cognitive shift in which the individual redefines the self-image to bring it in line with the dysfunctional behavior (e.g., redefining oneself as an addict or as being "out of control"). Since an intense AVE is usually associated with a generalized decrement in expectation of future coping, a global relapse is likely to ensue. Following the relapse, the individual may attempt to "save face" by shifting the attribution from one of internal causation to an external cause thought to be more "acceptable" by the self and others (e.g., shifting the blame to environmental or biological factors considered to be beyond one's control). The intensity of the AVE will also be affected by other factors such as whether or not a prior decision was made to relinquish abstinence, prior beliefs about the inevitability of loss of control following an initial lapse, duration of prior abstinence period, and so on (see Chapter 3 for details). The primary goal of the cognitive reframing process is to alter the individual's attributions and attitudes concerning reactions to the initial lapse. Before proceeding to a description of the cognitive intervention methods, a discussion of the issue of assessment of attributions follows.

Assessment of Attributions Related to the Abstinence Violation Effect

Since attributions are covert cognitive processes that are assumed to occur after the fact, they cannot be readily assessed prior to the occurrence of a lapse. As such, most assessment procedures for attributtions are, by necessity, retrospective. Retrospective self-reporting of attributions is fraught with methodological problems and difficulties in interpretation (cf. Kendall, 1981; Nisbett & Wilson, 1977). In addition to the usual problems of distortion of memory and incomplete recall, respondent bias may seriously impact the validity of the reported attributions. Since questions about an individual's attributions about the causes of a lapse or relapse obviously refer to material that is likely to evoke feelings of guilt or shame in the respondent, defense mechanisms may be evoked that will distort the validity of the response. The individual may provide the interviewer with responses that are considered to be socially desirable or face-saving as a result. Recent data showing that alcoholics give predominantly external attributions for the cause of a relapse occurring more than a year prior to the time of assessment supports the notion that a face-saving shift in attributions occurs over time (Vuchinich, Tucker, Bordini, & Sullwold, 1981).

Another problem concerns the assessment format used to measure attributions. Recent studies have found, for example, that when open-ended response formats are used instead of specific rating scales (based on the investigator's own theoretical model of attributions), some subjects either failed to make attributions (Diener & Dweck, 1978; Hanusa & Schultz, 1977) or they made fewer and very different attributions than expected based on prior theorizing (Harvey, 1981; Wong & Weiner, 1981). One recent study

(Pittman & Pittman, 1980) showed, however, that people are more likely to make attributions when they are deprived of control or are uncertain as to the cause of their behavior (as in the relapse situation). For a complete discussion of this and other methodological problems in the assessment of attributions, the reader is referred to recent volumes edited by Kendall and Hollon (1981) and Merluzzi, Glass, and Genest (1981).

Given these caveats, one must proceed with considerable caution in the assessment of attributions. As a starting point, it may be helpful to ask clients about a relapse that occurred sometime in the recent past, and to probe for causal attributions. Response to such inquiries, however, are likely to reflect self-serving biases and other attempts to "look good" (e.g., the gambling client who initially blamed his relapse on the external factor of the "downtown Reno" environment). In order to provide a more prospective assessment procedure, clients could be presented with descriptions of high-risk situations (identical to those used in the assessment of self-efficacy and coping responses) and asked to describe the causes of a lapse that might occur in that situation. Clients could first be asked to imagine themselves experiencing a lapse in that situation and then to give an account of the causes or reasons why the lapse might have occurred (Goldstein, Gordon, & Marlatt, 1984).

Alternatively, clients could be asked to imagine *someone else* experiencing a slip in that situation, and to provide reasons why that individual lapsed. As reported in Chapter 3, Jones and Nisbett (1972) found that actors (those actually experiencing a lapse in the present case) typically attribute the cause of their own behavior to external situational factors, whereas observers of the same behavior often attribute its cause to stable internal dispositions possessed by the actor. Since in the prospective assessment situation, clients are asked to assume the role of observer and predict their own responses in a future situation, the attributions given under both instructional sets (imagine you are in the situation vs. imagine someone else is experiencing the lapse) should be similar. A discrepancy between attributions made for the imagine–self versus imagine–other conditions may, therefore, reflect the client's own self-reporting bias (e.g., the client disclaims personal responsibility for a lapse while attributing personal failing as a cause for someone else's lapse). Until future research clarifies these assessment problems, however, the above reasoning must be considered speculative.

In addition to asking open-ended questions about the client's attributions, it may be useful to design rating scales as a more objective measurement procedure—keeping in mind, however, that the format for rating scales may reflect the theoretical bias of the investigator rather than tapping into the client's own unique attributions. As a rough predictor, however, such rating scales may be effective. Separate 7-point rating scales could be constructed based on the four attributional dimensions for relapse outlined in Chapter 3: difficulty of the high-risk situation, strength of factors beyond one's control such as addictive craving or emergence of loss of control symptoms, presence or lack of motivation or willpower, and occurrence of failure to exercise coping skills. A tendency toward making internal attributions would be reflected by attributions reflecting motivational deficit (lack of willpower) or uncontrollable internal biological factors such as craving or loss of control. On the other hand, external attributions would be reflected by causal ascriptions to the difficulty of the high-risk situation or to the exercise of coping skills in that situation. One additional advantage of using paper-and-pencil rating scales is that people may be more willing to reveal their own attributional bias because of the relative privacy of this method compared to the more public procedure of reporting responses overtly in the presence of the interviewer. Rating scale questionnaires have already been developed by some investigators to measure attributional style (cf. Peterson, Semmel, VonBaeyer, Abramson, Metalsky, & Seligman, 1982; Russell, 1982; Seligman, Abramson, Semmel, & VonBaeyer, 1979).

Cognitive Distortions and the Relapse Process

Some of the client's cognitive errors and distortions may increase the probability that an initial slip will develop into a total relapse. Many of these problems are similar to the cognitive errors made by depressed individuals as described in the recent literature (cf. Beck, Rush, Shaw, & Emery, 1979; Abramson, Seligman, & Teasdale, 1978). Beck and his associates have described a series of "depressogenic assumptions" that may lead to a variety of cognitive errors for depressed individuals. Each of these errors have parallel implications for RP. The following points are adapted from Beck's description of depressogenic assumptions and associated cognitive errors (Beck *et al.*, 1979, p. 261):

1. Overgeneralizing. The faulty assumption associated with this cognitive error is: "If it's true in one case, it applies to any case which is even slightly similar." Overgeneralization is probably the most common cognitive error that mediates the escalation from a single lapse to a total relapse. The lapse is taken as a sign or symptom of total relapse; the occurrence of a single, isolated event is overgeneralized as a sign of total failure, thereby increasing the probability of recurrence over time and situations.

2. Selective Abstraction. Here the faulty assumption is: "The only events that matter are failures, deprivation, etc. I should measure self by errors, weaknesses, etc." The occurrence of a single mistake or slip is selectively abstracted as an indication of total failure—there is an excessive focusing upon the immediate failure experience along with a relative neglect of all prior success experiences, including the progress and learning that have occurred prior to the time of the lapse. Suddenly, in the reaction to a single slip-up, all past accomplishments become worthless compared to the magnitude of the failure.

3. Excessive Responsibility. Here the client makes the faulty assumption: "I am responsible for all bad things, failure, and so on." This error corresponds to a tendency for some people to attribute the cause of a lapse to personal, internal failings such as lack of willpower or moral weakness. They assume total responsibility and therefore personal causality for the slip, making it more difficult to reassume control.

4. Assuming Temporal Causality. This error is the temporal equivalent to the overgeneralization problem described above. There is a tendency to generalize over time with the faulty assumption: "If it has been true in the past, then it's always going to be true." A slip is seen as the first event in a "domino effect" in which all future coping attempts are doomed to the same outcome as the original lapse. This error is similar to the "once a drunk, always a drunk" mentality expressed by some clients (and therapists).

5. Self-Reference. This error refers to the perception that a lapse will become the focus of everyone else's attention. The faulty assumption is: "I am the center of everyone's attention—especially my bad performances. I am the cause of misfortunes." Again, the person assumes personal responsibility for the lapse and is likely to think others will blame him or her for the event, thereby augmenting reactions of guilt and self-blame.

6. Catastrophizing. Here the error is assuming that the worst possible outcome will occur: "Always think of the worst. It's most likely to happen to you." Instead of thinking of how to cope successfully after the first mistake, the person instead focuses on the worst outcome imaginable—that the lapse will trigger a process leading to the depths of degradation and despair as the individual slides helplessly into the mire of addictive self-victimization.

7. Dichotomous Thinking. The final cognitive error is based on the assumption that "everything is either one extreme or another." The lapse is taken as a sign of dichotomous switch from the "white side" of abstinence and purity to the "black side" of relapse and failure. There is no "grey area" or room to maneuver back onto the track once a slip has occurred. All lapses are relapses; abstinence, once violated, can never be regained.

In addition to Beck *et al.*'s (1979) depressogenic assumptions, the following two variations that have particular significance for addictive behavior problems can be considered:

8. Absolute Willpower Breakdown. The faulty assumption is that "willpower is absolute—once willpower has failed, loss of control is inevitable." Any weakness takes on the all-pervasive power of original sin—one bite of the forbidden fruit is all it takes to bring down the wrath of God. There is no return to the "paradise" of abstinence after the fall from grace; there is no "second chance." Willpower failure means the Devil has won the battle of temptation.

9. Body over Mind. Here the client mistakenly assumes, "Once the deed is done and the drug is in my body, physiological addiction or disease processes take over that I am powerless to control." This is a powerful belief in our drug-oriented culture. Many people believe that a single shot of heroin is sufficient to produce a lifelong overpowering physical addiction that cannot be voluntarily overcome. Many alcoholics come to believe that alcohol, once it gets in the bloodstream, will trigger overwhelming craving and loss of control drinking. Smokers may believe that one or two puffs are sufficient to trigger a nicotine withdrawal syndrome that can only be sated by chain smoking. Although physical dependency may be reactivated after a period of more or less regular use, there is no firm evidence to support the claim that a single lapse (one drink, one cigarette, one slice of chocolate cake, etc.) is sufficient to undermine all voluntary attempts to regain control.

Cognitive Reframing and Reattributions for Lapses

In a recent review of attributional processes and health care, Janis and Rodin (1979) state:

Under certain conditions, emotional arousal in response to physical symptoms or other signs of threat can be reduced, rather than enhanced, by attributional processes. There is now considerable evidence showing that the degree of pain and the level of distress that people experience depend in large part on the labels and cognitions that are applied to physical states and are not intrinsic properties of the state itself (Beecher, 1959; Nisbett & Valins, 1971; Schachter & Singer, 1962). These labels, in turn, can further influence perceptions regarding both the source and the level of arousal. (p. 489)

Reactions to an initial slip or lapse are often encumbered with excess cognitive baggage that has the effect of weighing down the individual and making it harder to engage in constructive coping behavior. Attributional problems based on maladaptive assumptions and cognitive errors place an extra load on the person that go far beyond the intrinsic properties of the state itself and render the lapse much more difficult to deal with constructively. The purpose of the cognitive restructuring procedure is to reframe the lapse so as to lighten the load of maladaptive attributions and associated emotional reactions and make it easier to regain control. Before describing specific reframing techniques, some general principles outlined by other investigators should be mentioned briefly.

Beck and his colleagues have outlined a number of cognitive therapy procedures to remedy depressogenic assumptions, including the therapist's exposure of the client's faulty logic, presentation of alternative assumptions, challenging the validity of self-defeating beliefs by counter-examples and alternative conceptualizations, having the client keep a "log" of past successes, disattribution of personal responsibility, exposing the arbitrariness of assumptions, and so forth (for details, see Chapter 12 of Beck et al., 1979).

Similarly, Abramson et al. (1978) have detailed some general principles for cognitive restructuring with depressed clients. Among the principles advocated by these authors, the following have important implications for dealing with lapses. Concerning the attribution of "uncontrollability" (e.g., expecting that a lapse will inevitably trigger a loss of control reaction), Abramson and her colleagues suggest changing the expectation from uncontrollability to controllability; in addition to behavioral interventions such as skill training to augment self-efficacy, the therapist can attempt to "change attributions from inadequate ability to inadequate effort" and to change unrealistic attributions for failure toward external, unstable, specific factors instead of internal, stable, and general factors such as loss of willpower or the overpowering force of physical addiction (Abramson *et al.*, 1979, p. 69).

The influence of these general principles will become apparent in the discussion of specific reframing procedures to cope with slips. The following is a description of some general strategies of reattribution designed as interventions to counter faulty assumptions and cognitive errors associated with initial lapses. This material is followed by a list of specific techniques to be used with clients who have experienced a slip.

A lapse is similar to a mistake or error in the learning process. By defining habit change as a learning process, lapses can be reframed as mistakes, as opportunities for corrective learning, instead of as indications of total failure or irreversible relapse. Just as the novice bicycle rider profits from a painful slip (e.g., by learning not to take the next curve so fast, to apply the brakes more gently when coming to a stop, etc.), so the beginning ex-smoker learns from a slip what to do the next time (e.g., avoid going to bars with friends who smoke, slow down when feeling hassled at work, etc.). From this perspective, slips are considered a relatively *normal* experience instead of a symptom of psychopathology or volitional breakdown. The learning literature (e.g., in concept formation) supports the notion that more is learned more from mistakes than from continued successes, since each mistake contains more "information" than repeated success trials (cf. Kendler, 1964).

The occurrence of a mistake in a learning task is to be expected, since few learners are able to master a new skill without making errors, especially in the beginning states. In the reframing process, clients should be encouraged to make clear distinctions between a lapse as a mistake or error rather than a failure experience. Reframing lapses in this way helps counter the cognitive errors of selective abstraction (excessive focus on personal failure).

A lapse is a specific, unique event in time and space. In order to prevent the cognitive errors of overgeneralization and assuming temporal causality, the client can be encouraged to view a lapse as a unique, independent event occurring at a specific time and place. To help develop this perspective, the client can be instructed to focus on the *here and now* when a lapse occurs, instead of bringing in "excess baggage" from the past (e.g., "In the past, whenever I have experienced a slip, I have lost control") or by making projections into the future ("Now that I've had one cigarette, there is no way to stop—I might just as well smoke the whole pack"). Generalization errors are likely to occur to the extent that the client views the lapse as a sign or symptom of something "greater"—a symptom of recidivism, a sign of total volitional breakdown. From a here-and-now perspective, the lapse is just what it is: a momentary episodic event, a single act that occurs in a specific intersect of time and space. As a reminder of the overgeneralization problem, clients can memorize the old maxim, "One swallow doesn't make a summer." One swallow is just what it appears to be: a single swallow—it doesn't necessarily imply that one must therefore drink the entire bottle.

The lapse can be reattributed to external, specific, and controllable factors. As stated earlier, the magnitude of the AVE is hypothesized to increase if the individual attributes the cause of the lapse to internal, stable, and global factors such as lack of willpower or the influence of powerful physical factors (physical dependency or disease). Such attributions increase feelings of guilt and perceptions of loss of control (the lapse is rendered uncontrollable). The cognitive errors of self-reference (assuming one is to blame for the lapse due to deficiencies in willpower or constitution) and absolute willpower breakdown (assuming a single slip signals a total collapse of willpower) are related to these attributional patterns. Reattribution calls for a careful examination of the lapse episode to evaluate the influence of such factors as difficulty level of the high-risk situation, adequacy of the coping response (if any), transitory deficits in motivation (e.g., fatigue, excessive stress, unbalanced lifestyle, etc.), and the overall uniqueness of the situation. The purpose of this reattribution is to isolate factors that are *controllable*: The external situation can be modified, new coping responses can be learned, stress can be reduced, lifestyle habits can be changed—all factors that are external, specific, and changeable (vs. internal, global, and uncontrollable).

A lapse can be turned into a prolapse instead of a relapse. Here the point is that the eventual outcome of a lapse may not always be negative; it depends, to a large degree, on the client's perspective and philosophical framework at the time a lapse occurs. Catastrophizing is a cognitive error based on the faulty assumption that the lapse will lead to the worst possible outcome: lapse = relapse = collapse. On the other hand, the lapse may turn out to be a valuable learning experience, an event that raises consciousness and teaches the client information about sources of life stress that need attending to. For example, a lapse in response to marital distress may signal the need for professional help or marital counseling that may eventually lead to an improvement in interpersonal satisfaction. One client who experienced a smoking slip during a stressful workday realized his job was a continual source of tension and frustration and decided to seek out a less stressful and more personally satisfying job. In cases such as these where the eventual outcome of a lapse is beneficial, the lapse can be considered a *prolapse*; a fall "forward" instead of "backward." Wortman and Dintzer (1978) have noted that attributing special meaning to an otherwise negative event, or adopting an optimistic philosophical framework toward the event, may increase the client's ability and motivation to cope effectively. Seeing the "silver lining" in an otherwise totally negative event may help transform lapses into prolapses.

Abstinence or control is always only a moment away. One of the most problematic cognitive errors that clients make when experiencing a lapse is to assume that once the absolute rule of abstinence (or a controlled program) has been violated, even by a single discrete slip, abstinence cannot be regained. A closely associated cognitive error is based on the "body over mind" assumption: because once a drug enters the body, the chemical–pharmacological–physiological–addictive–disease process is triggered and the resulting biological symptoms (e.g., craving, subclinical withdrawal state, genetic predisposition, etc.) cannot be voluntarily controlled, relapse is the inevitable outcome. But the fact remains that abstinence or control is always only a moment away: *as long as the individual is not currently engaging in the taboo behavior* (e.g., after the initial lapse), *a state of abstinence exists.* Abstinence is a state that can be regained simply by not resuming the addictive behavior—a lapse does not mean that abstinence is forever lost. All one needs to do in order to abstain is to refrain from taking the next drink or the next cigarette. To be successful in this endeavor is to regain control. In this sense, the goal of the RP approach is always the same, regardless of whether or not a lapse has occurred—to prevent the occurrence of the next lapse–relapse. A lapse is best viewed as a temporary discontinuity in an otherwise ongoing journey of abstinence or controlled use. Just as a cloud that momentarily passes before the sun on an otherwise clear sunny day does not mean that weather has taken an inevitable turn for the worse, so a transitory lapse does not necessarily mean that the previous state of abstinence is lost forever. It can be regained at a moment's notice.

What to Do when a Lapse Occurs

The occurrence of a lapse cannot be viewed as a totally benign event. It is a moment of crisis in the way the Chinese view crisis—as a combination of danger and opportunity. The most dangerous period is the time immediately following the event. Table 4-2 contains a variety of recommended strategies to employ whenever a lapse occurs. Clients can be told to think of this list as a set of "emergency procedures" to be used in case a lapse occurs. The strategies are listed in order of temporal priority, with the most important immediate steps listed first. The main points of this information can be presented to clients in summary form by the use of a "reminder card" that should be kept handy in the event that a lapse occurs. Since specific coping strategies will vary from client to client, therapists may wish to prepare an individualized

Table 4-2.   Coping Strategies Recommended in Case of Lapse

1. Stop, look, and listen. The first thing to do when a lapse occurs is to *stop* the ongoing flow of events and to *look and listen* to what is happening. The lapse is a warning signal indicating that you are in danger. Think of it as similar to a railway crossing sign warning you of the danger of being hit by an approaching train unless you take appropriate precautions. Or think of a lapse as a flat tire. The first thing for the driver to do is to pull over to a safe place at the side of the road in order to deal with the situation. If possible, choose a "rest stop" or other quiet place where you will not be disturbed or distracted by various temptations. As soon as you have pulled over to the side of the road, consult your *Reminder Card* for instructions. These are specific instructions to follow when a lapse occurs to keep it from developing into a total relapse, just as a driver who experiences a flat tire or other mechanical problem consults the automobile manual or set of emergency procedures in order to cope with the problem.

2. Keep calm. Your first reaction to the lapse may be one of feeling guilty and blaming yourself for what has happened. This is a normal reaction and is to be expected—it is part of the Abstinence Violation Effect (AVE). The AVE is essentially a harmless normal reaction, unless you allow yourself to give in to it and give up control. Give yourself enough time to allow the AVE reaction to arise and to pass away, just like an ocean wave that builds in strength, peaks at a crest, and then ebbs away. Allow the AVE reaction to occur without evaluating it or yourself negatively. Simply assume the role of an objective observer and wait until the reaction passes. Whatever you do, try not to give in to temptations or urges to resume the old habit, since this will make the recovery process much more difficult. Remember the old saying: "One swallow doesn't make a summer"? Well, one slip doesn't have to make a total relapse, either. Just because you slipped once does not mean that you are a failure, that you have no willpower, or that you are a hopeless addict. Look upon the slip as a single, independent event, something that can be avoided in the future. A slip is a mistake, an opportunity for learning, not a sign of total failure.

3. Renew your commitment. After a lapse, the most difficult problem to deal with is your motivation. You may feel like giving up, saying to yourself, "What's the use—I've blown it already." Again, this is a normal reaction (part of the AVE) and it can be remedied by the following steps. Think back over the reasons why you decided to change your behavior in the first place. Think of the long-range benefits to be gained from this change. Are they worth giving up just because you had a transitory setback? Engage yourself in a dialogue about the reasons why you originally decided to change. To do this, you might consider "talking to yourself" or engaging in an inner conversation between the side of you that wants to stick to your original goal and the side that wants to give up and throw in the towel. Remember that you are attempting to change your habits in honor of yourself as a way of caring for yourself, your health, and your life. Look back at how far you have already come in the journey of habit change. Reflect optimistically on your past successes in being able to quit the old habit, instead of focusing pessimistically on your current setback. Do you really believe that a single slip cancels out all the progress you have made to date? Renew your commitment. Your actions are under your control, and you are the master of your fate.

4. Review the situation leading up to the lapse. Don't yield to the tendency to blame yourself for what happened. By focusing in on your own personal failings, you will increase your reactions of guilt and self-blame, making it all the more difficult to cope effectively. Instead, look at the slip as a specific unique event. Ask yourself the following questions: What events led up to the slip? Were there any early warning signals that preceded the lapse? What was the nature of the high-risk situation that triggered the slip? Ask yourself about the setting, the time of day, the presence or absence of others, your mood at the time, the activities that were going on at the time. Each of these questions may yield valuable information concerning sources of stress in your life. The fact that a slip occurred often is an event that tells you that something is going on that needs attending to. Did you make any attempt to cope with the situation before the lapse occurred? If not, why not? Was your motivation weakened because of fatigue, the effects of other drugs, social pressure from others, or other transitory factors? What could you do next time to cope more effectively? Imagine the whole scene happening again, except that this time, see yourself coping effectively and not giving in to the temptation. Beware of thoughts and feelings that suggest that the effects of the drug taken during the slip are going to overpower you and make it impossible for you to regain control. This feeling is often used as an excuse or cop-out to give up. In most cases, the physical effects of a single lapse are just not strong enough to overpower your ability to regain control. If you give in and "lose control," on the other hand, the physical effects of excessive use will in fact begin to "hook you" again and make it much more difficult for you to quit. It's always easier to quit now, just after the slip, than to give in and postpone indefinitely your plans for recovery.

5. *Make an immediate plan for recovery.* After a slip, it is true that "He who hesitates is lost." You must turn your renewed commitment into a plan of action to be carried out immediately. Your options will depend on the situation, of course, but the following guidelines may be of assistance. First, get rid of all drugs of other stimuli associated with the tempting habit. Throw away the rest of the pack of cigarettes; pour out the remaining booze from the bottle; flush your stash down the toilet. *Don't hesitate—do it now!* Second, remove yourself from the high-risk situation if at all possible. Check out, take a walk, leave the scene, split to a less tempting situation. If it is impossible to leave physically, leave psychologically. Close your eyes and meditate for a few moments, or take a few deep breaths to clear your mind. Relax and center yourself within instead of being "drawn out" by the external temptations and events. If necessary, find an alternative means of gratifying your need for satisfaction. Plan a substitute activity that will also meet your needs at the moment. Engage in robust physical exercise or other overt activity to drain off excess energy or negative feelings. Do something "good" for yourself to balance out the "badness" of the lapse (but refrain from the use of other drugs or activities that may make it harder to maintain control). If you are overcome with guilt and self-blame, do something that will serve as an "atonement" for your sin. Pay a fine, do a good deed for others, and so on, but avoid excessive self-punishment since this may backfire and cause you to "punish yourself" further by giving up and allowing a relapse to occur (e.g., "I'm no good, I deserve to die a hopeless drunk, so pass the bottle again").

6. *Ask for help.* Make it easier on yourself if you find that you need help: Ask for it! Ask your friends who are present to help in any way they can—by offering encouragement, providing alternative activities, suggesting ways of coping, or whatever. If you are alone, call your therapist or buddy and seek out their assistance and support. If you know about a crisis center or "relapse hot-line," give them a call for assistance. Don't be afraid to flag down a passing car when you're stuck on the road and find yourself unable to make the necessary repairs on your own.

---

reminder card for each client. The cards should be kept small enough to be carried in a wallet or purse.

Relapse Contracting

Therapists may wish to set up a "relapse contract" with some clients during the initial treatment phase. A relapse contract is an application of contingency management procedures (Bigelow, Stitzer, Griffiths, & Liebson, 1981) and represents a form of agreement between therapist and client concerning the steps to be taken in the event of a future relapse. In essence, the contract provides a method of formalizing or reinforcing the client's *commitment* to change. Use of a contract may be particularly effective with clients who express considerable ambivalence about changing their behavior, or those who have tried repeatedly but unsuccessfully to maintain abstinence or control their behavior. For these clients, the contract pins down the exact requirements and procedures to be followed in the event of a relapse. Similarly, the *response cost* of an initial slip can be increased by including a clause in the contract that specifies fines or other penalties to be paid in the event of a lapse. As mentioned earlier, however, the inclusion of fines or other punishments for slips can easily backfire once a slip occurs, increasing the chances that the lapse will escalate into a relapse. Some clients, once a slip occurs, may feel that the fine is a method of "paying off" the contract and therefore feel free to indulge after the contract is broken or nullified. Others may bridle at having their "hands tied behind their backs" by the use of a contract, and the resulting psychological reactance can provoke them into a mutinous relapse. Therapists should therefore use a relapse contract with caution, perhaps reserving it for particularly recalcitrant or resistant clients. Some of the points that might be incorporated into a relapse contract include the following:

1. In some circumstances, the contract can include a clause that specifies certain costs or fines for engaging in the prohibited behavior. For example, the client may agree to pay a fine for the first drink or cigarette (e.g., $25), and an even greater fine (e.g., $50) for the second use of the substance. The contract should include, in this case, a specified procedure for what is to be done with the fines involved (e.g., the therapist will send the fine to an agency or political campaign that the client finds particularly obnoxious).

2. The client agrees to *delay* taking the first drink, cigarette, or engaging in the addictive behavior for at least 20 minutes after the initial temptation to "give in." This delay period is to be used as a time to pause and reflect, to reconsider the situation, and to see the behavior as a clear *choice or decision*, rather than as a passive yielding to external pressures or internal urges. A review of the decision matrix (described in the final section of this chapter) would also be a helpful strategy at this time. A delay also decreases the probability that the first lapse, if it occurs at all, will occur at the peak of a high-risk situation. As previously stated, the most difficult type of relapse situation to cope with is one that is experienced as particularly stressful or overwhelming in intensity (e.g., sudden bad news or unanticipated misfortune). When people give in at the point of maximum intensity in this type of situation, it is likely that they will attribute magical coping properties to the activity or substance involved. They assume that without the help of the substance, it would be impossible to "make it through" the situation.

3. The client agrees that the first lapse (if otherwise impossible to prevent) will involve a single "dose" of the substance or activity. If smoking is the target behavior, for instance, the client agrees to borrow or otherwise obtain a single cigarette, rather than to purchase a full pack. For drinking, it is agreed that the client will obtain only a single drink (purchased at a bar or store, etc.), rather than a full bottle or six-pack. The dieter agrees to obtain a single food item instead of filling a whole grocery cart with fattening goodies. The principle behind the "single dose" agreement is an obvious one; it is much easier for smokers to stop or pause after one cigarette when they are not tempted by the remaining 19 cigarettes in the pack.

5. The client agrees to wait at least an hour before continuing to engage in the addictive behavior. The time immediately following the first lapse is crucial for the prevention of a total relapse, since this is when most people will experience the AVE. During the delay period, the client agrees to read a reminder card and to actively pursue the cognitive reappraisal procedures and other techniques described in the foregoing sections.

How long should the contract run? Choice of an expiration date is particularly important, since a contract that is too short may result in a reactance backfire effect as soon as it expires. A contract that is too long, on the other hand, may discourage clients from developing reliance on their own coping skills. The definition of too short or too long will depend on the individual client, but as a general rule the contract should not be any shorter than 1 week or longer than 1 month. In some cases, a shorter contract period can be renewed at the expiration date. It is important that the form of the contract and the specific clauses it contains is worked out cooperatively by both therapist and client until the final document meets with both parties' agreement. When in final form, the client and therapist should both sign and date the contract, with each party retaining a copy. Therapists should carefully prepare the clients for the expiration date of the contract, warning them of the possibility that they may experience temptations to relapse once the contracted behavior is "released." It is at the point when the contract expires that the client must accept full responsibility for the target behavior.

Relapse Rehearsal and Relapse Debriefing Procedures

Therapists can use the techniques described above throughout the treatment process. Prior to the initial quit date, or shortly after quitting, the material can be presented to the client in the form of a *relapse rehearsal*, described in Chapter 2. The relapse rehearsal provides an opportunity for the client to try out newly acquired coping skills and cognitive reframing procedures. Clients can be asked to imagine coping with actual high-risk situations (covert modeling) and to describe their intended behavior to the therapist who can provide necessary feedback and coaching. Once the client has embarked on the habit-change journey, serious temptation situations or actual slips can be processed and dealt with through the use of *relapse debriefing*. Relapse debriefing involves an in-depth exploration of a particular temptation or lapse conducted jointly by the therapist and client. All aspects of the temptation or lapse are explored in this process, including details concerning the high-risk situation, alternative coping responses, inappropriate and appropriate cognitive reactions, and so on. The format lends itself either to individual or group therapy. Shiffman and his colleagues provide an excellent detailed description of relapse debriefing procedures and a case study illustrating this method with a smoking client in Chapter 8.

The Programmed Relapse

By traditional definition, a relapse cannot be planned in advance. It is something that "just happens" to the individual, who feels in turn victimized by forces beyond volitional control. In contrast, the RP model emphasizes assuming personal responsibility in the relapse process and views the initial lapse and subsequent behavior as a *choice* instead of a *chance* event. The programmed relapse is a procedure designed to heighten the individual's sense of personal responsibility and choice in the self-management of an addictive habit.

The programmed relapse is a *paradoxical intention technique*, similar to methods described by Haley (1977) and other strategic therapists who often prescribe relapses to clients in order to emphasize their sense of personal choice and self-initiation for the behavior in question. In terms of addictive behaviors, a "relapse" can sometimes be construed as an event that gives the client permission to "lose control" and engage in unlimited indulgent gratification. Responsibility for the resulting binge can be attributed to the effects of the substance (e.g., "The alcohol made me lose control") and/or the influence of an overpowering physical or disease mechanism. In the programmed relapse, the client cannot "disclaim authorship" for the lapse, since the event is defined as a choice—an agreement made by the client to plan the "relapse" at a specific time and place.

A second advantage of the programmed relapse is that it removes the client's initial lapse from what might otherwise be a stressful high-risk situation. By programming the lapse to occur at a neutral time and place (such as the therapist's office), the client is less likely to ascribe "magical coping properties" to the addictive substance or activity compared to the attributions that would otherwise be made in a highly stressful situation. Planning the relapse for a stress-free time period and environment also enhances the opportunity for a disconfirmation of the client's positive outcome expectancies for the anticipated effects of the addictive activity. Since clients usually expect that the addictive substance will relieve the anxiety and tension of a high-risk situation, programming the lapse in a neutral, safe context renders these expectancies invalid since there is no stressful affect to be reduced by the drug or activity. A final advantage offered by the programmed relapse is that it provides the client a chance to experience behavioral and cognitive reactions to the lapse (the AVE) and to rehearse and practice corrective coping techniques. Although research has yet to validate the overall effectiveness of the programmed relapse method, this author's clinical experience with the method suggests at least three different applications of the procedure.

The first use of the programmed relapse is as a *last-ditch intervention strategy* to prevent a full-blown relapse. This application is recommended for use with clients who indicate that despite all efforts to the contrary, a relapse is imminent and otherwise unavoidable. The best way to illustrate this use of the procedure is to describe a recent case study as an example.

The client was a middle-aged male who came to me for help with his smoking. He was a chain-smoker who had smoked on a more or less continuous basis since his teens. As manager of an import–export firm, he described himself as a "workaholic" who smoked one cigarette after another in the hectic office environment. In a recent physical exam his physician advised him to stop smoking immediately because of a fast-developing emphysema condition. Motivated by a desire to improve his health (his father, also a heavy smoker, died in his mid-40s of lung cancer), he came to me for assistance. Despite our best efforts, the client (Mr. C) told me a few days after quitting that he felt it was impossible for him to maintain abstinence. He described his craving as "unbearably intense" and complained of an unusually stressful period at the office. "If I don't smoke, my whole life is going to fall apart," he said in an agonizing tone of voice. He also told me that this would be his last session and that he probably would not come back for more treatment. Clearly, I was on the verge of losing him as a client and he was on the verge of relapse. Instead of just letting him go, probably to smoke his first cigarette in a stressful work setting, I decided to see if he would agree to a programmed relapse. "Will you agree to waiting until Friday afternoon before you have your first cigarette?" I asked him. I told him that it was worth one more chance, since he had in fact been able to abstain for 4 days and should be able to make it for just an additional 2 days (I chose Friday, since this was the end of the work week). I also explained the rationale behind the use of this procedure and why it might work in his case. He reluctantly agreed to come in for the extra appointment. As he left, I told him: "Don't buy any cigarettes. I'll provide them for our session."

When he returned on Friday, 2 days later, he said he was "dying for a cigarette." I told him that it was really the other way around, that "cigarettes were for dying." Unamused by this comeback, he asked me when he could light the cigarette, explaining that his craving was so intense that he felt he would be able to inhale the entire cigarette in one huge drag. I asked the client to sit down in a chair in the middle of the room and to introspect for a few minutes, focusing on all the expectations he had concerning the physical and psychological effects of smoking the first cigarette. I turned on a tape recorder to record his responses (taped playbacks of the programmed relapse may serve as a useful therapeutic reminder for clients who are experiencing strong temptations to indulge). After thinking for a few minutes, he began to describe his outcome expectancies for smoking the cigarette. As I expected, his expectations were almost all positive, focusing almost exclusively on the immediate gratification effects. "As I inhale the first long drag, I expect my craving feelings to subside. This empty tight feeling in my stomach will smooth out and be replaced by the satisfying effects of tobacco," he went on in eager anticipation. "I can hardly wait for the feeling of relief. Relief is just a drag away. Can I light up now?" I handed him one of his favorite brand, a Lucky Strike, and a pack of matches. Before he lit up, I told him to focus on the feelings the cigarette produced—both the physical sensations and the psychological reactions—by closing his eyes and paying total attention to his internal reactions. He agreed and lit up his Lucky.

Mr. C took three very deep drags on the cigarette without saying a word. His eyes closed, he looked as though his insides were on fire, smoke streaming from his mouth and nostrils. After a few moments, he opened his eyes with a confused and perplexed look on his face. It was as though he had just experienced a mini-existential crisis of some kind. He coughed a couple of times and suddenly ground out the cigarette in the ashtray. "This isn't what I expected at all," he said despairingly. "In fact, this is ridiculous. Here I am just sucking it in, and then blowing it out. It all seems so . . . so crazy and worthless, killing myself this way. Besides, I don't feel good physically. I feel dizzy, my throat is hot and raspy, and my chest is tight. Do I really need this?" After we talked it over for the remainder of the session, Mr. C concluded that in fact he did *not* need it any more and he made a renewed commitment to abstinence. His magical expectations about smoking were dramatically disconfirmed by this experience. The Lucky struck out, and he was able to stick with his original goal to stop smoking.

The second application of the programmed relapse procedure highlights the *disconfirmation of positive outcome expectancies* (also illustrated in the previous example with Mr. C). In the following example, the client is a problem drinker.

A male in his early 30s, Mr. A described a history of heavy drinking dating back to his college days. Mr. A, now a successful lawyer, told me that he was firmly convinced that drinking was the only way he could relax after a hard day at the office. He claimed that he needed at least three to four beers after work in order to "unwind and relax at the end of the day. As I say to myself after I leave the office, out of these ropes, and into a good belt of booze!" He said that he had tried everything else to relax but that nothing worked as well as alcohol. "It's immediate, it cuts through my tension, and it's totally physical," he said. Once had a few beers, however, he found it difficult to stop drinking in the evening and complained of feeling tired and hungover the next morning. Since Mr. A seemed reluctant to explore the other means of relaxing after work that I suggested to him, including meditation and exercise, I decided to directly challenge his strongly held belief that only the physical effects of drinking could relax him. I set up our next session to be held in our experimental bar (BARLAB) and scheduled it for the late afternoon at the end of his workday. I told him to hold off on his daily happy hour until he arrived at the BARLAB and that I would provide the beer.

When he arrived at the BARLAB, Mr. A appeared tired and tense after his long day at the office. He was definitely in the mood for a couple of beers. As with the previous client, I told him to introspect while he was drinking a beer and to let me know when he began to feel more relaxed. I handed him a cold foaming glass of beer, and he downed half the glass in one continuous series of gulps. He then quickly polished off the remainder of the glass and asked for another, which I poured him from behind the bar. After consuming about a third of the second glass, he said, "Ahhhh, I feel it coming on now—kind of a letting go, an inner release. This is what I meant by relaxation. It's the real thing," he said with considerable satisfaction, wiping the foam from his upper lip. "What kind of beer is that anyway?" he asked me. "It's very good, although I can't place the brand," he continued, as I reached behind the bar to show him the empty beer cans. "It's called 'Near-Beer,'" I said, pointing to the label. "It contains no alcohol whatsoever. It's a nonalcoholic malt beverage, in fact." Mr. A reacted with considerable doubt and surprise. "It *must* have alcohol in it. I feel so relaxed," he protested. I handed him an unopened can of Near-Beer and asked him if he would like some more. He opened the can and tasted it. It tasted the same as the two he had already consumed. It took some doing, but Mr. A was finally convinced. "This means that I don't really need alcohol to get relaxed. I must somehow be relaxing myself," he concluded.

Once Mr. A realized that alcohol was not absolutely necessary as a means of producing relaxation, and that relaxation itself seemed to be a state of mind that could be triggered by his own belief system, he was more open to trying other methods of relaxing. His belief in alcohol as the sole means of coping with tension was dramatically disconfirmed by the programmed drinking experience. This case example illustrates the potential use of *placebos* in the programmed relapse technique. Placebos can be used instead of alcoholic drinks with clients for whom the actual use of alcohol would pose significant ethical problems (e.g., physically dependent alcoholics).

A third and final use of the programmed relapse technique is to *include programmed relapses as part of the maintenance program.* This use of the method has greatest application for addictive behaviors that do not require total abstinence as the treatment goal. Eating behaviors seem particularly appropriate for this approach, since any treatment program necessarily involves a reduction in consumption instead of abstention. Some clients are unable to persist with their diets or other weight reduction programs because of an intense feeling of deprivation—of having to stick to a diet without any release from constraint. Recent research on the psychological aspects of dieting suggest that individuals who are observing diets or who are chronically obsessive about their weight (restrained eaters) are more likely to show a *counterregulatory effect* when they consume food that exceeds their internal upper limits of permitted intake (Herman & Polivy, 1980). The actual caloric value of the excessive intake is unrelated to the magnitude of this effect, since studies using variants of the balanced placebo design show that the counterregulatory effect of excessive consumption can be triggered by foods *described* as high-calorie, regardless of their actual calorie content. In other words, excessive counterregulatory eating can be triggered by a low-calorie preload if it is described as being high in calories; conversely, a high-calorie preload may have no such effect provided subjects are told that the food contains few if any calories (i.e., it is below the threshold of what is considered to be excessive by the subject) (Herman & Mack, 1975; Polivy,

1976; Woody, Costanzo, Liefer, & Conger, 1981). Certain eating disorders (such as bulimia) may be triggered by similar psychological reactions (cf. Lowe, 1982; Polivy, Herman, Olmsted, & Jazwinski, 1983; Spencer & Fremouw, 1979).

The programmed relapse may provide a means by which the counter-regulatory effect can be deactivated. If the client plans ahead of time to engage in a binge eating session, the exacerbating effects of guilt and loss of control may be eliminated. The overall effect of such a procedure, despite its paradoxical nature, may be to enhance the long-term maintenance of weight loss. Although empirical support for this notion is currently lacking, a recent diet book capitalizes on this novel and unique approach. In a newspaper book review, the author, "Fats" Goldberg, and his diet book, *Controlled Cheating* (Goldberg, 1981), are discussed. Selections from the article follow.[1]

As you might have figured, Goldberg's guide to weight loss, "Controlled Cheating" (Doubleday), is, in his words, "not a book written by a skinny lady who decided to become a nutritionist." As you might never have deduced, Goldberg's scandalous and seductive eating program—on which he consumes pastrami omelets, Hostess Twinkies and Haagen-Dazs raisin ice cream—works. At least on Goldberg. It took him from 325 pounds (on freight and cattle scales) to 150 and has kept him there for more than 20 years. . . . Also known as the Goldberg Oasis Method of Weight Loss and Maintenance, Controlled Cheating is simple:

- Eat like a professional dieter (low-calorie, balanced foods eaten with knife and fork) for 14 days.
- Then cheat for one day, eating absolutely anything you want in any amount. "Bozo eating" or "ramming, jamming, stuffing, sliding and maneuvering all the delicious goodies you can get into your mouth at the same time" is permitted (but not advised) on Cheating Eating Day.
- Return to the "knife-and-fork prison" of traditional dieting for six days and cheat on the seventh day, repeating that weekly pattern until you are three-fourths of the way to goal weight.
- When you have dropped three-fourths of the weight, start feasting two days a week with several dieting days between them. Never change cheating days. In a section entitled "You Ain't Supposed to Mess with Your Controlled Cheatin' Day, No How," Goldberg explains why: "I know you because I'm just like you. When you start switching Controlled Cheating Days for every dog fight and worm wrestle [cf. high-risk situations], you're headed for big Trouble with a capital T. You'll not only cheat on that special Cheating Day, you'll cheat again on your regular Cheating Eating Day.
- When you have reached your goal weight, Cheating Eating Days occur every third day and are slightly more flexible. The time between cheating opportunities may be expanded but not condensed, and every six months the successful cheater wins an entire week's worth of bingeing.

1. Quoted material is from "Have Your Diet and Cheat It Too" by B. A. Krier, *Los Angeles Times*, October 22, 1981. Copyright 1981 by Los Angeles Times. Reprinted by permission.

But can you stay healthy eating like this? Goldberg, who was born in Kansas City, Mo., but has spent much of his life in New York running Goldberg's Pizzerias, insists that he is testimony to both the efficacy and safety of his plan . . . "No one ever sat down and figured out how fat people eat. I had to think it through because I was going nowhere with every other diet plan. If I didn't, I knew in my soul that I would keep blowing up until I was the size of the Goodyear Blimp and explode in a couple of years."

Goldberg even convinced Dr. Robert Bernstein, the medical director of the weight control unit of St. Luke's–Roosevelt Hospital Center in New York and a fan of Goldberg's pizza, to endorse his plan, saying that it is "consistent with the principles of good nutrition." . . . Goldberg adds, "I would like to do something spectacular in the diet industry because I see so much pain. I want to help because I see so many desperate people. I want to tell them the truth about weight and keeping it off, that going up and down is so stupid. You've got the pain of going up and the pain of going down." And now, in Goldberg's program, the joy of cheating days, which he believes will eventually help you eat the way naturally thin people do. "This diet is the way normal people eat," he says, finishing off his lunch with pie à la mode. "Normal people cheat and then they stop eating for a while." (Krier, 1981)

ON THE JOURNEY: STRATEGIES TO ENHANCE EFFECTIVE DECISION MAKING

Throughout the material presented in this and the previous chapter, we have emphasized *decisional* components of the relapse process. Decision-making processes come into play at every stage of the self-change journey: during the motivational and commitment stage (preparation for departure) when the individual decides to make a commitment to a behavior change goal; during the implementation of the commitment (deciding upon a day of departure and method of quitting); and during the postquit maintenance stage (the journey itself). In this section, the focus is on the latter stage and cognitive intervention strategies to enhance effective decision making during the maintenance stage will be described. Three areas are addressed in this regard: decision-making strategies to cope with weakened or unstable commitment to the initial goal; strategies to confront and cope with maladaptive decisional coping patterns such as defensive avoidance (rationalization and denial); and, finally, strategies to cope with relapse "set ups" and covert planning (e.g., coping with Apparently Irrelevant Decisions [AIDs] that lead to relapse).

Enhancement of Weakened Motivation and Commitment

Earlier in this chapter, a number of methods were described to strengthen the initial commitment to embarking upon the habit-change journey. Many of the same methods can be used to strengthen motivation and commitment (the will to maintain change) that have become weakened or challenged by exposure to temptation situations. Perhaps the main problem that weakens one's dedication to a prior commitment is that the original motivational matrix of incentives *changes over time*. There is a gradual shift of incentives as the individual proceeds through the maintenance phase. Factors that were important incentives because of their immediate negative effects at the time the original decision to change was made (e.g., experiencing health or social problems associated with the ongoing addictive behavior) lose their motivational impetus as time passes and the situation changes (e.g., the ex-smoker no longer experiences unpleasant congestion and coughing fits). In addition, the effects of some immediate positive consequences of quitting, such as receiving social reward and support from others, gradually fade away as other people take less notice of the individual's no longer engaging in the addictive habit (it is difficult for others to reward the "nonoccurrence" of a behavior). Long-range consequences also shift in valence, thereby weakening commitment. For example, after people have quit drinking or smoking for a period of time, they may feel a sense of false confidence (members of AA call this a "pink cloud" reaction) in that they feel freed up from the dangers of long-term negative consequences (e.g., a smoker is less influenced by fear of developing lung cancer after having quit for a while, thereby making it "safer" to experiment with the occasional cigarette). To the extent that the influence of long-range and immediate negative effects "wear off" in this manner, positive outcome expectancies for the effects of the addictive activity gain in strength, since they are no longer kept in check by the balancing influence of negative outcome expectancies. When this occurs, the individual is likely to waver in commitment and experience decisional conflicts that may increase the probability of relapse.

When motivation wavers and commitment weakens, it is important for the individual to review the initial goal and reasons for change. Vacillations in commitment are most likely to occur midway on the journey of change, since by this time the person is no longer experiencing the immediate negative consequences of the old habit pattern, and the long-term positive benefits of the change have yet to be fully experienced. Long-range positive benefits are less tangible compared to the lure of immediate (and tangible) gratification. The reduction of health risks that accumulate during each day of abstinence from tobacco, for example, may seem less rewarding than the anticipated satisfaction from a single cigarette (especially if the person rationalizes that smoking just one could not possibly endanger one's health). This apparent discrepancy in the cost–benefit analysis often leads to an increase in ambivalence and a weakening of commitment.

Review of the decision matrix, described earlier in this chapter in the section on motivation and commitment (see also Figure 1-9), serves as a reminder of the initial commitment and provides the client with an opportunity to review the anticipated positive and negative effects (both for immediate and long-term outcomes) associated with the original goal. After a careful review of the original decision matrix, filled out prior to the departure stage, an attempt should be made to update and revise the matrix in the light of recent and current developments. Successful outcomes already experienced should be noted with satisfaction; by the midway point of the journey, many accomplishments have already been achieved. Research indicates that recalling past success experiences may have the effect of shifting attributional patterns associated with initial failure (or the possibility of relapse) from an internal locus (self-blame) to an external locus (Teasdale, 1978).

Reviewing and updating the decision matrix is a particularly useful strategy for clients who tend to ignore past accomplishments and instead focus their attention pessimistically on current and anticipated difficulties. In addition to reviewing the person's progress to date, attention should be paid to the anticipated positive long-range consequences such as decreased risk of disease, a sense of self-mastery, and financial gain. (Concerning the latter, a recent newspaper article described a man who, after having quit smoking 10 years ago, recently purchased a brand-new Cadillac with the cash he had saved from not purchasing cigarettes during the past decade.) After all cells of the decision matrix have been updated, with new outcomes added and old outdated ones dropped, a renewed commitment to the original goal should be made.

A similar decision-making strategy to the decision matrix is the *decision balance sheet* procedure developed by Janis and Mann (1977). The primary assumption underlying this method is that "a person will not decide to embark on a new course of action or to continue an old one unless he expects the gains to exceed the losses (cf. gain–loss models of social behavior)" (Mann & Janis, 1982, p. 354). In this approach, there are four major kinds of expected consequences for each alternative course of action: utilitarian gains and losses for self, utilitarian gains and losses for significant others, self-approval or disapproval, and approval or disapproval from significant others. For each alternative course of action (e.g., stop smoking or resume smoking), all four of these expected consequences are rated for both anticipated positive and negative outcomes. According to the authors, an incomplete or defective balance sheet is predictive of problems in maintaining adherence to a decisional goal:

One of the main hypotheses that has grown out of our analysis of the balance sheets of persons making stressful decisions is that the more errors of omission and commission in the decision maker's balance sheet at the time he commits himself to a new course of action, the greater is his vulnerability to negative feedback when he subsequently implements the decision (Janis, 1959; Janis & Mann, 1977). We refer to this as the "defective balance sheet hypothesis." The defective balance sheet hypothesis asserts that the stability of a decision depends on the completeness and accuracy with which the decision maker has completed his decisional balance sheet before he begins to implement the decision. Errors of omission include overlooking the losses that will ensue from the chosen action; errors of commission include false, overoptimistic expectations about improbable gains. (Mann & Janis, 1982, p. 355)

The balance sheet method has been used successfully in studies of health-related decisions (see Janis & Mann, 1977, pp. 149–155, for a review of this research). In one recent study, for example, women attending a diet clinic who filled out a balance sheet dealing with the pros and cons of going on a recommended low-calorie diet showed significantly more adherence to the recommended plan than women who did not receive this procedure (Colten & Janis, 1981). In another study, use of the balance-sheet procedure was found to enhance attendance at an early morning exercise class (Hoyt & Janis, 1975). Clearly the use of decisional balance sheets is a useful adjunct to the commitment process.

Interventions for Maladaptive Decisional Coping Patterns

As noted in Chapter 3 in the section describing the role of decision making in the relapse process, the initial lapse can be viewed as a choice-point, a fork in the road along the journey of habit change. The "choice" of relapse involves a *decisional conflict* between two alternative courses of action: one associated with a desire for immediate gratification and the other associated with a fear of the long-range risks involved (cf. Ainslie, 1975). In addition, a second source of conflict involves the individual's self-esteem and reputation as a competent decision maker (Janis & Mann, 1977). Because of the stress involved with this decisional conflict, the individual is more likely to engage in maladaptive decisional coping patterns such as *defensive avoidance* (rationalization, denial, etc.). What can be done to modify these faulty cognitive defense mechanisms so as to reduce their influence?

One of the most seductive of all maladaptive decisional coping patterns is *rationalization*. As noted in Chapter 3, rationalization is a defensive avoidance maneuver in which "bolstering tactics" are used to distort the utility or value of a decisional outcome (cf. Janis & Mann, 1977). Bolstering tactics involved in rationalizations related to relapse decisions include the use of exaggeration (playing up the reward value of favorable consequences) and minimization (playing down the magnitude of loss from unfavorable consequences). Rationalizations involve the focusing of attention on selected desired outcomes (usually geared toward immediate gratification) to the neglect of other undesired outcomes (long-range costs).

One obvious cognitive intervention strategy is to make the individual more aware of the nature of the rationalization process and to confront the logic of the assumptions involved in making the rationalization. One method of this type is the awareness-of-rationalizations technique developed by Reed and Janis (1974). In this study, the authors attempted to modify the decisional balance sheet of heavy smokers by eliminating some of their rationalizations that served to bolster the decision to continue smoking. The experimenters hypothesized that if the smokers were given information refuting each rationalization, they would be less likely to use these rationalizations as cognitive defenses and would therefore be more responsive to warnings about the health risks involved. Subjects in the study were presented with a list of statements or "excuses" concerning smoking and asked if they were aware of their tendency to use these excuses to justify their own smoking behavior. The list contained these eight rationalizations for smoking:

1. "It hasn't really been proven that cigarette smoking is a cause of cancer."
2. "The only possible health problem caused by cigarettes that one might face is lung cancer, and you don't really see a lot of that."
3. "I have been smoking for a fairly long time now, so it is probably too late to do anything anyway."
4. "If I stop smoking, I will gain too much weight."
5. "Smoking just seems to be an unbreakable habit for me."
6. "I need cigarettes to relax. I will become edgy, or irritable without them."
7. "If I prefer to smoke, I am only hurting myself and nobody else."
8. "So smoking may be a risk, big deal! So is most of life! I enjoy smoking too much to give it up." (Reed & Janis, 1974)

To facilitate the subject's recognition of a tendency to resort to these rationalizations, the following questions were asked:

1. "Have you ever said this to excuse your smoking?"
2. "Has this excuse ever occurred to you?"
3. "Do you think that, deep down, you might possibly think that this just might be at least a reasonable or valid argument?"
4. "Have you ever heard anyone use this excuse?" (Reed & Janis, 1974; as cited in Janis & Mann, 1977, p. 346)

For each rationalization, the interviewer played a brief, tape-recorded statement that presented factual information designed to refute that excuse, whether or not the subject acknowledged using it. Results showed that subjects receiving this awareness-of-rationalization technique showed significant changes in smoking-related beliefs and an increased sense of vulnerability to the health risks involved, compared to control subjects (Reed & Janis, 1974).

An additional advantage of ferreting out a client's rationalizations and challenging their validity is that the confrontation makes it less likely that the client will be able to use the rationalization in the future. By putting the rationalization "on the table" and opening it up to the hard light of reality, the client will find it more difficult to selectively forget or "repress" the distorted logic involved. As a result, the rationalization may be seen for what it really is: a logically faulty excuse to justify an indulgent act. In this regard, it is important for the therapist to probe for each client's unique and idiosyncratic rationalizations in order to get them into the open and examine their validity. Rationalization is also an important component of the Apparently Irrelevant Decision (AID) process involved in relapse set-ups (described in the final section in this chapter).

Denial is another defensive avoidance coping pattern that can be used to justify a decision to resume an addictive habit. Another bolstering tactic, denial involves a tendency to ignore or deny the aversive aspects of the decisional outcome. Intervention strategies for denial involve having the client attend to the "denied" aspects of the outcome, such as the risk of long-range negative consequences. Confronting the client with the facts of the matter and challenging the validity of the logic involved may be an effective strategy. Rational–emotive techniques as described by Ellis and his colleagues (Ellis & Grieger, 1977) provide one model of how to challenge the client's errors in logic for both rationalization and denial.

Another technique that has been used with some success in breaking down denial of negative consequences is the *emotional confrontation via role playing* method described by Janis and Mann (1977). Based on the observation that some clients are able to suddenly drop all defensive strategies when confronted with an emotional experience that highlights the otherwise denied aspects of the decision (e.g., a smoker who visits a friend or relative who is dying of lung cancer), Janis and Mann explored the effectiveness of role-playing methods involving emotional confrontation. In one study (Janis & Mann, 1965), heavy smokers attending a smoking clinic were required to play the role of a lung cancer patient who received bad news from a physician. This role-playing procedure, an emotional ordeal that lasted just over an hour, proved to be effective in increasing the subjects' willingness and intention to stop smoking and was associated with a significant decrease in smoking rates at an 18-month follow-up (Mann & Janis, 1968). Thus this method shows considerable promise as a means of modifying denial and other defensive avoidance patterns. A related procedure described by Janis and Mann (1977) is called *outcome psychodrama*, in which the therapist presents a scenario that requires clients to project themselves into the future and to improvise a retrospective account of what has happened as a consequence of choosing one or another alternative course of action.

In addition to defensive avoidance (rationalization, denial, and other bolstering strategies), Janis and Mann (1977) discuss the problem of *hypervigilance* in which the decision maker, pressed by the emotional excitement and "hot cognitions" elicited in a high-stress situation, is likely to seize impulsively upon a hastily contrived solution that promises immediate relief. Hypervigilant reactions characterize the decisional coping patterns of many individuals when confronted with the stress and arousal of a high-risk temptation situation. The impulsive decision may be to engage in the addictive habit, since this promises immediate relief. In order to counter the maladaptive hypervigilant reaction, the client should be encouraged to adhere to the guidelines described in the previous section on coping with high-risk situations and initial lapses. First and foremost, the client should avoid or escape the high-risk situation as soon as possible, and pull into a "rest stop" in order to "cool down" the hot cognitions associated with the stressful situation. Detachment and disidentification strategies can be used in order to recenter oneself and renew one's commitment. Only when things have calmed down can one then review the situation objectively and engage in "vigilant" decision making characterized by careful unbiased appraisal of the alternatives before making one's final decision.

Coping with Apparently Irrelevant Decisions and Relapse Set-Ups

In the final section of Chapter 3 the process of relapse set-ups was described—the process by which some clients engage in covert planning to stage a relapse. The motivation for setting up a relapse in this manner derives from one's attempts to minimize the anticipated negative reactions of the self and significant others to the initial lapse. As Janis and Mann (1977) have stated, part of the stress of decisional conflict involves the decision maker's recognition that his or her personal reputation and self-esteem are at stake depending on the decision made. In addition to the threat of loss of self-esteem posed by a decision to resume an addictive habit following a period of self-imposed restraint, the individual must face the problem of negative reactions from significant others such as friends and family members. As such, any "planning" for relapse must be kept covert and any decisions made along these lines must be "justified" in the eyes of the self and others. Decisions may thus be influenced by the defensive strategy of *minimization of social surveillance* (Janis & Mann, 1977), in which the individual expects to "get away with something" that ordinarily entails personal and social responsibility. Relapse situations may be set up by the client in such a way as to *minimize surveillance* (e.g., to do it in "secret") and/or to *justify* the lapse as being relatively acceptable by the self and others (e.g., to put oneself in an impossibly tempting high-risk situation).

In the covert planning of a relapse set-up, the individual engages in a series of mini-decisions to set the stage for the ostensibly justifiable initial lapse. Each mini-decision must be justified by an "explanation" that satisfies the self and others and which does not "blow the cover" on the covert nature of the operation. The use of Apparently Irrelevant Decisions (AIDs) is crucial to this process of self-deception and minimization of social surveillance. At each choice-point, the client makes a decision that leads closer to the brink of relapse and justifies the decision that leads bolstering strategy such as rationalization or denial. As such, the decision is rendered "apparently irrelevant" to the goal of relapse. Each such "move" on the checkerboard leading to relapse can be thought of as a chain of AIDs culminating in the final set-up for the initial lapse. Eventually the individual arrives at a high-risk situation (e.g., the "downtown Reno" situation set up by our compulsive gambler described in Chapter 1). Indulgence at this point can be justified by the nature of the situation (e.g., "Everyone gambles in Reno"). Personal responsibility for the lapse is thereby minimized—along with the personal and social "costs" of the relapse.

The first step in teaching clients to intervene in the covert setting up of relapses is to help them recognize and understand the role of AIDs in the decision-making process. The client should be taught the principle of AIDs and how they are linked together in a chain of decisions leading to the brink of relapse. Clients need to understand that it is *much easier to intervene and break the chain at the early "links"* (choice-points) than it is to intervene later in the chain. Once the chain leads the client to the brink of relapse, self-control is much more difficult, if not impossible. Clients should be encouraged to *view AIDs as red flags that serve as early warning signals* for intervention. Upon noticing a red flag the client needs to slow down and assume a vigilant mode of decision making; each choice-point must be carefully evaluated and an alternative selected that leads the client further away from the risk of relapse.

Many clients have difficulty in assessing and evaluating the role of AIDs in their own relapse behavior. This difficulty is due to the fact that the "truth" of the AID and its ultimate purpose in setting the stage for relapse is masked by the client's defensive avoidance strategies. When asked about the events leading up to a covertly planned relapse, the client may deny the role of covert decision making, saying that the relapse "just happened" and there was no advance planning involved. How should this denial process be handled by the therapist? In the following example, a structured interview is described in which the therapist describes the role of AIDs in the relapse process. The client in this case is a pedophile who is being questioned about his past pedophilic behavior as part of a relapse prevention program for sexual offenders[2]:

During the interview, the concept of AIDs is formally introduced in the following manner. "Each of us makes many decisions every day which seemingly are so minor in importance that they could have absolutely no significant effect on an individual's life. But regardless of the apparent irrelevance, each one of these decisions profoundly alters the range of behaviors that are subsequently available to us. The cumulative effect of all of these Apparently Irrelevant Decisions has the potential to alter dramatically the final outcome of one's life. An example may clarify the actual importance of even a single AID. Imagine a pedophile, who emerges from the front door of his home to take a walk along the tree-lined street of his suburban residence. Nearing the sidewalk, he decides to turn left. After a brief excursion, he notices a school playground brimming with gleefully playing children, a definite high-risk

2. Quoted material is from "Relapse Prevention with Sexual Aggressives" by W. D. Pithers, J. K. Marques, C. C. Gibat, and G. A. Marlatt, in *The Sexual Aggressor* (pp. 225–226), edited by J. G. Greer and I. R. Stuart, New York: Van Nostrand Reinhold, 1983. Copyright 1983 by Van Nostrand Reinhold. Reprinted by permission.

situation for a pedophile. Since the individual probably was familiar with his neighborhood, he would have been cognizant that going to the left would take him by the school, whereas turning right would have led him away from that high-risk area. So, an AID was his choice to turn left, rather than right, onto the sidewalk. Clearly, his decision to walk to the left was only an apparently irrelevant one.

"Looking at the behavior you performed that got you into your current trouble, when did you make the *first* decision that started you toward your final decision to begin a sexual relationship with a female child?" At this point, the patient may provide any of a wide range of responses. In order to foster the atmosphere of cooperation that is critical, . . . the patient's response should not be challenged severely or ridiculed. If the patient responds with a statement such as, "I didn't make a decision to do it, it just happened," the therapist could reply: "It is really kind of difficult for me to imagine how anyone can perform any behavior without first having decided at some point that they were going to do it. Consider the person who is an alcoholic for example. Imagine him walking down a dimly lit city sidewalk close to midnight. As he walks, he reaches into his pocket for a cigarette and discovers that he is out. He anxiously looks around the streets for a store where he can buy some more. A flashing, red, neon light catches his eye and he begins walking briskly toward it. As he draws closer, he realizes that the red neon sign reads 'BEER.' He pauses only a moment to deliberate, deciding that he really needs a cigarette so he'll go into the bar to get a pack. He enters the bar and goes to the cigarette vending machine. Reaching into his pants pocket, he finds no coins. After asking two grey-haired men playing pool if they could change a dollar and seeing two heads shaking 'no' in unison, he turns toward the cash register near the bar to get change. Amid the clacking of billiard balls, he hears his name, 'George!' Turning toward the sound, he stares into drifting blue cigarette smoke and recognizes his foreman from the foundry. The foreman instantly turns to the bartender saying, 'Fill up a brew for George.' Debating only a second, George sips his first taste of foaming beer. That was only the first taste of many he had that night. . . .

"Now that you've heard the story, you may be able to see that George made a series of decisions which led up to his final decision to take a drink of beer. At each one of these choice-points, George could have made a different decision that would have taken him away from a dangerous situation. Did he really *have* to have a cigarette? Did he have no alternative but to enter the bar? Could he have said 'no' to the beer his foreman bought him? Instead, each decision that George made brought him closer to danger until he finally felt that he had no choice but to accept the drink that he was offered. So you can see that George made a series of decisions, each of which contributed in some way to his finally taking the drink of beer. Looking at your decision to have a sexual relationship with a female child in this way, can you tell me the earliest point at which you decided to seek out the relationship?" (Pithers, Marques, Gibat, & Marlatt, 1983, pp. 225–226)

Once the AIDs have been identified and ferreted out as contributory components in the setting-up process, the client can be helped to develop effective intervention strategies. One technique that is particularly effective is the use of self-talk or *internal dialogues with the self* (cf. Meichenbaum, 1977). The purpose of the internal dialogue is to highlight the AID as a choice-point or decision involving two competing alternatives: one leading closer to relapse and the other leading away from danger. As soon as the client has red-flagged an AID choice-point, a dialogue can be enacted between the part of the self that is attracted to the possibility of relapse and the part that wishes to maintain abstinence or retain control. Both points of view are made explicit by giving voice to them in the dialogue, thereby minimizing the distorting influence of rationalization, denial, or other defensive maneuvers. The internal debate between opposing motives can be further highlighted by the use of the Gestalt therapy "hot-seat" technique (Perls, 1971). In this procedure, the client first assumes the prorelapse role and argues this position to the opposed antirelapse side, presented as a personified image sitting on a chair directly in front of the client. After the prorelapse arguments have been made, the client switches places and assumes the antirelapse position and attempts to counter the arguments proposed by the prorelapse side. Through this process of debate, the rationalizations and other distortions of the prorelapse side can be brought into the open and effectively countered.

Relapse Road Maps

Once clients have learned to recognize existing Apparently Irrelevant Decisions and have mastered effective decision-making strategies to counter their influence, they are ready to move a step further and develop *prevention strategies* to minimize the impact of AIDs in the covert planning of future relapse episodes. The *relapse road map* is an imagery technique that can be used to facilitate prevention of relapse set-ups. An example of a relapse road map is presented in Chapter 1 (see Figure 1-6, p. 47), showing the sequence of events leading up to the downtown Reno relapse. In this example, several choice-points are indicated, including the first "early-warning junction" (a turn to the east leads to the Nevada border; a turn to the west leads to Placerville, the California "safe city" choice), the first rest stop on the Nevada side of the border (option for a U-turn and return to California), the "alternate route junction" before arriving in Lake Tahoe (option for taking the scenic bypass to the ski area), and the "last chance junction" just prior to entering Reno (option for a city bypass route, thereby avoiding the casinos of downtown Reno). Each of these decisional choice-points can be affected by the AIDs that increase the probability of relapse.

Clients can prepare their own relapse road maps by first identifying their own potential high-risk situations (events that are likely to cause problems in the future) and marking these events as "destinations" on the map. Events that are anticipated in the near future are marked as close destinations, whereas events likely to occur later on are represented on the map as more distant destinations (e.g., Lake Tahoe is "closer" than Reno, since Tahoe must first be passed through on the way to Reno). In this sense, "distance" on the map (mileage between high-risk situations) represents "time" in the client's future (1 mile = 1 minute at 60 mph). Once the proximal and distal high-risk situations have been identified on the map (e.g., a map of the upcoming week's events), the client should pay close attention to each intersection or junction (decisional choice-point) and identify the route that leads away from the high-risk destinations. Arguments to counter AIDs can then be planned for each choice-point and alternative courses of action devised. By engaging in such "advance route planning" on a regular basis (e.g., each Sunday night for the upcoming week's events), clients can learn to anticipate and prepare their reactions to each event or choice-point *before* they actually arrive.

There are many pitfalls and dead-ends along the journey of habit change. It is very easy to get lost along the way—to forget one's ultimate destination (Freedom Mountain) or be tempted by endless roadside attractions and temptations (downtown Renos). The best thing to do when lost is to consult a map. In addition to providing advance warning of upcoming high-risk situations (including those that are set up by the traveler), the relapse road map provides a useful metaphor for the entire journey of change, from the original point of departure (initial enactment of the commitment to change) to the final destination (stabilization and maintenance of the habit-change process). The road map provides the traveler with information both on past successes (the road already traveled) and on future risks (the road ahead). The map becomes a means of gaining perspective on alternative routes to the final destination. "A map *is not* the territory it represents, but, if correct, it has a similar *structure* to the territory, which accounts for its usefulness" (Korzybski, 1933, p. 58).

REFERENCES

Abramson, L. Y., Seligman, M. E. P., & Teasdale, J. Learned helplessness in humans: Critique and reformulation. *Journal of Abnormal Psychology*, 1978, *87*, 49–74.

Ainslie, G. Specious reward: A behavioral theory of impulsiveness and impulse control. *Psychological Bulletin*, 1975, *82*, 463–496.

Annis, H. M. *Situational confidence questionnaire*. Toronto: Addiction Research Foundation, 1982. (a)

Annis, H. M. *Inventory of drinking situations*. Toronto: Addiction Research Foundation, 1982. (b)

Bandura, A. Self-efficacy: Toward a unifying theory of behavior change. *Psychological Review*, 1977, *84*, 191–215.

Beck, A. T.. Rush, A. J., Shaw, B. F., & Emery, G. *Cognitive therapy of depression*. New York: Guilford, 1979.

Beecher, H. K. *Measurement of subjective responses*. New York: Oxford University Press, 1959.

Best, J. A., & Hakstian, A. R. A situation-specific model for smoking behavior. *Addictive Behaviors*, 1978, *3*, 79–92.

Bigelow, G., Stitzer, M. L., Griffiths, R. R., & Liebson, I. A. Contingency management approaches to drug self-administration and drug abuse: Efficacy and limitations. *Addictive Behaviors*, 1981, *6*, 241–252.

Birnbaum, I. M., & Parker, E. S. *Alcohol and human memory.* Hillsdale, N.J.: Erlbaum, 1977.

Blakey, R., & Baker, R. An exposure approach to alcohol abuse. *Behaviour Research and Therapy,* 1980, *18,* 319–325.

Brown, S. A., Goldman, M. S., Inn, A., & Anderson, L. R. Expectations of reinforcement from alcohol: Their domain and relation to drinking patterns. *Journal of Consulting and Clinical Psychology,* 1980, *48,* 419–426.

Christiansen, B. A., & Goldman, M. S. Alcohol-related expectancies versus demographic/ background variables in the prediction of adolescent drinking. *Journal of Consulting and Clinical Psychology,* 1983, *51,* 249–257.

Christiansen, B. A., Goldman, M. S., & Inn, A. Development of alcohol-related expectancies in adolescents: Separating pharmacological from social-learning influences. *Journal of Consulting and Clinical Psychology,* 1982, *50,* 336–344.

Clavell, J. *Shogun.* New York: Atheneum, 1975.

Colten, M. E., & Janis, I. L. Effects of self-disclosure and the decisional balance-sheet procedure in a weight reduction clinic. In I. Janis (Ed.), *Counseling on personal decisions.* New Haven, Conn.: Yale University Press, 1981.

Condiotte, M. M., & Lichtenstein, E. Self-efficacy and relapse in smoking cessation programs. *Journal of Consulting and Clinical Psychology,* 1981, *49,* 648–658.

Cooney, N. L., Baker, L., & Pomerleau, O. F. Cue exposure for relapse prevention in alcohol treatment. In R. J. McMahon & K. D. Craig (Eds.), *Advances in clinical behavior therapy.* New York: Brunner/Mazel, 1983.

DiClemente, C. C., Gordon, J. R., & Gibertini, M. *Self-efficacy and determinants of relapse in alcoholism treatment.* Paper presented at the annual meeting of the American Psychological Association, Anaheim, Calif., August 1983.

Diener, C. I., & Dweck, C. S. An analysis of learned helplessness: Continuous changes in performance strategies and achievement cognitions following failure. *Journal of Personality and Social Psychology,* 1978, *36,* 451–463.

Ellis, A., & Grieger, R. (Eds.). *Handbook of rational-emotive therapy.* New York: Springer, 1977.

Epstein, S., & Clarke, S. Heart-rate and skin conductance during experimentally-induced anxiety. *Journal of Experimental Psychology,* 1970, *84,* 105–112.

Girodo, M. Self-talk: Mechanisms in anxiety and stress management. In C. Spielberger & I. G. Sarason (Eds.), *Stress and anxiety* (Vol. 4). Washington, D.C.: Hemisphere, 1977.

Glass, D. C., & Singer, J. E. Behavior aftereffects of unpredictable and uncontrollable aversive events. *American Scientist,* 1972, *60,* 457–465. (a)

Glass, D. C., & Singer, J. E. *Urban stress.* New York: Academic Press, 1972. (b)

Goldberg, F. *Controlled cheating.* New York: Doubleday, 1981.

Goldfried, M. R., & Robins, C. On the facilitation of self-efficacy. *Cognitive Therapy and Research,* 1982, *6,* 361–380.

Goldstein, S., Gordon, J. R., & Marlatt, G. A. *Attributional processes and relapse following smoking cessation.* Paper presented at the annual meeting of the American Psychological Association, Toronto, Canada, 1984.

Goodwin, D. W. The alcoholic blackout and how to prevent it. In I. M. Birnbaum & E. S. Parker (Eds.), *Alcohol and human memory.* Hillsdale, N.J.: Erlbaum, 1977.

Gordon, D. *Therapeutic metaphors: Helping others through the looking glass.* Cupertino, Calif.: Meta Publications, 1978.

Haley, J. *Problem solving therapy.* San Francisco: Jossey-Bass, 1977.

Hanusa, B. H., & Schultz, R. Attributional mediators of learned helplessness. *Journal of Personality and Social Psychology,* 1977, *35,* 602–611.

Harvey, D. M. Depression and attributional style: Interpretations of important personal events. *Journal of Abnormal Psychology,* 1981, *90,* 134–142.

Herman, C. P., & Mack, D. Restrained and unrestrained eating. *Journal of Personality,* 1975, *43,* 647–660.

Herman, C. P., & Polivy, J. Restrained eating. In A. Stunkard (Ed.), *Obesity*. Philadelphia: W. B. Saunders, 1980.

Hodgson, R. J., & Miller, P. M. *Self-watching: Addictions, habits, compulsions*. New York: Facts on File, 1982.

Hodgson, R. J., & Rankin, H. Modification of excessive drinking by cue exposure. *Behaviour Research and Therapy*, 1976, *14*, 305–307.

Hodgson, R. J., & Rankin, H. Cue exposure and relapse prevention. In W. M. Hay & P. E. Nathan (Eds.), *Clinical case studies in the behavioral treatment of alcoholism*. New York: Plenum, 1982.

Hoyt, M. F., & Janis, I. L. Increasing adherence to a stressful decision via a motivational balance-sheet procedure: A field experiment. *Journal of Personality and Social Psychology*, 1975, *31*, 833–839.

Janis, I. L. *Psychological stress: Psychoanalytic and behavioral studies of surgical patients*. New York: Wiley, 1958.

Janis, I. L. Motivational factors in the resolution of decisional conficts. In M. R. Jones (Ed.), *Nebraska Symposium on Motivation* (Vol. 7). Lincoln: University of Nebraska Press, 1959.

Janis, I. L., & Mann, L. Effectiveness of emotional role-playing in modifying smoking habits and attitudes. *Journal of Experimental Research in Personality*, 1965, *1*, 84–90.

Janis, I. L., & Mann, L. *Decision-making*. New York: The Free Press, 1977.

Janis, I. L., & Rodin, J. Attribution, control, and decision-making: Social psychology and health care. In G. C. Stone, F. Cohen, & N. E. Adler (Eds.), *Health psychology: A handbook*. San Francisco: Jossey-Bass, 1979.

Jones, E. E., & Nisbett, R. E. The actor and the observer: Divergent perceptions of the causes of behavior. In E. E. Jones, D. E. Kanouse, H. H. Kelley, R. E. Nisbett, S. Valins, & B. Weiner (Eds.), *Attribution: Perceiving the causes of behavior*. Morristown, N.J.: General Learning Press, 1972.

Jones, M. Alcoholics go over the edge of a new high. *Seattle Times*, February 23, 1982, p. B1.

Kendall, P. C. Assessment and cognitive-behavioral interventions: Purposes, proposals, and problems. In P. C. Kendall & S. D. Hollon (Eds.), *Assessment strategies for cognitive-behavioral interventions*. New York: Academic Press, 1981.

Kendall, P. C., & Hollon, S. D. (Eds.). *Assessment strategies for cognitive-behavioral interventions*. New York: Academic Press, 1981.

Kendler, H. H. The concept of the concept. In A. W. Melton (Ed.), *Categories of human learning*. New York: Academic Press, 1964.

Kiesler, C. A. (Ed.). *The psychology of commitment*. New York: Academic Press, 1971.

Kleinknecht,. R. A., & Goldstein, S. G. Neuropsychological deficits associated with alcoholism: A review and discussion. *Quarterly Journal of Studies on Alcohol*, 1972, *33*, 999–1020.

Korzybski, A. *Science and sanity*. Clinton, Mass.: Colonial Press, 1933.

Krier, B. A. Have your diet and cheat it too. *Los Angeles Times*, October 22, 1981.

Lazarus, R. S., & Alfert, E. The short circuiting of threat by experimentally altering cognitive appraisal. *Journal of Abnormal and Social Psychology*, 1964, *69*, 195–205.

Levy, R. L. Relationship of an overt commitment to task compliance in behavior therapy. *Journal of Behavior Therapy and Experimental Psychiatry*, 1977, *8*, 25–29.

Loftus, E. F. Alcohol, marijuana, and memory. *Psychology Today*, March 1980, pp. 42–92.

Lowe, M. G. The role of anticipated deprivation in overeating. *Addictive Behaviors*, 1982, *7*, 103–112.

Mann, L., & Janis, I. L. A follow-up study on the long-term effects of emotional role playing. *Journal of Personality and Social Psychology*, 1968, *8*, 339–342.

Mann, L., & Janis, I. L. Conflict theory of decision making and the expectancy–value approach. In N. T. Feather (Ed.), *Expectations and actions: Expectancy–value models in psychology*. Hillsdale, N.J.: Erlbaum, 1982.

Marlatt, G. A., Goldstein, S., & Gordon, J. R. *Self-initiated attempts in smoking cessation: Process and outcome.* Unpublished manuscript, University of Washington, 1984.

Meichenbaum, D. *Cognitive-behavior modification.* New York: Plenum, 1977.

Merluzzi, T. V., Glass, C. R., & Genest, M. (Eds.), *Cognitive assessment.* New York: Guilford, 1981.

Miller, P. M. *Personal habit control.* New York: Simon and Schuster, 1978.

Mischel, W. A cognitive–social learning approach to assessment. In T. V. Merluzzi, C. R. Glass, & M. Genest (Eds.), *Cognitive assessment.* New York: Guilford, 1981.

Nisbett, R. E., & Valins, S. *Perceiving the causes of one's behavior.* Morristown, N.J.: General Learning Press, 1971.

Nisbett, R. E., & Wilson, T. D. Telling more than we know: Verbal reports on mental processes. *Psychological Review,* 1977, *84,* 231–259.

Ornstein, R. E. *The psychology of consciousness* (2nd ed.). New York: Harcourt Brace Jovanovich, 1977.

Parsons, O. A. Brain damage in alcoholics: Altered states of unconsciousness. In M. M. Gross (Ed.), *Alcohol intoxication and withdrawal.* New York: Plenum, 1975.

Perls, F. *Gestalt therapy verbatim.* New York: Bantam, 1971.

Peterson, C., Semmel, A., VonBaeyer, C., Abramson, L. Y., Metalsky, G. I., & Seligman, M. E. P. The Attributional Style Questionnaire. *Cognitive Research and Therapy,* 1982, *6,* 287–300.

Pirsig, R. M. *Zen and the art of motorcycle maintenance.* New York: William Morrow, 1974.

Pithers, W. D., Marques, J. K., Gibat, C. C., & Marlatt, G. A. Relapse prevention with sexual aggressives. In J. G. Greer & I. R. Stuart (Eds.), *The sexual aggressor.* New York: Van Nostrand Reinhold, 1983.

Pittman, T. S., & Pittman, N. L. Deprivation of control and the attribution process. *Journal of Personality and Social Psychology,* 1980, *39,* 377–389.

Polivy, J. Perception of calories and regulation of intake in restrained and unrestrained subjects. *Addictive Behaviors,* 1976, *1,* 237–243.

Polivy, J., Herman, C. P., Olmsted, M. P., & Jazwinski, C. Restraint and binge eating. In R. C. Hawkins, W. Fremouw, & P. Clement (Eds.), *Binge-eating: Theory, research, and treatment.* New York: Springer, 1983.

Pomerleau, O. F. Underlying mechanisms in substance abuse: Examples from research on smoking. *Addictive Behaviors,* 1981, *6,* 187–196.

Pomerleau, O. F., Fertig, J., Baker, L., & Cooney, N. Reactivity to alcohol cues in alcoholics and non-alcoholics: Implications for a stimulus control analysis of drinking. *Addictive Behaviors,* 1983, *8,* 1–10.

Rankin, H. J. Cue exposure and response prevention in South London. In W. M. Hay & P. E. Nathan (Eds.), *Clinical case studies in the behavioral treatment of alcoholism.* New York: Plenum, 1982.

Reed, H., & Janis, I. L. Effects of induced awareness of rationalizations on smokers' acceptance of fear-arousing warnings about health hazards. *Journal of Consulting and Clinical Psychology,* 1974, *42,* 748.

Rodin, J. Density, perceived choice, and response to controllable and uncontrollable outcomes. *Journal of Experimental Social Psychology,* 1976, *12,* 564–578.

Rohsenow, D. J. Drinking habits and expectancies about alcohol's effects for self versus others. *Journal of Consulting and Clinical Psychology,* 1983, *51,* 752–756.

Rose, G., & Hamilton, P. J. S. A randomized controlled trial of the effect on middle-aged men of advice to stop smoking. *Journal of Epidemiology and Community Health,* 1978, *32,* 275–281.

Rosen, S. *My voice will go with you: The teaching tales of Milton H. Erickson.* New York: W. W. Norton, 1982.

Russell, D. The Causal Dimension Scale: A measure of how individuals perceive causes. *Journal of Personality and Social Psychology,* 1982, *42,* 1137–1145.

Schachter, S. Recidivism and self-cure of smoking and obesity. *American Psychologist*, 1982, *37*, 436–444.

Schachter, S., & Singer, J. Cognitive, social and physiological determinants of emotional state. *Psychological Review*, 1962, *69*, 379–399.

Seligman, M. E. P., Abramson, L. Y., Semmel, A., & VonBaeyer, C. Depressive attributional style. *Journal of Abnormal Psychology*, 1979, *88*, 242–247.

Southwick, L., Steele, C., Marlatt, A., & Lindell, M. Alcohol-related expectancies: Defined by phase of intoxication and drinking experience. *Journal of Consulting and Clinical Psychology*, 1981, *49*, 713–721.

Spencer, J. A., & Fremouw, W. J. Binge eating as a function of restraint and weight classification. *Journal of Abnormal Psychology*, 1979, *88*, 262–267.

Staub, E., & Kellett, D. Increasing pain tolerance by information about aversive stimuli. *Journal of Personality and Social Psychology*, 1972, *21*, 198–208.

Tarter, R. E. Psychological deficit in chronic alcoholics: A review. *International Journal of the Addictions*, 1975, *10*, 327–368.

Teasdale, J. D. Effects of real and recalled success on learned helplessness and depression. *Journal of Abnormal Psychology*, 1978, *87*, 155–164.

Vuchinich, R. E., Tucker, J. A., Bordini, E., & Sullwold, A. F. Attributions of causality for drinking behavior made by alcoholics and by normal drinkers. *Drug and Alcohol Dependency*, 1981, *8*, 201–206.

Webster's new collegiate dictionary. Springfield, Mass.: G. & C. Merriam, 1983.

Weil, A. *The natural mind*. Boston: Houghton Mifflin, 1972.

Wilkinson, D. A., & Sanchez-Craig, M. Relevance of brain dysfunction to treatment objectives: Should alcohol-related cognitive deficits influence the way we think about treatment? *Addictive Behaviors*, 1981, *6*, 253–260.

Wong, P. T. P., & Weiner, B. When people ask "why" questions, and the heuristics of attributional search. *Journal of Personality and Social Psychology*, 1981, *40*, 650–663.

Woody, E. Z., Costanzo, P. R., Liefer, H., & Conger, J. The effects of taste and caloric perceptions on the eating behavior of restrained and unrestrained subjects. *Cognitive Research and Therapy*, 1981, *5*, 381–390.

Wortman, C. B., & Dintzer, L. Is an attributional analysis of the learned helplessness phenomenon viable? A critique of the Abramson–Seligman–Teasdale reformulation. *Journal of Abnormal Psychology*, 1978, *87*, 75–90.

5

LIFESTYLE MODIFICATION

G. ALAN MARLATT

ADDICTIVE LIFESTYLE: A CASE STUDY

Some time ago a client was referred to me for a drinking-related problem. The client, Mr. B, was an attractive, recently divorced man in his mid-30s who worked as a lawyer in a prestigious Seattle firm. Since I had previously worked with one of his colleagues in therapy, he decided to contact me for help. The incident that precipitated his calling me was that he had recently been arrested and charged with a DWI (driving while intoxicated) and reckless driving after driving his car into a telephone pole near his home. Although he had been alone at the time of the accident, and no one was hurt, he was quite distressed about the incident and decided that it was finally time to do something about his drinking (he also admitted that he hoped that seeing me would improve his case when the charges were brought to court). On the evening of his arrest, Mr. B had been driving home from the airport after a long flight from Atlanta. He had just completed a difficult business trip and wanted to unwind and relax on the flight to Seattle. During the 4-hour flight, he drank a couple of double Scotches before dinner, complimentary wine during the meal, topped off with an after-dinner Dubonnet on the rocks. By the time the plane arrived, late in the evening, and he was driving back to his apartment, he felt exhausted and could hardly keep his eyes open. About a mile from his destination, his eyes closed momentarily, and he found himself in a head-on collision with a telephone pole.

When I asked Mr. B about his drinking history, he said that he liked to drink as a way to relax but that his drinking had been "getting out of hand" in the past year since his divorce. He said that his wife used to complain about his drinking (even though he was rarely intoxicated), but that since the separation he lived alone and felt he could do anything he wanted, whenever he wanted, including drinking. He also said that work pressures had become more intense in the past year and a half, since he was in competition for possible promotion to a partnership in his law firm. Because there was no history of alcoholism in his family, and since he reported that most of his excessive drinking was of recent origin and appeared to be stress-related, I asked him to keep track of his alcohol consumption prior to the next treatment session. In order to assess the degree of stress and coping capacity in his daily lifestyle, I also asked him to keep detailed records of *all* of his activities for both a typical workday and weekend day. He recorded these activities on the Daily Want–Should Tally Form (to be described in detail later in this chapter), a self-monitoring record of all discrete daily activities from getting up in the morning to going to bed at night. For each activity listed (e.g., eating breakfast, driving to work, morning work conference, etc.) he was asked to rate on a 7-point scale the extent to which the activity was experienced as a "want" (something he liked doing and that was "for himself"), or a "should" (activities that he did not want to do and that were experienced as an external demand or hassle), or as something between the two (the midpoint on the scale was to be used for activities that felt "50–50" between a want and a should). In addition, I asked Mr. B to keep a detailed record of all drugs used during the day (alcohol, cigarettes, caffeine, tranquilizers, etc.) along with any mood changes (description of mood prior to and following use) associated with these substances. He agreed, commenting that his training as a lawyer would come in handy in keeping a detailed behavioral record.

At our next meeting, we carefully examined his self-monitoring forms. As we reviewed and discussed the events of the previous Monday, the day he selected as a typical workday, the following pattern emerged. The day began at 6:30 A.M. when his alarm went off—or at least that's when it was supposed to begin; as it turned out, Mr. B switched off the alarm and drifted back to sleep. The day before, he had decided that it was time to turn over a new leaf and begin a regular program of jogging, since he was generally feeling sluggish and somewhat overweight. He made plans late on Sunday afternoon to start his running program on Monday morning. On Sunday night, however, he was talked into going to a friend's house to play poker. Since he stayed up past midnight and consumed five beers during the game, he felt "too wiped out" the next morning to go running. When he finally did awaken, he had less than 45 minutes to get up, get dressed, and make it to the office for a 9:00 A.M. conference. Since there was no time to eat, he hurriedly boiled water for coffee, taking a large mug of extra-strong brew with him on the drive to work. On the way to the office, he found himself stuck in a freeway traffic jam and he began to feel anxious about the possibility of being late for his important client meeting. He turned on the AM radio, searched the dial for a traffic report that hopefully would inform him when the freeway would open up again. Instead, all he could get was frantic rock music and a talk show on the perils of the nuclear arms race. There was nothing to do but light up a cigarette, sip coffee, and wait impatiently until the traffic cleared.

When he finally arrived at his office 20 minutes late, he ordered coffee for himself and his client and immediately began the business of the day. His morning schedule was running behind due to the late start and he was unable to take any breaks until midway through the noon hour. (All business activities during the morning were rated as "shoulds" on his form.) Since arising, he had consumed four cups of coffee (upon query it turned out that his cup was a large 14-oz mug) and smoked eight cigarettes. Although he had only half an hour free for lunch due to an important court appearance scheduled for the early afternoon, he remembered feeling "jumpy, my nerves were on edge since I had eaten nothing since the evening before," and he stopped off at a quick-food restaurant on the way to the courthouse. While looking over the menu, the waitress came by and asked him if he would like a drink while he was waiting. He impulsively ordered a Manhattan on the rocks, anticipating relief from his edgy, tense feelings. "Shall we make that a 'special' Manhattan?" the waitress asked him, he recalled. "Why not," he said, even though he knew that "special" meant a double at a "special" price that was less than it would be if he had ordered two individual drinks—but since he did not have enough time for two drinks, the low-price double seemed a good deal in terms of both time and money saved. He also ordered a BLT with fries and a cup of black coffee to offset the effects of the alcohol. After gulping down his food and drinks and smoking a quick cigarette, he rushed out to his car in order to try to find a parking place convenient to the courthouse.

The afternoon was as stressful as the morning had been. To offset the feeling of fatigue brought on by the drink at lunch, Mr. B took time out for a cigarette and coffee break immediately after his session in court. At about 3:00 P.M., he experienced a brief period of skipped heart beats, which at first he attributed to excessive coffee consumption during the day. He then remembered that he had forgotten to take his daily medications for hypertension due to the early-morning rush and assumed that the extra systoles were a result of missing his morning pill. Since the extra heart beats made him feel additionally anxious, he decided to take a short walk around the courthouse for "a smoke and a breath of fresh air." By 4:00 P.M., he returned to his office and attempted to catch up with the day's mail and phone messages. The final 2 hours of his workday were spent in his office, making phone calls, dictating a legal brief, and smoking four additional cigarettes.

He left the office a little after 6:00 P.M., on his way to a 7:00 P.M. visit with his ex-wife and his two children. Visits with his former wife had recently become increasingly tense, since they often ended in a heated argument. While driving toward her house, he felt the familiar anxiety beginning to mount. Convincing himself that he needed a drink to settle his nerves before the visit, he stopped at a local restaurant where he knew they served generous doubles in the lounge during the Happy Hour. Sitting at the bar with a cigarette and a double Scotch on the rocks, he filled out his self-monitoring forms for the afternoon period. He rated the stopover in the bar as the most relaxing and enjoyable period of the day—a time-out from the mad rush of the day's activities. "This is the first thing I have done all day for *myself*," he wrote, "and I deserve this after the kind of day I've had." He described the bar as a kind of sanctuary, a place of relaxation and easy conviviality where he had no worries or immediate cares. The lights were dim and country music played softly in the background, as the bartender filled his glass with a second drink ("Two for the price of one—no wonder they call it the Happy Hour," he commented). Reluctantly, he left the bar at 7:30 P.M. knowing he would be late for dinner with his family, but "feeling no pain" as the glow of the two doubles spread through his empty stomach and eased his concern about the impending visit.

The evening visit did not go well. Mr. B's ex-wife was upset because he arrived late for dinner and the kids were on edge and raising a fuss. To make matters worse, she smelled liquor on his breath and accused him of trying to set up a fight since arguments were more likely to escalate when he had been drinking. Despite this concern, he convinced her that they should have wine with their meal. He ended up drinking almost two-thirds of the bottle. Although he felt loquaciously confident and in high spirits, the discussion eventually ran up on the rocks of an argument and the meal ended badly. His mood dramatically shifted from warm receptivity to angry rejection, and he finally stormed out of the house without saying goodbye to his children. He drove back to his apartment at a reckless pace, feeling vindictive and self-righteous. Although it was still relatively early in the evening and Mr. B had some important papers to prepare for work the next day, he felt too agitated to concentrate on his work. Since he had run out of anything to drink in his apartment, he decided instead to smoke a marijuana cigarette a friend had given him. The combination of the alcohol and the marijuana physically incapacitated him, and he felt too weak to do anything but watch television. He switched on the set, not caring what program he watched, and lay on his couch "just watching the colors change and the plastic people selling headache remedies." After an hour or so of lying there and smoking several cigarettes, he fell asleep on the couch with the television still on. Since he had not set the alarm, he awoke the next morning just as the *Today* show was signing off, and he was late for work again. Mr. B's record indicated that he had consumed a daily total of 24 cigarettes, 7 mugs of coffee, the equivalent of 10 single alcoholic drinks, and 1 joint.

Saturday, his typical weekend day, was also quite stressful, because he had no spare time during the week due to the press of his work and general lack of energy and had saved up all of his household chores until the weekend. Once again, a series of back-to-back should activities characterized the day: cleaning the apartment, doing the grocery shopping, paying bills, doing the laundry, and trying to catch up on some overdue paperwork. By Saturday night, he was more than ready to "tie one on and get stoned out of my mind." Most of Sunday was spent in bed nursing a hangover.

Just before the end of our meeting together, Mr. B asked me, "Tell me, do you think I'm an alcoholic? Some of my friends tell me that I should check myself into an alcoholism hospital for a couple of weeks. What do you think?" I told him that alcohol seemed to be but one thread in the stressful fabric of his addictive lifestyle, and that to concentrate only on his drinking would be to leave him vulnerable to the onslaught of his other health-threatening bad habits—smoking, excessive consumption of caffeine, lack of exercise, and the constant exposure to stress in both his professional and personal life.

At our next meeting, I confronted him with the seriousness of his situation. I told Mr. B that although I was concerned about his excessive use of alcohol, the possibility of his becoming an alcoholic was of less concern to me than the danger of his dying from an early heart attack, stroke, or lung cancer. "Crashing into the telephone pole is a clear warning signal that if you don't make some drastic changes in your lifestyle, you're headed for an early grave," I told him. "Drinking is only the tip of the iceberg. It indicates that there is enormous stress lying just below the surface of your lifestyle, and that unless you make some significant changes, your life is headed for the same fate as the Titanic." I reminded him about the many sources of stress in his life at work and with his estranged family, and that his attempts to cope with this stress were only adding to the load. His current lifestyle closely resembled what Friedman and Rosenman (1974) have termed the "Type A" pattern—a competitive, striving, time-pressured lifestyle that has been associated with increased risk of coronary disease. The probability of developing a serious life-threatening disease was exacerbated by his heavy reliance on "negative addictions" as a maladaptive attempt to cope with stress. His excessive reliance upon alcohol, caffeine, and nicotine, coupled with a poorly balanced diet, lack of exercise, and absence of positive social supports or access to counseling all added up to a frightening cumulative risk factor, especially since he had already been diagnosed as having essential hypertension.

We discussed his addictive habit pattern in detail. As we proceeded, Mr. B began to understand the interlocking nature of his habits. He used coffee to wake himself up in the morning and frequently as an attempt to cope with the excesses of the previous evening. But since he rarely ate anything in the morning, the stimulatory effect of several large mugs of coffee made him feel nervous and jumpy by midmorning. He admitted upon introspection that the first couple of cigarettes of the day actually increased his heart rate and general level of excitation, even though smoking "seemed to feel relaxing." Further discussion revealed that smoking seemed to have a relaxing effect not because of its intrinsic pharmacological effect, but because it provided him with a brief time-out period from work ("a mini-break," as he described it) and because of the contrast effect it produced relative to his prior arousal state. Rather than moving from a state of tension to one of relaxation, Mr. B began to see that a primary motive for engaging in one addictive behavior (e.g., smoking) was the attempt to ameliorate the aftereffects of a prior habit (e.g., drinking coffee) and that he was continuously moving from one state of stimulation to another, instead of waiting for the effects of the first activity to "wear off." Drinking was similar: although he drank at lunch or after work as an attempt to relax, the effect was a two-sided one. The initial stimulatory effect that appeared to counteract the cumulative effect of prior stress was soon followed by the downside of fatigue and loss of energy associated with the ultimately depressive action of alcohol. And so his habit pattern continued throughout the day—a rollercoaster of ups and downs, stimulants and depressants, each following the other in a vain attempt to cope with the sequela of the previous habit. Mr. B was, in short, trapped in an addictive lifestyle that posed a serious threat to his health. At the end of our second meeting, he was feeling both impressed and depressed with the impact of what we had discussed. But he was also very motivated to change, given the seriousness of his plight.

Mr. B's case illustrates the importance of *daily lifestyle* as a crucial factor in an individual's overall level of stress and the development of both mal-adaptive and adaptive coping responses. Recent reviews of the literature relating stress to physical and emotional disorders have emphasized the salience of lifestyle as an important etiological factor in the development of disease (cf. Hamilton & Warburton, 1979; Stone, Cohen, & Adler, 1979). Although much of the early literature focused in the impact of stressful life events such as divorce or major employment changes (cf. Billings & Moos, 1982; Holmes & Rahe, 1967; Johnson & Sarason, 1979), recent research has emphasized the influence of day-to-day events such as daily "hassles" and "uplifts"—the downs and ups of everyday existence (cf. DeLongis, Coyne, Dakof, Folkman, & Lazarus, 1982; Kanner, Coyne, Schaefer, & Lazarus, 1981). These daily stressors and associated behaviors appear to have more impact because of their proximal nature, compared to the more distal effect of isolated major life events. In Mr. B's case, he experienced stress from both sources: his recent divorce and separation from his family, along with the daily hassles of a competitive professional position. Although the major impact of the divorce itself was beginning to subside, stress was reactivated whenever he paid a visit to his ex-wife and children. The stress of his career, on the other hand, continued at a high level on a daily basis. On days when both sources of stress coincided, as on the Monday he described, the cumulative effect was particularly intense.

In addition to major life events and daily hassles as stressors, Mr. B's maladaptive attempts to cope with stress by his excessive indulgence in negative addictions served only to exacerbate his overall stress level. As with many individuals in our medication-conscious society, Bill expected that each time he used one of his many coping substances he would get a "quick fix" of relief from tension or fatigue. He was, however, unaware that many, if not most, of his quick fixes were in response to the after-effects of the substances taken earlier in the day. Stimulants were used to offset the downside of fatigue; depressants were used in an attempt to reduce the impact of the previous stimulants. Each occasion of use was reinforced by the immediate gratification associated with the initial effects of the substance (avoidance or escape from the prior aversive state). As the initial "positive" effect was gradually replaced by the negative after-effects (the second stage of the biphasic response), these unpleasant feelings served as the cue for the initiation of the next occasion of use. Each time this pattern was repeated, the addictive coping pattern was strengthened. As such, Mr. B's coping pattern represented a *vicious circle of addictive behaviors.*

Mr. B's increasing reliance upon negative addictions as a means of coping with stress was augmented by an almost total lack of compensatory "positive addictions" (such as a regular exercise or relaxation program). His daily schedule usually carried him from one should to the next, with few if any healthy wants interspersed in his schedule. As with the school teacher described in Chapter 1 who belted down a half-pint of vodka after work during the rush hour drive to her home, Mr. B accumulated a long chain of shoulds during the day that served as a partial justification for his excessive alcohol consumption after the day's work was over. Along with the cigarette and coffee mini-breaks at work, drinking at the end of the morning or in the early evening represented his only wants or self-indulgent activities. At one point in our sessions together, Mr. B mentioned that he felt that each time he completed a should during the day he accumulated points to use for justifying or rationalizing his indulgence in alcohol. It was as if he owed himself a high after the long succession of lows during the day. The more points he earned that day, the greater the allowable reward at the completion of the work day. Although there appeared to be a superficial equity or balance in his system of demands and pay-offs, Mr. B's health was the big loser in the long run.

If Mr. B had contacted a local alcoholism information center for a referral concerning his DWI arrest and his problems with alcohol, in all likelihood he would have been referred to a local inpatient alcoholism treatment center or to Alcoholics Anonymous. Once in the hands of these programs, Mr. B would probably be labeled as an alcoholic and urged to abstain from all future drinking. Little if any attention would be paid to his other addictive behaviors or the degree of lifestyle stress he experienced, since most traditional alcoholism workers would view Mr. B's drinking as the primary cause of his problems. In all likelihood, Mr. B's excessive use of tobacco and caffeine (along with his lack of exercise) would remain unchanged, if not actually increased by participation in these programs (most alcoholism treatment centers and AA meetings are notorious for their clientele's heavy consumption of coffee and cigarettes). Although it may be advisable in the long run for someone like Mr. B to abstain from all use of alcohol, it often makes more sense to first attempt to make changes in the client's overall lifestyle and pattern of substance use. By introducing additional positive habit patterns and balancing the shoulds and wants in his daily schedule, the intensity of the underlying stress that drives the negative addictions may be reduced significantly. As Mr. B comes to rely less on his previous bad habits as a means of coping with his problems, the vicious circle of using drugs to cope with the aftermath of prior substance use can be circumvented. As the intensity of stress diminishes and Mr. B learns new and effective methods of coping, his addictive lifestyle may be replaced by one characterized by *moderation* instead of excess. Lifestyle intervention can be used both for clients like Mr. B, who may be good candidates for a goal of moderation, and for other clients for whom abstention is the appropriate treatment goal. A balanced lifestyle is an important component of any relapse prevention program, regardless of the ultimate treatment goal.

The remainder of this chapter is devoted to a description of Relapse Prevention (RP) lifestyle intervention programs. In the next section, lifestyle assessment procedures are described, followed by a description of various lifestyle intervention strategies, such as relaxation and exercise, that are geared toward the modification of daily lifestyle activities. Mr. B's case will be discussed further as an example of how such programs can be implemented. The chapter concludes with a discussion of the underlying philosophy of this approach, with an emphasis on the principle of moderation as an important guiding assumption in lifestyle intervention.

LIFESTYLE ASSESSMENT PROCEDURES

Central to the assessment of lifestyle is the concept of *lifestyle balance*. A balanced lifestyle is characterized by a relative degree of balance in the individual's daily activities between sources of stress and one's resources for coping with that stress. The overall aim of the lifestyle assessment procedures described in this section is to establish the extent to which the client's daily activities contain a sufficient pattern of coping strategies to balance out or offset the impact of various life stressors. Sources of stress include major life events (illness, divorce, etc.), daily annoyances and hassles, and an imbalance between work and play activities (too many shoulds and too few wants). If these stressors are not balanced by sufficient stress management strategies, the individual is more likely to turn to addictive behaviors in an attempt to gain some relief or escape from stress. Clients who are attempting to refrain from an addictive habit are more likely to experience relapse if their lifestyle is an unbalanced one. Learning new ways of coping with stress, on the other hand, will reduce the motivational "need" to rely upon addictive habits and thereby reduce the probability of relapse.

This section begins with a discussion of assessment strategies that can be used to evaluate sources of stress in the client's life, including the impact of major life events, daily hassles, and the degree of daily balance between shoulds and wants. Assessment of coping strategies employed by the client to cope with these stressors is then described.

ASSESSMENT OF SOURCES OF STRESS

The primary arena for lifestyle assessment is the client's pattern of *daily activities*—the sources of stress and coping strategies for both a typical workday and a weekend day or holiday. Our emphasis on daily activities reflects the fact that most addictive behaviors are engaged in on a daily or almost daily basis, often with many repetitions throughout the day (e.g., cigarette smoking), or during a period of continued use at the same time period each day (e.g., drinking after work). Description of stressors or coping activities that occur infrequently during the year (e.g., filling out income tax forms or taking a 10-day vacation each year) are sometimes valuable, but they do not have the same impact as one's day-to-day activities. On the other hand, one's daily activities and moods are also influenced by the occurrence of major life events such as separation from one's spouse, a new job, moving to a new location. In this regard, it is important for the therapist to ascertain how the client is coping on a day-to-day basis with the onset or aftermath of such major events.

Major Stressful Life Events

As part of a general intake or diagnostic interview with any client, the therapist should make sure to inquire about significant life events that may increase or decrease stress experiences on a daily level. Areas to be probed include the obvious ones of personal relationships (changes in marital status, family problems, available social support from relatives, friends, or lovers), employment or career issues (loss of employment or new job, degree of satisfaction or frustration with one's career or lack of career, financial status), and physical and spiritual health (recent or ongoing illnesses, religious activities, etc.).

Since the early exploratory work of Holmes and Rahe (1967) on the impact of major life changes, other investigators have shown that these life stressors are often associated with changes in physical illness, mental health, and levels of personal effectiveness (cf. Dohrenwend & Dohrenwend, 1974; Johnson & Sarason, 1979; Rabkin & Struening, 1976). Although some studies have indicated a positive relationship between major stressful life events and the frequency of alcohol-related problems (e.g., Bell, Keeley, & Buhl, 1977; Bell, Keeley, Clements, Warheit, & Holzer, 1976), other reports have shown negative or mixed results (e.g., Morrisey & Schuckit, 1978). One obvious problem in the interpretation of these correlational studies is that it is very difficult to ascertain whether a particular stressful life event is a cause or an effect of alcohol abuse. Other critics have pointed to serious methodological problems associated with the early instruments used to assess major life events.

In response to methodological criticisms of the original questionnaire designed by Holmes and Rahe (entitled, Schedule of Recent Experiences), other investigators have developed psychometrically improved instruments to measure significant life events. One problem with the Schedule of Recent Experiences (Holmes & Rahe, 1967) is that it fails to distinguish between negative and positive major life events (e.g., death of a loved one vs. getting married). In an attempt to resolve this and other shortcomings with the original instrument, Sarason and his colleagues have recently developed the Life Experiences Survey (LES) (Sarason, Johnson, & Siegel, 1978). The LES is a 57-item self-report measure that allows respondents to indicate events they have experienced during the past year. The events listed refer to life changes common to individuals in a wide range of life situations (the final section is designed especially for use with a student population). For each item, the respondent is asked to indicate whether or not the event in question occurred during the preceding year (and if so, whether it occurred in the first or latter half of the year) and to rate the perceived impact of the event on a 7-point scale (ranging from extremely negative to extremely positive impact). Sample items include: marriage, detention in jail or comparable institution, death of a spouse, sexual difficulties, change of residence, breaking up with boyfriend or girlfriend, and so on. Spaces are provided for additional idiosyncratic items that are not included in the survey. Recent research using the LES indicates that events that are viewed as having a *negative* impact are more strongly associated with stress-related dependent measures than events that are viewed as having a positive impact (Johnson & Sarason, 1979; this reference also contains a complete version of the LES and instructions for scoring). In using this form as part of a lifestyle assessment battery for RP planning, the therapist should discuss the impact, if any, that each major life event has on the client's use of addictive substances or activities as a means of attempting to cope with this source of stress.

Daily Hassles and Uplifts

Recently, research on the impact of major life events on health has indicated that the long-range impact of such events on health status appears to be weak. As Rabkin and Struening (1976) point out, "In practical terms . . . life event scores have not been shown to be predictors of the probability of future illness" (p. 1015). Although research relating major life events and the occurrence of addictive behaviors or relapse episodes is sparse, one might postulate that although life events of this nature probably have their major impact at the time of actual occurrence, the long-term association may be a weak one. Perhaps of even greater influence on a day-to-day basis is the impact of daily hassles or annoyances. Some studies have shown a higher correlation between daily hassles and psychological and physical symptoms, compared to the relatively weak association found for major life events and these symptoms (DeLongis *et al.*, 1982; Kanner *et al.*, 1981).

Daily hassles have been assessed by Lazarus and his colleagues who have developed the Hassles Scale (Kanner *et al.*, 1981), a 117-item questionnaire.

Items on the scale reflect the content areas of work (e.g., dislike of work duties), family (e.g., not enough time for family), social activities (e.g., unexpected company), the environment (e.g., pollution), practical considerations (e.g., misplacing or losing things), finances (e.g., someone owes you money), and health (e.g., not getting enough rest). Respondents are asked to indicate the occurrence of any items that have hassled them in the past month. Participants also rate each hassle on a 3-point scale as having been "somewhat," "moderately," or "extremely" severe. From this information, two scores are derived: hassle frequency and intensity (mean severity for all items checked).

Along with hassles, Kanner et al. (1981) also assessed "uplifts" or positive experiences that are likely to occur in everyday life. The Uplifts Scale developed by these authors is similar in construction to the Hassles Scale, consisting of 135 items that tap into the same overall life domains including work (e.g., using skills well at work), family (e.g., children's accomplishments), activities (e.g., recreation), the environment (e.g., good weather), practical concerns (e.g., car running well), finances (e.g., saving money), and health (e.g., getting enough rest). Although Kanner et al. (1981) found a positive association between frequency of uplifts and psychological symptoms in women (but not for men), other investigators have failed to find a relationship between uplifts and physical health symptoms for either males or females (DeLongis et al., 1982). In terms of addictive behaviors, however, research has yet to be conducted on the association between daily hassles and/or uplifts and the use of addictive substances. One plausible hypothesis is that individuals with a high incidence of daily hassles and a relative paucity of normal uplifting events would be more likely to rely upon drugs or other addictive activities as a means of providing an immediate uplift in the form of a quick fix or getting high. Another hypothesis is that individuals with a high hassles score are more likely to relapse than others who have either a low hassles or high uplifts score. Research is needed to shed further light on these questions.

A related assessment procedure to the Uplifts Scale is the Pleasant Events Schedule (PES) developed by Lewinsohn and his colleagues in their study of determinants of depression (Lewinsohn & Graf, 1973; Lewinsohn & Libet, 1972). The PES is a 320-item inventory that can serve as a useful device for defining a client's ongoing or potential pleasurable activities.

Balance between Wants and Shoulds

As stated earlier, balance is defined here as the degree of equilibrium that exists in one's daily life between those activities perceived as external demands (the shoulds) and those perceived as activities the person engages in for pleasure or self-fulfillment (the wants). In this author's hypothesis, a lifestyle characterized by a preponderance of shoulds is often associated with a perception of self-deprivation and a corresponding need for self-indulgence. Probability of relapse is predicted to increase to the extent that the shoulds outweigh the wants, thereby increasing the likelihood that the individual will turn to an addictive activity as a maladaptive attempt to restore balance. Although this hypothesis is based largely on clinical case observations and is yet unsupported by empirical findings, some promising leads are emerging. In one recent dissertation study conducted in our laboratory, for example, significant positive correlations were obtained between the daily frequency of should activities reported by individuals and their daily consumption of cigarettes (Matheson, 1982).

Unlike the Hassles Scale and the Uplift Scale, both of which require the respondent to give a retrospective account of hassles and uplifts that have occurred during the past month, assessment of wants and shoulds involves an ongoing sampling of actual daily activities through the use of self-monitoring procedures. Instead of relying upon a predetermined item pool of activities developed externally (as in the Hassles and Uplifts Scales), the assessment of wants and shoulds requires the individual to provide his or her own accounting of daily events and their perceived quality as external demands or self-fulfilling activities. Any single event, such as performing a household cleaning task, may be viewed as a should by one individual and as a want by someone else. Or, as is often the case, the same individual could rate the same activity as a should on one particular day and as a relative want on another day, depending on the overall pattern of events and their appraised context.

A preliminary self-monitoring form to assess wants and shoulds that has been developed at the University of Washington is shown in Table 5-1. The Daily Want–Should Tally Form is given to clients who are asked to fill it out both for a typical weekday and a typical weekend or vacation day. Repeated daily assessments can be requested for more comprehensive evaluations of lifestyle. In the Tally Form, subjects are asked to provide the following information. For each day of recording, the subject is asked to keep an ongoing list of each discrete activity during the day, beginning with getting up in the morning and continuing until bedtime that night. For each activity listed (e.g., driving to work, lunch with a friend, meetings at work, etc.), the subject provides a rating on a 7-point want–should scale, with 7 representing a total should ("something you do because you feel obligated to do it and you get nothing or almost nothing out of it for yourself") and 1 representing a total want ("something you want and like to do for yourself, free from external demands or obligations"). A score of 4 represents a midway point, an activity that feels like an equal mixture of shoulds and wants; other points on the scale represent relative mixtures of shoulds and wants for each activity. For any given activity, the form requires the subject to list the time the activity began and ended, a brief description of the activity itself, and a corresponding want–should rating score. Additional comments

Table 5-1.   Daily Want–Should Tally Form

Instructions

People differ in the amount of time they spend during the day doing things they feel they have to do, versus things they want to do. Some of the things we do are "wants," things like reading a good book, going skiing, or relaxing in the sun. Other things we do are "shoulds," like doing our income tax return, paying bills, cleaning house, or taking out the garbage. Other things we do are a mix of want and should, like going to a party that we will enjoy but which is also a social obligation. During the next week we would like you to select a typical weekday and a typical weekend day. As you go through each of these days please list each activity you engage in under the appropriate time block. *Please do this and rate each activity at the time that each activity occurs.* Please include the following information:

1. The time you begin and end each activity.
2. A brief description of the activity.
3. The want–should rating, where 1 is a total want, something you do because you *want* to do it, 7 is a total should, something you do because you feel *obligated* to do it, 4 is an equal mixture, and 2–6 represent varying mixes of want and should. This is a subjective rating, there is no right or wrong answer.
4. A rating of your overall mood or satisfaction at the end of each time period, where 1 is the lowest satisfaction and 100 is the highest.
5. Finally, at the end of each day rate your overall satisfaction with the day on the same 1–100 scale.

Below is an example of a completed want–should tally form.

Time			Want–should rating						
			1 Want	2	3	4 Equal Mix	5	6	7 Should
From	To	Activity							
Morning									
6:30	7:30	Shower, dress, eat, get ready						×	
7:30	8:00	Drive to work							×
8:00	Noon	Work (paperwork)				×			
Satisfaction at end of morning (1–100):			60						
Afternoon									
Noon	2:00	Lunch with friend	×						
2:00	5:00	Work (meetings)							×
Satisfaction at end of afternoon (1–100):			40						
Evening									
5:00	5:30	Drive home							×
5:30	6:00	Relax, read paper	×						
6:00	7:00	Dinner with family		×					
7:00	11:00	Relax, talk with spouse		×					
Satisfaction at end of evening (1–100):			75						
Overall satisfaction rating for the entire day (1–100):			60						

concerning the activity (e.g., mood rating) can be placed on the form next to the want–should score. Subjects are also asked to rate their overall satisfaction level at three points during the day: at the end of the morning, afternoon, and evening, along with a fourth rating for the day as a whole. These subjective evaluations of satisfaction are rated on a 100-point scale.

The Want–Should Tally Form can be a useful aid to treatment planning for clients with addictive behavior problems. In reviewing the completed form with a particular client, the therapist should pay close attention to the overall pattern of daily activities and their ratings. Do the shoulds clump together during the morning and/or afternoon, with few want activities occurring prior to the evening hours? Are there sufficient want activities interspersed among the shoulds to yield a balanced pattern, or are all the wants relegated to the end of the day or to weekend days? Or, conversely, does the individual show a pattern of want activities early in the day such that the daily shoulds continue to be postponed until later in the day? How much time does the person spend in solitary compared to social activities? What is the nature of the want activities: does the person spend any time each day engaged in exercise, relaxation, alone times, time with friends, and so on? How flexible is the individual's pattern of activities? Can the shoulds be moved in the schedule or distributed in a more balanced fashion?

Information from the Want–Should Tally Form can be combined with daily self-monitoring of addictive behaviors (the Tally Form can be modified to include this information) for clients who are continuing to engage in addictive activities during the assessment period. When such information is available, the therapist and client can compare the occurrences of the addictive behavior with the preceding and contiguous pattern of wants and shoulds. Does the client show an increased tendency to indulge in an addictive habit when the day has been marked by a large number of should activities? Or does the person postpone indulgence until the weekend when pressing duties are reduced? Does the client tend to give a low or high priority to self-related activities such as exercise, relaxation, or spending time with a close friend? Information from the Want–Should Tally Form can provide a wealth of material that can be used in planning a lifestyle modification program for clients involved in a comprehensive RP program.

ASSESSMENT OF LIFESTYLE COPING STRATEGIES

The foregoing section discussed assessment of potential sources of stress in a client's daily lifestyle. How does the client cope with these stressors? In Chapter 2 we discussed specific coping strategies for dealing with high-risk relapse situations, for example, assertive responding in a specific anger-provoking situation. Here we turn our attention to the client's pattern of *global* coping strategies that serve to reduce stress arising from daily lifestyle sources. An underlying assumption is that these global coping strategies have a general impact across various life situations, including an enhanced capacity to cope with high-risk relapse situations. Many clients who regularly utilize these global coping strategies show a general increase in self-efficacy and associated coping responses. Because of their involvement in activities of this nature, they seem to be better "inoculated" against the stressful impact of both specific high-risk situations and the more diffuse stress elicited by general lifestyle factors.

Considerable information on lifestyle coping strategies can be obtained through examination of the structured assessment procedures described above. In particular, the daily self-monitoring of all activities required in the Daily Want–Should Tally Form is a valuable source of information, particularly if records are kept for a typical week. Examination of these records should show whether or not the client engaged in a regular program of exercise or relaxation, amount of time spent alone or working on hobbies, and so on. In order to flesh out this information and explore other areas of lifestyle coping, the therapist should take time to interview the client concerning how he or she copes in several key areas of life activities: health and exercise, relaxation, interpersonal relations, and spiritual life. Each of these life domains should be explored as part of a detailed lifestyle assessment interview.

Health and Exercise

Addictive problems often take their toll in increased health problems. Unless the client's overall health status is thoroughly assessed and appropriate remedial steps taken if necessary, the skill-training and cognitive reframing components of RP intervention may be rendered ineffective. For most clients, a complete *physical examination* is called for, particularly when there is a chronic addictive behavior pattern which may have caused physical damage. Clients who show signs of brain damage should be carefully evaluated by a neuropsychologist or neurologist in order to determine the extent to which they can profit from the practice of behavioral and/or cognitive coping responses. Clients who have cardiovascular problems must be evaluated by a physician prior to the assignment of rigorous exercise programs.

Nutrition is also a key area to explore. What is the client's normal diet and eating style? Are there indications of a past or present addictive eating pattern or other unusual problems associated with food (anorexia, bulimia, etc.)? To what extent does the client's consumption of alcohol, smoking, or other addictive behavior interfere with healthy eating habits? How much of the drinker's daily caloric intake is derived from alcoholic beverages? Does the smoker use smoking as an appetite suppressant? To what extent is eating or snacking used as a means of attempting to cope with stress? Is the client's general physique compatible with various exercise regimens?

Exercise is one of the most effective lifestyle coping strategies. Assessment of the client's utilization of exercise should be a central area of investigation prior to the introduction of lifestyle intervention procedures. What is the daily, weekly, and monthly pattern of the client's physical activities? Is there a regular daily or weekly exercise period, and, if so, what exercises are performed? Do the exercises focus on aerobic activity, such as jogging, running, swimming, bicycling, or participation in active competitive sports, or are they primarily isometric exercises such as weightlifting or gymnastics? How much "natural" exercise does the client get during the day—at home, on the job, or in between—in the form of walking, lifting, performing physical tasks or household chores? How does the client get around during the day: driving, walking, or riding a bike? Does the client have any social support for the exercise program, such as a regular exercise partner or participation in a team sport? What are the blocks and resistances to participation in exercise, if any, and how has the client attempted to deal with these in the past?

In addition to the present addictive behavior problem, does the client use any other drugs or medications on a regular or occasional basis? Are there prescribed medications for a particular physical or psychological problem? Are there problems or side effects? Does the client use tranquilizers, antidepressants, pain-killers, "wake-up" pills or sleeping pills, or other similar medications, and is this use under the supervision of a physician? How often does the client resort to such medications as a means of coping with life stress? What other drugs are used either as self-medication or for recreation (getting high)? In addition to alcohol, tobacco, and prescription medications, what is the use, if any, of other substances such as marijuana, cocaine, psychedelics or hallucinogens? Is there any indication of polydrug use or the interchangeable use of substances as an attempt to cope or get high? What is the social context of the client's drug use—do close friends or family encourage of discourage this behavior, and if so, how? One of the most commonly used drugs to cope with general lifestyle problems is caffeine. What is the client's regular use pattern for coffee, tea, and soft drinks and other substances containing caffeine? To what extent does the client use caffeine as a means of coping with the after-effects of other drug use? What are the client's beliefs and expectations concerning this drug use?

Relaxation

The opposite of feeling stressed is to feel relaxed. What methods does the client presently use to relax when feeling tense and agitated? To what extent is the target addictive behavior used as an attempt to relax, and is this pattern one of escape (the addictive behavior occurs *after* the onset of stress) and/or avoidance (use *prior* to the onset of anticipated stress)? What other resources are available to the client as a means of relaxing? To what extent are tranquilizers or other drugs used in order to feel relaxed? Does the client make use of formal relaxation procedures such as progressive muscle relaxation, biofeedback, meditation, self-hypnosis, or yoga? Does the client engage in physical exercise as a means of bringing on a state of relaxation?

The client can be asked what he or she usually does during the day, in the evening, on the weekends, and during vacation periods to relax. What are the client's typical recreational activities: how much time each day is spent in reading, watching TV or listening to the radio or stereo, or attending movies, plays, concerts, or sports events? Is the client engaged in hobbies or involved in arts or craft activities? Are there relaxing activities the client utilized in the past that might be reintroduced in the future? How does the client make use of vacation or holiday periods in terms of relaxation? Does the client make use of a relaxation procedure as a general preventive strategy or only when feeling under duress? Are these activities engaged in on a regular daily or weekly basis or is relaxation generally postponed until the end of the week or vacation periods? Is the client waiting until he or she retires before taking time off to relax (some individuals continue to postpone time for relaxation until toward the end of their lives, and then complain that they are too "burned out" to enjoy these activities).

Interpersonal Activities

The frequency and quality of interpersonal activities exert a tremendously important influence on an individual's general level of stress. Marital status and the quality of one's intimate personal relationships have been found to exert a significant influence on our capacity to cope with the stresses of life. What is the nature of the client's past and current interpersonal network? Who are the significant others in the client's life, and to what extent are these relationships contributing to or reducing the overall level of stress? If there are important marital or family problems, is the client presently receiving counseling or therapy? How satisfied is the client with his or her sexual activities or orientation? Does the client have close friends, both inside and outside the immediate family or living group, with whom he or she can confide and receive support? What is the nature of the client's overall social support network and how is this support obtained? Does the client belong to any self-help support groups, and are any of these related to the client's presenting problem (e.g., AA, Weightwatchers, etc.)? For each significant other in the client's life, what is that person's attitude and views concerning the client's addiction problem? Do these other persons collude in or share in the addictive activity (e.g., drinking partners), or are they willing to lend their support in helping the client change? To what extent will these significant others facilitate or impede the progress of treatment? How can the helpful folks be brought into the treatment program and the less helpful ones eased out? Are there new friends that could be made to replace the less helpful ones? What type of social pressure or other interpersonal sources of stress does the client think might increase the probability of a future relapse, and how might these potential problems be handled?

Religious Beliefs

An often neglected topic in the discussion of lifestyle issues is the amount of time spent during the day or week in spiritual activities. Perhaps this neglect is due to an assumption that religious or spiritual matters play little or no role in the development or modification of addictive behavior problems. In contrast, my own clinical work and related experiences have convinced me that this topic is of central importance for many people. The influence of religious beliefs is particularly salient for many individuals who have experienced drinking problems, although spiritual issues also often play a role with other addiction problems. Many alcoholics report that they have been able to stop drinking after going through a religious conversion experience, for example. Participation in AA often brings people in touch with their spiritual needs, both through the concept of allegiance to a "higher power" (and surrendering the notion of personal control) and the religious fellowship involved in AA "Twelve Step" work. Spiritual issues often come up with other addiction problems as well. I recently described a case study in which a heavy smoker was finally able to quit after years of unsuccessful attempts when he prayed to God for help and assistance (Marlatt, 1981).

One important reason to explore the client's involvement in religious or spiritual activities is that it may uncover important underlying beliefs or assumptions that may facilitate or impede the progress of therapy. Clients with fundamentalist beliefs or who have been associated with religious groups with stringent moral views may hold strong beliefs about the "sinful" nature of their addiction problem. Clients who believe that an addictive act is equivalent to "giving in to temptation" are more likely to experience strong guilt reactions whenever that behavior occurs. Reactions of self-blame and guilt to the "transgression" of an initial lapse or slip may make it more difficult for such clients to view the slip as a natural mistake in the learning process. In order to uncover such beliefs, the therapist can ask clients questions about their religious upbringing (including parental views) and current attitudes and activities. How does the client view the addiction problem in terms of its overall value or meaning: is it seen as a "bad" behavior or as a sign of moral weakness? To what extent does the client feel it is necessary to expiate the sinful behavior in order to obtain some form of inner peace or salvation? Does the emphasis on self-control and acceptance of personal responsibility for changing behavior (as in the RP approach) clash with the client's basic religious beliefs? If so, the mismatch of personal beliefs with the treatment program philosophy may lead to significant compliance problems in the course of treatment.

In addition to exploring areas associated with the client's formal religious orientation and beliefs, the therapist should also inquire about the client's general "philosophy of life" or basic orientation in terms of underlying values or meanings assigned to various life activities. What is the degree of congruence or fit between the client's value system and the addictive problem? Some clients see their addiction as a "foreign element" in their lives, like an unwanted illness or symptom of psychopathology, while others view it as a stage in their normal development through life, something they can learn from as they pass through it. Each of these views may be associated with a different outlook on the task of behavior change, from "fighting" a foreign influence, to acceptance of personal frailties and the gradual process of change.

Finally, the client should be asked about the amount of time spent in activities related to spiritual growth or self-discovery. How much time, if any, does the client spend alone each day or week? Is this alone time spent in self-related activities (such as keeping a personal diary, meditation or contemplation, spiritual reading, getting in touch with the "inner self," etc.) or is it devoted to the completion of should activities or mindless time-filling tasks? To what extent has the client participated or is open to involvement in various "New Age" activities or groups, such as *est*, meditation, holistic health and healings, or related concerns? Involvement in many of these spiritually related activities may facilitate motivation for and compliance with RP procedures, since one of the primary underlying assumptions of the New Age approach is that the individual must accept full responsibility for personal change and the development of a healthy lifestyle (cf. Cousins, 1981).

Clients with addiction problems often complain that they have no time to devote to themselves, that life is just "too busy" to pursue matters of the spirit or self-actualization. At the same time, however, these clients complain of a lack of inner value or meaning in their lives, and that they sometimes feel that their addictive activities are in response to this inner emptiness—a need to get high or to take time out from what they see as an otherwise mundane and often boring life. Spiritual pursuits and addictive behaviors often share a common element in that they are frequently associated with an altered state of consciousness that is quite different from the ordinary waking state of mind. For some clients, the need to experience this altered state with drugs or other addictive activities may mask an underlying need for a deeper and more satisfying spiritual life.

LIFESTYLE INTERVENTION PROCEDURES

There are several important goals of lifestyle modification. The primary goal in terms of the RP approach, of course, is to reduce the probability of relapse. Here, the lifestyle program is designed to achieve a better balance between the sources of stress and the repertoire of coping responses in the client's life. In contrast with the specific behavioral and cognitive coping skills designed to help the client deal with specific high-risk situations for relapse, lifestyle change strategies are intended to provide the client with more general or global coping skills that exert their effect over a wide variety of risk situations.

This transsituational enhancement of coping capacity is achieved in at least three ways. First, the incorporation of new and rewarding activities such as exercise and relaxation into one's daily lifestyle provides a resource of wants to balance off the excess of shoulds associated with an addictive lifestyle. In addition, the pleasure and sense of pride that accompany practice of these new activities will act to reduce the subjective sense of deprivation and personal loss associated with the termination of an addictive habit pattern. Second, the mastery of new lifestyle coping skills usually gives rise to an increased sense of self-efficacy. The prior self-image associated with engaging in the addictive habit, often characterized by a sense of passive reactivity and "giving in," is replaced by a perception of self-mastery and a proactive stance toward preventing relapse. Typically, the client will report that the self-efficacy associated with, for example, the development of a new exercise program, generalizes in the form of increased confidence in coping with high-risk temptation situations. Third, the regular practice of exercise and relaxation results in a variety of beneficial effects for the client's physical and psychological–spiritual well-being. The positive effects of exercise on the body's physiological state are well known and include such benefits as decreased weight and blood pressure, increased aerobic capacity, and so on. Similarly, the practice of relaxation has been found to be associated with lower indices of stress and an enhancement of planning and coping skills. These positive physical and psychological effects contrast sharply with the state of general debilitation and low energy typically associated with an addictive lifestyle.

POSITIVE VERSUS NEGATIVE ADDICTION

Positive lifestyle activities can themselves become "addictive" as they develop into regular habits. In contrast with a negative addiction (an activity that feels good in the short run but that has negative effects in the long run), a positive addictive habit frequently feels unpleasant in the short run (the novice jogger's first "short run" can be quite painful) but is associated with positive consequences in the long run (e.g., the feeling of a "warm glow" and enhanced well-being that follow a rigorous physical workout). William Glasser (1976) has coined the term *positive addictions* to describe lifestyle activities such as running and meditation. Glasser has noted the following six criteria that must be met in order for an activity to be defined as a positive addiction:

(1) It is something noncompetitive that you choose to do and you can devote an hour (approximately) a day to it. (2) It is possible for you to do it easily and it doesn't take a great deal of mental effort to do it well. (3) You can do it alone or rarely with others but it does not depend upon others to do it. (4) You believe that it has some value

(physical, mental, or spiritual) for you. (5) You believe that if you persist at it you will improve, but this is completely subjective—you need to be the only one who measures the improvement. (6) The activity *must* have the quality that you can do it *without criticizing yourself. If you can't accept yourself during this time the activity will not be addicting.* This is why it is so important that the activity can be done alone. Any time you introduce other people you chance introducing competition or criticism, often both. (Glasser, 1976, p. 93)

In essence, the goal of lifestyle modification in the RP approach can be summarized in these terms: to replace negative addictions with positive addictions (or to put it even more simply: to transform bad habits into good ones).

GENERAL PRINCIPLES IN WORKING WITH CLIENTS ON LIFESTYLE CHANGE

One might argue that to make significant changes in a client's lifestyle, particularly with clients who have a long history of giving in to the temptation of immediate gratification offered by drugs or other addictive behaviors, is a hopelessly idealistic task. Although it is certainly true that many clients will present significant compliance problems in the form of resistance when initially embarking on a program of lifestyle change, these problems may be overcome to a large degree by careful planning and continuing supervision and support by the therapist. Issues and strategies associated with overcoming resistance and increasing adherence and compliance with clients in general have been discussed in several volumes (see, e.g., Davidson & Davidson, 1980; Karoly & Steffen, 1980; Stuart, 1982; Wachtel, 1982). In addition to the above general references, the following points have been found to be helpful in our own work with clients. Utilizing one or more of the following suggestions may be of assistance in working with resistant clients.

As with all other aspects of the RP approach, the therapist should work with the client as a colleague or co-investigator in planning and developing a lifestyle change program that is tailor-made for the client. An individualized approach with careful supervision during the implementation and maintenance stages of the program is likely to be much more successful than simply giving the client some general advice to "get regular exercise" or "start jogging every day." Authoritative directives that are not followed up by the therapist may work for a short period but are unlikely to persist over time.

From the start, the therapist and client should participate together in the planning, selection, and implementation of the lifestyle change program. The focus should be not only on the development of a particular activity (learning how to meditate, etc.), but also on the various problems that may arise including scheduling time for the activity, possible roadblocks and other hindrances that might arise, exploring attitudes or fears that may be associated with the new activity (e.g., "Will meditation lead me to become emotionally detached from life?" or "I'm afraid that if I exert myself, my heart will give out!").

Although Glasser (1976) has stressed the need to perform positive addictions alone in order to avoid developing a stressful competitive attitude, there is much to be gained from performing these activities with the support of another individual or group, as long as the interactions involved do not focus on competition or interpersonal comparisons. Compliance in developing a regular exercise program such as jogging, swimming, or bicycling is often enhanced when the activity is performed with a close family member or friend. Similarly, membership in a meditation group or other social support system may also increase the likelihood that the activity will be maintained over time. On the other hand, some clients may prefer the time alone, away from the demands of others, while engaging in the lifestyle activity. For many individuals, the time spent alone in an exercise or relaxation program is the only time they are free from social obligations or other interpersonal demands. Again, the need for an individualized approach depending on the client's particular need is apparent.

Just as Rome was not built in a day, neither is a successful lifestyle change established in a relatively short period. It takes time to develop a new habit pattern in the same way that other new skills take time to master. The best strategy is to begin with a small, easily accomplished goal, and then to gradually work up to a more complete program over a period of several weeks or months. For someone who is out of shape physically and unused to engaging in aerobic exercise, it is best to begin with a modest goal such as engaging in a short period of brisk walking each day (e.g., 15 minutes). Later the periods of walking can be increased to half an hour daily, possibly followed by an eventual escalation to more demanding activities such as jogging or swimming depending on the particular client's background and needs. Similarly, rather than asking the client to start meditating for two 20-minute periods a day, a better strategy might be to ask for one 10-minute period a day during the 1st week, two such daily periods the 2nd week, and so forth. In this manner, self-efficacy is increased gradually and even the most resistant and unmotivated client may experience a sense of increased mastery that builds upon itself over time. One problem to avoid at all costs is to demand too much too quickly of the client. To require the client to begin with daily periods of aerobic exercise combined with two 20-minute meditation periods each day is to invite noncompliance and possible dropouts from treatment. A related issue involves the question of when to begin a lifestyle change program in the overall course of treatment within an RP program. Although the choice of when to begin will depend on the client (some clients will benefit immediately from an exercise or relaxation program introduced at an early stage of treatment), for most clients we recommend that lifestyle changes begin in the early stages of the maintenance phase (i.e., just after cessation of smoking or drinking), gradually increasing thereafter.

Whenever possible, the therapist should recommend the selection of activities that match the client's own needs or preferences. For clients who report experiencing considerable physical tension or somaticized stress, the best activity to begin with might be either aerobic exercise, progressive relaxation of the muscles, or a combination of the two. On the other hand, for clients who tend to experience stress primarily on a cognitive level, such as obsessive worrying or self-criticism, a beginning program of meditation may be advised (cf. Davidson & Schwartz, 1976). Similarly, if the client reports having enjoyed certain activities in the past (e.g., bike riding as a child), current participation in the same activities may reduce resistance and noncompliance. Choice of an activity may also depend on the target negative habit; for ex-smokers who are afraid of gaining weight, for example, a vigorous exercise program combined with dietary changes is recommended.

Whenever possible, the client should be given considerable flexibility in choosing an appropriate lifestyle change activity. Many individuals fail to maintain a regular program of change because they choose goals that are unnecessarily rigid, absolute, or overly idealistic. Making a strict resolution to run every day for 40 minutes, regardless of possible mitigating circumstances, is to invite failure. In this case, even a single slip (such as failing to run on the day of a big snowstorm or when the client has a bad cold) may result in a relapse from the exercise program. A better strategy would be to commit oneself to a general principle of engaging in at least three periods of lifestyle activity a week. Choice of a particular activity would depend on the circumstances of the day and the client's mood and physical condition. In this respect, the concept of *body time* may be an appropriate strategy. The individual makes a commitment to engage in body-time activities for, say, three times a week for a period of 1 hour each. Instead of selecting the same activity each period, the individual postpones choice of a particular activity until the prescheduled period begins. Then, perhaps after a brief period of meditation or self-introspection, a choice of a particular activity is made, depending on the person's mood, physical state, and the weather. On one occasion, the person may be feeling tense and anxious after a hard day at the office, and select a vigorous exercise such as jogging. At another time, a more appropriate choice might be to take a long, solitary walk, or to meditate. The main point about the body-time concept is that the individual makes a commitment to take a period of *time for oneself*, although the choice of activities within that time period remains flexible.

One of the main things to note in developing a lifestyle change program is to avoid situations in which performance of the particular activity becomes another should in the person's life. If the new behavior becomes a should instead of a want, the client may have difficulty in maintaining the activity over long periods of time. Reactance will develop and some sort of relapse is likely. To prevent this from happening, steps can be taken to make the experience pleasant and fun to participate in. As an example of this approach, consider the advice given by the syndicated columnist Richard Simmons, who advocates an occasional half-day "recharging" period as an enjoyable way to exercise and relax:

Everyone, no matter what age or what kind of physical condition, needs time to recharge. Recharging is both a physical and psychological process, but it mostly is psychological. What you need is to give yourself a change of pace . . . I don't mean the change of pace your travel agent offers you when he tempts you with trips. I mean the kind of change you get from going to a spa for a day or two. Now don't laugh. I know that not too many people can afford to go to one of those fancy spas you read about in magazines. But you can turn your home into a spa, and you can recharge there by yourself. And by yourself is what I mean. Recharging is best done alone. Farm the kids out to a friend's house, pack them off to grandma's for a weekend. Even if you can only get six hours alone, go for it.

- Start by stretching and getting in touch with your body. Assess your good parts and bad parts without getting too critical (don't get depressed or defensive, just take inventory).
- Take 40 to 60 minutes for exercise: brisk walking, bike riding, aerobics, whatever you choose. Exercise until you get that good feeling, but don't overdo it.
- Spend some time on "your beauty routine": shower, bath, sauna, hot tub or Jacuzzi. Be sure to moisturize your skin afterward . . .
- Eat a light but nutritious lunch. Listen to classical or relaxing music . . .
- Have a massage if you can afford it, or have a friend or spouse give you one.
- Go for a long (one hour) walk or meditate for one hour.
- Shower, rub down with moisturizer and relax.

You feel great, don't you? (Simmons, 1982, p. F8)

One of the main obstacles to maintaining a regular lifestyle change activity such as exercise is overcoming the resistance associated with beginning the activity (the "inertia" problem) and with the initial physical discomfort or psychological boredom that are associated with the early stages. The rewards associated with exercise are often delayed; unlike the immediate gratification associated with addictive behaviors, lifestyle changes often involve delayed gratification—the high feeling one experiences after exercising, improved health functioning, and reduced risk of disease. In order to help overcome the motivational deficits associated with starting and following through on a given exercise activity such as jogging, a combination of self-talk and positive imagery is recommended. Self-instructions and positive coping imagery often can bridge the gap between the immediate resistance (e.g., feeling too tired to get up in the morning and run) and the sought-after delayed rewards (e.g., feeling the glow of a work-out and the pride of accomplishment). As an example of the use of such procedures, I asked one of the most physically active colleagues in our research laboratory, Claudette Cummings (cf. Cummings, Gordon, & Marlatt, 1980), to share her own cognitive strategies she uses in her regular aerobics exercise program. In the selection below, she talks about overcoming the resistance associated with going jogging in the morning:

• *Stage I:* This morning dawns cold and wet. The rain sounds uninviting and I draw deeper beneath the night-long warmth of the bed covers. Then I remember that today is a "jogging day." Yesterday, after I finished swimming and while I was in the sauna, I decided when and what exercise I would do today. I plan my exercise day by day so that perhaps only 4 days each month are spent without exercise. And today, I remind myself that given my busy schedule, I either exercise early or not at all. The rain still falls and I really do not want to get out of bed. Suddenly, a now spontaneous axiom occurs to me: "I will ultimately feel better after I run than if I stay here and get 20 more minutes sleep." This cognition is a product of 8 years of experience with exercise. It has become an invariant truth that with the exception of physical illness, I will possess more energy, think more clearly, and experience a general heightened self-awareness after I exercise regardless of the condition I was in before. This is one of the few reliable methods in my life with which I can achieve a sense of well-being and centeredness using total self-control. I use exercise as an antidote for boredom, loneliness, fatigue, depression, post-food or alcohol binges, and a score of other states associated with the stress of my life. However, exercise is not a response limited only to negative emotions. It also adds increased appreciation to periods of pleasure, satisfaction, and joy.

This, then, is a description of the set of thoughts behind my abbreviated axiom which acts to counter my early morning monologue about sleeping the extra 20 minutes. I get out of bed, down a quick cup of coffee, dress, and am out into the grey early morning. Finally, after my obligatory set of warm-up stretches, I am ready. I run in place for a moment, and then with a deep and somewhat resigned breath, I am off. All is fine for the first 20 strides and then the hard part begins: the acclimatization to muscle exertion, oxygen depletion, and increased cardiac demands.

• *Stage II:* "God, my legs and feet feel like lead" and require more strength to move than I seem to easily have available. A new set of cognitions occurs. "Perhaps this morning I'll stop, shorten my run, or just walk the 3 miles." It is at this critical point that I activate a variety of images and cognitions on which I deliberately focus my attention. I do not know why I choose the particular one(s) in any exercise session. Sometimes, I guess, I use all of them and still wish I had more *tricks* up my "mental sleeve." The following is a nonexhaustive list of these "Stage II tricks":

1. Physical beauty: This is all I can do to maintain or improve my body's appearance in addition to diet and sleep.

2. Compensation for recent food and/or drink excesses.

3. Comparison of myself to others more or less fit (e.g., the handicapped, terminally ill, or fellow joggers): This results in either incentive to continue or pride over my current accomplishments.

4. Movement meditation: consciously letting go of thoughts; conscious attempt to create an altered state of awareness by intensely focusing my eyes a few feet ahead, feeling the sweat bead on my body, paying attention to the ambient environment (e.g., seasonal changes, clouds, light on water, tempera-

ture, feel of wind/sun/rain/fog on my face, etc.). Concentration on graceful movement; each step is the only one in the universe, thus make every movement count.

5. Classic techniques of pain control (e.g., relabeling pain as muscle strengthening).

6. Focus on work-related detail; brainstorming solutions to problems, planning and reviewing the day (caveat: I rarely use this trick since I conceptualize exercise as a time without external goal acquisition).

• *Stage III:* Usually near the end of my exercise session, and if I am lucky, another stage occurs. This stage feels as if I am no longer exerting effort to continue. I can observe and enjoy the process while my body autonomously maintains the pace without requiring volitional concentration or pain control. This brief experience is difficult to describe and I cannot predict its occurrence. It is a variable gift which I appreciate but do *not* seek as a motive for exercise. At the least, it is a period during which exercise is not aversive and at the best, it is close to transcendence through movement.

• *Stage IV:* At last, I am finished. Returning to a more normal metabolism, sweat clouding my vision, I walk while stretching and shaking out my arms and legs, and my breath comes slower. As a strong calm sense of satisfaction grows I tell myself "It's over, and didn't take that long or hurt that bad." I pour a glass of juice and head for the shower. During the shower, which is always sensational after exercising, I think of lots of self-efficacy statements. Finally, I think of tomorrow's schedule and plan how and when I can fit in another exercise session.

I will not detail in length the secondary gains that have accrued over the years as a result of regular exercise. Briefly they include increased self-control over food, alcohol, and drug intake, better posture, skin and muscle tone, sheer energy and endurance, better sleep and sexual functioning, regular and unconstipated bowel movements, and simply gobs of personal pride.

PLANNING A LIFESTYLE CHANGE PROGRAM

The elements of a lifestyle change program can be illustrated by returning to the case study described in the opening section of this chapter. Mr. B's addictive lifestyle encompassed a variety of target problems, all of which required attention in our clinical work together: excessive consumption of alcohol and caffeine, smoking, hypertension, and the life stress associated with his job and family life. The primary issue to be considered with clients such as Mr. B, whose lifestyle includes a variety of interlocking addictive behaviors, is: Where to start? As discussed in the previous section, it would be a mistake to try to tackle all of Mr. B's problems at once. Instead, he and I sat down together and discussed each problem in turn, including the health dangers involved and the relative difficulty expected for changing each behavior (his motivation and self-efficacy, etc.), and began to prioritize his goals for change. Together we agreed, based on a careful review of this information, to begin by working on his smoking. Although smoking was a firmly established habit in Mr. B's repertoire, he felt most highly motivated to change this behavior first, in view of its obvious implications for his health (especially the hypertension). Before embarking on an abstinence-oriented program based on RP principles for his smoking, we both were aware that he needed to make some basic changes in his daily activities, particularly for his typical workday at the office. By gradually introducing more want activities into his crowded schedule of shoulds, the stress of his hectic daily pace might be reduced.

We decided to pick want activities that would also make it easier for Mr. B to give up his nicotine habit. Since one of his concerns associated with stopping smoking was a fear of weight gain, we decided to begin by introducing two daily periods of brisk walking into his work schedule. After some juggling of his schedule, it was agreed that he would walk for half an hour each day at lunch time and again after the afternoon's work. As we began to introduce this rather modest change in exercise (based on his rather sedentary activity level prior to the program), Mr. B decided to "lock in" his motivation to comply with the walking program by parking his car in a parking lot located a half an hour's walk away from his office. After a week or so of this new activity, he began to report that he increasingly enjoyed these walks, since it gave him time to plan his day in the morning on the way to his office, and to review the day's activities in the afternoon on the way back to his car (living in Seattle, he also kept an umbrella and rain gear in his car so as not to be discouraged by the weather during his walks). After 3 weeks of the walking program, Mr. B reported feeling somewhat better physically but was beginning to become increasingly aware of his smoking and how it affected his physical capacity (he had been keeping self-monitoring records of his daily smoking patterns during this period). He felt ready to quit smoking.

Stopping smoking was easy—staying stopped was more difficult. As we began to examine the intensity of his urges to smoke during the week following his quit date (he quit "cold turkey" so we could begin immediately on the RP approach to maintenance), he reported that the strongest urges still occurred at work, particularly after a trying court case or when confronted with a pile of paperwork to complete before a pressing deadline. As a result, we decided to next implement a training program in relaxation; after a discussion of various relaxation procedures (described later in this chapter), Mr. B selected meditation. I instructed him in a simple form of mantra meditation and we practiced it together during several of our sessions together. Mr. B was able to clear his schedule so as to introduce brief "meditation breaks" just prior to or following a particularly stressful event at work. He placed a "Do Not Disturb" sign on his door and simply sat in quiet meditation for a period of 10–15 minutes (although on some occasions, he could only sit for about 5 minutes due to the press of his appointment schedule). He also learned to apply his meditation skills as a means of coping with urges to smoke. He particularly liked the "urge surfing" imagery while he meditated on the rising and falling of an urge (see Chapter 4 for a description of this technique).

During the first 3 weeks of his smoking cessation program, Mr. B reported two slips. On one occasion, he had a cigarette after a difficult court appearance when he met an old friend, a fellow lawyer, over coffee. His friend was smoking and he decided on the whim to bum a cigarette; "Coffee and cigarettes just go together like pepper and salt," he explained. In dealing with this slip, we worked on both the high-risk situation of social pressure (being in the company of another smoker and how to handle it) and the temptation provided by the strong association between smoking and drinking coffee. After some discussion about the harmful effects of excessive caffeine consumption (he was still drinking five to six mugs a day), particularly in terms of his hypertension (and related urge to smoke), he began to substitute decaffeinated coffee for his regular brew, although he still allowed himself a cup of "half-and-half" (half caffeinated, half decaffeinated) each morning to start the day. Within a week or two, Mr. B reported feeling more relaxed and less agitated than he could remember feeling in years. At the end of our 2nd month working together, he had increased his exercise program from daily walking periods to an aerobic program (a mix of jogging or swimming, depending on his mood and the circumstances), which he engaged in for 45 minutes, three times a week. He was meditating on the average of twice daily. He had also given up cigarettes (despite a couple of slips) and cut down drastically on his coffee consumption.

Mr. B's second smoking slip occurred after he had gone out with some friends for an evening of cards and drinking. He smoked two cigarettes late in the evening after he had consumed over six bottles of beer. His alcohol consumption had decreased to some extent since we had been working together, possibly as a result of his other stress-reducing lifestyle changes, but it remained a problem—particularly in certain high-risk situations (e.g., visiting his ex-wife and having an evening out with the gang). We decided to deal with his drinking problem as the final treatment goal—even though alcohol was the presenting problem when he first came in. After considerable discussion, we decided to choose a goal of moderation rather than abstinence, since the evidence suggested that his drinking was largely a response to stress situations. Mr. B agreed that he would abstain from all alcohol for a period of 30 days prior to embarking on the moderation program, in order to provide us with information concerning potential trouble spots down the road (intensity of urges to drink in various situations, etc.). We began this program at the beginning of our 3rd month of working together. After debriefing a number of slips during the 1st month, we instituted a program of moderation for his drinking. The program was based on principles described in Marlatt (1979) and Miller and Muñoz (1982). After various setbacks along the way, at the end of our fifth and final month of therapy, Mr. B's lifestyle had undergone a radical transformation: he was exercising and meditating regularly, and he continued to abstain from smoking and to moderate his use of caffeine and alcohol. He realized some of the long-range benefits of these changes: loss of 15 pounds, decreased blood pressure, and increased productivity at work. Although problems with his ex-wife continued, Mr. B felt better able to cope with the situation, particularly since he no longer drank to excess during their meetings. A 90-day follow-up visit revealed some slipping back and problems, but these were dealt with rather easily since Mr. B had by this time mastered many of the self-control skills and lifestyle changes and felt he could remedy his own deficiencies or problems as they occurred. In short, he had become his own "maintenance man."

In the following sections, several major lifestyle change activities are described. Most attention here is given to exercise and relaxation as primary "positive addictions" that are designed to replace negative addictive behaviors. In choosing among the various alternatives described, the therapist–client team should plan an individualized program of lifestyle change, based in part on the suggestions listed above and on the client's unique characteristics (age, physical strengths and weaknesses, personal preferences, etc.).

EXERCISE

According to the American College of Sports Medicine (ACSM), exercise refers to sustained increases in large muscle and cardiopulmonary activity, which, if performed with sufficient intensity, frequency, and duration, results in improved endurance (ACSM, 1978). For most RP programs, recommended exercises fall into the general category of aerobic exercise, including repetitive isorhythmic activities (e.g., brisk walking, jogging, cycling, rowing, and swimming), involving major muscle groups (such as the legs) in which energy is derived from metabolic processes using a constant flow of oxygen (Cooper, 1968; McArdle, Katch, & Katch, 1981). Other activities such as isometric exercise (e.g., weightlifting) have other benefits that are only tangentially related to our present discussion and so will not be included here.

How much aerobic activity is to be recommended to clients? According to the official policy of the ACSM (1978), the following guidelines are recommended to develop and maintain cardiorespiratory fitness and body composition in the healthy adult:

1. Frequency of training: 3 to 5 days per week.
2. Intensity of training: 60% to 90% of maximum heart rate reserve[1] or 50% to 85% of maximum oxygen uptake (VO_2 max).

1. To establish the advised rate of 60%–90% of maximum heart rate reserve, for a man or woman of a given age, the following formula may be applied as a rough index. For the lower 60% range, males should first subtract their current age in years from 220, females should subtract their age from 228, and then both multiply this figure by .60; the resulting heart rate figure represents approximately 60% of the maximum heart rate reserve for that age and sex. Similarly, to estimate the higher level of 90%, use the same subtraction as above and multiply the remainder by .90.

3. Duration of training: 15 to 60 minutes of continuous aerobic activity. Duration is dependent on the intensity of the activity, thus lower intensity activity should be conducted over a longer period of time. Because of the importance of the "total fitness" effect and the fact that it is more readily attained in longer duration programs and because of the potential hazards and compliance problems associated with high intensity activity, lower to moderate intensity activity of longer duration is recommended for the nonathletic adult.

4. Mode of activity: Any activity that uses large muscle groups, that can be maintained continuously, and is rhythmical and aerobic in nature, e.g., running, jogging, walking–hiking, swimming, skating, bicycling, rowing, cross-country skiing, rope skipping and various endurance game activities. (ACSM, 1978, p. 1)

According to many experts (e.g., Pollock, 1978), the exercise period should start with a 10- to 15-minute warm-up and muscle conditioning period, and end with a 5- to 10-minute cool-down. For clients who have rarely exercised in the past or for whom exercise may represent an increased health risk (e.g., clients with cardiovascular disease), a complete physical examination by a physician is mandatory prior to embarking on a new exercise program. All programs should, of course, begin slowly but surely, gradually building up to the levels recommended each week by the ACSM. Brisk walking on a daily basis is an excellent beginning exercise for many individuals, since it is pleasant, relatively easy to perform, and is less likely to be accompanied by compliance and adherence problems. For more intense aerobic activities, most clients should be advised to take a day's rest between workouts and to limit the duration of the activity to less than 30 minutes in the beginning stages.

Advantages of Exercise

There are several reasons why exercise is a highly recommended lifestyle change activity. These advantages should be shared with the client in order to enhance motivation and provide a rationale for embarking on an exercise program.

Aerobic exercises can become positively addicting (Glasser, 1976). The activity often becomes intrinsically rewarding over time and takes on the quality of a want instead of the should that most people associate with exercise. Consider the following description of cognitive states experienced by a runner (Jim Corey) described in Glasser's book:

I can describe two states of mind when I have settled into my runs. Sometimes both will occur during the course of a run, sometimes only one will occur when I am settled into a run. . . . The first mind state that I would describe is that of a rational cognitive nature and coincides with runs that are generally unsatisfactory in some way. The weather is hot, the dogs are harrassing me, and the course is becoming boring because I have been on it many times. The second mind state is . . . not cognitive or rational, instead it is ego-transcending. I simply perceive as I run. I react instinctively to obstacles which suddenly appear. I float. I run like a deer. I feel good. I feel high. I don't think at all. My awareness is only of the present . . . brain chatter is gone. (Jim Corey, cited by Glasser, 1976, p. 113)

Jim Corey's description of his second mind state while running (one that closely approximates the description cited above by Claudette Cummings) meets Glasser's definition of a positive addiction. The state is not unlike the high associated with the effects of many psychoactive drugs—a positive feeling tone, an altered state of consciousness, increased awareness of the here-and-now, often accompanied by decreased cognitive ruminations and concerns. Although some have postulated that the high effects sometimes associated with rigorous exercise are the result of increased output of the body's own natural opiates, the beta-endorphins (e.g., Apenzeller, Standefer, Apenzeller, & Atkinson, 1980), these effects are also frequently reported by meditators, and meditation seems to be on the opposite scale of physical arousal from exercise, a point we shall elaborate on in the next section. Some authors have even suggested that a meditation can be combined with running to produce a "running meditation response" (Solomon & Bumpus, 1978).

Participation in aerobic exercise is often incompatible with indulging in negative addictions. Runners who smoke, for example, often report that they become more acutely aware of the limiting effect their smoking habit has on physical endurance and breath capacity. As a result, their motivation to give up smoking (or the rewarding effects of having recently quit) is enhanced. Epidemiological studies indicate an inverse relationshp between smoking and habitual physical exercise (Criqui, 1980). Similarly, heavy drinkers often report that they feel less desire to drink *after* having completed a run at the end of the workday (Murphy, Pagano, & Marlatt, 1984). Aerobic exercise, such as jogging, is sometimes used as a component of alcoholism treatment programs (e.g., Gary & Guthrie, 1972). Individuals who are working on a weight problem often find that excessive food consumption is incompatible with participation in aerobic activities. Regular participation in aerobic exercise has been shown to produce weight loss for obese as well as normal-weight individuals (Epstein & Wing, 1980); weight loss associated with exercise may be mediated, in part, by decreased appetite (Bjorntorp, 1976; Brownell & Stunkard, 1980). In addition, exercise serves as a substitute for or time out from snacking as a maladaptive coping technique (Epstein & Wing, 1980).

Aerobic exercise appears to have a positive effect in reducing stress. Many individuals report informally that they find a vigorous workout to be the only effective way of cutting through the stress accumulated during a busy workday, particularly stress associated with worry and other cognitive ruminations. In a recent review of the literature on physical fitness training and mental health, Folkins and Sime (1981) report that regular exercise has been found to be associated with improved affect, an improved sense of well-being, improved sleep patterns, enhanced work performances, and so on. One study found beneficial mood changes in depressed patients who exercise (Greist, Klein, Eischens, Faris, Gurman, & Morgan, 1979). Similar effects have been reported anecdotally in alcoholic treatment programs that include running as an intervention procedure.

In addition to the short-term stress-reducing effects, considerable research has now accumulated indicating the positive long-range consequences of exercise on cardiovascular health. Recent reviews of this literature (e.g., Brownell, 1982; Martin & Dubbert, 1982) show that a systematic program of aerobic exercise has been shown to both improve cardiovascular efficiency and modify cardiovascular risk profiles in healthy, high-risk, and coronary patients. Exercise has also been found to be associated with reductions in harmful plasma triglycerides and LDL cholesterol and increases in the protective HDL cholesterol (Wood & Haskell, 1979); decreases in resting and active heart rate and blood pressure; and increases in stroke volume and oxygen utilization (Clausen, 1976). Exercise may also reduce blood pressure in hypertensives, independent of weight or dietary sodium reductions (cf. Horton, 1981). As Martin and Dubbert (1982) point out in their review of the exercise literature, however, many of the above results must be interpreted with caution, since much of the research in this area is still fraught with numerous methodological problems.

Inclusion of aerobic exercises as part of an RP program with addictive behaviors provides the client with a replacement or substitute activity for the previous negative habit pattern. An exercise program (or other lifestyle activity such as relaxation) may help offset the feeling of deprivation that often is experienced by clients who have recently given up a negative habit. Instead of feeling a sense of loss and emptiness, clients may begin to feel a sense of gain and accomplishment (increased self-efficacy) as they gradually master an improved healthy lifestyle. For those clients who may argue that they lack the time to participate in a regular program of exercise, the response is: How much time and energy did you put into the behaviors associated with your negative addiction? Often the time and energy put into an exercise program is *less* than that involved in the acquisition and consumption rituals associated with the addictive habit pattern.

Exercise Adherence Problems

Problems of compliance and adherence in maintaining a regular program of exercise appear to be equal to those encountered in maintaining abstinence or a controlled use pattern with addictive behaviors. In a review of the exercise adherence field, Martin and Dubbert (1982) conclude, in fact, that "examination of the exercise dropout/relapse pattern indicates a negatively accelerated curve not unlike that found for the negative addictive behaviors: The majority of dropouts/relapses occur within the initial three months, followed by continued deterioration, with attrition leveling off between 50% and 70% after 12 to 24 months" (p. 1008). In a review of factors found to be associated with increased adherence problems, these authors single out the following factors: motivational deficits, continuous smoking, lack of social support, higher intensity exercises (adherence is greater with lower intensity activities), and the like (Martin & Dubbert, 1982).

Investigators have only just begun to explore methods of increasing adherence among exercisers. Some of the most promising procedures reviewed by Martin and Dubbert include contracting and lottery procedures, increased support from significant others, stimulus control (reminders, prompts, etc.) and cognitive self-control procedures (self-monitoring, self-reward, self-contracting). In addition, flexibility of planning and choice among activities has been found to be important to exercise adherence (Thompson & Wankel, 1980). Aerobic exercise is particularly advantageous in this regard because it offers the client a choice among several different physical activities. When used in conjunction with the concept of body time (described above), the sense of choice and flexibility is further enhanced. Future research employing the general strategies of relapse prevention to the problem of exercise adherence may reveal additional effective strategies (e.g., anticipating and coping with high-risk situations that lead to a lapse from regular participation; cognitive reframing of lapses to prevent total dropout effects). A recent study by King and Frederiksen (1984), for example, compared the effectiveness of relapse preparation training and social support in increasing the number of participant-initiated jogging episodes among women who were not currently involved in exercise. Participants receiving either social support (running in a group) or relapse prevention initiated significantly more jogging episodes than control participants. At a 3-month follow-up, a significantly greater percentage of participants (83%) in the relapse prevention condition reported consistent jogging than did women in the other conditions.

RELAXATION

> Every man knows how useful it is to be useful;
> No one seems to know how useful it is to be useless.

The above quote, taken from the writings of Chuang Tzu (in Watson, 1968), a Taoist master and philosopher (399–295 B.C.), illustrates the importance and usefulness of "doing nothing"—for someone to have no particular "use" at a given time and place. Despite the Puritan ethic that views "not doing" as a sign of laziness and sloth, recent scientific evidence strongly suggests that various forms of relaxation can have profoundly positive effects on the physical, psychological, and spiritual well-being of individuals who regularly engage in them. As a result, members of our society are now offered a wide plethora of techniques and nonactivities that are claimed to enhance the capacity to relax. Contemporary behavior therapists often speak of the basic incongruity between states of stress and relaxation; relaxation is recommended as an antidote to stress and as a preventive procedure in stress-management programs. One might note, in fact, that the development of systematic desensitization in the early days of behavior therapy (Wolpe, 1958) utilized progressive muscle relaxation (Jacobson, 1929) as a technique for the "reciprocal inhibition" of anxiety or fear. In the past two decades, numerous other relaxation techniques have been introduced to the population at large. These procedures include the following: meditation, hypnotic relaxation and self-hypnosis, various guided imagery techniques, massage, deep breathing and other breathing procedures, as well as the latest in water-based techniques, from the ubiquitous hot tub to the "float to relax" flotation tank. Other individuals pursue a wide variety of recreational activities (from active sports activities to passive reading and television viewing) in order to relax and unwind from the daily stresses of life.

Until recently, it was thought that various relaxation procedures such as muscle relaxation, hypnosis, and meditation each had unique and separate effects. This hypothesis was based in part on the observation that different instructions and operational procedures are used in each method (e.g., physical relaxation of the musculature, trance induction, mental concentration on a fixed object of attention, etc.). Recent research comparing the effectiveness of several different relaxation procedures, both in terms of physiological and psychological–behavioral effects, has questioned the validity of the differential effectiveness hypothesis, however. In a research review of the physiological and clinical effects of meditation as compared to other relaxation techniques, Shapiro (1982) concludes:

Thus it appears that the original belief that we would be able to discriminate meditation as a unique physiological state has not been confirmed—on either an autonomic or a metabolic level or in terms of EEG pattern. Although it seems clear that meditation can bring about a generalized reduction in many physiological systems, thereby creating a state of relaxation, it is not yet clear from the available data that this state is differentiated from the effects of other relaxation techniques, whether they be hypnosis or deep muscle relaxation. Most studies have found that the constellation of changes is significantly different between meditation groups and placebo control groups, but not between meditation and other self-regulation treatments. . . . Meditation appears to be equally but no more effective than other self-regulation strategies for such problems as anxiety, anxiety in alcoholics, alcohol consumption, insomnia, and borderline hypertension. The self-regulation strategies compared with meditation included progressive relaxation, Benson's relaxation response, a pseudo-meditation treatment, antimeditation treatments, self-administered systematic desensitization, and cardiovascular and neuromuscular biofeedback. (pp. 269–270; original references deleted)

Shapiro's conclusions suggest that there may be an underlying commonality among the major relaxation procedures—at least for progressive muscle relaxation, meditation, and hypnotic relaxation. Each of the various relaxation techniques may be a different doorway leading to the same common response or relaxed mental state. Benson (1975) was among the first to hypothesize such a common response, which he termed the *relaxation response*: a "wakeful hypometabolic state" that can be differentiated from other major states of consciousness (normal awakeness, sleeping, dreaming) by a unique pattern of physiological responses (e.g., decreased sympathetic arousal, increases in alpha rhythm brain-wave amplitude, decreased oxygen consumption, etc.). Benson (1975) has described a noncultic form of meditation that he recommends as a standard method of eliciting the relaxation response (described below in the section on meditation techniques).

Other writers have focused on a psychological state common to several forms of relaxation. This common state has been variously referred to as "passive attention" (Bowers, 1982) or "choiceless awareness" (cf. Levine, 1979). Some investigators, notably Ornstein (1972, 1977), have hypothesized that meditation and other forms of deep relaxation may involve a shift in dominance in the cerebral hemispheres. Deep relaxation may inhibit dominant hemisphere activity, allowing the operations of the nondominant hemisphere to gain ascendance. As a result, the individual shifts from a linear, logical, verbal mode of consciousness to a more holistic, intuitive level of awareness. In this passive mode of consciousness, awareness remains clear (vs. in sleep) but the usual linkage between thoughts–intentions–actions is suspended. Instead, the relaxed individual is able to observe and be aware of mental processes without being "hooked" by them (or identifying with one's thoughts) or responding in the normal active mode of overt activity.

The state of passive attention engendered by deep relaxation often offers the individual new sources of creative inspiration and intuitive insight that are rarely obtained by more active modes of conscious control. The differences involved between active conscious control (e.g., as typically practiced in cognitive-behavior therapy) and the state of passive attention has recently been highlighted by Bowers (1982):

It has often seemed to me . . . that the cognitive-behaviorist's emphasis on cognitive control—of *doing* something to change one's thoughts, behavior, or circumstances— seems excessively organized around rational and willful efforts to produce significant change. There is, in contrast, a rich therapeutic tradition which argues that such willful attempts to control thought and feeling can sometimes be quite counter- productive, and indeed can often constitute a form of psychological resistance to significant psychological change. . . . A host of . . . early psychologists all realized that it was often beneficial to circumvent the patient's willful, active efforts to control thought and feeling, and instead to engender a psychological state of passive attention in their patients. The purpose of such mental passivity (which incidentally was often engendered by hypnosis) was to permit the patient to discover what thoughts, fantasies, or affects emerged—spontaneously, as it were. Such cognitive "emergents" often have surprise value, precisely because they, like dreams, are not the end product of willfully directed thought. Insofar as such unwilled emergents may help to define the patient's problem domain, the subsequent application of more active cognitive strategies can be more aptly targeted and sharply focused. (p. 76)

Advantages of Relaxation

As with aerobic exercise, there are a number of theoretical and practical reasons why relaxation is recommended as a lifestyle modification procedure for addictive behavior problems. These advantages are described below, followed by a description of the most commonly used relaxation procedures.

The state of relaxation is experienced by many individuals as an altered state of consciousness, different in quality from both ordinary wakefulness and sleep. The relaxed mind is similar in some ways to an automobile with its engine running but resting in neutral gear: the car is in a neutral but responsive state (passive attention), unlike when it is either fully running (ordinary wakefulness) or when the ignition is off altogether (sleeping). Thoughts, images, and feelings may come and go, but the mind is not "in gear" and responding to these stimuli with active cognitive processes or overt behavior. In most forms of relaxation, awareness or attention is focused on an internal, subjective stimulus (e.g., muscle tone, the breath, mantra, etc.) or on an external source of suggestion or guided imagery (hypnotic induction, relaxation tapes, etc.); awareness is not responsive to the usual demands in the outside world. Although the subjective experience of deep relaxation is ineffable and difficult to describe to others, it is frequently described as an altered state. Consider, for example, the following description given by a meditator cited in Glasser's book, *Positive Addictions*:

I used to feel myself sort of going into my head deeper and deeper. Now I am not aware of this but sometimes I am more aware of recent dreams during part of the meditation, like passing by them on the street. It is not at all like sleep. At times I am aware of slower breathing and reduced heart beat, sort of a suspended state but not like hypnosis. It is tremendously unique and a very personal experience, you just don't go out and rave about it to your friends. It is almost sacred but not religious at all. I have more energy, more determination, and really enjoy my every moment. I guess I am not aware at all of the meditation or of anything going on around me. I usually can't recall any memory of the meditation itself. I can meditate in front of the T.V. and not hear it at all. It is a very special part of my life. I hope to do it for the rest of my life but I don't promote it because I feel people will find it when they are ready for it. (Glasser, 1976, pp. 129-130)

People who practice a relaxation technique on a regular basis often describe the experience as a kind of high not unlike the effects of certain psychoactive drugs such as alcohol or marijuana. According to Andrew Weil, a noted authority on the subjective effects of drugs, most individuals have an intrinsic "need" to experience altered states of consciousness at various times in their lives; he argues that this is a *normal* need, part of the "natural mind," that can be satisfied by interchangeable activities ranging from use of psychoactive drugs to meditation and hypnosis (Weil, 1972). From this perspective, relaxation procedures may offer a substitute high or positive addiction to replace the addictive habit.

Addictive behaviors such as drinking or smoking often serve as discriminative stimuli for a "time-out" period from one's usual routine. Going to a bar at the end of the day or taking a cigarette break during a hectic work schedule are strongly associated with relaxation or escape from the humdrum of daily life activities. As such, these behaviors represent important "want" activities, significant periods of self-gratification. Without replacing such "wants" with an alternative time-out activity, the client's sense of deprivation may increase the temptation to return to the old habit pattern. Relaxation is an ideal substitute time-out since it is basically an effortless activity (unlike exercise) that often has a pleasant hedonistic quality. As with the addictive habits, relaxation is basically incompatible with "on task" behaviors such as work or other should activities. Similarly, since drugs typically elicit changes in conciousness that are nonlinear or less under conscious control and/or inhibition than normal wakeful consciousness (cf. Weil, 1972), substitute activities should also engender effects that are, in some ways, the opposite of normal conscious control. The passive attention associated with deep relaxation, along with the suspension of normal linear thought processes, makes it an ideal substitute in this regard.

As with exercise, there is considerable research evidence that documents the effectiveness of relaxation as a stress reduction activity (e.g., Bahrke & Morgan, 1978; Davidson & Schwartz, 1976; English & Baker, 1983; Glaister, 1982; Lehrer, Schoicket, Carrington, & Woolfolk, 1980). There are a number of theoretical explanations for the beneficial effects of relaxation. While some authors focus on the physiological benefits of deep relaxation (e.g., Benson, 1975; Jacobson, 1929), others have postulated psychological and behavioral mechanisms that may underlie, in part, the stress-reducing benefits. Goleman (1971) noted, for example, that meditation and other deep relaxation states may have beneficial effects because they resemble a form of "global desensitization":

The whole contents of the mind compose the meditator's "desensitization hierarchy." The contents of this hierarchy are organic to the life concerns of the meditator. . . . As in the desensitization paradigm, the "hierarchy" is presented coupled with the deep relaxation of deep meditation. Unlike the therapy, desensitization is not limited to those items which therapist and patient have identified as problematic, though those are certainly included, but extends to all phases of experience. . . . It is natural, global self-desensitization. (p. 5)

Recent theorizing by cognitive-behavior therapists such as Meichenbaum (1977) has stressed the role of verbal mediation in the elicitation and exacerbation of anxiety states. Deep relaxation, because of its nonverbal nature, may serve to extinguish or weaken the anxiety response. If anxiety is allowed to occur while the mind is in a state of passive attention, the agitation may arise and then subside again in the absence of verbal labels and mental judgments that might otherwise maintain or even increase the level of arousal. While relaxed, the individual can learn to simply *observe* the comings and goings of various feelings, thoughts, and images without "identifying" with them and acting on them in the usual manner. This process of "de-identifying" with one's thoughts helps the individual to adopt an objective, detached point of view—an attitude that may be a very effective cognitive strategy to combat stress. The process of "watching the mind" in this way is described by Levine in a recent book on meditation[2]:

For instance, if we watch the mind as though it were a film projected on a screen, as concentration deepens, it may go into a kind of slow motion and allow us to see more of what is happening. This then deepens our awareness and further allows us to observe the film almost frame by frame, to discover how one thought leads imperceptibly to the next. We see how thoughts we took to be "me" or "mine" are just an ongoing process. This perspective helps break our deep identification with the seeming solid reality of the movie of the mind. As we become less engrossed in the melodrama, we see it's just flow, and can watch it all as it passes. We are not even drawn into the action by the passing of a judgmental comment or an agitated moment of impatience. (Levine, 1979, p. 3)

The form of detachment described by Levine can be particularly effective in coping with urges and craving experiences after cessation of an addictive behavior (see the discussion of "urge surfing" as a cognitive intervention strategy in Chapter 4).

Although many different relaxation procedures have been described in the literature, four techniques stand out in terms of frequency of usage and clinical efficacy: meditation, progressive muscle relaxation, biofeedback, and hypnotic procedures. Although space does not permit a detailed description or research review for each, a brief discussion of these four techniques follows and includes references for further information. Problems of adherence and compliance with relaxation procedures in general are then discussed, followed by a final section describing research that has compared the effectiveness of several relaxation procedures and exercise in the modification of drinking behavior.

Meditation

It is easier to define meditation in terms of the process or procedures of meditation, rather than attempting to describe the experience of the meditative state itself. Although there are a number of different meditation tech-

2. Quoted material on this and following pages is from *A Gradual Awakening* by S. Levine, Garden City, N.Y.: Anchor/Doubleday, 1979. Copyright 1979 by Stephen Levine. Reprinted by permission of Doubleday & Company, Inc.

niques or procedures (see Goleman, 1977, for a review of various procedures), each of them is directed toward a common goal: to quiet the mind by entering a state of consciousness that goes beyond or transcends normal thought processes. Although some meditative procedures involve physical movement (e.g., Sufi whirling, Tai Chi, Hatha Yoga, and other movement meditations), most involve sitting quietly in a state of quiescence and restfulness. Several authorities have attempted to classify meditation procedures into three main categories: concentrative meditation, "opening up" or "insight" meditation, or a combination of the two (Goleman, 1977; Naranjo & Ornstein, 1977; Shapiro, 1980).

In concentrative meditation, the meditator directs his or her attention to a single stimulus. By focusing the attention on a single stimulus, such as the breath, a koan (Zen riddle or paradoxial question), a repetitive verbal mantra (Transcendental Meditation), or external object (e.g., candle flame or mandala), meditation is able to clear the mind of distractions stemming from the normal stream of ideation, feelings, and imagery. During the act of meditation, an attempt is made to be directly aware of the object in a nonanalytic way rather than by the use of normal cognitive processes. In contrast to the concentrative forms, the "opening up" type of meditation (also called insight or mindfulness meditation) includes procedures in which the meditator assumes a passive, open attitude toward all stimuli in the internal and external environment, without dwelling on any fixed stimulus. Attention is focused simply on what is happening in the here and now, with no attempt to focus one's thoughts in any particular direction. Frequently, training in concentrative meditation is a preliminary stage prior to advancing to mindfulness meditation. Other procedures involve elements of both concentrative and mindfulness meditation practices. For example, a person may focus attention on the breath or a mantra but be "open" to moving attention to other stimuli if they become predominant and then return to the "anchor" stimulus of the breath or mantra.

As Shapiro has noted (1980, 1982), the two types of meditation closely resemble the principal attentional systems in the brain which Pribram (1971) has described as similar to a modifiable camera lens: Either the focus can be similar to a wide-angle lens, a broad, sweeping awareness that takes in the entire field (mindfulness meditation); or a focus similar to a zoom lens that hones in on a single figure or stimulus in a restricted part of the field (concentrative meditation). Using attentional mechanisms as the basis for a general definition, Shapiro (1982) states that "meditation refers to a family of techniques which have in common a conscious attempt to focus attention in a nonanalytic way and an attempt not to dwell on discursive, ruminating thought" (p. 268).

Instructions on how to practice various meditation procedures and to teach clients to meditate have been described in a number of recent texts (e.g., Carrington, 1978; Levine, 1979; Shapiro, 1980). One of the simplest forms of concentrative meditation as a means of eliciting the relaxation response has been described by Benson (1975; Benson, Marzetta, Rosner, & Klemchuck, 1974). In the following instructions, the concentrative stimulus or mantra is the word "one":

1. Sit quietly in a comfortable position.
2. Close your eyes.
3. Deeply relax all your muscles, beginning at your feet and progressing up to your face. Keep them deeply relaxed.
4. Breathe through your nose. Become aware of your breathing. As you breathe out, say the word "one" silently to yourself, e.g., breathe in . . . out, "one"; in . . . out, "one"; and so on.
5. Continue, for 20 minutes. Occasionally open your eyes to check the time. When you finish, sit quietly for several minutes at first with closed eyes and later with opened eyes.
6. Do not worry about whether you are successfully achieving a deep level of relaxation. Maintain a passive attitude and permit relaxation to occur at its own pace. When distracting thoughts occur, ignore them and continue repeating "one." With practice the response should come with little effort. Practice the technique twice daily, and not within 2 hours after any meal, since the digestive processes seem to interfere with the elicitation of anticipated changes. (Benson *et al.*, 1974, p. 291)

One of the most significant effects of regular meditation practice is the development of mindfulness—the capacity to observe the ongoing *process* of experience without at the same time becoming "attached" or identifying with the *content* of each thought, feeling, or image. Mindfulness is a particularly effective cognitive skill for the practice of RP. If clients can acquire this ability through the regular practice of meditation, they may be able to "detach" themselves from the lure of urges, cravings, or cognitive rationalizations that may otherwise lead to a lapse. The distinction between awareness of the process versus the content of thought is nicely illustrated in the following quotation from Levine's book on meditation, *A Gradual Awakening:*

An image about practicing meditation that may be helpful is that of standing at a railroad crossing, watching a freight train passing by. In each transparent boxcar, there is a thought. We try to look straight ahead into the present, but our attachments draw our attention into the contents of the passing boxcars: we identify with the various thoughts. As we attend to the train, we notice there's supper in one boxcar, but we just ate, so we're not pulled by that one. . . . A few more boxcars go by with thoughts clearly recognized as thoughts. But, in the next one is a snarling lion chasing someone who looks like us. We stay with that one until it's way down the line to see if it got us. We identify with that one because it "means" something to us. We have an attachment to it. Then we notice we've missed all the other boxcars streaming by in the meantime and we let go of our fascination for the lion and bring our attention straight ahead into the present once again.

We stick to some and we don't stick to others. The train is just there—and the silent witness who's standing at the crossroads also seems to be there. Those are the first stages of trying to be mindful, trying to stay in the here and now. Then, as we're a bit more used to being aware of the contents, we start noticing the process of the train going by—just boxcar after boxcar—and our attention doesn't follow every stimulus: we don't keep getting lost down the track in the past or anticipating what's coming from the future. So, we're looking straight ahead, not distracted by any of the contents, when all of a sudden one of the boxcars explodes as it goes by. We're drawn out into that one, we jump into the action in that boxcar. Then we come back with a wry smile full of recognition that it was just an image of an explosion, just a boxcar thought. . . .

Then, we notice as we look straight ahead that we're starting to be able to see between the cars. And we begin to see what's on the other side of the train, what is beyond thought. We experience that the process is occurring against a background of undifferentiated openness, that, moment to moment, mind is arising and passing away in vast space. As we experience the frame of reference in which all this melodrama is occurring, it begins freeing us from being so carried away—even by fear [or by craving and urges]. We start seeing. "Ah, there's the exploding boxcar trick again," or "There's the angry boss one again." Whatever it is, we start seeing it as part of the process. We see it in context. The small mind that identified with all that stuff starts becoming bigger and bigger and bigger, starts encompassing even itself in a mind so vast it has room for everything and everyone, including the train and the observer. And, then, even that fellow standing at the crossroads watching turns out to be just the contents of one of those boxcars, just another object of mind. And awareness, standing nowhere, is everywhere at once. (Levine, 1979, pp. 29–31)

Interested readers may wish to consult additional reviews of the meditation literature: Woolfolk (1975) and Davidson (1976) have reviewed the physiological effects of meditation; Smith (1975) and Shapiro (1980, 1982; Shapiro & Walsh, 1984) have reviewed the therapeutic and clinical effects.

Progressive Relaxation

Originally developed by Jacobson (1929) as a method for reducing muscular tension, progressive relaxation and variations have been the most widely used relaxation procedures in the clinical literature. The individual initially practices muscle relaxation while lying down in a quiet room (or sitting back in a recliner chair), following the instructions given by a therapist, tape, or manual. By alternatively tensing and relaxing muscle groups, the client learns to recognize the sensations involved with muscle tension and practices eliminating this tension. In daily sessions, the subject practices making the discrimination of muscle tension and reducing that tension, while cycling through about 15 different muscle groups. Over time, a progressively larger portion of each session is spent relaxing the muscle groups, rather than discriminating tension in them. Finally, the subject practices progressive relaxation while sitting and then may attempt to incorporate this skill, as appropriate, into ongoing daily activities. In behavior therapy, progressive relaxation is frequently used to relax the client while items on a fear hierarchy are imagined successively. For detailed instructions on how to practice progressive relaxation or use it as a therapeutic strategy, the reader may refer to publications by Goldfried and Davison (1976) and Rosen (1978). A review of the psychobiological effects of relaxation is also provided by Davidson and Schwartz (1976).

Progressive relaxation and meditation, although they utilize different procedural methods, share a common element in that with both techniques, the individual is instructed to focus attention on a single stimulus object: meditators focus on the breath, mantra, or other meditation stimulus, and those practicing progressive relaxation focus their attention on the sensations and tone of the muscles. To the extent that both procedures may be effective because of this focusing of attention or awareness, this would support the hypothesis stated by Benson (1975), Shapiro (1982), and others that different relaxation techniques may produce a similar effect. Some investigators have noted, however, that long-term continued practice among patients who are instructed in a meditation technique may be superior to that associated with progressive relaxation; Glueck and Stroebel (1975) reported that psychiatric patients who were taught progressive relaxation discontinued practice of the procedure soon after instruction because it was considered rather laborious and a more difficult procedure than meditation.

Both meditation and muscle relaxation can be used in two major ways. The most common method is to engage in daily practice of a relaxation procedure (e.g., two 20-minute periods a day). The advantage of this method is that the individual develops a habitual pattern of relaxation that may serve as a global stress-reduction strategy, possibly with cumulative effects. Daily periods of relaxation also help build up a pattern of wants or self-time that become part of one's regular routine. The second application involves relaxation as a self-control strategy (cf. Goldfried, 1971). Here the client is encouraged to practice relaxation or meditation prior to or concurrent with an ongoing stress situation. This second method has clear import for relapse prevention. As soon as it becomes evident to the client that he or she is approaching a high-risk situation or anticipates a strong urge or temptation to lapse, a brief time-out period should be scheduled (e.g., pull over at a rest-stop) in order to relax and recenter one's energies. Often this will result in interrupting the chain of events that otherwise might lead to a lapse. Alternative coping strategies may occur to the client while in this relaxation break, even if only a few minutes are available to do this. Similarly, the client may be able to decrease tension and increase self-efficacy in the midst of an ongoing high-risk situation simply by redirecting attention inward to focus on the breath, a mantra, or on muscle tone (to release tension). Such "on the spot" relaxation draws the focus back to the individual's subjective center of control, instead of becoming increasingly pulled out by and "lost" in the external demands of the situation.

Biofeedback, Self-Hypnosis, and Other Relaxation Techniques

A number of other relaxation procedures have been described in the clinical literature. Although space does not permit full coverage of these additional methods, they will be briefly mentioned. Biofeedback, particularly with the electromyogram (EMG) (muscle-tone feedback) and the electroencephalogram (EEG) (alpha-wave feedback), has been described as an effective relaxation strategy for use with some addiction problems (e.g., Khatami, Mintz, & O'Brien, 1978). Some research has been done using EMG biofeedback and muscle relaxation as adjunctive treatment methods with alcoholics (e.g., Parker, Gilbert, & Thoreson, 1978; Steffen, 1975; Strickler, Bigelow, Wells, & Liebson, 1977). The main drawback with biofeedback procedures is that they require the use of biological monitoring systems and feedback apparatus that are often expensive and impractical for long-term use. Some therapists report that biofeedback may be a useful procedure when clients are initially being trained in, say, muscle relaxation (EMG feedback), particuarly with very tense or resistant clients, since the method is a novel one and gives them concrete feedback concerning their capacity to relax.

Self-hypnosis, guided imagery, and related procedures often provide a more structured experience than meditation, progressive relaxation, or biofeedback, since the individual progresses through a series of steps or images, often at the direction of some outside influence (e.g., following the instructions of a hypnotherapist or taped narrator). As such, these procedures may be more goal-oriented and purposive than the relaxation methods reviewed above.

A recent account of self-hypnosis was provided in an article by Thomas B. Morgan (1983), a writer who was experiencing writer's block. He visited a hypnotherapist in New York (Dr. Herbert Spiegel) who taught him a self-hypnotic technique. After first testing Morgan's suggestibility in a hypnotic session and then instructing him in the self-induction of a deeply relaxing state, Dr. Spiegel told his client to imagine a double screen in his mind. On the left side of the screen (as in a movie theater) he was to "see darkly" the nature of his problem (rewriting a novel). On the right side of the screen, he was told to visualize either an open field or a clear, blue sky. Morgan described seeing a bird appear in the blue sky portion of the screen. His therapist told him to "go with the bird. He's special. You should learn to talk with the bird or anyone else that appears on your screen. Discuss your problem there. Break it down. Go over it with them. Whenever you need help solving a problem, you will be able to consult the images on your screen" (Morgan, 1983, p. 79). Later in the article, Morgan describes a typical session of self-hypnosis:

Feet up, eyes closed, my left hand raised, it takes only a moment in my easy chair to imagine a peaceful field and a big sky behind the right side of my forehead. I people the scene with members of my family, old friends, and myself—that makes two of "me," one "I" watching as though offstage, talking to the others, including "myself," onstage. Sometimes I open my eyes, make a note on my clipboard, and close my eyes again, returning to the scene. I don't know what to call this: visual introspection? Internal brainstorming? Self-induced schizophrenia? Anyhow, the conversation rolls on, spontaneous but controlled by my goal. Now and again one of us will reformulate the problem, especially when I stand everyone on his head or turn the scene upside down. Sometimes, almost unbidden, the scene itself changes. We are at the beach, or in the sky. New people appear. A bird flies by. It is always the same bird, the one I first met in my second session with Spiegel. Okay, the bird talks. He has good ideas. Finally, a time comes when I feel that I've had enough. An insight may have occurred; usually there is nothing quite definite. I feel the real think-work is being done elsewhere. And since my sense of time and the world just the other side of actual awareness has continued, I seem to know when to stop the show. I lower my left hand, exhale, and return to normal consciousness. (Morgan, 1983, p. 85)

As with self-hypnotic procedures, guided imagery techniques provide a more structured format compared to meditation and deep muscle relaxation. Guided imagery often involves a goal or purpose, such as seeking wisdom or inspiration from inner "beings" or imagined entities. The subject usually follows a set of instructions taken from published materials or audiotapes, or as taught by a hypnotherapist, as in the foregoing case example. Although research in this field is generally lacking, future studies may reveal that self-hypnosis and related imagery techniques are a helpful adjunct to treatment with addictive behavior problems, particularly for motivational enhancement or creative problem solving. According to many recent popularized accounts of such procedures in the holistic health literature (e.g., in magazines such as New Age and the East/West Journal), these techniques enable people to tap into an "inner source" of energy and self-healing potential.

In addition to the relaxation procedures described above, many clients report that taking time out for themselves, self-time, is a refreshing and helpful lifestyle activity. In order to provide a replacement time-out period formerly created by addictive activities, clients can be encouraged to set aside a few hours each week just for themselves with no prescheduled activities or shoulds to get in the way. The time is to be spent doing a pleasant want activity, leaving the choice of activity until the beginning of the time-out period so that it can be determined by the client's mood and desires of the moment. Examples of options are listening to music, taking an exploratory walking tour, visiting an art gallery, or just sitting and watching the world pass by.

Of particular value are activities that permit the individual to step back and adopt an observing attitude—to see one's life from a meta-perspective. The use of a personal journal (written or recorded on cassette tapes) is highly recommended; major life themes may be revealed through the process of self-examination.

In some cases, keeping a journal can help an individual to make a major life change. In a recent autobiography, *Where Have I Been?*, comedian Sid Caesar (1982) described his own battles with the bottle during and after his successful television series. At one point he was drinking more than a fifth of whiskey a day, in a vain attempt to cope with the pressures and stress of his demanding career. After a long period of relative inactivity and multiple involvements with alcohol and other drugs (along with a corresponding decline in his career), Caesar spent 5 months in Paris while working on a small movie part. Prior to the trip, he had spent many years working on his drinking problems, including spending many sessions with various psychiatrists, all to no avail. Caesar's account of his experiences follows:

The repair of the mind. Some alcoholics and addicts do it through organizations like Alcoholics Anonymous. Some do it through therapy programs at chemical dependency centers in hospitals. A few manage to "white knuckle it" by themselves. *I* went to Paris. . . . On the morning of September 22, 1979, one week after I had arrived, I pulled out my cassette recorder and began a long series of daily conversations with myself. I was very self-conscious at first. For example, I had to have the radio on, playing music, before I could start talking. But even on that first day of taping, I realized I was doing a very interesting thing. I had split myself into two personalities, and I was Sid talking to Sidney. I wasn't aware of it until later, when I played those tapes over and over again, but, as Sid, I was using many of the techniques that had subliminally lodged in my mind from all the hours I had spent with psychiatrists. . . .

And so it started. I'd talk to the tape recorder when I woke up in the morning, I'd talk when I got home in the evening, and sometimes I'd have a third conversation between Sid and Sidney before I went to bed. I'm an audio person. I get more out of listening than reading. So when I played back the tapes, I could see the changes in me, the swings in mood between morning and night of the same day. Gradually the understanding came to me that I was in a good routine—that nobody is happy or sad all the time. If you are, something is wrong. And balance was what was lacking in my life. (Caesar, 1982, pp. 224–228)

In one of Caesar's conversations, he talked with himself concerning his desire for alcohol: Sid had a "knock-down-drag-out" encounter with Sidney who was craving a drink:

Well, so you want to take a drink? Let's talk about it. How about a nice good drink? You'll forget everything, heh? Then you'll think you're not responsible because then you're a little baby and not responsible, and you can get angry and do terrible things. Did it ever occur to you that you use up the same energy being angry as you do being happy? So do you think it's worth going through all this, with that boozing you have in mind? You say yeah, Sidney? Well, you're wrong. I went through it and it stinks. So you're wrong, Sidney, outright wrong. You idiot! You stupid shmuck! Why the hell are you even thinking like this? (p. 229)

According to Caesar's report, the self-therapy via cassette recordings worked. He maintained abstinence and continued to make daily entries on tape. Caesar discovered a very effective way of confronting himself (and his urges to drink) and making a drastic change in lifestyle by means of his self-analysis. It may be that keeping a journal or diary or just having conversations with oneself at regular intervals permits the individual to adopt a meta-level perspective and make significant life changes as a result. One wonders how many others have overcome addictive problems through a similar form of self-therapy.

Relaxation Adherence Problems

As with exercise, the regular practice of a relaxation technique is often difficult to maintain for a variety of reasons. In one of our own studies (described in the following section), we trained 44 college-age males (all heavy drinkers) in the practice of either meditation, progressive relaxation, or a quiet period of daily reading. All subjects were asked (and paid) to practice one of these procedures for a 6-week period; during a 7-week follow-up period, they were free to continue or to discontinue practicing their technique. The results showed that most of the progressive relaxation group either stopped practicing or practiced sporadically during follow-up. Seven of the 10 subjects in the meditation group reported some continued practice after treatment, as did 2 subjects in the progressive relaxation group and 3 in the quiet reading group. By the last 2 weeks of the follow-up period, however, only 3 meditators, 2 subjects in the progressive relaxation group, and 2 subjects in the reading group reported engaging in their assigned activity. Although the subjects in this study may have been less motivated to continue practice than the typical client in treatment, the high dropout rate remains a problem for many individuals (Marlatt & Marques, 1977).

Some of the same suggestions brought up regarding methods of increasing compliance and adherence in exercise programs apply to the long-term maintenance of a relaxation procedure. Clients should be encouraged to experiment with different procedures before they settle down with one that seems to work best. Expectations of immediate and dramatic changes in levels of tension or anxiety should be countered with information showing that improvement from the regular practice of a relaxation technique is often gradual and cumulative over time. Some clients complain that some relaxation sessions are less effective (or more boring, etc.) than others. Research on the physiological benefits of deep relaxation or meditation shows, however, that the beneficial results often appear to be generally equivalent, regardless of the subject's subjective appraisal of the quality of the session (cf. Wallace, 1970; Wallace, Benson, & Wilson, 1971).

For some clients, choosing a particular relaxation method from a "menu" of available strategies may enhance compliance. With some resistant clients, it may be a good idea to start with including one period of self-time a week, leaving the choice of activities up to the client. Later in the program, a particular procedure may be practiced on a regular basis. Other clients may prefer to use their relaxation technique as a means of coping with an impending or ongoing stressful situation, instead of the traditional method of practicing a technique at the same time each day (e.g., early morning and/or late afternoon). A few moments of watching the breath or engaging in deep breathing may be sufficient to recenter their energies and thereby cope more effectively with a high-risk situation. Another effective strategy is to have clients practice their relaxation technique in a group setting (e.g., in group therapy or in an inpatient setting), since many people report that their meditation or other relaxation experience is enhanced when it is practiced in a group format. Some clients have taught other family members to relax in a mutual relaxation period scheduled into their domestic routines.

RESEARCH ON LIFESTYLE INTERVENTION AND ADDICTIVE BEHAVIORS

What evidence exists showing that lifestyle intervention techniques such as relaxation or exercise have any effect on addictive behavior patterns? Research on this topic is sparse, probably due in part to the traditional conceptualization of addiction as a physiologically based response to excessive drug use (for which lifestyle change would seem to have little or no relevance). There are a few exceptions to this general pattern. In terms of smoking, for example, epidemiological studies indicate an inverse relationship between smoking and habitual physical exercise (Criqui, 1980) and there have been anecdotal reports that smokers who have begun intensive aerobic training programs often quit smoking (Morgan, 1981). In the alcohol field, preliminary survey studies reported that alcohol and drug use was reduced substantially in subjects who began a regular program of meditation (e.g., Benson & Wallace, 1972; Shafii, Lavely, & Jaffe, 1975). Most of these studies suffer from major methodological problems, however, and the results must be interpreted with considerable caution (Smith, 1975). Retrospective questionnaire surveys are frequently biased in terms of such problems as unreliable or invalid self-reports, motivational differences among subjects, lack of adequate control groups, and so on.

At our University of Washington laboratory, my colleagues and I have conducted two studies to date on the effectiveness of relaxation procedures and aerobic exercise as a lifestyle intervention procedure with heavy social drinkers. Both studies employed a prospective design, had appropriate control groups, and involved subjects who were not specifically motivated to either cut down on their drinking or to abstain. In the first study, we compared three different relaxation procedures and a no-treatment control. In the second study, we compared meditation with an aerobic exercise program and a no-treatment control group. The results of each study are briefly reviewed below.

In the first study (Marlatt & Marques, 1977; Marlatt, Pagano, Rose, & Marques, 1984), we investigated the effectiveness of participating in a daily relaxation program on the ongoing drinking behavior of male heavy social drinkers. Subjects who volunteered for the study agreed to keep a daily record of their drinking for a period of 15 weeks. We selected heavy drinkers instead of alcoholics as our subjects because we wanted to determine if the relaxation training would lead to a change in alcohol consumption for individuals who had expressed no particular desire to cut down or stop their drinking. After 2 weeks of pretreatment baseline recording, subjects were randomly assigned to one of four groups: progressive muscle relaxation, meditation training (using Benson's [1975] procedure), a "bibliotherapy" group, or a no-treatment control condition. Subjects in the progressive relaxation and meditation groups were asked to practice their techniques twice daily (morning and late afternoons) for a period of 6 weeks. Members of the bibliotherapy group, intended originally as an attention-placebo control condition, were asked to spend their daily relaxation periods quietly sitting and reading material of their own choosing. After the 6-week training period, subjects were followed for a period of 7 weeks, during which time subjects were free to continue or discontinue practice of their techniques.

The results, depicted in Figure 5-1, showed a significant reduction in alcohol use (approximately a 50% drop from pretreatment rates) for subjects in all three relaxation conditions, in comparison to the no-treatment control group. Subjects in these three groups also showed a significant shift toward a greater internal locus of control (using Rotter's [1966] measure) during the treatment period. This finding suggests that either the observed decrease in drinking is mediated by an increase in perceived internal control over one's behavior or that drops in alcohol consumption are associated with an increased perception of internal control. During the follow-up period, as mentioned earlier, almost all of the subjects discontinued practice of the procedures, perhaps because they were not as motivated to continue as other populations (e.g., clients in treatment). Overall, however, these results seem to indicate that taking regular time-out periods to relax, even if only for short periods each day, is associated with significant reductions in drinking rates.

In the second study in this series (Murphy, Pagano, & Marlatt, 1984), we decided to contrast the effectiveness of meditation as a relaxation procedure with aerobic exercise. Male heavy drinkers between the ages of 21 and 30 were recruited to participate in a 16-week research study consisting of a 2-week

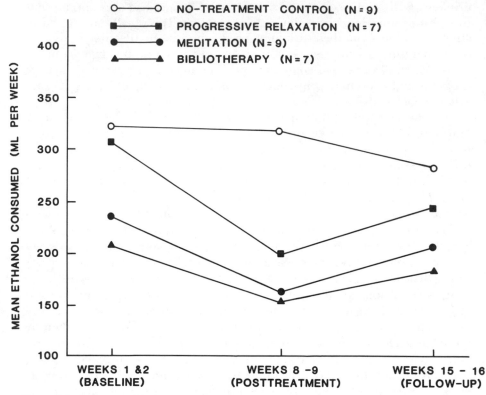

Figure 5-1. Average weekly reported alcohol consumption (ml/week) for no-treatment controls and for subjects who received training in progressive relaxation, meditation, or bibliotherapy. Data shown are for the pretreatment baseline period of 2 weeks, the last 2 weeks of treatment, and the last 2 weeks of follow-up. Only data from subjects who completed follow-up are presented. Based on data from Marlatt and Marques (1977).

baseline period, an 8-week treatment phase, and a 6-week follow-up period. As in the first study, the subjects indicated no desire to abstain or cut down on their drinking prior to participation in the study. In addition to completing various personality and behavioral assessment measures, all subjects kept an ongoing daily record of their drinking rates throughout the course of the study. Subjects were ranked and matched in terms of their pretreatment drinking rates and were then randomly assigned to one of three treatment conditions: aerobic exercise (running group), relaxation (meditation), or a no-treatment control condition.

During the treatment phase of the study, the subjects in the running condition met as a group four times a week. Each session was 70 minutes in duration and consisted of stretching and warm-up exercises before the run, the running period itself, and stretching and cool-down exercises after the run. The primary exercise modes included 30 minutes of a combination of walking and running or a full 30 minutes of running. Each subject was evaluated by the exercise leaders during each postexercise period and was given an individualized prescribed running level for the next session. Subjects in the meditation condition received instruction in a mantra meditation procedure developed by Carrington (1978). They were instructed to regularly repeat a soothing mantra for 20-minute periods at a time (once in the morning and once before dinner), sitting in a straight-back chair in a quiet, dimly lit room. Subjects also met and meditated as a group four times a week during the treatment phase. Subjects in the control group completed all the experimental measures but did not engage in any lifestyle change technique. During the follow-up phase, running and the practice of meditation were optional for all subjects, although they continued to monitor their daily drinking during this 6-week period.

The results of the study are depicted in Figure 5-2, which presents drinking rates for each group during the baseline period (weeks 1–2), the active treatment period (weeks 3–10), and the follow-up period (weeks 11–16). Statistical analyses revealed that during the treatment phase, although subjects in both the meditation group and the running group showed significant decreases in drinking compared to baseline drinking levels, only the running condition differed significantly from the control condition during this 8-week period. Results for the follow-up phase showed continued significant improvement (decreased drinking) for subjects in the running group, whereas those in the meditation group showed a gradual increase in alcohol consumption, relative to both the running and control groups. During the follow-up period, 62% of the subjects in the running group and 57% of the subjects in the meditation group continued practicing their techniques on a more or less regular period.

PRINCIPLES OF MODERATION

Moderation is the key to lifestyle balance. This final section includes a brief discussion of moderation as an underlying theme or guiding principle in lifestyle change. The concept of moderation is defined, and the advantages of this approach are highlighted. Moderation is then contrasted with the general concepts of control and addiction. Factors facilitating or impeding the development of moderation are outlined, followed by a discussion of how moderation methods can be developed in the treatment of addictive behaviors.

MODERATION: DEFINITION AND ADVANTAGES

Webster's New Collegiate Dictionary (1983) defines *moderate* (used as an adjective) as "avoiding extremes of behavior or expression" and "to lessen the intensity or extremeness" (used as a verb). In terms of addictive behavior,

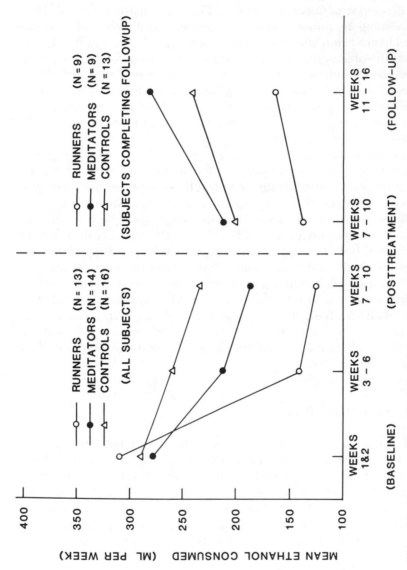

Figure 5-2. Average weekly reported alcohol consumption (ml/week) for no-treatment controls and for subjects who received training in meditation or running. On the left side, data are presented for all subjects; on the right side, only data from subjects completing the follow-up are presented. Based on data from Murphy, Pagano, and Marlatt (1984).

moderation can be defined as the midpoint or middle way, a position of balance between the extremes of either excessive control (restraint) and undercontrol (loss of control). To some, moderation represents the ultimate "cure" for an addictive habit; the goal of treatment, from this perspective, is to restore a normal or moderate pattern of use in the formerly addicted individual. To others, moderation will always remain an unacceptable if not impossible outcome that will never be appropriate for former addicts; total restraint (abstinence) is the only viable goal according to this view. The ongoing controversy about controlled or moderate drinking as a possible treatment goal for alcoholics or problem drinkers illustrates the degree of intense emotionality involved (Marlatt, 1983). Many individuals have raised the issue of whether *any* level of drug use can be considered moderate or safe (e.g., controlled tobacco smoking or the moderate use of alcohol by pregnant mothers). On the other hand, when it comes to the control of addictive behaviors such as obesity and other eating disorders (e.g., bulimia and anorexia), moderation is the *only* viable goal of treatment. One thing is certain: debates about moderation as an alternative to abstinence are themselves rarely moderate in content and tone.

Most of the debate hinges on the question of whether individuals who have been addicted to a substance or activity at one time in their lives can ever successfully moderate future use. There seems to be much general agreement that individuals who have *not* been formerly addicted can and do show moderation in the use of substances that other people have difficulty controlling. Social drinking is an obvious example. Recently, attention has also been paid to the moderate or "recreational" use of substances as strongly "addictive" as heroin and other narcotics by some individuals who show no signs of physical dependency (Zinberg & Harding, 1982). What are the determinants of moderation? Can moderation be acquired or learned, or is it the product of constitutional factors, other individual differences, environmental constraints, individual values and beliefs, or the pharmacological properties of the substance itself?

Many prominent philosophers and other public figures have long extolled the virtues of moderation (Benjamin Franklin stands out as a prime example). The middle way of moderation as an alternative to the extremes of excess and absolute restraint is also an important basic tenet of Buddhism, Taoism, and other Eastern philosophies. The Tantric teachings of Tibetan Buddhism perhaps represent the most advanced application of moderation principles in the spiritual realm (Blofeld, 1970; Guenther & Trungpa, 1975). Many contemporary Western beliefs (e.g., Christian fundamentalism), on the other hand, have adopted an absolute stance in which *any use* of taboo substances or activities (usually drugs and sexual behavior) is considered sinful, regardless of whether the user is a first-time experimenter or a chronic addict. As noted in Chapter 3, there can be no moderate partaking of Eden's forbidden fruit.

Perhaps the greatest advantage of moderation as a guiding credo in the field of addictions is embodied in what can be called the *pleasure paradox*. The pleasure paradox states that enjoyment and pleasure are inversely related to the amount of substance or activity engaged in by the individual. Smaller amounts of any potentially addictive substance or activity are usually associated with increased pleasure; the philosophy of "small is beautiful" (Schumacher, 1975) may gradually replace the consumer attitude of "more is better." Think of the enjoyment derived from a single glass of wine savored by a wine connoisseur or experienced by a gourmet in the midst of relishing a new culinary delight; contrast this with the image of a wino gulping a bottle of Thunderbird wine or an obese individual responding to a "big Mac attack." With moderation as the key, it is possible for people to actually have their cake and eat it too, as long as they take small, mindful bites, each savored for its unique taste and ingredients.

There are several reasons why moderation enhances pleasure at the least cost to the individual. The moderate user, in comparision with the addicted user, is likely to have a lower tolerance level for the euphoric effects of a particular substance or activity. Since it takes a smaller dose to produce a desired effect in the nontolerant user, the probability of overdosing and experiencing the associated discomfort and dysphoria of the aftereffects of a large dose is greatly decreased. As a result, the moderate user maximizes the hedonic quality of the initial phase of the usual biphasic response to most psychoactive drugs (the initial high) and minimizes the cost of the second, downside phase of the reaction. Whereas the heavy user often initiates a drug-taking episode in a dysphoric state (due to withdrawal from prior use or as an attempt to cope with negative emotional states, etc.), the moderate user is more likely to begin use when feeling a positive or at least neutral affective state. Consequently, the heavy user attains a lower ultimate level of positive effect compared to the moderate user. Moderation enhances an already positive state and the resultant pleasurable experience cannot be matched by the drug-dependent individual. The best and highest highs are those associated with moderation.

Moderate use of certain psychoactive drugs appears to be associated with the least harmful health effects. The effects of alcohol on the risk of cardiovascular disease is illustrative of this general relationship; several studies have now found that moderate daily consumption of alcohol is associated with less risk of cardiovascular disease as compared to the increased risk associated with either excessive consumption or total abstinence (Gross, 1983). In terms of many response systems, there appears to be an inverted-U relationship between frequency of drug use (or strength of a given dose) and the overall effects. Moderate use over time (or a smaller dose on a given occasion) is often associated with the most beneficial effects, compared with either a zero dose or an excessive amount. Alcohol and other psychoactive drugs often act as a stimulant at low dose levels and a depressant at higher levels; positive effects (enhanced arousal, fewer errors, etc.) are associated with the stimulatory effects only, perhaps because of the facilitating decrement in tension or anxiety associated with moderate use. For the moderate user, it is true that "a little goes a long way." Despite these advantages, the long-term maintenance of a moderate approach to drug use is not an easy task. For many individuals, the zone of moderation is but a passing blur on the pendulum's oscillating pathway between excessive restraint at one end of the extreme and addictive loss of control at the other.

MODERATION VERSUS RESTRAINT AND/OR CONTROL

Moderation represents a balance point or border area between the extremes of absolute restraint or control and loss of control (addiction). As illustrated in Chapter 1 (Figure 1-5), the person who shows a pattern of alternating periods of addiction (loss of control) and forced restraint (abstinence) is caught in an oscillation of perceived control. An individual caught in this revolving door between recidivism and restraint is likely to perceive an initial slip during a period of absolute restraint as a fatal flaw that triggers a return to the relapsed state. There is no "middle way" between the forces of control and indulgence in this pattern of oscillation. The person swings back and forth like a victim caught between the poles of an addictive magnet. The seesaw never comes to rest at the balance point.

In contrast, the person who is centered at the balance point of moderation is no longer a victim of oscillating forces but is in a position of meta-control, characterized by awareness, skills, choice, and the exercise of personal responsibility. Maintaining balance and a perspective of meta-control requires considerable practice and experience, particularly for those who are emerging from a prior pattern of addictive oscillation. Moderation and balance are skills that are characterized by a *flexibility of control* (vs. the absolute control of restraint)—an ability to withstand the pressures (or "roll with the punches") that would otherwise knock one off balance. Occasional slips do not lead inevitably to total loss of control. Errors are mistakes that can be learned from. They act as signals that provide corrective feedback to bring the individual back to the midpoint. The flexibility of control associated with balanced moderation is exemplified by jugglers and tight-rope walkers: either too little or too much control can result in a drop or fall; flexible adaptation maintains the balance. Another example of flexible balance in action is skiing. In a Sports Clinic column that appeared in a recent issue of *Esquire*, columnist Morten Lund notes that balance on skis can be acquired with practice and experience:

The "expert" skier, in this view, is one who most quickly senses, evaluates, and counters destabilizing motion. He can handle the relatively larger destabilizing forces of steep-slope skiing because he senses imbalance *sooner* and makes constant, small, imperceptible corrections to keep himself steady. . . . Much of it has to do with recognizing the obvious: once aware of the magnitude of his muscle tension, the skier is less tense and more flexible on the snow. When an expert skier hits a sizable bump, he lets the mogul push his skis up under him before dropping them again on the far side. He takes the bump like a car with supershocks. . . . Of course, nobody can function without some muscle tension, but the reason many skiers don't ski well is that they are frequently *overtense*. . . . When you float your center directly above the ankles, you are best equipped to counter imbalance from sudden acceleration or deceleration. You're right in the middle, keeping steady by minute balance corrections. . . . Skiing centered is the antithesis of skiing frozen: you *allow* your center to be pushed toward imbalance, but you are so aware of it that you make constant corrections toward balance. It's a matter of simply focusing your mind on your middle—you'll feel when you're centered and will be sensitive to the muscle tension that develops when you're *not*. (Lund, 1982, pp. 15–16)

Moderation and a flexible attitude toward control contrasts sharply with excessive restraint and *overcontrol*. Overcontrol occurs when the individual makes a tight, absolute commitment to change (i.e., to abstain or adhere to strict consumption limits) that presupposes a flawless performance, totally free from error. With this approach, the person often sets up an arbitrary division between the "self" (that aspect of the personality that "wills" or desires change) and the behavior or habit that is the target of the change program. Such an artificial dichotomy typically leads to an all-or-none evaluation process in which the "good" part of the self is at battle with the "bad" part that is in need of changing (cf. Bateson, 1972). In an effort to "keep the lid on," the individual who is locked into a self versus behavior struggle must expend considerable energy in restraining the unwanted behavior (often couched in terms of willpower vs. temptation). Such restraint must be vigorous and continually monitored, lest a momentary lapse occur that would undo the entire program of habit change. It is as though the person were trying to keep a dangerous snake locked up in a box; the box itself must be constantly monitored and guarded lest the snake somehow escape and wreak havoc. Any attempt to open the box (to feed the snake or to see if it is still alive) may precipitate an emergency situation if the snake escapes. From this perspective, the snake is the enemy and all effort must be expended to constrain its activities.

Rather than defining a bad habit as an enemy that must be vanquished, a moderation approach accepts the habitual behavior as part of oneself. Instead of attempting to keep the dangerous habit locked in its box, hidden from view, an alternative method based on the philosophy of moderation encourages the individual to "befriend" the enemy, to first get to know its actions and reactions on an intimate basis before embarking on a program of change. Paradoxically, the best way to control a behavior may be to first understand it (how it first develops and is maintained from both biological and psychological perspectives) and to accept it as part of oneself and one's overall pattern of activities. Such an attitude implies letting the snake out of its box (so that it can be observed and accepted) as a preliminary step to habit change—not keeping it penned up under the force of one's willpower. As the Zen teacher Shunryu Suzuki once stated, "To give your sheep or cow a large, spacious meadow is the way to control him" (Suzuki, 1970, p. 31).

The main problems associated with keeping the snake locked in the box are: (1) The snake (or bad habit) is viewed as an enemy and its activities are not well understood. (2) If the snake should happen to escape the box on even a single occasion (e.g., a lapse from abstinence), a disaster will ensue (loss of control). An individual who holds this absolute view will feel successful and in control only when the snake is locked firmly in its box. If the snake escapes, however, a pronounced swing to the loss of control side may occur. The degree of subsequent loss of control is probably in direct proportion to the degree of restraint previously employed to keep the snake locked up. Once the restraint is lifted, however, a rebound or "boomerang" effect is likely to occur as the snake springs free of its restricted environment. Overcontrol may backfire in the form of a pronounced relapse for any violation of control. A moderate approach provides a "spacious meadow" in which there is room for errors—errors which provide an opportunity to learn more about the "snake" and its varied ways, thereby allowing greater understanding and control in the long run.

The concept of moderation as defined in this context expands the boundaries of the mechanism of control beyond the usual definition of voluntary restraint or inhibition over the target behavior. From a moderation perspective, control implies *choice* instead of just forced restraint or *control over* the behavior in question. To exercise moderation, one must master both the skills of commission *and* of omission, depending on the situation and the choice of alternatives. True control in this sense implies a choice between committing an act (e.g., smoking or drinking) and refraining from or omitting that behavior; a choice between acting and "letting go" of the activity. Moderation implies learning to "take it or leave it" whereas control (and overcontrol) in the traditional sense implies only the option to leave (abstain) This line of reasoning provides a rationale for why many programs based on a goal of moderation (e.g., controlled drinking programs) require clients to initially master a period of abstinence (to learn not to respond) prior to teaching specific moderation skills (cf. Marlatt, 1983).

An additional point to be made here is the distinction between moderation as a "natural" state compared to the voluntary exercise of restraint or control over an otherwise "immoderate" behavior or act. As an illustration, consider two individuals, both of whom consume no more than three alcoholic drinks on a given day. While this relatively low consumption level can be defined as moderate for both individuals, the first person may be drinking this amount as a natural (or unrestrained) expression of his or her role as a social drinker, whereas the second person, a former problem drinker, may be voluntarily exercising restraint to adhere to a limit of no more than three drinks a day. Although it would be correct to say that the latter individual was engaging in controlled drinking, it would be inappropriate to apply this term in the former case, since no voluntary restraint or control over excessive use is implied. Along the same lines, it is appropriate to say that someone who smokes no more than three cigarettes a day is a controlled smoker only if the person had a history of smoking more than that amount. In other words, to say that a given behavior occurs in moderation does not necessarily imply that such behavior is under voluntary restraint or control.

In order to determine whether a given level of consumption is a product of voluntary restraint (control) or is a naturally occurring form of moderation, one must carefully investigate the *boundary conditions* for the behavior. To what extent are the upper and lower boundaries (the overall range of usage) for a given habit influenced by such factors as voluntary or learned methods of restraint, biological constraints (e.g., becoming physically ill over a certain limit of consumption), psychological and interpersonal factors (e.g., fear of negative evaluation or losing control), environmental constraints (e.g., availability of supply, cost, time of day, etc.), past learning history and exposure to models of moderation or excess, degree of experienced stress, and so on? Confusion over these issues is apparent in the debate about controlled drinking as an alternative to abstinence in the treatment of alcoholism. Participants in this debate often fail to distinguish between controlled drinking as a specific goal of treatment (backed up with a program of controlled drinking skills) and the occurrence of moderate or nonproblem drinking as a nonintended outcome of treatment programs in which abstinence is the intended goal (Marlatt, 1983). In this section, we have been dealing with the conceptual differences between moderation and the exercise of voluntary control or restraint. To further clarify the distinctions involved, one must also explore differences that exist between moderate and excessive (or addictive) levels of use.

MODERATION VERSUS ADDICTION

One way to distinguish between moderation and addiction is to focus on the affective consequences or changes in emotional state associated with taking a drug or engaging in an indulgent behavior of any kind. Of particular interest is the *change* in affect or hedonic state induced by the drug or activity relative to the emotional tone experienced by the individual prior to the indulgent act. Moderation is characterized by behaviors that serve to enhance or maintain a prior *neutral or positive* emotional state. Addiction, on the other hand, is characterized by the individual's attempt to alleviate or transform a prior *negative* emotional state. From a functional perspective, people take drugs to transform their level of emotional experience, to enhance good feelings, or to escape or avoid negative feelings. Most psychoactive drugs are experienced subjectively in terms of a change in physical sensations (the rush of euphoria, the relief from withdrawal, etc.) along with associated changes in mood and cognition. Even for addictive behaviors in which no endogenous drug is involved, such as compulsive gambling or sexual activity, there is a noticeable change in affect and mood associated with the intense physical excitement and arousal elicited by the behavior.

These changes in affect or physical sensations may be elicited by the unconditioned effects of the drug or activity itself (e.g., changes in neuro-chemical transmission or other nervous system alterations), or by conditioned stimuli previously associated with drug use. As mentioned in Chapter 3, the body may react to conditioned drug stimuli (the sight and smell of alcohol, for example) with a protective compensatory response that is opposite in hedonic quality to the unconditioned effects of the drug. The initial effects of a pharmacologically depressant drug such as alcohol may be excitatory and pleasurable, mediated by compensatory response effects that anticipate and compensate to some extent for the delayed depressant and dysphoric pharmacological effects of the drug.

The various transformations of affect associated with addictive versus moderate drug use is illustrated by the hypothetical model presented in Figure 5-3. In this figure, three stages of affect or hedonic quality are portrayed: affect or mood prior to drug use, and changes in mood that are associated with the initial and delayed effects of the biphasic response that follow use of the drug or activity. The upper half of the diagram illustrates the effects of moderate use and the lower half depicts addictive use. In moderate use, the individual chooses to engage in drug use only when the prior mood state is affectively neutral or positive (+). As an example, consider someone who is in a celebratory mood (+) at a wedding reception where champagne is being served. The initial effect of two or three glasses

Figure 5-3. Moderation versus addiction in the transformation of affective state: Hypothetical model.

	PRIOR MOOD	BIPHASIC DRUG RESPONSE		RESIDUAL MOOD
		IMMEDIATE EFFECT(+)	DELAYED EFFECT (-)	
MODERATION	+	+/+ ENHANCED POSITIVE (FEELING HIGH)	+/- NEUTRAL AFFECT	EQUILIBRIUM
ADDICTION	-	-/+ RESTORED NEUTRAL (NORMALIZATION)	-/- DELAYED NEGATIVE	DIS-EQUILIBRIUM

VICIOUS CIRCLE OF ADDICTION

of champagne consumed under these circumstances would most likely be marked by increased euphoria or enhanced positive feelings (+). Taken together, the prior positive mood state enhanced by the initial effects of alcohol (the first stage of the biphasic response) produces a double-positive "high" (+/+). If the person continues to moderate intake, thereby titrating a pleasurable blood-alcohol level, the delayed negative effects of drinking (−) will be minimal, perhaps limited to a mild feeling of fatigue or malaise associated with the second stage of the biphasic response. These negative aftereffects will be offset or neutralized by the combined positive effects of the prior mood state and the initial excitatory phase of the biphasic response. The end state following this drinking episode should be basically neutral (+/−) as a result; the final product is one of emotional balance or equilibrium. Moderation leaves no negative aftereffects. On the next drinking occasion, the individual is more likely to initiate use when experiencing a neutral or positive mood.

In the case of addictive use, however, the transformation of affect follows quite a different course. Addiction, from this perspective, represents an attempt on the part of the user to transform or cope with a prior negative mood state. Prior to use, the addicted individual is likely to be experiencing dysphoric feelings (−) arising from either a stressful life situation (high-risk situation) and/or the delayed effects of heavy prior drug use (e.g., physical discomfort, hangover, etc.). Drug use appears to offer instant relief (positive outcome expectancy) because of its initial positive effects (first phase of the biphasic response).

To illustrate, consider a businessman who goes out to a business luncheon meeting with some clients. Due to the residual effects of the past night's heavy drinking (ongoing hangover), he looks forward to his first martini as a little "hair of the dog" to alleviate physical discomfort. In addition, he is feeling some insecurity and doubt about his ability to secure a contract with his clients (high-risk situation) and he believes that a drink or two will fortify his confidence and lubricate the negotiations. His mood state prior to drinking is clearly negative (−). After downing his first martini, our friend may experience some temporary relief via the initial excitatory effects of alcohol (consumed prior to eating in order to maximize its effects). The degree of positive effect will be minimized to some extent, however, by the degree of tolerance involved. Heavy drinkers with pronounced tolerance may attempt to overcome this limiting factor by increasing drug dosage (ordering a "special" or double martini). Since the prior mood state is negative (−), the overall impact of the initial positive drug effect may be little more than a normalizing effect in which the person experiences a transformation from a negative to a neutral state. Our businessman may report feeling better after his second martini because the alcohol transformed his mood "upward" from a negative state to one of emotional neutrality (−/+).

The enhanced negative state (now neutral) is short-lived, however, due to the delayed negative effects associated with the biphasic response. After lunch is over, our businessman may begin to feel tired, restless, and unable to concentrate on his work as the delayed effects of his luncheon martinis intensify. As indicated in Figure 5-3, the cumulative effect is hedonically dysphoric $(-/-)$ and leads to a continued desire for alcohol as a means of providing temporary relief. The end state, in contrast with the equilibrium of moderation $(+/-)$ is one of disequilibrium or imbalance $(-/-)$. The negative aftereffects often linger on and provide the affective backdrop $(-)$ for the next occasion of drug use. The person in our example looks forward to his Happy Hour at the end of the day as the next opportunity to alleviate his continuing distress. He "craves" a drink (positive outcome expectancy) as a means of escaping or avoiding these unpleasant feelings. Guilt and concern about his increasing dependence upon alcohol provide further fuel for this ongoing dysphoric state.

A vicious cycle characterizes the addictive pattern; the disequilibrium experienced after one drinking occasion sets the stage for repeated use as an attempt to restore balance. Any short-term relief is quickly dispelled by the delayed negative effects which in turn give rise to another attempt to gain relief. The addicted individual is thus caught in a trap of his or her own making: The expected solution (more drugs) exacerbates the initial problem. How can we help the person escape from this addictive trap? Can the addicted individual be trained to exercise moderation? In the concluding section of this chapter, various determinants of moderation are described along with a brief discussion of how moderation principles can be developed in the treatment of addictive behaviors.

DETERMINANTS OF MODERATION

As mentioned above, just because moderate use of substances or other addictive activities often occurs on a natural basis does not necessarily imply that moderation can be inculcated by direct instruction and training, especially with individuals with a prior history of addictive use. In the discussion that follows, an attempt is made to identify various potential determinants of moderation. Some of these determinants are fixed and unchangeable (e.g., past history or genetic predisposition), while others are modifiable and presumably can be altered by outside intervention. Although research on this issue is still needed, the following factors appear to play significant roles in the development of moderation (or lack thereof).

Set and Setting Factors

Moderation is more likely to occur when the individual's "set" or network of outcome expectancies is emotionally neutral or positive in hedonic quality. Addiction is more likely to occur, on the other hand, when the person expects the drug or activity to positively transform a prior negative emotional state. Expectancy or set factors are subject to modification; people can be trained to adopt the "right attitude" toward the use of drugs by restricting their use to positive recreational settings (e.g., social gatherings, rituals and celebrations, wine with meals, etc.) and by avoiding any drug use that is an attempt to cope with stressful negative feelings. The individual's belief system about the possibility of moderation as an alternative lifestyle factor is also important. If someone firmly believes that moderation is an impossible goal in the treatment of addiction (due to biological, personal, or religious constraints), it is unlikely that a moderation approach will ever succeed. An open, inquisitive, and "friendly" attitude may have a beneficial effect in adapting a moderation approach, however. Setting factors are also significant: moderation is enhanced in certain settings (e.g., recreational drug use with other moderate users) and weakened in other settings (e.g., drinking alone in an attempt to relieve emotional distress). The use of appropriate stimulus control procedures (e.g., limiting availability of supply, restricting access to specific time and place) is also an important setting factor for moderation.

Coping Skills

An obvious determinant of moderation is the degree to which the individual has acquired effective coping skills to deal with various factors that would otherwise lead to excessive use. Among such skills would be the development of alternative coping behaviors, specific control skills (limit-setting, planning ahead for potential difficulties, titration of dose), enhanced awareness of drug effects and how to modify them, and self-monitoring of drug use across a variety of situations. A flexible orientation (not too much control nor too little) and a gesture of balance also will facilitate a moderate approach. Many of these skills can be taught and often serve as the basis for programs of controlled drug use. Related to this topic is the individual's use of specific *control styles* to regulate use patterns (Apsler, 1982). Research has shown that some individuals appear to regulate their consumption of food or drugs through the use of relatively safe control styles (e.g., drinking no more than one or two cocktails on any given occasion, or drinking no more than other people in the same situation). Excessive users, in contrast, often adopt a high-risk style that is more likely to be associated with problems (e.g., drinking in order to feel a certain way, or drinking until one feels one should stop).

History of Prior Use

One of the best predictors of moderation is the extent to which the individual has exhibited moderate use patterns in the past. A history of uncontrolled use despite prior attempts at moderation is not a good prognostic indicator of future successful moderation. For older individuals with a long history of excessive behavior (especially those with a family history of addiction and/or those with marked physical dependence), a goal of abstinence is usually recommended. Success in the moderation of one habit pattern (e.g., reduction of coffee drinking or successful weight loss) may increase the probability of success with a different behavior, however, and should be taken into consideration. Although past history, unlike the factors of coping skill and set setting, cannot be modified directly, many attitudes and beliefs concerning the likelihood of successful future moderation may be open to outside influence. A related factor in past history is the age of the client. Older individuals may show a "maturing out" process (cf. Fillmore, 1974) in which excessive use declines over time. In some cases, therefore, older clients may be more successful in attaining moderation than younger ones.

Lifestyle Balance and Stress

Earlier in this chapter it was noted that a condition of lifestyle imbalance (e.g., a lack of balance between daily wants and shoulds) may increase the likelihood of excessive drug use or other addictive habits. A balanced lifestyle should have the opposite effect and should enhance the possibility of successful moderation. Similarly, the degree of experienced stress (including major life stressors and daily hassles) will also influence the extent to which moderation is possible. Unless other means are developed to cope with stress, drug use may become excessive. Although sources of stress may be difficult if not impossible to control in an individual's life, the means used to cope with the stress are clearly open to modification.

Specific Substance of Use

A final factor to be considered here is the specific drug or activity used by the individual. With some substances (e.g., marijuana, cocaine, or alcohol) the goal of moderation may be to limit the number of occasions of use, as well as to control the amount of drug consumed on any given occasion, because of build-up of tolerance to specific drug dose levels over time. With substances such as tobacco, on the other hand, one must question whether *any* use of the substance is to be considered safe or desirable to control. Food consumption for addictive eaters, in contrast, can be successfully changed by balancing occasional overindulgence with restraint and adopting moderate use patterns most of the time.

In addition to the factors listed above, can we come to any general conclusions regarding the selection of a goal of moderation as compared to abstinence? Moderation is a desirable goal in many primary or secondary prevention programs. Despite its benefits, however, many contemporary educational or prevention programs continue to reject programs with this approach. Many authorities continue to hold the view that "responsible use" of drugs is an untenable concept and that any attempt to teach people how to use substances safely only provides a permissive atmosphere for immoral and immoderate behavior (the same argument is often raised in criticism of sexual education conducted in the school setting). Despite such opposition, research and program development aimed at fostering responsible decision making and moderate use patterns continue.

The most controversial application of a moderation approach concerns the use of these procedures with formerly addicted individuals. Is abstinence the only attainable goal for anyone who has experienced loss of control drug use in the past? Is abstinence the "upper ceiling" of change for these people? What about the possibility that someone could learn to abstain as an initial stepping stone to achieving eventual moderation? Perhaps, for some individuals, abstinence is a necessary way-station on the road to moderation, while for others abstinence is the only acceptable final destination. Figure 5-4 illustrates both of these possibilities. Various layers or zones are depicted, ranging from the lower loss of control zone to the higher zone of moderation and choice. The arrow moving upward through these zones illustrates the potential pattern of growth that can be followed in the course of recovery from an addictive habit.

Figure 5-4. The process of change from loss of control, "low" and "high" abstinence, to moderation: Hypothetical model.

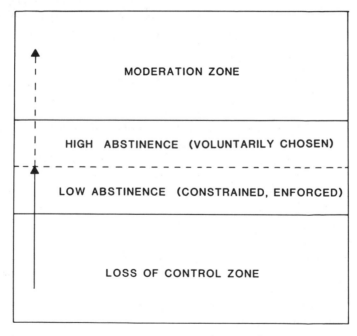

How does one move from the zone of loss of control to the zone of moderation? The first step in escaping from the zone of addiction is to make a commitment to abstain. To the extent that this commitment is seen as giving in to an external demand or a response to forces beyond one's control (as opposed to a fully accepted and internalized choice), the abstinence is likely to be short-lived and followed by frequent excursions downward to the zone of relapse and loss of control. To borrow a phrase from George Leonard (1983), who makes a similar distinction between "low" and "high" monogamy, we call this form of conformity to an externally imposed abstinence rule *low abstinence*. Low abstinence is characterized by a continued preoccupation with abstinence as an absolute dictum, a tendency to seek external aids to maintain abstinence (e.g., use of Antabuse or reliance on aversion treatment methods), and a high rate of relapse (most slips escalate into total relapses). For many individuals, particularly those with a poor prognosis for moderation (e.g., chronically addicted, older individuals), low abstinence should be considered as the primary and often only treatment goal.

For others with a good prognosis for moderation, abstinence can be defined as a necessary preliminary step to controlled use. For these individuals, abstinence provides an opportunity for new learning to occur. Because it is chosen voluntarily as the route to greater freedom of choice and control, we call abstinence of this kind *high abstinence*. In high abstinence, the ultimate goal is to build a foundation for greater choice and freedom which must also form the basis for eventual moderation should the individual choose that as a final goal. Abstinence of this type is a voluntary choice (not a forced giving-in) and is sought for its intrinsic challenge and sense of adventure. Slips and mistakes are viewed as temporary excursions from abstinence, errors to be learned from, rather than serving to plunge the person back into the depths of addiction. During the high-abstinence period, the person learns how to refrain from habitual use (learning to leave it instead of taking it), experiences the craving and urges as a source of information concerning areas of life stress, and a sense of drug free equilibrium is restored. Those individuals who ultimately wish to exercise moderation develop plans and deal with potential road blocks and hurdles during this period. Length of time to remain in high abstinence will depend on the individual, of course, but a minimum would seem to be at least 3 months (since this is the period of greatest risk for relapse). When the person is ready to embark on a program of moderation, occasional periods of high abstinence may be required as the new program stabilizes over time. Lapses in moderation are balanced by excursions into high abstinence—one moves "downward" into abstinence from the zone of moderation, rather than falling into the zone of relapse. As one becomes more accomplished in the moderation approach, greater sense of awareness develops, and one is able to foresee the consequences of one's acts and take appropriate remedial steps in advance.

It is only by developing a balanced, moderate lifestyle that one can be truly "cured" of an addictive habit. To oscillate back and forth between the zones of low abstinence and loss of control is to remain in the clutches of the addictive trap. It may take greater effort and ability in the long run to transform an addictive habit into a pattern of choice and awareness than it does to adhere to the rigors of low abstinence. The road to moderation is a long and difficult one, marked by a gradual strengthening of awareness. Progress is difficult, especially in the early stages when many mistakes occur. For many clients, the goal of moderation is an inappropriate one and should not be selected or attempted. For others, it is the high road to freedom.

The foregoing points on abstinence and moderation must be considered entirely speculative at this point, as there is little available research for any addictive behavior that identifies individuals who would benefit most from treatment with goals of either abstinence or moderation. Many contemporary addiction theories stress the progressive course of the addictive disease and insist that abstinence is the only way to arrest the insidious development of the underlying addiction. Others have argued that some individuals have successfully "cured" their addiction and are subsequently able to engage in moderate use of the previously addictive substance. Until further research provides firm empirical guidance on this sensitive and emotional issue, the safest and most conservative path in the treatment of most addiction problems (particularly those in which excessive use poses a high health risk) is to adhere to the goal of abstinence.

REFERENCES

American College of Sports Medicine. Position statement on the recommended quantity and quality of exercise for developing and maintaining fitness in healthy adults. *Sports Medicine Bulletin*, 1978, *13*, 1–4.

Appenzeller, O., Standefer, J., Appenzeller, J., & Atkinson, R. Neurology of endurance training: V. Endorphins. *Neurology*, 1980, *30*, 418–419.

Apsler, R. Measuring how people control the amounts of substances they use. In N. Zinberg & W. M. Harding (Eds.), *Control over intoxicant use.* New York: Human Sciences Press, 1982.

Bahrke, M. S., & Morgan, W. P. Anxiety reduction following exercise and meditation. *Cognitive Research and Therapy*, 1978, *2*, 323–333.

Bateson, G. The cybernetics of "Self": A theory of alcoholism. In *Steps to an ecology of mind.* New York: Ballantine, 1972.

Bell, R. A., Keeley, K. A., & Buhl, J. M. Psychopathology and life events among alcohol users and nonusers. In F. A. Seixas (Ed.), *Currents in alcoholism* (Vol. 2). New York: Grune & Stratton, 1977.

Bell, R. A., Keeley, K. A., Clements, R. D., Warheit, G. J., & Holzer, C. E. Alcoholism, life events and psychiatric impairment. *Annals of the New York Academy of Science*, 1976, *273*, 467–480.

Benson, H. *The relaxation response.* New York: William Morrow & Co., 1975.

Benson, H., Marzetta, B. R., Rosner, B. A., & Klemchuck, H. M. Decreased blood pressure in pharmacologically treated hypertensive patients who regularly elicited the relaxation response. *Lancet,* 1974(7852), 289–291.

Benson, H., & Wallace, R. Decreased drug abuse with transcendental meditation: A study of 1862 subjects. In C. J. Zarafonetis (Ed.), *Drug abuse: Proceedings of the international conference.* Philadelphia: Lea & Febiger, 1972.

Billings, A. G., & Moos, R. H. Stressful life events and symptoms: A longitudinal model. *Health Psychology,* 1982, *1,* 99–118.

Bjorntorp, P. Exercise in the treatment of obesity. *Clinics in Endocrinology and Metabolism,* 1976, *5,* 431–453.

Blofeld, J. *The Tantric mysticism of Tibet.* New York: Dutton, 1970.

Bowers, K. S. The relevance of hypnosis for cognitive–behavioral therapy. *Clinical Psychology Review,* 1982, *2,* 67–68.

Brownell, K. D. Behavioral medicine. In C. M. Franks, G. T. Wilson, P. C. Kendall, & K. D. Brownell, *Annual review of behavior therapy* (Vol. 8). New York: Guilford, 1982.

Brownell, K. D., & Stunkard, A. J. Physical activity in the development and control of obesity. In A. J. Stunkard (Ed.), *Obesity.* Philadelphia: Saunders, 1980.

Caesar, S. *Where have I been?* New York: Crown, 1982.

Carrington, P. *Freedom in meditation.* New York: Anchor/Doubleday, 1978.

Clausen, J. P. Circulatory adjustments to dynamic exercise and effect of physical training in normal subjects and patients with coronary artery disease. *Progress in Cardiovascular Disease,* 1976, *18,* 459–495.

Cooper, K. H. *Aerobics.* New York: Bantam Books, 1968.

Cousins, N. *Anatomy of an illness as perceived by the patient.* New York: Bantam, 1981.

Criqui, M. H. Cigarette smoking and plasma high-density lipoprotein cholesterol. *Circulation,* 1980, *62,* 70–76.

Cummings, C., Gordon, J. R., & Marlatt, G. A. Relapse: Prevention and prediction. In W. R. Miller (Ed.), *The addictive behaviors.* New York: Pergamon, 1980.

Davidson, J. Physiology of meditation and mystical states of consciousness. *Perspectives in Biology and Medicine,* 1976, *19,* 345–380.

Davidson, P. O., & Davidson, S. M. (Eds.). *Behavioral medicine: Changing health lifestyles.* New York: Brunner/Mazel, 1980.

Davidson, R., & Schwartz, G. The psychobiology of relaxation and related states: A multi-process theory. In D. I. Mostofsky (Ed.), *Behavior control and the modification of physiological activity.* New York: Prentice-Hall, 1976.

DeLongis, A., Coyne, J. C., Dakof, G., Folkman, S., & Lazarus, R. S. Relationship of daily hassles, uplifts, and major life events to health status. *Health Psychology,* 1982, *1,* 119–136.

Dohrenwend, B. S., & Dohrenwend, B. P. *Stressful life events.* New York: Wiley, 1974.

English, E. H., & Baker, T. B. Relaxation training and cardiovascular response to experimental stressors. *Health Psychology,* 1983, *2,* 239–259.

Epstein, L. H., & Wing, R. R. Aerobic exercise and weight. *Addictive Behaviors,* 1980, *5,* 371–388.

Fillmore, K. M. Drinking and problem drinking in early adulthood and middle age: An exploratory 20 year follow-up study. *Quarterly Journal of Studies on Alcohol,* 1974, *35,* 819–840.

Folkins, C. H., & Sime, W. E. Physical fitness training and mental health. *American Psychologist,* 1981, *36,* 373–389.

Friedman, M., & Rosenman, R. H. *Type A behavior and your heart.* New York: Knopf, 1974.

Gary, V., & Guthrie, O. The effect of jogging on physical fitness and self-concept in hospitalized alcoholics. *Quarterly Journal of Studies on Alcohol,* 1972, *33,* 1073–1078.

Glaister, B. Muscle relaxation for fear reduction of patients with psychological problems: A review of controlled studies. *Behaviour Research and Therapy,* 1982, *20,* 493–504.

Glasser, W. *Positive addictions.* New York: Harper & Row, 1976.

Glueck, B., & Stroebel, C. F. Biofeedback and meditation in the treatment of psychiatric illness. *Comprehensive Psychiatry*, 1975, *16*, 303–321.

Goldfried, M. R. Systematic desensitization as training in self-control. *Journal of Consulting and Clinical Psychology*, 1971, *37*, 228–234.

Goldfried, M. R., & Davison, G. C. *Clinical behavior therapy*. New York: Holt, Rinehart & Winston, 1976.

Goleman, D. Meditation as meta-therapy: Hypotheses toward a proposed fifth state of consciousness. *Journal of Transpersonal Psychology*, 1971, *3*, 1–25.

Goleman, D. *The varieties of the meditative experience*. New York: Dutton, 1977.

Greist, J. H., Klein, M. H., Eischens, R. R., Faris, J. W., Gurman, A. S., & Morgan, W. P. Running as treatment for depression. *Comprehensive Psychiatry*, 1979, *20*, 41–54.

Gross, L. *How much is too much? The Effects of social drinking*. New York: Random House, 1983.

Guenther, H. V., & Trungpa, C. *The dawn of Tantra*. Boulder, CO: Shambhala, 1975.

Hamilton, V., & Warburton, D. M. *Human stress and cognition: An information processing approach*. New York: Wiley, 1979.

Holmes, T. H., & Rahe, R. H. The Social Readjustment Rating Scale. *Journal of Psychosomatic Research*, 1967, *11*, 213–218.

Horton, E. W. The role of exercise in the treatment of hypertension in obesity. *International Journal of Obesity*, 1981, *5*, 165–171.

Jacobson, E. *Progressive relaxation*. Chicago: University of Chicago Press, 1929.

Johnson, J. H., & Sarason, I. G. Recent developments in research on life stress. In V. Hamilton & D. M. Warburton (Eds.), *Human stress and cognition*. New York: Wiley, 1979.

Kanner, A. D., Coyne, J. C., Schaefer, C., & Lazarus, R. S. Comparison of two modes of stress measurement: Daily hassles and uplifts vs. major life events. *Behavioural Medicine*, 1981, *4*, 1–39.

Karoly, P., & Steffen, J. J. (Eds.). *Improving the long-term effects of psychotherapy*. New York: Gardner Press, 1980.

Khatami, M., Mintz, J., & O'Brien, C. P. Biofeedback mediated relaxation in narcotic addicts. *Behavior Therapy*, 1978, *9*, 968–969.

King, A. C., & Frederiksen, L. W. Low-cost strategies for increasing exercise behavior: Relapse preparation training and social support. *Behavior Modification*, 1984, *8*, 3–21.

Lehrer, P. M., Schoicket, S., Carrington, P., & Woolfolk, R. L. Psychophysiological and cognitive responses to stressful stimuli in subjects practicing progressive relaxation and clinically standardized meditation. *Behaviour Research and Therapy*, 1980, *18*, 293–303.

Leonard, G. *The end of sex*. Los Angeles: J. P. Tarcher, 1983.

Levine, S. *A gradual awakening*. Garden City, N.Y.: Anchor/Doubleday, 1979.

Lewinsohn, P. M., & Graf, M. Pleasant activities and depression. *Journal of Consulting and Clinical Psychology*, 1973, *41*, 261–268.

Lewinsohn, P. M., & Libet, J. Pleasant events, activity schedules, and depressions. *Journal of Abnormal Psychology*, 1972, *79*, 291–295.

Lund, M. The steady skiier. *Esquire*, February 1982, pp. 15–16.

Marlatt, G. A. Alcohol use and problem drinking: A cognitive–behavioral analysis. In P. C. Kendall & S. D. Hollon (Eds.), *Cognitive–behavioral interventions: Theory, research, and procedures*. New York: Academic Press, 1979.

Marlatt, G. A. Perception of "control" and its relation to behavior change. *Behavioural Psychotherapy*, 1981, *9*, 190–193.

Marlatt, G. A. The controlled drinking controversy: A commentary. *American Psychologist*, 1983, *38*, 1097–1110.

Marlatt, G. A., & Marques, J. K. Meditation, self-control, and alcohol use. In R. B. Stuart (Ed.), *Behavioral self-management: Strategies, techniques, and outcomes*. New York: Brunner/Mazel, 1977.

Marlatt, G. A., Pagano, R., Rose, D., & Marques, J. Effect of meditation and relaxation training upon alcohol use in male social drinkers. In D. H. Shapiro & R. Walsh (Eds.), *Meditation: Classic and contemporary approaches.* New York: Aldine, 1984.

Martin, J. E., & Dubbert, P. M. Exercise applications and promotion in behavioral medicine: Current status and future directions. *Journal of Consulting and Clinical Psychology,* 1982, *50,* 1004–1017.

Matheson, C. M. *Exercise and meditation as a lifestyle intervention for addictive behaviors.* Unpublished doctoral dissertation, University of Washington, 1982.

McArdle, W. D., Katch, F. I., & Katch, V. L. *Exercise physiology: Energy, nutrition, and human performance.* Philadelphia: Lea & Febiger, 1981.

Meichenbaum, D. *Cognitive-behavior modification.* New York: Plenum, 1977.

Miller, W. R., & Muñoz, R. F. *How to control your drinking.* Albuquerque, N.M.: University of New Mexico Press, 1982.

Morgan, T. B. The power of the trance. *Esquire,* January 1983, pp. 74–81.

Morgan, W. P. Psychological benefits of physical activity. In F. Nagle & H. Montoye (Eds.), *Exercise, health and disease.* Springfield, Ill.: C. C. Thomas, 1981.

Morrisey, E. R., & Schuckit, M. A. Stressful life events and alcohol problems among women seen at a detoxification center. *Journal of Studies on Alcohol,* 1978, *39,* 1559–1576.

Murphy, T., Pagano, R., & Marlatt, G. A. *The effects of running and meditation upon alcohol consumption in male social drinkers.* Manuscript submitted for publication, University of Washington, 1984.

Naranjo, C., & Ornstein, R. *On the psychology of meditation.* New York: Penguin Books, 1977.

Ornstein, R. E. *The psychology of consciousness.* New York: Viking, 1972.

Ornstein, R. E. *The psychology of consciousness* (2nd ed.). New York: Harcourt Brace Jovanovich, 1977.

Parker, J. C., Gilbert, G. S., & Thoreson, R. W. Reduction of autonomic arousal in alcoholics: A comparison of relaxation and meditation techniques. *Journal of Consulting and Clinical Psychology,* 1978, *46,* 879–886.

Pollock, M. L. How much exercise is enough? *The Physician and Sports Medicine,* 1978, *6,* 50–64.

Pribram, K. *Languages of the brain: Experimental paradoxes and principles in neuropsychology.* Englewood Cliffs, N.J.: Prentice-Hall, 1971.

Rabkin, J. G., & Struening, E. L. Life events, stress, and illness. *Science,* 1976, *194,* 1013–1020.

Rosen, G. *The relaxation book: An illustrated self-help program.* Englewood Cliffs, N.J.: Prentice-Hall, 1978.

Rotter, J. B. Generalized expectancies for internal versus external control of reinforcement. *Psychological Monographs,* 1966, *80* (1, Whole No. 609).

Sarason, I. G., Johnson, J. H., & Siegel, J. M. Assessing the impact of life changes: Development of the Life Experiences Survey. *Journal of Consulting and Clinical Psychology,* 1978, *46,* 932–946.

Schumacher, E. F. *Small is beautiful.* New York: Harper & Row, 1975.

Shafii, M., Lavely, R., & Jaffe, R. Meditation and the prevention of alcohol abuse. *American Journal of Psychiatry,* 1975, *132,* 942–945.

Shapiro, D. H. *Meditation: Self-regulation strategy and altered states of consciousness.* New York: Aldine, 1980.

Shapiro, D. H. Overview: Clinical and physiological comparison of meditation with other self-control strategies. *American Journal of Psychiatry,* 1982, *139,* 267–274.

Shapiro, D. H., & Walsh, R. N. (Eds.). *Meditation: Classic and contemporary perspectives.* New York: Aldine, 1984.

Simmons, R. Time to recharge. *Seattle Times,* September 19, 1982, p. F8.

Smith J. C. Meditation and psychotherapy: A review of the literature. *Psychological Bulletin,* 1975, *32,* 553–564.

Solomon, E. G., & Bumpus, A. K. The running meditation response: An adjunct to psychotherapy. *American Journal of Psychotherapy*, 1978, *32*, 583–592.

Steffen, J. J. Electromyographically induced relaxation in the treatment of chronic alcohol abuse. *Journal of Consulting and Clinical Psychology*, 1975, *43*, 275.

Stone, G. C., Cohen, F., & Adler, N. E. (Eds.). *Health psychology*. San Francisco: Jossey-Bass, 1979.

Strickler, D., Bigelow, G., Wells, D., & Liebson, I. Effects of relaxation instructions on the electromyographic responses of abstinent alcoholics to drinking related stimuli. *Behaviour Research and Therapy*, 1977, *15*, 500–502.

Stuart, R. B. (Ed.). *Adherence, compliance and generalization in behavioral medicine*. New York: Brunner/Mazel, 1982.

Suzuki, S. *Zen mind, beginner's mind*. New York: Weatherhill, 1970.

Thompson, C. E., & Wankel, L. M. The effects of perceived activity choice upon frequency of exercise behavior. *Journal of Applied Social Psychology*, 1980, *10*, 436–443.

Wachtel, P. L. (Ed.). *Resistance: Psychodynamic and behavioral approaches*. New York: Plenum, 1982.

Wallace, R. The physiological effects of transcendental meditation. *Science*, 1970, *167*, 1751–1754.

Wallace, R., Benson, H., & Wilson, A. A wakeful hypometabolic physiologic state. *American Journal of Physiology*, 1971, *221*, 795–799.

Watson, B. (Trans.). *The complete works of Chuang Tzu*. New York: Columbia University Press, 1968.

Weil, A. *The natural mind: A new way of looking at drugs and the higher consciousness*. Boston: Houghton Mifflin, 1972.

Webster's new collegiate dictionary. Springfield, Mass.: G. & C. Merriam, 1983.

Wolpe, J. *Psychotherapy by reciprocal inhibition*. Stanford: Stanford University Press, 1958.

Wood, P. D., & Haskell, W. L. The effect of exercise on plasma high density lipoproteins. *Lipids*, 1979, *14*, 417–427.

Woolfolk, R. Psychophysiological correlates of meditation. *Archives of General Psychiatry*, 1975, *32*, 1326–1333.

Zinberg, N. E., & Harding, W. M. (Eds.). *Control over intoxicant use*. New York: Human Sciences Press, 1982.

PART II

APPLICATION WITH SPECIFIC ADDICTIVE BEHAVIORS

6

ALCOHOLIC RELAPSE PREVENTION AND INTERVENTION: MODELS AND METHODS

DENNIS M. DONOVAN AND EDMUND F. CHANEY

INTRODUCTION

Clinicians expend a considerable amount of time and energy in the treatment of alcoholics. However, this is often a frustrating undertaking. A primary goal in the treatment of problem drinking is reducing the probability of relapse. Yet, the empirical evidence suggests that this goal is seldom achieved, with approximately 50%–60% of alcoholics relapsing within the first 3 months after treatment (Hunt, Barnett, & Branch, 1971). Such "success rates" (or more accurately, "failure rates") often leave the clinician with a sense of personal helplessness and low personal efficacy. This often leads to the clinician's development of an expectation of the "unchangeability" of the alcoholic individual as well as dispositional attributions concerning the influence of factors such as "resistance" and lack of motivation. However, clinicians need not attribute the responsibility of an alcoholic client's outcome to their own abilities or competencies nor should negative outcome expectancies develop. Rather, it is important to try to understand the determinants of the alcoholic's return to drinking and to utilize this information to increase the effectiveness of treatment. This is one of the first steps in developing and implementing the types of Relapse Prevention (RP) strategies that form the primary focus of this book.

A complete and clinically useful understanding of the relapse process is sometimes difficult given the divergent philosophical and theoretical views that currently exist concerning the etiology of alcoholism and its treatment (Maisto & Schefft, 1977; Siegler, Osmond, & Newell, 1968; Robinson, 1972; Tarter & Schneider, 1976). Treatment attempts are guided by implicit or explicit assumptions about the causes of the target behavior. Incorrect, ill-defined, or incomplete frameworks cannot produce efficient therapy. Too little data are presently available to propose a comprehensive theory of relapse determinants. There are enough data, however, to suggest the outlines of the territory that such a theory should cover and to apply conceptualizations and hypotheses to clarify areas which current treatment attempts have neglected.

Traditionally, the determinants of relapse have been placed within the individual and conceptualized by the notions of craving and loss of control. In this narrow but consistent framework, drinking is a symptom of the disease of alcoholism. The use of alcohol is pathologic for the alcoholic; thus, one drink constitutes a relapse. Craving is the physiological or psychological need that motivates the alcoholic to take his first drink, and loss of control is the inevitable system alteration that compels him to continue drinking. With failure to find the physiological imbalance that is assumed to underlie the craving (Kalant, 1975; Kissin, 1974; Mendelson & Mello, 1976) and in the face of increasing evidence that one drink does not lead necessarily to loss of control (Engle & Williams, 1972; Ludwig & Wikler, 1974; Maisto, Lauerman, & Adesso, 1977), these concepts have undergone extensive modification.

An alternative approach to relapse places the determinants of excessive drinking in the environment. Subcultural norms and their attendant sanctions (Heath, Waddell, & Topper, 1981), modeling influences (Caudill & Marlatt, 1975), and the maintenance of equilibrium in systems (Bateson, 1972; Steinglass & Wolin, 1974) have been invoked to account for problem drinking. Approaches in this category have met with more success. Differences in rates of problem drinking are observable across cultural groups, and the influence of environmental contingencies on drinking has been demonstrated repeatedly. The utility of these approaches for treatment, however, is limited in two respects. First, they neglect individual differences, and second, they do not provide guidelines for RP without further elaboration.

Consistent with a growing body of evidence (Russel & Mehrabian, 1975; Endler & Magnusson 1976; Magnusson & Endler, 1977) that simultaneous consideration of person and situational variables explains more variance in human behavior than either does independently, an interactional approach is suggested. Situational aspects, discriminative stimuli, and consequences of relapse, as well as person variables, need to be considered within an internally consistent framework. This position is consistent with an emergent multivariate approach to alcoholism in which both person variables and situational factors are seen as contributing to the maintenance of drinking and to relapse. Within this context, alcohol dependence is viewed as a set of behaviors and cognitions that collectively produce different types of problems that contribute to the maintenance of or result from drinking behavior. However, these behaviors and cognitions are not thought to represent symptom manifestations of an underlying disease state (Caddy, 1978).

The person variables involved in the emergent approach to alcoholism are similarly not viewed as underlying personality trait dimensions. Rather, these variables represent dimensions of individual differences in behavior, cognitions, and beliefs, which are brought to bear within a given situation (Mischel, 1973, 1981). There is a continual dynamic interplay between person variables and situational factors. An individual's cognitive activities and behavior patterns are evoked, maintained, and modified by specific situational conditions; conversely, these latter conditions may be changed by the person's course of action (Mischel, 1981).

Mischel (1973, 1981) has suggested five categories of intrapersonal variables which influence a person's behavior in specific situations; these have been labeled *cognitive social-learning person variables*. These include the following: (1) cognitive and behavioral construction competencies, or what the person knows and can do; (2) encoding strategies and personal constructs, or how the individual appraises his or her world, and his or her characteristic ways of attributing responsibility for behavior; (3) cognitive expectancies or beliefs the individual holds about the outcome of his or her behavior or about his or her ability to execute a given behavior; (4) subjective values or preferences, or what is particularly reinforcing for the person; and (5) self-regulatory systems and plans, or the methods utilized to maintain goal-directed behavior even in the absence of external support. While these person variables were originally derived to understand, explain, and predict general behavior, they more recently have come to play a central role in the area of drinking behavior and alcoholism.

With the viewpoint that the person continuously generates and changes situations just as much as he or she is affected by them, our task is to link the stimuli that impinge on problem drinkers to the cognitive social-learning person variables that mediate drinking behavior and relapse. The purpose of this chapter is to provide such a link. Models of relapse among alcoholics will be reviewed, with an emphasis on key theoretical constructs. An attempt also will be made to integrate these constructs within the context of the person variables suggested by Mischel (1981) and to provide an overview of therapeutic strategies appropriate to each category.

COMPONENTS OF RELAPSE MODELS

Just as there are many different models of the etiology of problem drinking and alcoholism, there are also many models concerning relapse. As Tarter and Schneider (1976) noted, models represent attempts to explain complex and poorly understood events by placing them within a better understood system of factual events. As such, models provide a perspective and mode of representation. They provide a framework in which the relevance or irrelevance of events is determined, the manner and language with which events are conceptualized, and a foundation from which theory building may emerge. A feature of particular relevance to this chapter is that models change over time and reflect the dominant mode of thought at a given time in history.

During the recent past, the models applied to understanding relapse have undergone considerable change. This movement has not been without its difficulties. Proponents of different models have often assumed an adversarial stance with regard to the defense of their tenets against new and challenging data with a resultant increased polarization of views. Such is the "stuff" that leads to paradigm shifts (Kuhn, 1970). Often the outcome of such polemics parallels the evolutionary principle of "survival of the fittest." However, what often appears to be lost or overlooked in the scientific analogue of this process is that evolution also involves the passing on and incorporation of useful characteristics from predecessors. This factor should not be lost in the development of new models.

The philosophical, theoretical, and empirical "clash" most often encountered in the area of alcoholism and relapse has been between what have been labeled *medical–disease–physiological* and *behavioral–learning* models. The constructs most involved are those of *craving* and *loss of control drinking* (Maisto & Schefft, 1977; Nathan, 1981). These two constructs have served as the cornerstones of the model originally proposed by Jellinek (1960). Behavioral theorists have leveled criticism against these constructs due to the circularity and imprecision of their definitions, their lack of empirical validation, and their reification (e.g., Maisto & Schefft, 1977 ; Marlatt, 1978; Mello, 1972; Pattison, Sobell, & Sobell, 1977). While their construct validity may be questioned, the "face" validity of these constructs is confirmed through the reports of alcoholics. As Wallace (1977) noted, on an experiential and phenomenological level, a large percentage of alcoholics report experiencing a sense of unpredictability about where an initial drink will lead and a persistent recollection of the "glow" produced by alcohol. Regardless of the limitations involved, it is difficult to disregard completely such primary data. Another criticism of these constructs has involved the relative emphasis on hypothesized physiological underpinnings to the exclusion of more psychological variables. The redefinition of loss of control drinking by Glatt (1967, 1976) and Keller (1972) and the distinction made by Isbell (1955) between *nonsymbolic* (physiological) and *symbolic* (cognitive–psychological) forms of craving have led to an increased recognition of the role played by social, psychological, cultural, and situational factors in these processes.

At the other extreme, behavioral models of alcoholism can be criticized for their relative reluctance to acknowledge the possible influence that physiological factors exert on drinking behavior and relapse. The recent research in the areas of neuropsychological functioning (e.g., Chelune & Parker, 1981; Parsons & Farr, 1981) and on the behavioral correlates of alcohol dependence (Edwards, 1977; Edwards & Gross, 1976; Hodgson, Rankin, & Stockwell, 1979; Stockwell, Hodgson, Edwards, Taylor, & Rankin,

1979) are serving to rectify this deficiency. Another concern expressed by Litman (1980), a behavioral theorist, is that the same criticism concerning reification of constructs that has been leveled against the medical model might be brought to bear against psychological models which seem to reify cognitive control without specifying the conditions and mechanisms of the underlying processes. With the increased emphasis currently being given to cognitive constructs, these constructs must be operationalized and measured.

A way of stepping out of this controversy, in a manner consistent with Kelly's (1955) constructive alternativism, is to assume that neither position is completely correct or inclusive. Rather, while each set of models may have inherent limitations, each also may contribute to our further understanding of the relapse process. As the boundaries begin to blur somewhat, it may be appropriate to incorporate factors from each to enhance an emergent position that recognizes both physical and psychological components. Such a contention is consistent with the proposition made by Lindsmith (1968) concerning the process of addiction. He argues that neither cognitive–psychological nor physiological factors alone are sufficient to explain addiction. Rather, addiction appears to be an interactive product of learning in a situation involving physiological events as they are interpreted, labeled, and given meaning by the individual. Both the cognitive and physiological elements are indispensable features of the total experience and of the process of addiction. This proposition is also consistent with a truly multivariate approach to alcoholism and relapse, which implies multiple causality, multiple system involvement, and multiple levels of analyses.

As noted earlier, there have been a number of models presented in the area of relapse. In our attempt to incorporate applicable features from each, we have made a number of initial decisions. First, we will attempt to take an integrative rather than adversarial–competitive view of models presented by various proponents. We hope to avoid two risks that result from viewing each proponent's work as a unique model of relapse. The first risk is that such a formal model-by-model analysis reintroduces a sense of competition and polarization. Second, such an analysis would overlook the cross-fertilization and integration of thought that has occurred across such works. Therefore, we have chosen to view each proponent as contributing to an evolving, emergent model that is yet to be fully formalized. Such a meta-analysis assumes that the work of a given author represents a component that should be considered in any comprehensive explanation of relapse. A second decision was not to include a formal overview of what has been labeled the traditional disease model. This perspective has had a major impact on the field of alcoholism and relapse, and we feel that the readers have been exposed to its tenets. For those who have not, it would be most helpful to read the primary sources (Davies, 1976; Glatt, 1967, 1976; Jellinek, 1960; Keller, 1972) and recent critiques (Maisto & Schefft, 1977; Marlatt, 1978; Mello, 1972; Pattison et al., 1977; Robinson, 1972). We also hoped to avoid the possibility of establishing a "straw man"; that is not our intent. Third, we have decided to include those more recent multivariate formulations that view both person variables and situational variables as contributing to the relapse process. The components of relapse have been arranged in order along a somewhat arbitrarily defined continuum based upon the extent to which the primary person variables involved are relatively more physiologically oriented or more cognitively oriented. Such an arrangement does not suggest that a given component focuses on one form of person variable to the total exclusion of the other.

A final decision, which may initially appear contradictory to our stated intent, was to utilize cognitive social-learning theory as a core organizing principle in the present review. This choice is consistent with Tarter and Schneider's (1976) suggestion that individuals use a more familar and better understood frame of reference to explain more divergent and complex events. We view cognitive social-learning theory as providing a framework within which a wide and diverse set of data, both physiological and psychological, can be integrated. It also provides a framework from which therapeutic strategies can be generated. The review of the components of relapse begins with those that fall on the more physiologically oriented end of the continuum. Table 6-1 presents an overview of the relationship between the components of relapse addressed by the proponents to be reviewed and those cognitive social-learning person variables presented by Mischel (1981).

NEUROLOGICAL IMPAIRMENT

Gorski and Miller (1979) present a formulation of relapse for the purpose of guiding prevention counseling. It is based on observing and interviewing individuals who had received alcoholism treatment, left with a resolve to remain abstinent, but later resumed drinking. This model defines relapse as "a process that occurs within the patient which manifests itself in a progressive pattern of behavior that allows the symptoms of a disease or illness to become reactivated in a person that has previously arrested those symptoms" (p. 1).

The key elements of this definition are: "process," implying a dynamic situation which can be interrupted or changed; "within the patient," targeting attitudes, values, and behaviors for change; and "progressive . . . illness," endorsing a disease metaphor. Gorski and Miller take a holistic approach within a disease model framework and discusses physical, psychological, behavioral, and social components of relapse.

The core physical or, to be more specific, neurological consequence of drinking which predisposes a person to relapse is the "post acute withdrawal syndrome" (PAW). Gorski and Miller posit that the body, as in other chronic illnesses, adjusts to the effects of alcohol after prolonged use so that continued drinking actually has a normalizing effect on functioning. Thus, cessation of drinking, after the acute withdrawal symptoms have subsided, produces PAW, which is thought to surface in 1–2 weeks, peak at 1½–2 months, and subside over the next 3 months. It should be noted that this hypothesized time course is comparable to that which has been found to be maximally associated with relapse (Hunt *et al.*, 1971). Post acute withdrawal syndrome primarily affects higher level cognitive processes, producing impairment in abstract thinking, conceptualization, concentration, memory storage and retrieval, and increased emotionality or overreaction to stress. Thus, those cognitive attributes necessary for decision making are compromised at a time when psychological, behavioral, and social factors also create a relapse predisposition.

Gorski and Miller describe a "uniform pattern" of relapse beginning with attitude change long before the first drink. They label the initial symptom "apprehension about well being," or a sense of fear and uncertainty and lack of confidence in the ability to stay sober. This attitude is followed by other psychological and behavioral counterproductive coping processes such as denial, defensiveness, rigid and repetitive social and work involvement, isolation, avoidance, lack of planning and loss of specific objectives. These actions, combined with PAW, lead to confusion, breakdown in supportive social relationships, depression, loss of daily structure including sleep and meals, and abandonment of treatment involvement. The result is overwhelming loneliness, frustration, anger, tension, and the feeling that there are no remaining options but drinking, suicide, or insanity. A resumption of drinking leads to subsequent "loss of control."

Gorski and Miller feel that loss of control, like PAW, may be physiologically induced by the effects of alcohol on the central nervous system. An expectancy component is also discussed, however; the authors feel alcoholics are programmed to continue drinking after the first drink because they are taught that this is inevitable.

This neurologically based formulation of relapse leads to recommendations for the assessment of relapse proneness and for the composition of treatment strategies. Assessment of three areas is necessary: PAW, the personality dynamic, and the social context. Post acute withdrawal syndrome can be assessed clinically or objectively by using psychometric testing to explore brain–behavior relationships. Although the model does not specify what tests to use, presumably standard neuropsychological batteries would be appropriate. Both current severity and progressive course of the syndrome would be important. The "personality dynamic" includes memory of problem-solving strategies and the ability to apply strategies appropriate to a given situation. The social context assessment attempts to determine whether the individual's lifestyle supports abstinence.

In summary, the core of Gorski and Miller's relapse conceptualization is PAW, the post acute withdrawal syndrome. This construct has several functions within the formulation: PAW provides a disease model explanation

Table 6-1. Cognitive Social-Learning Person Variables Included as Components of Alcoholic Relapse Models Reviewed

Cognitive social-learning person variables	Components of relapse models						
	Neurological impairment	Psycho-biological	Opponent process	Cognitive appraisals	Self-efficacy	Inter-actional	Cognitive-behavioral
Cognitive and behavioral construction competencies	Post acute withdrawal syndrome	Insensitivity to interoceptive BAL cues resulting in "loss of control" Physical dependence		Coping abilities			Deficient social skills
Encoding strategies Constructs		Misattribution of mood states to conditioned withdrawal syndrome	Over-generalized B states	Appraisals		Rationalization, decreased cognitive vigilance	Attribution processes Rationalizations, AIDs

Cognitive social learning person variables		Influenced by temporal dynamics of opponent process		Self-efficacy versus outcome expectancies	Outcome expectancies	Self-efficacy, learned helplessness versus positive alcohol expectancies
Expectancies						
Subjective values and preferences	Craving	a and b processes				
Self-regulatory systems and plans	Apprehension about well-being		Cognitive coping strategies		Coping strategies	AVE, AIDs
Environmental demands and supports	Significant other involvement in RP and intervention planning	Setting events / CS_As and CS_Bs	High-risk situations categorization		High-risk situations categorization	High-risk situations categorization

of the alcoholic's aberrant behavior; PAW alerts the therapist to the fact that even though sober, the alcoholic may have impaired cognitive functioning and have difficulty benefiting from other than fairly concrete counseling; PAW also provides the alcoholic with a palatable explanation of unacceptable behavior, and explains the need to reduce stress and continue self-monitoring for warning signs of impending relapse.

PSYCHOBIOLOGICAL FACTORS

Ludwig and his co-workers (Ludwig & Stark, 1974; Ludwig & Wikler, 1974; Ludwig, Wikler, & Stark, 1974) have presented a formulation of relapse within what they describe as a psychobiological framework. To a large extent this formulation attempts to investigate constructs derived from the traditional disease model—particularly the concepts of craving for alcohol and loss of control—from a behavioral perspective. Craving represents a cornerstone of this formulation and is a particularly salient relapse precipitant.

Ludwig and Stark (1974) initially suggested that craving is psychobiological in nature; moreover, that it is multidimensional, consisting of cognitive, behavioral, physiological, and neurophysiological components. These authors, through survey methodology, attempted to determine factors that influence craving. It was found that 78% of the alcoholics surveyed reported craving alcohol. Of these, 42.5% described that construct in terms of wanting to achieve the desired effects of alcohol; the remaining 57.5% defined it as a need or desire. It was further found that both internal and external cues are related to the probability of experiencing sensations of craving. The external situations included those in which alcohol was available, those in which the person was under some form of stress, and those in which the individual felt as if he had failed in some personally meaningful area. The internal cues represented both negative affective states, such as anxiety, depression, loneliness, or boredom, and symptoms of an alcohol-withdrawal syndrome. Also, approximately 80% of the subjects reported some relative degree of loss of control drinking after they had been drinking steadily.

Ludwig and Stark (1974) interpreted these results to suggest that craving represents a conditioned "cognitive label." This label is attributed to most negative mood states experienced by the alcoholic, whether induced by external, situational cues or internal, intrapersonal cues. The presence of these states of negative arousal, perceived and interpreted as craving, channel the individual's focus and behavior toward the use of alcohol as a means of producing relief.

This conceptualization was expanded in a subsequent theoretical article by Ludwig and Wikler (1974). An attempt was made to explain sensations of craving within the context of classical conditioning theory. Craving for alcohol was viewed as the psychological or cognitive correlate of a "subclinical conditioned withdrawal syndrome." Through the process of temporal contiguity, craving and related sensations that are assumed to occur during withdrawal from alcohol become associated with stimuli experienced during the process of withdrawal. Ludwig and Wikler suggest that more frequent and severe withdrawal experiences in the past will lead to stronger sensations of craving in response to these conditioned stimuli. Furthermore, through a process of generalization, a broader range of stimuli become conditioned to and acquire the ability to elicit this subclinical withdrawal syndrome. These include both internal negative mood states and external cues associated with past drinking. If an abstinent alcoholic is exposed to such conditioned stimuli at some later date, the probability that he or she will experience craving is increased. The likelihood of drinking is also increased; drinking represents an instrumental response that would reduce the experience of the negative arousal state.

Ludwig and Wikler (1974) further describe the importance of the individual's cognitive processes in the experience of craving. They suggest that the way in which the alcoholic cognitively interprets and labels the elicited subclinical conditioned withdrawal syndrome will determine whether the concomitant sensations are experienced as craving. Those internal, interoceptive and external, situational cues that have been associated with past drinking provide a cognitive set conducive to the interpretation of arousal as a strong sense of craving. Miller (1976) has suggested that such cues represent *setting events*. These cues, through repeated association with the reinforcing effects of alcohol, have acquired secondary reinforcing properties. As such, their mere presence may precipitate drinking.

Ludwig and Wikler (1974) indicate that craving is the cognitive state that predisposes the individual to seek alcohol as a source of relief or pleasure; however, craving does not inevitably lead to drinking. Also, if one resumes drinking, this does not lead inevitably to loss of control. Loss of control is defined as a behavioral state initiated by craving and characterized by an inability to modulate alcohol intake. An hypothesized neurophysiological feedback dysfunction is thought to mediate loss of control drinking (Ludwig & Wikler, 1974). It is hypothesized that loss of control among alcoholics represents an inability to accurately utilize information from interoceptive cues (e.g., perceived intoxication or degree of speech or motor impairment) necessary to regulate the rate or quantity of alcohol consumed. Subsequent research by Ludwig, Bendfeldt, Wikler, and Cain (1978) provided support for this contention. They investigated the relative ability of alcoholics and social drinkers to maintain their blood-alcohol levels (BALs) within a predetermined range by focusing primarily on internal cues associated with BAL during a training session. In subsequent experimental sessions, individuals were given false exteroceptive feedback about their BALs (e.g., either underestimates or overestimates). They were asked, at 15-minute intervals, whether or not to accept a drink in order to maintain their BAL within the designated range. The results indicated that the alco-holics, relative to the social drinkers, consumed more alcohol, attained higher BALs, and had a greater average deviation from the targeted BAL range, with a greater tendency to drink in excess of this range. The alcoholics also evidenced a progressive inability to regulate their BALs over time and at higher levels of intoxication, regardless of the nature of the false feedback provided them. The relative deficits of alcoholics to modulate their alcohol consumption and subsequent BALs based upon interoceptive cues has been supported by other investigators (Nathan, 1978).

A variable that seems to fit within a psychobiological formulation of alcoholism and relapse is the severity of alcohol dependence (Edwards, 1977; Edwards & Gross, 1976). A major component of an alcohol dependence syndrome is the prior experience and severity of withdrawal phenomena and tolerance. These components are weighted heavily in the diagnostic differen-tiation between alcoholic versus nonalcoholic individuals (National Council on Alcoholism, 1972) and between alcohol-dependent persons versus alcohol abusers (American Psychiatric Association, 1980). While there are limitations inherent in such a dichotomous diagnostic system (e.g., Donovan & Marlatt, 1980), and while the concept of an alcohol dependence "syndrome" has been criticized (e.g., Shaw, 1979), there is an increasing body of evidence that promotes the clinical and predictive utility of this construct. Ludwig and Stark (1974), for example, found that the experience of craving was signifi-cantly related to prior alcohol withdrawal experiences. Ludwig and Wikler (1974), consistent with their formulation, argue that the more frequent and severe one's prior withdrawal experiences, the greater the predisposition to conditioned withdrawal symptoms with a resultant desire for relief through drinking (i.e., craving). Kaplan, Meyer, and Stroebel (1983) also found that alcoholics' decisions whether or not to consume a drink within a laboratory setting could be predicted from measures of their desire to drink, recent withdrawal symptomatology, and an increased heart rate in the presence of an alcoholic beverage. Recent alcohol administration studies have provided some further support for Ludwig and Wikler (1974). Hodgson et al. (1979) found that craving and a strong desire for alcohol were found in severely dependent alcoholics 3 hours after they had received a "priming dose"; no such priming effect was found among alcoholics judged to be moderately dependent. Rankin, Hodgson, and Stockwell (1980) also found that severely dependent alcoholics, in contrast to those who were moderately dependent, reported a stronger desire for a drink, consumed a fixed dose of alcohol more rapidly, and also drank more alcohol over a 30-minute drinking period.

Similarly, Stockwell, Hodgson, Rankin, and Taylor (1982) found that severely dependent alcoholics, following an initial priming dose, expressed a greater desire for and greater difficulty resisting the consumption of a sub-sequent drink than did moderately dependent alcoholics. In addition to consuming this drink more rapidly than the moderately dependent subjects, the severely dependent individuals also rated the actual drinking experience as more desirous and pleasant. An interesting interaction effect was also noted. The administration of the initial priming dose followed the balanced placebo design (Marlatt, Demming, & Reid, 1973), in which alcoholic and placebo beverages were administered under the instructional set suggesting that they either did or did not contain alcohol. It was found that the cognitive expectancy associated with the instructional set concerning the priming dose influenced the speed of subsequent drinking among the moderately dependent alcoholics. That is, those individuals who believed that the priming beverage contained alcohol, regardless of the actual content, consumed a subsequent drink more rapidly. On the other hand, the response of the severely dependent alcoholics was influenced more by the actual alcohol content of the priming dose. Thus, the level of alcohol dependence appears to mediate both self-reported and behavioral indices of craving and "loss of control" (Rankin, Hodgson, & Stockwell, 1979).

The severity of dependence may also contribute to relapse. There is a greater likelihood of severely dependent alcoholics to be either totally abstinent or uncontrolled with respect to their drinking, with less likelihood of controlled drinking (Orford, Oppenheimer, & Edwards, 1976; Polich, Armor, & Braiker, 1980). As Polich *et al.* (1980) noted, the presence of alcohol dependence symptoms (e.g., tremulousness, morning drinking, blackouts, missing meals), even at very low levels, is a serious indication and is predictive of continuing alcohol problems in the future. Similar considerations have led Miller and Caddy (1977) to rule out controlled drinking as a viable treatment goal for individuals who evidence a recent physiological addiction to alcohol, since dependence may occur more readily in persons with a history of withdrawal symptoms.

The extent to which alcohol dependence influences drinking and relapse directly or serves as an intervening variable is less clear. Heather, Rollnick, and Winton (1983), for instance, found that responses on the Severity of Alcohol Dependence Questionnaire (SADQ; Stockwell *et al.*, 1979), a self-report measure assessing prior withdrawal phenomena and tolerance, were significantly related to a measure of "subjective dependence." Thus, one's subjective estimate of the degree of dependence appears to be based to some extent on the presence of prior withdrawal and other physical indicators. Of particular relevance is that a major component of subjective dependence was the individual's belief about loss of control over drinking. Litman, Eiser, Rawson, and Oppenheim (1977) also found a positive relationship between the self-rated degree of alcohol dependence and the perceived threat or dangerousness of potential relapse situations. This was particularly true of those situations involving negative mood states, social anxiety, reduced cognitive vigilance, and the use of rationalizations. The more dependent individuals tended to utilize thinking of the negative consequences, guilt associated with drinking, and active behavioral avoidance of drinking-related situations as a means of dealing with potential relapse situations; however, only avoidance was judged to be an effective coping strategy.

The pattern of the previous results suggests that the severity of alcohol dependence is a salient component of relapse. As Hodgson (1980) notes, for the severely dependent person, the cessation of drinking may lead to actual or expected, real or conditioned withdrawal symptoms that may contribute to the alcoholic's experience of craving and impaired control. The probability of relapse appears to be increased further among severely dependent individuals due to the increased level of perceived threat in high-risk drinking situations in conjunction with a narrow range of effective coping strategies (Litman *et al.*, 1977).

OPPONENT PROCESS AND ACQUIRED MOTIVATION

Behavioral treatment strategies for problem drinkers have often ignored the fact that the effects of drinking change with repeated exposure. Psychophysiological processes manifested in tolerance and dependence alter the impact of alcohol on the individual depending upon his or her drinking history.

A model for the drinking history influence is suggested by Solomon (1980) in the opponent-process theory. Starting with the notion that an organism acts to moderate emotional influences of novel stimulation, the opponent-process theory has several characteristics. It postulates automatic processes, linking stimulation and behavior, whose parameters may change with repeated experience, but which are basically innate. The two processes are labeled a and b. The a process is triggered by stimulation of some sort and produces affective state A. The b process (the opponent process) is a "slave" process triggered by an a process and produces an affective state B that functions to oppose and decrease the A state. At any given moment, the affective state that the organism actually experiences is the sum of the A and B states. B states moderate or antagonize A states. As a result, the organism is responsive to stimulation but protected from extremes. The opponent-process theory is a general theory of affective dynamics with potential application to a wide variety of stimuli and circumstances, such as parachute jumping, cigarette addiction, electrical brain stimulation, and imprinting.

The a and b affective or hedonic processes are postulated to have certain temporal parameters. During the first stimulations of a novel sort, the organism experiences an initial affective state A with short latency that peaks, adapts to a steady level, and then declines to a peak of an opposite affective sign (state B), which then decays back to a neutral baseline (see Figure 6-1). These temporal characteristics are produced by the combination of an a process having short latency, duration limited to that of the stimulus event, and rapid decay, with an overlapping b process triggered by the onset of the a process. During the first few stimulations, the b process has a delayed

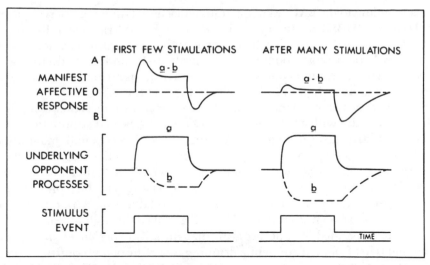

Figure 6-1. The comparison of the effects of opponent *b* processes for relatively novel stimuli and for stimuli that are familiar and have been repeated frequently. Adapted from "The Opponent-Process Theory of Acquired Motivation" by R. L. Solomon, *American Psychologist,* 1980, *35,* 691–712. Copyright 1980 by the American Psychological Association. Adapted by permission of the author.

and gradual onset and moderate magnitude and duration. Phenomenological perceptions at a cocktail party illustrate the process when alcohol is the stimulus:

We arrive at the party tired and emotionally drained from the day's activities and knock down a drink or two in order to loosen up quickly. Stress and strain begin to disappear. We feel relaxed, talkative, happy, even euphoric. . . . The party is becoming as noisy as it will ever get and life is a ball. Then the drinking slows down. The blood alcohol level begins to drop. The glow is fading, and people start to leave. Those who stay gradually become tired and sleepy. Conversation flags, smiles turn deadpan, and flashes of irritability soon appear. (Jones & Parsons, 1975, pp. 53–54)

As alcohol reaches the central nervous system, the *a* process produces a positive affective A state characterized by relaxation and social facilitation. After some delay, the *b* process begins to counter these positive feelings. When blood alcohol level begins to drop, the *a* process ceases to function, the *b* process becomes stronger than the *a* process, and the resultant emotional state B is negative. The social drinker experiences a letdown and perhaps discomfort. Thus the emotional effect of alcohol is in part a function of BAL for light to moderate drinkers. Ekman administered alcohol in varying doses and found that self-estimates of mood generally showed a curvilinear pattern corresponding to the BAL (Ekman, Frankenhaeuser, Goldberg, Bjerver, Järpe, & Myrsten, 1963; Ekman, Hagdahl, & Myrsten, 1964). Generally, mood variables changed in positive directions with increasing intoxication, reaching a high point corresponding with peak BAL, and then declining to baseline. However, mood and subjective intoxication ratings *decreased* with time more rapidly than did blood-alcohol concentration.

Opponent-process dynamics predict that hedonic effects of alcohol will change radically with prolonged use. After many repeated stimulations, the initial affective state (designated A′) may have a very small magnitude, declining rapidly to an intense peak of opposite affective sign (B′) which returns to a neutral emotional state very slowly. This difference with repeated stimulations is assumed to be a result of changes in the *b* process, that is, decreased latency, and increased intensity and duration. Opponent processes which have been strengthened by being evoked through repeated stimulation are designated *b′*. The alcoholic may initially experience some relaxation and relief from tension while drinking, but as he or she continues, often at a much higher rate than the social drinker (Nathan & O'Brien, 1971), the pleasant affect vanishes, to be replaced by heightened irritation or anxiety. If something interferes with the alcoholic's supply of alcohol and his or her BAL drops sharply, the alcoholic may experience intense discomfort lasting long after the BAL has dropped to zero. The *a* process responsible for the initial positive affect is assumed to be unchanged over many stimulations. The intensified *b′* process, however, counters positive feelings with less delay and with more strength and takes more time to return to neutral. For example, studies of programmed and free-choice experimental drinking with chronic alcoholics (Davis, 1971) show that during the first days of drinking in the laboratory, some subjects, following their first daily dose of alcohol, become more carefree and friendly and less depressed, hostile, anxious, and fatigued. As the days go by, however, there are significant decreases in carefree and friendly feelings with an increase in hostility.

Thus, for alcoholics, the psychophysiological effect of alcohol triggers an *a* process that initially results in an affectively pleasurable or neutral A state. At low levels of alcohol consumption, the attendant *b* process may not produce a noticeably negative hedonic state. With increasing levels of consumption and duration of use, however, the strengthened *b′* process manifests as depression, irritation, and sometimes anxiety. Also, the heavy drinker learns that the unpleasurable B state can be put off by continuing to drink. The more one drinks, the more important it is to continue drinking, because of the increasingly unpleasant consequences of stopping.

Not surprisingly, stimuli that accompany the act of drinking can come to evoke emotional reactions through conditioning. A recent experiment by Pomerleau, Fertig, Baker, and Cooney (1983) demonstrates the physiological and subjective responses to alcohol cues brought about by a history of chronic, heavy alcohol consumption. Alcoholics in treatment were compared to nonalcoholic controls by having subjects sniff their favorite alcoholic beverage. The physiological measure of swallowing (related to increased conditioned salivation) and the subjective desire to drink alcohol were elevated for alcoholics compared with nonalcoholics. The behavioral effects of the conditioning process are illustrated by Wellman's (1955) description of the development of problem drinking in a group of young men:

As their alcohol use increased, alcohol was deliberately used for the relief of external or internal stress and as a constant companion of conviviality of any kind. It was expected to diminish not only the tension which may arise from interpersonal situations, but also fatigue or chill or pain. (p. 721)

As the problem drinkers increased their intake, they were unhappy except when they were under the influence of alcohol and even the euphorias were of shorter duration than they had been previously. The relief from anxiety and tension was also of short duration. Depression was constant except when relieved by the adequate intake of alcohol. This total picture only developed after the pattern of regular drinking to drunkenness was followed by the alcoholic amnesia and intolerance of alcohol. (p. 724)

Opponent-process dynamics become relevant to relapse because it appears that A and B emotional states can be conditioned to previously neutral stimuli through repeated pairing, and thus the use of alcohol becomes connected with many facets of the problem drinker's life. Stimuli reliably present during the initial phase of drinking would come to elicit pleasurable A states and would be positive reinforcers, which should reinforce behavior and sometimes even temporarily eliminate the aversive B state. Solomon (1977, 1980) refers to stimuli of this type as CS_As. Conditioned stimulus events for the aversive B state would be aversive in themselves. They should have negative reinforcing properties and would energize escape and avoidance behaviors. Stimuli of this type are CS_Bs. To illustrate this, let us assume that a problem drinker has not been drinking. What might provoke a relapse? First, in a manner analogous to that proposed by Ludwig and Wikler (1974), the person may confuse emotional states, such as anxiety and agitated depression with alcohol withdrawal (the B state) and seek to reduce them with alcohol (the A state). Secondly, stimuli associated with the pleasurable A state (CS_As), such as handling a bottle of one's favorite beverage, may come to evoke an increment of the a process and therefore be opposed by the opponent process. For a social drinker, the resultant emotional state may be of pleasurable anticipation. For the experienced alcoholic drinker, the resultant state may be negative and require resumption of drinking for relief. Third, stimuli which have been associated repeatedly with withdrawal (CS_Bs), such as stimuli present when waking up with a hangover, should come to evoke directly a conditioned increment of the opponent b process, and again require alcohol for relief. In this view, although distinctive stimuli repeatedly associated with either previous intoxication states or withdrawal may provoke relapse, the two cases are quite different. Although visiting a bar or being around previous drinking companions may arouse some increment of the opponent b process indirectly, psychophysiological or environmental stimuli that have been associated with withdrawal for the individual should have a more direct, powerful, and immediate arousal effect.

No matter what the reason for resumption of drinking, it is highly likely that for most alcoholics descending BAL and associated stimuli (CS_Bs) have become a discriminative stimulus for further drinking to avoid the B' state. The longer and heavier the drinking history, the more evident "loss of control" will be. Even if the period of abstinence has been a lengthy one, for the person having experienced the B' hedonic state, continuing to drink is in large part an avoidance behavior and as such may be expected to be resistant to extinction. Nonalcoholic drinkers, not having to contend with a strengthened opponent process, should be able to stop when they want. As the individual repeatedly insults himself with excess alcohol consumption, difficulty stopping should increase with the strength of the b process.

Just as a simplistic disease model concept of craving suffers from conceptual confusion because it fails to distinguish between behavior that is positively and negatively reinforced, the concept of loss of control is confusing because it blurs two different conceptual levels. It seems to refer to the transition from positive to negative reinforcement in a drinking situation, but it also seems to refer to self-regulatory systems and plans. For the problem drinker, the use of alcohol as an emotional control mechanism may have become very important. Moreover, the more alcohol is used, the less control the individual has over its effects. As drinking increases, the individual's ability to titrate his drinking to stay within acceptable levels of intoxication may deteriorate because of the shifting relationship between alcohol and its emotional effects. The shifting subjective value of alcohol and the creation of an overdetermined network of stimulus–response expectancies of both positive and negative consequences in the drinking setting progressively limit the problem drinker's ability to make choices about his drinking.

COGNITIVE APPRAISALS

Sanchez-Craig and Walker's interst in the relapse process appears to have developed from an analysis of drinking episodes of patients in treatment at an alcoholic halfway house (Walker, Sanchez-Craig, & MacDonald, 1974). Of the drinking episodes identified, 43% were associated with an aversive social event (e.g. rejection, criticism, arguments, loss of a spouse, friend, or child). Of those episodes not immediately preceded by an aversive event, 37% were related to thoughts or feelings about social situations (e.g., negative interactions in the past or anticipated in the future, or feelings of social inadequacy). Of the remaining episodes, most were related to negative consequences of previous drinking (e.g., withdrawal symptoms, sleep disruptions, depression, worries about losing a job or going to jail). Only two episodes (3%) were associated with external, nonsocial events (e.g., loss of job and learning that a serious operation was required).

Based upon this initial analysis, Sanchez-Craig and Walker (Sanchez-Craig, 1975, 1976; Sanchez-Craig & Walker, 1975, 1982) developed a conceptualization of relapse that focuses primarily on cognitive appraisal processes, or the way in which the individual perceives and interprets situations. This focus has led to the development of "reappraisal therapy," a self-control strategy based on Lazarus's (1966) theory of psychological stress. The formulation suggests that it is mainly the individual's interpretation of situations, rather than the situations in and of themselves, which determine his or her behavior. Events can be appraised as neutral, as beneficial, or as harmful to the individual. If an event is evaluated as beneficial, the person will be likely to respond with some kind of approach behavior and to feel positively. But if the event is appraised as harmful, this will be accompanied by negative emotions (anger, depression, resentment) and the person may attack, avoid or withdraw. The response may be primarily behavioral (verbal or physical aggression) or cognitive (denial or rationalization). Appraisals are not necessarily either accurate or appropriate since they frequently occur in an automatic or undeliberated manner, and may neglect, or distort, or attribute nonexistent features to the stimulus situation. Appraisals are also not static, but open to change based either on further observations of the situation or the effects of one's actions in that situation. In addition to real or imagined features of the situation, appraisals are thought to be affected by the individual's repertoire of coping strategies. When faced with potentially threatening situations, the individual with adequate coping abilities may learn to react in a habitual, spontaneous, and effective manner. On the other hand, if coping strategies are not available, the individual will experience increasingly severe stress and negative emotions that will become more severe, generalized, and ingrained with repeated exposure to challenging situations.

Sanchez-Craig (1979) has applied this appraisal theory to alcohol problems and generated the following assumptions: (1) The problem drinker may appraise alcohol consumption as an aid for coping with a variety of aversive events (primarily social situations) or as a valued activity in itself. This appraisal may come about through experiences in which the alcohol serves to decrease the aversiveness of a situation (e.g., by making it easier to ignore a nagging spouse) or to increase the individual's confidence in his or her coping ability (e.g., to express emotions). (2) Prolonged use of drinking as a coping strategy in aversive situations can lead to habitual, automatic responding and interfere with the development of more appropriate responses. (3) Alcohol treatment may be initiated when new information (e.g., threat of loss of job) forces the individual to reappraise the deleterious effects of drinking. (4) When the individual attempts to abstain or reduce alcohol intake, a desire to drink is likely to be experienced, particularly in situations connected with alcohol use in the past. Unless the appraisal of alcohol as a negative stimulus is consolidated and reinforced, this learned desire will predominate and relapse will occur. Inaccurate or inappropriate appraisals can contribute further to a return to drinking in several ways. For example, the individual may focus on the immediate beneficial effects of alcohol and ignore negative long-term consequences. He or she may catastrophize aversive situations (e.g., "things are so bad, I may as well give up"). The individual may also justify a decision to drink through rationalization (e.g., "just one won't hurt"). Interventions to be reviewed later have been designed to facilitate the correction of such inaccurate appraisals.

SELF-EFFICACY AND OUTCOME EXPECTANCIES

Wilson (1978) has focused on cognitive expectancies as primary mediators of relapse. This perspective is based upon the earlier work of Bandura (1977) on perceived self-efficacy. Bandura (1977) has distinguished between an outcome expectation, analogous to Rotter's (1966) perceived locus of control, and self-efficacy. The former defines the belief that a given behavior will produce a certain outcome or result. The latter is a belief about oneself, that is, the extent to which the individual believes that he or she is capable of producing the behavior required to achieve the desired outcome within a given situation. Bandura (1977) suggests that self-efficacy expectancies predominate in predicting behavior in relation to outcome expectancies. If the individual doubts that he or she can perform the necessary behavior, knowledge about the contingent outcome is less relevant. Furthermore, the strength of the individual's self-efficacy expectations influences the probability of initiating coping behavior as well as the effort expended and the persistence of attempts to exert control in a given situation.

Bandura (1977) has suggested that the level of self-efficacy expectancies is dependent upon, among other things, the availability of interpersonal skills required to meet the demands of a given situation. Wilson (1978) argues that those forms of alcoholism treatment most frequently employed tend to minimize the alcoholic's self-efficacy expectations about coping with alcohol. Prominent "disease" approaches to alcoholism emphasize that the alcoholic is the passive victim of a chronic disease process which is characterized by an inability to exercise volitional control over consumption once drinking has begun. The alcoholic is further led to believe that he or she is different from nonalcoholics and is particularly vulnerable to the effects of alcohol. Thus, the alcoholic is provided with a set of beliefs and expectations that underscore a perceived lack of self-control over drinking. This set of cognitions is exemplified in the saying "One drink, a drunk." The individual develops a set of outcome expectancies that emphasize the inevitability of uncontrolled drinking following an initial drink. The first drink after abstinence is viewed by Wilson (1978) as a function of the faulty labeling of emotional or physical states in conjunction with the anticipated positive, short-term effects of alcohol. The desire for these immediately reinforcing consequences of drinking are often cognitively interpreted and labeled as craving. If drinking does occur following a period of abstinence, such beliefs concerning one's inability to maintain control may operate in the form of a self-fulfilling prophecy which will translate an initial "lapse" into a relapse. Also, given the perceived lack of control and the concomitant decrease in self-efficacy expectancies associated with the "lapse," the individual would be predicted within this context to refrain from any alternative coping strategies. Thus, such traditional forms of treatment, by minimizing positive self-efficacy expectancies, might inadvertently inculcate a form of "learned helplessness."

Rollnick and Heather (1982) have elaborated this self-efficacy component of drinking and relapse. They indicate that abstinence-oriented treatment has both positive and negative outcome and efficacy expectancies. The positive outcome expectancy is that life-long abstinence will lead to the elimination of one's drinking problem; the negative counterpart is that if the alcoholic resumes drinking, this will lead to an uncontrolled relapse. The positive efficacy expectancies develop concerning one's treatment-induced mastery over drinking and the resultant ability to remain sober. As noted by Wilson (1978), the negative counterpart focuses on the individual's lack of control and inability to cope with drinking in the future.

Rollnick and Heather (1982) note a number of problems in the process of treatment. The first is that the individual's initial belief in abstinence as an outcome is often not assessed at the beginning of treatment. However, treatment personnel often assume that clients have abstinence as a primary goal. The authors suggest that the possible discrepancy between client and therapist beliefs in this goal creates problems in the therapeutic process. This is particularly notable when the client does not hold abstinence as an outcome expectancy. Such clients are often labeled as "resistant" and lacking in "motivation." This problem can be overcome by more adequately assessing clients' outcome expectancies and negotiating appropriate forms of treatment in those cases where abstinence is not the primary goal.

A second problem in therapy is the form of treatment most often employed in traditional treatment settings. Both Rollnick and Heather (1982) and Wilson (1978) note that verbally mediated approaches such as individual and/or group insight-oriented therapies represent the modal form of intervention. However, Bandura (1977) has indicated that such therapies, based on "verbal persuasion," are relatively ineffective in enhancing a sense of mastery or self-efficacy. In the case of alcoholism, Rollnick and Heather (1982) suggest that the outcome of such verbally mediated interventions may be an increased sense of willpower to remain abstinent. In the absence of the requisite coping skills, however, such willpower may represent a nonveridical "illusion of control" that will prove inadequate across a number of situations frequently found to precipitate relapse. Both Rollnick and Heather (1982) and Wilson (1978) therefore suggest a variety of performance based cognitive–behavioral interventions to enhance one's perceived self-efficacy.

Rollnick and Heather (1982) also relate both the outcome and efficacy expectancies to drinking and relapse. They view the return to drinking as a two-stage process. The first phase consists of the events that take place prior to the initial drink being consumed; the second represents those events that occur after the first drink. They note that both positive and negative outcome and efficacy expectancies are communicated to a client during the course of treatment. It is suggested that belief in the *positive* expectancies (e.g., the belief in the need for lifelong abstinence and in one's mastery over drinking) is related to the first of these two phases: the more strongly held these beliefs, the longer the period of abstinence. The belief in the *negative* expectancies (e.g., the inevitability of relapse following a first drink and one's inabilty to exert control) predicts behavior in the second phase: the more strongly held these beliefs, the greater the probability of relapse after the first drink. Some recent empirical support has been provided concerning the mediating influence of these negative expectancies. Heather, Winton, and Rollnick (1982) found that alcoholics who held the belief of "one drink, a drunk" reported less confidence in their ability to drink socially and also were found to be drinking in a less controlled fashion at a 6-month follow-up period than those who did not hold this belief. Heather, Rollnick, and Winton (1983) also found that acceptance of this belief was more predictive of posttreatment relapse than was a measure of the severity of alcohol dependence.

Rollnick and Heather (1982) stress the extent to which the mixed messages (e.g., both positive and negative outcome and efficacy expectancies) the client acquires during treatment represent a double-edged sword. However, Wilson (1978) indicates that expectancies alone cannot account fully for alcoholics' relapses. It is necessary to conduct a more thorough assessment of other social learning factors such as the individual's incentives for continued sobriety, the adequacy of the individual's behavioral coping skills, and the availability of an environmental support system that reinforces sobriety.

PERSON–SITUATION INTERACTION

Litman, Eiser, and Taylor (1979) initially became interested in the relapse process in response to previously published reports concerning relapse rates across different forms of addictions (e.g., Hunt *et al.*, 1971). The results of such studies, which showed marked relapse rates within the first 3 months following treatment, were interpreted as supporting a "decay" of the extinction of the addictive behavior that had been accomplished through treatment. Litman, Eiser, and Taylor (1979) criticized the methodology employed in conducting such survival analyses, as well as the inferences drawn from them. Additionally, it was argued that relapse is an individual process that cannot be described adequately by the type of group data that had been employed. Furthermore, data presented by Litman, Eiser, and Taylor (1979) indicated that there were marked individual variations in both the time at which alcoholics first resumed drinking and the patterns of drinking that occurred following an initial slip.

Subsequent research by Litman and her co-workers has attempted to elucidate the factors that contribute to this individual variation in the relapse process. Litman, Eiser, Rawson, and Oppenheim (1977) formulated an approach to relapse described as an interactional perspective (Litman, 1980). Relapse was conceptualized as an interaction among the following factors: situations that are perceived by the individual as dangerous and therefore represent a high risk of relapse; the availability of an adequate repertoire of coping strategies to deal with these situations; and the individual's perception of the potential effectiveness and appropriateness of the behaviors available. The judged effectiveness of these coping strategies, as well as the probability of the individual's attempting to use them, was further thought to be mediated by the degree of "learned helplessness" with which he or she viewed the situation. This conceptualization is quite similar in many ways to the cognitive-expectancy and cognitive–behavioral approaches presented by Marlatt (1978) and Wilson (1978). Thus, the likelihood of relapse would be enhanced in those high-risk situations where the individual felt helpless to cope (e.g., a low level of perceived self-efficacy) due to the lack of effective and/or appropriate behaviors.

Litman *et al.* (1977) conducted a survey of alcoholics to assess those situations which were most likely to precipitate relapse, coping behaviors within the individual's repertoire, and the perceived effectiveness of these behaviors. Four primary high-risk situations were derived through factor analysis. These included negative mood states such as depression and anxiety, external situations or environmental settings that previously had been associated with drinking, social–interpersonal anxiety, and decreased cognitive vigilance and the use of rationalizations to justify taking a drink. The first three of these categories are comparable to ones found by Marlatt and Gordon (1980) to precipitate relapse. The fourth category (decreased cognitive vigilance and rationalizations) is similar to the Apparently Irrelevant Decisions (AIDs) Marlatt discusses in this volume that bring the individual closer to the point of relapse. It was also found that individuals who rated themselves as more dependent on alcohol perceived each of the four high-risk relapse situations as more dangerous to their sobriety than subjects who were less dependent; this was particularly true for lessened cognitive vigilance and rationalizations.

In addition to these high-risk situations, four primary coping strategies were identified. These included two forms of cognitive self-control methods. The first represented positive thinking in which the individual either thought of the benefits of sobriety or challenged faulty motivations. The second involved thinking of all of the negative consequences resulting from drinking. The remaining strategies were behavioral in nature. These included distraction–substitution, in which the individual engaged in behaviors incompatible with drinking, and active avoidance, in which the individual kept away from people or situations associated with drinking in the past.

A subsequent study (Litman, Eiser, Rawson, & Oppenheim, 1979) investigated factors that differentiated alcoholics with a recent episode of drinking from those who had remained sober for at least 6 months. Those subjects who had been drinking perceived significantly more situations as dangerous or as a threat to continued sobriety than did the abstainers. This was particularly true of situations involving negative mood states and external events or cues previously associated with drinking. The two groups did not differ with respect to the judged risk of social anxiety or lessened cognitive vigilance. Coupled with this enhanced risk, the relapsed subjects also appeared to have a more restricted range of coping strategies available to them. This was particularly true of the use of positive thinking as a means of coping, with the abstinent subjects employing this strategy significantly more frequently than those who had relapsed. Finally, the perceived effectiveness of those coping strategies available was lower among the relapsed subjects. The single best discriminator between the two groups was cognitive control as an effective coping strategy. This category included both positive and negative thinking. The abstinent subjects were significantly more likely than those who had relapsed to utilize such cognitive controls in an effective manner. The groups did not differ in the extent to which avoidance and distraction–substitution were perceived as effective methods of coping. Thus, the individual likely to relapse views more situations as threatening to sobriety and has fewer effective ways of dealing with these situations.

As noted earlier, this conceptualization is similar in many respects to that of both Marlatt (1978) and Wilson (1978). It differs from these in some ways, however. While a major component appears to involve the individual's self-perception, the construct of self-efficacy, while implied, is not formally integrated into the model. Also, Litman does not address the mediating role of the individual's expectancies concerning the positive effects of alcohol. A final difference, noted by Litman (1980), has to do with the clinical implications. She notes that the cognitive–behavioral approaches, at least in their early formulation, stressed the importance of social skills training as a primary mode of intervention. However, the interactional perspective emphasizes the flexibility of coping skills and the development of cognitive controls. This latter therapeutic approach would appear to place a relatively greater emphasis on techniques such as cognitive restructuring, rational emotive therapy, covert sensitization, and covert rehearsal. Also, the results of Litman and Oppenheim (1980) suggest that those alcoholics who have remained sober have acquired different coping strategies at different points during the process of recovery. This finding suggests that therapeutic interventions should allow the gradual acquisition of coping behaviors in a hierarchical fashion.

COGNITIVE–BEHAVIORAL FACTORS

Marlatt's conceptualization of relapse (Cummings, Gordon, & Marlatt, 1980; Marlatt, 1978; Marlatt & Gordon, 1980) appears to be the most comprehensive and integrative of those reviewed (see Part I of this book for an updated, revised model). The formulation of this model derived from the evaluation of the relative effectiveness of differing forms of aversive conditioning procedures in the treatment of alcoholism (Marlatt, 1973). It was found that approximately 75% of the subjects had experienced one or more drinking episodes during the 3-month posttreatment follow-up period. A subsequent analysis investigated those emotional and situational factors present at the time the individual took his or her first drink. Four categories, accounting for over 80% of these initial drinking episodes, emerged as broadly defined determinants of relapse. These included feelings of frustration and anger that remain unexpressed, an inability to resist social pressures to drink, intrapersonal negative mood states such as anxiety, depression, loneliness, and boredom, and intrapersonal temptations to drink.

The first three of these categories represented the initial empirical cornerstone from which subsequent research was generated and around which the present formulation evolved. Clinical analogue studies have subsequently validated the extent to which social anxiety (Higgins & Marlatt, 1975), unexpressed anger (Marlatt, Kosturn, & Lang, 1975), and interpersonal peer pressure and modeling (Caudill & Marlatt, 1975) influence alcohol consumption among heavy social drinkers. Subsequent clinical analyses of relapse situations indicate the reliability of these general categories for alcoholism as well as for other addictive behaviors (Chaney, 1976; Cummings et al., 1980; Marlatt & Gordon, 1980).

These identified situational categories represent *high-risk* situations that facilitate return to an initial drink after a period of abstinence, or a *lapse*. Both behavioral and cognitive–expectational components appear to enhance the risk experienced in such situations. On a behavioral level, it appears that some individuals are deficient in those social skills and interpersonal competencies necessary to deal with demands placed on them within these situations. Other individuals may have such skills in their repertoire but may be inhibited from performing them in the high-risk situations. Many alcoholic individuals appear to be characterized by such social skills deficits (Chaney, 1976; Chaney, O'Leary, & Marlatt, 1978; O'Leary, O'Leary, & Donovan, 1976). Peter Miller and his colleagues have demonstrated that alcoholics, in contrast to social drinkers, have difficulties in the area of appropriate assertive skills, particularly the expression of negative feelings. The inability to express such feelings was found to be significantly related to drinking among the alcoholics (Miller & Eisler, 1977; Miller, Hersen, Eisler, & Hilsman, 1974). Similarly, Chaney (1976; Chaney et al., 1978) found that the inability to deal effectively with negative mood states, express anger and resentment, and fend off peer pressures within the high-risk situations is predictive of relapse following treatment.

Three primary sets of cognitions appear to result from, or interact with, these behavioral deficits to further enhance the probability of a "lapse" (Donovan & Marlatt, 1980). The first set of cognitions involves the level of stress and sense of control experienced within the high-risk situation. Sells (1970) and Lazarus, Averill, and Opton (1970) note that the level of stress experienced within any situation is dependent upon the individual's appraisal of the demands of the situation within the context of the perceived availability of coping skills to deal with these demands. When the individual is deficient in the requisite behavioral skills, or has cognitive distortions (e.g., faulty appraisal) or low self-efficacy, the level of perceived stress is increased. Sells (1970) also noted that such stress is interpreted and experienced as a loss of personal control. The decreased perception or experience of control appears to be a second set of the primary cognitions that enhance the probability of drinking (Donovan & Marlatt, 1980; Donovan & O'Leary, 1979, 1983). Furthermore, the lack of adequate behavioral skills compounds a reduced sense of self-efficacy (Bandura, 1977). The belief that one is not capable of executing those behaviors necessary to appropriately resolve a stressful situation will inhibit attempts to exert control in the future. This decreased perception of self-efficacy, combined with behavioral deficits, produces a form of "learned helplessness" which, in addition to enhancing perceived stress levels, also leads to feelings of dysphoria and lowered self-esteem (Abramson, Seligman, & Teasdale, 1978; Litman et al., 1977).

Within this context, the third set of primary cognitions emerges. These have to do with positive expectations individuals hold concerning alcohol and its effects (Brown, Goldman, Inn, & Anderson, 1980; Deardorff, Melges, Hout, & Savage, 1975; Donovan & Marlatt, 1980; Farber, Khavari, & Douglass, 1980). Individuals develop a set of positive outcome expectancies concerning the functional utility of alcohol. These include the enhancement of one's sense of perceived personal and interpersonal control, the escape from or avoidance of unpleasant emotional states, and the facilitation of social assertion and inclusion. These expectations appear to have been associated with and shaped by the initial stimulant effects of alcohol's biphasic response curve prior to the onset of the more negative affective states associated with continued drinking (Marlatt, 1978, 1979). This proposition is consistent with Solomon and Corbit's opponent-process theory (Solomon, 1977; Solomon & Corbit, 1973). It further appears that these anticipated positive effects of alcohol, rather than the actual outcomes, provide both the primary motivation for and reinforcement of drinking among many individuals.

While these anticipated positive outcomes may, in fact, differ from the actual effects of alcohol, they appear to exert a considerable degree of control over drinking behavior and may mediate a return to drinking. As Lindsmith (1968) noted, an individual vividly recalls the efficacy of mind-altering substances such as alcohol even after prolonged periods of abstinence. This may be particularly true in those situations where the individual's own level of self-efficacy is low. When an individual is confronted by such situations, these expectations may be evoked. The presence of internal arousal states and/or environmental cues associated with past drinking, in addition to having secondary reinforcing properties (e.g., Miller, 1976) or eliciting a subclinical withdrawal state (e.g., Ludwig & Wikler, 1974), serves to strengthen and enhance the salience of the positive outcome expectations of drinking. Within this context, the individual's strong desire for the anticipated effects of alcohol may be cognitively interpreted as or attributed to a state of craving (Marlatt, 1978). Consistent with this proposition, Eastman and Norris (1982) found that alcoholics with an abstinence orientation, who maintained positive expectations concerning drinking behavior and drunken states, had a higher probability of relapsing than did alcoholics who did not hold such expectations.

Based upon this formulation (Marlatt, 1976; Marlatt & Donovan, 1981, 1982) the probability of returning to drinking is an interactive function of the situational demands or stresses experienced by the individual, the availability and implementation of effective social skills and coping strategies, the concomitant level of perceived personal control and self-efficacy, and the anticipated positive effects of alcohol. If the individual is confronted by a situation that is appraised as stressful and for which no adequate coping response is available, there is a resultant decrease in the perception of control and self-efficacy. Given these preconditions, in conjunction with the belief that alcohol is an effective means of both decreasing perceived stress and enhancing one's sense of personal control, the probability of drinking is high.

According to Marlatt's perspective (Cummings et al., 1980; Marlatt, 1978; Marlatt & Gordon, 1980), the transition from an initial drink following abstinence (a lapse) to continued drinking (a relapse) is mediated by one's perception of and reaction to the first drink. This mediating process has been termed the Abstinence Violation Effect (AVE) (see Chapter 3 of this book for an updated revision of the AVE). The relative impact of the individual's violation of a voluntary period of abstinence is dependent upon the level of commitment to remaining abstinent and the length of time one has remained sober; the longer the abstinence period and the greater the commitment, the greater will be the intensity of the subjectively experienced AVE.

Two component cognitive–affective processes are subsumed within the AVE construct and are assumed to contribute additively to the individual's reaction and to the probability of continued drinking. The first is a cognitive dissonance effect (Festinger, 1964). During the course of sobriety, the individual develops a self-image based upon the perception of being an abstinent ("recovering") alcoholic; the strength of this perception is enhanced with prolonged sobriety. However, a return to drinking directly confronts and challenges the validity of this self-image. The resultant cognitive dissonance is experienced as an internal conflict characterized by a negative state of arousal involving guilt, depression, and lowered self-esteem. Festinger (1964) suggests that such a state will motivate the individual to engage in behaviors to minimize the experienced dissonance. The same beliefs concerning alcohol's positive outcomes that may have contributed to the initial lapse may, under these circumstances, contribute to continued drinking. This result would be likely to the extent that the individual believes alcohol will serve to minimize the negative mood states associated with the dissonance. Subsequent drinking might also serve to reduce the dissonance by modifying the individual's cognitions and self-image to be consistent with no longer being abstinent.

The second cognitive process involved in the AVE is a personal attribution effect. The individual may have a tendency to attribute the cause of the initial lapse to personal weakness or failure (e.g., stable, internal attributes) rather than to situational factors. The attribution of one's failure to control the outcome of significant life events to personal deficiencies is a defining feature of learned helplessness (Abramson et al., 1978) and would be expected to result in increased dysphoria and a decreased motivation to exert control. This personal attribution process would also result in a decrease in the individual's level of perceived self-efficacy, further reinforcing the belief that he is not capable of coping effectively. To incorporate the work of Wilson (1978) and Rollnick and Heather (1982), the negative components of both the outcome and efficacy expectancies are operative following the initial lapse: the inevitability of relapse following a first drink and one's inability to exert control over drinking. The probability of continued drinking is further enhanced by the individual's beliefs concerning the positive effects of alcohol. In particular, if the individual expects alcohol to minimize negative mood states and to increase one's sense of perceived control, the likelihood of a full-blown relapse is quite high.

COGNITIVE SOCIAL-LEARNING PERSON VARIABLES AND INTERVENTIONS

The previous review indicates that recent models of relapse view both situational and person variables as significant contributors to the relapse process. While it is possible to address aspects of the alcoholic's social situation during the course of treatment, it is more common to find attention focused on thoughts, feelings, and behaviors. As noted previously, certain situations may represent a higher risk of relapse than others. However, it is not the situation in and of itself that is important. Rather, it is the individual's cognitive, affective, and behavioral reactions as they interact with the situational demands that are of relevance. The following section presents suggestions for therapeutic interventions at the level of those cognitive social-learning person variables felt to be of primary salience in the return to drinking.

COGNITIVE CONSTRUCTION COMPETENCIES

Mischel (1973, 1981) indicated that a primary predictor of later social and interpersonal adjustment is the individual's cognitive ability or level of intellectual functioning. Gorski and Miller's (1979) conceptualization of relapse is the only one of those reviewed to take this factor into account. They argue that the PAW negatively impacts on the alcoholic's neuro-psychological processes, particularly those involved in abstract thinking, conceptualization, and concentration. This proposition is consistent with a growing body of evidence that documents the deleterious effect of chronic drinking on neuropsychological functioning. While the alcoholic's verbal abilities remain relatively intact, those skills involved in problem solving, planning, foresight, and the ability to utilize information to make appropriate decisions are markedly impaired (Chelune & Parker, 1981; Goldstein, 1976; Parsons & Farr, 1981). Both age and the length of heavy drinking also influence the level of impairment. Older alcoholics and those who have a longer history of abusive drinking evidence a greater level of impairment (Chelune & Parker, 1981).

Fitzhugh, Fitzhugh, and Reitan (1965) suggested quite some time ago that the nature of alcoholics' neuropsychological deficits may be involved in poor prognosis. Treatment staff easily might come to expect a patient to do well based upon the intactness of verbal skills, but fail to appreciate fully the difficulties involved in trying to adapt to the complexities of posttreatment living. The good verbal facade often masks the more subtle deficits in neuro-psychological functioning (Goldstein, 1976). Chelune and Parker (1981) present a scenario that suggests the way in which such deficits may precipitate relapse. The alcoholic leaving treatment, as part of his or her desire to recapture lost time and encouraged by well-wishing family members and employers, often takes on tasks and assumes responsibilities that may over-tax his or her current adaptive abilities. Often, the individual is not capable of adequately handling all that he or she has taken on. The alcoholic's failure may result in a sense of discouragement, frustration, and inadequacy. These feelings may be enhanced further by the individual's perceived inability to live up to the expectations of others. The felt frustration and dysphoria may precipitate relapse. Chelune and Parker (1981) argue that this outcome may be particularly true among those individuals who have poor problem-solving skills and see no alternative but to return to more established and reinforcing means of dealing with problems, namely drinking.

A number of authors have recently investigated the predictive utility of neuropsychological functioning among alcoholics. Guthrie and Elliot (1980) found that a battery of tests assessing verbal learning, verbal memory, and visual memory was predictive of outpatient aftercare group therapy involvement, with those subjects who were unimpaired at the time of inpatient treatment being more likely to follow through. Also, there appeared to be an inverse relationship between the level of impairment and abstinence. Only 17% of those subjects in the most impaired group were abstinent at a 6-month follow-up period; this contrasted with the 67% abstinence rate among the nonimpaired group. O'Leary, Donovan, and Chaney (1979) found a trend consistent with that of Guthrie and Elliot (1980). Alcoholics who were initially impaired on an index of adaptive problem-solving abilities tended to have more drinking episodes, shorter average periods of total abstinence, and higher average consumption rates of alcohol at a 1-year follow-up period than less impaired individuals. Berglund, Leijonquist, and Horlen (1977) also found that a group of alcoholics whose drinking at follow-up was judged to be improved had a significantly lower score on a pretreatment index of neuropsychological impairment than did a group whose drinking was judged to be unimproved. Gregson and Taylor (1977) also found pretreatment neuropsychological status to predict both drinking and work behavior at follow-up. Furthermore, the level of impairment was found to be more predictive than social and demographic variables that previous research had found to account for the majority of variance in outcome following treatment. More recent research (Donovan, Kivlahan, & Walker, in press; Walker, Donovan, Kivlahan, & O'Leary, 1983) suggests that while neuropsychological impairment is predictive of outcome, other aspects of the alcoholic's psychosocial functioning and posthospitalization support system may be more predictive of subsequent treatment success.

From the perspective of treatment, this body of findings has a number of implications. The first is that verbally mediated, insight-oriented therapy may be relatively inappropriate for neuropsychologically impaired alcoholics. Schau and O'Leary (1977) and Guthrie and Elliot (1980) suggest that such therapies, which appear to be the modal form of treatment, may require more abstracting and conceptualization ability than the individual is capable of handling. Rather, these authors suggest that structured interventions focusing on the development and rehearsal of social and behavioral coping skills might lead to more efficacious outcomes. In a sense, this approach trains the individual in skills that help to *compensate* for the neuropsychological deficits. Second, individuals who are more impaired may require a more prolonged hospitalization period in order to benefit maximally from treatment (Guthrie & Elliott, 1980; O'Leary & Donovan, 1979). Thus, treatment programs may need to be flexible to the extent that is programmatically possible in tailoring length of stay to the level of adaptive abilities. Third, there is evidence that the level of neuropsychological impairment decreases with longer periods of abstinence (Chelune & Parker, 1981; Eckhardt, Parker, Paulter, Noble, & Gottschalk, 1980; Parsons & Farr, 1981). These findings are directly relevant to the timing of various interventions and their potential effectiveness (Chelune & Parker, 1981). Treatment strategies should be introduced sequentially, moving from greater structure and concreteness initially to greater abstractness in accordance with the individual's level of function. This suggestion is consistent with the finding of Litman and Oppenheim (1980) that alcoholics who have remained sober without treatment have utilized different strategies at different stages of recovery. Often they began by behavioral avoidance of drinking situations but were later able to utilize more cognitively sophisticated methods. These latter two clinical implications (e.g., tailoring treatment length to level of impairment and sequential introduction of interventions) appear to be directed at helping to *accommodate* the level of neuropsychological impairment. A fourth implication focuses on helping the individual actively to *overcome* alcohol-induced deficits (e.g., Diller & Gordon, 1981). Cermak (1980) and Hansen (1980) have provided initial overviews of procedures potentially applicable in the cognitive retraining of neuropsychologically impaired alcoholic patients.

Gorski and Miller (1979) have derived a treatment approach based upon the conceptualization of the neuropsychological components of relapse. It appears to follow the first and third of the principles outlined above. The intervention focuses on the development of compensatory problem-solving skills and is sequential in nature. Treatment is divided into relapse prevention and relapse intervention (after the first drink). Relapse prevention has three major emphases: training the individual, involving significant others in the treatment process, and arranging follow-up and reinforcement. The actual clinical intervention is divided into three sequential phases. The first phase of individual training consists of instruction, exploration of individualized events in the relapse chain, and development of a list of personalized warning signs. The second phase consists of daily self-monitoring for the occurrence of warning signs that would suggest the beginning of a relapse chain.

The most extensive component of the relapse prevention training is introduced in the third phase. This consists of problem-solving training and is called *response training*. The procedures are analogous to those outlined by D'Zurilla and Goldfried (1971). Individuals are trained to recognize that a problem exists, define the parameters of the problem, generate a number of behavioral alternatives to the problem, evaluate the short- and long-term consequences of each, choose the most appropriate alternative, and practice it through response implementation. Intagliata (1978) found that alcoholics involved in groups that focused on the development of such skills evidenced significantly higher levels of interpersonal problem-solving abilty than those in a control group. Similarly, the former subjects also had better and more appropriate discharge plans for dealing with impending real-life problems than did the control subjects.

Gorski and Miller (1979) advocate the involvement of significant others in the training process to apprise them of the individual's warning signs and prevention strategies that have been developed and particularly to develop a "denial intervention plan" to specify how others should handle situations in which they are aware of warning signs the patient denies.

Relapse intervention planning is similar in technique to RP, but focuses on ways of dealing with the potential loss of control associated with drinking. Warning signs are identified, appropriate counter plans are developed, and significant others are informed and involved. Since relapse does occur and loss of control may result, Gorski and Miller (1979) suggest that the alcoholic may have occasion to use relapse intervention strategies even if he or she is highly skilled in RP techniques.

BEHAVIORAL CONSTRUCTION COMPETENCIES

A related competency suggested by Mischel (1973, 1981) represents the individual's level of social competence or repertoire of behaviors necessary to cope adequately with a variety of situational demands. Such competencies incorporate interpersonal and emotional problem solving abilities. A number of previous investigations and reviews suggest that deficits in such skills may contribute to drinking problems (e.g., Marlatt et al., 1975; Miller & Eisler, 1977; Miller et al., 1974; O'Leary, O'Leary, & Donovan, 1976). Furthermore, the models presented by Litman et al. (1977) and Marlatt (Cummings et al., 1980; Marlatt, 1978; Marlatt & Gordon, 1980) argue that deficits in one's repertoire of coping skills, particularly those specific to high-risk situations, may contribute to relapse among alcoholics.

Within this context, a primary therapeutic goal would be to increase the alcoholic's repertoire of social skills (Miller, 1978b). Social skills training procedures for alcoholics have been reviewed elsewhere (Van Hasselt, Hersen, & Milliones, 1978; Miller & Hester, 1980), and controlled outcome studies support their efficacy. For example, Jackson and Oei (1978) compared social skills training, cognitive restructuring, and traditional supportive therapy with inpatient alcoholics selected for low social skills. The results indicated that skills training and cognitive interventions were superior to supportive therapy at discharge and follow-up as assessed by interview, staff rating, and self-report measures including alcohol intake. In addition, at the 3-month follow-up, the cognitive restructuring group appeared to be doing better than the skill-training group. Their skill-training intervention consisted of direct training of a variety of social and assertive skills with no direct manipulation of cognitions. The cognitive restructuring group involved direct manipulation of cognitive beliefs but no direct skill training.

The authors concluded that although both approaches were individually useful, maladaptive cognitions may inhibit the individual's use of new responses, suggesting that a combination of the two approaches would be advisable at least for some alcoholics.

Intagliata (1978, 1979) reported on 64 male veterans in inpatient alcoholism treatment assigned to a control group or to 10 sessions of behavioral group therapy specifically designed to improve interpersonal problem-solving thinking skills. Therapy was conducted in small groups and consisted of a rationale, training in problem recognition, definition, generation of alternatives, decision making, and role playing of solutions. Patients reported that learning a logical way to look at problems, not jumping to conclusions, and thinking about more than one way to solve a problem were the most useful aspects of training. Evaluation at program discharge found that problem-solving training subjects had made significantly more improvement on the Means–Ends Problem Solving measure (MEPS; Platt & Spivack, 1975) than controls. Follow-up at 1 month indicated that of the 22 treatment subjects contacted, 14 described using the problem-solving methods to deal with specific real life problems.

Chaney and his colleagues (Chaney et al., 1978) evaluated an eight-session skill-training group intervention with hospitalized male alcoholics. Groups were designed to teach the problem-solving steps of (1) orientation, (2) definition, (3) generation of alternatives, (4) decision making, and (5) verification. The teaching used instruction, modeling, behavioral rehearsal, and coaching, both of actual response behavior and of the cognitive process for generating the response.

Goldfried and D'Zurilla's model (1969) was used to generate relevant training and testing tasks. These were assembled into a manual and the Situational Competency Test (SCT), a role-playing instrument designed to assess the skillfulness of verbal behavior. Forty subjects were assigned randomly to one of three groups: skill-training, discussion control, or no additional treatment control. The three most important findings were that the skills-training subjects showed significant improvement as compared with the other groups in handling difficult tasks as measured by the SCT. Secondly, during the 1-year follow-up period, the skill-training group, on the average, drank one fourth as much as the pooled control groups, spent one sixth as many days drunk, and had an average drinking period length less than one eighth as long. Finally, measures from the predischarge SCT were comparable or superior to demographic and drinking history measures in predicting drinking behaviors during the 1-year follow-up period, accounting for from 16% to 53% of the variance of specific indices. In other words, pretreatment social skill level was an important determinant of treatment outcome. Using a measure like the SCT to assign patients to individualized treatment, may increase cost effectiveness. Further discussion of the Chaney et al. (1978) study can be found in Chapter 2 of this book.

Additional information about the relationship of performance on the SCT and relapse is provided in an independent investigation by Rosenberg (1983), who studied relapsed and nonrelapsed alcoholics who had attended residential treatment. He found that the SCT significantly differentiated between these two groups, although for his sample the relationships were not as strong. He points out that since he gave the SCT after relapse it may be that his findings reflected the influence of relapse on social skill rather than the converse.

Jones, Kanfer, and Lanyon (1982) partially replicated the Chaney *et al.* (1978) study by randomly assigning 20 female and 48 male alcoholic in-patients to skill-training, discussion control, or no additional treatment groups using the training procedures developed by Chaney. Subjects' problem-solving skills were assessed using the Adaptive Skills Battery (ASB; Jones & Lanyon, 1981), an instrument similar to the SCT but scored somewhat differently. Jones *et al.* (1982) found that all three groups showed a significant increase in level of coping skills during treatment. The 1-year follow-up found that both the skill-training and discussion groups drank less and had fewer days drunk than the control group. Unfortunately, the follow-up comprised only 46% of the sample. The authors suggest that their sample may have been sufficiently well functioning prior to treatment to benefit equally from either identifying problematic situations or actually practicing solutions.

In summary, there are sufficient controlled evaluations of assertion or social skills training in alcohol RP to warrant the conclusion that training to improve behavioral construction competencies is effective with at least certain problem drinkers. Many procedural and prescriptive questions remain to be answered. Which clients need skill training? Socially skilled alcoholics may not need behavioral training but may benefit from cognitive restructuring. At the other pole, cognitively impaired alcoholics may not be able to retain and benefit from skills training. What should alcoholics be trained to do? As yet there is little information about what behaviors are most effective in preventing relapse in particular types of situations. Perhaps the major problem in attempting to answer these questions has been the lack of shared formulation of the concept of social skills, which would allow the results of independent studies to be directly compared. To illustrate possible pitfalls, if *social skill* is thought of as a trait, then investigators ask questions like whether alcoholics are more or less socially skilled than other psychiatric patient groups (Monti, Corriveau, & Zwick, 1981). Such a question is too general to be helpful in refining treatment strategies. If, however, the assessment and treatment of social skills deficits focus solely on specific behaviors in particular situations, there are no guidelines for "chunking" situations in order to be able to predict whether a person's performance in one situation will relate to that in any other situation. A *task* analysis of behavior (McFall, 1982; Schwartz & Gottman, 1976) appears necessary. "To assess how adequately a person has performed a particular task, one must understand these important features of that task, its purpose, its constraints, its setting, the rules governing task performance, the criteria for distinguishing between successful and unsuccessful performance, and how the task relates to other aspects of the person's life-system" (McFall, 1982, p. 16).

Although the most widely used model for assessing social competence (Goldfried & D'Zurilla, 1969) has been used productively for group comparison treatment studies, to make sure the results of assessment are useful in treating a particular individual, it is necessary to determine which tasks are relevant to that person. Thus, continued refinement of instruments such as the SCT (Chaney et al., 1978) and the ASB (Jones & Lanyon, 1981) is necessary. One promising improvement is being explored by Annis (Annis, 1984; Annis, Davis, & Levinson, 1981) and Baker (1981) who are attempting to incorporate Bandura's (1977) ideas about self-efficacy and Marlatt's (Marlatt & Gordon, 1980) categorization of relapse situations into assessment instruments. Annis (1984), for example, has developed two scales currently undergoing psychometric evaluation. The first, the *Inventory of Drinking Situations*, assesses the extent to which the individual drank heavily across a wide variety of interpersonal and intrapersonal situations. The second, the *Situational Confidence Questionnaire*, assesses the individual's perceived ability to resist the urge to drink heavily across the same set of situations. DiClemente, Gordon, and Gibertini (1983) are also developing a scale to measure alcoholics' temptation to drink (cue strength) and their confidence that they would not drink (self-efficacy) in a number of drinking situations. Such measures may ultimately be useful in determining alcoholics' needs for skills training and as a means of evaluating the outcome of such training (Annis et al., 1981; Rist & Watzl, 1983).

How should training components be combined to make a cost-effective package for a specific group of clients in a particular treatment setting? As the studies reviewed above suggest, problem drinkers no doubt differ not only in their need for skill training, but also in their ability to benefit from specific treatment components. It has been amply demonstrated that more therapy is not necessarily better therapy (Miller & Hester, 1980). It will require both improved methods of assessing social skills and the optimization of elements of current skill-training packages to specify particular training techniques for particular skills deficits in people faced with particular task demands.

ENCODING STRATEGIES AND PERSONAL CONSTRUCTS

Mischel (1973, 1981) indicates that behavior depends on the "stimulus as coded." Individuals respond to situations as they are perceived, appraised, and interpreted. This theme is found across a number of the models of relapse reviewed. Negative emotional or arousal states often appear to be interpreted as craving, particularly in the presence of prior drinking cues (Ludwig & Wikler, 1974; Marlatt, 1978; Sanchez-Craig, 1975, 1976; Wilson, 1978). The perceived stressfulness of high-risk relapse situations is enhanced when the individual appraises and comes to believe that he or she does not have an appropriate set of coping skills, thus leading to a lowered self-efficacy expectancy and increased subjective helplessness (Lazarus et al., 1970; Litman, Eiser, Rawson, & Oppenheim, 1977, 1979; Marlatt, 1978; Sanchez-Craig, 1976; Wilson, 1978).

The relapse model presented by Sanchez-Craig (1975, 1979) has led to a treatment approach directed at the individual's encoding strategies and personal constructs that may contribute to drinking behavior. This *reappraisal therapy* combines components involving the development of behavioral competencies and cognitive restructuring. Given an analysis of alcohol abuse in terms of how individuals appraise situations, the treatment procedure that Sanchez-Craig developed has the following goals: (1) to enable the person to recognize those situations in which he or she has a tendency to drink; (2) to enable the person to realize that he or she can cope with those situations without drinking; (3) to inhibit the immediate, unthinking tendency to drink; (4) to deliberately change the appraisal of formerly stressful sitautions; and (5) to make an active attempt to change the situation where possible.

The treatment procedure has four facets: identification of drinking episodes, exposure to the stimulus situation in imagination, generation of alternative coping strategies, and cognitive rehearsal of new coping responses. The client is first directed to analyze previous drinking episodes. A focus is placed on antecedents and setting events, the interpretations and feelings about the events, whether the decision to drink was conscious, how it was made, whether faulty thinking was involved, and short- and long-term consequences of drinking for the individual and significant others. After analysis of six to eight drinking episodes, a pattern usually emerges allowing common elements to be identified.

In a more recent version of the treatment (Sanchez-Craig, 1979), three instruments are introduced to facilitate identification of drinking episodes. The *Drinking Diary* is used to keep a record of abstinent and drinking days and drinking behavior. A *Drinking Episodes Questionnaire* is used to elicit descriptions of past drinking episodes which resulted in negative consequences. Finally, during treatment, the *Urges to Drink Questionnaire* is used to specify situations and responses in which the client had a craving to drink but was able to cope with the situation successfully.

For each episode identified, the client is directed in a reappraisal of his or her ability to cope with the situation without drinking. This is done by imaginally recreating the situation and focusing the client's attention on negative elements and on bodily responses, feelings, and thoughts. The goal is to elicit as strong an emotional reaction as possible in order to demonstrate to the client that he or she can in fact tolerate these feelings. The client is then assisted in generating alternative interpretations and positive self-statements and selects the most effective self-statement. Three general types of self-statements are elicited: (1) those which serve as a cue to inhibit immediate action; (2) those which lead to reappraising the actual aversiveness of the situation (e.g., "Are things really all that bad?"); and (3) those which motivate the client to positive action. As the last step in training, the client is instructed to reimagine the formerly aversive situation and practice using the new self-statements. This sequence is repeated for each identified drinking episode.

Reappraisal therapy resembles other multifaceted behavioral approaches to alcohol abuse (Miller, 1978a; Miller & Muñoz, 1976; Sobell & Sobell, 1973). The primary differences are that Sanchez-Craig's approach emphasizes the use of cognitive procedures in coping with "craving" and in the use of successful coping events as a means of identifying strengths in the client that can lead to desired outcomes in the future. Reappraisal therapy can also be compared to Ellis's (Ellis & Harper, 1970) cognitive restructuring techniques with the emphasis on correcting mistaken beliefs. A number of other investigators have focused more specifically on the maladaptive thinking patterns among alcoholics (e.g., Brandsma, Maultsby, & Welsh, 1980; Emery, 1981; McCourt & Glantz, 1980; Whelan & Prince, 1982).

McCourt and Glantz (1980) noted that the maladaptive thought processes of alcoholics are similar to those found among clinically depressed individuals. These include such cognitive styles as arbitrary inferences, dichotomous evaluations of people or situations, overgeneralizations, and thinking that is either overly global and abstract or overly narrow and concrete. Such thought processes tend to taint one's perception, appraisal, and interpretation of themselves, their abilities, the expectations they have of others, and situations with which the individual must deal. McCourt and Glantz (1980) indicate that alcoholics who think in this way are often "locked into" a given pattern of responding, unable to consider or generate other alternatives or to change their perspective. Within this context, alcohol use or relapse may result from such maladaptive cognitions and may represent the only means perceived by the individual for altering his or her experience of problems.

The focus of the cognitive restructuring procedures, or rational-behavior therapy (Brandsma et al., 1980), is to directly challenge and change unrealistic or maladaptive thought processes. A related target for intervention might be those cognitive strategies often referred to as intellectualization, rationalization, and denial. Gorski and Miller (1979) indicate that such defenses are components of a "uniform pattern" that leads to relapse. Similarly, Litman et al. (1977) found that decreased cognitive vigilance and rationalizations were related to relapse. The use of such defenses may underlie individual's making Apparently Irrelevant Decisions (AIDs; Marlatt, 1979) that lead the individual closer to or covertly "set up" a relapse. Litman (1980) has suggested the appropriateness of cognitive restructuring techniques to counter the relapse-enhancing nature of such defenses. In addition, the results of Litman, Eiser, Rawson, and Oppenheim (1979) suggest that the risk of relapse would be reduced by training the individual to use self-statements that challenge faulty motivations, reiterate the positive benefits of sobriety, and/or recognize the negative consequences of drinking.

A final target for possible therapeutic intervention within this general area involves the misattribution process by which negative arousal states are interpreted and cognitively labeled as "craving" (Ludwig & Wikler, 1974; Marlatt, 1978; Sanchez-Craig, 1979; Wilson, 1978). Alcoholics have been described in clinical literature as being deficient in their ability to recognize, differentiate, and label mood states. Within the context provided by both Ludwig and Wikler (1974) and Solomon and Corbit (1973), this deficit may contribute to a tendency to overgeneralize in this interpretation process, cognitively labeling a wide range of internal states as craving. This proposition may be particularly true of individuals who have higher levels of alcohol dependence. The higher incidence of craving reported by highly dependent individuals may reflect both an overgeneralization (similar to an acquired equivalence of classes) or a lack of discrimination of arousal states arising from a variety of sources. An intervention that would focus on the accurate identification and labeling of mood states, as opposed to the automatic interpretation of such states as craving, would be helpful. This might be accomplished by a detailed self-monitoring of the internal and external events the individual associates with craving (e.g., Kennedy, Gilbert, & Thoreson, 1978). The use of Sanchez-Craig's (1979) *Urges to Drink Questionnaire* would appear to facilitate this assessment. Such an analysis would allow the individual to become more aware of the antecedents of internal states and to develop a more differentiated, analytical perspective. The desired outcome of such a procedure would be the reduction of the automatic nature of the misattribution process. Brandsma *et al.* (1980) have described craving as such an automatic process. That is, the individual immediately moves from a perceived event (e.g., negative arousal state) to a felt response (e.g., "craving"). Within the context of rational–emotive therapy (Ellis & Harper, 1970), this represents an "A-to-C" process in which the intermediate cognitive–analytical step is bypassed. The proposed intervention serves to reinstate this previously missing cognitive component.

COGNITIVE EXPECTANCIES

Mischel (1981) indicated that when one turns from what people can do and how they categorize their world to what they actually do, the focus shifts from cognitive and behavioral construction competencies and encoding strategies to the selection and execution of behavior in specific situations. An important set of cognitive social learning person variables in this regard is the individual's expectancies concerning behavioral alternatives in that situation. As such, Mischel (1981) argues that such expectancies or beliefs are central person variables. This tenet also applies to the relapse models reviewed, in that a variety of expectancies are hypothesized to mediate the initial resumption of drinking as well as continued consumption (Donovan & Marlatt, 1980; Donovan & O'Leary, 1979, 1983; Marlatt, 1978; Rollnick & Heather, 1982; Wilson, 1978). These expectancies might be categorized broadly as self-efficacy and outcome expectancies. The influence that these cognitions have on drinking appears to be amenable to a variety of cognitive–behavioral interventions.

Self-efficacy expectancies represent the individual's beliefs concerning his or her ability to execute a behavior needed to produce a desired outcome (Bandura, 1977). The models presented by Marlatt (1978), Rollnick and Heather (1982), and Wilson (1978) suggest that many alcoholics have lowered self-efficacy expectancies secondary to deficits in their repertoire of adaptive coping skills, particularly those required in dealing effectively with high-risk relapse situations. The belief that one is unable to cope effectively may lead to a passive "giving in" to the situational demands and to a reduced likelihood of attempting to exert control in the future. Thus, the probability of relapse is increased.

As noted by Rollnick and Heather (1982) and Wilson (1978), the forms of treatment, as well as the philosophical underpinnings, found in traditionally oriented alcoholism programs may inadvertently reinforce the person's belief in his or her inability to exert control over drinking. Bandura (1977) argued that verbally mediated, insight-oriented therapies are less effective than behaviorally oriented therapies in modifying self-efficacy expectancies. Bandura (1977) noted that performance accomplishments, or successful coping with difficult situations, is a particularly salient source of efficacy information because it is based upon personal mastery experiences. Thus, an appropriate therapeutic intervention would involve training the individual in those behavioral and emotional problem-solving skills necessary to successfully master situations that previously had been beyond the individual's control. The relevant target situations for intervention might be identified through assessment techniques such as self-monitoring of drinking prior to the onset of treatment, self-monitoring of the antecedents of the desire to drink (e.g., "urges," "craving"), relapse fantasies, responses to Chaney's (Chaney et al., 1978) SCT, or ratings of the perceived degree of difficulty the individual anticipates in dealing with high-risk situations (e.g., efficacy estimates; Annis, 1984; DiClemente et al., 1983). Once delimited, behavioral skills are trained through the procedures previously described in the section on behavioral construction competencies. The acquisition of such coping skills is believed to produce a stronger and longer lasting sense of self-efficacy than might be produced by a variety of other techniques appropriate to the modification of these expectancies (Bandura,

1977). Marlatt (1979) has suggested that once the individual has acquired the appropriate coping skills in treatment, providing the individual with the opportunity to practice these skills in actual high-risk situations under therapist supervision (e.g., "dry runs") would potentially increase generalization. The assumption underlying such techniques is that the increased behavioral competence will lead to a corresponding increase in self-efficacy expectancies. The availability of coping skills, and the belief that one can utilize them effectively, would be predicted to minimize relapse.

The results of Rist and Watzl (1983) are of interest. Female alcoholics were provided skills training during the course of a 3-month inpatient treatment program. The focus of the training was to enable patients to reduce the impact of social pressure to drink, and to reject alcoholic beverages. Both before and following the skills training, subjects rated the difficulty involved in not drinking (relapse risk) and the discomfort they could expect to feel (specific assertiveness) in 16 situations of social temptation to drink. They also rated the degree of discomfort they would expect to feel in non-alcohol-related situations requiring an assertive response (general assertiveness). Subjects evidenced significant improvements over all three measures over the course of training. However, differential findings were noted with respect to subsequent drinking outcome at a 3-month follow-up. No differences were found between abstinent and relapsed subjects with respect to the level of general assertiveness. However, both at pretreatment and posttreatment assessments, the abstinent subjects rated themselves as expecting less discomfort and as being less at risk to relapse under social pressure to drink. The authors note that general assertiveness appears to be less useful than alcohol-related assertiveness in predicting later drinking status. In a similar manner, the beliefs one holds about the ability to perform adequately and exert control (self-efficacy expectancies) in high-risk drinking situations would appear critical to relapse (Donovan & O'Leary, 1983; Rollnick & Heather, 1982).

While performance accomplishments represent a major source of information about self-efficacy, Bandura (1977) noted that there are a number of other avenues through which such expectancies can be modified. The first of these is vicarious experience, involving both live and symbolic modeling. An added advantage of the "dry run" suggested by Marlatt (1979) is that the individual observes other alcoholic clients utilizing acquired coping skills within high-risk situations. The relapse rehearsal technique described by Marlatt (1979), which is analogous to the procedures described by Sanchez-Craig (1979), represents a symbolic, covert rehearsal process in which the individual imagines or visualizes himself or herself engaging in appropriate adaptive behaviors. These modeling and covert practice experiences may instill the belief that if others can cope effectively, then the individual is able to achieve some improvement also. This belief can be reinforced further by verbal persuasion techniques, which represent an additional source of efficacy information (Bandura, 1977). The negative cognitive set accompanying low self-efficacy expectancies may need to be challenged through techniques such as cognitive restructuring. Through such a process, the individual is led to believe on a cognitive–attitudinal level that he or she is able to cope effectively with situations that previously had been beyond his or her control. Furthermore, in order to minimize the debilitating influence that low self-efficacy expectancies might exert on actual attempts to engage in adaptive problem-solving behavior, the individual might be trained in self-instructional and self-reinforcement techniques (e.g., Meichenbaum, 1977). These intervention strategies would provide self-directed guidance and increased incentive to persist in executing coping behaviors in the face of lingering doubts about one's ability which are based upon past experiences of failure.

A final source of efficacy information involves the experience and interpretation of emotional arousal (Bandura, 1977). As noted previously, the lack of available skills needed to cope effectively with high-risk situations may result in an increased perception of stress, arousal, tension, or anxiety (Lazarus et al., 1970; Sells, 1970). This may lead to a reduced sense of personal control, further reinforcing the individual's belief that he or she is unable to cope (e.g., reduced self-efficacy). It is anticipated that the acquisition of requisite coping behaviors would lead to a reduction in the level of perceived stress. Bandura (1977) noted that perceived self-competence reduces one's susceptibility to self-arousal, thereby reducing the frequency and/or intensity of negative cognitions that typically interfere with performance. Thus, the likelihood of performance successes is increased and, in turn, leads to a strengthening of self-efficacy. Sanchez-Craig's (1979) therapy approach appears to deal more directly with the perceived stress on a cognitive level. Imagery techniques are employed to elicit intense emotional reactions in relation to past or anticipated relapse situations, allowing the individual to experience these feelings and to learn that they are tolerable. Additionally, the individual is assisted in reinterpreting, reappraising, and reattributing the nature, causes, or consequences of the perceived stress. This procedure is similar to the technique of induced affect originally developed by Sipprelle (1967). In this technique, which has evolved into a cognitive–behavioral self-control strategy (e.g., Smith, 1980; Smith & Ascough, in press), the individual is trained to utilize deep breathing, relaxation, and coping self-statements to reduce high levels of arousal while maintaining the symbolic representation of the affect-inducing situation. Thus, the individual is able to exert control over emotions that previously were believed to be beyond personal control.

The second broad category of expectancies represents outcome expectancies, which Bandura (1977) argues are conceptually distinct from self-efficacy. Outcome expectancies represent the belief that a particular behavior will produce certain outcomes. Two subsets of this larger class of expectancies are involved in the relapse models reviewed. The first represents the positive expectancies individuals hold concerning the perceived benefits of drinking. The second involves the expectations an individual holds concerning the outcome of an initial drink after a period of abstinence. Marlatt's (1978) model has placed the greatest emphasis on the perceived benefits of drinking as a mediator in the relapse process. Individuals have come to believe that alcohol can serve a variety of positive functions, such as mood alteration, social facilitation, and the enhancement of perceived control (Brown *et al.*, 1980; Donovan & Marlatt, 1980). The anticipated functions appear to fall along two primary dimensions (Farber *et al.*, 1980). The first is an escape-drinking/negative-reinforcement dimension in which the person drinks in order to avoid or escape unpleasant internal and/or external stimuli. The second is a social-drinking/positive-reinforcement dimension, involving drinking in response to social pressures or as a means to achieve certain social goals such as peer acceptance or approval.

It is hypothesized that the salience of these positive drinking-related outcome expectancies is increased in those situations which have been associated with drinking in the past and for which the person has no adequate coping skills (Donovan & Marlatt, 1980; Marlatt & Donovan, 1981). Thus, it would be anticipated that the acquisition of behavioral competencies (as well as the accompanying increase in self-efficacy) would reduce the salience of these expectancies. Other interventions might address these expectancies more directly. Emery (1981) has identified a number of common "thinking errors" that lead to alcohol use: (1) escape from feeling bad ("I can't stand feeling bad"), (2) dealing with hopelessness ("There's nothing else for me"), (3) replacing social skills ("I can deal better with people after a few drinks"), and (4) escape from stress ("The arguing, yelling, and lack of money won't bother me"). It is felt that each of these beliefs is an appropriate target for cognitive restructuring techniques. Marlatt (1979) has suggested that an educational approach might also be employed, utilizing the basic framework of Solomon and Corbit's (1974) opponent-process model. Thus, clients are instructed concerning alcohol's biphasic response pattern and that drinking, while temporarily producing a positive state, typically results in affective states directly opposite from those expected and desired.

The second subset of outcome expectancies pertains to beliefs associated with an initial lapse. The negative outcome expectancy is that if the alcoholic resumes drinking this will lead to an uncontrolled relapse (Rollnick & Heather, 1982; Wilson, 1978). According to Gorski and Miller (1979), alcoholics are "programmed" to continue drinking because they have been taught that this is an inevitable outcome. The task of the therapist is to remove the "fulfillment" from an otherwise self-fulfilling prophecy. Again, cognitive restructuring techniques can be utilized to challenge the validity of this belief system, providing the client with scientific and clinical information that counters the contention. Adjunctively, former clients who have experienced an initial lapse but successfully prevented a subsequent bout of uncontrolled drinking might be called upon to share their experiences; rather than providing a "drunkalogue," they instead can present "self-controlalogues." A final technique in this area is represented by Marlatt's (1979) programmed relapse procedure. Although not applicable in a number of treatment settings where alcohol administration is not feasible, this technique allows the client the opportunity for "hypothesis testing" under controlled and supervised conditions. The hypothesis under consideration is "one drink, a drunk." By removing a number of the environmental cues and setting events associated with past drinking, as well as the cognitive, expectational, and affective components related to high-risk relapse situations, the individual is better able to objectively experience and explore the impact of and reactions to drinking. The purpose of such a "clinical trial" is to minimize factors that typically lead to "experimentor bias" among alcoholics who otherwise would "experiment" with drinking under "uncontrolled" conditions. The hope of the therapist is that the "null hypothesis" obtains, that is, the client will obtain no "significant effects" from drinking. This outcome is predicated upon past research that has demonstrated that alcohol consumption in the absence of drinking-related cues and/or cognitive sets does not lead to an increase in craving or uncontrolled drinking (Engle & Williams, 1972; Ludwig & Wikler, 1974; Ludwig et al., 1974; Maisto et al., 1977; Marlatt et al., 1973).

Although not properly defined as an expectancy, the final cognitive factor to be discussed in this section is the attributional process associated with the AVE (Marlatt, 1978; Marlatt & Gordon, 1980). While this process might be classified more appropriately as an encoding strategy or personal construct, its operation directly influences expectancies that the individual generates following an initial lapse. It is hypothesized that the individual attributes the resumption of drinking to personal factors such as a lack of willpower or internal weakness. The attribution of failure to control the outcome of significant events to such internal, stable factors is a defining characteristic of personal helplessness (Abramson et al., 1978). Abramson et al. (1978) noted that personal helplessness is related to both efficacy and outcome expectancies; personal helplessness involves a low self-efficacy in conjunction with a high outcome expectancy. In Rollnick and Heather's (1982) model, this would correspond to the belief that one is not able to control drinking in the future (e.g., negative efficacy expectancy), and therefore will not be able to maintain the desired goal of lifelong abstinence (e.g., positive outcome expectancy).

In addition to the depression and lowered self-esteem accompanying personal helplessness, a particularly relevant motivational deficit also occurs. The belief that outcomes are uncontrollable retards the initiation of potentially adaptive coping responses. This feature is also comparable to the contention of Bandura (1977) that lowered self-efficacy expectancies impede both the initiation and persistence of coping behavior. Phenomenologically, the cognitive and motivational sets appear to translate into one of the categories of "thinking errors" that Emery (1981) suggests is related to drinking among alcoholics: "What's the use? There's nothing else for me." Marlatt (1978) argues that such a cognitive set, resulting from the attribution of failure to stable personal causes rather than to changeable situational factors, increases the individual's expectancy for continued failure. As such, the probability that the initial lapse will continue into a prolonged relapse also increases.

Marlatt and Gordon (1980) have outlined a behavioral intervention aimed at reducing the likelihood of transition from lapse to relapse. This involves the negotiation of a set of rules and guidelines that govern behavior surrounding an initial drink. These might involve agreeing to delay taking the first drink for a specified period of time after an urge to begin drinking, agreeing to limit an initial lapse to a single drink, and taking a "time out" period following an initial drink to reconsider the continuation of drinking. Clients are also given reminder cards that specify the steps to take following an initial drink.

Cognitive restructuring techniques again appear appropriate to deal with the helplessness associated with the personal attribution process. Abramson *et al.* (1978) have outlined a number of relevant intervention strategies based upon the learned helplessness model. If an individual has the requisite behavioral coping skills available in his or her repertoire, then the therapist attempts to modify the client's distorted expectation that these responses will fail. The goal is to change the expectation from one of uncontrollability to controllability. A second focus is to change the actual attribution away from internal, stable, and global or generalized factors. The literature reviewed by Abramson *et al.* (1978) suggests that the attribution of failure to external, unstable, and specific factors reduces the severity, chronicity, and generality of the affective, cognitive, and motivational consequences of helplessness. This reattribution process is similar to that suggested by Marlatt in Chapter 4 of this book. The individual is instructed to review the situational factors that may have contributed to or precipitated the lapse (e.g., external factors). The individual might also attribute the drinking to a momentary lapse in motivation or a lack of skills that can be acquired through further practice (e.g., unstable factors). Finally, the lapse is viewed as a unique, independent event that occurred within a specific situational context (e.g., specific factors).

SUBJECTIVE VALUES AND PREFERENCES

Mischel (1981) notes that the behaviors individuals choose to perform depend, in part, on the subjective values of the outcomes they expect. With respect to drinking behavior, it appears somewhat difficult to make a clear distinction between the expectancies one holds concerning the perceived benefits of alcohol consumption and one's subjective values and preferences. However, Rotter (1966, 1975) and others (e.g., Donovan & Marlatt, 1980; Donovan & O'Leary, 1983) have attempted to provide such a conceptual distinction. Donovan and Marlatt (1980) have suggested that the value attached to a given outcome is both subjective and relative in nature, and is defined as the degree of preference an individual has for a given outcome. When a person consistently behaves in such a way as to obtain a certain reinforcing outcome from a number of alternatives available in a given situation, then that reinforcer is prepotent or has the highest level of perceived value. This contention appears to have particular relevance to alcoholics who choose to engage in drinking rather than in other behaviors incompatible with drinking that might lead to equally reinforcing outcomes. Thus, it appears that drinking has acquired a subjectively valued positive valence for the alcoholic.

Attempts to change alcoholics' subjective preference for alcohol have the longest history in the behavioral treatment literature and, with qualifications, have generated some of the most impressive results. The general premise has been that if alcohol-related cues could be conditioned to evoke immediate unpleasant affect, drinking would be deterred. Aversive techniques including apneic paralysis, chemically induced nausea, electric shock and more recently cognitive techniques such as covert sensitization and videotaped self-confrontation of intoxication have been applied (Baker & Cannon, 1979; Miller & Hester, 1980). In a review of the aversive conditioning literature over a decade ago, Bandura (1969) suggested that the prevalent respondent conditioning theory was too simplistic and that evidence supported the existence of cognitive mediation. Thus, in successful aversion training, external stimuli come to activate a self-stimulation mechanism which, in turn, produces the aversive reactions. The utility and effectiveness of the aversion will depend more on cognitive factors than precision of the conditioning paradigm.

Opponent-process theory suggests that alcohol's valence is a function of drinking history and that it changes from positive to negative reinforcement as the individual becomes habituated. For a given individual, hedonic a processes remain relatively constant over time and repeated occurrences. It is the b process that grows stronger. From this point of view, learned aversion, no matter what the operational paradigm used, has two potential uses for the alcoholic: (1) counteracting a positive reinforcer (the alcoholic A state); and (2) counteracting arousal stimuli for drinking. In the latter process, the negative hedonic state produced by the aversive stimulation may become associated to cues previously associated with drinking and must be stronger than the positive drinking a process to be effective in relapse prevention. To the degree that addictive behavior is composed of avoidance and escape behavior motivated by the aversive alcoholic B′ state and phenomenologically similar states, punishment might simply intensify the urge to drink and indeed this often seems to take place in self-confrontation of drinking behavior. Patients may become so aroused viewing their own past drinking behavior that they leave treatment and return to drinking. Given that the B′ state which is hypothesized to motivate the avoidance operants has been weakened, successful aversive conditioning should have two results. The stimuli surrounding the initiation of drinking behavior should become less pleasant. If the individual then avoided these stimuli, he or she would be avoiding drinking situations. By experiencing these previously positively valenced stimuli less often, the individual also would experience the conditioned aversive opponent process less often. If he or she did drink, the conditioned aversion should produce an immediate, unpleasant affect, aborting further drinking. Aversive conditioning would not be expected to have a direct effect on the drinking behavior components of escape, the avoidance of cues previously associated with withdrawal, or similar overgeneralized B states (i.e., anxiety or stress from other sources). Thus, as Bandura points out, the individual must have incentives in the form of other sources of positive reinforcement (and the necessary skills) if aversion therapy is to be helpful rather than harmful.

Aversion therapy appears most useful with individuals having intact jobs and marriages who presumably have alternative behaviors in their repertoire to take the place of drinking. Even for fairly well functioning individuals, however, booster sessions may be necessary to maintain the effect (Vogler, Lunde, Johnson, & Martin, 1970). With regard to technique, there have been few direct comparisons of chemical and electrical aversion (Jackson & Smith, 1978), and their relative effectiveness is unknown. Chemical aversion techniques in particular are well developed (Bandura, 1969) and it is doubtful that procedural modifications have much to offer in the way of increased utility. Cognitive and verbal aversion techniques are newer and, by comparison, less well developed and evaluated. However, such techniques are more congruent with the view of aversion training as a self-control procedure. For instance, results of covert sensitization procedures, the primary verbal aversion method to date, have been mixed. It appears that there is a person-by-treatment interaction in that subjects who develop conditioned nausea (i.e., become nauseous to images of alcohol alone) have better outcome than those who are only able to develop nausea upon demand (Elkins, 1977). This suggests that the conditioning process itself is important. Another technique, self-confrontation of videotaped drunken behavior, can be a very unpleasant experience with the danger of increased stress and early treatment drop out, but with the potential of synergistic effect when combined with skill training (Baker, Udin, & Vogler, 1975). Again, it appears necessary that subjects have skills sufficient to achieve alternate reinforcement.

A more recent approach to changing the valence of stimuli related to alcohol consumption is to focus on the negatively reinforcing aspects of drinking, that is, to try to do something about the propensity of withdrawal-related cues to trigger "craving." Pickens, Bigelow, and Griffiths (1973) appear to be the first investigators to have presented a systematic method for extinguishing cues associated with the aversive B state (CS_Bs). One component of treatment in this single-case study was a procedure in which stimuli that had been associated with past drinking were presented to the patient immediately before some scheduled activity such as a meal, so that the patient was given a choice between drinking and performing an incompatible response. CS_Bs were presented in a hierarchy progressing from drinking situations to sniffing and testing alcohol in increasingly large amounts until at the end of the program the patient was able to drink two drinks without going on to further drinking. This type of extinction technique should receive further investigation as a means of decreasing the overdetermined nature of relapse by weakening conditioned cues for drinking. Hodgson and Rankin (1976) also present a case study suggesting that CS_Bs can be extinguished, and have proposed a more extensive treatment regimen based upon cue exposure (Rankin & Hodgson, 1977).

Recently, Rankin, Hodgson and Stockwell (1983) presented a controlled evaluation of this technique in hospitalized alcohol-dependent individuals. The experimental group received six sessions of *in vivo* cue exposure and response prevention training. In these sessions subjects were given two priming drinks of their preferred alcoholic beverage and then were instructed to resist consuming a third available drink. The control subjects received no alcohol during their six sessions. Rather, they were instructed to imagine drinking scenes and mentally practice resisting drinking in those situations ("imaginal cue exposure"). Only one of the experimental subjects consumed the third drink when it was available. In comparing performance on behavioral drinking tests before and after the respective interventions, experimental subjects showed significant increases in their drinking time whereas control subjects did not. This result was interpreted as indicating a differential decrease in craving, since the authors measured craving in terms of speed of consuming alcohol. The finding is also consistent with and supported by the experimental subjects' decreases on subjective measures of desire for a drink and difficulty in resisting. Although this study indicates that cue exposure methodology could be a useful adjunct to treatment, the extent to which results would generalize to the natural environment still is unknown.

In summary, from an interactional perspective, it appears that in most cases, the change mechanism involved in manipulations of the subjective value of alcohol is cognitive in nature. It appears to depend on the individual having adopted self-regulatory systems and plans consistent with using responses learned in aversive conditioning, punishment or extinction paradigms as self-control strategies when later faced with drinking cues. In any event, the subjective value of alcohol for the experienced drinker is a complex and overdetermined variable, not likely to be treated effectively with aversion therapy alone.

SELF-REGULATORY SYSTEMS AND PLANS

The last of the cognitive social-learning person variables described by Mischel (1981) is the individual's self-regulatory systems and plans. These represent cognitive and behavioral strategies relevant to the generation and maintenance of goal-directed behavior even in the absence of environmental supports. The development of such strategies appears to be particularly important for alcoholics attempting to remain abstinent following treatment, since the environments to which they return are often more conducive to drinking than to sobriety.

By this point in the treatment process, it is assumed that the client will have been well trained in specific techniques to minimize the probability of relapse. However, as Marlatt (1979) notes, it is not sufficient to train the individual in specific skills appropriate to a limited number of personally defined high-risk relapse situations. While the use of generalized problem-solving skills is likely to increase the individual's ability to deal with a somewhat broader range of situations, the development of more global intervention strategies appears necessary. Marlatt (1979) argues that such a global, comprehensive intervention package should involve at least three components: (1) intervening in the client's overall lifestyle with the goal of increasing one's ability to cope with generalized stress and high-risk situations with an increased sense of self-efficacy; (2) identifying and responding to situational, interpersonal, and intrapersonal cues that should serve as early-warning signals; and (3) exercising self-control strategies to reduce the relapse-enhancing potential of any situation the individual encounters.

A number of recent generalized self-control strategies would appear well-suited to the last of these three goals. Marlatt and Gordon (1980) have found that situations involving negative affect, particularly depression or unexpressed frustration and anger, account for a large percentage of relapse. While the development of situation-specific skills has been found to be an effective intervention (e.g., Chaney et al., 1978), the availability of more generalized mood-management strategies might enhance treatment outcome. With respect to depression, two complementary interventions might be employed. The first involves learning depression self-management skills. These might include increasing involvement in pleasant activities, learning to relax, becoming more socially skillful in interpersonal relationships, controlling negative self-defeating thoughts, increasing positive self-reinforcing thoughts, providing oneself with appropriate coping-oriented self-statements, and gaining constructive problem-solving skills (Lewinsohn, Muñoz, Youngren, & Zeiss, 1978). The second strategy would involve general assertiveness training. Such training would provide the individual with an appropriate avenue for expressing aspects of covert hostility, particularly resentment, that appear to accompany depression. The acquisition of assertive behavior has been shown to result in a decrease in depression (Sanchez & Lewinsohn, 1980).

Novaco (1975, 1976, 1977) has developed a cognitive–behavioral program that seems particularly suited to those individuals for whom situations involving unexpressed frustration and anger represent a high risk of relapse. The goal of the intervention is to enable the individual to recognize anger and its source in the environment and then communicate the anger in a nonhostile form. The acquisition of the cognitive, physiological, and behavioral self-control skills leads to a decrease in the levels of arousal and irritability, reduces the accumulation of anger, prevents an aggressive overreaction, and provides a means for adaptively changing the situation that caused the anger (Novaco, 1977).

It appears that the decrease in depression and anger and increase in assertiveness produced by these intervention strategies are accompanied by an increased perception of personal control and self-efficacy (Kazdin, 1979; Novaco, 1977; Zeiss, Lewinsohn, & Muñoz, 1979). The individual is provided with a set of skills that can be employed to deal effectively with a specific problem area. However, as the person gains increased confidence in the ability to handle such problems, the effects begin to generalize to other life difficulties (Bandura, 1977). The increased perception of control is likely to result in decreased drinking.

A similar outcome could be predicted for a variety of stress-management techniques. As noted previously in the discussion of cognitive expectancies, the technique of induced affect has been promoted as a cognitive–behavioral self-control strategy in which the person gains mastery over arousal states and emotions which previously were believed to be beyond personal control (Smith & Ascough, in press). Generalized relaxation and meditation techniques may operate along similar lines (see Chapter 5). With respect to drinking behavior, Marlatt and Marques (1977) found that heavy social drinkers who engaged in either deep muscle relaxation or a meditative technique showed a significant reduction in alcohol consumption compared to a no-treatment control group. It was also found, somewhat unexpectedly, that an "attention control" group whose members spent a comparable amount of time in recreational reading evidenced a similar reduction in drinking. The reduced alcohol consumption across these three groups appears to have been mediated by an increased level of perceived personal control. It may be that merely taking time out from the rigors of normal life stress, regardless of the nature of the specific stress-reducing activities, is an important feature in minimizing the probability of drinking. Such strategies may contribute to the lifestyle balance that Marlatt and Gordon (1980) argue is a necessary component of RP. As noted in Chapter 5, if the individual does not provide himself or herself with sufficient opportunities to take time out, he or she may begin to experience the burdens of the day (e.g., a high shoulds-to-wants ratio) and feel increasingly justified in taking a drink. This chain of events may be facilitated by Apparently Irrelevant Decisions (AIDs) and rationalizations. The general stress-management skills are meant to interrupt this cognitive–behavioral chain. Similarly, Marlatt (Marlatt & Marques, 1977) has suggested that both meditation and relaxation training provide the individual with a greater sense of objectivity and detachment. This cognitive set may lead to a more accurate appraisal of situational demands and may minimize the likelihood of being "hooked" into habitual response patterns by arousal states that in the past were interpreted as craving. Also, from the perspective of the opponent-process model, the cognitive and physiological states produced by such techniques may be phenomenologically comparable to the hedonic A state previously achieved through drinking.

Finally, the individual must have a plan that insures the utilization of those specific and general skills that he or she has acquired. Emery (1981) notes that such a plan should be comprehensive in nature. It should include attempts to solve those problems that contribute to one's drinking, plans to avoid situations that in the past have led to the problem, ways to think and behave differently if one finds oneself in a high-risk situation, awareness of and cognitive correction for thinking errors and beliefs that may enhance the desirability of drinking, an alertness or vigilance with respect to critical incidents (e.g., a moment that requires making a decision that will affect one's attempt to remain abstinent), and caution against making AIDs that might lead one closer to relapse. The client should have a thorough knowledge of and competence in the execution of the components of his or her individually tailored plan, allowing a relatively automatic series of responses when needed. The mobilization and implementation of the plan would appear to be crucial when the individual begins to experience "apprehension about well-being" (Gorski & Miller, 1979). Gorski indicates that this sense of fear, uncertainty, and lack of confidence in one's ability to stay sober, which appears to be somewhat analogous to a decrease in self-efficacy expectancies, is often the first event in a behavioral chain leading to relapse.

The relapse road map technique described by Marlatt in Chapter 4 of this book represents such a comprehensive plan of action. During the early developmental phases of abstinence suggested by Litman and Oppenheim (1980), or when the individual feels particularly vulnerable, one might utilize stimulus control and avoidance strategies. The individual "steers clear of" and minimizes contact with prior drinking acquaintances, drinking-related cues, and high-risk relapse situations. These techniques are similar to the active avoidance and substitution–distraction factors that Litman *et al.*

(1977, 1979) and Sjöberg, Samsonowitz, and Olsson (1978) found to be primary means of coping among recovering alcoholics. The individual also must be aware of the presence of factors, both situational and intrapersonal, that may represent warning signals of impending relapse precipitants. Failure to do so may lead to decreased cognitive vigilance, increased rationalization, and an increased likelihood of making AIDs, all of which may increase the probability of relapse (Litman, Eiser, Rawson, & Oppenheim, 1977, 1979; Marlatt, 1979). Gorski and Miller (1979) also emphasize the importance of involving significant others at this stage and instructing them in how to deal with warning signs that they observe but that the client denies. An additional component of the plan involves the use of the cognitive self-control methods found by Litman *et al.* (1977). These include thinking of the positive benefits of sobriety, referred to by Rollnick and Heather (1982) as the positive treatment outcome expectancies, and thinking of the negative consequences of drinking. This process is comparable to the use of a more structured decision matrix presented by Marlatt (1979). In this procedure (also described in Chapter 4), the client reviews both the immediate and delayed positive and negative consequences associated with the choice either to resume drinking or to remain abstinent. The hope is that such a review, with an emphasis on the delayed effects, will counter the individual's focus on the immediate positive effects of drinking and thus reduce the probability of responding based upon a desire for immediate gratification. Within the relapse road map procedure, the individual is able to utilize the above techniques to identify early warning signals, predict or anticipate potential high-risk situations before they occur, and plan alternative strategies to cope with them.

The goal of both the specific and global strategies is to help the individual gain increased cognitive and behavioral control that will minimize the probability of relapse. However, the actuarial statistics suggest that a large percentage of individuals will return to drinking. It is at this point that one's approach must shift from relapse prevention to relapse intervention in which the individual must mobilize strategies to deal with the potential loss of control associated with a first drink (Gorski & Miller, 1979). This would involve a number of specific counterplans, including the previously discussed cognitive restructuring strategies to deal with the attributional processes and the affective components of the AVE (see Chapter 4). Also, the individual should be provided with a reminder card that provides a detailed outline of the previously negotiated behavioral contract specifying the steps to take in order to regain control and to seek therapeutic support. Gorski and Miller (1979) suggest that involvement of significant others in the development and implementation of relapse intervention strategies may be of particular importance. The goal of these interventions is to keep the individual from crossing over the threshold from an initial lapse to a full-blown relapse.

SOCIAL SUPPORT SYSTEMS

As several of the models discussed above point out, person variables interact with the environment to determine whether and when relapse will occur. Studies of remission of problematic drinking in the absence of formal treatment (incorrectly termed spontaneous remission) suggest that availability of nonalcohol-related leisure activities, support from family and friends, and the existence of a relatively stable social and economic situation are important factors in the maintenance of behavior change (Billings & Moos, 1983; Tuchfeld, 1981). Unfortunately, in many cases the problem drinker's environment may exacerbate his or her difficulties.

With regard to the effects of such factors on alcohol consumption, the two most studied social roles are work and family. Roman and Trice (1970) illustrate the interrelationship between person and situation factors in drinking with their analysis of occupational risk factors for excessive drinking. They delineate several situational types that present a risk that social drinking will become excessive drinking. These are situations in which: (1) clear performance goals are absent; (2) hours of work and schedules of output are flexible and at individual option; (3) task requirements keep one away from the view of supervisors; (4) work addiction is encouraged; (5) occupational obsolescence occurs; (6) regular drinking is required as part of work role performance; (7) pathological drinking patterns accrue benefits to others; and (8) there is a transition from a setting in which social control is present and heavy drinking is an accepted means of releasing tension into a setting in which the stresses are still present, but the controls are absent. Any of these situations would presumably make it more difficult for the heavy drinker to abstain or to moderate his or her drinking. A comprehensive individualized RP treatment package would have to take cognizance of such situational demands.

The importance of the family environment in shaping and restricting the behavioral options of the problem drinker also has been studied. For instance, Steinglass (1979) applied a general systems approach to the alcoholic's family or group. The alcoholic's reference group or family can be viewed as a working system in which each member carefully selects or manipulates each other member and adjusts his or her own behavior so that there is a complementary relationship of needs, strengths, and values. The purpose of such maneuvering is to maintain the solidity of the family group ensuring that the members of the system stay together. Drinking behavior may be both a sign of stress in the system, and an integral part of one of the working programs within the system. On the basis of observation of hospitalized couples allowed access to alcohol, Steinglass suggests that for some couples, excessive drinking by one or both individuals temporarily reduces tensions within the family system, and the success of this behavior tends to reinforce continued drinking. Change in the drinking behavior of one member may pose a threat to marital solidity and may be countered by behavior of other members of the unit. The frequency of coping behavior by wives of alcoholics has been found to be related to their husband's drinking outcome (Orford, Guthrie, Nicholls, Oppenheimer, Egert, & Hensman, 1975), suggesting that there is a relationship between the spouse's response to drinking behavior and the individual's success in moderating it.

Attempts to intervene in the marital relationship of problem drinkers as part of multimodal interventions have received empirical support (Hedberg & Campbell, 1974; McCrady, Paolino, Longabaugh, & Rossi, 1979; Steinglass, 1979). However, relationship-oriented behavioral techniques developed with other populations have not yet been systematically integrated and evaluated as relapse prevention strategies (Chaney, 1978; Chaney & Ostrow, 1979; O'Farrell & Cutter, 1979).

Gorski and Miller (1979), for instance, propose that significant others may have had harmful reactions to the patient's previous relapses and need to be brought into treatment to be informed of and involved in the patient's RP strategies and in relapse intervention strategies. A *denial intervention* plan could be created, getting the patient to specify how others should confront him with behavior indicating imminent relapse. Significant others can also be involved in the relapse intervention plan; specifically, based on the patient's unique history, how should family members respond to a relapse? Gorski suggests that these plans and agreements needs to be refreshed and renewed for at least 1–2 years following treatment. For many families, these techniques are likely to be insufficient. Couples' assertiveness and communication training and contracting for behaviors to enhance marital satisfaction also may be necessary.

The most comprehensive research to date on the combined effects of environmental stressors and supports on alcoholics' posttreatment functioning is that of Moos and his colleagues (Billings & Moos, 1981, 1983; Bromet, Moos, Bliss, & Wuthmann, 1977; Cronkite & Moos, 1980; Moos, Finney, & Chan, 1981). One set of Moos's data consists of long term follow-up information from approximately 120 relapsing and nonrelapsing alcoholics treated in one of five residential programs who came from and returned to a family setting. One study (Moos et al., 1981) compares the alcoholics to community controls matched for sex, age, ethnicity, religion, education, and family size. Relapsed alcoholics were found to experience more negative and fewer positive life events than recovered patient and community controls. Successfully treated alcoholics appear to create relatively benign conditions for themselves such as developed social support networks, cohesion and low conflict in family relationships, and low time-urgency and pressure in work settings, all of which may help to prevent relapse.

There have been very few attempts to help alcoholics systematically modify their postdischarge environment. Hunt and Azrin (1973) evaluated a community reinforcement program designed to rearrange the vocational, family, and social reinforcers of the alcoholic in such a way that time out from reinforcement would occur if he or she began to drink. In the area of vocational counseling, a variety of techniques were used to increase the patient's job-finding skills until he or she did, in fact, get a job. In the area of marital and family counseling, a contingency contracting approach was employed. For patients who were neither married nor living with their family, attempts were made to arrange a synthetic or foster family. In the area of social counseling, a former tavern was converted into a self-supporting social club for clients. In addition, attempts were made to provide such enrichments as a driver's license, telephone service, and a newspaper subscription where absent. Follow-up over a 6-month period indicated that the community reinforcement patients remained more sober than controls, spent more time gainfully employed, with their families and out of institutions, earned twice as much, and spent more time on weekends in socially acceptable activities. An important aspect of the treatment as it actually took place seems to have been providing new operants by systematically training and actively programming reinforcement in areas of social, family, and vocational activities. Not only were external sources of reinforcement manipulated, but new skills and environments decreased the probability of exposure to situations in which drinking had previously occurred. More recently Azrin (1976) has presented a modified community-reinforcement approach incorporating the use of Antabuse, an early-warning notifications system to alert the counselor if problems are developing, group counseling to increase treatment cost effectiveness, and a neighborhood friend–advisor to continue social support after the initial counseling period. Although attempts to modify the alcoholic's posttreatment environment are difficult and expensive, for many clients, this may be a *sine qua non* of relapse prevention.

SUMMARY AND DISCUSSION

The previous review, while not exhaustive, has clearly indicated that relapse among alcoholics is a highly probable, complex, multifaceted phenomenon. Psychobiological, behavioral, cognitive-expectancy, attributional, and appraisal components appear to contribute to the relapse process. Previous models that have attempted to explain addiction or relapse in terms of only one of these primary variable classes appear to provide limited, incomplete, and ill-defined frameworks. Much as Engle (1977) identified the need for a more comprehensive biopsychosocial model in the biomedical sciences, Lindsmith (1968) appears to have anticipated the need to integrate a broader range of constructs in an attempt to understand addiction more fully. He argued that neither psychological nor physiological factors alone were sufficient to explain addiction. Rather, addiction appears to develop and be maintained by an interaction between these two classes of variables. Both physiological factors and the acquired meaning or interpretation given them by the individual are indispensable features of the total experience and process of addiction. While this assertion was made with respect to opioid addiction, the review in this chapter suggests that it applies with equal validity to alcohol dependence. Since alcoholism and relapse appear to be multidimensional processes, it is necessary to approach them in a multivariate manner.

From a clinical standpoint, a number of issues emerged during the course of the review. The first is that relapse must be viewed as a two-stage process, involving the chain of events that leads to a lapse and the chain of events that moderates the probability of the initial drink escalating to a more serious relapse. In the past it appears that much therapeutic time and energy has been directed at the first of these two processes, with only a minimal focus on the second. In order to achieve successful therapeutic outcomes it will be necessary to modify treatment staffs' orientation to view each of these two components of relapse as equally important. Such an approach may have secondary benefits in addition to those directly related to the client's treatment. Such a reorientation, focusing on both relapse prevention and relapse intervention, may reduce the negative stigma that treatment personnel often implicitly attach to an individual's return to drinking. Treatment staff frequently communicate their displeasure with a client who relapses, which may contribute to the client's already self-induced feelings of failure, guilt, and shame. Others may also try to help the client reconceptualize his or her relapse as yet another phase in the progressively deteriorating course of the disease of alcoholism. Such well-meaning interventions may inadvertently reinforce the individual's beliefs about his or her inability to exert control over drinking. The reorientation that would accompany the adoption for a relapse prevention–intervention approach might suggest to both the client and clinician that relapse need not be inevitable and totally devastating. Rather, it would encourage attributions regarding controllability, the role of effort, and the need to pursue additional treatment avenues to reduce the probability of relapse and its impact if one does violate a personal commitment to abstinence.

A second issue concerns the clinical tasks implied in a multivariate, multimodal approach to alcoholism and relapse. One implied task involves assessment. Given the wide variety of psychobiological and situational components and cognitive social-learning person variables in the relapse process, the extent and breadth of the factors assessed must be expanded. This represents a somewhat imposing task, particularly for those variables that are more cognitive in nature (e.g., appraisals, attributions, efficacy and outcome expectancies, and coping ability). Such variables appear to be difficult to operationalize within the framework of assessment (Donovan & Marlatt, 1980). Thus, the increased move toward RP as a therapeutic approach also ushers in an increased need for the development and validation of assessment techniques focusing on person variables and situational factors. The recent work on the development of self-report measures focusing on aspects of alcohol dependence and its correlates (Kaplan *et al.*, 1983; Raistrick, Dunbar, & Davidson, 1983; Skinner & Allen, 1982; Stockwell, Hodgson, Rankin, & Taylor, 1979, 1982; Stockwell, Murphy, & Hodgson, 1983), on alcohol-related efficacy expectancies (Annis, 1984; DiClemente *et al.*, 1983), and on behavioral and self-report measures of one's ability to cope with high-risk relapse situations (Chaney *et al.*, 1978; Jones & Lanyon, 1981; Litman, Stapleton, Oppenheim, & Peleg, 1983) should serve as models for others who undertake such a task. This chapter's review also suggests the importance of components that fall more on the physiological end of the continuum. Therefore it is important to include measures of factors such as neuro-psychological status, the severity of alcohol dependence, and craving in an assessment battery. A theoretically coherent approach to multivariate assessment, including measures of each of the major person–situation classes outlined above, would provide a systematic basis for pretreatment evaluation, individualized therapy, and the identification of future threats to the client's sobriety.

Clinical assessment is conducted with a purpose. In addition to delimiting salient parameters of the problem, a primary goal of assessment is to aid the clinician in differential treatment planning. This represents the second general clinical task implied in a multivariate approach to alcoholism and relapse. The wide variety of factors contributing to relapse necessitates a multimodal approach to treatment based upon the assessed strengths and deficits of the client. A number of points are relevant to this task. First, the two-stage process of relapse suggests that different therapeutic strategies need to be employed to help the client deal with each of the stages. Thus, the term *relapse prevention* (RP) is too narrow in scope. Rather, as Gorski and Miller (1979) suggest, it is necessary to train the individual (as well as significant others in the social support network) in those skills falling within the categories of RP and relapse intervention. Second, it appears important to present therapeutic interventions in a sequential fashion commensurate with the individual's ability to understand and effectively implement them. In most cases this may mean a movement from more concrete behavioral strategies early in treatment to more abstract cognitively oriented ones across time. This continuum appears to follow the "natural course" of recovery employed by individuals who were able to achieve and maintain sobriety without formal treatment (Litman & Oppenheim, 1980). Finally, while therapeutic interventions must initially focus on those deficits targeted through assessment, it is necessary to provide the individual with a set of general skills (e.g., self-regulatory systems and plans) that will allow him or her to cope effectively with a wide variety of potential problem areas. Rather than providing the individual with specific skills to master specific problems, the clinical task should involve increasing both the extent and flexibility of coping skills, as well as efficacy expectations regarding their appropriate application. Such an orientation focuses on the generalization of coping to increase the maintenance of therapeutic gains.

A final issue is more general in nature and deals with the role played by psychological models. Cognitive social learning theory has provided a framework within which to conceptualize alcoholism and relapse. As such, it has served many of the functions suggested by Tarter and Schneider (1976) as appropriate for a psychological model. However, one such function is yet to be fulfilled. A primary function of a model is to guide hypothesis generation and empirical tests, which constitute the foundation from which theory building may emerge. As noted in the introduction, there currently are insufficient data available to propose a comprehensive theory of relapse. However, there are sufficient data to suggest the outlines of the territory that such a theory should encompass. It has been our task to outline these general areas; our task has been completed. It is now the task of the clinician and researcher to generate hypotheses and test them. It is only in this way that the model of relapse presented in this volume can be validated and built into a viable theory. Litman (1980) has warned that without appropriate operationalization and empirical validation of constructs, psychologically oriented models of alcoholism will be as open to criticism as previous medical models have been. Thus, without continued effort the currently emergent cognitive social-learning model of alcoholism may suffer a lapse (or relapse?) into a state of disrepute similar to that experienced by its predecessors in the process of scientific evolution.

ACKNOWLEDGMENTS

The preparation of the present chapter was supported in part by the Health Services Research and Development Service of the Veterans Administration. Appreciation is expressed to Daniel Kivlahan for his review of and insightful comments on previous versions of the manuscript.

REFERENCES

Abramson, L. Y., Seligman, M. E. P., & Teasdale, J. Learned helplessness in humans: Critique and reformulation. *Journal of Abnormal Psychology*, 1978, *87*, 49–74.

American Psychiatric Association. *Diagnostic and statistical manual of mental disorders* (3rd ed.; DSM-III). Washington, D.C.: American Psychiatric Association, 1980.

Annis, H. M. A relapse prevention model for treatment of alcoholics. In D. Curson & H. Rankin (Eds.), *Alcoholism relapse*. London: Logos Alpha, 1984.

Annis, H. M., Davis, C., & Levinson, T. *The prevention of alcoholic relapse: A research proposal*. Unpublished manuscript, Addiction Research Foundation, Toronto, Ontario, Canada, 1981.

Azrin, N. H. Improvements in the community-reinforcement approach to alcoholism. *Behaviour Research and Therapy*, 1976, *14*, 339–348.

Baker, L. H. *Relapse prevention in alcoholics: Process and outcome*. Unpublished manuscript, Veterans Administration Medical Center, Newington, Conn., 1981.

Baker, T. B., & Cannon, D. S. Taste aversion therapy with alcoholics: Techniques and evidence of a conditioned response. *Behaviour Research and Therapy*, 1979, *17*, 229–242.

Baker, T. B., Udin, H., & Vogler, R. E. The effects of videotaped modeling and self-confrontation on the drinking behavior of alcoholics. *International Journal of the Addictions*, 1975, *10*, 779–793.

Bandura, A. *Principles of behavior modification*. New York: Holt, Rinehart & Winston, 1969.

Bandura, A. Self-efficacy: Toward a unifying theory of behavioral change. *Psychological Review*, 1977, *84*, 191–215.

Bateson, G. *Steps to an ecology of mind*. New York: Ballantine, 1972.

Berglund, M., Leijonquist, H., & Horlen, M. Prognostic significance and reversibility of cerebral dysfunction in alcoholics. *Journal of Studies on Alcohol*, 1977, *38*, 1761–1770.

Billings, A. G., & Moos, R. H. The role of coping responses and social resources in attenuating the stress of life events. *Journal of Behavioral Medicine*, 1981, *4*, 139–158.

Billings, A. G., & Moos, R. H. Psychosocial processes of recovery among alcoholics and their families: Implications for clinicians and program evaluators. *Addictive Behaviors*, 1983, *8*, 205–218.

Brandsma, J. M., Maultsby, M. C., & Welsh, R. J. *Outpatient treatment of alcoholism: A review and comparative study*. Baltimore: University Park Press, 1980.

Bromet, E., Moos, R., Bliss, F., & Wuthmann, C. Posttreatment functioning of alcoholic patients: Its relation to program participation. *Journal of Consulting and Clinical Psychology*, 1977, *45*, 829–842.

Brown, S. A., Goldman, M. S., Inn, A., & Anderson, L. R. Expectations of reinforcement from alcohol: Their domain and relation to drinking. *Journal of Consulting and Clinical Psychology*, 1980, *48*, 419–426.

Caddy, G. R. Toward a multivariate analysis of alcohol abuse. In P. E. Nathan, G. A. Marlatt, & T. Løberg (Eds.), *Alcoholism: New directions in behavioral research and treatment*. New York: Plenum, 1978.

Caudill, B. D., & Marlatt, G. A. Modeling influences in social drinking: An experimental analogue. *Journal of Consulting and Clinical Psychology*, 1975, *43*, 405–415.

Cermak, L. S. Improving retention in alcoholic Korsakoff patients. *Journal of Studies on Alcohol*, 1980, *41*, 159–169.

Chaney, E. F. *Skill training with alcoholics*. Doctoral dissertation, University of Washington, 1976. (University Microfilms No. 77-557)

Chaney, E. F. *Development and evaluation of a behavioral marital therapy program for outpatient alcoholics*. Paper presented at the annual meeting of the Western Psychological Association, San Francisco, 1978.

Chaney, E. F., O'Leary, M. R., & Marlatt, G. A. Skill training with alcoholics. *Journal of Consulting and Clinical Psychology*, 1978, *46*, 1092–1104.

Chaney, E. F., & Ostrow, F. *Descriptive time-series examination of behavioral marital therapy for alcoholics*. Paper presented at the annual meeting of the Western Psychological Association, San Diego, Calif., 1979.

Chelune, G. J., & Parker, J. B. Neuropsychological deficits associated with chronic alcohol abuse. *Clinical Psychology Review*, 1981, *1*, 181–195.

Cronkite, R. C., & Moos, R. H. Determinants of the posttreatment functioning of alcoholic patients: A conceptual framework. *Journal of Consulting and Clinical Psychology*, 1980, *48*, 305–316.

Cummings, C., Gordon, J. R., & Marlatt, G. A. Relapse: Prevention and prediction. In W. R. Miller (Ed.), *The addictive behaviors*. New York: Pergamon Press, 1980.

Davies, D. L. Definitional issues in alcoholism. In R. E. Tarter & A. A. Sugerman (Eds.),

Alcoholism: Interdisciplinary approaches to an enduring problem. Reading, Mass.: Addison-Wesley, 1976.

Davis, D. Mood changes in alcoholic subject with programmed and free-choice experimental drinking. In N. K. Mello & J. H. Mendelson (Eds.), *Recent advances in studies of alcoholism.* Washington, D.C.: U.S. Government Printing Office, 1971.

Deardorff, C. M., Melges, F. T., Hout, C. N., & Savage, D. J. Situations related to drinking alcohol: A factor analysis of questionnaire responses. *Journal of Studies on Alcohol,* 1975, *36,* 1184–1195.

DiClemente, C. C., Gordon, J. R., & Gibertini, M. *Self-efficacy and determinants of relapse in alcoholism treatment.* Paper presented at the annual meeting of the American Psychological Association, Anaheim, Calif., 1983.

Diller, L., & Gordon, W. A. Interventions for cognitive deficits in brain injured adults. *Journal of Consulting and Clinical Psychology,* 1981, *49,* 822–834.

Donovan, D. M., Kivlahan, D. R., & Walker, R. D. Clinical limitations of neuropsychological testing in predicting treatment outcome of alcoholics. *Alcoholism: Clinical and Experimental Research,* in press.

Donovan, D. M., & Marlatt, G. A. Assessment of expectancies and behaviors associated with alcohol consumption: A cognitive–behavioral approach. *Journal of Studies on Alcohol,* 1980, *41,* 1153–1185.

Donovan, D. M., & O'Leary, M. R. Control orientation among alcoholics: A cognitive social learning perspective. *American Journal of Drug and Alcohol Abuse,* 1979, *6,* 487–499.

Donovan, D. M., & O'Leary, M. R. Control orientation, drinking behavior and alcoholism. In H. M. Lefcourt (Ed.), *Research with the locus of control construct* (Vol. 2: *Development and social problems*). New York: Academic Press, 1983.

D'Zurilla, T., & Goldfried, M. Problem-solving and behavior modification. *Journal of Abnormal Psychology,* 1971, *78,* 107–126.

Eastman, C., & Norris, H. Alcohol dependence, relapse and self-identity. *Journal of Studies on Alcohol,* 1982, *43,* 1214–1231.

Eckardt, M., Parker, E. S., Paulter, C., Noble, E., & Gottschalk, L. Neuropsychological consequences of post-treatment drinking behavior in male alcoholics. *Psychiatry Research,* 1980, *2,* 135–147.

Edwards, G. The alcohol dependence syndrome: Usefulness of an idea. In G. Edwards & M. Grant (Eds.), *Alcoholism: New knowledge and new responses.* London: Croom Helm, 1977.

Edwards, G., & Gross, M. M. Alcohol dependence: Provisional description of a clinical syndrome. *British Medical Journal,* 1976, *1,* 1058–1061.

Ekman, G., Frankenhaeuser, M., Goldberg, L., Bjerver, K., Järpe, G., & Myrsten, A. Effects of alcohol intake on subjective and objective variables over a five hour period. *Psychopharmacology,* 1963, *4,* 28–38.

Ekman, G., Hagdahl, R., & Myrsten, A. Subjective and objective effects of alcohol as functions of dosage and time. *Psychopharmacology,* 1964, *6,* 399–409.

Elkins, R. L. A therapeutic phoenix: Emergent normal drinking by "failures" in an abstinence-oriented program of verbal aversion therapy for alcoholism. *Scandinavian Journal of Behavior Therapy,* 1977, *6* (Suppl. No. 4), 55. (Abstract)

Ellis, A., & Harper, R. A. *A guide to rational living.* Englewood Cliffs, N.J.: Prentice-Hall, 1970.

Emery, G. *A new beginning: How you can change your life through cognitive therapy.* New York: Simon & Schuster, 1981.

Endler, N. S., & Magnusson, D. Toward an interactional psychology of personality. *Psychological Bulletin,* 1976, *83,* 956–974.

Engle, G. The need for a new medical model: A challenge for biomedicine. *Science,* 1977, *196,* 129–136.

Engle, K. B., & Williams, T. K. Effect of an ounce of vodka on alcoholics' desire for alcohol. *Quarterly Journal of Studies on Alcohol,* 1972, *33,* 1099–1105.

Farber, P. D., Khavari, K. A., & Douglass, F. M. A factor analytic study of reasons for drinking: Empirical validation of positive and negative reinforcement dimensions. *Journal of Consulting and Clinical Psychology*, 1980, *48*, 780–781.

Festinger, L. *Conflict, decision and dissonance*. Stanford: Stanford University Press, 1964.

Fitzhugh, L. C., Fitzhugh, K. B., & Reitan, R. M. Adaptive abilities and intellectual functioning in hospitalized alcoholics. *Quarterly Journal of Studies on Alcohol*, 1965, *26*, 402–411.

Glatt, M. M. The question of moderate drinking despite "loss of control." *British Journal of Addiction*, 1967, *62*, 267–274.

Glatt, M. M. Alcoholism disease concept and loss of control revisited. *British Journal of Addiction*, 1976, *71*, 135–144.

Goldfried, M. R., & D'Zurilla, T. J. A behavior analytic model for assessing competence. In C. D. Spielberger (Ed.), *Current topics in clinical and community psychology* (Vol. 1). New York: Academic Press, 1969.

Goldstein, G. Perceptual and cognitive deficit in alcoholics. In G. Goldstein & C. Neuringer (Eds.), *Empirical studies of alcoholism*. Cambridge: Ballinger, 1976.

Gorski, T. T., & Miller, M. *Counseling for relapse prevention*. Hazel Creste, Ill.: Alcoholism Systems Associates, 1979.

Gregson, R. A. M., & Taylor, G. M. Prediction of relapse in men alcoholics. *Journal of Studies on Alcohol*, 1977, *38*, 1749–1760.

Guthrie, A., & Elliot, W. A. The nature and reversibility of cerebral impairment in alcoholism: Treatment implications. *Journal of Studies on Alcohol*, 1980, *41*, 156–158.

Hansen, L. Treatment of reduced intellectual functioning in alcoholics. *Journal of Studies on Alcohol*, 1980, *41*, 156–158.

Heath, D. B., Waddell, J. O., & Topper, M. D. (Eds.). Cultural factors in alcohol research and treatment of drinking problems. *Journal of Studies on Alcohol*, 1981 (Suppl. No. 9).

Heather, N., Rollnick, S., & Winton, M. A comparison of objective and subjective measures of alcohol dependence as predictors of relapse following treatment. *British Journal of Clinical Psychology*, 1983, *22*, 11–17.

Heather, N., Winton, M., & Rollnick, S. An empirical test of "a cultural delusion of alcoholics." *Psychological Reports*, 1982, *50*, 379–382.

Hedberg, A. G., & Campbell, L. A comparison of four behavioral treatments of alcoholism. *Journal of Behavior Therapy and Experimental Psychiatry*, 1974, *5*, 251–256.

Higgins, R. L., & Marlatt, G. A. Fear of interpersonal evaluation as a determinant of alcohol consumption in male social drinkers. *Journal of Abnormal Psychology*, 1975, *84*, 644–651.

Hodgson, R. J. The alcohol dependence syndrome: A step in the wrong direction? A discussion of Stan Shaw's critique. *British Journal of Addiction*, 1980, *75*, 255–263.

Hodgson, R. J., & Rankin, H. J. Modification of excessive drinking by cue exposure. *Behaviour Research and Therapy*, 1976, *14*, 305–307.

Hodgson, R. J., Rankin, H. J., & Stockwell, T. R. Alcohol dependence and the priming effect. *Behaviour Research and Therapy*, 1979, *17*, 379–387.

Hunt, G. M., & Azrin, N. H. A community-reinforcement approach to alcoholism. *Behaviour Research and Therapy*, 1973, *11*, 91–104.

Hunt, W. A., Barnett, L. W., & Branch, L. G. Relapse rates in addiction programs. *Journal of Clinical Psychology*, 1971, *27*, 455–456.

Intagliata, J. C. Increasing the interpersonal problem-solving skills of an alcoholic population. *Journal of Consulting and Clinical Psychology*, 1978, *46*, 489–498.

Intagliata, J. C. Increasing the responsiveness of alcoholics to group therapy: An interpersonal problem-solving approach. *Group*, 1979, *3*, 106–120.

Isbell, H. Craving for alcohol. *Quarterly Journal of Studies on Alcohol*, 1955, *16*, 38–42.

Jackson, P., & Oei, T. P. S. Social skills training and cognitive restructuring with alcoholics. *Drug and Alcohol Dependence*, 1978, *3*, 369–374.

Jackson, T. R., & Smith, J. W. A comparison of two aversion treatment methods for alcoholism. *Journal of Studies on Alcohol*, 1978, *39*, 187–191.

Jellinek, E. M. *The disease concept of alcoholism.* New Haven, Conn.: Hillhouse Press, 1960.

Jones, B. M., & Parsons, O. A. Alcohol and consciousness: Getting high and coming down. *Psychology Today,* 1975, *8,* 53–58.

Jones, S. L., Kanfer, R., & Lanyon, R. I. Skill training with alcoholics: A clinical extension. *Addictive Behaviors,* 1982, *7,* 285–290.

Jones, S. L., & Lanyon, R. I. Relationship between adaptive skills and outcome of alcoholism treatment. *Journal of Studies on Alcohol,* 1981, *42,* 521–525.

Kalant, H. Direct effects of ethanol on the nervous system. *Federation Proceedings,* 1975, *34,* 1930–1941.

Kaplan, R. F., Meyer, R. E., & Stroebel, C. F. Alcohol dependence and responsivity to an ethanol stimulus as predictors of alcohol consumption. *British Journal of Addiction,* 1983, *78,* 259–267.

Kazdin, A. E. Imagery elaboration and self-efficacy in the covert modeling treatment of unassertive behavior. *Journal of Consulting and Clinical Psychology,* 1979, *47,* 725–733.

Keller, M. On the loss-of-control phenomenon in alcoholism. *British Journal of Addiction,* 1972, *67,* 153–166.

Kelly, G. A. *The psychology of personal constructs: A theory of personality.* New York: W. W. Norton, 1955.

Kennedy, R. W., Gilbert, G. S., & Thoreson, R. A self-control program for drinking antecedents: The role of self-monitoring and control orientation. *Journal of Clinical Psychology,* 1978, *34,* 238–243.

Kissin, B. The pharmacodynamics and natural history of alcoholism. In B. Kissin & H. Begleiter (Eds.), *The biology of alcoholism* (Vol. 3). New York: Plenum, 1974.

Kuhn, T. S. *The structure of scientific revolutions* (2nd ed.). Chicago: University of Chicago Press, 1970.

Lazarus, R. S. *Psychological stress and the coping process.* New York: McGraw-Hill, 1966.

Lazarus, R. S., Averill, J., & Opton, E. Towards a cognitive theory of emotion. In M. Arnold (Ed.), *Feelings and emotions.* New York: Academic Press, 1970.

Lewinsohn, P. M., Muñoz, R. F., Youngren, M. A., & Zeiss, A. M. *Control your depression.* Englewood Cliffs, N.J.: Prentice-Hall, 1978.

Lindsmith, A. R. *Addiction and opiates.* Chicago: Aldine, 1968.

Litman, G. K. Relapse in alcoholism: Traditional and current approaches. In G. Edwards & M. Grant (Eds.), *Alcoholism treatment in transition.* London: Croom Helm, 1980.

Litman, G. K., Eiser, J. R., Rawson, N. S. B., & Oppenheim, A. N. Towards a typology of relapse: A preliminary report. *Drug and Alcohol Dependence,* 1977, *2,* 157–162.

Litman, G. K., Eiser, J. R., Rawson, N. S. B., & Oppenheim, A. N. Differences in relapse precipitants and coping behavior between alcohol relapsers and survivors. *Behaviour Research and Therapy,* 1979, *17,* 89–94.

Litman, G. K., Eiser, J. R., & Taylor, C. Dependence, relapse, and extinction: A theoretical critique and a behavioral examination. *Journal of Clinical Psychology,* 1979, *35,* 192–199.

Litman, G. K., & Oppenheim, A. N. *A model for alcoholism survival.* Unpublished manuscript, Addiction Research Unit, Institute of Psychiatry, London, England, 1980.

Litman, G. K., Stapleton, J., Oppenheim, A. N., & Peleg, M. An instrument for measuring coping behaviors in hospitalized alcoholics: Implications for relapse prevention treatment. *British Journal of Addiction,* 1983, *78,* 269–276.

Ludwig, A. M., Bendfeldt, F., Wikler, A., & Cain, R. B. "Loss of control" in alcoholics. *Archives of General Psychiatry,* 1978, *35,* 370–373.

Ludwig, A. M., & Stark, L. H. Alcohol craving: Subjective and situational aspects. *Quarterly Journal of Studies on Alcohol,* 1974, *35,* 899–905.

Ludwig, A. M., & Wikler, A. "Craving" and relapse to drink. *Quarterly Journal of Studies on Alcohol,* 1974, *35,* 108–130.

Ludwig, A. M., Wikler, A., & Stark, L. H. The first drink: Psychobiological aspects of craving. *Archives of General Psychiatry,* 1974, *30,* 539–547.

Magnusson, D., & Endler, N. S. (Eds.). *Personality at the crossroads: Current issues in inter-actional psychology*. Hillsdale, N.J.: Erlbaum, 1977.

Maisto, S. A., Lauerman, R., & Adesso, V. J. A comparison of two experimental studies investigating the role of cognitive factors in excessive drinking. *Journal of Studies on Alcohol*, 1977, *38*, 145–149.

Maisto, S. A., & Schefft, B. K. The constructs of craving for alcohol and loss of control drinking: Help or hindrance to research. *Addictive Behaviors*, 1977, *2*, 207–217.

Marlatt, G. A. *A comparison of aversive conditioning procedures in the treatment of alcoholism*. Paper presented at the annual meeting of the Western Psychological Association, Anaheim, Calif., 1973.

Marlatt, G. A. Alcohol, stress, and cognitive control. In I. G. Sarason & C. D. Spielberger (Eds.), *Stress and anxiety* (Vol. 3). Washington, D.C.: Hemisphere Publishing, 1976.

Marlatt, G. A. Craving for alcohol, loss of control and relapse: A cognitive–behavioral analysis. In P. E. Nathan, G. A. Marlatt, & T. Løberg (Eds.), *Alcoholism: New directions in behavioral research and treatment*. New York: Plenum, 1978.

Marlatt, G. A. Alcohol use and problem drinking: A cognitive–behavioral analysis. In P. C. Kendall & S. D. Hollon (Eds.), *Cognitive–behavioral interventions: Theory, research, and procedures*. New York: Academic Press, 1979.

Marlatt, G. A., Demming, B., & Reid, J. B. Loss of control drinking in alcoholics: An experimental analogue. *Journal of Abnormal Psychology*, 1973, *81*, 233–241.

Marlatt, G. A., & Donovan, D. M. Alcoholism and drug dependence: Cognitive social learning factors in addictive behaviors. In W. E. Craighead. A. E. Kazdin, & M. J. Mahoney (Eds.), *Behavior modification: Principles, issues, and applications* (2nd ed.). Boston: Houghton Mifflin, 1981.

Marlatt, G. A., & Donovan, D. M. Behavioral psychology approaches to alcoholism. In E. M. Pattison & E. Kaufman (Eds.), *Encyclopedic handbook of alcoholism*. New York: Gardner Press, 1982.

Marlatt, G. A., & Gordon, J. R. Determinants of relapse: Implications for the maintenance of behavior change. In P. O. Davidson & S. M. Davidson (Eds.), *Behavioral medicine: Changing health lifestyles*. New York: Brunner/Mazel, 1980.

Marlatt, G. A., Kosturn, C. F., & Lang, A. R. Provocation to anger and opportunity for retaliation as determinants of alcohol consumption in social drinkers. *Journal of Abnormal Psychology*, 1975, *84*, 652–659.

Marlatt, G. A., & Marques, J. K. Meditation, self-control and alcohol use. In R. B. Stuart (Ed.), *Behavioral self-management: Strategies, techniques and outcomes*. New York: Brunner/Mazel, 1977.

McCourt, W., & Glantz, M. Cognitive behavior therapy in groups for alcoholics: A preliminary report. *Journal of Studies on Alcohol*, 1980, *41*, 338–346.

McCrady, B. S., Paolino, T. J., Longabaugh, R., & Rossi, J. Effects of joint hospital admission and couples treatment for hospitalized alcoholics: A pilot study. *Addictive Behaviors*, 1979, *4*, 155–165.

McFall, R. M. A review and reformulation of the concept of social skills. *Behavioral Assessment*, 1982, *4*, 1–34.

Meichenbaum, D. *Cognitive-behavior modification: An integrative approach*. New York: Plenum, 1977.

Mello, N. K. Behavioral studies of alcoholism. In B. Kissin & H. Begleiter (Eds.), *The biology of alcoholism* (Vol. 2). New York: Plenum, 1972.

Mendelson, J. H., & Mello, N. K. Behavioral and biochemical interrelations in alcoholism. In W. P. Creger, C. H. Coggins, & E. W. Hancock (Eds.), *Annual review of medicine* (Vol. 27). Palo Alto, Calif.: Annual Reviews, 1976.

Miller, P. M. *Behavioral treatment of alcoholism*. New York: Pergamon, 1976.

Miller, P. M. Behavior therapy in the treatment of alcoholism. In G. A. Marlatt, & P. E. Nathan

(Eds.), *Behavioral approaches to alcoholism.* New Brunswick, N.J.: Rutgers Center of Alcohol Studies, 1978. (a)

Miller, P. M. Alternative skills training in alcoholism treatment. In P. E. Nathan, G. A. Marlatt, & T. Løberg (Eds.), *Alcoholism: New directions in behavioral research and treatment.* New York: Plenum, 1978. (b)

Miller, P. M., & Eisler, R. M. Assertive behavior of alcoholics: A descriptive analysis. *Behavior Therapy,* 1977, *8,* 146–149.

Miller, P. M., Hersen, M., Eisler, R. M., & Hilsman, G. Effects of social stress on operant drinking of alcoholics and social drinkers. *Behaviour Research and Therapy,* 1974, *12,* 67–72.

Miller, W. R., & Caddy, G. R. Abstinence and controlled drinking in the treatment of problem drinkers. *Journal of Studies on Alcohol,* 1977, *38,* 986–1003.

Miller, W. R., & Hester, R. K. Treating the problem drinker: Modern approaches. In W. R. Miller (Ed.), *The addictive behaviors.* New York: Pergamon, 1980.

Miller, W. R., & Muñoz, R. F. *How to control your drinking.* Englewood Cliffs, N.J.: Prentice-Hall, 1976.

Mischel, W. Toward a cognitive social learning reconceptualization of personality. *Psychological Review,* 1973, *80,* 252–283.

Mischel, W. A cognitive–social learning approach to assessment. In T. V. Merluzzi, C. R. Glass, & M. Genest (Eds.), *Cognitive assessment.* New York: Guilford, 1981.

Monti, P. M., Corriveau, D. P., & Zwick, W. Assessment of social skills in alcoholics and other psychiatric patients. *Journal of Studies on Alcohol,* 1981, *42,* 526–528.

Moos, R. H., Finney, J. W., & Chan, D. A. The process of recovery from alcoholism: 1. Comparing alcoholic patients and matched community controls. *Journal of Studies on Alcohol,* 1981, *42,* 383–402.

Nathan, P. E. Studies in blood alcohol level discrimination. In P. E. Nathan, G. A. Marlatt, & T. Løberg (Eds.), *Alcoholism: New directions in behavioral research and treatment.* New York: Plenum, 1978.

Nathan, P. E. Nonproblem drinking outcomes: The data on controlled drinking. *Advances in Alcoholism,* 1981, *2*(12), Whole No. 12.

Nathan, P. E., & O'Brien, J. S. An experimental analysis of the behavior of alcoholics and nonalcoholics during prolonged experimental drinking: A necessary precursor of behavior therapy? *Behavior Therapy,* 1971, *2,* 455–476.

National Council on Alcoholism (Criterion Committee). Criteria for the diagnosis of alcoholism. *American Journal of Psychiatry,* 1972, *129,* 127–135.

Novaco, R. W. *Anger control: The development and evaluation of an experimental treatment.* Lexington, Mass.: D. C. Heath, 1975.

Novaco, R. W. Treatment of chronic anger through cognitive and relaxation controls. *Journal of Consulting and Clinical Psychology,* 1976, *44,* 681.

Novaco, R. W. Stress inoculation: A cognitive therapy for anger and its application to a case of depression. *Journal of Consulting and Clinical Psychology,* 1977, *45,* 600–608.

O'Farrell, T. J., & Cutter, H. S. G. A proposed behavioral couples group for male alcoholics and their wives. In D. Upper & S. M. Ross (Eds.), *Behavioral group therapy, 1979: An annual review.* Champaign, Ill.: Research Press, 1979.

O'Leary, D. E., O'Leary, M. R., & Donovan, D. M. Social skill acquisition and psychosocial development of alcoholics: A review. *Addictive Behaviors,* 1976, *1,* 111–120.

O'Leary, M. R., & Donovan, D. M. Male alcoholics: Treatment outcome as a function of length of treatment and level of current adaptive abilities. *Evaluation and the Health Professions,* 1979, *2* 373–384.

O'Leary, M. R., Donovan, D. M., Chaney, E. F., & Walker, R. D. Cognitive impairment and treatment outcome with alcoholics: Preliminary findings. *Journal of Clinical Psychiatry,* 1979, *40,* 397–398.

Orford, J., Guthrie, S., Nicholls, P., Oppenheimer, E., Egert, S., & Hensman, C. Self-reported coping behavior of wives of alcoholics and its association with drinking outcome. *Journal of Studies on Alcohol*, 1975, *36*, 1254–1267.

Orford, J., Oppenheimer, E., & Edwards, G. Abstinence or control: The outcome for excessive drinkers two years after consultation. *Behaviour Research and Therapy*, 1976, *14*, 409–418.

Parsons, O. A., & Farr, S. P. The neuropsychology of alcohol and drug use. In S. B. Filskov & T. J. Boll (Eds.), *Handbook of clinical neuropsychology*. New York: Wiley-Interscience, 1981.

Pattison, E. M., Sobell, M. B., & Sobell, L. C. (Eds.). *Emerging concepts of alcohol dependence*. New York: Springer, 1977.

Pickens, R., Bigelow, G., & Griffiths, R. An experimental approach to treating chronic alcoholism: A case study and one-year follow-up. *Behaviour Research and Therapy*, 1973, *11*, 321–325.

Platt, J. J., & Spivack, G. *Manual for the means-ends problem solving procedure (MEPS): A measure of interpersonal cognitive problem-solving skill*. Philadelphia, Penn.: Hahnemann Community Mental Health/Mental Retardation Center, Department of Mental Health Sciences, Hahnemann Medical College and Hospital, 1975.

Polich, J. M., Armor, D. J., & Braiker, H. B. *The course of alcoholism: Four years after treatment*. Santa Monica, Calif.: The Rand Corporation, 1980.

Pomerleau, O. F., Fertig, J., Baker, L., & Cooney, N. Reactivity to alcohol cues in alcoholics and non-alcoholics: Implications for a stimulus control analysis of drinking. *Addictive Behaviors*, 1983, *8*, 1–10.

Raistrick, D., Dunbar, G., & Davidson, R. Development of a questionnaire to measure alcohol dependence. *British Journal of Addiction*, 1983, *78*, 89–95.

Rankin, H. J., & Hodgson, R. J. Cue exposure: One approach to the extinction of addictive behaviors. In M. Gross (Ed.), *Alcohol intoxication and withdrawal* (Vol. 3b). New York: Plenum, 1977.

Rankin, H., Hodgson, R., & Stockwell, T. The concept of craving and its measurement. *Behaviour Research and Therapy*, 1979, *17*, 389–396.

Rankin, H., Hodgson, R., & Stockwell, T. The behavioral measurement of alcohol dependence. *British Journal of Addiction*, 1980, *75*, 43–47.

Rankin, H., Hodgson, R., & Stockwell, T. Cue exposure and response prevention with alcoholics: A controlled trial. *Behaviour Research and Therapy*, 1983, *21*, 435–446.

Rist, F., & Watzl, H. Self assessment of relapse risk and assertiveness in relation to treatment outcome of female alcoholics. *Addictive Behaviors*, 1983, *8*, 121–127.

Robinson, D. The alcohologist's addiction: Some implications of having lost control over the disease concept of alcoholism. *Quarterly Journal of Studies on Alcohol*, 1972, *33*, 1028–1042.

Rollnick, S., & Heather, N. The application of Bandura's self-efficacy theory to abstinence-oriented alcoholism treatment. *Addictive Behaviors*, 1982, *7*, 243–250.

Roman, P. M., & Trice, H. M. The development of deviant drinking behavior: Occupational risk factors. *Archives of Environmental Health*, 1970, *20*, 424–435.

Rosenberg, H. Relapsed versus non-relapsed alcohol abuses: Coping skills, life events, and social support. *Addictive Behaviors*, 1983, *8*, 183–186.

Rotter, J. B. Generalized expectancies for internal versus external control of reinforcement. *Psychological Monographs*, 1966, *80*(1, Whole No. 609).

Rotter, J. B. Some problems and misconceptions related to the construct of internal versus external control of reinforcement. *Journal of Consulting and Clinical Psychology*, 1975, *43*, 56–67.

Russel, J. A., & Mehrabian, A. The mediating role of emotions in alcohol use. *Journal of Studies on Alcohol*, 1975, *36*, 1508–1536.

Sanchez, V., & Lewinsohn, P. M. Assertive behavior and depression. *Journal of Consulting and Clinical Psychology*, 1980, *48*, 119–120.

Sanchez-Craig, M. A self-control strategy for drinking tendencies. *Ontario Psychologist*, 1975, 7, 25–29.

Sanchez-Craig, M. Cognitive and behavioral coping strategies in the reappraisal of stressful social situations. *Journal of Counseling Psychology*, 1976, 23, 7–12.

Sanchez-Craig, M. *Reappraisal therapy: A self-control strategy for abstinence and controlled drinking.* Paper presented at the Taos International Conference on Treatment of Addictive Behaviors, Taos, N.M., 1979.

Sanchez-Craig, M., & Walker, K. I feel lonely but that doesn't mean I have to drink. *Addictions*, 1975, 22, 3–17.

Sanchez-Craig, M., & Walker, K. Teaching coping skills to chronic alcoholics in a coeducational halfway house: 1. Assessment of programme effects. *British Journal of Addiction*, 1982, 77, 35–50.

Schau, E., & O'Leary, M. R. Adaptive abilities of hospitalized alcoholics and matched controls. *Journal of Studies on Alcohol*, 1977, 38, 403–409.

Schwartz, R. M., & Gottman, J. M. Toward a task analysis of assertive behavior. *Journal of Consulting and Clinical Psychology*, 1976, 11, 910–920.

Sells, S. B. On the nature of stress. In J. E. McGrath (Ed.). *Social and psychological factors in stress.* New York: Holt, Rinehart & Winston, 1970.

Shaw, S. A critique of the concept of the alcohol dependence syndrome. *British Journal of Addiction*, 1979, 74, 339–348.

Siegler, M., Osmond, H., & Newell, S. Models of alcoholism. *Quarterly Journal of Studies on Alcohol*, 1968, 29, 571–591.

Sipprelle, C. N. Induced anxiety. *Psychotherapy: Theory, Research, and Practice*, 1967, 4, 36–40.

Sjöberg, L., Samsonowitz, V., & Olsson, G. Volitional problems in alcohol abuse. *Göteborg Psychological Reports*, 1978, 8(5), 1–38.

Skinner, H. A., & Allen, B. A. Alcohol dependence syndrome: Measurement and validation. *Journal of Abnormal Psychology*, 1982, 91, 199–209.

Smith, R. E. Development of an integrated coping response through cognitive-affective stress management training. In I. G. Sarason & C. D. Spielberger (Eds.), *Stress and anxiety* (Vol. 7). Washington, D.C.: Hemisphere, 1980.

Smith, R. E., & Ascough, J. C. Induced affect in stress management training. In S. Burchfield (Ed.), *Stress: Psychological and physiological interactions.* Washington, D.C.: Hemisphere, in press.

Sobell, M. B., & Sobell, L. C. Individualized behavior therapy for alcoholics. *Behavior Therapy*, 1973, 4, 49–72.

Solomon, R. L. An opponent-process theory of acquired motivation: IV. The affective dynamics of addiction. In J. Maser & M. E. P. Seligman (Eds.), *Psychopathology: Experimental models.* San Francisco. W. H. Freeman, 1977.

Solomon, R. L. The opponent-process theory of acquired motivation: The costs of pleasure and the benefits of pain. *American Psychologist*, 1980, 35, 691–712.

Solomon, R. L., & Corbit, J. D. An opponent-process theory of motivation: II. Cigarette addiction. *Journal of Abnormal Psychology*, 1973, 81, 158–171.

Solomon, R. L., & Corbit, J. D. An opponent-process theory of motivation: I. Temporal dynamics of affect. *Psychological Review*, 1974, 81, 119–145.

Steinglass, P. Family therapy with alcoholics: A review. In E. Kaufman & P. N. Kaufman (Eds.), *Family therapy of drug and alcohol abuse.* New York: Gardner Press, 1979.

Steinglass, P., & Wolin, S. Explorations of a systems approach to alcoholism. *Archives of General Psychiatry*, 1974, 31, 527–532.

Stockwell, T. R., Hodgson, R. J., Edwards, G., Taylor, C., & Rankin, H. J. The development of a questionnaire to measure severity of alcohol dependence. *British Journal of Addiction*, 1979, 74, 79–87.

Stockwell, T. R., Hodgson, R. J., Rankin, H. J., & Taylor, C. Alcohol dependence, beliefs and the priming effect. *Behaviour Research and Therapy*, 1982, *20*, 513–522.

Stockwell, T. R., Murphy, D., & Hodgson, R. The severity of alcohol dependence questionnaire: Its use, reliability and validity. *British Journal of Addiction*, 1983, *78*, 145–155.

Tarter, R. E., & Schneider, D. U. Models and theories of alcoholism. In R. E. Tarter & A. A. Sugerman (Eds.), *Alcoholism: Interdisciplinary approaches to an enduring problem.* Reading, Mass.: Addison-Wesley, 1976.

Tuchfeld, B. S. Spontaneous remission in alcoholics: Empirical observations and theoretical implications. *Journal of Studies on Alcohol*, 1981, *42*, 626–641.

Van Hasselt, B., Hersen, M., & Milliones, J. Social skills training for alcoholics and drug addicts: A review. *Addictive Behaviors*, 1978, *3*, 221–233.

Vogler, R. E., Lunde, S. E., Johnson, G. R., & Martin, P. L. Electrical aversion conditioning with chronic alcoholics. *Journal of Consulting and Clinical Psychology*, 1970, *34*, 302–307.

Walker, K., Sanchez-Craig, M., & MacDonald, K. *Teaching coping strategies for interpersonal problems.* Paper presented at the North American Congress on Alcohol and Drug Problems, San Francisco, 1974.

Walker, R. D., Donovan, D. M., Kivlahan, D. R., & O'Leary, M. R. Length of stay, neuropsychological performance, and aftercare: Influences on alcohol treatment outcome. *Journal of Consulting and Clinical Psychology*, 1983, *51*, 900–911.

Wallace, J. Alcoholism from the inside out: A phenomenological analysis. In N. J. Estes & M. E. Heinemann (Eds.), *Alcoholism: Development, consequences, and interventions.* St. Louis: Mosby, 1977.

Wellman, M. Toward an etiology of alcoholism: Why young men drink too much. *Canadian Medical Association Journal*, 1955, *73*, 717–725.

Whelan, M., & Prince, M. Toward indirect cognitive confrontation with alcohol abusers. *International Journal of the Addictions*, 1982, *17*, 879–886.

Wilson, G. T. Booze, beliefs, and behavior: Cognitive processes in alcohol use and abuse. In P. E. Nathan, G. A. Marlatt, & T. Løberg (Eds.), *Alcoholism: New directions in behavioral research and treatment.* New York: Plenum, 1978.

Zeiss, A. M., Lewinsohn, P. M., & Muñoz, R. F. Nonspecific improvement effects in depression using interpersonal skills training, pleasant activity schedules, or cognitive training. *Journal of Consulting and Clinical Psychology*, 1979, *47*, 427–439.

7

THE PROBLEM DRINKERS' PROJECT: A PROGRAMMATIC APPLICATION OF SOCIAL-LEARNING-BASED TREATMENT

BARBARA S. MCCRADY, LARRY DEAN, EDMUND DUBREUIL, AND SUZANNE SWANSON

PROLOGUE

Bill walked into the Problem Drinkers' Project thinking, "Here I am, 36 years old and in an alcoholism program. I've never needed anything like this before. All I need to do is not drink. What's the big deal?" It was 9:00 A.M. on a Thursday morning. Bill had just spent 4 days in detoxification, and he was going to go home that evening after completing his 1st day in the program. As he walked into the Day Hospital, a staff member met him and walked him down a hall to a room with a closed door. She said that the first group had just begun and that the group was "goal setting." His palms were sweaty and his stomach felt queasy as he thought, "Goal setting—I've never done that in my life."

As she opened the door, Bill walked in and saw familiar faces of people he had met during detoxification. "Hi, Bill, glad you're here." He was also greeted by a staff member who had talked with him about the program earlier in the week. The others in the room introduced themselves as well but the names were quickly forgotten and the faces became a blur. He decided, "I'll give this a day, but I probably won't be back. I'm just here to stop my wife from nagging me."

Bill watched as everyone blew into a machine, and was told that the machine tested whether people had been drinking or not. He noticed that when one person had a positive reading nobody criticized him. The staff member said, "We'll help you look at what happened that you drank, and how you could have handled it without alcohol." Bill was amazed.

As Bill sat back, he watched a staff person write on a large white wallboard, using colored markers. Group members were talking about things like "triggers, feelings, thoughts, and alternatives." He became curious and tried to listen. It was still hard to concentrate these days, but the writing on the board seemed to make it easier. People were talking about things they planned to do over the next few days. This seemed to be "setting goals." One man said he was going to call his wife and ask her to come in to couples group later in the day. Bill thought, "Good grief, my wife and I haven't any problems when I'm not drinking. Why should she get involved? She's been through enough." However, he agreed to ask his wife to come in since the other clients' spouses were coming in for group. After an hour, the group was over, and one of the clients offered to show him around the unit.

"Bill" was beginning treatment in a day hospital treatment program for problem drinkers located in a private psychiatric hospital (Butler Hospital, Providence, Rhode Island). The program, called the Problem Drinkers' Project (PDP), includes both group and individual sessions, and is run from 9:00 A.M. to 3:30 P.M., Monday through Friday. Clients attend general, behaviorally oriented therapy groups for 8 hours/week, attend a social skills training group 2 hours/week, couples or family groups 3 hours/week, and see one film and attend one lecture on medical aspects of alcoholism each week. Clients participate in group recreational activities once each week and either cook or clean up from lunch each day. Figure 7-1 shows the program schedule.

A treatment manual with exercise sheets is used to supplement the groups. Clients are encouraged to read this and complete the work sheets during free time on the unit or at home. The clients retain this manual and often refer to it after completion of the program. The staff is a multidisciplinary treatment team of psychiatrists, psychologists, nurses, social workers, mental health workers, occupational therapists, and volunteers. All of these people work together along with the client to identify treatment goals and develop individualized therapeutic approaches to complement the program's basic design.

Sixteen clients, approximately two thirds of whom are men, participate in this program for an average of 3 weeks after detoxification. The majority of the clients in the program have a primary diagnosis of alcohol dependence or alcohol abuse; one quarter have additional psychiatric diagnoses. Most have had previous treatment for their drinking problems and have been in trouble with alcohol for an average of 15 years. They have been drinking heavily for most of the 6-month period preceding treatment. Many have job-related problems as a result of their drinking. Most have a full-time form of employment, however, are married, and average about 40 years of age (the age range is from 13 to 80 years). (See Longabaugh, McCrady, Fink, Stout, McAuley, Doyle, & McNeill, 1983, for a more complete description of the population.)

The majority of clients participate in treatment on a partial hospitalization basis. Clients are excluded from the program if they are acutely suicidal, homicidal, or psychotic. Occasionally a person's psychiatric, medical, or insurance status warrants their using the program while remaining in the hospital on a 24-hour basis.

A controlled evaluation of the effectiveness of the program was begun in 1979. Over a 13-month period, 174 clients entered the research project. While

Time	Monday	Tuesday	Wednesday	Thursday	Friday
9:00–9:30	Blood-alcohol levels	Community meeting	Medical education	Blood-alcohol levels	Community meeting
9:30–10:00	Goal setting			Goal setting	AA
10:00–10:30					
10:30–11:00	Social skills	Functional analysis group	Social skills	Movie and discussion	
11:00–11:30					
11:30–12:00					
12:00–12:30	Lunch	Lunch	Lunch	Lunch	Lunch
12:30–1:00					
1:00–1:30	Functional analysis group	AA group	Women's group	Functional analysis group	Functional analysis group
1:30–2:00					
2:00–2:30		Community activities	Alcohol discussion group		
2:30–3:00					
3:00–3:30	End-of-the-day meeting	End-of-the-day meeting	End-of-the-day meeting	End-of-the-day meeting	End-of-the-day meeting
3:30–4:00					
4:00–4:30	Family group				
4:30–5:00		4:45-5:45 Couples group		4:45-5:45 Couples group	
5:00–5:30					
5:30–6:00					
6:00–6:30					
8:00–9:00					AA, Alateen, Al-Anon

Figure 7-1. Weekly program schedule for the Problem Drinkers' Project.

all subjects participated in the same treatment program, one third did so while receiving 24-hour hospitalization; two thirds received their treatment as day patients. Results of the first 6 months of follow-up (Longabaugh *et al.*, 1983) found few differences between the two groups. However, patients were abstinent approximately 85% of the time during follow-up; average alcohol intake of absolute ethanol dropped from about 8 oz/day to 1 oz/day, and subjects and correspondents reported significant improvements in their subjective well-being and interpersonal relationships. About one quarter of the subjects had brief rehospitalizations during this time period. The only area of poor outcomes related to occupational status—fewer subjects had full-time jobs 6 months after treatment than prior to treatment. Thus, the evaluation suggested that treatment was feasible in the day hospital setting, and at least as effective as comparable treatment delivered in the context of a 24-hour hospitalization. Moreover, since the absolute level of outcomes was so positive, we decided that presenting the program in some detail would be useful to other clinicians and clinical researchers in the alcohol field.

INTRODUCTION

This chapter has several goals. While other chapters in this book focus on research and theoretical aspects of Relapse Prevention (RP), this chapter will present an actual problem drinkers' treatment program that utilizes an RP approach. The chapter will first present a theoretical rationale for using partial hospitalization to treat problem drinkers, followed by a discussion of the goals of this particular program and the cognitive–behavioral model used to implement those goals. The remainder of the chapter describes the actual components of the program, with a practical presentation of different group therapy topics, as well as a discussion of the problems of implementing a behavioral RP approach in actual clinical practice.

Partial hospitalization has been available as a treatment modality since the 1930s (Luber, 1979), although systematic studies of partial hospitalization have been conducted only since the 1960s. A number of studies (e.g., Beigel & Feder, 1970; Craft, 1959; Finzen, 1974; Fotrell, 1973; Fried & Brull, 1972; Guy, Gross, & Hogarty, 1969; Rabiner & Lurie, 1974; Washburn, Vanicelli, & Longabaugh, 1976) have found that partial-hospitalization treatment is a clinically effective alternative to a 24-hour hospitalization for a large proportion of patients who present for inpatient treatment. This population includes all patients who are not acutely homicidal, suicidal, or unable to care for themselves. Patient groups treated in the partial hospital have compared favorably on outcome measures such as readmission rate, total duration of hospitalization, occupational and social role functioning, experienced family burden, and patient and family satisfaction with treatment. Further, partial hospitalization has also been found to be less costly to patients and third-party insurers (Fink, Longabaugh, & Stout, 1977). Considering this generally encouraging literature on partial hospitalization, it would be reasonable to hypothesize that similar results might be found when treating alcoholics in this setting. Treatment should be equally effective, and less costly.

Partial hospitalization has not been widely used in the treatment of alcohol abuse and alcoholism, despite the increasing emphasis on cost effectiveness in treatment programs. There are, however, a few enthusiastic clinical reports about the use of this setting for problem drinkers (e.g., Fox & Lowe, 1968; Pallett, 1976; Powell & Viamontes, 1974; Ruprecht, 1961; Ryan, 1981). The lack of use of partial hospitalization is somewhat surprising, considering the history and successful use of this setting for other types of psychological and psychiatric problems.

RATIONALE FOR PARTIAL-HOSPITALIZATION APPROACH

Four key elements in social-learning-based treatment approaches (e.g., Marlatt & Gordon, 1980; Miller, Taylor, & West, 1980; Sobell & Sobell, 1980) make partial hospital treatment for drinking problems particularly attractive. First, clients need to be able to recognize that changing their drinking behavior is necessary, but can be a difficult task that requires new skills. Clinical observation suggests that after detoxification many alcoholics feel well physically, feel convinced that they will "never" start drinking again and subject themselves to the same painful experiences, and report that they have "no desire" to drink. Relapse rates contradict this optimistic view. It is understandable that clients feel this way since, in an inpatient hospital, they are rarely exposed to cues for drinking, and do not have to cope with a variety of daily situations without alcohol. Family visits are often benign (families being on their "best behavior" when visiting a "sick" person in a hospital), employers are often relieved and supportive, and drinking buddies rarely come to the hospital bringing gifts of alcohol.

Thus, so-called problem "denial" is high and is supported by the 24-hour inpatient setting. In the partial-hospital setting, on the other hand, clients are home every day, see friends, have to go by their old drinking haunts, and have to handle a host of minor daily ups and downs without alcohol. Since this is a difficult task, the prediction would be that denial would be weakened by exposure to cues to drink, and clients should have a more realistic view of the difficulties of remaining abstinent when in a partial-hospitalization program.

A second key element is the necessity for exposure to the natural environment when assessing drinking patterns. In the partial hospital, clients are exposed to drinking cues on a daily basis. This should result in a more accurate assessment by the clinical staff and the client of environmental cues for drinking, as well as cognitive and emotional antecedents to drinking. Clients' capacity to recognize high-risk situations should be enhanced.

The third advantage to partial hospitalization is the increased opportunity for rehearsal of new skills in the natural environment. Leaving each day gives the client opportunities to seek out drinking cues and rehearse new responses, implement alternative ways of thinking and reacting to certain cues, and learn to avoid certain settings, people, or interpersonal interactions, while receiving the daily support and treatment interventions of the clinical staff. Clients often experience drinking urges during treatment, or have drinking episodes. Learning to cope with these during intensive treatment facilitates generalization of skills to similar situations encountered after treatment is terminated.

A fourth advantage of partial hospitalization, when compared to the inpatient setting, is the increased opportunity to teach clients how to anticipate and solve problems. If part of the program each day is geared toward discussion of what problems or difficult situations may occur each evening, or each weekend, clients can begin to learn to anticipate such situations and develop coping strategies. The lack of exposure to the natural environment in inpatient programs prohibits this process.

PROGRAM GOALS

Based on the preceding rationale, the PDP has several goals for treatment. The six major goals are as follows:

1. Provide clients a social learning framework within which to understand their drinking, and help decrease the guilt and shame about their drinking behavior which many problem drinkers experience.

2. Assist clients to make a realistic assessment of the extent and severity of their drinking problems, to label their drinking as a problem behavior, and to recognize the necessity of abstaining from the use of alcohol.

3. Help clients to identify environmental, cognitive, and affective antecedents to their drinking.

4. Teach clients skills to facilitate maintaining abstinence, such as problem solving, environmental restructuring, social–interpersonal skills, cognitive restructuring, methods of dealing with urges to drink, and relaxation.

5. Rearrange consequences of drinking by (a) helping clients to change their positive expectancies about the effects of alcohol and to access reinforcers without drinking, and (b) developing social systems to support and reinforce abstinence.

6. Teach clients about relapses and relapse management.

The program stresses abstinence from alcohol rather than individualized drinking goals for several reasons. First, a large proportion of our clients have had medical sequelae of their drinking that would make even moderate drinking inadvisable. Also, the majority of clients have been physically addicted to alcohol, making controlled drinking a more difficult goal to achieve. Since most of the therapy is delivered in groups, it was judged that having controlled drinking goals for a subset of the clients would diminish the support and modeling functions of group treatment.

PROGRAM APPLICATION OF THE FUNCTIONAL ANALYSIS

To achieve program goals, the program elements are derived from a stimulus–organism–response–consequences (S-O-R-C) model of behavior (e.g., Kanfer & Philips, 1970). However, this basic behavioral model has been extended in its application to include many cognitive elements, and is compatible with contemporary cognitive theorizing. This model is also used as a clinical tool to facilitate working with some of the difficult clinical problems that a problem-drinker population presents, such as the often observed tendency to underestimate the seriousness of their problems or the need for behavior change.

The functional analysis is a behavioral model that attempts to demonstrate to the client the "function" that alcohol plays in one's life. A primary goal in using the functional analysis is to encourage problem drinkers to begin perceiving their drinking problem not as a totality, but as a group of problems identifiable by looking at drinking episodes with common features. These episodes are defined by behavior chains that demonstrate to clients the relationships between events or environmental settings, their internal responses to these, their drinking, and the consequences of their drinking.

The functional analysis begins with an introduction to the components of a behavior chain, including antecedents, behavior, and consequences, as illustrated in Figure 7-2. Antecedents are further broken down into three components. First is an external stimulus, which is the identified starting point of any drinking episode. The external event initiates the sequence of events that make up a behavior chain. The second component is the cognitive reaction to the external stimulus. Cognitions include one's perceptions of the environment, expectations regarding the future, and thoughts about the need to make a behavioral response. The final component of the antecedent portion of the chain is the affect generated from the perceived external stimulus and cognitions. The second general category includes the behaviors that follow from these antecedents. In the case of a problem drinker, this behavior is drinking alcohol.

The consequence components are categorized as positive and negative. A positive consequence is the desirable end that the drinker associates with the consumption of alcohol in a situation. A negative consequence is the

Figure 7-2. Components of a behavioral chain used in the functional analysis.

final component of the drinking behavior chain, and may be directly or indirectly related to the use of alcohol. A negative consequence is an undesirable result of alcohol consumption affecting the physical, psychological, social, or occupational well-being of the individual. For the client, consequences are described as desirable or undesirable to emphasize their expectancies about the effects of alcohol, rather than the conditioning aspect of consequences.

General Relationships between Components

The relationships between the components of a behavioral chain are of both sequence and influence. Although the behavior chain is presented as a linear model, there is often interplay between cognitions and affect before the sequence is complete. For example, the problem drinker may have cognitions that elicit an affective response. Because of this response, the individual may evaluate the generated emotional response. This interplay may continue for some time before the person engages in overt behavior.

Figure 7-2 illustrates that the occurrence of each component is dependent upon the occurrence of the preceding component. When an individual describes the sequence of events of a drinking episode, it is also assumed that these events have been experienced repeatedly, so that the cognitive–affective–behavior–consequence sequence described is representative of the client's drinking problem.

Relationship between Antecedents

As stated earlier, external stimuli are the identified starting points of a drinking episode. These stimuli could include drinking environments, arguments with significant others, social situations, or certain days of the week. These events are incorporated into the functional analysis only if the problem drinker responds to these events by consuming alcohol. The discrimination helps the problem drinker separate alcohol issues from other problem issues. These external events will likely elicit specific cognitive and affective responses. For example, a problem drinker may be exposed to a drinking cue such as a bar and think, "Boy, it would be nice to have a drink." This thought may elicit feelings of contentment, a result of anticipated positive consequences. The functional analysis assumes that each time the problem drinker is exposed to the external cue, it is likely that he or she will think about drinking and experience a sense of contentment.

Secondly, a relationship between the cognitive and affective components exists, which is also important to the functional analysis. Affect is conceptualized as a result of cognitions; negative thinking will produce negative emotions and positive thinking will produce positive emotions. When incorporated into the functional analysis, the assumption is that a problem drinker engages in specific thoughts that produce emotions that cue drinking, and that control over drinking is a function of changing negative thought patterns.

Relationship between Behavior and Consequences

This relationship is more complex, due to the direct and indirect relationship between the behavior, drinking alcohol, and its consequences. There are specific positive and negative consequences that are a direct result of alcohol use. For example, alcohol can directly alter one's arousal level, produce intoxication, interfere with biological functioning and damage vital organs. Other consequences are not direct physiological consequences of drinking alcohol, but are mediated by the expectancies of the individual consuming the alcohol. For example, alcohol will alter mood, but the direction of change may be a function of the drinker's expectancies about alcohol's effects; alcohol may be expected to produce sleep, but it actually interferes with sleep.

Relationship between Positive Consequences and Behaviors

Positive consequences tend to become associated with drinking over time because they occur quickly and repeatedly. Because the positive consequences follow the drinking behavior, the drinker expects positive consequences to be experienced when drinking. Positive consequences are expected before the person drinks any alcohol. The problem drinker has thoughts about an external stimulus and has an emotional response to these thoughts. These thoughts often include a plan of action, which may include alcohol. The expectation of positive consequences influences the person's decision to use alcohol.

For example, the problem drinker may be responding to an external event such as inability to sleep. Part of the cognitive process will be to decide what action to take to deal with the problem. The drinker may realize from past experience that alcohol produces relaxation and sleep, and then choose alcohol as a way to handle insomnia. This example demonstrates to clients both that positive consequences occur after the drinking behavior, and that they are an *expected* result of the behavior. Because the problem drinker expects these consequences, he or she may decide to drink in response to problems.

Relationships Surrounding Negative Consequences

The negative consequences have a minimal influence on the other components of the behavior chain, because they tend not to be anticipated or utilized during the cognitive portion of the chain. (Delayed punishment generally has been shown to have minimal influence on preceding behaviors.) Positive consequences usually closely follow the behavior, with the negative consequences occurring later. There may also be a time interval between the occurrence of the positive consequences and that of the negative.

In the previous insomnia example, the individual drank and experienced the positive consequence of getting to sleep. The next day, the person would awaken unrefreshed, with an upset stomach, and morning vomiting. These negative consequences, however, occur anywhere from 6 to 8 hours later, a time interval that weakens the cognitive and conditioning association between alcohol and the negative consequences. It is probable that the problem drinker would not associate these negative consequences with the previous night's drinking. On the contrary, he or she would probably say, "If it were not for the alcohol, I would not have slept at all."

This minimal association between drinking alcohol and the negative consequences is apparent when examining the cognitive portion of any drinking episode. These negative consequences are rarely anticipated, and do not tend to influence the decision about whether or not to drink. If they are considered, the association is too weak to counter the strong positive association between drinking and the positive consequences.

Through an understanding of these basic components of the functional analysis and the relationships among the components of the behavioral chain, an individual can begin to functionally analyse his or her drinking problem.

In the preceding discussion, the components of a behavioral chain and the relationships that make up the functional analysis have been presented, utilizing professional terminology. In order for this model to be an effective teaching tool, simpler terminology is used in the therapy groups. Antecedents become *triggers*, cognitions become *thoughts*, affect becomes *feelings*. These terms are utilized in the following sections in descriptions of how these concepts are used with clients in individual and group therapy.

THERAPY GROUPS AND TECHNIQUES

In this section, each topic covered in the therapy groups is described. The topics are selected to address the major goals of treatment. The relationships between these goals and the therapy groups and other program elements are summarized in Table 7-1. Therapy groups are presented in some detail to facilitate readers using such groups in their own treatment programs. Figure 7-3 represents an optimal time sequence for the therapy groups.

Table 7-1.   PDP Program Goals and Therapy Groups

Treatment goal	Therapy groups/program elements
Providing a framework; decreasing shame and guilt	Learning theory and alcoholism Films
Assessing extent and severity of drinking problem	Behavior chains Films Medical education What prevents seeking treatment—what brought you into treatment? Alcoholics Anonymous (AA) Volunteers Positive consequences of sobriety—negative consequences of drinking
Identifying antecedents to drinking	Brainstorming antecedents Behavior chains Self-recording of urges or drinking Irrational thinking Expressing feelings
Skills acquisition	Drink-refusal training Assertiveness training Alternatives Goal setting Couples group Evening and weekend planning Rational alternatives
Consequence control—developing support systems	Positive consequences of sobriety—negative consequences of drinking Couples group Employer involvement Alternatives Self-reinforcement Use of AA Aftercare planning
Relapse management	Slips

The behavior chains group presents the functional analysis, which clients learn to use to examine their drinking. The other groups focus on understanding or changing how clients deal with each element of the behavior chain (e.g., rearranging environments; developing means of socializing without alcohol). These groups, in combination with individual work, address the program goals listed in Table 7-1. Before illustrating the specific PDP groups, some general comments will be made about the type of group atmosphere we attempt to achieve.

	Monday	Tuesday	Thursday	Friday
Week 1				
9:00	Goal setting	——	Behavior chains	——
10:30	——	What prevents seeking treatments	——	——
1:00	Learning theory	——	Brainstorm triggers	Do two individual chains
Week 2				
9:00	Goal setting	——	Expressing feelings	——
10:30	——	Rational alternatives	——	——
1:00	Irrational thinking	——	Do two individual chains	Positives of sobriety— negatives of drinking
Week 3				
9:00	Goals—theory and doing	——	Do two individual chains	——
10:30	——	Putting environ- mental alternatives into action	——	——
1:00	Alternatives	——	Slips	Do two individual chains

Figure 7-3. Optimal time sequence for therapy groups.

Given the cognitive emphasis on the program, clients need to discuss internal events, as well as environmental situations related to drinking, and learn to become "problem solvers." An atmosphere is required in which self-exploration and learning are reinforced and encouraged. This atmosphere is accomplished in many ways, including by frequently giving verbal reinforcement for group preparation, using easy questionnaires, and giving diplomas for completion of the program.

Clients can also be encouraged to think of treatment as an experiment in learning abstinence and other new behaviors, and that the client's involvement needs to be positive in order for him or her to want to continue the "experiment." This is done by repeatedly reinforcing clients for seeking and staying in treatment, for not drinking when they could easily leave the hospital or sneak drinks, and providing as positive and accepting an atmosphere as possible.

Another guiding premise is that societal attitudes about alcoholism create shame and guilt, which interfere with the problem drinker's seeking treatment. Moralistic concepts are avoided because they are seen as punishing and are often antecedents to drinking. In the event a given client's moralistic belief about self (e.g., "I drink because I'm weak") is a cognitive antecedent to drinking, then the refutation of such a concept is necessary. Presenting drinking behavior as learned and explaining that feeling guilty changes nothing (except maybe their blood-alcohol level) is discussed repeatedly.

Also consistent with our conceptual framework is the recognition that clients ultimately make the decision about whether to drink or use alternative behaviors based upon their expectations of the immediate and long-term consequences of drinking or alternative behaviors (see Chapter 3). The staff's role is to facilitate client understanding of the alternatives and consequences, and to maximize the likelihood of reinforcement for abstinence. If a client has doubts about the desirability of not drinking or developing behaviors alternative to drinking, then these doubts are dealt with via the functional analysis, and are not responded to by punishment or interpreted as denial.

In contrast to a disease model, this conceptual framework also suggests that each individual is unique with respect to antecedents, consequences of drinking, and viable alternatives to drinking. This diversity is developed in groups by the therapist listening and asking questions in order to gather as much data as possible about each client before helping the client develop alternatives.

At the same time, similarities between group members are stressed. The functional analysis illustrates that everyone drinks in response to antecedents, that alcohol changes cognitive and affective states, and that there are many similarities in negative consequences of drinking. These similarities encourage group members to discuss their drinking antecedents and consequences with other group members, help them to identify more aspects of their drinking, and result in close emotional ties with one another. This approach also seems to be successful in discouraging group members from seeing themselves as unique or despicable because of their drinking.

MOTIVATION AND DENIAL

As discussed above, one of the first goals of the program is to help clients to develop a framework for understanding their drinking problems, and to enable them to assess the extent and severity of their drinking problems, in order to recognize the need to remain abstinent. The first part of this process is similar to what traditional programs call dealing with denial. In the social-learning framework used in this particular program, psychodynamically motivated denial is not considered, but it is often observed that many clients tend to underestimate the extent and severity of their drinking problems, or tend to underestimate how difficult it will be for them to change their behavior to successfully avoid the use of alcohol, or may not recognize the need to develop new skills to support abstinence.

The program utilizes a variety of formats to assist the client in making a decision about drinking as well as to illustrate the need for cognitive and behavioral changes to support abstinence. Films are shown weekly. "True-to-life" dramas are presented on the screen to illustrate the negative consequences of drinking and to show behavior patterns common to those with drinking problems. Clients often begin to recognize emotionally the painful results of their drinking. Identifying with people in the films often helps the client to recognize and accept the severity of the alcohol problem and the need to make major life changes in order to not drink. Table 7-2 lists the films shown most often.

While there may be some drawbacks to setting a strong expectancy that abstinence is necessary, our population consists primarily of alcohol addicts and people with medical consequences of drinking, so that setting a strong abstinence expectation is stressed.

Medical education is used similarly in this process. Lectures, films, and impromptu discussions about the medical aspects of alcoholism help to decrease the belief that drinking is a relatively harmless behavior. Clients are encouraged to discuss any current medical problems they have, and to learn how further use of alcohol is apt to cause additional physical difficulties. It is very important in this process of decreasing denial for the problem drinker to talk with and listen to other clients who have recognized the full implications of their drinking, as well as to those who have successfully changed.

The variability of group experiences is an asset in terms of its effect on denial. Clients will present arguments about why they are not in trouble with alcohol. A common theme of these arguments is a list of responsibilities that in the past have not been neglected, for example, "I never missed a day's work." One of the most effective approaches to dealing with this denial is to expose that person to a group of problem drinkers who accept that they have problems with alcohol. In many cases these individuals are responsible individuals and, in some cases, highly successful. These individuals do not fit the stereotypic definition that a particular client may hold. This forces the problem drinkers who have been denying the problem to take a new look at their original definition of problem drinker and modify it to include those

Table 7-2.   PDP Program Films

Medical Aspects of Alcohol Part I
    Southerby Productions, Inc.
	The Other Guy
	    Blue Cross/Blue Shield

Medical Aspects of Alcohol Part II
    Southerby Productions, Inc.
	Alcohol, Pills & Recovery
	    FMS Productions

The Secret Love of Sandra Blain
    Southerby Productions, Inc.
	Conspiracy of Silence
	    RMI Medion Productions, Inc.

The New Life of Sandra Blain
    Southerby Productions, Inc.
	Guidelines
	    FMS Productions

people who acknowledge their drinking problem and are also responsible human beings. This new definition may facilitate their including themselves.

The program uses abstinent volunteers, who previously had drinking problems, to assist and to give reassurance that "it can be done!" They discuss the many relapses and near lapses they have experienced and what they did to cope. They also help the problem drinker to learn how to deal with "day-to-day" drinking situations in a realistic and nonthreatening manner.

Despite the strong behavioral approach, Alcoholics Anonymous (AA) is encouraged in order to facilitate clients' recall of negative consequences of drinking, to expose them to nondrinking models, and to involve them in a support system that will reinforce not drinking. Once a week, the clients attend an AA meeting outside of the hospital. They also participate in a weekly discussion group led by an AA member. Several of the volunteers who are AA members hold a weekly group to teach clients how to use AA in conjunction with the skills learned in the program. Specific types of AA meetings as well as their locations are reviewed.

The PDP uses additional formal and informal approaches to help clients recognize the severity of their alcohol problem, that cognitive and behavioral changes are needed, and that abstinence is a goal. Staff and other clients label denial when it is apparent at any time throughout the program. One group is used to brainstorm a list of the positive consequences of abstinence and the negative consequences of drinking. Each client writes out his or her behavior chains, which include lists of negative consequences of alcohol. Clients are asked to keep these and their own lists of positive consequences of sobriety and negative consequences of drinking for future reference. In addition, another group focuses on each client's denial techniques and their detrimental effects. Two lists are generated on the board: a list of reasons that kept each client from seeking treatment earlier, and a list of reasons for seeking treatment now. On completion of this exercise, clients are able to recognize their own denial and the need to decrease its intensity in order to develop new skills to remain abstinent. Further approaches to denial are discussed later in the chapter.

The problem drinker's willingness to engage in behavior change should increase as the intensity of the denial diminishes. The client becomes more and more aware of the need to recognize drinking antecedents and develop alternate responses to facilitate not drinking. The functional analysis assists with this process by introducing a model that helps take all of the components of a confusing drinking problem and places them into an understandable scheme. The functional analysis offers a tool to the problem drinker to help make some sense out of a drinking problem and develop control over abstinence. In the next section, we discuss how clients are taught to view their drinking as a learned behavior, and how they are taught to analyze their drinking into behavior chains.

LEARNING THEORY AND PROBLEM DRINKING

One subset of therapy groups deals with learning and alcohol use. There are two major groups in this subset. The first group on drinking, reinforcement, and learning starts with the therapist giving a few examples of simple behavior chains (e.g., antecedent [cold room] → behavior [turn up thermostat] → consequence [warm room]), pointing out the relationship between consequences and the likelihood of the behavior recurring. Next the behavior chain in its totality is presented (i.e., trigger → thoughts → feelings → behavior → positive consequences → negative consequences). Simple drinking chains are developed with special attention given to defining the specific components of the chains and illustrating the temporal sequence (e.g., trigger [11:45 P.M. and in bed and not asleep] → thoughts ["I'm not going to fall asleep tonight with alcohol"] → feelings [anxiety] → behavior [drink alcohol] → positive consequences [drowsy, sleep] → negative consequences [wake up early, jittery]). The immediate reinforcing qualities of alcohol are pointed out.

At this point, three principles of learning are given: (1) The more positive or rewarding an experience you have as a consequence of a behavior, the more likely you are to repeat it. (2) The more rewarding trials you have with a behavior, the more likely it is to be repeated. (3) The time between the behavior and experience of its consequences is important (e.g., "If you experienced a hangover immediately after drinking instead of the next day, chances are you wouldn't drink").

The second major therapy group presents a learning-theory framework for understanding the development of problem drinking. One benefit of this group is an awareness of the many environmental influences that contribute to one's use of alcohol. It also tends to minimize guilt and shame associated with a moralistic view of alcoholism. Moreover, as opposed to a disease model, the learning-theory perspective gives clients more of a sense of how to stay sober by learning behaviors alternative to drinking.

This group typically starts with the therapist asking a question such as, "Why do you think some people develop drinking problems?" The group brainstorms (without evaluation) as many possible causal factors as they can. Usually, the brainstormed answers fit into the following categories: (1) life stresses (e.g., retirement, death of loved one); (2) emotional–physiological (e.g., chronic anxiety, depression, chronic pain); (3) other people's behavior (e.g., unfaithful spouse, recalcitrant business partner, alcoholic parent); (4) drinking environments (e.g., "All my friends drink"); (5) heredity and early socialization (e.g., "My father is an alcoholic"); and (6) positive consequences (e.g., "I could socialize better"). After the brainstorming, the different ideas are organized into categories (similar to those in the preceding list) to illustrate similarities among group members' ideas.

Next, responses that fit into categories 1–4 are labeled as antecedents; answers that fit category 6 are labeled as reinforcement and referred back to the behavior chain. At this point group members are asked: "There are a lot of people who have encountered major stresses in their lives, such as divorce, death of loved one, or who have suffered from emotional problems such as depression who have not developed 'alcoholism' or become problem drinkers. Why? What's different about them or you?" Two different types of answers are usually provided: "We're weak," or "We learned that alcohol helped us cope."

It is important for the therapist to point out that all human beings need to find ways of coping with stress, emotion, and pain, that these ways of coping are learned, and that they have nothing to do with weakness or stupidity or morality. It is also suggested that part of the reason that alcoholism is so widespread in our society is that it is an acceptable and widely advertised method of coping that offers quick relief with few immediate and obvious negative consequences. Since most people view alcoholism as a moral weakness, they have no reason to suspect that their own alcohol use may eventually lead to problems.

At this point, the therapist moves to a discussion of factors that contribute to developing drinking problems. First, the effects of environment on attitudes are discussed. To illustrate, it is pointed out that society glamorizes the use of alcohol. Alcohol advertisements clipped from magazines are passed around, and group members discuss the different messages given by ads. Other environmental influences on attitudes, such as family, friends, neighborhood, culture, and religion are also noted.

Second, it is pointed out that beliefs affect behavior. As illustrations, either different countries or religious groups with different rates of alcoholism are presented. The therapist points out that countries and religions that perpetuate attitudes condoning or condemning intoxication tend to have high rates of alcoholism. The explanation suggested to explain this phenomenon is that people do not learn ways of drinking safely.

The group discussion then moves from the societal level to the individual by discussing modeling. To illustrate modeling, it is pointed out that children of alcoholics are at high risk to develop alcoholism, even though many of these children vow that they will never drink like their alcoholic parent. The group is asked: "How do you explain their eventual alcohol abuse? What did they learn?" The therapist may suggest that seeing an alcoholic parent get drunk after marital arguments or after a stressful day at work teaches the child that alcohol can be used to deal with problems. Later in life the child, now adult, who encounters similar problems may use alcohol just as the parent did.

The third topic covered is the relationship between *life stresses* and rates of alcoholism. Examples offered include alcoholism after retirement, among people who live in economically disadvantaged areas of the country, and among people who have experienced unique stresses such as Vietnam veterans.

The final concept presented in the group is that coping skills are learned just as drinking is learned. Failure of an individual to learn effective nonchemical coping skills leaves the individual with unmet needs. Given sufficient stress and an introduction to alcohol, then the likelihood of continued drinking and the development of alcohol problems becomes much higher.

ANTECEDENT IDENTIFICATION

The second subset of therapy groups teaches clients how to identify antecedents to drinking. In addition to the groups, clients are encouraged to monitor and report urges to drink, and some discussion of antecedents is included in most groups. For example in the couples group, a client might realize that she frequently drinks when her husband criticizes her. Clients are also given the Drinking Patterns Questionnaire (Zitter & McCrady, 1979), which lists more than 200 possible antecedents of drinking, to facilitate clients' antecedent identification.

The most basic of antecedent groups involves having the whole group brainstorm antecedents. This can be done in a number of ways. The most useful is to write "triggers → thoughts → feelings" on the board and ask group members to brainstorm environmental and organismic antecedents. This approach is useful in making group members aware of the many possible antecedents to drinking and also clarifies distinctions between environment, cognitions, and affect.

In a similar group, each client brainstorms his or her own antecedents to drinking, which are written under their names. The group focuses on one individual until a long list of his or her antecedents is written on the board. The therapist asks leading questions to clarify their responses and teach them to think in behaviorally specific terms. For example, if a client says: "My husband is a trigger," she might be asked: "In what way is he a trigger? Do you always drink when you are around him or think of him? If not, what are the specific circumstances?" Support and help can be elicited from the group. Since group members spend a lot of time talking to one another between groups, their knowledge and perceptions of each other can be very valuable.

Some basic diagnostic questions that guide the therapist in this group are: (1) Can clients identify antecedents under all categories (triggers, thoughts, feelings)? (2) Is there an awareness of the relationship between components (e.g., someone may readily recognize an association between anger and drinking but have little awareness of environmental stimuli or cognitive mediators)? (3) Which antecedents are major problems to focus on in treatment? (4) What cognitive changes are needed (e.g., does an individual tend to project responsibility, or have problems with simple goal setting, or have problems with catastrophizing)?

The third major antecedent group is called *self-destructive thinking* or *irrational thinking* (Ellis, 1962; Mahoney, 1974) and focuses on cognitions as antecedents to drinking. The relationship between external stimuli and one's cognitive appraisal of these stimuli and related inferences is examined, with particular emphasis on "errors" in reconstruction and inference. Furthermore, the relationship between cognitions and affective states is explained, along with the behavioral results. This group is extremely important, not only in helping clients with particularly self-destructive cognitive styles, but also in helping clients learn alternative responses to unmalleable aspects of the environment.

After a brief introduction to the purpose and content of the group, relationships between triggers, thoughts, and feelings are introduced. This is done by again writing "triggers → thoughts → feelings" on the board and giving examples that would clarify that cognitions are necessary mediators between triggers and feelings, and that the same trigger may be construed differently by different people, resulting in different feelings.

Clients are then asked to brainstorm the irrational thoughts one person might have about a trigger, and compare these to the rational thoughts another person might have about the same situation. After brainstorming, the group is asked to describe the differences between the two types of thinking (rational vs. irrational). To illustrate these differences, lists similar to the following are presented.

Person A	*Person B*
1. Came to conclusions based upon little information (assumptions).	1. Came to conclusions based upon as much information as possible.
2. Did not think of ways to test out conclusions.	2. Thought of ways to test out conclusions.
3. Did not test out conclusions.	3. Tested out conclusions.
4. Conclusions resulted in negative feelings and/or self-destructive behavior.	4. Conclusions held up and did not result in destructive behavior.

After presenting and discussing these lists, a formal definition of irrational thinking is written on the board: "Making assumptions (or having thoughts, beliefs, and attitudes) not based on reality, and therefore not tested out, which result in harm to you (e.g., depression, fear, anxiety, drinking, social isolation, etc.)."

Next, "categories" of irrational thinking are presented and group members provide personal examples of how they have thought irrationally for each category. The categories are: (1) negative self-statements, (2) unrealistic expectations of self, (3) unrealistic expectations of others and life in general,

(4) assuming the worst about one's own health, (5) assuming the worst about one's situation ("Bad luck . . . things always go wrong"), (6) assuming the worst about other people (with particular emphasis on "mind reading"), (7) catastrophizing, and (8) "There is nobody like me (as bad, weak, or insecure)."

The success of the brainstorming is enhanced when the therapist: (1) is aware that group members will only reluctantly divulge their more irrational ("stupid, crazy") thoughts; (2) develops hypotheses about how each group member thinks irrationally; (3) illustrates irrational thoughts in a supportive way; (4) provides examples of irrational thoughts; (5) uses experienced group members as models; and (6) uses humor, sometimes by overstating the irrationality of someone's thoughts (e.g., a client once explained that she drank a whole pint bottle of vodka because she would then no longer have to worry about it. The therapist responded with a smile and said, "It's a good thing you weren't in the liquor store"). Irrationality is in large part a tendency to lose perspective, which often leads to being overly self-critical. Humor, a good means of regaining perspective, is often more supportive than a matter-of-fact statement, which may be interpreted as a criticism.

Throughout the group, the therapist helps clients to identify current irrational thoughts, particularly those associated with urges to drink. For example, a client may talk about how after a marital argument, he or she catastrophized about continued marital discord and considered drinking as a means of dealing with the situation.

The fourth major antecedent group presents the affective component of the behavioral chain, and is called *expressing feelings*. The goals of this group are to teach clients: (1) how to become aware of their affective states; (2) that affective states are often antecedents to drinking and other destructive behaviors; (3) that affect is "normal" or functional and needs to be responded to; (4) that one has choices in how to respond to unpleasant affective states; (5) that denial of, and/or not expressing affect, is ultimately destructive and ineffective in terms of symptom relief (i.e., relief from unpleasant affect); (6) that there is a link between thoughts and feelings, as taught in the irrational thinking group; and (7) that affect can be used as a signal that cognitive or behavioral changes are necessary.

The group starts with a brief definition of feelings, to differentiate feelings from opinions and beliefs. An effective and simple way to define feelings is to write a number of feelings on the board (e.g., anger, fear, anxiety, depression, joy, etc.) and to point out they all seem to have a physiological component (e.g., rapid heart beat, lethargy). The therapist also points out that not expressing feelings is ineffective, and leads to long-term negative consequences. This is done by drawing a picture of a steam kettle on the board and noting that if you heat it sufficiently without releasing some pressure, the steam will build up and the kettle will explode. It is suggested that the same phenomenon happens with human beings—if we try to ignore and do not express feelings we will eventually experience negative consequences. A brainstormed list of negative consequences ("ways in which the kettle explodes") is written on the board (e.g., hypertension, chronic anxiety, ulcers, headaches, physical abuse of family members, suicide, self-hatred, etc.), with the link between not expressing feelings and the specific negative consequences carefully explained. All throughout this group, drinking is pointed out to be a learned response to unpleasant feelings. Clients are encouraged to discuss urges to drink that are associated with unpleasant feelings.

At this point, it is important to emphasize that although unpleasant feelings are not enjoyable, they are necessary signals to change, and without them, positive functioning is not possible. To concretize the above, examples of how group members used feelings as signals to use alternatives are pointed out, such as a person using anxiety about being away from the hospital for a full weekend as a signal to develop activities and emergency plans for the weekend.

By the time the environmental, cognitive, and affective antecedent groups are completed, most clients have a fairly complete assessment of the external and internal antecedents to their drinking, and understand the concept of problem drinking as a learned behavior. Figure 7-4 is an example of a completed antecedent portion of the drinking chain for an individual client as it may be written on the board.

After clients have learned to view drinking as a learned behavior and have assessed their drinking in terms of behavior chains, they have a good idea of what environmental situations, thoughts, and feelings they need to learn to respond to. They are then ready to learn new behaviors and cognitive responses. In the PDP, these are called *alternatives*. The next section presents specific groups, each focusing on altering the responses made by problem drinkers in situations which in the past have influenced the drinking behavior. These groups focus on goal setting, cognitive alternatives, drink refusal and assertiveness, relaxation, support systems, and slips. The groups are presented here in this manner for the sake of clarity, which does not imply a therapeutic sequence. In a clinical setting the order and the degree of focus on any group or groups would be determined by the needs of the patient population.

LEARNING ALTERNATIVE BEHAVIORS

One group session is devoted to introducing clients to the concept of learning alternative behaviors. This session begins by asking group members to offer specific drinking episodes previously identified in their functional analysis. A detailed behavioral chain is then placed on the board. The first question proposed to the group is: What alternative behavior could have been chosen

Bill's Drinking Chain:

Trigger →	Thoughts →	Feelings →	Behavior →
4:30, driving home from work and seeing favorite bar (Jakes).	"That boss of mine, no matter what I do I can't please him. . . . He always finds something to complain about. . . . I wonder if Jim is at Jakes. . . . It would be nice to stop and have a few beers to relax. I deserve a few drinks after the day I've had. . . . Oh, I almost forgot, Mary's [wife] mother is coming over for dinner. . . . That's all I need is to have to listen to her complaining all night. . . . Well, if I have a few drinks it will be easier to listen to her. . . . Mary will be upset if I stop for a few, but then she's always upset lately. . . . I can't seem to please anyone. . . . Sometimes I think life is hopeless."	Anxiety Anger Depression Hopelessness	Stopped at bar and drank

Bill's Completed Drinking Chain Would Include:

Positive consequences →	Negative consequences
Anxiety reduction Stopped thinking about work Stopped thinking about marital and family situation Intensity of hopelessness and anger decreased	Missed dinner Blackout Driving while intoxicated Verbally abusive toward wife Minor withdrawal symptoms in morning Late to work Wife angry and afraid of me Felt guilty about drinking and abusive behavior Felt fear over loss of control of drinking and blackout More angry and hopeless thoughts about work and marriage Physical damage due to toxic effects of alcohol

Figure 7-4. A client's behavioral chain for drinking.

in this situation? Group members will begin to offer suggestions. For example, using the case vignette from Figure 7-4, several suggestions might be presented. Instead of drinking, the individual could have taken a different route home, gone home to discuss the boss with his spouse, rewarded himself with a meal at a nice restaurant, taken a nap in order to relax, or discussed not seeing his mother-in-law. The important concept to demonstrate is that alternative behaviors were available.

The next step is for the therapist to select one of the suggested alternative behaviors, and help the group generate a list of possible positive and negative consequences of choosing this particular alternative behavior. For example, if the group decided on going home to discuss the boss with his spouse, the group might develop the following list of consequences: (1) positive consequences—avoiding the bar and intoxication, avoiding an argument with spouse about drinking, getting this matter "off his chest," and together developing ways to improve the situation with the boss; (2) negative consequences—getting into an argument with his wife, his wife might be unavailable to talk, fear that friends will call him "henpecked," and becoming aware of poor communication skills.

The analysis continues with a comparison between the positive and negative consequences derived from drinking in this situation and the positive and negative consequences of choosing the alternative behavior in this situation. First, the group members compare the positive consequences of the two behaviors. Clients can clearly see that drinking alcohol provides some very powerful consequences that are very difficult to duplicate with alternative behaviors. It is important that the group members understand this point. The group is asked, "Will the specific alternative used in this situation provide you with the same positive consequences as alcohol did?" The group will likely acknowledge that the alternative response will provide some of these, but not all. This is an important point, so the problem drinker must be encouraged not to accept the inadequacy of this alternative behavior. It is assumed that alternative behaviors must provide some positive consequences that are comparable to the positive consequences of drinking.

When the problem drinker acknowledges that alternatives do not provide all that alcohol provided, it is likely that he or she will deny the need for these positive consequences. The problem drinker may state that he or she does not need, for example, to avoid going to his or her in-law's, or to avoid facing his or her spouse, or to detach himself or herself from the marital situation. The message is directly stated that the reinforcing consequences of alcohol are powerful, and that it is therefore important that alternative behaviors are also strongly reinforcing. For clients, positive reinforcement sometimes is explained by saying that positive consequences meet one's own needs. It is stressed that needs are a part of a person. While it is difficult to alter the means one uses to fulfill needs, attempting to alter what is needed is next to impossible. It can be said that the risk of drinking increases in any given trigger situation when attempted alternative behaviors fail to fulfill the problem drinker's needs. While the concept of needs is not commonly used in social-learning formulations, it often seems easier for clients to understand.

At this point, the group is informed that the alternative chosen in this situation is inadequate. The group is asked to continue to brainstorm alternative behaviors that would fulfill as many as possible of the "needs" fulfilled by drinking in this situation. The comparison between drinking and alternative behaviors helps to demonstrate the process of developing, assessing, adding, and deleting alternative behaviors in order to attempt to duplicate the effects of alcohol in that situation.

The group is then asked to compare the negative consequences of drinking to the negative consequences of the alternative behavior. One of the most obvious conclusions one can draw from such a comparison is the absence of some extremely negative consequences of drinking. For example, choosing the alternative behavior will avoid an argument with spouse, a blackout, withdrawal symptoms, further inflammation of the liver due to alcohol, family disruption, excessive amounts of money being spent at the bar, and negative feelings about drinking and self. The important message here is that alternative behaviors can avoid negative consequences that are directly related to drinking. Elimination of negative consequences is added to the notion that alternative behaviors fulfill needs and becomes an important criterion for assessing behavioral alternatives: does the alternative behavior fulfill needs and eliminate negative consequences that are directly related to alcohol consumption?

A similar analysis is applied to several drinking episodes of different individuals, and group members are encouraged to do so with all the behavioral chains that make up their drinking problem. It is emphasized that the alternative behaviors needed to change drinking episodes have to be specific, and must be chosen in relation to the information presented in the behavioral chains from the client's original functional analysis.

This process of altering can be applied to the trigger, thought, and feeling portions of the behavioral chain as well as to the actual behavior. In the case of triggers, the individual is taught to alter the external environment through stimulus-control procedures. For example, many problem drinkers identify drinking episodes that begin with particular environments, such as a bar, restaurant, or party. A problem drinker may decide that altering environments is a helpful approach. For many, altering means avoiding situations, which is encouraged. It is also recognized that avoidance of environmental triggers is not always practical. The group is encouraged to think of ways to alter environments to make them more conducive to abstinence. For example, not all drinking environments are the same: a men's bar may be more conducive to heavy drinking than an elegant French restaurant. Being in a bar with a special date may be more conducive to abstinence than being in the same bar with heavy drinking buddies. It is stressed that altering environments does not mean just avoiding environments that influence drinking, but also changing the conditions of those environments. If a problem drinker avoided all drinking environments, the individual would avoid a great deal of life. To avoid becoming isolated, the drinker may want to frequent bars or lounges on occasion, but go to those where the primary focus is dinner and entertainment, rather than heavy drinking. The problem drinker may also seek out new, nondrinking environments where organized activities are the focus, or may only go to bars when with friends who drink in a controlled manner.

It is important to remember when altering environments to do so through the information presented in the functional analysis. For example, going to bars or lounges with friends who are moderate drinkers is a valid alternative only if the problem drinker can say with some certainty that specific people have influenced his or her drinking in the past. This information will be presented in the thought portion of the functional analysis. A problem drinker will have identified thoughts such as, "If I don't drink my friends will think me weak," or "This engagement is important to my wife so I'll watch my drinking." These thoughts may indicate that expectations about others are important and can influence the problem drinker's behavior, so that surrounding oneself with people who support abstinence may be a way to alter an environment in order to make it conducive to abstinence.

At times, the alternative chosen does not fit the situation. For example, an individual might choose bowling as an alternative to drinking environments. The problem drinker would be encouraged to try this during treatment and might discover that he or she doesn't like bowling, or that the availability of alcohol is another trigger.

The thoughts and feelings portion of the behavioral chain are also focal points of the alternatives concept, although in this portion avoidance is probably an impossible strategy. The message to the clients is that they are not predestined to think and feel a specific way in response to a particular stimulus. Clients are given the opportunity to apply the concepts introduced in the irrational thinking groups earlier in treatment. Avoidance is discouraged because negative thoughts and feelings often lead to urges to drink. One purpose of the alternative groups is to teach problem drinkers to perceive these thoughts and feelings as threats to sobriety. The group members are taught that dealing with drinking urges early in the sequence gives one an advantage in resisting drinking. One technique taught is to counter irrational thinking with rational thinking (discussed later in this chapter).

At this point, the group has been exposed to how the concept of alternatives can be applied to the various components that make up behavioral chains. It is appropriate in the final part of the group to direct attention to applying this process to the problem drinker's natural environment. Group members take their original functional analysis, which illustrated the choices they had made that led to drinking, and develop an alternative functional analysis that graphically represents choices that can be made to decrease the likelihood of drinking. Each member is asked to attempt these alternative behaviors when exposed to drinking cues in their natural environment.

Because putting these alternatives into actual practice is very difficult, the program offers specific groups to allow the problem drinker to develop skills to implement these alternatives, assess their effectiveness, and refine them. One subset of alternatives groups teaches clients general skills needed to implement behavior change, including such skills as problem solving, goal setting, and self-reinforcement. The first two of these skills are taught through structured groups; the third is introduced in either of the two types of structured groups.

GOAL SETTING

Goal setting is used to facilitate clients implementing changes in environments, thoughts, or behavior. Goal setting facilitates the problem drinker's assuming responsibility for his or her behavior and developing a sense of control. It teaches the client to plan ahead and think through methods of accomplishing short-term objectives that lead to long-term achievements.

Persons in the PDP are presented the rationale and steps for setting realistic and manageable goals. Formalized hourly goal-setting groups are held twice a week to teach this material, and to assist the problem drinkers in actually setting goals. They are asked to report back on goal achievement during each session. Outside of group, the treatment team and other group members help the problem drinker with goal setting whenever the opportunity arises. There are many natural opportunities in treatment for goals to be set and completed. Examples include: calling an employer to discuss returning to work, asking a spouse to come to couples group, reading a portion of the program manual, or calling for an appointment for follow-up care.

When introduced to goal setting, clients are taught that setting realistic and manageable goals helps them to be more successful and less self-defeating. Several examples are used to point out the advantages. It is explained that it can be quite overwhelming to "stay sober the rest of my life" and that this goal can actually be a trigger in itself. If one breaks this larger seemingly impossible goal down into more manageable steps, such as playing tennis instead of going to a bar after work today, the goal is more apt to be accomplished. The group leader explains that in order to reach a goal, one must have an exact description of what it is one wants. In addition, four main characteristics of good goals are discussed: (1) goals should be stated in terms of the *client's own behavior*, (2) goals should be *measurable*, (3) goals should be somewhat, but not too *risky*, (4) goals should be *time phased*.

The first point is illustrated through examples: getting a raise is not a good goal because the boss, not the client, has control over giving out raises. If getting a raise is important to the client, he or she could set the following goals: "I will ask my boss for a raise and let him know why I think I deserve one." This is stated in terms of the client's *own behavior*. Regardless of whether or not the boss gives him or her a raise, the client can feel good about asking and letting the boss know why the client thinks he or she deserves one, thus completing the stated goal.

Second, clients are taught that a good goal will be observable to themselves and others, and therefore the goal can be *measured*. It is explained that "happiness" is something we all would like to have, but it is not a good goal to set because it cannot be measured. If one cannot measure the goal, then one cannot know how successful one has been at meeting the goal.

The staff explain to the group that goals should have *some risk* so that they feel good about accomplishing the goal, but not so much risk that they are sure to fail. Most people set superhuman goals for themselves and feel badly if they do not accomplish the impossible. They may think that "Everyone must like me," "My children must always act nicely in public," "I must never get angry," or "I must never argue with my spouse." Discussion centers around how easy it is to feel defeated for not being able to meet such unrealistic goals or expectations.

Setting a time limit on when the goals are expected to be completed is the fourth characteristic of good goal setting. "Staying sober for the rest of my life" is not *time phased* because one has to die before achieving it. Saying "I will ask my boss for a raise by the end of the week" is time phased because at the end of the week one either did or did not ask for a raise. It is explained that it is easy to put off unpleasant tasks and then to feel badly about doing so. Setting dates for meeting goals not only puts pressure on people to accomplish the goal, but allows one to set new goals as well. Having goal-setting meetings twice each week during treatment facilitates learning time phasing. This introduction to goal setting is completed with the following example: If a person wanted to be a long-distance runner (ultimate goal), he or she would not start out by entering the Boston Marathon. He or she would fail, possibly get hurt physically, and most likely give up running. If, however, the person started out by first walking, then jogging short distances, he or she would work up to long distance by setting good goals.

Lectures, board work, and discussions are used to teach clients the components of goal setting. A section in the PDP manual reviews these steps and complements the group and individual work. After the introduction to goal setting, clients set specific goals to accomplish between one group and the next. Goals are recorded on sheets, as illustrated in Figure 7-5. As depicted, these sheets include spaces for the actual goal description, time by which it will be completed, a line for comments, and a box to record if and

As you go along in PDP you will be asked to think about and set your own goals. The following are work sheets which will help you with your goals.

Problem or trigger	Goal	Date	Met
1.			
2.			
3.			

Example:

Ultimate goal or ideal	Current goals	Date	Met
1. To be assertive.	1. Attend PDP groups.		
	2. Read and learn the social skills section.		
	3. Role play being assertive to my spouse in social skills group.		

Ultimate goal or ideal	Current goals	Date	Met
1.			
2.			
3.			

Figure 7-5. Sample goal-setting sheet.

when the goal is completed. Using these sheets and reporting back to the group during the next session reinforces accomplishing goals.

To follow up on the goal setting, as well as to help clients anticipate and solve day-to-day problems, a half-hour meeting is scheduled at the end of each day.

END-OF-THE-DAY MEETINGS

During these meetings, clients are encouraged to think about which people, situations, or problems they might encounter during the evening. The focus is partially on helping clients consider whether they are likely to encounter triggers. They then discuss how they might cope with or avoid such situations. Back-up planning is encouraged, in case the original plans cannot be executed.

Evening and weekend planning is also a format to help people consider how to develop and use support systems. Clients are encouraged to spend time with family members and friends, try out AA meetings or follow-up groups, and experience different leisure activities. An added advantage of the group approach is that clients learn from one another as they make suggestions, listen to progress reports, and give support to one another.

To help clients actually follow through on plans, self-reinforcement techniques are introduced. Most clients anticipate that there are numerous positive consequences of abstinence. At the beginning, however, people are taught that they will have to plan their rewards to reinforce sobriety. It is explained that there are two kinds of rewards: short-term and long-term rewards. Short-term rewards are rewards for daily successes. People are taught to cognitively reward themselves for successfully handling urges to drink. They are encouraged to "pat themselves on the back" by thinking, for example, "That was great that I didn't drink. It was tough and I'm proud of myself."

More concrete short-term rewards are encouraged as well. Clients are taught to reward themselves with special "treats" for positive behavior. A few suggestions include having a favorite dessert, reading a book, going to a movie, or soaking in the tub. An exercise sheet is available for people to list potential reinforcers.

Long-term rewards for larger accomplishments are also introduced. For example, a person might calculate how much money he or she spent on alcohol daily and monthly, and would be asked to add up how much money would be saved if sober for 6 months. Then the person would set a goal of buying a special item or going on a trip with some of the money, if still sober at the end of 6 months. Again, an exercise sheet is used for people to plan long-term reinforcers.

COGNITIVE ALTERNATIVES

A second approach to alternatives is to teach clients skills to manage cognitions that often lead to drinking. These skills are not taught in a single group, but rather are woven into several different groups.

An alternatives group called *steps to rational thinking* presents a specific exercise that clients can use. The steps are presented on the board and explained. The steps include: (1) STOP: "Use uncomfortable feelings as signals to examine your thoughts"; (2) AWARE: "Become aware of your assumptions"; (3) DISPUTE: "Challenge the assumptions that may be irratonal"; (4) TEST: "Test out the validity of these assumptions"; and (5) POSITIVE: "Think positive thoughts about yourself and the situation." Next, the steps are used in group to deal with current examples of irrational thinking of individual group members. The primary goal of this group is to teach clients to respond to negative emotional states by cognitively using these steps.

In addition to this particular group, the theme of rational thinking is interwoven through many groups. The antecedent group on irrational thinking can be viewed as an alternatives group to the extent that becoming aware of irrational thoughts helps clients change these thoughts. The functional analysis group often focuses on cognitive change. Irrational thoughts are identified in these groups and rational–cognitive alternatives are suggested by the therapist and other group members. In general, throughout all PDP groups and individual time, clients are encouraged to test out their irrational thoughts.

COPING WITH URGES

Learning to identify and cope with urges to drink may be introduced in any of the groups. Sometimes, clients do not experience such urges, do not recognize them as such, or do not report such urges because they believe that they "shouldn't" be having thoughts about wanting to drink. Yet it is important for the problem drinker to identify these urges while in treatment in order to have a chance to rehearse methods of dealing with them (see also Chapter 4). The program staff encourages people to monitor these urges while in the clinical setting or in their natural environments during the evening and weekend periods. Self-recording charts are sometimes given to patients to mark down specific details relating to each urge. This practice helps the patient to not only identify drinking cues but also focus on cognitive–behavioral alternatives to avoid or deal with the cues while still in treatment. Clients are encouraged to accept urges as natural feelings which serve as a cue that some kind of action is called for.

If a client does experience strong urges to drink, several interventions are used, including: (1) encouraging the client to complete a behavior chain to analyze what is contributing to the urge; (2) suggesting an alternative behavior such as discussing the urges or engaging in an enjoyable activity that is also incompatible with drinking; or (3) rehearsing the positive consequences they have experienced from abstinence, as well as the negative consequences they had experienced as a result of drinking. In order to have lists available of positive–negative consequences, one group session may be devoted to brainstorming these lists. Group members are asked to think of as many positive aspects of abstinence as they can, and these are written on the board. Then a similar listing is made of negative experiences or consequences of drinking. These lists usually are quite lengthy. Clients are encouraged to write down these lists and keep them in their wallet or a convenient place, review them frequently, and to recall the lists as a way of handling an urge to drink.

DRINK REFUSAL AND ASSERTIVENESS TRAINING

The third component of teaching alternatives involves alternate skills training in drink refusal, assertiveness, and deep muscle relaxation. Due to the limited number of available therapists, the social skills group includes all clients in the program, with a maximum of 16. Because of the large group size, role playing or other forms of behavioral rehearsal are particularly difficult to incorporate, so novel ways of doing role playing have been developed. Also, since clients are admitted to the program on a rolling basis, the group usually includes two to three new clients each session. Thus materials need to be repetitive, and each session has to provide useful information and experience on its own, without relying heavily on material from previous sessions. The group meets twice weekly, resulting in most clients receiving six group sessions of this particular group. The group has two main content areas—drink refusal and assertiveness training.

Drink refusal (e.g., Foy, Miller, Eisler, & O'Toole, 1976) is covered in two group sessions. In the first, clients are introduced to the idea that they will need to refuse drinks, and that it takes skills to do so. Usually, a few clients have already had to refuse drinks, and their experiences are incorporated into this discussion. Next, in order to help clients appreciate the necessity of learning this skill, they are encouraged to brainstorm situations in which they have had to refuse drinks, or situations in which they have been offered drinks. This list is often quite long and includes situations ranging from visiting friends, watching sports events with friends, being in a local bar, to being at a wake or funeral. During this discussion, some clients state that the only person they have to refuse is themselves. However, by the time the whole situations list is generated, they are usually able to identify some situations in which they might have difficulty with refusal. Each client is then asked to state which situations would be most difficult for them, and each person's name is written next to the situations they mentioned. Usually, these situations relate to those identified in their functional analyses.

Next, the clients brainstorm ways in which people offer or push drinks. This list also is long and is written on the board. Examples include, "Would you like a drink? How come you're not drinking? What's the matter—you too good to drink with us?" and many others. The group leader tries to elicit a range from low to high pressure comments. This part of the discussion helps clients recognize ways that others attempt to pressure or embarrass them into drinking. Hopefully this recognition will make it easier to resist subtle pressures to drink. Next, the group generates a list of goals that they wish to accomplish in refusing a drink. This is a new notion to most group members, and they often hesitate after saying that the goal is to not drink. However, with some prompts or examples from the leader, they usually state that other goals are: to feel comfortable with refusal, to reinforce their personal commitment to not drinking, and to establish with other people that they have decided to stop drinking. Finally, a list of ways to refuse drinks is generated. This list usually includes many comments that may be viewed as excuses for not drinking, such as "I'm on medication," as well as positive refusals such as "I don't drink," "I'll have a ginger ale," or "I've quit drinking." After the list is completed, the leader helps the group to go through the list and evaluate each comment against the goals for refusal. Usually, the "excuses" are eliminated at this point. At the end of this group, one group member is asked to copy the list of refusal statements, and the group leader has this list photocopied to distribute during the next group.

The next group begins with a brief review of the previous group, and the list of refusal statements is distributed. This allows new members to become oriented to the topic. Then, role playing is introduced. The rationale for role playing, as explained to clients, is that it gives them an opportunity to put their ideas about refusing into practice in a safe environment where mistakes do not mean relapse. A sheet of guidelines for role playing is distributed, and a sample role play of drink refusal is carried out with all group members present. Then the group divides into small groups of three to four members and each small group goes into a separate room and practices role playing. Usually, two group therapists are available for the four small groups and must float between groups. However, most clients are able to carry out this task successfully, role playing and giving each other feedback. The group reconvenes for 5–10 minutes at the end of the hour, and each small group does one sample role play for the larger group. Clients are then encouraged to practice these skills outside of treatment hours, and report on their successes or difficulties.

The other four sessions of the social skills group focus on assertiveness and expressing feelings (e.g., Chaney, O'Leary, & Marlatt, 1978). When clients learn about behavior chains, they are introduced to the notion that there often is a relationship between feelings and drinking behavior. The social skills groups are designed to introduce information about ways of expressing feelings, and to reinforce the relationship between not drinking and expressing emotion. This series of groups has both a behavioral and a cognitive focus. In the first group, clients are presented with the three words, *passive, assertive*, and *aggressive*. Definitions of each word are brainstormed, and are written on the board. Often, clients have trouble discriminating between passive and calm. They also often think of aggressive as being determined about one's work, or ambitions. These confusions are clarified so that the two main dimensions that discriminate the three concepts are whether feelings are not expressed (passive), or are expressed (assertive and aggressive), and whether the other person's feelings are taken into account (assertive) or not (aggressive). Patients then are asked to discuss the ways in which their drinking changes how they express feelings, and if they could characterize themselves as mostly using one of the three defined response styles the majority of the time. Many clients characterize themselves as passive much of the time when not drinking, and aggressive when drinking. Many report that they "store up" angry thoughts, and express these when drinking. Some clients, in contrast, report that drinking enables them to forget angry feelings and be calmer. Some report no difficulties in this area, but can contribute to the group by talking about how they handle their own feelings.

In the next group session, the above definitions are reviewed briefly. The primary goals of this session are to illustrate how cognitive processes affect the decision to express feelings, to go through an exercise in disputing irrational thoughts about expressing feelings, and to go over guidelines for assertive behavior. The behavior chain is the vehicle for accomplishing this. Clients are asked to provide an example in which a person was passive but wished he or she had not been. Then a behavior chain is completed on the board. After writing down the situation, the group leader asks the group to identify as many thoughts as possible that would lead them to be passive. Thoughts are common ones, such as "If I say something, he won't like me," "It's silly for me to be upset," and so on. The passive behavior is then described, and positive and negative consequences of the passive behavior are generated and written on the board. Then the leader goes back to the passive thoughts and asks the group how they would dispute each of these thoughts in order to be assertive instead. The assertive thought is written in under each passive thought. The assertive behavior is then described, and the positive and negative consequences are also listed. The group concludes with a discussion of guidelines for assertive behavior. These include: (1) use "I feel" statements; (2) criticize behavior, not personality; (3) make specific requests for change; (4) say something positive about the person or situation; (5) make eye contact and use "good body language."

The next two group sessions are devoted to role playing for assertiveness. As with drink refusal role playing, guidelines are distributed, a sample role play is held in the large group, and the group divides into smaller subgroups to practice. A range of situations are role played. For example, a client may role play expressing dissatisfaction to his or her doctor, or talking to a co-worker who has been making mistakes and letting the client take the blame, or telling a spouse that something he or she is doing is annoying. After these topics are rehearsed, clients then try their new skills immediately with the relevant person. While specific assignments are not made at the end of the group, patients are encouraged to practice at home, and to then report back at the next group meeting or to their therapist. After some discussion of these experiences, the group spends a second session on role playing. At the conclusion of this second session, the group reconvenes to do sample role plays for each other. Again, assertion is reviewed in the daily group therapy, and further successes or problems are addressed there.

RELAXATION TRAINING

Relaxation training is another technique used to provide the problem drinker with skills that can serve as alternatives to drinking (see also Chapter 5). Clients who have used alcohol in an attempt to decrease anxiety and tension often are unaccustomed to experiencing these feelings and taking other action to reduce them.

Relaxation skills are taught to selected individuals who identify anxiety or tension as being strongly associated with drinking or urges to drink. Relaxation tapes are available to use during free time. On occasion, a staff member will create an individualized tape for a client to use, although time does not allow for this to be done routinely. Clients can make copies of the standard tape for their own use. The rationale for relaxation as an alternative to alcohol is explained to the client. Instructions about appropriate settings, body posture, attire, and imagery are presented. Clients are encouraged to practice daily and report their progress to the staff and other clients. Relaxation practice may be set as a goal and eventually should become an integral part of the clients' repertoire of alternative behaviors to drinking. Some groups like to listen to the tapes and practice together. Tapes and group practice are helpful to the program staff, who are often pressed for time and find it difficult to provide this rather time-consuming and repetitive treatment on an individualized basis.

This section has presented the concept of cognitive and behavioral alternatives to drinking, and how these are used in the clinical program. We now consider how these techniques were helpful to a client, "Bill."

The End of the Day for Bill. Bill was sitting with his group during the last meeting of the day on a Friday afternoon. Each group member was planning out the weekend, identifying potentially difficult times and situations, trying to decide how to handle them. Bill appeared restless, was tapping his feet and wiping his hands on his jeans. He said he was having a strong desire for a drink as he listened to others make weekend plans. He mentioned that he was accustomed to drinking after work on Friday afternoons, and that he did not think he would be able to drive past his favorite bar on his way home without having a drink. He said, "I'm so uptight I feel like I'm going to jump out of my skin!"

Immediately, the group members let Bill know that they understood how difficult it was to feel the way he was feeling. Someone mentioned that he had a choice about whether he drank or not and asked him if he wanted to give up how good he was feeling for a hangover, facing his wife, and maybe having a fight at the bar. The group also helped him recognize that it was natural to feel the way he was feeling. Bill talked about how much calmer he would feel if he drank, but recognized that although he would feel better temporarily, it was probably not worth the risk. He decided to take a different route home, by-passing the bar. He planned to play catch with his two boys after dinner, and agreed to meet one of the fellow group members at a nearby AA meeting at 7:30 that evening. He said he would ask his wife to come as well. The group wished him luck and said that they would see him on Monday morning.

On Monday, Bill said that he had managed to avoid the bar, played with his kids, and went to AA as planned. He, his wife, and some AA friends stopped for ice cream sundaes on the way home. He said that he felt proud of himself for getting through a day when he would usually have done a lot of heavy drinking.

SUPPORT SYSTEMS GROUP

So far, the discussion of the groups has presented educational information and skills training provided for the individual problem drinker. However, numerous studies have demonstrated the crucial role of external environmental supports in helping clients maintain changes in their drinking behaviors (e.g., Azrin, 1976; Hedberg & Campbell, 1974; Hunt & Azrin, 1973). This section describes ways that environmental supports for clients are involved in the treatment. The supports described here include spouse, children, other relatives, intimate friends, and employers. They are involved in a variety of settings, including twice weekly couples group, weekly family meetings, individual sessions with the program social worker, and telephone contacts. Basic alcohol information is provided, alcohol-related issues are addressed, and individualized techniques are developed for families and other supports to help the client to maintain abstinence and to improve the quality of relationships. Work with the client's support system has both a behavioral and cognitive focus. Network members are asked to read the manual and complete the written exercises. This helps familiarize them with some of the terminology, approach, and topics used in the PDP.

Couples and Families

The couples and family groups tend to be less structured than many of the other groups. Thus, the presentation of these groups will focus more on issues or topics that may be addressed at some point during a couple's participation in the program, rather than providing a group-by-group blueprint for couples' treatment. Couples and families are given a chance to explore their attitudes and discuss their feelings about the client's drinking. This is an important step, as couples and families often enter treatment with mixed and ambivalent feelings toward the client. Some are not sure they can improve their relationships, or maintain their marriage at all. Others are not sure that they want to attempt changes, for fear these attempts will fail. These attitudes are understandable, considering that many have experienced previous unsuccessful attempts at change. Spouses may also feel guilty and resentful because they have tried to control their partner's drinking, but to no avail. These feelings must be addressed in order to begin to work on other changes. The various family and couples groups are conducive to sharing and identifying with other people having similar thoughts and feelings. It can give family members a sense of relief to realize that having these feelings is understandable and that they are not alone in experiencing them.

Since making changes is difficult, risky, and time consuming, couples need to consider what they have at stake as they attempt to decide whether or not to enter treatment. Couples are asked to list negative consequences they will avoid if they work together to maintain abstinence and make positive changes. Couples are then asked to consider the immediate and more long-term positive consequences they have to gain if they become involved in attempting constructive changes. As a result of this exercise and the ensuing discussion, couples are often willing to become involved in the program. The couples group sessions address several areas, including couple problems that may be antecedents to drinking (e.g., communication problems); cognitive and affective issues, such as trust or feelings about family roles; generally increasing the reward value of the relationship and developing specific contingency contracts about drinking; and alcohol-specific issues such as urges and relapses.

Couples are taught some communication skills and problem-solving techniques. They are able to rehearse these skills outside of the program and discuss the results upon return to the group. The communication training is enhanced by the problem drinker's exposure to the social skills group. Role playing and modeling are useful tools to enhance this process.

An important area that is a common concern of many couples is trust. Many unpleasant situations have occurred within the family over the years, and it takes a long time before trust is established. Trust may have been replaced by suspicion. This is natural and is recognized and discussed by couples. They are taught that if spouses are suspicious or anxious that the problem drinker is drinking, it is constructive for the spouse to express this in a concerned way by stating the specifics that have been noticed. For example, a spouse might say, "You've been working hard not to drink. I've enjoyed being with you during this time. However, you were late coming home from work several nights this week and you seem rather worried. I'm wondering if you're drinking again." Spouses are told that this positive supportive approach could encourage their mate to discuss the situation far better than if they were to nag, smell his or her breath, check up on him or her, or keep their concerns to themselves. It is explained that it might be a support to the problem drinker to let him or her know that his or her spouse has liked being with him or her during abstinence and is still there for support. This intervention also allows the problem drinker a chance to reassure the spouse if there is no drinking. Thus, this can prevent unnecessary worrying for the spouse as well.

Another common concern is that of family roles. Since family members learn to assume particular roles within the system in response to one another's behavior (e.g., Steinglass & Robertson, 1981), it is very important for families to redefine and negotiate these roles and responsibilities once the problem drinker becomes abstinent and more involved in the family. Discussions are held for couples to share the feelings they have about giving up their roles as well as assuming new ones and making compromises. One example of this would be the situation where the wife has become the primary person who meets the children's needs, since her husband began to abuse alcohol. Once he became abstinent, he became more involved in his children's lives. The wife might discuss her fears, apprehensions, and regrets about sharing parenting responsibility with her husband once again. He in turn would be encouraged to talk about his feelings related to assuming a new family role. Further negotiations might take place to help this become a smoother transition.

A number of group topics serve to modify consequences of drinking and abstinence. Some spouses and family members are ready to set very clear and definite contingencies regarding the problem drinker's abstinence and potential relapse. Writing down the consequences of drinking that the family will implement can be useful to avoid misunderstanding and confusion. For example, one spouse stated that she wanted to continue with their marriage as long as her husband remained in treatment with her and continued to work on his abstinence. She said that if he slipped, but resumed abstinence and treatment, she would not leave him. She did say that if he resumed drinking, stopped treatment, and ceased trying to stop drinking, she would not be able to live with him and would leave him. The therapist asked the problem drinker to restate his wife's plan, and if he agreed with it. The therapist asked the wife if her husband seemed clear in his understanding of her plan. The couple then was asked to write this out to avoid any misunderstandings in the future. The written agreement would also be used as a reminder to the client of the negative consequences of a relapse.

Other spouses and family members may not be ready or able to set such contingencies, yet must be taught how to recognize the difference between a slip and relapse (see the following section) and their role in each. They are taught to recognize specific cognitive, emotional, and behavioral changes to identify both a slip and a relapse. They are also helped to develop their own set of alternatives, to assist them to keep the drinking episode in perspective, to remain as calm as possible, and to support the problem drinker's alternate behavior and not reinforce drinking behavior. The importance of making a decision for themselves, if active drinking should recur, is stressed, and support systems for the family are advised. These will be discussed when aftercare planning is described at the end of this section.

An Antabuse (disulfiram) contact can be used as an additional support for abstinence, as well as a supportive technique for the spouse. The problem drinker would agree to take Antabuse daily in the presence of the spouse, and at a specific time convenient to both. The spouse would agree to this and to a particular course of action to take if the problem drinker did not take the Antabuse. For example, the spouse might contact the therapist and agree to meet with the problem drinker and the therapist if the contract should be broken. An Antabuse contract may be made either verbally or in writing. A written agreement is encouraged, to prevent misunderstanding about the contingencies.

Couples and families are able to discuss and try out simple reciprocity assignments. As previously mentioned, couples are encouraged to find new mutually enjoyable activities. They are helped with other reinforcements, such as giving compliments and rearranging the consequences of drinking and nondrinking behavior. For example, a female client might feel sad and resentful that her husband is out late at various meetings a number of evenings a week. She may let him know she would like him home more, but have no success in changing his behavior. She may attempt to cope with her anger and loneliness by drinking and telephoning her husband. In turn, the husband may return home earlier and even skip meetings when she is drinking. However, as soon as his wife stops drinking, he returns to his nightly schedule again. Drinking resumes as his behavior changes and precipitates his wife's anger and loneliness. Clearly, the drinking is being reinforced by the husband's attentiveness when his wife drinks. This couple would be helped to change their communication, and the husband might be encouraged to modify his schedule in response to his wife directly expressing her desires and not in response to her drinking. He would be asked to show her attention more frequently when she is abstinent, but to detach from her if she is drinking. The wife would be asked to agree to remain abstinent if her husband is showing more attention, and both would compromise on the number of meetings he attended. She also would be encouraged to deal with her feelings without resorting to alcohol, even if he does not completely fulfill the agreement. Each partner also would be instructed to compliment the other when a positive change is made.

A variety of alcohol-related issues are addressed in couples and family groups. Couples discuss whether they will keep alcohol in their home, whether spouses will drink alcohol, how they can handle specific social situations where drinking is involved, and what they will tell people about their drinking problem and treatment. Families are taught that the problem drinker has the responsibility of choosing his behavior and that it is not the spouse's responsibility to control the drinking or to protect the problem drinker from experiencing negative consequences.

Family members often become anxious when the problem drinker experiences an urge to drink. They sometimes think that this means the client is *going* to drink. At these times, families may fall back on old methods in an attempt to prevent this from occurring. The family is helped to view an urge to drink as a natural feeling and to understand that an urge to drink does not mean that he or she will drink! The family is encouraged to think of ways to support the problem drinker during an urge. Because alternate responses are discussed and planned while the family is in treatment, some of the client's alternatives can include a family member. Other alternate responses do not involve the family, but anxiety is often reduced significantly if the family knows how the problem drinker is dealing with urges.

The following is an example of how a spouse might help a problem drinker with an urge to drink. The antecedent to this client's urge was coming home from work at 5 P.M. after a difficult day at work. He was thinking, "I never do anything right." He was feeling tense and hopeless. His thought was to have a drink to stop his thinking and to feel more relaxed. His wife was aware of her husband's tension, as well as alternatives they had discussed. She responded by reminding him of how he was falling into negative thinking and that he could develop more positive thoughts, could discuss his feelings more, and they could go for a walk together to unwind. She remembered to remain calm herself and keep the situaton in perspective without overreacting. The couple went for a leisurely walk before supper. They talked of their feelings for a while and ended their conversation on a positive and lighter note. The problem drinker and his spouse thus got through this urge by recognizing cognitive–emotional antecedents and utilizing cognitive–behavioral alternatives. The spouse was supportive, yet left the decision and responsibility to drink or not to drink up to her husband. Thus, the couples and family program has both a skills training component as well as contingency management procedures.

Employers

Incorporating the support of the employer can be another useful way of reinforcing the client's sobriety. Initially, the employer expresses support, since he or she is relieved that the employee is now in treatment. However, the support can be expanded further by the employer becoming involved with the treatment team by attending a meeting or by telephone contact. It can be helpful if the employer tells the problem drinker why he or she is valuable to the job and that the employer would like to see the problem drinker continue employment as long as he or she utilizes treatment and works at remaining sober. Sometimes the employer or company nurse might contract to witness the problem drinker's taking of Antabuse several times a week. Periodic discussions between the employer and aftercare therapist can be used to assess progress, support constructive change, identify potential lapses, and deal appropriately with relapses. Consistent with the general program philosophy that a drink should not mean catastrophe, employers are educated about the possibility of relapse and are given guidelines for effective responses to drinking episodes.

Self-Help Groups

Some clients and families are strongly encouraged to use AA, Al-Anon, and Alateen meetings while in the program. All clients attend at least three AA meetings before completion of the program. Weekly AA meetings are held on the grounds of the hospital. Since certain aspects of these meetings are antithetical to a behavioral approach, clients are taught to use the AA meetings primarily as a way of meeting nondrinking people, gaining support, and structuring time.

Aftercare

Even though the clients gain some initial skills to maintain abstinence, and rehearse these skills during treatment, maintenance of these skills and generalization to new situations and environments is an important continuing issue. Our goal is to involve all clients in some form of aftercare treatment after they complete their PDP day treatment. The clients are assisted by staff in choosing whatever combination of treatment and support systems best meets the family's needs. However, many clients feel confident that they need no further help. A weekly group as well as individual sessions and weekly staffings address the rationale for aftercare and available resources. Modeling in groups is an important step to encourage follow-up treatment. Often the group includes one member who had previously received PDP treatment, and relapsed. Many of these clients state that lack of involvement in aftercare contributed strongly to their relapse. The statistics on the frequency of relapse in the first 3 months following treatment (Hunt, Barnett, & Branch, 1971) are also used as a reason why aftercare treatment is important. When a client agrees to follow-up treatment, every attempt is made for the client to have an appointment at the aftercare agency prior to discharge. A staff member also may call a client after his or her first scheduled outpatient visit to discuss how it went.

Clients who wish follow-up treatment often want to continue with the treatment or therapist with whom they were involved in the program. Unfortunately, there are no agencies in the community that provide behaviorally oriented outpatient treatment. The staff on the unit are heavily committed to their day hospital responsibilities and have extremely limited time to provide follow-up treatment. Some workshops have been held to attempt to educate community agency personnel about the PDP approach to treatment, but most of these agencies still use a disease model approach. Because of staff dissatisfaction with the types of aftercare available, a long-term attempt was made to convince the hospital administration of the need for aftercare programming within the hospital. After a survey of the results of referrals to aftercare agencies showed that most clients did not continue unless they were seeing someone from the hospital, and after innumerable memos about the rationale for such a program, the hospital agreed to allocate funds for aftercare program personnel and for a training program for hospital clinical staff so that they could continue the treatment begun in PDP. The aftercare program at the hospital currently includes individual adult therapy and groups for individuals or couples.

In summary, a major treatment goal is to identify and engage the client's support systems. These might include spouses, children, other relatives, close friends, and employers. The purpose is to relay basic alcoholism information, and teach individualized techniques to help maintain sobriety. Short-term and long-term strategies can be developed to improve communication and rearrange the positive consequences of abstinence and the negative consequences of drinking. Members of these support systems are taught how to recognize drinking antecedents and to support alternative behaviors. Environmental changes can be made together to further deal with drinking cues. Since developing and rehearsing new skills are a long-term requirement for sobriety, aftercare is an essential treatment component to promote during the rehabilitation phase.

SLIPS GROUP

The entire structure of the PDP is designed to help clients and their families develop skills to avoid relapses and to minimize the length and severity of drinking episodes. However, it was also felt that the issue of slips should be addressed directly in one group session.

The term *slip* has been used to refer to drinking alcohol after a period of abstinence. Marlatt (Chapters 3 and 4) has taken this concept and expanded it by distinguishing three categories of slips: relapse, lapse, and prolapse. The PDP subscribes to this notion of slips, but also adds an additional element consistent with our orientation. The concept of a slip is not only related to behavior and its consequences, but it is also related to the chain of events that precede the drinking behavior.

In the slips group, each group member is asked to define the term slip by considering two basic questions: (1) What do I do if a slip occurs? and (2) What must happen in order for me to realize that a slip is about to occur?

The group begins with the group leader presenting information about what has happened to others after completing treatment for alcoholism. This is first approached by presenting the relapse curve (Hunt, Barnett, & Branch, 1971) presented in Chapter 1, Figure 1-3. It is pointed out that by 2 weeks after treatment, 33% of those treated consumed alcohol. At the end of 3 months, 60% drank. At the end of 8 months, 63% of the treated people slipped, and by the end of the 12 months 67% of the treated people slipped.

One could conclude that this information is destructive, leading group members to wonder, "What's the use, my chances for success are slim." Although many problem drinkers do question their ability to remain abstinent, this is an important question for them to ask. The information presents a realistic picture of the difficulty of remaining abstinent. It is hoped that this information will motivate individuals to utilize treatment to the fullest and will encourage them to use aftercare treatment once they have completed the day treatment program. It is also hoped that presenting information on relapses will help decrease guilt if the problem drinker has a slip. These statistics are intended to minimize guilt by demonstrating that slips are a part of the recovery process.

The statistics also have implications for treatment after hospital discharge. It is stressed that within the first 3 months following treatment, 60% of treated problem drinkers may slip. This seems to imply that the first 3 months are critical, and that taking active steps to avoid relapses is crucial. To dramatize the relationship between abstinence and active behavior change, the group is asked to brainstorm behaviors that they think are demonstrated by individuals who are likely to slip and behaviors of those likely to stay abstinent. Group members suggest that people who are likely to slip will go to bars, rely on willpower to remain abstinent, discontinue Antabuse after discharge, and discontinue outpatient counseling. The group, with help from the leader, will describe individuals likely to remain abstinent as continuing in counseling, stopping going to bars, participating in AA, taking Antabuse after discharge, increasing family or social system involvement, and developing interests in nondrinking activities. This exercise is useful in that it gives the problem drinker the opportunity to evaluate how he or she relates to the characteristics in each list. It also helps to minimize the negative effects of the statistics by implying that slips may be related to behavior, rather than destiny.

Once slips are presented as a common occurrence and the relationships between slips and the need for specific behaviors is illustrated, the group begins to consider what to do if a slip occurs. The focus is on developing a plan of attack for each group member if a slip should occur. At this point the group is asked: "Say that you have a lapse in your abstinence; are you going to stop the drinking episode or are you going to choose to continue to drink until you have had a complete relapse?" This question helps to demonstrate that lapses do not constitute failure, and that there is a choice between continuing drinking or stopping.

The group is asked to brainstorm ways of stopping a drinking episode. They are encouraged to write down the suggestions that they think will be effective in preventing the continuation of drinking, and are encouraged to carry this list for reference in case a lapse occurs. An example of such a list is: put down the drink; remove oneself from the lapse situation; review written lists of negative consequences of drinking and the positive consequences of abstinence; implement alternatives such as going to an AA meeting or seeking out a designated supportive person; think, "A drink is not a failure— I can still choose not to drink."

The group also addresses the second question raised above: How does one recognize that a slip is imminent? The program introduces problem drinkers to the notion that events prior to drinking can also be seen as a slip. Adding this component to the definition of a slip is important if problem drinkers are going to benefit from slip prevention. Group members are asked: "What is it that must happen in order for you to conclude that a slip is about to occur?" Some will respond by saying, "I must drink a great deal for a long time," others will indicate, "I must drink one beer." For others, one swallow is enough to constitute a slip. These responses show that they associate slips with drinking, but not with behaviors that precede drinking.

To address this issue, a group member is asked to share an experience where a slip occurred or almost occurred. The slip is written as a behavior chain on the board. One example often presented is when a person was lonely because he or she was avoiding a normal source of socializing, the bar. The slip occurred due to a sequence of events beginning at the point that the individual considered returning to the bar. The sequence may be outlined in the following manner.

- *Event 1:* The individual sits at home, lonely and feeling deprived of social contact. He or she might think, "I'll just go to the bar, see my friends, play cards and drink soda."
- *Event 2:* The person drives to the bar thinking about how good it will be to see friends, having no intentions of drinking, and not questioning his or her ability to refuse alcohol.
- *Event 3:* He or she pulls into the parking lot, stands in front of the bar, trying to avoid being aware of sweaty palms and increasing anxiety.
- *Event 4:* The individual walks in, looks around, and is engulfed in the atmosphere—the smell of alcohol, the loud conversation, smoke, people drinking, and laughter.
- *Event 5:* The individual begins entertaining thoughts such as, "One bottle of beer won't hurt. After all, I used to drink a quart of Jack Daniels. I've been sober for 3 months. I can control my drinking."
- *Event 6:* The bartender calls out the person's name and sets up his or her usual drink.
- *Event 7:* He or she sits in front of the drink.
- *Event 8:* The person picks up the drink and puts it to his or her lips.
- *Event 9:* The individual pours the alcohol into his or her mouth.
- *Event 10:* He or she swallows the alcohol. The question posed to the group is: "At which event do each of you think you would be most likely to ask for help or to avoid the drink?"

The leader would identify the event for each group member by writing their names next to the identified event. For the most part, group members will identify events early in the sequence, although occasionally an individual identifies event seven as the point to avoid the slip. This particular choice is usually discussed, because many problem drinkers believe that they need to test themselves in order to prove that they can refuse the drink. This thinking is discouraged by pointing out that it is obvious that problem drinkers do not do well on tests where there is alcohol involved. It is explained that the better test is learning to identify that one is slipping early in the sequence. To demonstrate the advantage of dealing with a slip by altering the events early in the sequence, the group will further analyze event seven and an earlier event, such as event one. The group is asked: "How would you deal with event seven to avoid drinking?" A group member may state, "I'll use my willpower and refuse." This is usually challenged by the group leader, or a group member who had failed such tests many times in the past. It doesn't take long for the group to be willing to abandon the idea that slip prevention is best at event seven.

The group finds that they have an easier time dealing with event one. A group member will focus on the individual sitting at home alone. He or she might note the danger of being alone, and refer to incidents in their own life when being alone influenced drinking. Members of the group may offer suggestions, such as calling or visiting a friend, or going shopping. Another group member may focus on the thought, "I'll just go to the bar, see my friends, play cards and drink soda." This individual may question the rationality of such a thought. The group may find it amusing to think that they would go to a bar for any reason other than to drink. In this situation, the suggested alternative would be related to concepts that the group has been learning in groups dealing with irrational thinking. The group may recognize that altering this thought may decrease the chance of getting into the car and driving to the bar.

This exercise attempts to sensitize problem drinkers to the notion that slipping can be defined in terms of events that occur long before the alcohol is consumed. It also demonstrates how altering events can stop the sequence of events, once recognized as likely to lead to drinking.

At this point, the group is asked to recognize how they have successfully dealt with slips in the recent past. For example, a group member could recognize how he or she prevented a complete relapse by coming into the hospital, or prevented slipping by not getting involved with a drinking situation the night before. It is important that group members be able to recognize that they are successfully dealing with slips, and to identify what they did that contributed to that success. For example, it is not by chance that members of the group remained abstinent over the weekend or did not drink the night before.

PROGRAMMATIC PROBLEMS AND SOLUTIONS

In the preceding sections of the chapter, we have described the PDP treatment philosophy and how this is implemented through the structured group program. The final section of the chapter addresses issues in designing and maintaining an ongoing clinical program when using a fairly structured behavioral approach to treatment. Our current attempts to solve these problems are also presented.

POPULATION VARIABLES

Alcohol problems can affect persons from a variety of educational, occupational, and social backgrounds. Similarly, the presenting symptoms can vary greatly. Because of this, a treatment program must be prepared to deal with a heterogeneous client population. The following section presents a sample of variables that can complicate treatment, and ways of dealing with them.

One issue facing any alcohol program is the question of whether clients participating in the treatment program are doing so while under the influence of drugs. The most commonly abused drugs are marijuana, minor tranquilizers such as Valium (diazepam) and Librium (chlordiazepoxide), barbiturates, and amphetamines. These drugs are like alcohol because they alter mood. The presence of drugs can have negative effects on the client using the drug, others in the treatment group, and the alcohol treatment program in general. The most common negative effects of using drugs are: (1) perpetuating a client's belief that drugs are a major way of handling life stresses; (2) interfering with the correct diagnosis of the cause of presenting symptomatology; (3) the danger created by prescribing medications without the knowledge that the client is abusing other medication; (4) decreasing cognitive functioning, which would affect the client's ability to benefit from the treatment program; (5) producing confusion in group members who are struggling with the difficulties of abstinence while seeing others anxiety free because of the drugs they are using; (6) damage to the program's reputation in the eyes of potential clients and referring physicians.

Because of the above concerns, detecting mood-altering drugs is an important responsibility of the treatment staff. Two techniques for detection are teaching the treatment staff the behavioral symptoms common to specific drugs and using drug screening tests. The latter approach eliminates suspicion and allows the treatment team to focus on the issue of treatment rather than the presence of nonprescribed drugs. The results of positive drug screens are shared with the client, which usually begins a therapeutic process of finding out why drugs are used and how treatment can be supportive until alternatives can be developed. The results of negative drug screens can be viewed as a form of external control that encourages clients to refrain from the use of nonprescribed medication, and can be used as an objective indication of success in treatment.

Another kind of problem encountered in a heterogeneous population is the occurrence of certain medical and psychiatric problems that appear or persist after alcohol withdrawal is completed. When this occurs, the staff will ask for a psychiatric consultation in order to determine medical and/or psychiatric needs. In some cases, the individual may need transfer to another treatment setting. In other situations, the psychiatric or physical problem can be treated simultaneously. In either case, it is important that the additional problems do not cause the treatment team or the consulting physician to lose sight of the fact that an alcohol problem does exist and treatment is required.

Another population variable that faces the staff in treating problem drinkers in a group is the variability in cognitive functioning. This variability can be a function of a variety of factors, such as level of education, age, sex, intelligence, cultural differences, language sophistication, level of motivation to participate, and other interfering problems. Because of the variability in cognitive functioning among group members, one may think that group treatment is an impossibility. On the contrary, it is this variability that makes group treatment most valuable. The task for the group leader is to utilize these varying experiences and skills to generate a group understanding of concepts being presented. For example, in any group the level of comprehension can vary from people who comprehend at a very concrete level to those who can comprehend complex abstractions. The concept that drinking is a learned behavior can be presented by using very theoretical terms such as behavior, expectations, reinforcement, and contingencies, or the concept can be presented in concrete terms such as, "You drink again because the last time you drank you liked it." The leader may present both these variations to the group in order to generate a group discussion in which each member learns from the various levels. The group usually produces a third variation of the original concept that will include technical terms, slang, street talk, and cursing. The variability of language includes all members in the discussion, giving the message that comprehension is what is important, however it can best be achieved.

To facilitate comprehension of theoretical concepts, specific techniques are used. First and most obvious is the use of behavioral chains. The chains are written down on a marker board to make the concepts as concrete as possible. Different colored markers are used to emphasize important components and relationships, or to contrast ideas. Repetition is also an important element in facilitating comprehension. It is normal for a group member to experience presentation of specific aspects of the program (such as behavior chains, alternatives, and goals) on more than one occasion. This is done because of the newness of the language and the difficulty of some of the skills being learned and to help those who may have memory problems. The program further relies on alternative teaching modalities such as lectures, groups, individual meetings, role playing, and audiovisual presentations.

A manual was also written by the PDP staff as a supplement to the group therapy. The manual contains approximately 125 pages and presents a variety of topics, ranging from an introduction to the functional analysis, an introduction to alternatives to drinking, and social skills techniques, to concepts relating to alcohol and medical complications, and issues relating to families. Homework assignments and exercises are included. Clients can use the manual during treatment and as a reference after treatment.

In this section, we have focused on client variables that affect the delivery of the treatment program. The next section describes administrative and structural variables that affect the program.

PROGRAMMATIC VARIABLES

There are myriad difficulties in running an ongoing treatment program, particularly in a hospital, that are not present when delivering treatment in a research project. In addition, there are some difficulties in treatment of alcoholics and problem drinkers in the day hospital that are not present in an inpatient treatment setting.

One of the most persistent problems is that clients must be admitted on a rolling basis, whenever the program has an opening. With rolling admissions, clients enter the program at any point in the sequence of treatment. Thus, some clients in the group may be familiar with behavior chains, may have already made significant changes in their marital situation, and have found a new activity to occupy themselves after work, while others may still be uncertain whether or not they have a drinking problem. The group leaders never have a group of clients who have all had the same information and experiences in the groups and, in fact, cannot even be assured that all the clients had participated in the previous day's group. These problems are dealt with in several ways. First, the content of each group is designed to communicate information on its own, without requiring prior knowledge in order for the group to be useful. Second, behavior chains are presented, and examples are worked repeatedly for clients. The behavior chain allows clients to have some framework for understanding what is being discussed in a particular group and for quickly being able to identify in what areas they need to make behavior changes. Thus, wherever in the sequence of groups they begin, once they learn about behavior chains, clients can begin to apply cognitive, affective, or behavior change groups to their own drinking problems, and understand how the various groups relate to drinking behavior.

A second way of handling the rolling admissions problem has been to not make the sequencing of the groups absolutely rigid. Thus, if a number of clients are nearing discharge, a group might be repeated that is particularly relevant to them, or which they had not previously participated in. There are some disadvantages to this flexible sequence, as some groups are not covered as frequently or systematically as would be ideal, but the flexibility is useful for the rolling admissions dilemma. Additionally, the content of the groups is somewhat redundant and repetitive, with many of the groups beginning with a review either of the previous group or of behavior chains, and the relationship between a particular group and behavior chains is usually mentioned.

Finally, clients who have been in the group longer are used to introduce new clients to the program. The older client will show the new person around the unit, and accompany him or her to groups. Sometimes, more experienced clients sit down with new people and explain behavior chains or other aspects of the group to them. They may go over parts of the treatment manual, or just talk. This is helpful to the person who has been in treatment longer and also seems to help the new person feel more comfortable.

The next set of problems is directly related to the fact that this is a day treatment program. Since clients go home every day and are home all weekend, there are increased opportunities for them to drink or use drugs during treatment, or to completely relapse and discontinue treatment. Getting accurate information about their behavior outside of treatment hours sometimes becomes difficult. Clients are often reluctant to report drinks or even thoughts about wanting to drink. Sometimes, this seems to stem from their previous experience of being punished by those around them if they drank. Also, since many disease model alcoholism treatment programs discharge clients immediately if they drink, and since many of our clients have participated in such programs, it is not surprising that they do not willingly or easily report their drinking.

A number of techniques are used to minimize drinking episodes during treatment to increase honesty and to maximize the likelihood that the treatment staff is obtaining accurate information about the client's behavior outside of treatment. To help clients remain abstinent, much of treatment focuses on short-term ways of staying sober. For most, drink-refusal training comes early in treatment. Clients learn how to do behavior chains early and are encouraged to analyze drinking urges using these chains. Time structuring is discussed regularly; the end-of-the-day meeting addresses plans for the evening or weekend and helps clients anticipate possible drinking situations and how they can avoid or manage them successfully without drinking. This daily focus on *how* to stay sober appears important. Some clients are quite concerned that they will not be able to avoid drinking. For some, Antabuse is prescribed. They are still exposed to the same cues for drinking, but are forced to find some behavior alternative to drinking because of the fear that they will become ill if they drink while on Antabuse. Clients also are breath tested on a regular basis. The breath testing is done at the first meeting of the day, allowing the staff to detect morning drinking, or heavy drinking from the previous evening. Because the breath testing is done in a group setting, there is strong social pressure not to drink, since all members of the group would know. The breath testing also contributes to the staff's obtaining accurate information about drinking. As noted above, clients who have a history of using or abusing drugs also have regular blood or urine screens as well.

Involvement of the family in the treatment is also important to the process of supporting abstinence and getting accurate information. All clients who have available family members, roommates, or close friends are approached by the social worker and asked to agree to allow their significant other to be contacted. Most agree. When the correspondent comes in for an initial interview, information about the client's drinking history and other problem areas is obtained. The way that the correspondent has responded to these problems also is explored. Finally, the person is strongly encouraged to participate in the family or couples group meetings. As discussed previously, since much of the focus of these meetings is on how to support abstinence, how to discuss drinking urges, and how to manage drinking episodes, the spouse or significant other quickly becomes available as a support for the patient outside of treatment hours. Hopefully the person has skills to be supportive and also has a relationship with the treatment staff, so that drinking will often be reported by the significant other even before the client has acknowledged it.

Finally, to help honesty clients are told explicitly during some of the groups that drinking occurs in problem drinkers, that the most important aspects of having a slip are managing it to minimize its length and severity, and to learn from it. Then, if a client has a slip during treatment and reports it, has a positive breath-test reading, or a significant other tells the staff about the drinking, the client is encouraged to work an individual behavior chain around the drinking episode, and it is discussed in group. Other group members may be encouraged to brainstorm ways of avoiding similar slips, and may also discuss their own experiences with slips or relapses, as a way to minimize the punitive aspects of discussing the drinking episode. However, for clients who return to daily or addictive drinking, rehospitalization may be recommended, followed by at least a brief course of Antabuse while in the PDP. Clients who engage in frequent but not addictive drinking and who do not seem committed to sobriety may be put on a treatment contract that requires abstinence, with a series of contingencies for continued drinking, the ultimate consequence being discharge from the program. However, even if a client is discharged in this manner or discontinues treatment to return to drinking, that person would still be readmitted if he or she sought further treatment. Again, this is in marked contrast to disease-oriented programs, which may state that the person has not yet "hit bottom" and therefore is not ready for treatment.

Separate from the problems of the program and interfacing with the hospital is the extremely important issue of staff morale and the possibility of staff burnout. The clients turn over rapidly in the program, the content of the groups becomes repetitive, clients relapse and return for further treatment, the schedule is heavy, many people are putting conflicting demands on the staff, and many clients are irritable, uncertain about whether or not they want to or need to stop drinking, or have memory and comprehension deficits and are confused and therefore difficult to work with. Staff are on the unit with the clients for 6½ hours/day, with only short breaks.

Frequent supervision and case reviews help staff to discuss treatment plans, gain perspective on difficult clients, and discuss their frustration in working with certain clients. The program chief lets staff know that frustration and difficulty in maintaining a therapeutic stance with some clients is acceptable. She may discuss her own reactions to difficult clients, and enlist feedback and support from other staff members. Staff meetings to discuss program planning and program changes are also held weekly. Staff are extremely active in generating new ideas for program changes, and for evaluating the success of certain program activities. They also look for and discuss problems encountered by alcoholic clients elsewhere in the hospital. This vigilance increases their alliance with the program, and gives them an awareness of the importance of their role in assuring that problem drinkers throughout the hospital get quality care. Staff meetings and supervision are often quite humorous. Many jokes are cracked, often having absolutely nothing to do with the clients or the program. Staff will gently tease each other when a staff member is doing something that is bothering other staff. Feedback about problems that different staff have as therapists is also delivered in a supportive, sometimes teasing way. Staff often put their feet up on extra chairs, or tip their chairs back against the wall during such meetings (as does the program director). This informality, joking, tangentiality, and teasing allows for a break from the pressured day, and also creates an atmosphere of caring and involvement that allows staff to feel more comfortable to discuss difficult issues as therapists.

Staff are actively involved in providing educational programs for the rest of the hospital. Regular case conferences are held, led by the unit staff, and the themes are often creative ideas that staff generate (e.g., a case conference entitled "Your Slip Is Showing" to illustrate our model of lapse and relapse and how to manage it). The staff also suggested writing a treatment manual and wrote much of it on their own time. Several of the content groups were developed by unit staff, and three are participating in coauthoring this chapter. In general, the relaxed, supportive atmosphere, the joking, the high staff involvement in planning and contributing to the development of the program, and a treatment model that allows clients to make mistakes all contribute to high morale under difficult circumstances.

Another major problem for an alcoholism treatment program that operates within a general psychiatric facility is that of interfacing with the admissions office and the inpatient service in order to identify problem drinkers and to facilitate the referral of such clients.

Most clients usually have their first contact with the hospital through the admissions office, where a decision about a person's need for treatment and level of care (i.e., inpatient, outpatient, or Day Hospital) is made. For clients who are not in need of 24-hour care initially, a direct referral is made to the PDP. Most of the program referrals, however, come from the inpatient service, since most of the people who present themselves to our facility are in need of a brief detoxification period or inpatient intervention. The potential PDP referral, therefore, is initially evaluated by and under the care of a treatment team that is not directly a part of the PDP. The initial treatment team can and does make decisions about a problem drinker's treatment independent of the PDP staff.

Other treatment staff in the hospital are not always aware of indirect indicators of drinking problems and may not know clinical strategies to assess such problems. However, even when staff recognize an alcohol problem, they may believe that no treatment can help an alcoholic, and therefore they may not work hard to get a client to begin in treatment on the PDP. They may also believe that unless a person is "motivated" or "has hit their bottom," then treatment is useless. Our philosophy is, of course, that a problem drinker's decisions about abstinence and the need for change can be affected by appropriate treatment methods.

Some clinicians may believe that alcoholism programs treat clients for their alcohol abuse independent of any other problems they may have. In their view, a client who seems "primarily depressed" would not receive adequate treatment in PDP. Also, clinicians who have not had a lot of experience with problem drinkers may tend to accept the stereotype of alcoholics as male, skid-row bums, and be reticent to diagnose and refer someone who does not fit their stereotype.

The last attitudinal problem involves the belief that returning to drinking and seeking readmission is indicative of a treatment failure and lack of "motivation" on the client's part. Any of the above beliefs, particularly when coupled with ambivalence on the part of the client, can result in the client not using the PDP.

After a period of trial and error, a set of solutions that seem most effective has been adopted. The solutions fall into two categories—a formal inservice education program and informal contact between the PDP liaison staff and the inpatient and admissions staffs.

The inservice education program consists of a series of films, videotapes, and occasional lectures and discussions, which all new staff are required to attend. The hospital also has an ongoing education program. One part of this program consists of case conferences in which a treatment team presents a client's problems and history, the specific treatments used, and the outcome. This affords us with the opportunity to educate other staff not only about alcoholism and what can be done in treatment, but also about our philosophy regarding relapses and relapse prevention.

The second major part of the ongoing education program is a rotation (as group observers) of inpatient staff through PDP. This involves the unit staff members being away from their unit and in PDP for only about 5 hours/week. Unit staff often observe clients who detoxified on their unit in groups and can see their progress through treatment. PDP staff also make themselves available to go to inpatient unit staff meetings to explain the program and philosophy.

The second solution to the problems with referrals involves the PDP liaison staff person. The liaison not only screens clients and offers consultation on referrals, but also troubleshoots for problems at the various steps in the referral process and makes himself available to give advice on problematic referrals. This type of informational education is very effective because it involves a current problem with specific therapeutic techniques. Also, if the advice is effective, considerable credibility is attributed to PDP consultations and therefore to the PDP.

The final program problem has been that of establishing positive community relationships when the program does not use a disease model approach. Many alcoholism counselors were suspicious of the behavioral model, equated it with controlled drinking, and did not like the research focus of the unit. The program director and many of the other staff joined community committees for alcoholism planning, and sat on many panels to discuss alcoholism treatment and resources and to present the program. One member of the staff became active in the local Alcoholism Counselors Association. Some clients are strongly encouraged to attend AA meetings, and AA, Alateen, and Al-Anon meetings are held on the grounds of the hospital. The community is quite aware of the program's use of AA and animosity has abated somewhat. However, most disease-oriented alcoholism counselors prefer not to refer to our program, referring instead to one of the inpatient, AA-oriented alcoholism rehabilitation hospitals in the area.

CONCLUSIONS

Social-learning approaches to the treatment of problem drinkers can be innovative, exciting, and compassionate. Deriving such treatments from theoretical and empirical literature is challenging, but applying these concepts to a heterogeneous population in a complex natural clinical setting is equally or more challenging. Developing ways of handling the myriad challenges has been a gradual process and continues. We have attempted in this chapter to give the reader specific techniques and warnings about major pitfalls so that others who want to develop clinical programs will have some guidelines. The data about the program indicate that the effectiveness of the treatment is high, which is encouraging in suggesting that treatment can be derived from a research base, applied in a relatively uncontrolled setting, and still result in robust results.

POSTSCRIPT

Bill had been out of the PDP for 3 months. Abstinence had been fairly easy and manageable much of the time. Yet, at times his urges to drink were strong, and he worked hard to think them through and use alternatives to drinking. His use of support systems, begun when he was in PDP, was extremely important and helpful. Bill attended a PDP couples aftercare group once a week on Monday evenings. He attended one AA meeting a week as well. Bill returned to work. He and his wife were spending more time together and with their children. They were all making gains in the quality of their communication and mutual leisure time. They still had times when each would resort back to old behaviors. He would withdraw and "bottle up" his feelings on occasion. She tended to nag him during these periods, trying to get him to discuss issues. But in general their conversations were more open and direct.

As the weeks passed, Bill continued to feel "good." He and his wife quit the couples aftercare group. He even skipped his weekly AA meeting every few weeks. After all, he thought, "I haven't been drinking for nearly 6 months. I don't really think my problem with alcohol was really that bad!"

The holiday season was beginning to unfold. Bill and his wife were busy with Christmas shopping and decorating their home. The kids were excited and his wife thought to herself, "I hope we have the best holiday season ever." Bill was working overtime these days so they weren't spending as much time together quietly talking. He stopped going to his AA meetings altogether so he could help with the preparations. Several parties were being held and there just was not enough time for everything! He told one friend, "I don't need to go to AA anymore as I don't have problems with drinking now."

Bill and his wife attended his company Christmas party. He was feeling a bit awkward because so many of his co-workers knew he had stopped drinking. As he was going for refreshments, several buddies walked up and slapped him on the back, pushing him quickly forward to the bar. One had the money out in his hand and was speaking loudly to the bartender, "Give this man a beer. He thinks he can't drink and he's wrong. One beer won't hurt him!" Bill tried to back away and decline, but his thoughts were becoming confused and his two buddies continued to push and shout. He took the beer and thought, "Okay, well, I guess I can have a beer or two tonight. I'm okay." He walked back to his table and his wife was off talking to several friends she had not seen since the party a year ago. He drank the beer down quickly before she would return and notice. However, except for one more beer later on that night, he drank club soda throughout the remainder of the party.

Bill was leaving work several days later. Several of the men who had encouraged him to have the beer at the party raced toward him as he was getting into his car. They said, "Stop by the club with us for a while on the way home. You haven't joined us in a long time." He agreed to stop for just a short while. He thought, "I drank two beers at the party and had no problems. I'll do the same and be home in time for dinner." As Bill walked into the club, several of his buddies began to cheer and shout, "Come have a beer with us." Several people he knew were playing pool in the corner. They stopped to welcome him back and asked him to play the winner. He agreed and soon decided to spend several hours before going home. He drank 8 or 10 beers before leaving, and by the time he arrived at his house, dinner was over and his wife and children had gone out. A note from his wife was on the counter saying she had gone to a meeting and the children were staying at a friend's house. He had several mixed drinks and went to bed.

The next morning, Bill did not get up for work. His head hurt and his stomach felt queasy. As he lay in bed he thought of the important business meeting he was missing by not being at work. He remembered his boss telling him when he was in PDP that he wanted him back in the company as long as he did not drink. He began to think of how much better his relationship with his wife and children had been since he stopped drinking. He was feeling better physically as well. He got out of bed and telephoned the staff member who had worked with him in the program. He discussed the positive consequences of his sobriety with her.

He talked about the problems that could result if he continued to drink. He decided to remain abstinent. He planned out the remainder of the day and evening and called his wife at work to invite her out for dinner. He told her of his decision not to drink and how much he had learned about his thoughts and behavior as he looked back at his recent lapse.

REFERENCES

Azrin, N. H. Improvements in the community-reinforcement approach to alcoholism. *Behaviour Research and Therapy*, 1976, *14*, 339–348.

Beigel, A., & Feder, S. L. Patterns of utilization in partial hospitalization. *American Journal of Psychiatry*, 1970, *126*, 1267–1274.

Chaney, E. F., O'Leary, M. R., & Marlatt, G. A. Skill training with alcoholics. *Journal of Consulting and Clinical Psychology*, 1978, *46*, 1092–1104.

Craft, M. Psychiatric day hospital. *American Journal of Psychiatry*, 1959, *116*, 251–254.

Ellis, A. *Reason and emotion in psychotherapy*. New York: Stuart, 1962.

Fink, E. B., Longabaugh, R., & Stout, R. Partial hospital under-utilization. In R. Luber, J. Maxey, & P. Lefkovitz (Eds.), *Proceedings of the annual conference on partial hospitalization*. Boston: Federation of Partial Hospitalization Study Groups, 1977.

Finzen, A. Psychiatry in the general hospital and the day hospital. *Psychiatry Quarterly*, 1974, *48*, 489–495.

Fotrell, E. M. A ten years' review of the functioning of a psychiatric hospital. *British Journal of Psychiatry*, 1973, *123*, 715–717.

Fox, V., & Lowe, G. D. Day hospital treatment of the alcoholic patient. *Quarterly Journal of Studies on Alcohol*, 1968, *29*, 634–641.

Foy, D. W., Miller, P. M., Eisler, R. M., & O'Toole, D. H. Social skills training to teach alcoholics to refuse drinks effectively. *Journal of Studies on Alcohol*, 1976, *37*, 1340–1345.

Fried, Y., & Brull, F. Intensive psychotherapy for acute psychiatric patients in a day hospital setting in Israel: Theoretical considerations. *British Journal of Psychiatry*, 1972, *131*, 635–639.

Guy, W., Gross, G. M., & Hogarty, G. E. A controlled evaluation of day hospital effectiveness. *Archives of General Psychiatry*, 1969, *20*, 329–338.

Hedberg, A. G., & Campbell, L. A comparison of four behavioral treatments of alcoholism. *Journal of Behavior Therapy and Experimental Psychiatry*, 1974, *5*, 251–256.

Hunt, G. M., & Azrin, N. H. A community-reinforcement approach to alcoholism. *Behaviour Research and Therapy*, 1973, *11*, 91–104.

Hunt, W. A., Barnett, L. W., & Branch, L. G. Relapse rates in addiction programs. *Journal of Clinical Psychology*, 1971, *27*, 455–456.

Kanfer, F. H., & Phillips, J. S. *Learning foundations of behavior therapy*. New York: John Wiley & Sons, 1970.

Longabaugh, R., McCrady, B., Fink, E., Stout, R., McAuley, T., Doyle, C., & McNeill, D. Cost-effectiveness of alcoholism treatment in partial vs. inpatient settings: Six month outcomes. *Journal of Studies on Alcohol*, 1983, *44*, 1049–1071.

Luber, R. F. (Ed.). *Partial hospitalization: A current perspective*. New York: Plenum, 1979.

Mahoney, M. *Cognition and behavior modification*. Cambridge, Mass.: Ballinger, 1974.

Marlatt, G. A., & Gordon, J. R. Determinants of relapse: Implications for the maintenance of behavior change. In P. O. Davidson & S. M. Davidson (Eds.), *Behavioral medicine: Changing health lifestyles*. New York: Brunner/Mazel, 1980.

Miller, W. R., Taylor, C. A., & West, J. C. Focused versus broad-spectrum behavior therapy for problem drinkers. *Journal of Consulting and Clinical Psychology*, 1980, *48*, 590–601.

Pallett, A. Alcoholic day treatment unit; Herbert Day Hospital, Bournemouth. *British Journal of Addictions* (Notes and News), 1976, *71*, 99–100.

Powell, B. J., & Viamontes, J. Factors affecting attendance at an alcoholic day hospital. *British Journal of Addictions*, 1974, *69*, 339–342.

Rabiner, C., & Lurie, A. A case for psychiatric hospitalization. *American Journal of Psychiatry*, 1974, *131*, 761–764.

Ruprecht, A. L. Day-care facilities in the treatment of alcoholics. *Quarterly Journal of Studies on Alcohol*, 1961, *22*, 461–470.

Ryan, W. A new approach to employee alcoholism. *New England Business*, June 1, 1981, pp. 32–36.

Sobell, L. C., & Sobell, M. B. *Clinical aspects of a behavioral treatment program for problem drinkers.* Paper presented at the annual meeting of the Association for Advancement of Behavior Therapy, New York, 1980.

Steinglass, P., & Robertson, A. The alcoholic family. In B. Kissin & H. Begleiter (Eds.), *The biology of alcoholism* (Vol. 7: *Psychosocial pathogenesis of alcoholism*). New York: Plenum Press, 1981.

Washburn, S. L., Vanicelli, M., & Longabaugh, R. A controlled comparison of psychiatric day treatment and inpatient hospitalization. *Journal of Consulting and Clinical Psychology*, 1976, *44*, 665–675.

Zitter, R., & McCrady, B. S. *The Drinking Patterns Questionnaire.* Unpublished manuscript, 1979.

8

PREVENTING RELAPSE IN EX-SMOKERS: A SELF-MANAGEMENT APPROACH

SAUL SHIFFMAN, LAURA READ, JOAN MALTESE, DAVID RAPKIN, AND MURRAY E. JARVIK

Smoking kills. In the United States alone, *1000 people die each day* of smoking-related disease. While they live, people who smoke (55 million in the United States) suffer more illness, hospitalization, and work disability than nonsmokers. Quitting smoking reduces or eliminates all of these ill effects. The longer ex-smokers are abstinent, the more their health approaches that of nonsmokers (U.S. Public Health Service, 1979).

Yet most people who quit smoking relapse. Smoking cessation programs are quite effective in helping people stop smoking; cessation rates of 70% are typical and 100% "quit" rates are not uncommon. Within 6 months, however, 75%–80% of these "successes" are smoking again (Hunt & Matarazzo, 1973). Mark Twain put it succinctly: "Quitting smoking is easy—I've done it a hundred times."

The key to successful treatment of smoking is relapse prevention. While smoking cessation is clearly a necessary condition for long-term maintenance of nonsmoking, cessation by itself has nearly become a trivial clinical achievement. "Better" smoking cessation methods are not likely to produce substantial improvements in maintenance. We need clinical methods that address the core of the problem—Relapse Prevention (RP).

This chapter presents a clinical approach to RP in smokers and ex-smokers. Our aim is to provide guidelines for the working clinician involved in the treatment of cigarette smoking. While much of what we propose is supported by clinical research, many aspects of our approach have yet to be rigorously tested. Such is the state of the art; research on RP is in its infancy and the clinical enterprise must proceed based on provisional conclusions. We have used, extrapolated from, and cited relevant research where it exists. Much of our thinking is based on our clinical experience with smokers who were facing the challenges of maintenance. Over several years, as part of a clinical research program on long-term maintenance of nonsmoking, we have operated an RP hot line for ex-smokers. The Stay-Quit Line (SQL),

472

which is described in detail later in the chapter, provided counseling for ex-smokers undergoing relapse or near-relapse episodes. Our work with hundreds of ex-smokers who called the SQL was the clinical laboratory in which our methods were developed and tested. Before proceeding with a description of our clinical approach, we will develop its theoretical and empirical underpinnings.

THEORY

While smoking may be a physical addiction to nicotine, we believe that the best approach to clinical treatment of smoking does not focus on this aspect of smoking behavior. We approach the modification of smoking behavior as a problem in self-control or self-management. The traditional emphasis on personal pathology or personal traits is replaced with a focus on critical situations and on personal self-management skills.

These are two hallmarks of our RP approach: a situational focus and an emphasis on coping skills. The introductory chapters have already outlined this point of view. We wish only to add here that research has not supported the importance of personality traits in the maintenance of nonsmoking. Many attempts have been made to identify the traits associated with recidivism. With minor exceptions these attempts have failed (Smith, 1970). This "trait" approach attributes relapse to some stable process, quality, or deficit in the ex-smoker and thus focuses on discovering *who* will relapse. This ignores the fact that relapses are concrete events and that the first cigarette must be smoked at a specific time and place under particular circumstances. We believe that a focus on these "critical incidents" is more productive. Thus, the core of our approach is a focus on events and situations that trigger relapse.

Clearly, however, no situation is sufficient to cause relapse. In order for a relapse to occur, the situational cues and the craving they engender must overwhelm the ex-smoker's capacity to cope or resist. Relapse occurs at the intersection of a triggering situation and a deficient coping response. Indeed, our work shows that the ex-smoker's coping response may be the critical factor in bringing about relapse. The development of skills for coping with relapse-facilitating situations is the major focus of our clinical approach.

An important characteristic of the RP approach is its emphasis on *self-management*. This is a broad and ambitious conception of treatment. The RP approach does not promise or offer magical cures for smoking. It assumes that these are impossible because it sees the control of smoking as a problem of self-control. The RP model assumes that success in maintenance depends on the client, and aims to teach clients an approach to regulating their own behavior and their lifestyle. The client is not passively acted upon but is the active agent of treatment.

RELAPSE CRISES

The core of RP lies in anticipating and coping with relapse-facilitating situations, which we call *relapse crises*. (The word *crisis* may be deceiving here, since some of these situations are quite pleasant and unstressful. The situations need only be critical with regard to maintenance.) A relapse crisis is an event in which the ex-smoker experiences a threat to abstinence. Another definition of relapse crises reflects the joint importance of situational antecedents and coping responses: crises are high-risk situations in which impulses tax the person's coping resources.

Our concept of *relapse crisis* differs somewhat from the concept of a *high-risk situation* as defined in Chapter 2, though there is much overlap. *High-risk situation* focuses on the situation, while our concept focuses on the ex-smoker's experience or response in the situation. A cocktail party, for example, is a high-risk situation for most smokers. This high-risk situation produces a crisis only some of the time, when it brings the ex-smoker to (or over) the brink of smoking. Relapse crises occur in a subset of high-risk situations (and lapses in a subset of crises). This difference in terminology is a difference in emphasis, rather than one of fundamental theory, and the terms will be used nearly interchangeably.

In discussing maintenance, we prefer to focus on relapse *crises*, rather than relapse episodes. Focusing on relapse crises allows us to become familiar with success as well as failure in maintenance. Also, our work with ex-smokers has shown that there is little reason for distinguishing between lapses and near lapses: their situational antecedents and emotional consequences are surprisingly similar. In a study of callers to our smoking cessation hotline, we found that relapse crises tend to have similar emotional consequences for the ex-smoker, regardless of their outcome (Shiffman, Read, & Jarvik, 1981). Marlatt (Chapter 3) predicts that successful coping with a high-risk situation will enhance an ex-smoker's self-efficacy, while relapse or failure to cope will precipitate the Abstinence Violation Effect (AVE) (see Chapter 3), including diminished self-efficacy. Among the ex-smokers we studied in our smoking hotline study, relapse crises had uniformly negative emotional impact, regardless of their outcome. Ex-smokers who had successfully coped with the crisis were just as likely as those who had lapsed to report feelings of failure and lowered self-efficacy. This may be an artifact of our method, since ex-smokers who experienced a surge in confidence would be unlikely to call a hotline for help. We believe, however, that these findings reflect a more important process. Ex-smokers don't expect to experience relapse crises—they naively expect that a successful maintenance is one free of difficulty or struggle. Given this standard, they count all crises—even successfully managed ones—as "failures." (Bandura, 1977, has emphasized the importance of internal standards as determinants of self-efficacy.) This highlights the importance of instilling appropriate expectations regarding maintenance. Ex-smokers who measure their performance against an unrealistic standard are bound to become demoralized and ultimately to relapse.

In our analysis of hundreds of relapse crises, we also found few differences in the situations that precipitated relapse and those in which relapse was averted (Shiffman, 1982). The situation precipitates a relapse crisis but does not determine its outcome; relapse crises can be defined as phenomena in their own right independent of outcome. Relapse crises have common situational antecedents and emotional consequences, regardless of their outcome.

The outcome of a relapse crisis is determined by the ex-smoker's response to the crisis. Ex-smokers who produced coping responses were generally successful in maintaining abstinence in the face of strong temptations to smoke. Nearly one out of five ex-smokers did not attempt to cope with the relapse crisis, and these noncopers were the most likely to relapse. Any coping response was better than none. Thus, crises are situational, but relapses depend on the failure of the ex-smoker's coping capacity.

COPING WITH RELAPSE CRISES

The greatest single cause of relapse is failure to attempt coping in relapse crises. In order to formulate a program of RP, it is useful to understand how these failures to cope come about. While the production of a coping response in a particular situation appears simple, the underlying sequence of events is relatively complex. First, the ex-smoker must recognize the risk of relapse and thereby cue the remainder of the sequence. This stage requires an awareness of craving and a recognition that some action is required ("Uh-oh, I'm in trouble here—I really want a smoke. I'd better do something."). Many ex-smokers are lost at this first juncture, "Before I even knew I wanted one, I was smoking."

Once the ex-smoker is aware of the relapse crisis, other processes may interfere with the production of coping responses. Inhibitory anxiety may derail the process. Intoxication may inhibit further action. Low self-efficacy (the expectation that one is incapable of doing anything) may lead to inaction. Or, the ex-smoker may make a conscious, deliberate decision to smoke.

If the ex-smoker survives these tests, he or she is then faced with a problem in *meta-coping*—deciding what coping response to use. This involves evaluation of the situation and of one's coping repertoire and a match between the two. (Obviously, these processes are nearly instantaneous and largely implicit.) In evaluating the situation, the ex-smoker must consider motivations for smoking, the urgency and danger of the impulse, and available options. In choosing a coping response, one implicitly considers one's repertoire by asking which might help, which is best for the situation, and whether the response is likely to be effective. Failure in these considerations will result in inadequate coping, inappropriate coping, or no coping.

Finally, assuming that the preceding steps have been successfully negotiated, a specific coping response is produced. Unfortunately, this does not guarantee success. In our analyses, nearly a third of the ex-smokers who attempted coping nevertheless smoked (Shiffman, 1982). Not all coping is adequate or successful. How quickly the coping response is produced may be important. In a laboratory analogue study, Chaney, O'Leary, and Marlatt (1978) found that alcoholics who were slower to produce coping responses on the Situational Competency Test (SCT) were more likely to relapse. Our work suggests that coping responses become less effective when ex-smokers are depressed or have been drinking, perhaps because the coping is enacted half-heartedly (Shiffman, 1982). The coping response may be incomplete or inadequate. Multiple coping responses are more successful than single coping responses (Shiffman, 1982). In a pilot of a study similar to Chaney et al.'s (1978), we also found that recidivists' coping responses were of lower quality; they were vaguer and less appropriate for the situation (Shiffman, Maltese, & Jarvik, 1983). Thus, while any coping response is better than none, some coping performances are better than others.

Given a crisis, the person's response to it, and an outcome, the future of the person's attempts at maintenance is determined by his or her attitudes and feelings about these events. One's expectations and standards will color one's response. If one takes the crisis in stride as an anticipated struggle, analyzes the crisis and learns from it, resolves to continue one's efforts and feels confident in that endeavor, then one is likely to recover from the experience. If the AVE leads to feelings of guilt and incompetence, and if these feelings then keep one from confronting and analyzing one's difficulties and allow one to justify further indulgence, then return to baseline smoking will be the likely result. Each stage in the resolution of a relapse crisis thus holds the potential for failure and the promise of successful intervention.

RESEARCH FINDINGS

Because this approach to relapse prevention is new, it has not been thoroughly researched. Situational antecedents of relapse have attracted the most attention from investigators. Other studies have tested a number of propositions of the RP model. The role of self-efficacy has also been investigated.

RELAPSE DETERMINANTS

Several different research groups have studied the situational determinants of relapse in ex-smokers. Cummings, Gordon, and Marlatt (1980) report on data collected by Marlatt's group on the precipitants identified by relapsed smokers who had undergone outpatient treatment. According to the classification scheme described in Chapter 2, negative emotional states account for 37% of the relapses, and interpersonal conflict accounts for 15%. Thus, the majority of relapses are associated with negative affect. Social pressure, which includes the indirect pressure of others' smoking, accounts for an additional one third of relapses. The contributions of other determinants were relatively minor.

Lichtenstein, Antonuccio, and Rainwater (1977) described relapse episodes in 84 unassisted quitters using Marlatt's coding scheme. Their data differ from those of Cummings *et al.* (1980) in that urges and temptations (18%) and social pressure (48%) were more prevalent, while negative emotional states were less prevalent. Perhaps unassisted quitters differ from clinic members. Differences notwithstanding, the studies show that negative affect and social pressure are overwhelmingly the most important relapse precipitants.

Lichtenstein *et al.* (1977) also report that more than a third of relapses occurred when the ex-smoker had been drinking alcohol and nearly two thirds occurred when other smokers were present. The smokers were evenly divided on the experience of smoking itself—equal numbers found it pleasant and unpleasant. Most experienced guilt or regret, and most tried to regain control of their smoking following the lapse.

In our studies of relapse episodes and crises, we analyzed the reports of 183 ex-smokers calling the Stay-Quit Line (Shiffman, 1982). Negative affect or stress were cited as precipitants by a majority of the sample (52%). Frustration and anger seemed to play especially significant roles. Surprisingly, depression was associated with about one out of five relapse crises. Congruent with Cummings *et al.* (1980), nearly a third of the hotline callers cited other smokers or smoking paraphernalia as the trigger for their relapse crisis. Most crises occurred in association with food or alcohol consumption (60%). Many of these took place when the ex-smoker was socializing. Withdrawal symptoms seemed to play a surprisingly small role in precipitating relapse crises, being absent about 50% of the time.

A preliminary cluster analysis of our data suggests that there are five major types of relapse situations, three marked by positive affect and two by negative affect (Shiffman, Read, & Jarvik, in press). The clearest positive affect situation is a social gathering, often a party, at which the ex-smoker is drinking in the presence of other smokers. The others' smoking triggers the relapse crisis. Another situation occurs when the ex-smoker relaxes at home in the evening, usually after dinner. Here, the associations with eating or relaxation precipitate the episode. The third situation is the only one marked by withdrawal symptoms. The episode usually occurs at work and is marked by discomfort and severe cravings. Negative affect situations fall into two types: high and low arousal. The high-arousal situation usually occurs at work, where the ex-smoker feels pressured, frustrated, or anxious. In the low-arousal condition, the ex-smoker is usually at home and is feeling bored or depressed. Thus, we can identify a relatively small set of situations in which the risk of relapse is high. Relapse prevention depends on preparing ex-smokers to cope with these high-risk situations.

RESEARCH ON COPING WITH RELAPSE CRISES

Our telephone hotline study highlights the importance of coping responses in relapse prevention (cf. Shiffman, 1982). Situational data were insufficient to predict smoking in relapse crises; the principal determinant of relapse was the ex-smoker's coping response. Ex-smokers who did not cope had a relapse rate two and a half times greater than those who did attempt coping. Among those who coped, we differentiated between behavioral and cognitive coping responses. Behavioral responses involve doing something—leaving a situation, eating, and so on. Cognitive responses involve thinking—reminding oneself how hard it was to quit, imagining a smoke-blackened lung, and so on. Both types of coping were effective and a combination of the two was most effective. The data show, however, that behavioral coping responses are affected by the ex-smoker's state of arousal during the crisis, while cognitive responses are not.

Alcohol consumption inhibits behavioral coping and this may mediate its role in relapse. Our study found that ex-smokers who had been drinking were much less likely to perform behavioral coping, but alcohol had no effect on cognitive coping (Shiffman, 1982). Even among those ex-smokers who coped, those who had been drinking were less effective in avoiding relapse. Depression also diminished the effectiveness of behavioral coping. While depressed ex-smokers used behavioral coping as frequently as non-depressed ex-smokers, their efforts were less effective. Cognitive coping was not affected by depression. These findings point to the importance of a broad repertoire of coping responses, and they emphasize the importance of cognitive coping responses in RP.

While these data highlight the importance of coping responses, some of our preliminary work has not demonstrated the effect of coping *skills* in maintaining nonsmoking. Six months to a year after they had quit, we tested the coping skills of 45 ex-smokers, some of whom had relapsed (Shiffman *et al.*, 1983). In the Smoking Situational Competency Test (SSCT), we asked them to write down how they would cope with each of 10 high-risk situations. Their responses were counted and rated for quality by expert judges. Despite encouraging trends, differences between recidivists and maintainers were not reliable.

Findings on another measure, the Coping Response Survey (CRS), were more encouraging (Shiffman *et al.*, 1983). Respondents reported their use of each of 24 coping responses. The successful maintainers reported heavier use of cognitive coping responses, while the recidivists reported greater reliance on behavioral coping responses. Murphy (1983) similarly reported that only cognitive or verbal coping strategies distinguished successful from unsuccessful self-initiated quitters. Thus, data from diverse sources consistently indicate that the use of cognitive coping strategies is a critical element in successful maintenance. The implications for treatment are clear: the treatment must emphasize the development of diversity in the coping repertoire and ensure the inclusion of cognitive coping strategies.

The CRS also underscored the importance of the meta-coping processes. One important component of meta-coping involves using the most effective coping responses most frequently. On the CRS, each respondent stated how frequently he or she used each coping response and how helpful it had been. The correlation between these two measures reflects the respondent's discrimination among coping responses based on their efficacy. Successful maintainers showed better discrimination than recidivists on the CRS. Thus, both meta-coping and coping response skills are instrumental in preventing relapse.

PROGRAMMED RELAPSE

Among the most intriguing clinical applications of the RP model is the programmed relapse described in Chapter 4. Marlatt (1978) posits that the feeling of being out of control following a lapse may trigger a full-blown relapse. Perhaps giving clients an experience of controlled relapse might function to inoculate them against the AVE. In this procedure, the therapist directs abstinent clients to smoke a single cigarette in the treatment setting and follows this with a discussion of their feelings, and so on, presumably providing an opportunity to learn and practice slip-recovery skills.

Cooney and Kopel (1980) conducted a randomized clinical trail of this procedure. Clients in a programmed relapse condition were compared to clients in an absolute abstinence condition in which the importance of avoiding even the slightest slip was emphasized. The process data were encouraging. The programmed relapse increased self-efficacy ratings and decreased reported craving. Follow-up data, however, revealed that the programmed relapse clients were somewhat *more* likely to relapse than were the absolute abstinence clients, though not significantly so. Moreover, the more a client's self-efficacy was enhanced by the procedure, the more likely he or she was to relapse. This suggests that the programmed relapse procedure may have made some clients overly confident. In our studies of self-efficacy, we have observed that recidivists sometimes have higher self-efficacy than survivors just prior to a relapse crisis (Shiffman et al., 1981). Confidence without competence produces failure.

Perhaps this procedure might prove effective when utilized as an emergency intervention in circumstances when relapse seems imminent, as suggested by Cummings et al. (1980). In other words, when the choice is between an uncontrolled relapse and a programmed relapse, the latter might avert much of the AVE and allow the therapist to use the relapse as an occasion for teaching the client how to analyze and recover from a lapse, thus enhancing maintenance. The effectiveness of the programmed relapse procedure has yet to be empirically tested, however.

SELF-EFFICACY AND MAINTENANCE

Research on the relation between self-efficacy and maintenance is among the most exciting recent developments in research on the smoking relapse process. Since Bandura's (1977) introduction of self-efficacy theory, it has been proposed that self-efficacy is an important cognitive mediating factor between treatment and maintenance. Several independent studies have shown that self-efficacy ratings can be used to predict maintenance. Condiotte and Lichtenstein (1981), DiClemente (1981), and Colletti, Supnik, and Rizzo (1981) achieved prospective prediction of maintenance using three different self-efficacy scales with three populations. In each case, subjects with lower self-efficacy during or soon after treatment were more likely to resume smoking. Condiotte and Lichtenstein's (1981) study went considerably further than this and deserves detailed discussion. Condiotte and Lichtenstein asked 78 smokers entering smoking cessation programs to estimate their ability to maintain abstinence in each of 45 situations sampled by Best and Hakstian's (1978) Smoking Situations Questionnaire. Measures were obtained pre- and posttreatment and subjects were followed closely. Subjects' self-efficacy rose as a result of treatment. Posttreatment self-efficacy scores not only predicted who would relapse, but also accounted for half the variance in the length of abstinence. Condiotte and Lichtenstein reasoned further that clients' self-efficacy ratings would be situation-specific, implying that ex-smokers will relapse in situations for which their self-efficacy is lowest. Condiotte and Lichtenstein performed a cluster analysis of their Posttreatment Confidence Questionnaire, arriving at a typology of situations. They then asked recidivists to identify the situation in which they experienced their first slips. Condiotte and Lichtenstein found a remarkable degree of agreement between situational self-efficacy ratings and actual relapses. Ex-smokers were most likely to relapse in situations similar to those in which their self-efficacy was low. In essence, Condiotte and Lichtenstein could predict who would relapse and when. This has great clinical potential, as it could allow treatment to focus specifically on each client's relapse vulnerabilities. Research on the relapse process is thus contributing to improved RP.

TREATMENT APPROACH

Our approach to RP emphasizes three major processes: education, assessment, and coping skill development. Education orients the smoker to the quitting process and encourages realistic expectations. Assessment determines in which situations relapse is likely and identifies deficiencies in clients' coping repertoires so that they can be corrected.

After discussing each of these processes we will describe and demonstrate what we consider to be the centerpiece of our clinical method: the relapse debriefing. A relapse debriefing is a review of a relapse episode or crisis in order to assess relapse vulnerability, evaluate and teach coping skills, and combat the AVE. The relapse debriefing thus embodies all of the treatment processes we discuss. We strongly urge the reader to give special attention to the section on relapse debriefing and to adopt this method in clinical practice.

In the final sections of the chapter, we discuss the importance of lifestyle and lifestyle change in the maintenance of nonsmoking and present an outline of treatment in an RP clinic. Finally, we introduce several methods for extending treatment beyond the normal clinic structure and describe the telephone hotline, SQL, as an example of these methods.

ORIENTATION TO QUITTING

While skills training is the most prominent active ingredient in smoking cessation treatment, reorientation of clients' attitudes toward the quitting process is also important. It is helpful to provide the client with general guidelines and information about the quitting process. These guidelines are important in orienting the client toward (1) realistic expectations of quitting smoking, (2) recognition of the difference between initial quitting and maintenance stages, (3) the use of self-observation in maintenance, and (4) the use of coping strategies and responses in maintenance.

We have said that clients often have inaccurate expectations of the quitting and withdrawal processes. Frequently, their criteria for satisfactory progress are so unrealistically high that they become discouraged almost before they begin. Clients who by objective standards are quite successful in dealing with cravings may become upset because they fall short of their high expectations. Many clients expect a successful quitting effort to be free of struggle and are disappointed when they encounter difficulties. "I should be able to handle this without difficulty," or "It shouldn't be this hard for me. I must be doing something wrong," or "I guess I'm just not as strong as I thought," are common sentiments that reflect demoralizing and self-defeating attitudes. The fact that cravings are felt, that some situations are stressful, or that cigarettes are missed is interpreted as failure. In effect, these clients experience some aspects of the AVE even before they have violated abstinence.

A more realistic expectation of what will take place during the process of quitting and staying off cigarettes can facilitate the course of treatment and make demoralization less likely. Clients may be less likely to misinterpret reasonable difficulties as failure if they expect them, know that they are "normal," and know that they can learn to cope with them. Knowing that cravings may reappear after they have subsided for a while, for example, may allow the person to deal with cravings more effectively. Instead of experiencing panic and guilt over feeling the urge to smoke "just when things were going better," the person may be able to recognize the cravings as a "normal" event and interpret them as a signal that coping is needed.

Information also often serves to normalize the client's experiences. Callers to our hotline were often just as concerned with how "normal" their experiences were as with the experienced difficulties themselves. Many clients were greatly relieved to know that their experiences were similar to others' and that they were not "doing anything wrong."

In a sense, the function of the initial orientation is to dispel clients' myths about quitting and maintenance. In the following discussion and in Table 8-1, we have contrasted a number of common misconceptions with more factual information regarding the course of quitting and maintenance.

1. Extreme generalizations about quitting are the source of much

Table 8-1. Myths and Facts Regarding Smoking Cessation

Myth	Fact
Quitting is either easy or it is impossibly difficult.	Some people have very few withdrawal symptoms and find quitting to be fairly easy. Others may experience withdrawal symptoms or intense cravings that make quitting more difficult.
Quitting does not take any extra effort or time.	It is usually helpful to allocate extra time and energy to quitting.
Cravings for cigarettes last forever.	Individual cravings are typically short and decrease in frequency, while the intensity may not change.
If the initial quitting is hard, maintaining abstinence is equally difficult.	Quitting and maintaining abstinence are different and may require different strategies.
If you have any difficulty, it probably means you cannot quit or did not really want to. You might as well smoke.	Most people can expect some difficulty in quitting.
Feeling proud or successful after getting through a difficult time is a waste of time. After all, the battle is not over yet.	It is important to recognize and reinforce progress rather than interpret crises as signs of failure.
There is not much to know about quitting— it just takes wanting to.	There are definite coping skills and strategies that can be learned to manage quitting.
If you have had a hard time quitting in the past you can expect it to be hard in future quitting attempts.	Successive attempts at quitting are not necessarily the same. In fact, previous quits may provide insights and skill development for future quits.
It does not make any difference when you try to quit, or, it is best to wait for the "perfect quit date."	Timing may be an important consideration that may affect a client's success in quitting.

mythology. Quitting is thought of as either easy or impossible. Statements such as "I've seen other people quit without any problems; I shouldn't have any problems with it either," or "Some people just can't quit. Why try to fight it?" are common. Actually, the experience of quitting is not the same for everyone. It is important for clients to realize that what happened to a spouse or friend when he or she quit may not apply to them. Unrealistic expectations of the quitting process lead to unrealistic planning. Clients for whom quitting is difficult may need to make changes in work or social schedules to arrange for resources to deal with the added stress. In some circumstances, arranging for time off from work may be appropriate. Other clients may need to make less dramatic preparations such as having gum or snacks available or allowing themselves frequent breaks during the day. Clients should expect to adjust their lifestyles in order to accommodate the quitting process.

2. Smokers often have inappropriate attitudes about the timing of quitting. "It never seems like the right time to quit," and "I should be able to quit at any time," are both heard. In fact, timing is often an important consideration and may affect a client's success in quitting. Clients who are dealing with other stressful events in their lives—divorce, work problems, or any major lifetyle change—might appropriately postpone smoking cessation to a time when they can devote more energy to the effort. On the other hand, waiting for that perfect moment when one's life is entirely settled is risky; the time may never arrive. Usually, the best time to quit is now.

3. Another common misconception is that "Craving goes on forever." Often, when people are distressed by cravings or withdrawal, the first thing they want to know is "How long do I have to deal with this?" To some, the cravings seem never-ending and they may say to themselves, "All I think about is cigarettes or trying not to smoke. It's taking up all of my time. I need to get on with my life, I can't keep this up."

Actually, withdrawal symptoms usually subside after the first couple of weeks (Shiffman, 1979). Also, though the intensity of cravings may remain constant, their frequency usually diminishes as abstinence proceeds. Clients unaware of this may experience the return of an intense craving as an indication that they have made no progress. Craving may sometimes subside for weeks and then reappear with the intensity of the first week. This recurrence of cravings, however, is usually of short duration.

4. There is also a misconception regarding the duration of cravings. People report "constant craving that seems to go on indefinitely." When they attend more closely to the craving sensation, they usually find that the cravings last only about 3–5 minutes. This information seems useful because some clients find it easier to deal with or wait through each craving when they know it is time limited rather than never-ending.

5. Few people realize that there is a difference between quitting and maintaining abstinence. Clients need to know that these two phases of

treatment require different approaches. Early on, when the likelihood of withdrawal symptoms and cravings is high, clients may need to maintain almost constant vigilance. They may need to adjust their daily routines or social calendars (avoiding parties, for example) to accommodate the additional stress and vulnerability to relapse. Fortunately, client morale and commitment is at its peak during this period.

As cravings and withdrawal symptoms subside, less vigilance is required. However, clients must avoid overconfidence or negligence. They should be aware that the urge to smoke may still occur and that coping responses must be readily available. We often recommend that clients carry a "menu" of coping skills with them for some time after quitting. This menu, written on a $3'' \times 5''$ card, lists behaviors or thoughts that the client has previously found helpful in resisting the urge to smoke. When a craving occurs, the client need only reach for his or her card to be reminded of effective coping responses.

Continued long-term vigilance also dictates planning in advance for difficult situations. For instance, a client who has been abstinent for a few weeks and is no longer experiencing much craving should still anticipate the occurrence of extraordinary stressors. Plans to attend a party at which smokers will be present should cue the formulation of a coping plan. The client might plan to limit his or her alcohol intake or to take along a nonsmoking companion. The point is to educate clients about the intermittent nature of relapse crises and to the protracted period of risk.

6. Clients tend to be excessively attentive to failure and considerably less attentive to success. This imbalanced view lowers morale and self-efficacy. "It never seems to get better. I thought I was doing okay until the craving came back. I guess I just can't do it. I might as well smoke." Clients need to be oriented to their successes and to value successive approximations to the goal. While many of the assessment procedures we have recommended focus on identifying vulnerabilities, it is important that clients also recognize and reinforce progress.

The importance of the attitude which the client brings to self-observation cannot be overestimated. A realistic and nonjudgmental attitude allows clients to examine crises without viewing them as failures. Clients who expect maintenance to be an ongoing coping process without magical or perfect solutions can accept crises as situations that are particularly difficult and require extraordinary vigilance. They do not expect to master each situation with equal ease; effective coping is seldom achieved in a single, giant step. Clients with realistic attitudes expect to learn from their experiences and to gradually approach effective coping. Their expectations are consistent with a coping model rather than with an unrealistic mastery model (Meichenbaum, 1971). (In the Meichenbaum study, subjects exposed to a coping model who struggled to cope with a threatening situation performed better than those exposed to a mastery model who succeeded immediately.)

In summary, we think that realistic expectations and a nonjudgmental attitude are keys to success in maintenance. It is important that ex-smokers recognize and monitor their progress, whether it is recognizing decreasing frequency of cravings, successful negotiation of a crisis, or learning about a vulnerable situation through a slip. Optimal preparation for quitting includes (1) expecting some degree of difficulty; (2) allocating sufficient time and energy to quitting; (3) anticipating vulnerabilities or potentially difficult situations; and (4) identifying cravings as signals to engage in coping strategies, rather than as failures. The successful client is armed with a plan for quitting and a willingness to learn from his or her "mistakes."

ASSESSMENT OF RELAPSE RISK

"Forewarned is forearmed" might be the rallying cry of the RP model. Assessment is a tool of forewarning or anticipation and thus plays a critical role in relapse prevention. Assessment guides and focuses intervention. In the absence of appropriate assessment, planning and intervention become diffuse and ineffective. The goal of assessment is to identify the client's vulnerabilities to relapse in a way that allows them to be addressed.

Although the central goal of assessment is to serve as a foundation for appropriate intervention, the assessment process also has other subsidiary but important functions. Self-observation or self-monitoring are highly reactive procedures. Observation of a target behavior tends to change that behavior in the desired direction. Self-monitoring thus becomes not only an assessment procedure but a first step in intervention (McFall, 1970, 1977; Fredericksen, Martin, & Webster, 1979; Abrams & Wilson, 1979).

The assessment process also functions as a training vehicle for the client. Clients must learn self-management skills that they can apply when the therapist's instruction and support are unavailable. Since self-observation is a critical part of self-management, the assessment provides the therapist an ideal opportunity to model appropriate self-observation. Wherever possible, the client should have an opportunity to understand the rationale and basis for each assessment procedure. The therapist should also describe how the client can apply each assessment procedure during maintenance.

A final nonspecific function of assessment is to foster in clients a sense of control over their smoking behavior. Counting, measuring, and defining their smoking behavior tend to remove it from the realm of uncontrollable and unacceptable behavior into the realm of the manageable.

Methods of assessment for relapse prevention vary according to their target (*what* is observed) and their method (*how* it is observed). Examples of targets are smoking, urges to smoke, and coping responses. We will describe three assessment methods: (1) self-observation, in which the client directly observes and records a target behavior, (2) self-report, in which the client reports his or her impression of the target behavior, presumably based on past self-observations, and (3) analogue methods, in which the target is observed directly, not in its natural environment, but in a situation that one hopes is analogous to the natural situation and that allows one to make predictions about behavior in the real world.

Self-Monitoring

The sequence of assessment follows the sequence of treatment and addresses the client's current circumstances or needs. When clients first present themselves for treatment, they are usually still smoking. This provides us with an opportunity to get data about their smoking behavior. Self-monitoring of smoking behavior is easily accomplished through the use of a self-monitoring form such as that reproduced in Figure 8-1. The form is carried wrapped around the pack of cigarettes (thus earning the nickname *wrap sheet*) and an entry is made for each cigarette consumed. A direct benefit of this procedure is that an accurate estimate is made of the current magnitude of the smoker's habit.

Self-monitoring often has a strong emotional impact on smokers and makes them aware of how much and how often they smoke. This is clinically useful, particularly with clients who are initially ambivalent about changing their smoking behavior. The self-monitoring form also provides information about the distribution of smoking behavior in relation to activities and affects. This provides useful data regarding the cues that stimulate a person's desire to smoke. As an initial step in characterizing the smoker's habit, it is useful to have the smoker tally, for example, the percentage of cigarettes smoked in negative affect situations. This may suggest the extent to which the smoker can anticipate difficulty with such situations.

Where gradual reduction is the method of treatment, self-monitoring becomes a central component of the process. It is used to monitor the progress of the reduction regimen and can be used to select targets for further reduction. One might note the distribution of cigarettes during the day and suggest, for example, that no cigarettes be smoked an hour before bedtime, then 2 hours before bedtime, and so on. Similarly, situations can be targeted for reduction. After noting the number of cigarettes smoked in association with food or alcohol consumption, for example, the clinician and smoker might set a goal of eliminating smoking in those situations. Treatment then proceeds by progressively targeting each smoking situation in turn.

Self-Reports and Self-Efficacy

It is also useful to assess smoking behavior through self-report. By far the most common instrument for this is the smoking typology developed by Tomkins (1966) and Horn (Ikard, Green, & Horn, 1969; U.S. Public Health Service, 1969). Some items in this measure focus on the situations in which the person smokes, while others focus on the reason that the person smokes

Name _____ Date _____ Page _____

Day of week _____

Time	Food and/or alcohol	Relaxation	Work	Social, Recreational	Other	Activity	Angry	Anxious	Bored	Depressed	Frustrated	Happy	Relaxed	Tired	Need rating Most				Least
1															1	2	3	4	5
2															1	2	3	4	5
3															1	2	3	4	5
4															1	2	3	4	5
5															1	2	3	4	5
6															1	2	3	4	5
7															1	2	3	4	5
8															1	2	3	4	5
9															1	2	3	4	5
10															1	2	3	4	5

Wrap this Daily Cigarette Count around your pack of cigarettes and hold it fast with a rubber band. When you are about to take a cigarette, but *before* you actually put it in your mouth and light up, (1) check the activity you are doing; (2) check the word or words that best describes your feeling at the time; and (3) indicate how important that particular cigarette is to you at the time:

1. most important
2. above average
3. average
4. below average
5. least important

Figure 8-1. Daily cigarette count.

487

or the gain he or she gets from smoking. A score is derived for the strength of each of the following motives for smoking: (1) stimulation, (2) tension reduction, (3) enhancement of pleasure or relaxation, (4) sensorimotor experience of handling a cigarette, (5) dependence or addiction, and (6) automatically, out of habit.

An alternative instrument for self-report of smoking behavior is the Smoking Occasions Questionnaire. Its advantage is that it is situation-focused and thus dovetails well with the situationally oriented intervention model which we will emphasize. An additional advantage is that these item stems have proven their validity in Condiotte and Lichtenstein's (1981) research on the use of self-efficacy ratings to predict relapse. The use of the same items to assess smoking behavior and self-efficacy provides an elegant and convenient parallelism of form.

Table 8-2 shows the items of the Smoking Occasions Questionnaire, grouped into seven scales. We drew the items from Best and Hakstian's (1978) and McKennel and Thomas's (1967) and McKennel's (1970) assessment instruments. We administered the resulting scale to 167 smokers entering smoking cessation programs and factor analyzed their responses. After eliminating clinically irrelevant distinctions, the following factors remained (see

Table 8-2.   Item Stems from Smoking Occasions Questionnaire, by Factor

Negative affect

When you feel frustrated

When you feel angry

When you feel tense

When you feel worried

When you feel upset

When irritable

When you feel annoyed

When you are angry with yourself

Positive affect

When you are resting

When you want to relax

When you feel really happy

When you are doing something interesting

Bored

When you are trying to pass time

When you feel restless

When you feel bored

When alone

When you are waiting for someone or something

Social

In company

When talking

Food substitute

When you want to avoid eating sweets

When you want to keep slim

Alcohol

When you are drinking an alcoholic beverage

Eating

When you have finished a meal or snack

When you are drinking coffee or tea

Chapter 2 for the relationship between this typology and Marlatt and Gordon's [1980] typology of relapse precipitants):

- *Eating* is a frequent stimulus for smoking and a prominent antecedent of relapse (Shiffman, 1982). Smoking after meals or coffee is so common that these occasions must be considered high risk for all smokers.

- *Negative affect* situations are also frequently associated with smoking and relapse. In these situations, the smoker seems to use cigarettes to blunt unpleasant affect.

- *Alcohol* consumption is strongly associated with smoking. Smokers are almost always drinkers and laboratory experiments have demonstrated that drinking facilitates smoking (Mello, Mendelson, Seller, & Kuehnle, 1980; Griffiths, Bigelow, & Liebson, 1976). In our studies of relapse, drinking was one of the most powerful causes of relapse (Shiffman, 1982).

- *Social* situations are also common triggers for smoking. In addition to being cued by other smokers, many smokers seem to use smoking to manage feelings of awkwardness in social situations.

- *Boredom* is also associated with smoking. Smokers who are bored may see it as "something to do" or may seek the stimulating pharmacological action of nicotine. In our experience, boredom is often used to describe a condition of mild depression.

- *Positive affect.* While smoking is more common under negative affect, some smokers are especially likely to smoke when feeling good, claiming that smoking accentuates their positive feelings.

- *Food substitution* is another function cigarettes often serve. Smokers sometimes have a cigarette instead of food. Fears (sometimes justified) of weight gain after quitting often undermine clients' motivation to stay abstinent.

While there is much overlap between classification systems, the system in the preceding list differs from the clusters reported by Condiotte and Lichtenstein (1981) in their work on self-efficacy assessment. The items in their clusters seem too heterogeneous for clinical application. This presented a dilemma. The Condiotte and Lichtenstein scaling was empirically proven as a predictor of relapse, but not readily applicable. Our scaling was readily applicable, but unproven in relapse prediction. In suggesting the use of the latter scaling, we are inferring that prediction of relapse from self-efficacy is robust and does not depend on Condiotte and Lichtenstein's scaling.

While it seems reasonable to assume that smokers are most likely to relapse in situations in which they were likely to smoke, there are no data linking the distribution of smoking to the distribution of relapse vulnerability. Given this, we recommend that clients' self-reports on the Smoking Occasions Questionnaire be used cautiously in identifying their areas of relapse vulnerability. While assessment of smoking behavior is useful, the real work of RP requires assessment of *abstinence* behavior and its correlates. Once the smoker has given up smoking, even partially, the same techniques used to assess smoking can be used to assess urges to smoke, shifting the target while leaving the methods intact. A formal "quit date" scheduled early in treatment permits assessment and intervention in abstinence. This is more directly relevant to relapse prevention, because urges to smoke are precursors of relapse.

Assessment of self-efficacy may be the most clinically powerful RP assessment tool. With relatively modest effort, the clinician can accurately predict the situation in which smokers are likely to relapse. Stated simply, the way to discover the situation in which smokers will relapse is to ask them which situations they cannot handle. More specifically, clients can rate their confidence in their ability to successfully manage each situation in the Smoking Occasions Questionnaire. As we noted earlier, these ratings not only predict the probability of relapse, but also identify the situations in which relapse is likely to occur. "Forewarned is forearmed."

Relapse History

Self-efficacy ratings are prospective; they ask the client to predict to hypothetical, future situations. Retrospective data are another major source of information for assessment. Most smokers who seek treatment have made at least one previous attempt to quit smoking; many have had several "failures." It is useful to ask each client to recall in as much detail as possible the circumstances surrounding past relapses. This should help the client anticipate difficulties in maintenance; past behavior is often the best predictor of future behavior. Later in this chapter, we devote a section to techniques for debriefing relapse episodes or crises. Analysis of these critical incidents may be the most powerful component of RP treatment.

While the assessment techniques we have described differ in method and target, all have a common purpose: to identify the situations in which the client is most vulnerable to relapse so that intervention can be focused. By and large, smoking cessation programs have used a shotgun strategy, attempting to prepare each client equally to deal with any and all high-risk situations. This diffusion of effort produces clients who are inadequately prepared to handle many critical situations they will face. We believe that a targeted strategy in which clients master a smaller but more relevant set of competencies is preferable. In this approach, effort is concentrated on learning to deal with those situations that present the greatest risk for relapse. Thus a client who smokes primarily in positive affect situations, who previously relapsed at a party, and whose self-efficacy scores are lowest for social and alcohol smoking situations is instructed to spend little time on relaxation skills (which may be important to his or her neighbor), but to concentrate on mastering assertion and other "party-relevant" skills. In a subsequent section on interventions, we discuss the matching of situational vulnerabilities and relevant coping skills. We believe that such targeted treatment is the key to RP.

Coping Skills Assessment

Coping skills are at the core of RP. High-risk situations and ex-smokers' vulnerability to them tell only half the story of relapse. Relapse occurs at the intersection of a high-risk situation and a coping skill deficit. In principle, given adequate coping responses, high-risk situations would be irrelevant. More practically, clinicians are seldom in a position to affect the prevalence of high-risk situations. Our ability to affect outcome in maintenance thus depends on our ability to modify the other side of the equation, the ex-smokers' responses. Since intervention without adequate assessment is intervention done blindly, the assessment of coping skills is a critical component of RP.

Coping skills can be assessed with the same processes applied to the assessment of smoking behavior: self-monitoring, self-report, and analogue methods. We will review the use of the CRS, a self-report measure; the SSCT, an analogue measure; and the use of in-session role-playing methods in the assessment of coping skills.

The CRS is a self-report and self-monitoring instrument for assessment of ex-smokers' actual coping behaviors. The core of the CRS is a list of coping responses as shown in Table 8-3. These items serve as an aid to clients in observing and recording their coping behaviors. To obtain a broad overview of clients' coping patterns, clients can estimate how frequently they use each of the listed responses and how effective they feel each has been for them. In a more focused use of the CRS, clients are asked to keep weekly records of coping responses and their efficacy. In the very early stages of abstinence, even daily records may not be excessive.

Analysis of the CRS reveals the client's style of coping. Favored responses will readily stand out, as will underutilized responses. The breadth of the client's *enacted* coping repertoire (as opposed to the latent repertoire of responses he or she can do but may not actually do) will be evident. The CRS is divided into cognitive and behavioral responses, so that the client's relative reliance on each is readily estimated. This is one of the important uses of the CRS. In our pilot work, we have found that clients who were successful in maintaining abstinence were distinguished by more frequent use of cognitive coping responses (Shiffman *et al.*, 1983). The CRS can thus identify clients who are at risk of overreliance on behavioral coping.

The efficacy ratings on the CRS are useful in focusing clients on their strengths by identifying the coping strategies that work for them. Too often, clients do not attend to the empirical "track record" of a particular response

Table 8-3. List of Coping Responses from the Coping Response Survey

Things You Might Think

1. Thinking about the positive benefits of not smoking (health, pride, etc.)
2. Thinking about the negative effects of smoking (bad taste, expense, etc.)
3. Giving yourself commands ("Don't do it!"; "Stop!")
4. Encouraging yourself ("C'mon, you can do it.")
5. Reminding yourself how hard it was to quit in the first place
6. Telling yourself "I don't really want to smoke."
7. Imagining something relaxing, like a favorite spot (the ocean or mountains, etc.)
8. Imagining the bad effects of smoking (black lung, etc.)
9. Imagining yourself as a successful ex-smoker
10. Distracting yourself by thinking about other things
11. Going over your reasons for quitting
12. Telling yourself "I just need to get through the next few days."
13. Recognizing the difficulty of quitting
14. Imagining your friends' or family's reactions if you were to smoke

Things You Might Do

1. Having something to eat or drink
2. Getting high or intoxicated (alcohol, marijuana)
3. Physical exercise
4. Slow deep breathing to relax
5. Distracting yourself by doing something else like going for a walk or occupying your hands with something
6. Avoiding high-risk situations (e.g., other smokers, parties)
7. Delay—putting off having a cigarette
8. Getting support from others
9. Treating yourself with rewarding or comforting activities

and continue to use coping strategies that have not been effective. In our work with the CRS, we found that for successful ex-smokers there was a strong relationship between how effective they thought a response was and how frequently they used it. They seemed to note what worked and then use it. The recidivists showed a weaker relationship between efficacy and frequency of use; their choice of coping responses was less dictated by considerations of efficacy. Analysis of the CRS can be used to detect this dysfunctional pattern. Use of the CRS as a self-monitoring instrument also acts to correct this pattern by making the track record of each response obvious to the client.

The SSCT is probably the most useful tool for coping skills assessment. Building on a method developed by Chaney *et al.* (1978) for use with alcoholics, we have developed the SSCT for use with smokers (Shiffman *et al.*, 1983).

The SSCT tests the smoker's responses to a range of high-risk relapse-facilitating situations. The client is orally presented with narratives of 10 relapse-promoting situations as shown in Table 8-4. The client is given 30 seconds to write down what he or she would say, do, or think in order to cope with each situation. The time limit is meant to model reality, where one must often respond quickly to be effective.

Responses on the SSCT are scored according to three criteria, each assigned a weight of five points. (1) *Logic and concreteness of the response.* Is the response specific and detailed? Does the response refer to elements of the particular situation? Does the person specify what he or she will do, with what, and to whom? Is the response logical in this situation? (2) *The appropriateness and likely effectiveness of the response.* Can the coping behavior be done in the situation? How effective is it likely to be in this situation? Are alternatives listed? (Points are subtracted for movement toward smoking, e.g., experiencing others' cigarettes vicariously or breathing their smoke or

Table 8-4.   Situational Narratives for Smoking Situational Competency Test

Negative Affect

1. You've just picked up your car from the mechanic and the bill is twice as much as you expected it to be. As you drive home you find that the very thing you took the car in for is still not fixed. The car stalls in rush-hour traffic. You feel angry and frustrated; you crave a cigarette.

2. You're at work and you've been pressured all day, the phone has been ringing and you haven't been able to handle all the calls and still get your work done. Finally you get home and you want to relax but you are still tense from work—a cigarette would help.

3. A traffic jam on the freeway kept you in stop-and-go traffic for half an hour. Now you're late for your appointment and you're still not exactly sure of the directions. You start to feel very anxious, and you imagine a cigarette could relax you.

4. Your boss has been pressuring you to finish the project you've been working on. You know you'll be pressured all day. A cigarette might ease the pressure so that you could work better.

Positive Affect

5. You're sitting on the back patio with a few friends on a warm evening. You are relaxing and enjoying the company. One of your friends lights a cigarette. It looks so refreshing.

6. You're at a party with friends. People are smoking and drinking. You're having a glass of wine and intense conversation. You always used to have a cigarette with your drink. It looks good.

7. You've just finished dinner and you're feeling relaxed. You push back your chair and suddenly, you really crave a cigarette.

Neutral Affect

8. While waiting at the market checkout stand, you find yourself next to the cigarette stand and you notice that the market carries your old brand of cigarette. Boy, do those cigarettes look good—you can almost taste one!

9. You are home, alone. You feel bored. There isn't anything you have to do, and nothing you think of seems particularly appealing—except maybe a cigarette.

10. You are at a restaurant waiting for your friend who promised to meet you for lunch. Your friend is already 30 minutes late. You've had a drink and a few breadsticks. You think a cigarette would help pass the time.

for drinking alcohol. (3) *The extent to which the response is specific to the stimulus situation.* Is the effect sought from smoking explicitly addressed? Is the stressor (or precise cue) dealt with?

The simplest use of the SSCT is to assess clients' overall coping competency, which is measured by the total SSCT score. This can identify those clients who are in need of additional intervention. Repeated administration of the SSCT before and after treatment can be used to test the effectiveness of skills-training procedures. While global scoring is useful, it blurs together diverse sources of information. In our work with the SSCT, we have found that clients' scores on the 10 situations of the SSCT are not highly inter-correlated. Although the scale appears to be unidimensional, the average correlation between any two situations is only .45. Thus, ex-smokers' coping competencies appear to be relatively situation-specific. Detailed interpretation of SSCT responses can yield a wealth of additional clinically useful information. Clients vary in the degree to which particular situations tempt them to smoke. Each of the situations also requires somewhat different coping responses; a client who deals adequately with pressure at work may have difficulty coping with a party.

The SSCT provides an overview of the client's coping repertoire. One useful procedure is to note the number of different responses the client applies to the 10 situations. Clients who rely on a few coping responses should be encouraged to broaden their repertoire. The breadth of the client's coping repertoire should be evaluated in other ways as well. It is particularly important to ensure that clients employ a mix of behavioral and cognitive coping. The typical deficit is an underutilization of cognitive responses. The SSCT protocol should also be scored for the number of responses the client can produce for each situation. Clients who can only produce a single response need additional help, even if that one response seems good. Thus, the SSCT can be used as a guide for intervention, and as a global measure of competence.

While the written format of the SSCT makes it efficient for assessment, more realistic analogue methods probably have greater validity and the additional advantage of linking more directly with skills training interventions. *Role-playing analogues* can be used to present clients with realistic representations of high-risk situations, and clients can be asked to enact their coping responses. (Note that the SSCT is a rich source of stimuli on which to base role-plays. If scoring of the SSCT reveals that many clinic members are deficient in their responses to the party situation, for example, the clinician might initiate a role-play of a party as a lead-in to teaching skills appropriate to that situation.) In this format, the clinician can more readily evaluate the client's capacity to engage in appropriate coping behavior. The SSCT tests clients' *knowledge* of appropriate coping responses. While knowing good coping responses is a necessary condition to using them, it is not sufficient.

Good coping also requires behavioral skill in enacting the coping responses one knows. Role-playing analogues provide the clinician with an opportunity to assess these behavioral skills. The use of role-playing to assess coping skills is part of a broader use of role-playing for both assessment and intervention. It is described in more detail below in the section on relapse debriefing.

STRATEGIES FOR COPING WITH TEMPTATIONS TO SMOKE

While we shall propose that coping is most effective when it is matched to the specifics of the situation, there are a few basic coping strategies that are so broad that they are nearly universally applicable and constitute a first line of defense in almost any situation. Generous use of these first-line strategies should minimize the use of the more elaborate procedures described below. The first-line strategies are to avoid, escape, distract, and delay.

Avoidance

If one could avoid all of the situations associated with smoking, maintenance would be easy. Of course, clients may be able to avoid some of the more dangerous situations, especially during the first few weeks of quitting when the probability of relapse is high.

For example, parties are among the most risky situations for ex-smokers. Seeing others smoking and knowing that cigarettes are within easy reach, combined with the relaxing effects of alcohol, make relapse likely. We often recommend that new quitters forego parties for the first few weeks of maintenance. A well-planned avoidance strategy can go a long way toward averting relapse crises. This depends on identifying high-risk situations and eliminating them. If idle time is troublesome, one can plan to be constantly active; coffee breaks can be eliminated if they are troublesome, and so on.

Though avoidance is one of the most effective coping strategies, it is not always the method of choice. Some high-risk situations cannot be avoided—one cannot always be shielded from the sight of people smoking nor can most of us easily eliminate work pressure. Some high-risk situations cannot be anticipated and the client may not be willing to forego others. Alternatives are critical.

Escape

If a high-risk situation has not been avoided, escape is often the most effective strategy. Taking a break from a stressful meeting, moving to another room at a party to avoid smokers, or taking a brief walk out of the office at peak stress times are examples of how this strategy is used. In addition to the therapist's "permission," some clients may need help with assertion skills to master the craft of escape.

Distraction

Cravings often occur in situations where escape would be difficult. Examples include waiting in line, driving a car, and stressful interactions. In many instances, a change in mental or physical activity may be helpful. In a work setting, refocusing attention, perhaps to a detail of the task at hand, or changing tasks is helpful. One client reported that he could distract himself from wanting a cigarette by humming to himself, which he could do while driving or even while standing in the line at the market. Distraction may be accomplished either cognitively (e.g., thinking of an upcoming vacation or imagining a waterfall) or behaviorally (e.g., tackling the dishes or a crossword puzzle).

Delay

Simply delaying or "waiting out" the craving is often an effective way to keep from smoking. Most cravings last only a few minutes and waiting till the craving has passed may make the situation easier to manage. Self-talk such as "I'll wait 5 minutes then decide" or "I'll wait till I finish what I'm doing, then see how I feel" gives some relief from the pressure of abstaining. It may be easier to say "no" for a few minutes than forever.

COGNITIVE AND BEHAVIORAL COPING SKILLS

When these general coping strategies are unavailable or inadequate, the ex-smoker must turn to more elaborate coping responses. In this section, we describe coping responses useful in averting relapse. Each response is best suited to particular circumstances. In the next section, we reintroduce a typology of relapse situations and suggest coping responses that seem best suited to each. *Cognitive coping responses* include imagery, cognitive restructuring, and other self-talk.

Imagery can be a potent technique for self-management. Imagery need not be exclusively visual. While many people experience visual imagery, others hear, feel, touch, or otherwise sense. Indeed, the more sensory modalities involved in an image, the greater its potency. Images may be spontaneous or deliberately invoked; either can be potent. Craving is usually associated with a spontaneous image of smoking as a pleasurable experience. This image of "a satisfying smoke" may incline the person to smoke.

Deliberate, maintenance-oriented images can be planned in advance. They can draw upon the negative consequences of smoking and the positive consequences of maintenance that are most salient for the individual. For some clients, imagining blackened and damaged lungs due to smoking is a useful aversion tool, while for others an image in which they are healthy, long-lived, breathing easily, and enjoying the loving company of good friends may be more useful. Aversive images can be immediate (e.g., imagery that the smoke will cause pain in one's throat and make one sick and dizzy), or more long range (e.g., imagining oneself hospitalized for surgery). In the same way, positive images can be immediate (e.g., imagining the pride and satisfaction one may feel at controlling one's habit, or the congratulations of one's family members). Such images can be used in any crisis.

The potency of an image can be increased by preceding it with a few minutes of relaxation. Relaxation can also be the primary goal of the image. A vivid image of a favorite vacation spot, complete with all its sights, sounds, smells, and moods, can produce a profound sense of relaxation. Such relaxation imagery is an excellent way to deal with a tension-induced crisis and generally is a powerful stress-reduction technique.

Cognitive restructuring is a deliberate change in one's perceptual set or view of a situation. One way to restructure one's view of the situation is to redefine one's cravings. There are a number of steps to be followed in restructuring thoughts: (1) Identify the source of stress or evaluate the situation associated with the craving. (2) Reevaluate the situation (e.g., "What's really going on in this situation? Is the problem or my craving really that bad?" and "What will smoking a cigarette do for me?"). (3) Redefine the situation and one's reaction to it (e.g., "I don't want to smoke, I want to relax").

Other thought restructuring includes construing the situation in a favorable light such as reminding oneself that "things have been or could be worse—this isn't so bad," or concentrating on something good that might develop from the situation. Thus, a tense interlude waiting for a friend might be redefined as an opportunity to relax quietly.

Other self-talk includes anything that people might say to themselves to keep from smoking. Some of the most common types of thoughts are going over reasons for quitting; reviewing positive consequences of being abstinent (better health, family's pleased reaction) or negative consequences of smoking (illness, social stigma); remembering how hard it was to quit, devaluing others' smoking ("They would quit too, if they could") and statements of determination ("I won't smoke," "I can do this," or "I am a nonsmoker").

Behavioral coping responses may include relaxation, physical activity, alternative consummatory behavior, and assertion skills. The principle here is to identify and then satisfy the need underlying the craving for cigarettes.

Relaxation techniques (see Chapter 5) range from taking deep breaths to learning progressive muscle relaxation. A number of sources are available for teaching oneself relaxation skills that can be useful when trying to quit smoking (Rathus & Nevid, 1977). Other ways of relaxing include imagery and creating a relaxing environment, such as a quiet room, a hot bath, or a favorite chair.

Physical activity is useful as a substitute for smoking. Any large-scale movement such as calisthenics, running, brisk walking, cleaning, or gardening can serve to release tension (see Chapter 5). Exercise also engages one in activity incompatible with smoking.

Alternative consummatory behavior as a substitute is limited because many people who quit smoking are concerned about excessive weight gain. Eating low-calorie foods such as celery, carrots, seeds, and popcorn may be helpful. Also tea, coffee (if it is not part of a smoking routine), and non-alcoholic beverages are good substitutes. Chewing gum, sucking hard candy, or putting pens, straws, and toothpicks in one's mouth are also reported as effective substitutes.

Assertion skills are also often important in maintenance. The ability to refuse cigarettes when offered, to ask others not to smoke, or to seek support during a crisis can often make the difference between abstinence and relapse. Assertion skills can also facilitate action to reduce stress, e.g., asking for a reduced workload at work.

MAKING COPING RESPONSES TO SPECIFIC HIGH-RISK SITUATIONS

Earlier, we recommended the use of the Smoking Occasions Questionnaire and its associated typology for assessment of smoking and self-efficacy. These assessments allow the clinician to predict the situations in which the client is most vulnerable to relapse and permit the clinician and client to concentrate on those coping skills that are most appropriate to the client's vulnerabilities. In this section, we suggest coping responses that are most suitable for each of the situations described by the Smoking Occasions Questionnaire (Table 8-2).

Although using the relapse typologies developed by Marlatt and Gordon (1980) or by Shiffman *et al.* (in press) might seem natural, it would fail to provide any connection between assessment and intervention planning. Since the Smoking Occasions Questionnaire is recommended for assessment of smoking and self-efficacy, it is clinically practical to base one's intervention strategy on it. The following pairings of situations and coping responses are also depicted in Table 8-5 and are based on our clinical judgment; they have not been tested. Also, they are not meant to be rigid rules, but rather heuristic suggestions.

Negative affect—feelings of frustration, worry, anxiety, embarrassment, anger, and depression—are often perceived by the smoker as a need for a cigarette, which is expected to reduce these negative feelings. Coping skills that are used to manage negative affect include relaxation, calming self-talk, physical exercise, and cognitive restructuring, especially reevaluation of the presumed calming effect of cigarettes.

Table 8-5. Summary of High-Risk Situations and Effective Coping Skills

Situation	Basic			Cognitive			Behavioral				
	Leave situation	Distraction	Delay	Imagery	Cognitive restructuring	Self-talk	Physical activity	Relaxation	Consummatory behavior	Other rewards	Assertion skills
Negative affect					X	X	X	X		X	X
Relaxed–happy		X		X	X	X		X	X		
Waiting–bored	X	X	X		X	X	X		X		
Food substitute		X			X				X	X	
After meals	X				X		X				
Social	X				X	X			X		X
Other important variables											
Other smokers	X				X	X	X				X
Withdrawal symptoms		X	X	X	X	X	X	X	X	X	
Alcohol	X							X	X		

Feeling relaxed or happy may also signal the desire for a cigarette. Cognitive restructuring is helpful in helping clients to reevaluate what they really want from the cigarette. Other relaxing activities may be just as satisfying. Reviewing reasons for quitting or remembering how hard it was to quit may also be used to combat the urge to smoke in this situation.

Waiting or feeling bored often cue a desire to smoke. When smoking has been used to help pass the time, the act of smoking may seem "automatic." Advanced planning is critical. When these situations cannot be avoided, planning activities to fill free time adequately is critical. Physical exercise, consummatory behavior, and focusing on distracting thoughts may provide a quick substitute for the cigarette. Recognizing the time limit of the situation may also be helpful (e.g., "It's just ten more minutes—I can hold off").

Food substitutes may be used; when smoking has been used as a food substitute for hunger suppression, frequent craving may result. Chewing gum, drinking tea or water, snacking on nonfattening foods, or even chewing on straws or toothpicks may help.

Distracting thoughts and behaviors are also useful in this situation. Cognitive restructuring may provide insight into actual desired effect such as need for comfort or reward. Other substitutes can then be considered.

After meals is a time typically associated with smoking. Leaving the situation is the most effective strategy. Clearing the table, washing dishes, taking a walk, or moving to a different room may be sufficient to break the routine.

Social situations are among the most vulnerable times for ex-smokers. Avoiding or leaving parties as the desire to smoke increases is advisable. Coping skills that can be employed in the social setting include limiting alcoholic intake to one drink or abstaining completely, eating or drinking in lieu of smoking, seeking out other non- or ex-smokers, and avoiding groups where several people are smoking. Self-talk, such as devaluation of other smokers (i.e., thinking "They look like they enjoy it, but I bet they'd stop if they could"), remembering reasons for quitting, and assertively refusing cigarettes when offered are also helpful.

Our work suggests that a few factors not included in the Smoking Occasions Questionnaire typology are important elements in relapse-promoting situations. It should be noted that smokers often provide the ex-smoker with both a stimulus and an opportunity to smoke. Smokers may also impose direct or subtle social pressure to smoke. In addition to the coping skills described above, these situations often call for assertion skills in refusing cigarettes or rebuffing hostile or teasing comments. Another factor is the experience of withdrawal symptoms, which sometimes motivate ex-smokers to return to smoking. One response is to deal with the symptoms directly, relaxing in the face of anxiety or irritability, taking aspirin for headaches, and so on. Another response is to remind oneself that the symptoms will soon disappear and that smoking will only reinstate and prolong them. Finally, alcohol consumption often makes ex-smokers more vulnerable to relapse. Drinking alcohol is often associated with situations that are already of considerable risk to ex-smokers. The consumption of alcohol is likely to increase the desire for a cigarette and lower one's ability to resist or actively cope with the craving. Finding other methods for relaxation or substituting nonalcoholic beverages is advisable.

Coping skills are the key to successful self-management. Armed with a broad repertoire of well-practiced and appropriately chosen coping skills, an ex-smoker is likely to remain an ex-smoker.

SLIP RECOVERY AND RELAPSE CRISIS DEBRIEFING

Many ex-smokers slip. A critical part of maintaining abstinence from cigarette smoking is the ability to recover from such slips or limited episodes of smoking. Clients are seldom prepared for slips; the quitting process does not allow for backsliding. Yet, many smokers are able to recover from slips and become permanent ex-smokers. How lapses are handled can make the difference between success and relapse.

The clinician's open, accepting attitude toward lapses serves as an important model for clients' slip-recovery efforts. This can be conveyed through debriefing of relapse episodes, which is discussed in the next section. (See also Chapters 3 and 4 for a discussion of the AVE and interventions to prevent or ameliorate it.)

Among the most powerful tools for promoting maintenance is the relapse crisis debriefing. By this we mean a review of the circumstances surrounding a relapse crisis experienced by a clinic participant. This procedure provides a means of assessing the participant's relapse vulnerability and intervening in the processes that facilitate relapse. It also provides an ideal context for teaching and practicing coping skills. Indeed, relapse debriefing is so useful and flexible a procedure that it should be considered an important feature of any RP program. In this section, we describe the process of relapse crisis debriefing. This is followed by an annotated transcript of a debriefing that conveys more of the clinical flavor of the procedure.

The debriefing process rests on the identification of an incident in which the ex-smoker was confronted with a serious threat to abstinence. These incidents may be culled from various sources. Clinic members may be asked to recall past relapses, thus putting past "failures" to good use. Conversely, clinic members should regularly be asked to anticipate high-risk situations they may encounter between sessions. These can be worked on in the session through imaginative role playing. Finally, participants' current experiences can be harvested as grist for the debriefing mill. It is useful in each session to do a round-robin review of participants' status and progress. Out of this or other disclosures will come material relating to relapse crises or actual lapses that can be debriefed. It is particularly important that at least one instance of a "slip" be debriefed in each clinic so that anti-AVE attitudes and slip recovery can be modeled. In this section, we will focus primarily on debriefing of clinic members' recent experiences, but most of what is said is applicable to all debriefing.

A good deal of clinic time should be devoted to discussion of the difficulties participants are experiencing in maintaining abstinence. Devoting most of the last half of a clinic program to this activity would be appropriate. It is tempting and common for clinic facilitators to ignore clinic members' difficulties during this period. Dwelling on difficulties seems embarrassing, demoralizing, and seems to violate the principle of focusing on the positive. This avoidance has two unfortunate consequences: (1) An opportunity to teach skills for analyzing and coping with such difficulties is missed. (2) It models a critical and defensive attitude toward these difficulties, which is bound to hamper participants' ability to deal appropriately with them. The cost of the therapist being judgmental and impatient regarding lapses cannot be overestimated.

Detailed debriefing of relapse crises serves multiple purposes. The most straightforward is to collect information regarding the relapse vulnerabilities of the person whose difficulties are under discussion and to make specific suggestions to improve that person's coping responses. A second purpose is to model for others in the group the procedures involved in problem solving for relapse prevention. In addition to modeling the intellectual skills of analyzing a high-risk situation, identifying a *trigger*, and arriving at appropriate coping responses, the debriefing can also model an appropriate attitude of nonjudgmental, positive curiosity.

The group leader should listen to the discussion with an eye (ear) toward identifying lapses or crises that may be usefully debriefed. Often, these will not be clearly identified by the participants, who may be embarrassed about them or unskilled in defining them. Statements such as "This has been a hard week for me," often signal relapse crises. The leader should develop these by inquiring into the timing and nature of the difficulty in a manner that does not convey criticism or disappointment in the group member's performance, but rather an eagerness to grapple with the problems of maintenance. Positive, reinforcing statements about the value of bringing up such incidents are in order.

The group leader can then engage the client to develop a complete picture of the relapse crisis. Setting the scene is the first order of business. What sort of day was it? Restful? Stressful? Where did the crisis take place? Who else was there? What was the client doing? How was he or she feeling? Developing this information completely, without moving too quickly to conclusions about the nature or cause of the crisis, is important. With the stage set, focus shifts to the crisis itself, with a view toward identifying the crisis trigger. In some cases, the onset of craving is sudden and the client can easily identify the critical instant. More often, the onset is vague and a moment-by-moment account of the sequence of events and feelings helps locate the precipitating stimulus. The leader should encourage the client to imagine himself or herself in the relevant situation (e.g., "What do you feel now as you think about and remember that?"). If the situation is interpersonal, role playing is useful.

The precipitant of the crisis should be identified clearly and explicitly. "So you were feeling okay until he offered you a cigarette, and that's when you started to feel a strong craving. It was being faced with an actual offer that made it hard." The client's experience of "craving" should also be carefully analyzed. How was the craving experienced? Were there any physical sensations? Did the client entertain images or fantasies about how it would feel to smoke? What did the client expect to get from smoking? Making these processes explicit helps the client to recognize cravings and provides material for developing cognitive coping responses to combat the craving (e.g., evaluating the realism of one's expectations of smoking).

The client's coping responses to the situation should be carefully explored. What did he or she consider doing or actually do or think? If responses that were considered were not enacted, what inhibited them? In discussing the client's coping responses, the leader's attitude is crucial. While the debriefing will invariably bring out deficits in the client's coping response, it can also pinpoint the client's attempts to cope effectively. It is important that the leader reinforce these successive approximations, rather than punish "failure." Even if the client enacted no coping response at all, his or her thoughts about coping should be valued and reinforced.

Wherever possible, the client should be asked to say or do what he or she reported saying or doing in the real-life situation. This provides an opportunity to assess the quality of the coping response. If the client reports having "refused a cigarette," for example, ask that this be demonstrated, using the words and tone used *in vivo*. Often, ex-smokers express their refusals halfheartedly, undermining them with a hesitant or longing tone. Others refuse a cigarette with a tone of insulting superiority that elicits a retaliation from the offering smoker and ultimately makes a lapse more likely. Only by eliciting the behavior in specific detail will these difficulties (which call for assertiveness training) become evident.

The next step in the sequence focuses on the effect of the client's coping response. What was the effect on the client's craving and on his or her resolve? What effect did the response have on others? It is important for both client and leader to be willing to acknowledge that some coping responses will fail some of the time. This recognition opens the door to a search for responses that might have been more effective.

Exploring the sequelae of the crisis or lapse is a final step. If the client smoked, how did this feel? How did other people respond? In this sequence, the leader must walk a fine line. In order to remain credible, the leader must be willing to acknowledge positive aspects of the client's smoking experience and to convey an attitude of acceptance toward the lapse. At the same time, the leader should focus on developing awareness of negative experiences or disappointments that the client may be suppressing. After even a brief period of abstinence, many ex-smokers will have lost much of their tolerance to smoking and will reexperience many of the aversive feelings they had when they first started smoking. The leader should draw the client's attention to these sensations. Did the smoke burn in his or her throat? How did his or her lungs feel? Did he or she experience any dizziness? Did the smoking really fulfill the smoker's expectations and accomplish what he or she expected of it? How did the situation proceed after the client smoked? Did the anxiety, anger, and/or depression dissipate? Was the pleasure, energy, and/or relaxation much enhanced? Research suggests that lapses to smoking are experienced as pleasant only about half of the time. Even when they are pleasant and accomplish some of what the ex-smoker wants of them, they rarely meet the ex-smoker's exaggerated expectations.

An account of the emotional and cognitive sequelae of a crisis should also be developed, with a view toward identifying the AVE. To what did the client attribute the relapse crisis or lapse? What were its effects on his or her self-esteem and self-efficacy? Did the client feel guilty, worried, defeated, or proud (if the crisis was overcome)? Has the client smoked more since the initial lapse because he or she considered the "defeat" final?

Once the debriefing has been completed, the leader presents an integration or summary of the account that has been developed, focusing especially on the situational precipitants, the client's coping, and the AVE. This summary sets the stage for problem solving. The focus here is on "What might you do differently next time?" The client will usually be able to formulate several alternatives. Other group members can also be involved in brainstorming alternatives. It is useful, too, to elicit from other group members whether they have been in similar crisis situations. This lifts some of the onus from the group member who is serving as an example and makes explicit the vicarious learning from which other group members may profit.

After this discussion, the leader should help the client formulate a specific coping plan for the relevant situation. If the plan includes skills that have not yet been covered in the clinic or if the role play has demonstrated a skill deficit that is not peculiar to this one client, the leader may use this occasion to introduce and teach the relevant skill. The leader should encourage immediate rehearsal of the coping plan through role playing, and assess the client's adequacy and self-efficacy. Repeated instruction and rehearsal may be necessary to bring the coping skill to an adequate level of performance. Other group members should also use this opportunity to rehearse these skills.

Finally, the client and other group members should be encouraged to anticipate whether and when the situation in question might arise again. Some clients will be overly concrete in their thinking and must be explicitly encouraged to consider variants of the situation that has just been debriefed (e.g., being offered a cigarette at work instead of in a bar). Plans can then be tailored specifically to fit the anticipated situation. The leader may also invite the clients to report back on "how it went" in the anticipated situation.

The debriefing procedure is time-consuming. A half hour is probably a rock-bottom minimum for a complete run-through. Relapse debriefing warrants this heavy investment of time because it effectively serves many of the agendas of RP. Properly conducted, debriefing is a healthy mix of individualized attention and group discussion. It is an effective means of assessment of situational vulnerabilities and coping response adequacy. It provides an effective context in which to teach and rehearse new coping responses. It encourages both retrospective review and anticipatory planning. It provides an opportunity for modeling appropriately nonjudgmental attitudes and anti-AVE thinking. Most importantly, relapse debriefing models the way in which all of these processes are integrated into a functional sequence. The crowning value of relapse debriefing is its potential to teach ex-smokers precisely the process they will need to employ on their own if they are to be successful in maintenance.

RELAPSE DEBRIEFING: A CASE HISTORY

Our description of the relapse debriefing process cannot really convey the flavor of the interaction. Here we present a transcript of an interaction between a clinic therapist (*T*, the senior author) and client (*C*). This client was particularly cooperative and introspective; many clients would present greater difficulty than she did. *T* first addresses *C* during a round-robin checking on the status of each member. Our comments on *T*'s actions are in brackets.

T: How's it going?

C: Well, okay.

T: Just okay? [Picks up discouraged tone.]

C: Well, I was naughty once.

T: Naughty. Do you mean you smoked?

C: Yeah. I just . . . you know, I just don't seem to be able to hold out when it gets rough.

T: Hmmm. You had a rough time and you smoked. How many did you smoke? [Probably too specific too quickly. But we hold to a "coping" model for therapists, too.]

C: Ah, I had several.

T: Just a few. [Restructures with emphasis on the positive.]

C: Yeah, but . . .

T: Great! So this gives us a chance then to kind of look at what gives you some trouble. [Models nonjudgmental attitude and eagerness to "learn from mistakes."]

C: Not smoking.

T: Not smoking. That's the hard part, huh? Well, I think it would be helpful here to review the details of what happened. That way we'll get a sense of the dangers that tripped you up, and then we can think about things you could do. Let's focus on when you first had a cigarette. When was that?

C: Well, it was just the one time.

T: Great! So there was just this one limited occasion. [More emphasis on successive approximation.]

C: It was yesterday, but I'm feeling kind of, you know, not so sure about today. I could have smoked.

T: Yeah, you feel like you've blown it since you smoked last night and maybe you'll smoke today and maybe you'll smoke tomorrow. [Reflects *C*'s lowered self-efficacy expectations.]

C: Yeah, and this is going to be just like all my other attempts to quit.

T: You're feeling pretty demoralized. Like it's a wildfire. Like once it starts there's no way of stopping it. [Continues highlighting AVE.]

C: Yeah, well, one puff does it.

T: Really? I think that's not necessarily true. I'm impressed that you smoked yesterday, and yet from what you're saying it was just on one occasion. And actually since then you haven't smoked. Is that accurate? [Confronts with evidence for positive viewpoint.]

C: (*Brightly*) Yeah! Right, right. I didn't smoke today. But I felt so shitty, so stupid.

T: You really kicked yourself for it. [Highlights *C*'s AVE-promoting cognitions.]

C: Yeah.

T: Does that help? How does it feel?

C: . . . to kick myself? Not good, not good.

T: Naw, naw, just kind of gets you down. You know, my experience is that one puff isn't the end of it, and that the fact that you smoked in some situation—we haven't had a chance to find out yet which—doesn't mean you're going to have trouble with every situation, and that one of the things we can really do now is look at that situation and see what was special about it. I'm guessing that there was something special about it that made it especially difficult for you. [Anti-AVE education.]

C: Hmm. Well, I'd just come home from work and I felt pretty tired and . . .

T: It had been a long day and you were pretty worn out.

C: Yeah, I just felt too tired to do anything. You know, I'm working so hard at quitting and everything, that I just felt like "Oh, I don't want to go through that."

T: You were just exhausted. Let's start right there when you feel like you've got nothing left. Okay, so we get home from a hard day at the office. [Focuses on critical incident.] Kind of a stressful day?

C: Well, there wasn't any one particular thing, but there were lots of things to do around the house and I've been keeping myself busy, but I was too tired to do that.

T: So one of the things that happened was that some of the things you were doing that had been helping you—keeping yourself busy—[highlights previous coping] weren't available because you were just too exhausted to be busy. So there was a little crack in your defenses right there. [Suggests circumscribed attribution of slip.]

C: Uh-huh. That's mainly what I've been doing, you know, I've been going to movies and stuff, but this time I really just wanted to relax. You know, I didn't want to start fixing dinner. I had been going home and immediately starting dinner just to keep myself busy.

T: After a while keeping yourself that busy starts to get kind of thin. [Sympathizes with reasons for failing to cope, rather than judging.]

C: Yeah, yeah.

T: So set the scene for me a little bit. About what time is it? I guess it's after work so it's evening. You arrive at your front door. Then what happens? [Focusing.]

C: Well, I go in and I start toward my chair where I usually sit to kind of unwind before I quit smoking, and then I get up because you told me I'm not supposed to sit in that chair anymore. I just went over to the couch and started thinking about what I had to do around the house and just started thinking that a cigarette would be real nice because I could just relax and unwind and . . .

T: That's when the craving really hit you, when you started to relax and feel how exhausted you were. [Underlines precipitating cause of episode.]

C: Yeah, and I remembered, at first I thought, I really thought about having a cigarette, and I thought. . . . Oh, you see a couple days ago, I hardly ever do this, but I went down to the store near my house and I noticed that they had my brand, my old brand. Seeing it there I almost kicked myself because I never realized it was so convenient down there and I think that had something to do with it.

T: That was in the background; you were sort of feeling nostalgic.

C: Yes, and I knew that it was pretty readily available.

T: Yeah, that it was right there.

C: So I started thinking about that it was there and that it was close and . . .

T: Let me slow you down a little bit. You were talking about wanting a cigarette, feeling as though it would be good and right close by. What did you want? What was your fantasy about how good it would be? [Does not let "craving" go unanalyzed. Attempts to translate it into specific expectancy.]

C: I just thought it would be great to pull in that hot air and just kind of surround myself in this kind of haze.

T: What would it do for you? [Doesn't accept ready answer; pressing for more.]

C: I think, I think it would let me kind of block out the day and just kind of have time.

T: Hmmm, it would be a way to almost raise a flag that says "I'm done working and I'm relaxing now and I'm letting go."

C: yeah.

T: That would be nice. You were kind of hoping a cigarette would help you do that. [Nonjudgmentally sympathizes with *C*'s desires.]

C: It would be kind of my way to say, you know, I need this time to myself. That always was my way of taking a break, you know.

T: And here when you were feeling especially exhausted and feeling like you especially needed a break. You know, you talked about sitting down in your smoking chair and then getting right up, which was real sharp of you to catch that. [Reinforces attempts to cope.] Maybe you were feeling that even this quitting stuff is just more work. "Here I come home from a hard day of work and I can't even sit in my smoking chair."

C: Yeah, and I just don't feel like getting busy and what else to do. And then I remembered that somebody had brought Russian cigarettes for us all to try about a year ago.

T: Russian cigarettes?

C: Russian cigarettes and God they're awful! I remembered I started going through cabinets where I thought I had left them, and I finally found them. I mean, I threw out all my cigarette things when I quit, you know. I remembered these and their being there was like . . .

T: These were your ace in the hole. [Teasingly points out *C*'s role in setting up the relapse.]

C: Well, I didn't know. I forgot them actually; I forgot that they were in the house at the time when I was getting rid of everything.

T: How convenient. [Said teasingly—as though sharing a joke.]

C: Right! It almost seemed that if I can't find them I won't smoke.

T: They're practically staring at you in the back of the cabinet. . . . I'm teasing you. [Again emphasizes *C*'s active role. Does not accept account in which *C* is passively victimized.]

C: Well it was a sign for me. It's stupid but I was saying if I can't find them then I won't smoke and if I can . . .

T: That was the test. You would let nature decide, fate decide. That's where you gave up, huh? [Emphasizes *C*'s choice and decision.]

C: Yup. You know after I smoked, they weren't good, you know. They were stale and I felt dizzy.

T: From the face you're making it was pretty unpleasant. [Emphasizes aversion.]

C: Yeah.

T: One of the things you said you were hoping they would do for you is help you sort of block out this relaxing break time. Did it do that for you? [Encourages comparison of expected and actual effects.]

C: Well, they kind of did, but I got so feeling guilty about having smoked, that I really, and they weren't that pleasant so that . . .

T: So really, right now, with your commitment to quit, they really didn't do very much for you.

C: No, they really didn't, because I just felt bad because I'd blown it, but I couldn't resist.

T: Well, we've already heard about some things you did to resist. You got up out of your smoking chair. What other things did you try when you were thinking, "God, I've got to have a cigarette"? [Highlights coping and prompts for more reports of coping.]

C: I didn't really do anything. I just, well, I was thinking about how they were available and probably said to myself "No, don't smoke" or . . .

T: So you did kind of, just by talking to yourself in the head, kind of, try to deal with the situation?

C: I hadn't really thought of them as, but I guess so.

T: Yeah, those are kind of hard to catch, they're fleeting thoughts rather than something you go out and do.

C: Yeah. Normally I would have gotten involved or busy in some activity.

T: Yeah. That's one of the things that seems striking here. If I'm remembering correctly, you quit a couple of weeks ago, so you've been doing all this stuff which has really worked for you—keeping yourself busy—and that part of what made this situation so very difficult was not only was it one in which you really wanted a cigarette, but it was one in which what you've been doing to help yourself just wasn't available or didn't work. You just were not up to keeping yourself busy and so it's like the little smoking gremlin found this chink in your armor, this little loophole in your coping. [Summary.]

C: Yeah, that's really true.

T: You tried some stuff, but this situation was one that you weren't quite prepared for.

C: No. I don't know what I should have done.

T: Well, let's look at it. What might you have done? [Picks up agenda of exploring alternatives, but puts responsibility on C at first.]

C: Well, I could maybe have not gone home.

T: What would that do? [Rejects response offered as an easy out.]

C: Well, I really didn't have this craving real strong till I was home. Maybe I could have gone out again.

T: So one thing you could have done was just sort of bail out, say this is . . .

C: Yeah, gone over to a friend's house or something.

T: You're not sounding too enthusiastic about it. Would that have worked for you in that situation? [Confronts C's halfheartedness in brainstorming alternatives.]

C: Well, I was just so tired. I don't know.

T: Part of what I hear you saying is that "When I'm feeling that tired and exhausted, I'm just not up to doing any big things like leaving." What you were after was some . . .

C: Something to relax . . .

T: You're saying, "Don't take that away from me." Sure, you could have gone to the movies or friends or cooked dinner, but you just weren't up to it. [Sympathizes with C's position, which seems to resolve impasse.]

C: I really haven't found any other way that is as relaxing as coming home and sitting in the special chair. You know, I just have that one chair that sort of signals this for me. Maybe petting my cat and the whole kind of routine, evening routine.

T: Yes, and part of what you were wanting was that sense of sort of deep relaxation, letting down.

C: Yeah, and I don't want to eat because I'm worried about gaining weight.

T: So that's one other method of relaxing that we don't want to use. Let's think about what else do you do that relaxes you. Petting your cat is one . . . [Prompts for positive solutions.]

C: Yeah. Well, I like walking and like a hot drink, I guess. Although I'm not having coffee because it reminds me of cigarettes.

T: So, you'd need to have some hot drink that wasn't related to smoking for you.

C: Yeah. I guess some tea or something.

T: What else? Maybe I can come in with some suggestions and other people in the group can, too. I don't know if you noticed but several people were nodding their heads as you were going through this and maybe they have some ideas about what works for them. [Helps *C* use group support. Also involves group in problem solving.]

GROUP MEMBER: I call a friend and talk when I get home and just tell them how tired I am and everything.

T: (*to group member*) Oh, and that relaxes you. (*to C*) Would that work for you? [Won't accept solution without acceptance by *C*.]

C: I guess I could do it; I don't want to bend anybody's ear off.

T: Yeah, you don't want to burden them.

C: Yeah.

T: Do you think you're close to being a burden right now? [Prompts for realistic evaluation.]

C: No. You know, I guess I could do it.

T: You know, there was a time when I went through a period where I really needed my friends and I was afraid of getting too burdensome, and I called them when I wasn't feeling tired or anything and I said, "Boy, I'm going through this hard time, but I'm worried about being too dependent. Is it okay if I call you now and again?" I was really surprised; I was touched that people really welcomed my calling them. So that's something you might use to reassure yourself that . . . [Uses self-disclosure to normalize and express empathy for *C*'s predicament as well as to suggest a solution.]

C: Call them when I'm not feeling real bad.

T: Tonight maybe and say . . . [Pushing for a specific, immediate action.]

C: Is it okay if I do it in the future?

T: Yeah. You could even say your leader in the smoking clinic suggested you might do that, but you wanted to check it out with them first.

C: Yeah. I think they would respond to that better than just calling and saying, "Oh, I'm so tired" and everything. Kind of give them some warning.

T: Yeah. They'd know what was going on. Let's also think of some things that you can do on your own so you don't feel entirely dependent upon other people. We've done those breathing exercises at the beginning of the clinic a couple of times. How do you feel when you do those? Do they relax you?

C: Yeah, they do, especially here in the clinic. I really didn't try them at home, but they were relaxing.

T: It kind of works here, but you haven't transferred it. How can we help you transfer it out of the clinic? The thing that I have in mind is just like with your friends. Where we're going to prepare them, I have in mind preparing you, like maybe having you practice some of that breathing at home when you're not feeling any craving and seeing if it works for you at home.

C: Yeah that would help because, you know, I do have energy to try new things but at that particular time, you know, I'm just . . .

T: Can we try it now? Can we . . . [Pushing for immediate action.]

C: Just breathe?

T: Yeah, I'll do it with you. Actually we could do it as a group and you could just keep track of what you do and remind yourself of how it works. [Attempts to defuse threat.]

C: Now?

T: It's embarrassing. [Picks up on *C*'s resistance.]

C: Yeah.

T: Would it help if we all did it? [Offers compromise and structures group practice of an important skill.]

C: Yes.

(Group practices deep breathing for about one minute.)

T: You've got good timing. You're taking real deep breaths slowly. [Specific positive feedback on performance.] Okay, so let's review so far. We had this tough situation in which you really wanted to relax. Some of the things you'd been using very successfully to cope weren't avaliable to you. In addition to that, cigarettes were in the house. [Focuses on specific extenuating circumstances.] Where are the Russian cigarettes now, by the way? [Looking for other actions which may be needed.]

C: They're all in me.

T: They're all in you. You've gotten rid of them that way. Okay, so that's one thing we won't have to worry about is cigarettes being . . .

C: I don't know if I would have smoked if they weren't in the house, you know. For me I really can't have them there. It's just too much of a temptation.

T: Yeah, it makes it too easy. I'm hoping other people in the group are listening if they have a few stashed away somewhere. In terms of planning for the future, I'm guessing that you're going to have more hard days at work and come home and not feel like being very active. [Anticipates future crises; avoids unrealistic "happily ever after."] We've talked about you maybe calling a friend for relaxation and support and doing deep breathing. I'd like to get a sense from you of whether you think that will be enough to give you the feeling of relaxation you need, so that you won't smoke in order to get it. [Prompts for self-efficacy evaluation.]

C: I think that will help. I think also just doing some of the other things, like maybe walking . . . I'd like having a spot where I relax kind of.

T: Yeah, I'm glad you mentioned that. I think that's something to look at, too. You used to have your smoking chair and that was real relaxing and you were very attentive to that in not letting yourself sink into that. Then you went to the couch, which maybe is a place where you used to smoke too? [Focusing on stimulus control of smoking.]

C: Well, the whole house is, except maybe the kid's room, but . . .

T: So the kid's room is a place where you never smoked.

C: Yeah, but that's not relaxing.

T: Did you smoke in bed, when you smoked?

C: No. Yeah, I could just come home and . . .

T: That would combine real well with the relaxing breathing, for you to kind of lie in bed and . . .

C: . . . just take a nap.

T: Yeah, it would be a way for you to get your relaxation in a way that wouldn't even suggest smoking.

C: So when I'm tired, take a nap. That makes sense. Well, I think that might work. Then I have a phone in my bedroom, too, so I could just do . . .

T: So you could do everything at once. Tell you what I'd like you to do. Since this is the first time you're trying it, and, who knows, it may work wonderfully or it may need adjusting, I'd like you to try it tonight, whether you need it or not, and then call your buddy. [Making specific assignment and extracting commitment. Also leaves door open for difficulty.] Who's your buddy in the clinic? [See section on Extensions of Treatment for description of the buddy system.]

C: Joe.

T: Joe. (*to Joe*) Joe, can you be home? (*to C*) Okay. Why don't you try it and then call Joe and just, no big deal, just kind of tell him how it went, and he might have some ideas to discuss with you about adjusting things that you didn't do quite right. [Structures contact between buddies. Assignment will also serve as practice in mutual problem solving.]

C: Okay.

T: Then, next week we'll find out how it went. How are you feeling now about. [Again, seeks self-efficacy statement.]

C: I feel better, more relaxed about the whole thing. Because I can't be busy all the time.

T: No, that would be crazy.

C: And this will give me an alternative.

T: Sounds to me that right now you're feeling a little more hopeful that you haven't blown it forever. It's not like you're . . .

C: I've had some cravings today, but I haven't smoked.

T: That's not surprising. Since you've smoked last night your body is a little confused. It sort of says, "Well, maybe we're back to smoking, maybe I should want one." It's kind of a confusing signal. [Re-attribution of cravings.] Really, what's impressive is you've had cravings but managed not to smoke. [Reinforces positive action, successive approximations to complete abstinence.]

   C: That's true. It was tougher today than before, but I just kind of waited through them.

   T: So you were just holding off.

   C: Yeah.

   T: Sure doesn't sound like a lost case to me. Let's move on.

LIFESTYLE INTERVENTIONS

Changing smoking behavior is not enough to ensure the endurance of smoking cessation. The ex-smoker's lifestyle must also be changed. A lifestyle that supported smoking is unlikely to support nonsmoking. People may have used smoking to reduce or manage feelings of frustration and deprivation. Some lifestyles may be chronically unsatisfying, making return to smoking all too tempting. Smoking may also mask underlying chronic problems that surface on cessation. Combined with the stress of smoking cessation itself, these may tax the resources of some clients.

   Cigarettes are important in the lives of most smokers and serve many functions. They may be used as sources of stimulation or relaxation, as tension reducers, as appetite suppressants, or simply as punctuation marks that define transitions between activities. The need for these functions continues after cessation and the ex-smoker may not readily develop new ways of meeting them. Ignoring these legitimate needs sets clients up for relapse. Smokers come to treatment with a strong association between these needs and smoking. Usually, they are not even aware of the underlying need; they simply feel they want a cigarette. One function of treatment is to sever the link between legitimate needs and smoking and to substitute other, more functional ways of meeting them.

   Since smoking is often used to mask needs, smokers are often out of touch with important needs. This hampers selection of appropriate alternatives. Clients need help in labeling their needs and in finding other ways of satisfying them. In the section on coping skills, we discussed a number of substitutes that may be effective in reducing craving. Early in treatment, many substitutes may be used in lieu of having a cigarette. Many of these substitutes cannot be used for long periods of time without harmful side effects, however. Eating sweets or taking tranquilizers may be appropriate as stopgap measures, but create problems in long-term use. Such substitutes also perpetuate the cycle of deprivation, craving, and dependence. Clients need appropriate skills for satisfying the needs flagged by craving without smoking. A more satisfying, need-fulfilling lifestyle also makes craving for cigarettes less likely. The assumption here is that other behaviors can satisfy these needs at least as effectively as smoking and can therefore displace smoking as a valued activity.

Some lifestyle interventions aim to help the smoker develop immediate substitutes for smoking.

On admission to the smoking cessation clinic, Mrs. S smoked 45 cigarettes a day. Review of her self-monitoring forms showed that the bulk of these were smoked while she was anxious. Her Smoking Occasions Questionnaire confirmed this. In the clinic, she often seemed jittery and talked so quickly she was difficult to understand. Mrs. S successfully quit over a weekend, but resumed smoking when she returned to work. She was assigned to practice deep muscle relaxation using a prerecorded cassette. (Since most of the other clinic members did not have comparable difficulties with anxiety, the therapist decided against spending much clinic time on relaxation training.) After a week of practice on her own, she demonstrated her relaxation techniques in the clinic and received additional instruction. She was also instructed to initiate her relaxation routine whenever she wanted a cigarette. A month later, Mrs. S was able to stop smoking. She continued to practice relaxation and was still abstinent at 2 months.

Other interventions may be broader. In extreme cases, smoking may have masked relatively severe underlying problems or lifestyle deficits that emerge in full force on cessation. If not addressed and treated, these problems usually lead to relapse. The smoking cessation clinician should also be sensitive to such situations because they can occasionally be severe enough to warrant referral for psychological treatment.

Mr. K, 69 years old, was referred by his cardiologist for help with his smoking 3 years after his wife's death. Since his wife's death, Mr. K had become increasingly lonely. The core of his social life became the local senior citizens' center, where the older men gathered to talk and smoke. Mr. K was initially very successful in quitting smoking cold turkey, but began to experience increasing difficulty not smoking. In particular, he had a strong craving when he was alone. A self-monitoring diary showed that he was spending a great deal of time alone. Discussion brought out that he found it difficult to be around his smoking friends from the senior citizens' center. He felt "odd" not smoking with his old buddies and had trouble making conversation. The last time he visited with these friends, he smoked.

Mr. K's maintenance efforts were complicated by an underlying social and lifestyle deficit. With the death of his wife, he had lost most of his social contacts (his wife had been the outgoing, "social" one). Before quitting, he dealt with his loneliness by socializing at the park, where smoking facilitated social contact. On cessation, he experienced his loneliness more forcefully. Mr. K was encouraged to join another club where he shared more interests with the members. He was also given very brief instruction on how to strike up a conversation and encouraged to raise his quitting as a conversational gambit. His social contact increased somewhat and he was successful in maintaining nonsmoking.

This case history illustrates the use of interventions that are not directly targeted to smoking behavior, but which influence maintenance indirectly.

The following discussion and case history illustrate lifestyle interventions even further removed from smoking behavior.

Mr. L, who had been ordered by his doctor to stop smoking, was a veteran of several smoking cessation programs. Each time he applied himself vigorously to quitting, but was not able to maintain abstinence for very long. He complained that, after a while, not smoking so interfered with his ability to work that he was "forced" to start smoking again. A discussion of Mr. L's self-monitoring data was a stimulus for a discussion of his lifestyle. Mr. L was a classic "workaholic." He typically worked 12-hour days 6 days a week and found little time for anything else. He reported that he nearly always felt rushed and that the interludes between work activities were spent anticipating the next round of activity. He agreed that his two-pack-a-day habit helped him maintain this lifestyle.

A "want–should" analysis (see Chapter 5) of Mr. L's life showed a nearly total absence of wants. While Mr. L easily identified several behaviors that might become wants for him (gym workouts and tennis were high on the list), he claimed that all were too time consuming given his busy schedule. Mr. L's therapist forcefully pointed out that this issue was critical to Mr. L's success in quitting smoking, and that he had been willing to commit substantial time and energy to this project. Mr. L contracted to work out three times a week on a trial basis. With Mr. L's permission, the therapist contacted Mrs. L and encouraged her to engage Mr. L in positive conversation about his workouts. Mr. L reported a slight decrease in tension on the workout days. When the clinic ended, Mr. L was unwilling to commit firmly to continuing his workouts. However, his wife reported that he seemed to be enjoying them and thought he would continue.

The reader is referred to the section on lifestyle change in Chapter 5 for further discussion of these interventions.

We would like to say a final word about lifestyle interventions. We have emphasized that smoking is often intricately intertwined with lifestyle and personality issues and have recommended that these be addressed in treatment. This might leave the impression that smoking cessation depends on deep personality changes, that psychotherapy is a prerequisite to successful quitting, or that much of the smoking clinician's work is focused on these broad issues rather than on smoking itself. These conclusions would be mistaken. Smoking cessation is and should be a focused, limited form of treatment aimed solely at modifying smoking behavior. Realistically, there is seldom time to make any but the most limited intervention into underlying processes. One can only point out connections or identify directions for change. There is an ethical issue here, too. Clients enter the clinic with an implicit contract to focus on their smoking behavior and not necessarily to expose their souls or lifestyles to examination and reevaluation. The clinician who pushes this boundary must do so with the utmost care and sensitivity. We do not mean to endorse a model in which smoking is treated indirectly. Rather, we wish to endorse a model in which smoking is treated with an awareness of its role in the context of the client's life.

EXTENSIONS OF TREATMENT

Treatments extending beyond the smoking cessation clinic are important supplements to clinic treatment, which is limited by its relatively short duration. It is neither practical nor economical to run clinics as long as 6 months. Yet, the first few months comprise a critical period for relapse. In this section we introduce extensions of treatment that have been used to address this problem.

Although they have long been proposed as solutions to the relapse problem, booster sessions, in which the client is given an extra dose of treatment, have produced disappointing results (Colletti & Kopel, 1979; Bernstein & Glasgow, 1979). Perhaps boosters that review coping skills, slip recovery, and other maintenance techniques would be more successful. Ex-smokers may be more receptive to the information after they have had some experience with maintenance. A practical difficulty with this approach is that the most needy clients are often reluctant to return for boosters.

Prerecorded phone messages that provide encouragement and tips appear to be somewhat helpful (Dubren, 1977); such messages have the advantage over booster sessions of being available *ad lib* when the client is in crisis. Clients can also be given a maintenance diary with messages to be read each day and spaces to record their responses (e.g., American Health Foundation, 1980; Powell & McCann, 1981).

While these media messages can boost morale or provide information, they cannot respond to the ex-smoker's individual needs. One solution, pioneered by Janis and Hoffman (1970), is to assign clinic members to "buddies" who provide *ad lib* support in maintenance. Janis and Hoffman showed that such a procedure improved maintenance among those who used it. It is helpful if buddies are assigned during the beginning of the clinic and are required to telephone their buddies. This makes it likelier that the smoker actually will use his or her buddy. Assigning clinic members to triads makes it more likely that one of the buddies can be reached and less likely that a smoker loses all support when a buddy relapses.

THE STAY-QUIT LINE

The extended treatment of choice would combine the availability of the buddy system with the skillfulness of a trained counselor. The telephone hot-line, SQL, originated as part of our research on when and how smoking relapses occur. A hot line proved to be an ideal mechanism for observing the process of relapse and also provided an opportunity to intervene at critical transitions. Ex-smokers were encouraged to call the line whenever they experienced a relapse or relapse crisis. The SQL was strictly concerned with maintenance; only callers who were abstinent for 2 days or more were counseled. Some called while struggling with cravings, and others called a day or a week after they had started smoking. During the lifetime of the hot line, over 400 ex-smokers received relapse crisis counseling.

Counselors at SQL were clinical professionals or seasoned parapro- fessionals. Their clinical training was supplemented by education regarding smoking and smoking cessation and by supervised training in relapse pre- vention. The SQL's counseling approach reflected the RP model we have been describing. Indeed, much of this approach evolved in the course of our telephone counseling work. The SQL relied heavily on the debriefing of relapse crises as an assessment and intervention procedure. Calls typically lasted 20–30 minutes. The relapse debriefing presented above conveys the flavor of most hot-line calls. The unique feature of the hot line was its immediacy and its ability to reach people not otherwise reachable. Ex- smokers called us from home, work, bars, and sidewalk phone booths. The urgency of their struggle and the intensity of their feelings were often impressive. Much of the counselors' task was to help the callers define and focus their concerns so that they could move from generalized distress to specific problem solving. We attempted to do this by insisting that the caller focus on one specific problem situation. This was sometimes difficult.

Given a receptive ear, many callers wandered far afield from the agenda. Sometimes they disclosed other significant problems. Discussing a relapse crisis brought on by a marital spat easily shaded into discussion of marital difficulties. We responded to these disclosures sympathetically but brought the caller back to the agenda at hand. Occasionally these discussions led to a request for referral to psychotherapy. Referrals were made only when the caller made the request. On a few occasions, we encountered callers who were suicidal and required immediate crisis management and referral.

Callers often seemed to expect ready advice from a hot line and some had difficulty seeing the function of assessment. An analogy to medical treatment ("Your doctor wouldn't prescribe anything until he or she is sure what's wrong") was helpful here. The lesson implicit in this ("Base your course of action on a thorough assessment") may have been as impactful as anything else we did.

Callers' response to the SQL was overwhelmingly positive. In a follow- up, 95% of those contacted said they would recommend the hot line to a friend who was quitting smoking. About 65% thought the hot line was "extremely helpful." Almost all thought it at least "somewhat helpful." In response to an open-ended query about what had been helpful, the coun- selors' supportiveness and their specific suggestions were cited most often.

The hot line also seemed to help callers stay off cigarettes. We attempted to contact callers 2, 4, 6, 12, and 24 weeks after their initial call to ascertain their smoking status. Our actual follow-up proved to be considerably more erratic than this, and some callers were contacted only once as long as a year after their call. (An attempt to conduct a more rigorous randomized evalua- tion of the hotline proved impossible.) Despite the limitations of self-report data obtained from this select sample, the results were encouraging. Let us first consider a group of SQL callers who had not yet smoked at the time of their call, and who were reached 2 weeks later. Of this group, 74.3% were still abstinent, despite having been "on the verge of relapse" 2 weeks earlier. At the time of our last follow-up contact with each of them (an average of 5 months later), 63% were still abstinent.

Examination of the callers who called the SQL after they had smoked tests the hotline's ability to help ex-smokers recover from a slip. Marlatt and Gordon (1980) report that 92% of slips led to full-blown relapses. Of the lapsed SQL callers we reached after 2 weeks, only 63.2% were smoking. The final follow-up ($\bar{X} = 20.8$ months) showed this figure to be stable. Thus, despite methodological flaws too numerous and obvious to belabor, these data suggest that the SQL was effective in promoting maintenance and provides a model for RP efforts. Relapse prevention demands patience, insight, foresight, energy, and skill. Without them, quitting and relapse become an endless cycle. With them, maintenance becomes possible.

ACKNOWLEDGMENTS

This work was supported by USPHS Grant No. DA 01986 from the National Institute on Drug Abuse.

REFERENCES

Abrams, D. B., & Wilson, G. T. Self-monitoring and reactivity in the modification of cigarette smoking. *Journal of Consulting and Clinical Psychology*, 1979, *47*, 243–251.

American Health Foundation. *The American Health Foundation stop smoking system.* New York: Mahoney Institute for Health Maintenance, 1980.

Bandura, A. Self-efficacy: Toward a unifying theory of behavioral change. *Psychological Review*, 1977, *84*, 191–215.

Bernstein, D. A., & Glasgow, R. E. The modification of smoking behavior. In O. F. Pomerleau & J. P. Brady (Eds.), *Behavioral medicine: Theory and practice.* Baltimore: Williams & Wilkins, 1979.

Best, J. A., & Hakstian, A. R. A situation-specific model for smoking behavior. *Addictive Behaviors*, 1978, *3*, 79–92.

Chaney, E. F., O'Leary, M. R., & Marlatt, G. A. Skill training with alcoholics. *Journal of Consulting and Clinical Psychology*, 1978, *46*, 1092–1104.

Colletti, G., & Kopel, S. A. Maintaining behavior change: An investigation of three maintenance strategies and the relationship of self-attribution to the long-term reduction of cigarette smoking. *Journal of Consulting and Clinical Psychology*, 1979, *47*, 614–617.

Colletti, G., Supnick, J. A., & Rizzo, A. A. *An analysis of relapse determinants for treated smokers.* Paper presented at the annual meeting of the American Psychological Association, Los Angeles, Calif., August 1981.

Condiotte, M. M., & Lichtenstein, E. Self-efficacy and relapse in smoking cessation programs. *Journal of Consulting and Clinical Psychology*, 1981, *49*, 648–658.

Cooney, N. L., & Kopel, S. A. *Controlled relapse: A social learning approach to preventing smoking recidivism.* Paper presented at the annual meeting of the American Psychological Association, Montreal, Canada, September 1980.

Cummings, C., Gordon, J. R., & Marlatt, G. A. Relapse: Prevention and prediction. In W. R. Miller (Ed.), *The addictive behaviors.* Oxford: Pergamon Press, 1980.

DiClemente, C. C. Self-efficacy and smoking cessation maintenance. *Cognitive Research and Therapy,* 1981, *5,* 175–187.

Dubren, R. Self-reinforcement by recorded telephone messages to maintain nonsmoking behavior. *Journal of Consulting and Clinical Psychology,* 1977, *45,* 358–360.

Frederiksen, L. W., Martin, J. E., & Webster, J. S. Assessment of smoking behavior. *Journal of Applied Behavior Analysis,* 1979, *12,* 653–664.

Griffiths, R., Bigelow, G., & Liebson, I. Facilitation of human tobacco self-administration by ethanol: A behavioral analysis. *Journal of Experimental Analysis of Behavior,* 1976, *25,* 279–292.

Hunt, W. A., & Matarazzo, J. D. Three years later: Recent developments in the experimental modification of smoking behavior. *Journal of Abnormal Psychology,* 1973, *81,* 107–114.

Ikard, F. F., Green, D., & Horn, D. A scale to differentiate between types of smoking as related to the management of affect. *International Journal of Addictions,* 1969, *4,* 649–659.

Janis, I. L., & Hoffman, D. Facilitating effects of daily contact between partners who make a decision to cut down on smoking. *Journal of Personality and Social Psychology,* 1970, *17,* 25–35.

Lichtenstein, E., Antonuccio, D. O., & Rainwater, G. *Unkicking the habit: The resumption of cigarette smoking.* Paper presented at the annual meeting of the Western Psychological Association, Seattle, Wash., April 1977.

Marlatt, G. A. Craving for alcohol, loss of control, and relapse: A cognitive behavioral analysis. In P. E. Nathan, G. A. Marlatt, and T. Løberg (Eds.), *Alcoholism: New directions in behavioral research and treatment.* New York: Plenum, 1978.

Marlatt, G. A., & Gordon, J. R. Determinants of relapse: Implications for the maintenance of behavior change. In P. O. Davidson & S. M. Davidson (Eds.), *Behavioral medicine: Changing health lifestyles.* New York: Brunner/Mazel, 1980.

McFall, R. M. Effects of self-monitoring on normal smoking. *Journal of Consulting and Clinical Psychology,* 1970, *35,* 135–142.

McFall, R. M. Parameters of self-monitoring. In R. B. Stuart (Ed.), *Behavioral self-management: Strategies, techniques, and outcomes.* New York: Brunner/Mazel, 1977.

McKennel, A. C. Smoking motivation factors. *British Journal of Social and Clinical Psychology,* 1970, *9,* 8–22.

McKennel, A. C., & Thomas, R. K. *Adults' and adolescents' smoking habits and attitudes.* United Kingdom: Ministry of Health, 1967.

Meichenbaum, D. Examination of model characteristics in reducing avoidance behavior. *Journal of Personality and Social Psychology,* 1971, *17,* 298–307.

Mello, N. K., Mendelson, J. N., Seller, M. L., & Kuehnle, J. D. Effects of alcohol and marijuana on tobacco smoking. *Clinical Pharmacology and Therapeutics,* 1980, *27,* 202–209.

Murphy, M. *The self-help process in smoking cessation.* Paper presented at a meeting on the role of self-help in smoking prevention and cessation, National Cancer Institute, Bethesda, Md., February 1983.

Powell, D. R., & McCann, B. S. The effect of a multiple treatment program and maintenance procedures on smoking cessation. *Preventive Medicine,* 1981, *10,* 94–104.

Rathus, S. A., & Nevid, J. S. *Behavior therapy: Strategies for solving problems in living.* New York: New American Library, 1977.

Shiffman, S. The tobacco withdrawal syndrome. In N. M. Krasnegor (Ed.), *Cigarette smoking as a dependence process.* Washington, D.C.: National Institute on Drug Abuse, Research Monograph 23, Department of Health, Education and Welfare, 1979.

Shiffman, S. Relapse following smoking cessation: A situational analysis. *Journal of Consulting and Clinical Psychology,* 1982, *50,* 71–86.

Shiffman, S. M., Maltese, J., & Jarvik, M. E. *Coping skills and coping styles in the maintenance of nonsmoking.* Manuscript in preparation, 1983.

Shiffman, S. M., Read, L., & Jarvik, M. E. *Self-efficacy changes following relapse crises.* Paper presented at the annual meeting of the American Psychological Association, Los Angeles, Calif., August 1981.

Shiffman, S., Read, L., & Jarvik, M. E. Smoking relapse situations: A preliminary typology. *International Journal of the Addictions,* in press.

Smith, G. M. Personality and smoking: A review of the empirical literature. In W. A. Hunt (Ed.), *Learning mechanisms in smoking.* Chicago: Aldine, 1970.

Tomkins, S. S. Psychological model for smoking behavior. *American Journal of Public Health,* 1966, *56,* 17–20.

U.S. Public Health Service. *Smokers' self-testing kit.* Washington, D.C.: Public Health Service Publication No. 1904, 1969.

U.S. Public Health Service. *Smoking and health: The report of the U.S. Surgeon General.* Washington, D.C.: U.S. Department of Health, Education and Welfare, 1979.

9

RELAPSE IN WEIGHT CONTROL: DEFINITIONS, PROCESSES, AND PREVENTION STRATEGIES

BARBARA STERNBERG

In the field of weight control, one of the most distressing facts is that while only a small percentage of dieters succeed in losing weight in the first place, an even smaller percentage succeed in keeping the weight off for any significant period of time. Why the ability to maintain is so elusive is not understood. This chapter examines the issue of maintenance by focusing on the processes involved in the failure to maintain, or relapse. It is hoped that by exploring the issues and recent research, new avenues of investigation into this problem will be opened.

THEORETICAL ISSUES AND PROBLEMS

ABSTINENCE IS NEVER A GOAL

In the treatment of obesity, controlled food use, rather than abstinence, is the goal. But what is "controlled food use"? The concept is vague and difficult to define. Abstinence is a discrete variable; it can be easily defined and measured. Controlled eating, on the other hand, is a continuous variable. It is difficult to define because there is no clear-cut demarcation between controlled and uncontrolled eating. It is difficult to define specific rules by which a dieter should govern his or her eating. The difficulties posed by the unavailability of an abstinence criterion can be seen by comparing treatment for cigarette smoking with treatment for obesity. For the smoker who adopts abstinence as a goal, definition of appropriate behavior is easy: Smoke no cigarettes. Violation of this rule is also easy to detect, as an occurrence of cigarette smoking is readily observable. For the dieter, however, defining controlled eating is more difficult. A dieter on a 1200 calories/day diet may lose weight by eating even as many as 1300 or 1400 calories/day. Although consumption of 4500 calories may be a clear example of uncontrolled eating, small differences in caloric intake may produce no noticeable differences in rate of weight loss, at least on a short-term basis.

WEIGHT LOSS IS NOT A BEHAVIOR

For many substances with high rates of abuse, such as cigarettes and alcohol, evidence points to a direct relation between behavior (use of the substance) and damaging effects on the body. Cigarettes, for example, have been shown to have direct damaging effects on the pulmonary, cardiovascular, and other systems of the body. Alcohol, when consumed in sufficient quantity over extended time periods, has been shown to bring about adverse changes in the liver, brain, and other organs. The behavior, then, of smoking a cigarette, or having an alcoholic drink, can be defined, essentially, as self-administration of pharmacologically active agents with relatively direct physiological consequences.

Weight loss differs from these examples in several ways. First, food is not a drug. Second, the relationship between changes in behavior and reduction of body mass is not direct, nor well understood. Third, unlike smoking cessation and alcohol treatment, the goal of obesity treatment—weight loss—*is not a behavior*. Obesity treatment focuses upon producing change in selected target behaviors which are at best imperfectly related to reduction of body mass. In addition, the relationship between selected target behaviors and weight reduction is only assumed. No studies have succeeded in demonstrating a relationship between changes in target behaviors, such as record keeping or slowing down rate of eating, and reduction of body weight. Mahoney (1975) has pointed out that behavioral weight-reduction approaches *assume* the existence of an obese eating style that includes overeating, rapid eating, and so on. When treatment is successful, it is then inferred that the eating style has been altered, and that this in turn has led to weight loss. But the direct demonstration of this causal chain has not been made. In fact, one study that monitored daily changes in eating behavior found no relationship between changes in eating behavior and weight loss (Jeffery, Wing, & Stunkard, 1978).

WEIGHT LOSS IS SUBJECT TO PHYSIOLOGICAL INFLUENCES

While the desired outcome in obesity treatment is physiological change, the focus of intervention is behavior. These are only imperfectly related. It is well known that individuals differ in ease of and rate of weight loss. Such individual differences are poorly understood and often overlooked in obesity treatment, especially in treatments that offer a standard program to all dieters. Differences in metabolism and metabolic changes during dieting, while formerly considered minor, have received renewed attention as potentially important variables in explaining individual differences in weight-loss success (Wooley, Wooley, & Dyrenforth, 1979). Differences in percentage of lean muscle mass may be associated with differences in metabolism, and other aspects of physiological functioning may also influence rate and ease of weight reduction. Yet treatment for obesity is not usually individualized on the basis of these or related variables.

In addition, the form of weight-loss treatment often implies to the dieter that regular, linear weight loss is both expected and desired. Weight-loss programs typically meet on a regular schedule (usually weekly), and clients develop the expectation that their weight losses should follow this same regular schedule. It is not unusual to see clients feeling disappointed and discouraged when weight loss does not occur evenly and regularly on a weekly basis. But because of fluctuation in physiological processes, weight loss is often erratic. This situation may further complicate dieting efforts because desired behaviors are not the only behaviors that are positively reinforced. Because of fluctuations in physiological state, inappropriate eating behaviors will sometimes be followed by weight loss, and appropriate eating behavior by weight gain. Clinicians who treat obese individuals are familiar with the dieter who gets off the scale feeling relieved at having lost weight despite a lack of adherence to the diet. In this way, physiology "interferes" with the direct relationship between behavior and desired outcome.

PROBLEMS IN DEFINITION

In weight control, a relapse can occur either during the weight-loss process, when someone who has made a commitment to a weight-loss program fails to adhere to its dietary prescriptions and fails to lose weight, or after weight loss has occurred. In the latter situation, relapse can be considered a weight regain. The Relapse Prevention (RP) model can be applied in both situations as the postulated causal mechanisms are identical. Although not necessarily more important, the term *relapse* is most frequently used to mean weight regain following weight loss. Definitions of this second meaning of relapse will be explored below.

Defining Relapse

The term *relapse* might best be understood in relation to its opposite: maintenance of weight loss. *Maintenance* can be defined as weight loss that is kept off over time. Conversely, a *relapse* can be defined as weight loss that is subsequently regained.

These definitions are difficult to quantify. How long must weight loss be kept off to be considered maintained? How much weight must be regained to be considered a relapse? No general agreement exists as to how to quantify these constructs, and the literature contains numerous definitions utilized by different investigators. These definitions include:

- Successful losers: individuals who lost 20 or more pounds and kept it off for a year or longer (Leon & Chamberlain, 1973a, 1973b)
- Regainers: individuals who lost weight, but regained 20% or more (Wing & Jeffrey, 1978)
- Maintainers: individuals who regained less than 20% (Wing & Jeffery, 1978)
- Poor maintainers: individuals who regained more than 50% of weight previously lost (Gormally, Rardin, & Black, 1980)
- Good maintainers: individuals who regained less than 30% of weight previously lost (Gormally et al., 1980)

These definitions, chosen by the investigators, may not correspond with the dieter's *own* perception of success or failure at maintenance. Few if any reported studies have asked dieters to assess their own levels of success. Yet it is likely that individuals differ in their subjective assessments of success and failure. Two individuals who have each lost 30 pounds and regained 10 pounds, for example, may differ in satisfaction with their performance. This difference may affect feelings of self-efficacy, which can in turn affect future performance. According to Bandura's self-efficacy model (Bandura, 1977), appraisal of one's performance influences magnitude, generality, and strength of future action. A negative assessment of one's past and current performance in maintaining weight loss may lead to diminished belief in one's ability to maintain weight loss in the future, and hence, to weight regain. Perception of oneself as successful (especially if success is perceived as resulting from one's own skills rather than from chance or some external source) may lead to enhanced self-efficacy and continued effort directed toward weight loss or maintenance. The cognitive–behavioral RP model builds upon the self-efficacy construct and utilizes it as an explanatory concept in understanding how an initial rule violation is likely to influence further substance use and relapse.

A final definition of relapse is based upon the common assumption that changes in target behaviors such as rate and amount of food consumed lead to weight loss. These target behaviors function as rules governing eating. Accepting this assumption, maintenance could be defined as continued use of rules governing eating behavior. Relapse could be considered the violation of one or more such rules. Asking dieters to state the techniques they have used most frequently (and with perceived success) during weight loss, and examining levels of continued adherence to these techniques after weight loss, could potentially provide valuable information about the role of target behaviors in the maintenance–relapse process. Using such a process, Gormally et al. (1980) found a difference between maintainers and regainers in reported rate of adherence to a self-nominated critical dietary technique. Results of this study indicate that this definitional approach may be useful in understanding maintenance–relapse processes. However, behaviors critical for maintenance may differ from those critical for weight loss.

Definitions of Initial Slip

The cognitive–behavioral RP model defines a *slip* as the first occurrence of target substance use after a period of abstinence. When the treatment goal is controlled substance use, the model requires examination of an initial un-controlled use following a period of controlled use. This period of controlled use must have stemmed from a decision to control substance use. This model would not apply, then, to an individual who ate little food but lost weight due to illness, because the volitional aspect is lacking. Examining an initial period of uncontrolled use permits exploration of affective and cognitive reactions to the event, changes in self-efficacy, level of cognitive dissonance and methods of resolving it, and other key issues. Examining these issues in regard to eating requires defining an "appropriate" equivalent of a first cigarette or first alcoholic drink, which is easy to do when a prescribed diet involves strict adherence to a given calorie level or to food lists. An initial slip, within this context, can be considered failure to adhere to the prescribed daily calorie intake level, or consumption of foods other than or in addition to those on the prescribed food list. When a weight-control program is more flexible, however, as many behavioral programs are, defining an initial slip is more difficult.

In behavioral weight-control programs, the focus is placed upon changing eating and exercise habits. Often a specific calorie level is not prescribed, and individuals are given considerable latitude in choice of foods and daily caloric intake. For such a program, an appropriate definition of an initial slip might be more subjective, such as any instance of unplanned and uncontrolled eating in which an individual ate more than expected or planned and without prior compensatory plan. An alternative definition might be eating that is not in accordance with a commitment to lose or maintain weight. If concepts such as controlled and uncontrolled eating have been introduced and discussed within the treatment program, such definitions should prove usable for later investigation of maintenance and relapse processes.

A COGNITIVE-BEHAVIORAL ANALYSIS OF THE RELAPSE PROCESS AMONG DIETERS

Despite difficulties of definition, the RP model can be used to examine relapse and maintenance processes in weight loss. It is assumed, according to the model, that a dieter, while following a set of rules governing eating and exercise behavior, experiences a sense of personal control (self-efficacy) over these behaviors. This perception of control will continue until the dieter encounters a high-risk situation. High-risk situations, by definition, pose threats to the dieter's sense of control over his or her eating. High-risk situations found to be especially prevalent among dieters include negative affective states such as boredom and depression and positive affective states occurring in social situations such as parties. In a high-risk situation, the dieter is likely to feel helpless or powerless, but the likelihood of a slip (i.e., unplanned overeating) will depend upon the ability to engage in some adequate coping behavior. If the dieter does cope effectively (e.g., asserts himself or herself in resisting social pressure), the probability of a slip in that immediate situation will decrease. In addition, the dieter will regain a feeling of control and an expectation of being able to control eating in similar situations in the future.

If, on the other hand, the dieter does not cope effectively and eats more food than is consistent with his or her weight-loss or maintenance goals, it may be due to one of two reasons. First, the dieter may not have the skills needed to cope adequately in the high-risk situation. Some dieters, for example, may not be aware that it is appropriate, when at a restaurant, to ask for food prepared in a specific way, such as broiled rather than fried. Alternatively, the dieter may have the skills but be prevented from using them by anxiety or fear. For example, many dieters do not assert themselves with individuals who apply direct social pressure upon them to eat, because of anxiety. But regardless of the reason, failure to perform an adequate coping response is likely to lead to decreased self-efficacy, an increased sense of helplessness, and diminished belief in one's ability to cope. Expectancies for being able to cope in similar situations in the future would also decrease as the dieter comes to feel "I can't handle this," and gives in to urges to overeat.

The temptation to succumb will increase further if the dieter has positive expectancies about the effects of food. The dieter may selectively recall positive aspects of overeating, such as the initial taste of a highly palatable food and pleasurable sensations of fullness. He or she may anticipate these effects and at the same time not attend to the negative effects such as feeling bloated and uncomfortably full. For example, an individual who has habitually responded to feelings of loneliness and depression by eating calorically dense foods may recall only the pleasurable bodily sensations attendant upon devouring a chocolate cake and fail to recall the feelings of being very full, uncomfortable, and out of control, which follow consumption.

In addition, the dieter is likely to respond to instances of overeating with cognitive dissonance: His or her perception of self as a dieter or controlled eater may be in direct conflict with the overeating behavior. He or she is also likely to attribute the cause of the overeating to "lack of willpower" and other internalized constructs, rather than to lack of coping strategies. These phenomena, comprising the individual's reaction to an inappropriate eating event or slip, make up the Abstinence Violation Effect (AVE). For a dieter who is committed to a 1200 calories/day diet, for example, and who, without prior preparation, eats 2500 calories in a day, the dissonance component of the AVE will vary in intensity depending upon such factors as duration of the diet, how public the person's commitment to lose weight was, how many previous high-risk situations he or she successfully or unsuccessfully encountered, and so on. According to cognitive dissonance theory, dissonance is experienced as a negative emotional drive state and can motivate behavior or cognitions that reduce the dissonance (Festinger, 1964). Continued overeating may be particularly effective in reducing dissonance, as eating has been shown to be a high-probability behavior for many dieters experiencing negative affective states such as anxiety, boredom, and depression. After overeating, the dieter can change his or her cognitions to match the newly resumed uncontrolled eating pattern: "I guess I really am not a person who can control my eating and my weight—I'm destined to be fat all my life."

In addition, a dieter who blames himself or herself for uncontrolled eating may attribute this "failure" to internal weakness and personal shortcomings. People often draw inferences about their internal states (emotional and cognitive) through observations of their own behavior (Bem, 1972). Thus, if a slip occurs, a dieter may infer lack of willpower or lack of personal control as the determinant. The dieter's expectancy of continued failure in dieting attempts will increase as a result. This expectancy of failure may mediate decrements in future performance. Hence, if the dieter now considers himself or herself to be "weak-willed" and "powerless in the face of tempting foods," the expectation of being able to resist the next temptation will probably be lower, mediated by cognitions such as: "I guess I'm destined to be fat all my life, so I might as well give in and eat all I want. I can't stop myself, anyway."

UNDERSTANDING AND PREDICTING RELAPSE AND MAINTENANCE

CORRELATES OF MAINTENANCE

Several studies have looked for correlates of maintenance and its opposite, relapse. Leon and Chamberlain (1973b) studied predominately female participants of a weight-reduction club who had successfully maintained weight losses for 1 year or longer. Successful maintenance was defined as a weight regain of less than 20% of weight lost. These individuals reported being less likely to eat calorically dense snack foods, eating fewer calories while watching television, and engaging in fewer activities outside the home than regainers. In a second study, Leon and Chamberlain (1973a) found that regainers reported eating in response to a larger number of emotional states than did maintainers.

Wing and Jeffery (1978) studied 42 males and 22 females who had lost 20 or more pounds and maintained the loss for 1 year or longer. They found that maintenance was accomplished by close monitoring of weight and modification of food intake. Gormally *et al.* (1980) conducted a 7-month follow-up evaluation of individuals who had participated in a behavioral weight-reduction program. Successful maintainers, defined as those who regained less than 30% of total weight lost, reported greater confidence in their ability to control eating urges and weight, greater adherence to a self-nominated critical dietary habit, and greater frequency of exercise than regainers.

Findings from the preceding studies suggest that numerous factors may be involved in the maintenance process. Adherence to changes in diet and exercise patterns, which may be accomplished by self-monitoring and other behavioral means, appears important. Cognitive and affective factors such as self-efficacy and response to emotional arousal may be important as well.

INNOVATIVE STRATEGIES FOR IMPROVING MAINTENANCE

Periodic booster sessions have been advocated for maintenance of behavior change and have been used in treatment of obesity (Wilson, 1979; O'Leary & Wilson, 1975). Kingsley and Wilson (1977) found that booster sessions used during a 3-month posttreatment period were effective in producing additional weight loss during that time period. Other studies, however, were unable to replicate this effect (Ashby & Wilson, 1977; Wilson & Brownell, 1978, 1980). Brownell, Heckerman, and Westlake (1979) found evidence suggesting that booster sessions may facilitate maintenance of weight loss. However, as only 49% of their subject sample completed a 6-month follow-up evaluation, it is not possible to draw conclusions for the entire sample. Beneke and Paulson (1979) found that a fading out and a continuous contact booster procedure were equally affected in enhancing maintenance. At this time, results of research on booster sessions for maintenance of weight loss appear mixed.

A second strategy tried in recent years has been the inclusion of a significant other, usually a spouse, in treatment. This procedure could improve maintenance if the significant other became a source of ongoing support and positive reinforcement. Results of research in this area are suggestive, but inconclusive. Wilson and Brownell (1978) included husbands in the treatment of overweight women, but found no differences at posttreatment or follow-up in weight lost by these women compared with women whose husbands did not participate.

O'Neill, Currey, Hirsch, Riddle, Taylor, Malcolm, and Sexauer (1979) compared weight losses of male and female dieters who participated in treatment with or without a spouse. Again, no differences were found due to spouse participation. Rosenthal, Allen, and Winter (1980) included husbands in all, part, or none of the treatment sessions for overweight women. Results showed that any level of husband involvement was associated with greater weight loss than no husband involvement at post-treatment and at a 6-week follow-up, but the effects engendered by husband involvement had dissipated by a 3-year follow-up. Although findings in this area are inconclusive (see also Brownell & Stunkard, 1981), some researchers suggest that focusing upon increasing social support for newly developed eating and exercise behaviors, both in the home and in other settings such as the work site and community, may foster increased maintenance and should be included in treatment (Brownell, 1982).

COGNITIVE PROCESSES IN MAINTENANCE AND RELAPSE

In recent years, increased attention has been focused on the role of cognitions in the process of behavior change, including the area of weight reduction and maintenance. It has been argued that cognitive variables must be considered because problems presented by clients are complex and require multifaceted treatment approaches (Wilson, 1979), and because lasting treatment effects require focus upon all modalities of psychological functioning (Lazarus, 1976). Yet few studies have investigated the role of cognitions in the process of weight reduction.

Mahoney, Rogers, Straw, and Mahoney (1977) found a direct relationship between dieters' self-statements about their ability to carry out weight-reduction procedures, and weight loss. They conclude that an individual's belief in the value of his or her weight-loss efforts may be more important than the procedures used. This conclusion supports Bandura's contention that self-efficacy statements seem to be a determinant of behavior and effort in a variety of situations (Bandura, 1977). Bandura postulates that the critical determinant of behavior is not so much an individual's ability to perceive the relationship between a specified behavior and an outcome, but rather the individual's expectancies regarding his or her ability to successfully carry out the behaviors leading to the desired outcome. The findings of Gormally et al. (1980), described earlier, also support the hypothesis that self-efficacy is an important dimension of weight loss and maintenance. In this study, maintainers reported greater confidence in their ability to control eating urges and weight than regainers. In their review of the role of predictor variables in the behavioral treatment of obesity, Cooke and Meyers (1980) conclude that cognitive factors are among the few variables that appear to bear a significant relationship to success in treatment.

Few studies have investigated the effects of adding cognitive components to behavioral treatments for obesity. Dunkel and Glaros (1978) compared a cognitive treatment procedure (self-instruction), a behavioral treatment procedure (stimulus control), a combination of the two, and a relaxation control group. In the cognitive component, dieters were taught to talk to themselves in ways that might lead to better coping with feelings of hunger, frustration of the desire to eat, and fatigue and boredom related to physical exercise. At posttreatment, the combined cognitive–behavioral group lost more weight than the behavioral group, and the cognitive group lost more weight than the control group. At 7-week follow-up, more dieters who received either the combined or cognitive intervention continued to lose weight than did those who received either the behavioral or control treatment. Although longer follow-up periods are needed, the results of this study are at least encouraging.

Collins (1980) compared cognitive, behavioral, and combined cognitive–behavioral treatment approaches in an 8-week weight-reduction program. In the cognitive-therapy group, participants were taught to recognize and change negative thoughts and self-statements about their weight, weight loss efforts, and food. Techniques included cognitive restructuring, self-instructional training, and rational–emotive therapy. Results through a 7-month follow-up showed that the behavioral treatment group lost more weight than the control group. The difference between the cognitive–behavioral and control groups was marginally significant, and the cognitive group did not differ from the control group in amount of weight lost. During the first 3 months of maintenance, participants in all four groups continued to lose weight, with the greatest average weight loss occurring in the cognitive–behavioral group.

The findings of the above two studies suggest that cognitive interventions may offer some promise for the treatment of obesity, especially when combined with more standard behavioral approaches, and may be especially useful for the enhancement of maintenance. Further investigation is needed.

In a clinical report of "volitional breakdown," or "failure to adhere to values and commitments in relation to weight loss," Sjoberg and Persson (1977) describe reported cognitions and feelings of nine overweight individuals treated at a weight-reduction clinic in Sweden. On the basis of interviews conducted at various points during and following treatment (up to 4 months after the initiation of treatment), Sjoberg and Persson concluded that moods and emotional stress led to breakdowns and these were preceded by distorted reasoning. Those patients who were most successful at losing weight reported few negative self-statements or negative affects following diversion from the diet. Those who were least successful reported numerous negative self-statements and low feelings of self-efficacy in regard to weight-loss ability. These case reports support Bandura (1977) and others who consider cognitions to be key components of behavior change processes. None of Sjoberg and Persson's patients who lost significant amounts of weight reported feelings of guilt or self-blame or negative self-statements while they were dieting. These individuals appeared to have high degrees of self-efficacy in relation to their weight-reduction efforts. Unsuccessful dieters, on the other hand, reported feelings of depression and guilt as well as negative self-statements in regard to ability to control eating behavior and weight.

EXPLORATION OF RELAPSE PROCESSES

DETERMINANTS OF INITIAL SLIPS AMONG DIETERS

The findings of Sjoberg and Persson (1977) conform strikingly with the hypotheses of the RP model. In my first attempt to investigate patterns and determinants of relapse among successful dieters (Rosenthal & Marx, 1981), my colleague and I interviewed 28 female participants of a behavioral weight-reduction clinic at 60 days posttreatment. Each dieter participated in a 1-hour structured interview adapted from the assessment procedures described by Marlatt (1976) for the investigation of relapse processes among smokers, alcohol abusers, and heroin abusers. The interview consisted of questions about weight regain and further loss since termination of the weight-control clinic, methods and techniques used by the dieter to control her weight and eating behavior, and details about the circumstances, cognitions, and affects surrounding first and second dietary slips. A slip was considered to have occurred when a dieter did not use any method to control her weight during a 24-hour period. For example, a slip was considered to have occurred if a dieter who reported ordinarily keeping careful records of foods eaten and calories consumed and exercising daily did not do so for a period of 24 hours. A relapse was considered to have occurred if a dieter reported a weight regain of 5 pounds or more during the 60-day posttreatment period. Dieters were categorized as having relapsed regardless of whether or not weight regained was subsequently lost.

Interviews were analyzed via the classification system described by Marlatt in Chapter 2 for examination of relapse determinants and processes among alcohol abusers and smokers. In this system, the initial slip is categorized, first as *intrapersonal* or *interpersonal*, depending upon the salience of other people in causing the slip. Within each of these two major categories are subcategories that occur within either one: coping with negative emotional states (e.g., frustration, anger, and depression); coping with negative physical states (e.g., pain, illness, and fatigue); enhancement of positive emotional states (e.g., celebrations and travel); testing personal control; giving in to temptation and urges; and reactions to social pressure. Each occurrence of an initial slip is assigned to both a major category and a subcategory, based upon interview responses.

All 28 participants reported having had at least one initial slip during the first 60 days posttreatment. All interviews were coded by two independent raters. Interrater reliability (calculated by comparing number of agreements) was .93. Table 9-1 shows the determinants of initial slips by category.

Intrapersonal determinants accounted for 48% of initial slips. Two thirds of these were subcategorized as due to coping with negative emotional states of anxiety, boredom, and depression.

Interpersonal determinants were primary in 52% of initial slips for dieters. The subcategory enhancement of positive emotional states accounted for 32% of all initial slips. Interpersonal conflict accounted for 10% of initial slips for dieters, and social pressure accounted for another 10%. Finally, eating in response to negative physical states (e.g., pain, illness, and fatigue) accounted for only 5% of initial slips.

These findings point to two major types of high-risk situations for individuals trying to lose weight or maintain weight losses. Negative affective states occurring when the individual is alone, predominantly anxiety, boredom, and depression, were associated with one third of the initial slips and thus appear to be difficult for a large number of dieters to handle effectively. Positive emotional states involving other people, such as celebrations, parties, and social gatherings, are another type of high-risk situation for many individuals attempting to control their weight.

Of the 28 subjects who completed interviews, 67% had regained 5 pounds or more and thus by our criterion were classified as having relapsed during the 60-day posttreatment period. Two separate patterns emerged from cluster analysis, based upon amount of weight fluctuation between posttreatment and the 60-day interview. One pattern involved considerable weight fluctuation during this time period. These 10 individuals lost weight during treatment ($\bar{X} = 11.1$ pounds), regained 5 pounds or more within 60 days, but also within the same 60 days lost additional weight. The second pattern showed less fluctuation. These 9 individuals lost weight during treatment ($\bar{X} = 14.9$ pounds), regained 5 pounds or more during the 60-day posttreatment period, but then stabilized at the higher weight. A third group of 9 nonrelapsers showed a pattern of weight loss during treatment ($\bar{X} = 13.8$ pounds) and only minimal weight regain during the 60-day posttreatment period ($\bar{X} = 1.8$ pounds).

These three groups differed in regard to several items on the 60-day interview. The high-fluctuation group reported having felt guiltier during and immediately after the initial slip than did the more stable weight regainers or the nonrelapsers. According to the cognitive–behavioral relapse model described in Chapter 3, feelings of guilt could lead to reduced feelings of self-efficacy, and thus to further subtance abuse. The finding that stronger guilt feelings surrounding an initial dietary slip are associated with weight regain, supports this hypothesis.

Of the nonrelapsers, 89% reported relying upon record keeping and calorie counting as primary means of controlling weight regain posttreatment. Only 53% of participants who regained 5 pounds or more reported utilizing this method. This finding suggests that feedback stemming from record keeping and calorie counting may be very useful for weight-loss maintenance, or that participants who adhered compulsively to a target weight-control behavior may be more successful than those who did not. The latter interpretation is consistent with Gormally et al. (1980). Successful maintainers in Gormally et al. (1980) reported a 73% adherence rate to a critical dietary habit that they had identified as especially helpful in their

Table 9-1. Analysis of Relapse Situations with Dieters, Alcohol Abusers, Smokers, and Heroin Addicts

Situation	Dieters (n = 48)	Alcoholics (n = 70)	Smokers (n = 35)	Heroin addicts (n = 32)
Intrapersonal determinants	48%	61%	57%	53%
Negative emotional states	32%	38%	43%	28%
Negative physical states	5%	3%	—	9%
Positive emotional states	11%	—	8%	16%
Testing personal control	—	9%	—	—
Urges and temptations	—	11%	6%	—
Interpersonal determinants	52%	39%	43%	47%
Interpersonal conflict	10%	18%	12%	13%
Social pressure	10%	18%	25%	34%
Positive emotional states	32%	3%	6%	—

Note. Data for dieters from Rosenthal and Marx (1981) are compared with data from Marlatt and Gordon (1980) for alcohol abusers, smokers, and heroin addicts.

weight-control efforts. Only 46% of regainers reported adherence to a critical dietary habit.

In our study, individuals who relapsed tended to experience their initial slip in the evening after 5 P.M. (Rosenthal & Marx, 1981). For those who did not relapse, only 33% of initial slips occurred in the evening, with the majority (56%) occurring in the afternoon, between noon and 5 P.M. It may be that when a slip occurred during the evening, fewer external demands (e.g., a job) were available to distract the individual from continued eating. When a slip occurred in the afternoon, other activities may have helped the individual end the eating episode more quickly. Setting of the initial slip did not differentiate relapsers from maintainers. For both, initial slips usually took place either at home (41%) or in a restaurant (37%).

DETERMINANTS OF INITIAL SLIPS IN WEIGHT CONTROL, SMOKING, ALCOHOL, AND HEROIN USE: A COMPARISON

Hunt, Barnett, and Branch (1971) have pointed out that the temporal pattern of relapse is very similar for smokers, alcoholics, and heroin abusers. The commonality of relapse rates in all three of these substance abuse areas is striking: Approximately two thirds of all relapses occur within the first 90 days following treatment.

Findings from the Rosenthal and Marx (1981) study of determinants of relapse among dieters showed that 100% of the dieters interviewed had had at least one slip, and two thirds had regained 5 pounds or more within 60 days posttreatment. These findings suggest that the relapse pattern among dieters may be similar to that among smokers, alcoholics, and heroin abusers. Mechanisms underlying the relapse process in weight-loss maintenance might also be similar. If so, determinants of initial slips for individuals attempting to control their weight should resemble those for the other three substances. Table 9-1 summarizes and compares determinants of initial slips for the four substance use categories. The first category, intrapersonal determinants, accounted for 48% of initial slips for dieters. This is slightly less the percentage of initial slips due to intrapersonal factors found for alcoholics (61%), smokers (57%), and heroin abusers (53%). Two thirds of dieters' initial slips (32%) were subcategorized as due to coping with negative emotional states. This same category accounted for 38% of total initial slips for alcoholics, 43% for smokers, and 28% for heroin abusers, again showing similarity across the various substances. In addition, 83% of initial slips due to intrapersonal negative emotional states among dieters, and 85% for alcohol, heroin, and cigarette users, were subcategorized as being due to states of anxiety, boredom, and depression. Across all four substance abuse areas, it appears that uncontrolled substance use is a common response to painful or uncomfortable feelings experienced when alone.

Interpersonal determinants were primary in 52% of initial slips for dieters versus 42% for the other substances. The greatest difference between dieters and users of the three other substances falls under the subcategory of enhancement of positive emotional states. This subcategory accounted for 32% of initial slips among dieters, in contrast to only 3% for the other three substances. This difference may reflect the fact that although cigarette smoking and alcohol consumption are acceptable behaviors within our culture, food and eating activities permeate our culture to an extent unmatched by the other three substances. Not only is food more widely available than any of the three other substances, but it is a central focus for many social events, such as holidays, parties, celebrations, and even vacations. This difference may be reflected in the higher percentage of dieters whose initial slip occurred in such situations, relative to users of the three other substances.

The higher percentages of initial slips due to enhancement of positive states for dieters may also be due to high levels of indirect social pressure. Indirect social pressure can operate via modeling of rate and amount of food consumed (social facilitation), and was often scored as a secondary determinant of initial slips among dieters. In comparison, social pressure was scored as the primary determinant of initial slips for 18% of alcohol users, 25% of smokers, and 34% of heroin users versus only 10% for dieters.

Interpersonal conflict accounted for 10% of initial slips for dieters, roughly comparable to the mean of 15% for alcohol, cigarette, and heroin users. Finally, eating as a method of coping with negative physical states, including pain, illness, and fatigue, accounted for 5% of initial slips for dieters and 6% for users of the other three substances.

The similarities in determinants of initial slips across the four substance abuse areas—alcohol, heroin, cigarettes, and food—point to similarities in mechanisms underlying relapse for these areas and perhaps for consummatory behaviors in general. Although similarities in relapse rate have been traditionally viewed as evidence of common underlying physiological processes, Marlatt and Gordon (1980) argue that similarities in cognitive and affective processes might alternatively explain these similarities.

A COMPARISON OF A STANDARD AND A RELAPSE PREVENTION WEIGHT-CONTROL PROGRAM

The finding in Rosenthal and Marx (1981) that two thirds of initial slips falls into two categories—response to negative emotional states occurring when the individual is alone, and response to positive emotional states occurring in social situations—suggests that additional emphasis upon these situations might be incorporated into weight-control programs. Teaching skills for managing these situations as well as the cognitions and feelings that lead to them might increase maintenance of weight loss. To examine this hypothesis, R. D. Marx and I conducted a study of 43 individuals, predominantly female, who participated in both a 9-week behaviorally oriented weight-reduction program and a 60-day posttreatment interview.

Participants were students and staff at a small regional university who were recruited via advertisements appearing in campus publications. They were among an original pool of 65 participants in a weight-reduction program who were randomized into a standard behavioral or RP condition and further randomized into one of two identical groups within each condition.

The Standard Behavioral Weight-Reduction Program

Although it is incorrect to imply that there is one single "standard" behavioral weight-control program, most programs today do seem to contain similar elements. The treatment program used in our study (Rosenthal & Marx, 1979) was based upon one developed by Hagen (1974) and revised by Smith-Scott (1976). It included record keeping, stimulus control procedures, methods for slowing down eating rate, satiation and hunger-control techniques, use of rewards, chaining procedures, methods of obtaining social support, and assertiveness training. The program consisted of nine weekly 2-hour sessions. The 1st hour involved weigh-ins and presentation of new material in a large group format. The 2nd hour was devoted to small-group discussion.

The Relapse Prevention Program

Participants in the RP program met conjointly with standard treatment participants for the 1st hour of each session (Rosenthal & Marx, 1979). Thus they received instruction in the behavioral techniques listed above. Like the standard treatment participants, these individuals met for the 2nd hour of each session in small groups. Total group and therapist contact time for all participants was equal. However, new information was presented during the first 20 minutes of the small group, and discussion focused around cognitive RP material. The major emphasis of this component was upon changing cognitions and self-statements in regard to problem eating situations. Components of this program are discussed briefly following.

Analysis of High-Risk Situations

We defined high-risk situations as situations that are commonly associated with overeating for an individual (Rosenthal & Marx, 1979). Participants were told about the most frequent high-risk situations (intrapersonal negative emotional states and interpersonal positive situations). They were taught to label and monitor their own high-risk situations and classify them into general problem categories ("difficulties with feelings," "difficulties with social situations," etc.). Discussions focused upon alternative strategies for handling these situations. Often, role play was used as a tool to develop skills.

Want–Should Ratio

Marlatt and Gordon (1980) have described the importance of including in one's daily schedule periods of "time out" for reinforcing activity. The want–should ratio is a rough index developed to assess amount of wants and shoulds interspersed during the day. Participants kept an activity record for 1 weekday and 1 weekend day each week for 2 weeks and labeled each activity on the basis of the amount of want and should it entailed (most activities are a combination of wants and shoulds). These records were examined during small-group sessions, and participants were encouraged, where necessary, to achieve better balance of these two types of activities (Rosenthal & Marx, 1979).

Apparently Irrelevant Decisions

Marlatt and Gordon (1980) have suggested that a person headed toward a slip makes numerous small decisions over time which, although seemingly small and irrelevant at the time they are made, actually bring the individual closer to the brink of the slip. For example, it is not uncommon for dieters to purchase desserts and other calorically dense foods for the supposed purpose of "having something around in case company drops by," or baking cookies "for my children," and so on. In making such decisions, the individual begins slowly to set the stage for a slip by decreasing the chain of behaviors ending in food consumption. Also, individuals appear to have little awareness of the relationship between these decisions and the occurrence of the slip. These small decisions have been called Apparently Irrelevant Decisions (AIDs). Participants in our program were taught to examine their thoughts when tempted to purchase or cook a food that might bring them closer to a slip, and were encouraged to take personal responsibility for thinking through the decision and weighing its potential costs and benefits.

Discussion of Slips, Relapse, and Self-Efficacy

Most weight-reduction programs make little mention of the possibility of a slip or a relapse, or how to handle one if it occurs. This effectively deprives dieters of the opportunity to develop skills for coping with these situations and/or minimizing damage should one occur. In our study (Rosenthal & Marx, 1979), these phenomena were openly and repeatedly discussed within the small-group context. Participants described past slips and relapses and their reactions to them. They were encouraged to examine their feelings and cognitions before, during, and after slips. Alternative cognitions were suggested and practiced in the group and between sessions. In addition, the concept of self-efficacy was explained to participants, and they were encouraged to describe their own levels of self-efficacy with regard to weight reduction at the present time and during past unsuccessful weight-loss attempts.

Abstinence Violation Effect

The AVE has been defined by Marlatt and Gordon (1980) as the cognitive and emotional reactions to an initial slip following a period of controlled substance use or abstinence. This effect was explained to participants (Rosenthal & Marx, 1979), who then discussed diet-related experiences within this framework. For example, they were told "You can expect to feel guilty and disappointed with yourself after you overeat, but these feelings do *not* mean that you are a failure at dieting. If you wait and do not overeat further, these feelings will pass." Group members' experiences with such phenomena were then solicited and discussed. Participants were given specific suggestions and techniques for handling the reactions that make up the AVE. They were encouraged to view a slip as an opportunity to examine remaining difficulties and practice new coping strategies.

Approximately 50 days posttreatment (Rosenthal & Marx, 1979), participants were contacted by telephone and asked to come in for a 40-minute interview and weigh-in. Interviews were conducted by senior undergraduate psychology majors and a graduate student in counseling psychology. A slip was defined as "a violation of rules governing food intake that had been used as part of your weight-control program." This definition, while less precise than that of Rosenthal and Marx (1981), permitted greater flexibility of interpretation. Otherwise, the interview was identical to that used in Rosenthal and Marx (1981). Following the interview, participants were weighed on a physician's scale that had been used throughout the weight-reduction program.

Behavioral Findings

As predicted, participants in the two conditions did not differ in weight change from pre- to posttreatment (RP group, $\bar{X} = -10.9$ pounds; standard treatment group, $\bar{X} = -10.1$ pounds; $t (34) = .45$, n.s.). Nor did they differ in percentage body weight lost from pre- to posttreatment (RP group, $\bar{X} = -7\%$; standard treatment group, $X = -6\%$; $t (34) = .77$, n.s.). The two conditions did differ, however, in weight lost between pretreatment and the 60-day follow-up interview (RP group, $\bar{X} = -13.9$ pounds; standard treatment group, $\bar{X} = -8.7$ pounds; $t (34) = 2.08$, $p < .05$). Expressed in terms of percentage body weight lost pretreatment to follow-up, RP participants lost more ($\bar{X} = -9\%$) than did standard treatment participants ($\bar{X} = -5\%$; $t (34) = 2.23$, $p < .05$). The means and standard deviations for these weight data are presented in Table 9-2, and the data are depicted graphically in Figure 9-1.

More participants in the RP condition continued to lose weight posttreatment than did those in the standard treatment condition (41% vs. 22%). More participants in the RP condition maintained their posttreatment weight losses with no additional loss or gain than did standard treatment participants (27% vs. 14%). Finally, twice as many participants in the standard condition regained weight during the 60-day posttreatment interval. These

Table 9-2. Means ($\bar{X}$) and Standard Deviations (SD) of Difference Scores in Pounds and Percentage Weight Loss for Relapse Prevention and Standard Treatment

	Pretreatment to posttreatment		Pretreatment to follow-up	
	$\bar{X}$	SD	$\bar{X}$	SD
Difference in pounds				
Relapse prevention ($n = 22$)	−10.9	5.1	−13.9	8.2
Standard treatment ($n = 14$)	−10.1	5.0	−8.7	6.4
Difference in percentage weight loss				
Relapse prevention ($n = 22$)	.07	.04	.09	.05
Standard treatment ($n = 14$)	.06	.03	.06	.04

Note. Data from Rosenthal and Marx (1979).

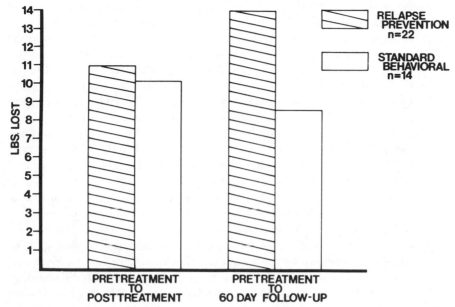

Figure 9-1. Pounds lost pretreatment to posttreatment and pretreatment to follow-up for participants in the standard behavioral and RP conditions. Based on Rosenthal and Marx (1979).

findings suggest that the RP program was effective in producing superior maintenance and continued weight loss. These data are presented in Table 9-3.

None of the participants in the RP program were heavier at follow-up than at pretreatment as compared with three (14%) of the standard treatment participants. Three (21%) of the RP participants had lost 21 or more pounds between pretreatment and follow-up as compared with none in the standard treatment program. These data suggest that magnitude of weight loss was superior for individuals receiving the RP package.

The number of participants who slipped (i.e., experienced at least one instance of violation of rules governing eating) during the 60-day post-treatment period differed in the two conditions. One hundred percent of the participants in the standard treatment condition slipped compared with 80% of the RP participants. A z test for differences between proportions showed this is to be a borderline significant difference ($z = -1.7$, $p < .10$). Of those who did slip at least once, 56% of those in the RP program reported that the decision to overeat was deliberate as compared with only 40% of those in the standard treatment condition. These findings, depicted in Table 9-4, suggest that the RP program was effective in reducing incidence of slips and in changing some aspects of individual's perceptions of the experience.

The RP model generates several hypotheses about cognitive and affective reactions to dietary slips. It predicts that individuals who slip would attribute the cause of the slip to internal failings and weakness and that they would feel guilty following a slip. Individuals who received the RP techniques were expected to experience fewer of these reactions than those who received the standard program. Participants in the RP program were taught to look for environmental determinants of their slips, rather than intrapersonal determinants. These predictions were tested by a nonparametric statistic, the Sign Test, and 80% of the predictions were supported ($p = .05$). Relapse prevention participants reported feeling less guilty and tended to attribute the cause of the slip to external environmental pressures and situational circumstances. They reported that the external circumstances preceding the slip were more stressful than did standard treatment participants. Finally, they indicated feeling less influenced by lack of willpower and internal weakness.

The results of this investigation suggest that specific intervention strategies based upon the cognitive–behavioral RP model may help prevent a relapse and/or mitigate its damaging effects, on a short-term basis. Participants in the RP condition showed superior maintenance of weight loss, more frequent additional weight loss following treatment termination, and greater magnitude of weight loss at 60 days posttreatment, than did standard treatment participants. As predicted, participants in the RP program did not differ from standard treatment program participants in magnitude of weight loss during or at the end of treatment. The cognitive strategies thus seemed to be selectively effective *after* the treatment program had ended. Individuals who received the RP package also differed from standard treatment participants in several affective and cognitive responses to an initial slip. Relapse prevention participants rated the situation in which they slipped as being more stressful, and attributed a major cause to situational pressures and environmental factors. They were more likely to view a slip that did occur as deliberate, rather than as an experience over which they had no control. These attitudes and feelings had been encouraged in the RP participants. It is not clear if these increased external attributions caused the superior weight loss and maintenance found in RP participants. Nor can specific components of the RP program be identified as more or less effective. However, during the 60-day follow-up interview, participants rated components of the pro-

Table 9-3. Posttreatment to Follow-Up Changes for Relapse Prevention and Standard Treatment Conditions

	Relapse prevention	Standard treatment
Lost further weight	9 (41%)	3 (21%)
No change	6 (27%)	2 (14%)
Weight regain	7 (32%)	9 (64%)

Note. Data from Rosenthal and Marx (1979).

Table 9-4. Sign Tests for Behavioral and Questionnaire Predictions for the Relapse Prevention (RP) and Standard Behavioral (S) Treatment Groups

Measure	Relapse prevention		Standard behavioral	Prediction	Predictions met?[a]
Lost further weight posttreatment	9 (41%)		3 (21%)	RP > S	+
Maintained losses posttreatment	6 (27%)		2 (14%)	RP > S	+
Gained weight posttreatment	7 (32%)		9 (64%)	RP < S	+
Pounds lost during treatment	$\overline{X}$	10.9	10.1	RP = S	0
	SD	5.1	5.0		
Used RP techniques to control weight		13%	0%	RP > S	+
Was relapse deliberate? (yes)		56%	40%	RP > S	+
How guilty during?	$\overline{X}$	4.1	4.5	RP < S	+
	SD	2.0	1.8		
How guilty after?	$\overline{X}$	4.7	4.9	RP < S	+
	SD	2.0	2.0		
How influenced by environmental pressures? (1 = very much influenced)	$\overline{X}$	2.0	4.0	RP < S	+
	SD	1.3	1.8		
How influenced by lack of willpower? (1 = not influenced)	$\overline{X}$	2.8	3.7	RP < S	+
	SD	1.7	1.9		
How much in control prior? (1 = not in control)	$\overline{X}$	4.0	4.2	RP > S	−
	SD	1.8	1.6		
How much in control after? (1 = not in control)	$\overline{X}$	3.7	4.1	RP > S	−
	SD	1.9	1.9		
How stressful was the situation? (1 = not stressful)	$\overline{X}$	4.4	3.3	RP > S	+
	SD	2.3	2.5		

Note. Data from Rosenthal and Marx (1979).
[a]+ − yes; − − no; 0 = no difference.

gram for frequency of use both during and after treatment. Analysis of high-risk situations was listed most frequently, followed by balancing wants and shoulds.

Although the findings of this study (Rosenthal & Marx, 1979) permit cautious optimism, maintenance was evaluated for a short time period (60 days). The effectiveness of RP intervention strategies for long-term maintenance has received support in a recent study by Perri, Shapiro, Ludwig, Twentyman, and McAdoo (1984).

FUTURE DIRECTIONS FOR RESEARCH

The processes involved in maintenance and relapse in weight control are far from fully understood. While we have a fairly detailed understanding of the situations in which a dieter is likely to be at high risk for overeating, we are not yet able to predict who is likely to continue overeating (i.e., experience a relapse) and who is not. In his work on relapse among ex-smokers, Shiffman (1982) found that only a few components of an initial slip situation (which he termed a *relapse crisis*) were actually predictive of continued smoking (i.e., relapse). In particular, those relapse crises that occurred in the presence of other persons were found to be more likely to lead to a relapse than those that occurred when the ex-smoker was alone. Also, consumption of alcohol during the relapse crisis was associated with a higher relapse rate than those crises that occurred without the use of alcohol. Shiffman has suggested that rather than looking to the characteristics of the relapse crisis situation for predictors of relapse, the ex-smokers' methods of coping with the relapse crisis should be examined. He has divided the exploration of the relapse process into two components: (1) the relapse crisis (analogous to the high-risk situation discussed in this chapter), and (2) the outcome of the relapse crisis (relapse or continued abstinence). Shiffman has found that when an ex-smoker made some attempt to cope with a relapse crisis, either behaviorally (e.g., by leaving the situation) or cognitively (e.g., by mentally reviewing reasons to quit smoking), he or she was far less likely to continue to smoke than when no attempt to cope was made. Shiffman concluded that for ex-smokers, situations can induce relapse crises, but the outcome of a relapse crisis (relapse vs. maintenance) is better predicted by use or nonuse of coping responses (see Chapter 8). This notion deserves investigation in weight control as well. Examination of this issue, in addition to examination of cognitive and affective reactions to an initial slip, might enhance our ability to predict who is likely to relapse, triggered by what circumstances.

In addition, the ability to predict who is likely to relapse could facilitate development of more specifically tailored treatment programs for weight loss than are currently available. Most approaches to obesity treatment tend to be of the "kitchen sink" variety; they are broad-spectrum approaches designed to offer something to everyone. But if coping styles were found to differentiate individuals who experienced an isolated slip from those who relapsed, as Shiffman found with ex-smokers, programs could be tailored to address the needs of individuals with different coping styles. One interesting finding of Shiffman's that might be relevant to weight control is that effectiveness of coping was dependent upon affective state. Behavioral coping attempts were twice as effective when the ex-smoker was not depressed during the relapse crisis.

Examination of the timing of RP strategies is also needed. Should RP strategies be included as part of behavioral obesity treatment programs? Or might RP strategies be more effective if taught *after* weight loss has been achieved, during booster sessions, when the dieter is more likely to be truly concerned about such issues?

What is also needed is the study of the relapse process as it is occurring, rather than retrospectively. Direct study is preferable to retrospective study because it is less subject to distortions of memory and selective recall. Shiffman has pioneered such an approach by the development of a telephone hot-line for ex-smokers who were experiencing or had experienced a relapse crisis within the past 48 hours (see Chapter 8). Also desirable would be the inclusion of a second source of data regarding the incident, perhaps from a spouse, child, or close friend. Studies of maintenance and relapse often suffer from lack of reliability assessment, as these are difficult to perform (e.g., when an individual experiences a relapse crisis when alone). However, reliability assessments are highly desirable.

The RP model has proven itself to be of heuristic value in the study of relapse in weight control. However, the fit between the model and the data is imperfect. The data analyzed in this chapter suggest that while some aspects of the model appear to correspond with "real-life" relapse situations, other aspects do not. The model would predict that a dieter who felt in control during an initial slip would be less likely to experience a full-blown relapse than a dieter who did not. Such a difference was not found. On the other hand, dieters who reacted to an initial slip with high levels of guilt did relapse more frequently than those who felt less guilty, as the model predicts.

Open-ended interviews of dieters who have experienced an initial slip could shed light on the predictive utility of the RP model. Do dieters express their feelings, thoughts and understanding of the situation in ways that follow the model's predictions? Are initial slips described by dieters in ways that permit categorization of responses according to the RP model?

Some work along this line has been undertaken in the area of alcohol abuse, with a categorization system for initial slips derived from open-ended interviews. Similar work needs to be done with dieters. It cannot be assumed that our language and coding systems, or those developed for use with alcohol abusers, adequately capture the experiences of dieters.

It will also be important for studies of RP strategies to do more than compare outcome differences between treatment and control groups. Changes in cognitions need to be demonstrated rather than inferred to support the RP model. The RP model is difficult to test because of its focus upon indirectly observable events such as cognitions and feelings. Attempts to validate the model's predictions are difficult to design and implement, but therein lie the ultimate demonstrations of the model's value.

CONCLUDING COMMENTS

1. *Relapse* and *maintenance* are difficult to define. Difficulties in definition should not, however, deter much needed research efforts.

2. A focus on long-term maintenance of weight loss should be given greater emphasis in all weight-loss programs.

3. Investigations of relapse and maintenance should focus on the multiple techniques used by the dieter, and the affects and cognitions surrounding successful and unsuccessful maintenance efforts.

4. Investigations of maintenance and relapse should examine coping strategies used by dieters in high-risk situations.

5. The process of maintenance appears to be different from the process of weight loss. Investigation into the nature of these differences is needed.

6. The RP model has heuristic value in the study of relapse in weight control. It has been especially valuable in describing components of relapse situations and permitting comparison of relapse situations across different addictive behaviors.

REFERENCES

Ashby, W. A., & Wilson, G. T. Behavior therapy for obesity: Booster sessions and longterm maintenance of weight loss. *Behaviour Research and Therapy*, 1977, *15*, 451–466.

Bandura, A. Self-efficacy: Toward a unifying theory of behavioral change. *Psychological Review*, 1977, *84*, 191–215.

Bem, D. J. Self-perception theory. In L. Berkowitz (Ed.), *Advances in experimental social psychology* (Vol. 6). New York: Academic Press, 1972.

Beneke, W., & Paulson, B. Long-term efficacy of a behavior modification weight loss program: A comparison of two follow-up maintenance strategies. *Behavior Therapy*, 1979, *10*, 3–13.

Brownell, K. D. The addictive disorders. In C. M. Franks, G. T. Wilson, P. C. Kendall, & K. D. Brownell, *Annual review of behavior therapy* (Vol. 8). New York: Guilford, 1982.

Brownell, K. D., & Stunkard, A. J. Couples training, pharmacotherapy, and behavior therapy in the treatment of obesity. *Archives of General Psychiatry*, 1981, *38*, 1224–1229.

Brownell, K. D., Heckerman, C., & Westlake, R. The behavioral control of obesity: A descriptive analysis of a large-scale program. *Journal of Clinical Psychology*, 1979, *35*, 864–869.

Collins, B. L. *Comparative efficacy of cognitive and behavioral approaches in weight reduction.* Unpublished doctoral dissertation, State University of New York at Stony Brook, 1980.

Cooke, C., & Meyers, A. The role of predictor variables in the behavioral treatment of obesity. *Behavioral Assessment*, 1980, *2*, 59–69.

Dunkel, L., & Glaros, A. Comparison of self-instructional and stimulus control treatments for obesity. *Cognitive Therapy and Research*, 1978, *2*, 75–78.

Festinger, L. *Conflict, decision and dissonance.* Stanford: Stanford University Press, 1964.

Gormally, J., Rardin, D., & Black, S. Correlates of successful response to a behavioral weight control clinic. *Journal of Counseling Psychology*, 1980, *27*, 179–191.

Hagen, R. L. Group therapy versus bibliotherapy in weight reduction. *Behavior Therapy*, 1974, *5*, 222–234.

Hunt, W. A., Barnett, L. W., & Branch, L. G. Relapse rates in addiction programs. *Journal of Clinical Psychology*, 1971, *27*, 455–456.

Jeffery, R. W., Wing, R. R., & Stunkard, A. J. Behavioral treatment of obesity: The state of the art in 1976. *Behavior Therapy*, 1978, *9*, 189–199.

Kingsley, R. G., & Wilson, G. T. Behavior therapy for obesity: A comparative investigation of long-term efficacy. *Journal of Consulting and Clinical Psychology*, 1977, *45*, 288–298.

Lazarus, A. A. *Multimodal behavior therapy.* New York: Springer, 1976.

Leon, G., & Chamberlain, K. Comparison of daily eating habits and emotional states of over-weight persons successful or unsuccessful in maintaining a weight loss. *Journal of Consulting and Clinical Psychology*, 1973, *41*, 108–115. (a)

Leon, G., & Chamberlain, K. Emotional arousal, eating patterns and body image as differential factors associated with varying success in maintaining a weight loss. *Journal of Consulting and Clinical Psychology*, 1973, *40*, 474–480. (b)

Mahoney, B. K., Rogers, T., Straw, M., & Mahoney, M. J. *Results and implications of a problem-solving treatment program for obesity.* Paper presented at the meeting of the Association for Advancement of Behavior Therapy, Chicago, December 1977.

Mahoney, M. J. Fat fiction. *Behavior Therapy*, 1975, *6*, 416–418.

Marlatt, G. A., The Drinking Profile: A questionnaire for the behavioral assessment of alcoholism. In E. J. Mash & L. G. Terdal (Eds.), *Behavior therapy assessment: Diagnosis, design, and evaluation.* New York: Springer, 1976.

Marlatt, G. A., & Gordon, J. R. Determinants of relapse: Implications for the maintenance of behavior change. In P. O. Davidson & S. M. Davidson (Eds.), *Behavioral medicine: Changing health lifestyles.* New York: Brunner/Mazel, 1980.

O'Leary, K. D., & Wilson, G. T. *Behavior therapy: Application and outcome.* Englewood Cliffs, N.J.: Prentice-Hall, 1975.

O'Neill, P. M., Currey, H. S., Hirsch, A. A., Riddle, F. E., Taylor, C. I., Malcolm, R. J., & Sexauer, J. D. Effects of sex of subject and spouse involvement on weight loss in a behavior treatment program: A retrospective investigation. *Addictive Behaviors*, 1979, *4*, 167–177.

Perri, M. G., Shapiro, R. M., Ludwig, W. W., Twentyman, C. T., & McAdoo, W. G. Maintenance strategies for the treatment of obesity: An evaluation of relapse prevention training and post-treatment contact by mail and telephone. *Journal of Consulting and Clinical Psychology*, 1984, *52*, 404–413.

Rosenthal, B. S., Allen, G. J., & Winter, C. Husband involvement in the behavioral treatment of overweight women: Initial effects and long-term followup. *International Journal of Obesity*, 1980, *4*, 165–173.

Rosenthal, B. S., & Marx, R. D. *A comparison of standard behavioral and relapse prevention weight reduction program.* Paper presented at the meeting of the Association for Advancement of Behavior Therapy, Chicago, December 1979.

Rosenthal, B. S., & Marx, R. D. Determinants of initial relapse episodes among dieters. *Obesity and Bariatric Medicine*, 1981, *10*, 94–97.

Shiffman, S. M. Relapse following smoking cessation: A situational analysis. *Journal of Consulting and Clinical Psychology*, 1982, *50*, 71–86.

Sjoberg, L., & Persson, L. A study of attempts by obese patients to regulate eating. *Gotesberg Psychological Reports*, 1977, *7*, 12.

Smith-Scott, J. *Revision of Hagen et al. weight reduction manual.* Unpublished manuscript, Western Washington University, 1976.

Wilson, G. T. Current status of behavioral treatment of obesity. In N. A. Krasnegor (Ed.), *Behavioral analysis and treatment of substance abuse.* Washington, D.C.: National Institute on Drug Abuse, Research Monograph 25, Department of Health, Education and Welfare, 1979.

Wilson, G. T., & Brownell, K. D. Behavior therapy for obesity: Including family members in the treatment process, *Behavior Therapy*, 1978, *9*, 943–945.

Wilson, G. T., & Brownell, K. D. Behavior therapy for obesity: An evaluation of treatment outcome. *Advances in Behaviour Research and Therapy*, 1980, *3*, 49–86.

Wing, R. R., & Jeffery, R. Successful losers: A descriptive analysis of the process of weight reduction. *Obesity and Bariatric Medicine*, 1978, *7*, 190–191.

Wooley, S. C., Wooley, O. W., & Dyrenforth, S. R. Obesity treatment re-examined: The case for a more tentative and experimental approach. In N. A. Krasnegor (Ed.), *Behavioral analysis and treatment of substance abuse.* Washington, D.C.: National Institute on Drug Abuse, Research Monograph 25, Department of Health, Education and Welfare, 1979.

AUTHOR INDEX

SUBJECT INDEX

22